THE WORLD'S BEST

The Ultimate Book
For The International Traveler

Prepared by the staff of
International Living

www.InternationalLiving.com

The World's Best

Published by Agora Ireland Publishing & Services, Ltd., 5 Catherine Street,
Waterford, Ireland.

Publisher: Kathleen Peddicord
Editor: Fiona Hegarty
Product Editor: Lynn Chestnutt
Proofreaders: Robbie McDonald and Emily Furlong
Graphic Designer: Shannon Roberts

Cover design by: Susan Redmond
Printed by: Victor Graphics

ISBN: 0-9547754-3-0

120B000435

CONTENTS

SECTION 1: THE WORLD'S BEST DESTINATIONS

SECTION 2: THE WORLD'S BEST HONEYMOON DESTINATIONS

SECTION 3: THE WORLD'S BEST BEACHES

SECTION 4: THE WORLD'S BEST SPORTING DESTINATIONS

SECTION 5: THE WORLD'S BEST SHOPPING

SECTION 6: THE WORLD'S MOST SCENIC DRIVES

INTRODUCTION

WHO THAT IS BUSY TO MEASURE AND COMPARE
THE HEVYN AND ERTH AN THE WORLDE LARGE
DESCRYBYNGE THE CLYMATIS AND FOLKE OF EVERY PLACE
HE IS A FOLE AND HATH A GREVOUS CHAGE.
—*Alexander Barclay,* The Ship of Folys, *1509*

Consider for a moment how much bigger the world is today than it was in 1986, when we published the first edition of *The World's Best*. How many more people there are. How many more places open to foreign travelers. How many more opportunities. The original *World's Best* was but 207 pages. The book you are now reading is more than 700 pages. And still I would caution that this new and expanded *World's Best* is far from comprehensive.

We have tried to include bests in every corner of the globe…in Bucharest and Buenos Aires…in Nepal and Nova Scotia…in Washington, D.C. and Wales…but we realize that we have but skimmed the surface.

To create this new edition, we called upon our regular correspondents all over the world (more than 200 of them) and asked that they send us their personal world's bests—their picks for the world's best art museum, sunset, surfing, scuba diving, opera house, ski resort, canyon, champagne, castle, nightclub, island, garden, market, train ride, travel bargains, restaurants, cafés, and neighborhoods. To their lists we added our own superlatives—our choices for the biggest, the oldest, the smallest, the cheapest, the grandest, the prettiest, the tallest, the coziest, the most remarkable…

Anyone who sets out to name the world's best this or the world's best that, does indeed have a "grievous charge." Who's to say what's best?

We are, we decided. And on that authority, we offer a collection that is neither complete nor objective.

What we have attempted to do is to draw forth for you a small sampling of the wealth our world has to offer.

Enjoy.

Sincerely,

Kathleen Peddicord
Publisher, *International Living*

P.S. Details, details.

Prices throughout this book are, for the most part, given in U.S. dollars based on the current exchange rate at the time of going to press. This is meant only to give you an idea of the current pricing. Remember, exchange rates fluctuate daily. Furthermore, hotels and restaurants typically raise their prices every season. And inflation in some countries rages wildly.

SECTION 1:

THE WORLD'S BEST DESTINATIONS

Austria • Britain • Bulgaria • Croatia • Czech Republic • France Germany • Greece • Hungary • Ireland • Isle of Man • Italy Montenegro • Poland • Portugal • Romania • Scandinavia • Spain Switzerland • Commonwealth of Independent States • China • India Indonesia • Israel • Japan • Southeast Asia • Africa • North Africa Australia • New Zealand • United States • Canada • Caribbean Belize • Costa Rica • Honduras • Mexico • Nicaragua • Panama Argentina • Brazil • Chile • Ecuador • Peru • Uruguay • Venezuela

THE BEST OF AUSTRIA

AUSTRIA IS SWITZERLAND, SPEAKING PURE GERMAN AND
WITH HISTORY ADDED.

—J.E. Morpugo, 1963

Austria—the land of Mozart, Strauss, Schubert, and Mahler—is the
music capital of Europe. Instead of Muzak, classical music is played in
elevators and offices. School children learn to play musical instruments at an
early age. And Austria's yearly classical music festivals draw music lovers
from around the globe.

Vienna alone supports four major symphony orchestras, two opera
houses, and a host of theaters.

The world's best music festivals

The **Salzburg Festival** is the world's leading and most famous festival
(we'll tell you more about the Salzburg Festival on page 10). Two other
charming festivals, which are held in Vienna, are the **Haydn Festival** and
the **International Chamber Music Festival**. Tickets to these music festivals
are cheapest if you purchase your tickets in Austria. *Tickets for Events in
Austria* is an information sheet which is available from the **Austrian National
Tourist Office**, *tel. (212) 944-6880; website: www.austria-tourism.at.*

THE BEST OF VIENNA

Vienna, the capital of the Hapsburg empire for 600 years, is one of the
loveliest cities in the world. Magnificent palaces, theaters, and ballrooms
from its days of glory remain throughout the city. The best way to explore
Vienna is on foot, and the best place to begin is the **Ringstrasse**, affectionately known as the Ring.

The most beautiful avenue in Vienna

One of the most beautiful avenues in the world, the Ring circles
Vienna's old quarter. Most of Vienna's major sights line this shaded, tree-
lined boulevard created by Emperor Franz Josef in December 1857.

You can walk the most picturesque section of the Ring in 45 minutes.
(You can walk the entire Ring in two hours.) Begin at the 600-year-old
Vienna University, near the Schottentor (Scottish Gate), and work your way
around the Ring past the Stadtstheater, Europe's leading German-language
theater; the neo-Gothic *Rathaus*; the Greek-style Parliament building; the

1

Hofburg Palace; the Natural History Museum; and the Art History Museum. Then continue past the great opera house, the Imperial Hotel, and the town parks (as well as the airline bus terminal).

Vienna's number-one attraction

The most important sight in Vienna is the **Hofburg Palace** (known as the Hofburg), once the winter residence of the Hapsburgs. Built in the 13th century, it has been embellished with every architecture style up to modern day. More a city than a palace, it is now filled with museums and government offices.

The great entranceway to the Hofburg, the michaelertor, is on the Michaelerplatz flanked by two grand fountains. On the left as you enter are the Imperial Apartments, where you can see the exercise equipment of Emperor Franz Josef's beautiful, reclusive wife Sisi, who was obsessed with her figure (more than 100 years before it was fashionable to be so).

Beyond the courtyard to the left is the gateway to the Schweizerhof, the original nucleus of the Hofburg. The 13th-century Schweizerhof was named for the Swiss Guards who watched over the ruler. The Hofburgkapelle (the chapel), where Mozart and Schubert played, is in the courtyard of the Schweizerhof. Today, the Vienna Boys' Choir sings here on Sundays during the summer and on holidays.

The Hofburg also contains the **Imperial Treasury**, where you can see the ancient Imperial Crown, encrusted with gems and dating back to 962 A.D.; objects said to be made of unicorn horn; the elaborate cradle designed for Napoleon's son; and an agate bowl once thought to be the Holy Grail.

In the Augustinerkirche of the Hofburg is the **Chapel of St. George**. It contains 56 urns holding the hearts of the Hapsburgs. However, the chapel is not just a place of death. Maria Theresa and Francis of Lorraine were married here, as was Napoleon, by proxy, to Marie Louise.

The world's best horsemanship

The **Spanish Riding School**, located in Hofburg, trains the noble white stallions that descend from the Spanish horses imported to Austria by Emperor Maximillian II in the 16th century. The horses dance to Viennese music, guided by expert riders wearing the traditional gold-buttoned brown uniform and gold-braided black hat.

Performances are held at the school on Sunday mornings at 10:45 a.m. and occasionally on Wednesday nights at 7 p.m. from March to June and September to December. Purchase tickets six months in advance by writing to the **Spanische Reitschule**, *Hofburg, A-1010 Vienna, Austria; tel. (43)1-533-9031; website: www.spanishridingschool.com.*

Gothic architecture at its best

The most important gothic structure in Austria is the early 12th-century

St. Stephen's Cathedral. Most of the Gothic touches were added in the 14th and 15th centuries. Climb the 345 steps to the top of the 450-foot church spire for a view of Vienna.

Inside, the black marble baroque altar is carved with illustrations of St. Stephen being stoned to death. The pulpit, designed by Anton Pilgram between 1510 and 1515, is carved with the heads of the early fathers of the church (Augustine, Gregory, Jerome, and Ambrose), as well as animals symbolizing the sins. Pilgram's own face peers out from the stairs.

Another masterpiece is contained in the theater: the tomb of Frederick III, created by Nikolaus of Leyden from 1467 to 1513. It is covered with carvings representing good and evil and topped with a marble statue of the emperor in his coronation robes.

Beneath the cathedral in the catacombs are the internal organs of 56 Hapsburgs minus the hearts, which are in the Church of the Augustin Friars. The bodies are in the Imperial Burial Vault at the Church of the Capuchin Friars. (The reason behind separating the body parts was that if one church burned down, not all the Hapsburg remains would be lost.) You also can see the foundations of the original basilica, which burned in 1258.

Maria Theresa's favorite place

Schönbrunn Palace, west of town, was the summer home of the Hapsburgs from 1695, when it was built, to 1918, when the last Hapsburg emperor, Charles I, abdicated. Marie Theresa ruled Austria from here while raising 16 children (Marie Antoinette was one of them) and fighting a war for her right to the throne. She redesigned the palace, and today it is much as she left it.

Often compared to Versailles, the Schönbrunn contains 1,441 rooms (45 can be visited) and a vast baroque garden. The rococo palace theater, once the stage for Max Reinhardt's famous acting school, still houses a drama school. See the collection of royal carriages; the room where Napoleon stayed; the Millions Room, a highly ornate rococo room with gold-framed mirrors and Indian paintings; and the Great Gallery, with its frescoed ceilings. The Schonbrunn is also home to the oldest zoo in Europe, designed in 1752 by Jadot. It is probably the only baroque-style zoo in the world.

The favorite park of the Viennese

Prater Park, across the Danube River, is famous for its Ferris wheel, the Riesenrad. (The best view in Vienna is from the top.) The park was the royal hunting ground until 1766, when Emperor Joseph II opened it to the public.

The three-mile-long Hauptallee leads through the center of this garden-filled park. Lined with chestnut trees, this road is a great place to bike ride. Avoid the Krieau section, where thieves lurk.

Austria's greatest museum

If you see only one museum in Vienna, make it the **Kunsthistorisches Museum** (Art History Museum), which is across the Ringstrasse from the Hofburg. The greatest museum in Austria, it houses the paintings, sculptures, jewels, and bibelots collected by the Hapsburgs from 1500 to 1918.

The Kunsthistorisches Museum looks more like a palace than a museum, with its columned windows, enormous doors, broad central staircase, heraldic patterns, painted ceilings, and high cupola. Spread through seven buildings, it can be confusing, and the easiest way to see it is to ramble. Be sure to see the works of Pieter Brueghel the Elder in Gallery X, Dürer's works in Room 15, Giuseppe Arcimboldi's surreal works in Room 19, the Titians in Gallery I, The Tintorettos in Gallery II, the Raphaels in Gallery III, and Vermeer's works in Gallery VIII.

Vienna's other top museums

The **Österreichische Galerie** (Austrian Gallery), *Prinz Eugenstrasse 27*, contains modern, baroque, and church art. Located in the baroque Belvedere Palace, which was built by Hildebrandt between 1714 and 1723, the gallery is divided into three parts. Modern artworks are kept in the Upper Belvedere. Look for the works of Gustav Klimt (1862-1918), many of which are embellished with gold. The Lower Belvedere, where the beloved Prince Eugene (who protected his country from the Turks) once lived, is now the Museum of Austrian Baroque. The Orangerie houses the Museum of Medieval Austrian Art.

The **Graphische Sammlung Albertina** (Albertina Graphic Arts Collection), near Augustinerbastel, has the greatest collection of drawings by old masters in the world. The etchings of Durer are the biggest attractions. Also here are works by Rubens, Fragonard, and other masters. (Reproductions are usually on display, for conservation reasons.)

The **Naturhistorisches Museum** (Natural History Museum), across the street, houses the world's oldest-known sculpture, the *Willendorf Venus*, created in Moravia about 2900 B.C. You'll find this ancient fertility figure in Room 11. The five-inch limestone carving of a plump woman represents the mother goddess.

The **Akademie der Bildenen Kunste** (Academy of Fine Arts), near Getreidemarkt, is the respected art school that rejected the young Adolf Hitler after he failed the entrance exams. Some say this rejection fueled Hitler's anti-Semitism. (He claimed Jewish professors kept him out.) Established in 1692, the academy houses the impressive triptych *The Last Judgment* by Hieronymus Bosch.

Neue Hofburg, a wing of the Hofburg, has a collection of Roman sculptures from the ancient city of Ephesus, which were found on the western coast of Turkey. The museum also houses musical instruments, including the pianos of Beethoven, Schubert, and Mahler.

The world's best boys' choir

The world-famous **Vienna Boys' Choir** performs every Sunday and religious holidays from January 1 through late June and mid-September through December 31. The performances are held in the Imperial Chapel of the Hofburg. Tickets range from 35 euro to 48 euro ($46 to $63) and can be purchased at *www.mondial.at/english/boys.html* or call **Vewaltung der Hofmusikkapelle** at *(43)1-533-9927*. Purchase your tickets in advance and get to the church early to get a good seat.

Austria's finest musical experience—and Europe's most beautiful opera house

A night at the **Staatsoper** is the finest musical experience you will have while traveling in Austria. This opera house is regarded as the most beautiful in Europe. The Vienna State Opera, one of the finest opera companies, is accompanied by the Vienna Philharmonic, one of the world's finest orchestras.

If you plan on attending this magical experience in June, September, October, or May, order your tickets two to three months in advance. Call the ticket information office at the tourist board, *tel. (43)1-515-33135;* don't send money—you pay for the tickets when you arrive in Vienna. You can also visit the website at *www.staatsoper-berlin.org/en/intro.htm.* You should pick your tickets up four days before your chosen performance time and remember to bring your passport and confirmation letter. The cheapest tickets are sold at the ticket booth an hour before the performance.

Café culture at its coziest

The Viennese have gotten the café down to an art. Cafés have been a way of life in Vienna since the Turks retreated in 1683, leaving their sacks of coffee beans outside the walls of the city. People spend hours in cafés, sipping coffee, chatting with friends, and reading newspapers. (Cafés usually supply an assortment of international newspapers.)

Café Hawelka, *tel. (43)1-512-8230* is a dark café with black chairs, coat racks, seats upholstered in red and brown stripes, and heavy curtains. It draws an assortment of people including students, old people, artists, and businessmen. Caricatures and drawings line the walls of this café, once frequented by Trotsky and his contemporaries. Orson Welles came here to soak up atmosphere and prepare for his role in the film *The Third Man.* English and American newspapers are available.

Café Central, *tel. (43)1-53-33-763* is another cozy place that was an intellectual hangout at the turn of the century. It is decorated with frescoes, marble columns, and fountains and is in an enclosed courtyard. It serves the best *Topfenstrudel* in Vienna.

Café Schwarzenberg, *tel. (43)1-512-73-93* is a 120-year-old café with oak-paneled walls, mirrors, and a white tile ceiling. They have a pianist that always draws a crowd.

Vienna's best restaurants

Gottfried, *tel. (43)1-713-82-56*, awarded a coveted Michelin star, specializes in fish and Rohe Rinderfiletscheiben mit Ruhrei und Schalottenrahm (raw beef with scrambled eggs and shallot-flavored whipped cream). Make reservations in advance. The restaurant is closed Saturday and Sunday at lunch.

Hauswirth, *tel. (43)1-587-1261* is a wonderful place to try their specialties of Roulade von der Bachforelle (baked trout), Kalbsbriesrose mit Ganseleber im Blatterteig (sweetbreads and goose liver in a puff pastry), or Rehruckenfilet in der Semmelhulle auf Wacholdersauce (venison filet in juniper sauce). Reservations are required. The restaurant is closed on Sundays and on bank holidays.

Sacherstube, the Hotel Sacher's restaurant, *tel. (43)1-51-45-60*, is a lovely surprise to those who think hotel restaurants are just mediocre. The food is good and the atmosphere is pleasing. Men should wear a tie. Reservations are advised.

Zu den Drei Husaren, *tel. (43)1-51-21-092*, is the essence of old Vienna, serving first-rate hors d'oeuvres and desserts. Opened 50 years ago, the restaurant is decorated with stag horns, antique busts, Gobelin tapestries, and old portraits. They have the dessert to end all desserts called the Preiselbeeren omelette with praline sabayon. Reservations are necessary.

The world's best pastries

Vienna's *Konditoreien* (pastry shops/cafés) produce the world's most delectable pastries—seductive arrays of tempting cakes, dripping with icing and whipped cream. Imagine a horseshoe-shaped Kipferl with shredded almonds or a Schifferl, shaped like a small boat, with tiny strawberries as passengers. Sweet lovers can be spotted on any afternoon lingering in *Konditoreien* over savory confections and a cup of coffee or tea.

Vienna's *Konditoreien* are as colorful and varied as the pastries they serve. **Demel's**, from its exalted position on the Kohlmarkt, calls itself *K.K. Hofzuckerbackerei* (imperial and royal sugar baker). **Gerstner**, with its enviable position overlooking the Kaerntnerstrasse, also claims royal recognition: Emperor Franz Josef prophetically remarked more than 100 years ago, "Gerstner will have a great future." Another landmark, famous for its dainty china and delicious cakes, is **Heiner's**, with *Konditoreien* on both the Kaerntnerstrasse and the Wollzeile.

The best of Viennese nightlife

The **U4**, *tel. (43)1-85-83-07*, is our favorite nightclub in Vienna. So named because it is downstairs from an elevated subway stop on the U4 line, it is populated by a mature, sophisticated crowd.

Queen Anne, *tel. (43)1-512-0203*, is the most popular disco in town.

Jazzland, *tel. (43)1-533-25-75*, is the best place for good, sultry jazz. The atmosphere is funky and smoky. Famous bands sometimes play here.

Reiss Bar, *tel. (43)1-512-7198*, is the hot spot for the executive type. The champagne flows with ease in this art-retro spot where executives rub shoulders with other executives.

Griechenbeisl, *tel. (43)1-533-1941*, claims to be the oldest tavern in Vienna, dating back to 1500. The local food is great and they have live music every evening. The beer is always on tap and the wine flows with ease.

Vienna's best hotel

The Imperial, *tel. (43)1-501-100*, is a deluxe hotel located in a former palace. Built in 1869 for the duke of Württemberg, it was turned into a hotel in 1874. Wagner lived here for two months during the productions of his operas around the corner. Elizabeth Taylor stayed here with her three dogs and two cats, her mother, and her servants. Other noted guests have included Ormandy, Nureyev, Fonteyn, Domingo, and Carreras. During World War II, the Nazis used the Imperial as a guesthouse, and Hitler stayed here several times. When the war was over, the hotel served as the Russian headquarters.

Rooms at the Imperial are furnished with antiques and have wall safes. The magnificent central staircase of red, yellow, and black marble is supported by reclining gods and goddesses. Gobelin tapestries and portraits of Emperor Franz Josef and Empress Elizabeth hang on the walls.

Three top-rung hotels

The Bristol, *tel. (43)1-51-51-60*, is a luxurious, traditional hotel across the street from the opera house. It has large, beautifully furnished bedrooms and one of the best hotel bars in Europe. The Bristol's restaurant, the Korso, received a star from Michelin for its terrific food.

The Sacher, *tel. (43)1-51-45-60*, is a first-class place with lovely rooms that are furnished with antiques. Musicians and music lovers stay at this hotel, which is next door to the opera house. The concierge is said to be able to get tickets to almost any of Vienna's musical events—for a handsome fee of course.

The Hotel im Palais Schwarzenberg, *tel. (43)1-78-45-15*, is in a converted 17th-century baroque palace in a quiet location. Its restaurant has a Michelin star. Once a palace, it has ceiling frescoes and elaborate chandeliers and is furnished with antiques. Surrounded by a 37-acre park in the center of Vienna, the hotel has very good service.

The most affordable hotels

Amadeus, *tel. (43)1-638-738*, is consistently good and centrally located, with private baths and telephones.

Kaiserin Elisabeth, *tel. (43)1-515-260*, toll free in Europe *tel. (800)90-66-90-66;* toll free in USA *tel. (1)800-780-5734*. The hotel is situated in a pleasant 14th-century building that is centrally located. Prices start at $99 for a single room for the weekend. Rooms must be booked by phone.

Vienna's most tragic site

A chapel in **Mayerling**, in the middle of the Vienna woods, marks the place were Crown Prince Rudolf, son of Emperor Franz Josef, and his mistress Baroness Mary Vetsera committed double suicide. The Emperor had refused to allow Prince Rudolf to end his unhappy marriage.

Heurigen, or little wine bars, are located in Grinzing and other villages in the woods. A sprig of pine above the door of one of these bars means new wine, less than a year old, is ready to be drunk.

The best taverns (and best views of Vienna)

The little-known *Heuriger* is a unique style of east Austrian tavern with origins that go back more than 1,200 years. In 1784, Emperor Joseph II passed a decree allowing all farmers and winegrowers in this region to sell their own produce (although he was only officially recognizing a tradition started in A.D. 795). Each winegrower would only open for business a few weeks at a time, ensuring that there was always an open tavern to be found somewhere. *Heurigen* that continue to operate this way are now called *Buschenschanken* (bushel taverns) because of the pine bushel above the doorway that tells you they're open. But most Heurigen can be enjoyed year-round, usually in the outer districts of Vienna.

One of the best *Heurigen* is a cozy inn called **The Huber**, in Vienna's 16th district (**Die Huber**, *Roterdstrasse 5, 1160 Wien*). Its bare wooden tables and long benches are typical of Heurigen, as are the waiters and waitresses that wear traditional Austrian costume: Lederhosen for the men, Dirndl for the women. But this is not a show put on for tourists—all the patrons are locals, and most know the owner by name.

Food is inexpensive and plentiful; beware the huge portions served in Heurigen—one portion of *wiener schnitzel* is more than enough for two people (unlike most Austrian restaurants, in a Heuriger, it is perfectly acceptable to take food home). *Heurigen* also offer excellent table wine, usually served in an open carafe—a half-liter won't cost more than four euro ($5).

Heurigen are generally open from late afternoon until midnight and most have live Viennese music. In summer, sitting outside in the *Schrebergarten* is a treat. For the best views of Vienna, we recommend **Weingut am Reisenberg**, *Oberer Reisenbergweg 15, 1190 Wien*, but it can get crowded on weekends and most of the summer. If it's too busy, you'll find the second best views of Vienna at **Heuriger Leitner**, *Sprengersteig 68, 1160 Wien.*

INNSBRUCK: THE PRETTIEST ALPINE CITY

Innsbruck, the capital of Tyrol, is one of the prettiest cities in the world. It is also one of the biggest ski centers in Europe. The towering Alps can be seen from almost every street corner. The **Nordkette**, a steep alpine head-wall, is the closest and most dramatic of the mountains that surround the city. **Maria-Theresien-Strasse**, the main street, has an especially inspiring view of the mountains.

Miles of cross-country ski tracks can be found outside Innsbruck, as well as the Olympic bobsled run, a ski jump, and a large ice-skating rink and hockey arena.

(See more about skiing in Austria in Section 4: The World's Best Sporting Destinations.)

Gothic architecture (the pointed, arched, and vaulted style prevalent in Europe from the 13th to 15th centuries) can be seen throughout 800-year-old Innsbruck. Much of it was built by order of Empress Maria Theresa and Emperor Maximilian I. Gothic arcades, forerunners of modern malls because they kept shoppers out of the weather, can be found off Herzog Friedrichstrasse.

Innsbruck's treasures

The **Goldenes Dachl** (Golden Roof) is the symbol of Innsbruck. The ornate Gothic balcony, built in 1500 by Maximilian I to commemorate his wedding, was used by the royal couple to watch armor-clad knights jousting below. The regal balcony has sculpted crests and heroic wall paintings. A roof made of 2,657 gold-plated tiles tops the balcony.

Next to the Golden Roof is the **Goldener Adler** (Golden Eagle Inn), the oldest hostelry in the city. Andreas Hofer, the leader of the Tyrolean uprising against Napoleon, gathered his small and poorly armed troop of volunteers here. His troops, despite their poverty, managed to defeat the well-equipped French and Bavarian armies in three battles.

Hofkirche (the court church), on the Renweg, is known as the Tyrolean Westminster Abbey. It was commissioned by Emperor Ferdinand I as a cenotaph dedicated to his grandfather Maximilian I (who was buried at Wiener Neustadt). Built from 1553 to 1563, it contains a white marble tomb with a monumental bronze statue of the kneeling Maximilian on top. Standing vigil are 28 enormous bronze statues of royal figures. It also contains the tomb of Andreas Hofer.

Across the Inn River is the **Hungerburgbahn** (a funicular) that will carry you to the peaks with the best views of Innsbruck. It crosses the Inn and ascends the mountainside to Hungerburg, a lofty section of the city. An aerial tram continues from here to Seegrube and Hafelaker, affording breathtaking overlooks on the Nordkette.

Downhill from here is the **Alpine Zoo**, which contains species already extinct in the Eastern Alps, as well as rare animals and birds seen only by hunters in the high mountains. Wildcats, wolves, bears, bison, otters, beavers, griffons, vultures, owls, and eagles are kept in surroundings as similar as possible to their natural habitats. The zoo is open from 9 a.m. to 6 p.m. You can get here from Innsbruck via Bus Z.

The best way to explore the mountains

Club Innsbruck arranges daily hikes and ski trips in the mountains outside Innsbruck. You don't have to be a member; you get a Club Innsbruck card when you register at a hotel in town for at least three nights. Sign up for club Innsbruck's programs at information centers or at your hotel before 4 p.m. the day before you plan to participate.

From June to September, the club offers daily guided hikes, with a free loan of hiking boots and a rucksack. Bus transportation to the starting point of each day's tour and back from the end point is free, as are the services of experienced, licensed guides.

During the winter, the club provides free ski buses to the five main ski areas surrounding Innsbruck and a daily cross-country ski bus. Winter hiking trips with guides are scheduled Monday through Friday. If you would rather hike on your own, pick up the map called *Innsbruck and Umgebung*. Many of the best trails start at Hungerburg. The blue trails can be followed in good walking shoes, but don't try the red ones without sturdy climbing boots.

Innsbruck's finest inn

The 600-year-old **Goldener Adler** *tel. (43)512-586-350*, set in the heart of Old Town, is said to be the best inn in Innsbruck. Request a room with antique trappings.

THE BEST OF SALZBURG

Mozart's birthplace, dominated by a 12th-century fortress called the Hohensalzburg, is a baroque city surrounded by mountains. The Salzach River divides **Salzburg** into two worlds. On the left bank are narrow streets and ancient buildings that date back to the 13th to 15th centuries. The right bank is a modern city in the shadows of the Kapuzinerberg Mountain.

The Salzburg music festival

The **Salzburg Festival** is the world's leading and most famous festival. This is a perfect time to visit this musically based town. The festival is held from late July to August. Advance ticket sales normally end by January. For more information contact the **Austrian National Tourist Office**, *tel. (212) 944-6880; website: www.austria-tourism.at* or the **Ticket Office of the Salzburg Festival**, *Festspielhaus, A-5010 Salzburg, Austria*. You can also reserve tickets through a travel agent in the United States.

The old quarter

The best place to begin your exploration of Salzburg is in the **old quarter**. In the shadows of the castle, it is a maze of winding old streets with little shops, medieval wrought-iron signs, and fountains. Explore on foot — cars are banned here.

The main thoroughfare, Getreidegasse, leads into **Judengasse**, once the Jewish ghetto. Today, it is a picturesque neighborhood with five- and six-story houses. Continue on to the **Alter Markt** (Market Square), where flower stalls scent the air and a 16th-century fountain splashes.

The top sights of Salzburg

Mozart was born at *Getreidegasse 9* in 1756 and he lived here for his first 16 years. Early editions of his works (he began composing when he was five) and models of sets of his most famous operas are on display at the house, which is open every day. (The house where Mozart lived from 1773 to 1787 is on the other side of the river at Makatplatz 8, but it is only open in the summer.)

The **Dom** (cathedral), with its two towers, marble façade, and massive bronze doors, is also in the old quarter. Look for its blue terracotta dome. Consecrated in 1628, the early baroque structure was modeled on St. Peter's in Rome.

Across from the cathedral is the **Residenz**, a series of buildings that once comprised the palace of the prince-archbishops. On the first floor are 15 staterooms decorated with frescoes and paintings. A gallery of European paintings from the 16th through 19th centuries on the second floor contains works by Rembrandt, Rubens, and Breughel.

The **Glockenspiel**, in front of the Residenz, is a 35-bell carillon constructed in the 18th century. The bells are played every day at 6 a.m., 11 a.m., and 7 p.m.

The magnificent **Mirabell Palace**, with its elaborate formal gardens, is on the other side of the river. Built in 1606 by Archbishop Wolf Dietrick for his mistress (and the mother of his 12 children), it is known for its grand ceremonial staircase, which is decorated with marble angels, and its Marble Hall. The gardens are filled with statues, pools, and flowers of every shade and variety. Candlelight chamber music concerts are held here.

Guarding Salzburg from a great rock 400 feet above the city is the **Hohensalzburg**, a fortress built between 1077 and 1681. This stronghold of the bishops of Salzburg is filled with Gothic woodcarving, coffered ceilings, and intricate ironwork. To get to the fortress, which offers the best view of the city, walk or take the funicular from Festungsgasse, near St. Peter's Churchyard. Tours of the castle are scheduled every 15 minutes.

Outside Salzburg is the 17th-century **Hellbrunn** Palace, built by the archbishop and prankster Markus Sittikus, who used hidden nozzles in the benches, walls, sculptures, floors, and ceilings to spray unwary guests. The palace is open to the public everyday from April through October.

The best eating in Salzburg

The two best restaurants in the Salzburg area are **Weisses Kreuz**, *tel. (43)662-845-641* and **Eschlböck-Plomberg**, *tel. (43)662-31660*, five miles northeast of Salzburg in Mondsee. Weisses Kreuz offers garden dining. It is closed every Tuesday and for two weeks in February.

Eschlböck-Plomberg is located on a beach and it also serves meals on the terrace. It is closed Monday during the winter.

Stiftskellar Sankt Peter, *tel. (43-662)841268*, is located near the cathedral. It is a 16th-century wine cellar that serves wines from its own vineyards. The restaurant is divided into eight rooms, which serve traditional Austrian dishes at a reasonable price.

Salzburg's best affordable hotels

Hotel Schone Aussicht, *tel. (43)662-6406-080*, is a chalet hotel on the hill with a view of Salzburg and the Alps. It has a pool, tennis courts, a sunny terrace, and a cozy, beamed bar. Some of the rooms have balconies. Service is friendly and fresh flowers decorate the rooms. However, the walk from the bus stop is up three steep hills, so it's best to have a car if you stay here.

Hotel Kaserbrau, *tel. (43)662-842-445*, is a small hotel nestled in the shadows of the Hohensalzburg. The building dates back to 1342, and some of the rooms have been furnished in baroque style. Others are furnished in pinewood.

Hotel Elefant, *tel. (43)662-843-397*, is a medieval townhouse in the historic heart of Salzburg. The tall, narrow building is on a quiet pedestrian street five minutes from the opera house. The public rooms have inlaid furniture and old paintings. The floors on the first floor are marble, and the rooms are decorated with antiques. The upper floors are less elegant; some of the rooms are small and plain. About half have private baths.

Salzburg's castle hotels

Gastschloss Monchstein, *tel. (43)662-848-5550*, is a many-tiered, ivy-covered castle on a mountaintop above Salzburg. Once a guesthouse for archbishops, it became a retreat for scholars from the University of Salzburg in 1654. Today it is a hotel. You can take an elevator to the castle from the streets below. The hotel is open May through January.

Schloss Haunsperg, *tel. (43)6245-2662*, is a 14th-century castle hotel just south of Salzburg. The spacious rooms are furnished with antiques, and guests can use the tennis courts on the grounds. The castle is near the Autobahn that runs south from Salzburg past the airport; exit at Hallein and follow the signs to Oberalm and the castle.

The best hotel outside Salzburg

Just east of Salzburg is the **Simony Hotel**, *tel. (43)6134-231*, where you can get a true feel for old Austria. The rooms look out over a lake, and the cuisine at the hotel restaurant is marvelous.

The world's best salt mines

The salt mine at **Hallein**, located 10 miles south of Salzburg, is a bit like a roller coaster. To get around inside the tunnels, you slide down a series of long wooden chutes at 40 miles per hour. To visit, you must put on a special uniform, which consists of baggy white overalls with a white hood and a leather backside.

The mine contains sketches of the 1,000-year-old body of a man found in 1666 perfectly preserved in salt. And at midlevel is a salt lake, which, during the off-season, you can raft across to see a cathedral-like cavern 270 feet long and 150 feet wide.

Europe's best tobogganing

Don't leave Austria before you visit the Lake District, an area about 30 minutes east of Salzburg. In the winter, Austria's 200 lakes are covered with ice skaters, and the surrounding mountains with skiers. In the summer, these lakes are filled with sailboats. (Motorboats are not allowed.)

The area around **Wolfgangsee** is especially popular. You can't really explore the Lake District without a car. If you don't have a rental car, join a tour. If you're lucky, your guide will introduce you to the little-known sport of mountain tobogganing. To participate, you pick up a metal, saucerlike toboggan and then take a chair lift to the top of the mountain, carrying the toboggan with you. At the top, place the toboggan on the metal track that curves its way down to the bottom, sit cross-legged on the toboggan, and push off. It is like riding a roller coaster, only better because you can go as fast or slow as you want. (A stick in the front acts like a break.) It takes about five minutes to get to the bottom.

After the trip down the mountain, drive to **St. Gilgen**, a small resort town near Lake Wolfgang. It is a favorite spot among the people of Salzburg, who come here for weekend getaways. St. Gilgen is a small place with only a few restaurants and small shops—but that is as it should be. The charm of this lakeside village would be lost if someone built condominiums here.

If planning to spend time at Wolfgansee, find a room in one of the inns situated on the side of the mountain overlooking the lake. Ask when you arrive in the area; a local should be able to point the way to a good one.

Austria's strangest tradition

The men of the little town of **Landeck** climb to the top of the rocky crags that loom above Landeck and light huge bonfires that can be seen for miles. Then they set fire to circles of wood dipped in tar, roll them down the hill, and then ski downhill, racing the fiery disks at insane speeds.

The highest waterfall in Europe

Krimml Waterfall splashes down 1,250 feet through the mountains, 30 miles east of Innsbruck. You know when the fall is close; it fills the valley with mist.

Kitzbühel, the prettiest ski town

A treasure of a ski village is **Kitzbühel**, a friendly, uncrowded town with slopes for skiers of all experience and enough activity to keep even snow haters happy. This is the place to go to avoid irritating crowds and the ridiculously high prices often found in the Alps. It has well-groomed slopes, a casino, and plenty of nightlife.

Kitzbühel is worth visiting even if you don't ski. An ancient walled town, it has crooked, narrow streets and Tyrolean architecture, with gabled stone-and-stucco houses that date back to the Middle Ages.

The skiable part of the Kitzbühel Alps reaches as high as 7,750 feet. The greatest vertical drop here is 4,150 feet. These heights may seem small compared with those at other Alpine resorts; however, the smooth pastures of these mountains require less snow for good skiing than the rockier slopes of other ski areas. And the weather is milder than in other areas. Kitzbühel's 60 ski lifts and trails provide an overwhelming choice of trails, all accessible by a single ski pass called the Kitzbühel Ski Circus.

THE BEST OF BRITAIN

THE WAY TO ENSURE SUMMER IN ENGLAND IS TO HAVE IT FRAMED
AND GLAZED IN A COMFORTABLE ROOM.

—*Horace Walpole, 1774*

Britain is a land of perfectionism. Shirts must be made with precision. Suits are of good English wool. Tea must be made just so. And politeness is practically law.

The land itself is a place of wonders—mighty castles, charming villages with thatched cottages, ancient cathedrals, pre-historic stone circles, misty lakes, and dramatic shorelines.

Although hundreds of regions throughout Britain demand a visit, the number-one destination is London. Here, many of the world's most famous playwrights and artists blossomed; history's most bloody and fascinating tales unfolded; and the outcome of World War II was sealed. We begin our look at the best of Britain, then, in this remarkable city.

⭐ LONDON, THE MOST MEMORABLE CITY

"What has made London the most poignantly memorable city of the world is its continuing ability to recognize the human condition," writer Richard Condon once said. "From Battersea to Woolwich, across the 32 boroughs of the city, humans reign in perpetual celebration of one of the most complex multilayered communities on the planet… Quirky, steeped in the past but actively and civilly pursuing the present, London—and Londoners—continue to honor all that is human. And 1,250 years after its founding, visitors are still drawn to the city's idiosyncrasies—all those facets that endure and enrich life."

Top sights in London

Big Ben, the most famous sight in London, is usually misidentified. Many people believe, incorrectly, that Big Ben is the clock in the Parliament tower; it is actually the 13-and-a-half-ton bell.

The home of **Parliament**, beneath Big Ben, is a huge complex of Victorian buildings that covers eight acres and includes 1,100 rooms. The guided tour is said to be definitely worth your time.

Westminster Hall, built from 1394 to 1402, is a part of the palace. Admission is free, but donations are accepted. The donations go toward restoration funds.

English kings and queens begin and end their careers at **Westminster Abbey**, where royal coronations and burials have been held since the time of William the Conqueror. **Poets' Corner** in the south transept contains the tombs of Geoffrey Chaucer, Charles Dickens, Robert Browning, and Thomas Hardy.

The **Tate Gallery** has the best collection of works by British painters, including Turner, Blake, Hogarth, and Constable. It also contains works by French Impressionists Manet, Monet, Cézanne, and Degas, as well as sculptures by Rodin, Picasso, and Henry Moore. The gallery is located on Millbank Street, near Pimlico underground station.

Whitehall, where fiery King Henry VIII once had his palace, is now an efficient, modern-day government center that runs between the Thames River and St. James' Park. **Number 10 Downing Street**, where the prime minister lives, is part of Whitehall. The War Rooms at 70 Whitehall served as Churchill's subterranean headquarters during World War II. The rooms are open to the public from 10 a.m. until 5 p.m.

The **Banqueting House** in Whitehall is where Charles I was beheaded. Today the building is used for government receptions. Rubens decorated the house with nine allegorical ceiling paintings. A bust of Charles I on the staircase marks the position of the window the king walked through to get to the scaffolding where he was beheaded.

Surrounded by four regal lions, the mighty **Nelson Column** rises from the heart of Trafalgar Square, a monument to Admiral Nelson. (Nelson died in battle with the French off Cape Trafalgar. Here, he spurred his men on to victory with the inspiring words "England expects every man to do his duty.")

Concerts are held Sundays at noon in the templelike **St.-Martin-in-the-Fields** (1721-1726), also on the square. Nearby is the **National Gallery**, with works by Vermeer, Turner, Botticelli, Michelangelo, Holbein, El Greco, and Delacroix. Take a look at the gallery's controversial annex.

Europe's largest medieval fortress

The **Tower of London**, the largest medieval fortress, has witnessed foul deeds and grand spectacles. Inside the fortress, on Tower Green, innumerable heads rolled, including those of Anne Boleyn, Lady Jane Grey, Sir Walter Raleigh, and the Earl of Essex, Queen Elizabeth I's rejected lover. In the Bloody Tower, as it is known, Richard III supposedly murdered 13-year-old King Edward V and the king's little brother.

The **Crown Jewels** are kept in the Tower of London. The Cullinan diamond here is the largest ever found. It was sent to London from Transvaal in a brown paper package via third-class mail.

London's oldest church

Any visit to the Tower of London should include a visit to the **Chapel of St. John**. The chapel was built in 1080, making it the oldest church in London.

The most famous sea clipper

The **Cutty Sark**, the most famous sea clipper ever built, rests on the waterfront in Greenwich. Built in 1869, it was one of the few sailing ships to survive despite the dawn of the steam age. Rescued from oblivion and restored, the *Cutty Sark* houses an interesting collection of figureheads and full-scale cabin relics. It is open Monday through Saturday from 10:30 a.m. to 6 p.m. and Sunday 2.30 p.m. to 6 p.m.

London's best post office

The **Trafalgar Square Post Office**, *tel. (44)20-7930-9580*, is London's best—and it's also open the latest. It is open until 8 p.m. Monday through Saturday, and Sunday until 5 p.m.

The worst place to tell secrets

St. Paul's cathedral has a **Whispering Gallery** where you can hear a word whispered on the other side of the dome as loudly as if the person was standing right beside you. Prince Charles and Lady Diana were married here.

The best changing of the guard

The best changing of the guard in London isn't at Buckingham Palace, as you might expect. It is in the middle of **Whitehall**, where the red-suited Horse Guards are stationed. The changing of the guard here is as picturesque as at Buckingham Palace and a good deal less crowded. (Tourists visit Buckingham Palace by the millions.)

The best place for repartee

The best entertainment in London is a session at the **House of Commons**, on Parliament Square, where insults are exchanged freely and with wild abandon. Florence Horsbrugh, once minister of education, suffered the following insult: "I do not know what the Right Honorable Lady, the Minister of Education, is grinning at. This is the face that sank a thousand scholarships." And Winston Churchill, when accused of being drunk by a female political foe, replied, "And you, Madam, are ugly. But tomorrow I shall be sober!"

You can observe these verbal battles from the gallery. The 156 seats are filled on a first-come, first-served basis. You can wait for a spot Monday through Thursday after 4.15 p.m. or Friday after 10 a.m. at the St. Stephen's entrance. (Incidentally, admission to the **House of Lords** is at this same spot.)

London's strangest sight

Cleopatra's Needle is the most surprising monument in London. This Egyptian obelisk dates back to 1500 B.C. Set in the shadow of Waterloo Bridge on the edge of Thames embankment, it bears the carvings of two of Egypt's greatest rulers: pharaohs Thothmes III and Ramses II. Offered to England in the 19th-century by the ruler of Egypt, the obelisk actually had nothing to do with Cleopatra—it was transported down the Nile into the Mediterranean aboard a boat called *Cleopatra*.

When the Needle reached the Bay of Biscay on Oct. 14, 1877, it fell overboard during a storm. Six men volunteered to recover the monument and drowned trying to save it. (Their names are inscribed on the south face of the base.) Several days later, the monument was rescued by a freighter that lugged it to London.

The world's spookiest walks

As the night sets in and the long shadows fall, travel into the crooked, cobbled alleyways of Whitechapel to follow Jack the Ripper's bloodstained trail of terror. The **Jack the Ripper Haunts Walk** takes place every night at 7.30 p.m. and lasts about two hours. Meet the guide outside Tower Hill Underground station. No need to reserve in advance; the cost is $7.90 ($6.30 for students). Website: *http://london.walks.com*.

London's liveliest corner

Piccadilly Circus is as crazy and colorful as its name. Crowded with people and filled with brightly colored billboards, the square is centered around a small statue of Eros and known as a pickup spot and favorite spot for pickpockets. But don't worry about the criminal elements—Piccadilly is also crowded with ordinary citizens and tourists and is perfectly safe.

Piccadilly is also where you'll find the **Royal Academy of Fine Arts**, the **Ritz**, and **St. James' Church**, which offers concerts during the summer.

The artiest neighborhoods

Covent Garden, where professor Higgins met Eliza Doolittle in *My Fair Lady*, has become the city's favorite hangout for yuppies. It's home to the London Transport Museum, the Theatre Museum, the Theatre Royal and Royal Opera House, and a crafts market. The area is used as an impromptu stage for clowns, mimes, musicians, and other entertainers, who perform and then pass the hat.

Bloomsbury was once the home of the literary and intellectual "Bloomsbury Group," which included Virginia Woolf, John Maynard

Keynes, and E.M. Forster. This charming area offers the British Museum, the Courtland Institute Galleries, and Pollock's Toy Museum.

Soho is home to London's red-light district, but it's also lined with little restaurants and shops. Like Piccadilly, its criminal element is pretty harmless, because there are always so many people around. The square, which is home to nightclubs and London's biggest cinemas, is being renovated.

Soho's **Berwick Street** has a great produce market. **Leicester Square** was the home of painters Hogarth and Reynolds. **Hampstead** is a writers' and artists' quarter on a hill overlooking the city. Here you can rummage in antique stores and bookshops before enjoying afternoon tea in a café in the area. Visit **Keats'** home on Wentworth Place and **Freud's** home at 20 Maresfield Gardens.

London's most romantic park

The most romantic park in central London is off Guilford Street in Bloomsbury. But it has a strange restriction—no adult, a sign by the gate announces, may enter unless accompanied by a child. **Coram's Fields** is six acres of playground on the site of the Foundling Hospital for abandoned children, set up by Captain Thomas Coram more than 250 years ago.

The best place to rant and rave

Amateur orators spout forth at **Speakers Corner** in Hyde Park every Sunday. If you feel the urge to speak from a soapbox, this is the place. If you'd rather just listen, be prepared. You never know what you might hear—anarchists, religious zealots, racists, communists, or vegetarians!

Hyde Park is worth a visit even if you aren't interested in all the ranting and raving. On a pretty day, you can go boating in the park or just take a long stroll.

The world's best waxworks

Madame Tussaud's, *tel. (44)207-935-6861*, located on Marylebone Road, is just about as touristy as you can get in London, but if you like waxworks, these are the best in the world. Madame Tussaud began her museum in Paris in the late 18th century, but revolutionary events drove her to London in 1802. The Chamber of Horrors is still the most interesting section of all, but rock stars, politicians, sports personalities, and royalty are certainly equally well-presented.

The world's best theater

London is the world's theater capital. Most of the major theaters are in the West End, a short walk from Trafalgar Square, in Covent Garden, or in Leicester Square. Notable exceptions are the National Theatre complex on the South Bank, next to the Royal Festival Hall, and the splendid

Barbican Centre for the Arts, permanent London home of the Royal Shakespeare Company.

You can get half-price tickets to major shows at the **Leicester Square Ticket Booth** (right in Leicester Square). Tickets are available for same-day West End shows only and you'll rarely find tickets for recent hits. What is available is posted on the boards next to the booth, but the line is normally long and the tickets go fast, so keep an eye on the board as you wait.

You can also get discounted tickets by going to the theater lobby right before the performance—although you may find yourself running from theater to theater. Last-minute tickets are sometimes also available for sold-out shows, although not at discounted prices. Tickets are always discounted for students with international student identification cards and senior citizens.

The world's best fringe theater

London's so-called fringe theaters are far removed from the neon lights and star-studded marquees of the fashionable West End. Yet, these small (each seats less than 100 people), out-of-the-way theaters offer some of the city's most inspired, innovative, and imaginative theatrical performances.

One of the best-known fringe theaters in London, and for good reason, is the **Albany Empire**, *tel. (44)20-8691-3333*, located on Douglas Way. It offers two plays simultaneously year-round.

The three best ways to spend a Sunday afternoon

Where should a bargain hunter in London head on a Sunday afternoon? The **Bayswater Road Art Exhibition**. From modern art to detailed still lifes, baroque to Romantic, portraits to landscapes, watercolors to oils, copper etchings to pastels—it's all at Bayswater, one of the largest open-air exhibitions in the world. The exhibits stretch for eight-tenths of a mile, beginning at Clarendon Place and continuing until Queensway, and they are open every Sunday, rain or shine, 8 a.m. until 5 p.m. The Queensway and Lancaster Gate Underground stations bring you right to the heart of the area.

The second best place to spend a Sunday afternoon is **Camden Lock**, London's largest, gaudiest, and most unpredictably varied flea market. It's cheap and friendly—and for dedicated "people watchers," it offers a never-ending flow of exotic youth. To get there, take the Northern Line to Camden Town or Chalk Farm.

And the third best way to spend a Sunday is to take a tour of **Little Venice**. You come upon it unexpectedly—it's just a short walk from Warwick Avenue tube station to the little bridge over the canal. Here Regent's Canal meets the Grand Union Canal, forming a wider stretch of water flowing around a tree-covered island. The nickname "Little Venice" was first coined by the famous poet Robert Browning, who once lived nearby. Sycamore trees line the banks of the canals, and the Nash-designed houses, with their distinctive white stucco facades and lawns and gardens sweeping down to the water's edge, boast an 18th-century elegance.

One of the best outfits offering tours to Little Venice is **Jason's Trip**, *tel. (44)207-286-3428*. Another good tour company is **Waterbus Company**, which departs hourly from the intersection where Grand Union Canal and Regent's Canal cross. The Waterbus Company lands at the zoo; it offers a reduced ticket price—and none of the waiting lines found at the main gate. Both tours pass Browning's Island, Regents Park, the zoo, the Maida Hill tunnel, and Camden Locks.

London's best flea market

Petticoat Lane Flea Market, held Sundays in Middlesex Street, is brimming with bargains. The lively outdoor market has antiques as well as inexpensive new goods (especially clothing and appliances), bric-a-brac, and used items. The real bargains are found before 8 a.m. Take the underground to Liverpool Street and then walk up Bishop's Gate to Middlesex Street. (You won't find Petticoat Lane on the map; it's a nickname for Middlesex Street.)

The most entertaining flea market

One of the largest and most entertaining flea markets in Europe is held every Sunday on **Portobello Road**. To get there, take the underground to Notting Hill Gate and then walk down Pembrook Road to Portobello Road. On Saturdays, the road is lined with street performers and part-time vendors selling everything from rock group buttons to antiques. Fine hats and shoes that once bedecked Britain's elite can be found here at pauper's prices. If you aren't interested in buying, just watch the people.

Antique hunting at its best

Since it opened in the late 1960s, **Antiquarius**, *134-141 Kings Road, London SW3*, has been one of the best places in London to shop for antiques. More than 200 stalls offer a splendid array of items from the Georgian, Victorian, Edwardian, and art nouveau periods, including fine jewelry, china glass, books, prints, and antique clocks. This is a wonderful place to get lost for an afternoon.

Camden Passage is another great place for antiques—it has more than 100 shops. Decorative and Victorian antiques are of especially good quality in this corner of London, so don't expect knockdown prices. Take the underground to the Angel Islington stop and then walk up Islington High Street. An early morning flea market is held here Wednesday and Saturday.

Serious antique hunters flock to the **New Caledonian Market** (Bermondsey) at the London bridge underground station. This huge market has quality silver, china, jewelry, memorabilia, and *objets d'art*. It is open Friday 5 a.m. until 1 p.m. Arrive early for the best buys.

The best antiquarian bookdealer

A Mr. Maggs still owns **Maggs Brothers**, *tel. (44)207-493-7160*. This bookdealer specializes in illuminated manuscripts, first editions, and autographed letters of English authors. Many priceless works are in stock, and the bibliophile (with clean hands) is welcome to stop in and see the treasures. For instance, you can inspect one of the original privately printed editions of T.E. Lawrence's (Lawrence of Arabia) Seven Pillars of Wisdom. The lover of fine books will find no worthier shrine.

The best brass rubbing center

The best place for brass rubbing in London is the **London Brass Rubbing Centre** itself, *tel. (44)207-930-9306*. Located in a magnificent 18th-century church, famous for its lunchtime concerts of chamber and choral music, this is one of the few places in London where you can still make your own brass rubbings. The center is open Monday through Saturday 10 a.m. until 6 p.m. and Sunday noon until 6 p.m.

The world's best maze

Hampton Court Palace, *tel. (44)870-752-7777*, (for ticket sales *tel. (44)870-753-7777*), located at East Molesey, Surrey, contains England's oldest and most popular maze. The labyrinth is bounded by high hedges and reinforced with railings to prevent cheating. Arrive by boat from Westminster Pier or by train from the Waterloo station in London (a distance of 10 miles). The palace, which dates from the early 1500s, is open Tuesday through Sunday 9.30 a.m. until 6 p.m. and Monday 10.15 a.m. until 6 p.m. The last entry is at 5.15 p.m.

The best place to go fly a kite

The **Kite Store**, *tel. (44)207-836-1666*, was the first shop of its kind in Europe, and it now stocks more than 200 kinds of kite, as well as boomerangs and Frisbees. Once you've purchased your kite, the best place to fly it is on Hampstead Heath, which offers a tremendous view of the city below.

The most magical toy store

Hamley's, *188-196 Regent Street; tel. (44)870-333-2455; website: www.hamleys.com*, is packed with every imaginable form of entertainment for both children and adults. The store is open Monday through Friday 10 a.m. to 8 p.m., Saturday 9.30 a.m. to 8 p.m., and Sunday noon to 6 p.m.

London's oldest cheese store

Paxton & Whitfield, *93 Jermyn Street*, is the oldest and best cheese store in London; it came to Jermyn Street in 1797. With more than 300 European cheeses (including 40 to 50 British varieties), Paxton & Whitfield assuredly will have the kind you are looking for. (The cheeses are stocked not according to price but according to tradition.) There's absolutely no risk of buying an off-brand wheel of Brie, for instance. The counters are also stacked with preserves, pickles, and fine wines.

The best stuffed shirts

The stuffed shirts of the world know the best shirt shopping is along Jermyn Street in London. Here, traditional shirts are made of Sea Island cotton or two-fold poplin. The collars are perfectly shaped and stitched, as are the cuffs. The buttons are mother-of-pearl. The cut is generous, and the shirttails are long.

Hildich & Key, *87 Jermyn Street*, produces the finest and most expensive shirts in London. Made of soft cotton, they have hand-sewn buttonholes, removable collar stays, and double cuffs.

Turnbull & Asser, *71 and 72 Jermyn Street*, has shirts with collars roomy enough for T&A's generous ties. And the cut of the shirts makes them extra comfortable.

The finest linens in the world

Despite its tiny interior, the **Irish Linen Company**, *35-36 Burlington Arcade; tel. (44)207-493-8949*, has a beautiful selection of some of the finest handworked linens you can find anywhere. Price-conscious shoppers will be most interested in the decorative tablecloths and napkins.

London's best tailor

Stovel & Mason, *32 Old Burlington Street*, is a London tailor who offers Saville Row quality at more moderate prices. (Always have suspenders or brace buttons attached to the inside of your pants, and insist on 13-inch-deep pockets and jacked cuffs that unbutton.)

London's finest shoemakers

The three best shoemakers in London are **Lobbs**, *9 St. James Place, London SW1* (the waiting list is long); **Wildsmith**, *Prince's Arcade, Piccadilly*, which makes the best old-fashioned shoes in London; and **Tricker's**, *67 Jermyn Street*.

The best brollies

Swaine & Adney in Piccadilly makes umbrellas by hand. The very best brolly (a favorite in the House of Lords) is a Brigg.

The city's best lace market

Nottingham holds the best lace market at Sneinton. The market is open Monday, Wednesday, Friday, and Saturday 10 a.m. until 4 p.m. To learn about the history of lace or to see demonstrations about how lace is made, visit **Lace Hall**, *High Pavement*, or **Severn's Building**, *Council Road*. Both are open daily 10 a.m. until 5 p.m.

The best ways to explore London

Walking is the best way to see the city if you don't have money to blow on a private guide. And on foot, you can see London in greater detail and mingle with the British. You can make your own way through the city using a guidebook and map, or you can join one of London's many walking tours. One of the best is offered by **And Did Those Feet...** (formerly Citisights of London), which offers history and archeology walks of Roman, Saxon, and medieval London. The two-hour tours are led by professional archeologists.

London Walks, *tel. (44)207-624-3978*, takes you in the footsteps of Jack the Ripper, Shakespeare, Dickens, Virginia Woolf, and other notables.

If your feet get tired, rest a while on a double-decker bus or London's famous subway, known as the tube or the underground. The underground is the world's oldest and most extensive rapid transit system, with more than 250 stations and 750 miles of track.

Fares are set according to the length of your ride. On buses, you can pay the conductor, but you must buy an underground ticket before you get on the train. And make sure you don't throw away your ticket—you'll need it to leave the station at the other end of your journey.

A **London Travelcard** ticket allows you unlimited travel on the London bus and tube systems. It is available from travel agents, at any subway station, and at the London Regional Transport Travel Information Centre.

Tour buses depart Victoria Station and Piccadilly Circus daily at 9:30 a.m., 11:00 a.m., and 2:30 p.m.

London double-decker bus tours also are available, *tel. (44)207-222-1234*. The open-topped buses depart Piccadilly Circus, Victoria Station, and Marble Arch daily 9 a.m. until 4 p.m. The tours last about two hours and 20 minutes. A free map is included. Reservations aren't necessary.

The best places to take tea

In a city known for its tea, a few places stand scones and Devonshire cream above the rest. The most elegant place to enjoy a pot of hot tea with scones is the **Dorchester Hotel** on Park Lane.

The coziest place for tea would be **Brown's**, a Victorian Hotel on Dover Street. Rudyard Kipling once stayed here. Men must wear a tie to take tea at Brown's after 4 p.m. (And they should take a moment to glance into the men's room before they leave; the scale is an extremely rare antique.)

Another good place to take tea is the department store **Fortnum and Mason**, *181 Piccadilly, London W1*. If the fashionable Fountain Room is too crowded, go upstairs to the more discreet St. James Restaurant—few people know about it.

A quiet, modest place to have tea, especially if you are shopping, is **Liberty's** on Regent Street. Of the two restaurants here, the one upstairs is the prettiest.

The best restaurants in London

The **Grill Room** at the **Connaught Hotel**, *16 Carlos Place, London W1Y 6AL; tel. (44)207-499 7070*, is the best restaurant in London. This elegant establishment serves traditional French and English food to cabinet ministers and art dealers. As an hors d'oeuvre, try the mouth-watering *croustade d'oeufs de caille Maintenon* (quails' egg yolks in a pastry boat). Also try the seafood with shrimp and lobster in a wine sauce. Order coffee following your dinner—it comes with sugar-glazed grapes and strawberries dipped in chocolate. Opening hours are Tuesday through Friday from 12:30 p.m. to 2:30 p.m. and 6 p.m. to 10:45 p.m., Saturday 6 p.m. to 10:45 p.m.

Mr. Frascati Italian restaurant, *Spring Street* (near the Paddington Rail and Tube Station), is a courtly bit of Italy in the heart of London. Chef Nino Di Fonzio and co-owner Maurizio Del Guidice bought the restaurant after working there as manager and head chef for 10 years. Try the Italian wild mushrooms sautéed in fresh tomato, garlic, wine, and parsley, or thinly sliced beef filets flavored with olive oil, anchovies, capers, and gherkins, and topped with parmesan cheese. All pastas are home made. Mr. Frascati stays open later than most London restaurants and is open until 10:30 p.m. on Sunday nights.

The best service in London

The **Terrace Restaurant** at the **Dorchester Hotel**, *53 Park Lane, London W1; tel. (44)207-629-8888*, has one staff member for every two guests. This marble-columned, elegantly lit institution serves exquisite nouvelle cuisine, served in a series of leisurely courses.

The best roast beef in London

At **Simpson's in the Strand**, *100 Strand; tel. (44)207-836-9112*, a maître d'hôtel dressed in tails ushers diners into the paneled dining room. Six 30-pound four-rib loins are roasted simultaneously. Roast beef and saddles of mutton are wheeled directly to guests' tables and carved there. The cattle are chosen by Simpson's agents at auctions in Scotland. The Duke of Wellington and Margaret Thatcher are said to prefer Simpson's.

The best kosher eateries

One of the best ethnic restaurants in London is **Reuben's**, *20 Baker Street; tel. (44)207-935-5945*, a kosher eatery. Reuben's serves food in the Anglo-Continental style, although it does offer a wide variety of traditional foods as well.

Another good kosher eatery is **Bloom's**, *90 White Chapel High Street; tel. (44)207-247-6001*.

The best Indian food

Bombay Brasserie, *140 Gloucester Road*, next to **Bailey's Hotel**, *Courtfield Close*, is the best of the upscale Indian restaurants in London. Especially good are the Goan fish curry, the aromatic chicken dishes, and the bean curries.

A more economical choice is the **Diwana Delicatessen**, *114 Drummond Street, NW1*. This restaurant is open daily noon until 10 p.m. but is closed Mondays.

The best Southeast Asian restaurant

The small, comfortable room at **Nam Long**, *40 Frith Street, London W1*, features Vietnamese specialties. Although the décor is unremarkable from the outside, inside the elegant wallpaper and tile floor convey a feeling of well-being. The food is well prepared, and the sizzling dishes are served in containers set in varnished wood. The service is attentive.

London's best nightlife

One of the trendiest of London's wine bars is **Ebury Wine Bar**, *139 Ebury Street, Belgravia*.

If you'd prefer something rowdier, **Brahms and Liszt**, *19 Russell Street*, is the best place for a rip-roaring good time. (*Liszt* is Cockney slang for *pissed*, meaning drunk.)

The funniest place in London

The Comedy Store, *1a Oxendon Street; tel. (44)207-930-2949* hosts a great mixture of talent; it is said that the cream of the crop of stand-up London comedians have performed here and still do. Tickets can be purchased through Ticketmaster, *website: www.ticketmaster.com*, or *tel. (44)207-344-0234*.

London's best pub

London's heart is in its pubs. They are located on nearly every street corner and are an integral part of British life. Each has its own inimitable character.

Choosing London's best pub is a big task—everyone has his or her own favorite. Our favorite is **Anchor Tavern**, *34 Park Street, Southwark, tel.*

(44)207-407-1577, on the south side of the Thames. This cozy riverside pub was once frequented by writer Samuel Johnson, as well as smugglers, rivermen, and wardens from the nearby Clink Prison. (The slang word for prison comes from the Clink.)

The Anchor Tavern originally was built near the site of Shakespeare's Globe Theater; it was rebuilt about 170 years ago. The low-beamed rooms are many and varied.

Legend has it that a special brew known as Russian Imperial Stout was prepared at the pub for the empress of Russia. Besides beer, try the roast forerib of beef or the steak and mushroom pudding. The Anchor is open noon until 2 p.m. and 7 p.m. until 10 p.m. It is closed Sunday evenings.

The Flask, *77 Highgate West, Hampstead*, is our second choice for a best pub in London. (You couldn't expect us to pick just one.) The Flask is tremendously popular among Londoners, primarily because of its friendly atmosphere.

London's best live storytelling

The best live storytelling and poetry reading events in London are organized by **ABC Tales**, *tel. (44)207-209-2605; website: www.abctales.com*, to showcase new writers and performers before live audiences. You can even perform yourself. Admission is $8.50. The quality of the writing and performing is high—at least as good as anything you'll find in the West End.

The best hotels in London

The **Connaught Hotel**, *16 Carlos Place, London W1Y 6AL; tel. (44)20-7499-7070; website: www.savoy-group.co.uk*, is the best in town, with old-fashioned elegance and perfect service. The exterior of the Connaught is elegant, with a gracefully curving façade. Flowers brighten the porch. The interior is cozy, with wood paneling, Oriental rugs, and upholstered chairs.

A magnificent staircase with dark wood banisters leads to bedrooms on the upper floors. The spacious rooms have cheery wallpaper, brass beds, and antique desks. And the bathrooms are luxurious, with grand tubs, fine soaps, thick towels, and a cord ring for the maid. Breakfast, including fresh orange juice, is brought to your room on a cloth-covered table and served in fine china. Write to request a room on the Carlos Place side. Book dinner reservations six weeks in advance. **Claridge's**, *Brook Street, London W1A 2JQ, tel. (44)20-7629-8860; website: www.claridges.co.uk*, in the heart of Mayfair, is a close second to the Connaught Hotel. It boasts a Hungarian Quartet that has been playing in the lobby for most of this century. Liveried attendants greet you at the door, and dress-maids are available to help you choose what you'd like to wear for the evening. Rooms have fireplaces, bells to ring for the maid or valet, and royal-sized bathtubs.

The **Beaufort**, *33 Beaufort Gardens, London SW3; tel. (44)207-584-5252*, is an early Victorian house converted to an elegant guest residence in 1985. Each room is decorated in a different style, but all have telephones and color televisions. It's like staying in someone's home—but enjoying the amenities of a luxury hotel, including fluffy robes, wooden and silk hangers, a dish of chocolates, a personal decanter of brandy, and a Sony Walkman.

Last, but not least, is **Brown's**, *19-22 Dover Street, London W1A 4SW; tel. (44)207-493-6020*. The building dates back to 1660; it opened for business as Brown's in 1837. Teddy Roosevelt was married at Brown's, Kipling wrote here, and Queen Victoria visited Queen Wilhelmina here. From 1924 to 1935, it was the official court of the king of Greece. Oak paneling, 19th-century prints, antiques, and stained glass add atmosphere to the 12 connecting buildings that make up Brown's.

The oldest pub in the world

The **George and Vulture** is the oldest pub in the world. The original, called the George, was built in the 12th century. Sir Richard Wittington, the "thrice-round mayor of London," visited here in the 1500s, just as Chaucer (and Chaucer's father) had done earlier. Daniel Defoe, Jonathan Swift, and Charles Dickens were frequent customers at this historic pub.

The Pickwick Club meets at the George and Vulture quarterly, and members quote from the many Dickens passages about the place. The fictional Mr. Pickwick, when asked where he spent his leisure time, replied that he was "at present suspended at the George and Vulture." A framed check written by Dickens to the proprietor hangs on the wall.

Other historic pubs

Ye Olde Cheshire Cheese was opened in 1538 and rebuilt in 1667 after the Great Fire of London. The Cheese was a favorite of Goldsmith and Johnson and was mentioned by Dickens in A Tale of Two Cities. It is one of London's few remaining 17th-century chophouses.

The Cheese has sawdust on the floors (changed twice daily), and tables are boxed in, with a bench for three diners on each side. An open fire cheers the original bar in winter, which, until recently, was reserved for men only. Try the savory baked cheese and Guinness on toast, the steak and kidney pie, and the Yorkshire pudding.

One of the oldest riverfront pubs, the **Prospect of Whitby**, was popular with painters Whistler and Turner. While drinking here, Hanging Judge Jeffreys watched his sentences being carried out at nearby Execution Dock.

The **Trafalgar** is located on the Thames at the place where time begins—Greenwich mean time, that is. The Greenwich observatory and maritime museum are also located here. The food is good but expensive. The view is superb—and free. Take a ferry from Tower Bridge to Greenwich.

Britain's smallest pub

The **Nutshell Pub**, *Bury St., Suffolk* is the smallest pub in Britain, holding up to six people. The rest of the customers have to take their chances with the weather and drink outside. There is also a genuine mummified cat hanging from the ceiling—a lost relic from the days of witch burning.

The best hotels for the money

11 Cadogan Gardens, *Sloane Square, London; tel. (44)207-730-3426*, near the intersection of Sloane Square and Draycott Place, is so popular that you must book a room months in advance. Bookings from travel agents are not accepted. This Victorian hotel is filled with mahogany and silver. A butler serves breakfast and tea.

Ebury Court, *26 Ebury Street, London SW1*, is quaint, with white wood-work and chintz curtains. It has a steady British and American clientele.

The **Cranley Place Hotel**, *1 Cranley Place, South Kensington, London SW7*, is in a Regency-style house near Harrods. Bedrooms are decorated Laura Ashley-style and furnished with antiques. Breakfast can be taken in the dining room or in your hotel room.

The **Wilbraham**, *1 Wilbraham Place, Sloane Street; tel. (44)207-730-8296* feels more like a small country inn than a London hotel. It is a converted Victorian house in Belgravia, near Sloane Square Station.

The **Inverness Court**, *1 Inverness Terrace, London; tel. (44)207-229-1444*, was built for Lily Langtry by Edward VII and truly stands out from countless others in the neighborhood. For a truly royal experience, rent the Langtry Suite, which comes with a four-poster bed and a decadent sunken bath.

The best side trips from London

Most travelers to Britain see little more than London. Yet it's outside London that you see the real England. The easiest way to get to the sights outside London is by rail or bus (or coach, as the British say). London has eight main train stations, each dealing with a different region—so make sure you are leaving from the right station. Each has an information office.

Buses are the least expensive way to take side trips. London has two main bus services: **National Express** and the **Green Line**. The main station for National Express is **Victoria Coach Station** (NOT Victoria Train Station, which is nearby), *Buckingham Palace Road, London SW1*. The main station for the Green Line is **Eccleston Bridge**, just down the street. If you are in a hurry, take a National Express bus. The Green Line makes more stops and is slower. However, the Green Line does have some express buses (called Rapid Buses).

CAMBRIDGE — THE PRETTIEST TOWN

Cambridge is the prettiest of England's two rival university towns. A serene place, Cambridge was originally a Roman crossing over the River Cam. At the time of the Domesday Book (1086), Cambridge was a small trading village. Scholars gathered here in 1209 after being ousted from Oxford by irate townspeople. They opened a series of colleges that eventually became the university. The lovely old city (in Britain, any town with a cathedral is called a city) did not always see eye to eye with the university — riots were staged in 1381. The phrase "town and gown" indicates some of the old animosity.

The most impressive Gothic structure

The magnificent architecture of Cambridge and the beautiful surrounding countryside are good reasons to spend several days here. **King's College Chapel** is one of the most impressive Gothic structures in England. Be sure to see "Evensong" on Sunday, sung by a boys' choir at the chapel.

The best punting

A punt is a kind of boat, and punting is one of the most enjoyable ways to while away a sunny summer's afternoon — drifting under the Bridge of Sighs, the Mathematical Bridge, and down the mile-long stretch of the river Cam known as "The Backs."

The Cam is one of the most glorious of England's waterways and the best views of the colleges are from the river. "The Backs" is so-called because it runs behind many of the university buildings. Plus you'll see things from another angle; the imposing architecture of King's Chapel, the Wren Library at Trinity, and all those dreaming spires. Punts are a quintessential part of the Cambridge experience. Between 9 a.m. and dusk they can be hired for around $18 per hour. **Scudamore's Punting Company**, *tel. (44)1223-359-750*, has stations at Mill Lane (near Queen's College and Laundress Green), Jesus Green, and Magdalene Bridge, and they also offer chauffeured punts of between 45 minutes and two hours duration.

Oxford—the oldest University

Oxford University, with its 34 colleges and thousands of students, draws visitors from around the world. The college's 100 acres includes lawns, gardens, water walks, and a private deer park where the famous Magdalen deer can be spotted. New College, built in the late 14th century, is one of the most inviting colleges on campus, with its medieval cloisters and peaceful gardens. A section of the old city walls can be found here.

While the university was founded in the 12th century, the town itself dates back to A.D. 912. The hero of many Dorothy Sayers mystery stories, Lord Peter Whimsey, studied at Oxford.

Oldest museum in Britain

The oldest public museum in Britain, the **Ashmolean**, is located in Oxford. It has a great collection, including works by French Impressionists and Renaissance artists Raphael and Michelangelo. It also contains historical curios, such as the lantern Guy Fawkes carried when he tried to blow up Parliament in 1605.

The best inn

The **Bear Inn**, *6 Alfred Street, Oxford; tel. (44)1865-728-164*, is the best place to stay in Oxford. The establishment is over seven-centuries-old and has oak beams and low ceilings. Rooms on the upper stories have sloping floors, and the steps are uneven.

The Bear Inn is an important part of Oxford tradition—students meet here to sing university songs and to hold parties. The famous collection of neckties hanging on one wall here includes more than 4,200 ties donated by customers since 1951. Each bears the owner's signature. The collection includes ties from members of rowing clubs, cricket teams, student societies, the police, and the military. The ties are displayed according to nationality.

British silks at their best

A visit to Gloucestershire, just west of Oxford, is a real treat. **Beckford Silk** is a silk mill where you can watch hand-screen printing of fabrics and talk to the printers about their skills.

Just a stone's throw away in the little village of Kemerton, another talented craftsperson also works in silk: **Tilly M**, *Stables Cottage, Kemerton GL20 7AY*, an artist who is eager to chat with visitors about her designs.

The best cheeses—and the craziest sport

In addition to its silks, **Gloucestershire** is also world-famous for its cheeses and for its cheese-rolling rituals. Originally, these rituals were associated with the rites of Midsummer. At one time they were common throughout Gloucestershire and Wiltshire; now they are only kept up in Cooper's Hill and Randwick.

In Randwick, three cheeses play a role in two celebrations. At 10:30 a.m. on the first Sunday in May, the cheeses are taken to the village church, St. John's, for a short service. From there, they are rolled three times around the church, and then one of them is cut up and distributed among the congregation.

The other two cheeses reappear the following Saturday, known as Wap, or Mayor's Day (May 11). Displayed on litters, they occupy a place of honor in a colorful procession that also includes a Wap Queen, a band, and the Wap Mayor, accompanied by his sword-bearer and a sheriff.

The entire procession makes its way to the Mayor's Pool, where the Wap

Queen officially welcomes the Mayor, who is then ceremoniously thrown into the water. After the dunking, the crowd accompanies the Mayor and the Queen to the hill near the village school, where the cheeses are rolled down the slope to open the Wap Fair.

Cheese rolling at Cooper's Hill involves a much steeper slope. The ceremonies here take place on Spring Bank Holiday (May 27). Races are staged at half-hour intervals, beginning at 6 p.m. For each race, six to 10 runners line up at the top of the hill, set their cheeses, (usually seven-pound Double Gloucesters) rolling downhill, and then take off after them in hot pursuit. The cheeses have been known to pick up such speed on their way down the hill that they have bounded right over the roof of the house at the bottom. The winner of the race keeps his cheese.

The best ecclesiastical maze

Grey's Court, near Henley-on-Thames in Oxfordshire, has the best example of an ecclesiastical maze in all England. Based on an ancient pagan design, it is formed by brick paths running through turf. At its center are two crosses—one Roman, one Byzantine. Made to celebrate the enthronement of the present Archbishop of Canterbury in 1982, the maze is said to represent the path of life and to symbolize pilgrimage.

The best racetrack in England

Known as the horse racing capital of the world, **Newmarket** is renowned not only for its racetrack—with some of the best flat racing to be found anywhere—but also for its many training establishments and stud farms close by. It's a charming little town just 60 miles (about two hours drive) from London and is a must for anyone interested in horses and racing.

Newmarket has two courses: the Rowley Mile and the July Course. The three major race meetings are in spring (April/May), summer (July/August), and autumn (late September/October), with the most famous events being the One Thousand and Two Thousand Guineas (late April), the Cambridgeshire (early October), and the Caesarewich (mid-October).

The town is also home to the **National Horseracing Museum**, *tel. (44) 1638-667-333; website: www.nhrm.co.uk/home.html;* which presents exhibits that bring to life the social history of racing and includes pictures and sculptures by such masters of the genre as Stubbs and Munnings. The museum has five galleries, a coffee bar, a restaurant, and a gift shop and shows videos of famous races.

The best antique shopping outside London

Strangers usually visit Hungerford for one reason—to browse and to buy in the many antique shops. Here the collector can concentrate on the business at hand, undistracted by any other major attractions. The **Hungerford**

Arcade on High Street has more than 80 stalls to investigate. There's some pretty junky stuff there, but treasures can still be found. For quality antique kitchenware, try **Below Stairs**, across the road from the Arcade. Over the Kennet and Avon Canal, where High Street turns into Bridge Street, is a whole collection of quality silver and Edwardian to Georgian wine labels.

A bit farther on is **Pandora's Box**, where Joan Gleave stocks mainly Victoriana and specializes in Staffordshire pottery figures. The latter were often made to commemorate historic events (note the delightful group from the Crimean War) or a famous personality (generals and royalty were favorites).

On Charnham Street is **Bow House Antiques**, where upstairs Mrs. Herrington has a nursery of toys, dolls, teddy bears, and some bewitching dollhouse furniture. On the same street is an old cottage called **The Collector's Shop**, which has a wide variety of stock from different dealers that is well worth rummaging through.

The world's only rocking horse workshop

Situated in the small Shropshire village of Wem, about 150 miles from London, is a workshop that makes nothing but rocking horses, *1 Drayton Road, Hodnet, Shropshire; tel. (44)1630-685-888; website: www.rockinghorses.co.uk/index.htm.* These beautiful, large-eyed creatures were a popular feature of many Edwardian and Victorian nurseries. David and Noreen Kiss have made a profession out of restoring old horses from the 18th and 19th centuries, and the barn in their garden has become the world center for these wooden chargers of old. The rocking horses are made in a variety of woods, and visitors can view the entire process of reviving the rockers; everything is on display, from a basic block of timber to the full-colored model horse on its curving runners.

The oldest inhabited manor house in England

New Hall, *tel. (44)121-378-2442*, isn't new. It's a 12th-century manor house, destined to become a more than worthy rival to the rather soulless conference hotels in nearby Birmingham—and a pleasant relief from the hotels in London. There are 65 rooms in the house, all with private baths.

Britain's most charming village

The village of **Shanklin**, on the Isle of Wight off the southern coast of England, is charming—just what you'd imagine a British village should be. Thatched-roof cottages, many of them restaurants, pubs, and gift shops, line the streets. St. Blasius, the old parish church, dates in part from the 14th century. Climb down into the Shanklin Chine, a narrow ravine with a waterfall.

The Isle of Wight is accessible from Portsmouth or Southhampton on the mainland by hydrofoil or ferry.

The largest inhabited castle in the world

Windsor Castle, still used by royalty after 850 years (construction of the castle was begun by William the Conqueror in the 11th century), is the largest inhabited castle in the world. Many of Britains kings and queens are buried in St. George's Chapel here.

Located on the River Thames, Windsor is a picturesque Victorian town. Across the river from Windsor is Eton College, the most exclusive boys' school in Britain. Founded in 1440, it has educated many of the nation's leaders.

Canterbury: Chaucer's favorite

St. Augustine established Christianity in Canterbury in A.D. 597, and in 1197 the martyr Thomas Becket was murdered in the cathedral here. Canterbury has been a settlement since the Iron Age. Visit **Canterbury Cathedral**, the mother church for the Anglican faith and a center for pilgrimages (including one Chaucer wrote about). The structure was begun in 1070 and completed in 1503.

The world's most famous cliffs

The white cliffs of **Dover** are world-famous for their brilliant white color and their sheer drop into the sea. The best view of the cliffs is from the ferry that crosses the English Channel on its way to France.

Dover is home to the **White Cliffs Experience**, an exhibit that outlines thousands of years of British history, from the Roman invasion of Britain in 55 B.C. to the air raids during World War II. It's adjacent to the Dover Museum, which is on Market Square; *tel. (44) 1304-201-066; website: www.dover.gov.uk/museum.*

THE MOST PICTURESQUE REGION: THE SOUTHWEST PENINSULA

The southwest peninsula—Devon and Cornwall—is for people who like to breathe tangy sea breezes, explore fishing villages, walk harbor walls, swim in the sea, and wallow in England's maritime history. The southern coast faces the English Channel, which affords a mild climate with gentle waves softly lapping the secluded bays and ancient smugglers' coves. The northern coast of the peninsula faces the full force of the Atlantic.

All along the peninsula are little villages that appear to tumble down the hillsides. Inland are the granite moors. Dartmoor, Exmoor, and Bodmin are designated National Trust areas, protected from development.

Cornwall—the least changed region

Cornwall is one of the last genuinely unchanged counties in England, located 300 miles from London . (The train journey takes about five hours.)

This region, the one-time hideout of smugglers and pirates, is also the location of Tintagel, the legendary home of King Arthur. The tiny village of Camelford is supposedly the original Camelot. You can partake in a medieval banquet in the Great Hall at Tintagel, surrounded by the colors and banners of the Knights of the Round Table.

The best outdoor theater

Penzance, a colorful old South Cornish town of pirates and smugglers, is nearly 300 miles from London. In the summer, open-air opera, including the apt Gilbert and Sullivan work of *Pirates of Penzance*, is performed at **Minack Theatre** at Portcurno.

The Minack Theater is carved out of a cliff. The audience watches the performances in the open air looking over the Atlantic. Take along a warm sweater and a blanket. For information *tel. (44)1736-810-181; website: www.minack.com.*

The prettiest Cornish town

St. Mawes, on the southern coast of Cornwall, is one of the prettiest towns in Britain. Located at the mouth of Percuil Creek, it is known for its fine sailing and its castle, which was built by King Henry VIII from 1540 to 1543. The castle is shaped like a cloverleaf for good luck.

Cornwall's best hotels

The best seaside hotel in Cornwall is the **Falmouth Hotel**, *tel. (44)1326-312-671; e-mail: info@falmouthhotel.com; website: www.falmouthhotel.com.* Overlooking Pendennis Point and Pendennis Castle, it was opened in 1865 and has accommodated Edward VII and stage stars Anna Neagle and Herbert Wilcox.

Allhays Country House, *Talland Bay, Looe, Cornwall; tel. (44)1503-272-434* or *(44)1503-273-188; e-mail: info@allhays.co.uk; website: www.allhays.co.uk,* is one of the best B&Bs in the region.

Truro Farm, *Park Farm, St. Clements, Truro, Cornwall*, is a rambling stone house constructed in a jumble of periods from the 16th through the 18th centuries. Rooms have lovely antiques ranging from Georgian to Victorian.

A footpath leads to the village of Malpas, from which you can take boat trips downriver to Falmouth.

The best moor: Dartmoor

In the heart of Devon is the 365-square-mile **Dartmoor National Park**, *tel. (44)1626-832-093, www.dartmoor-npa.gov.uk*, which embodies the country's mystery and beauty. Dartmoor is the setting of *The Hound of the Baskervilles*, as well as the location of the notorious Dartmoor Prison. Its desolate moors are relieved by cozy villages and rolling hills.

Wild ponies canter through Dartmoor's fields of wild flowers. Thatched cottages dot the landscape, and towns here—Widecombe-in-the-Moor, Ashburton, Okehampton, and Chagford—are all within walking distance of the moors. Try to be in the area during a village fair or stock show. You will think time has stood still.

If you want to explore the wilds of Dartmoor National Park, pick up an ordinance map of the park, don your waterproof boots, and set out.

After hiking all day in the moor, stop in at **Barton's** in Chagford, where you can enjoy an authentic Devonshire tea, complete with scones, straw-berry preserves, and thick Devonshire cream.

The best stone rows

Dartmoor has the country's best example of stone **rowsyard**—high rocks set in a line. The rocks are sometimes covered with circular designs. Look carefully, they are often hidden by heather. The rows lead to round barrows or cairns (burial mounds).

The best Bronze Age village

Grimspound in Manaton is one of the best examples of a fortified Bronze Age village on the moor. It is also the largest, with 24 hut circles in a 150-yard enclosure. The protecting wall was originally 10 feet high and had three entrances. The hut circles had cooking holes, stone platforms, and flat center stones that supported the roof poles.

The most luxurious hotel in Devon

The most luxurious place to stay in Dartmoor National Park is **Gidleigh Park**, *tel. (44)1647-432-225; website: www.gidleigh.com*. This peaceful country manor has blazing fires, chintz-covered furniture, and oak-paneled walls. The hotel has 12 rooms and an exceptional restaurant and is surrounded by 30 acres. The hotel is rather expensive, but worth it.

The coziest B&B by the moor

Burrator House, *tel. (44)1822-853-1211*, is a Georgian house on 20 acres. It is on the B3212 Road and has a trout pool, a miniature waterfall, a swim-ming pool, and a Victorian snooker table. (Snooker is a form of pool.)

THE BEST OF THE COTSWOLDS

The "Heart of England" lies just an hour and a half (by train) west and slightly north of London. Here, a softly rolling ribbon of hills enfolds rustic villages of another, more romantic age. This region, known as the **Cotswolds**, was the prosperous hub of the wool trade in the 13th through

16th centuries, and you can still glimpse an occasional flock of sheep. Towns and villages nestling in these hills are made up of houses built of the local stone, with steep slate roofs.

The most charming village

Tetbury is the most charming village in the Cotswolds, an old market town with hilly streets that weave and curve around the Old Market House, built in 1655. Early in the morning, bottles of milk with cream on top sit outside the doors of the town's quaint houses.

Tetbury has a beautiful church, St. Mary the Virgin, some antique shops—and little else.

Shakespeare's favorite

Stratford-upon-Avon, Shakespeare's home town, sits at the northeast tip of the Cotswolds. Despite its commercialized, touristy flavor, Stratford is pretty, with authentic Tudor buildings on practically every street.

You're cheating yourself if you don't make it to one of the Royal Shakespeare Company's productions. Also worth a stop is the Dirty Duck Pub, where actors hang out between shows. It is across from the theater, right up from the McDonalds.

Stratford-upon-Avon Brass Rubbing Centre is the best brass rubbing center in the area. It traces the history of commemorative brasses from the 12th through 17th centuries.

The best of Cheltenham

Cheltenham, the tourist base of the Cotswolds, is a melange of old and new. Georgian terraced houses with flower-draped, wrought iron balconies stand beside gray cubelike office buildings and utilitarian storefront strips.

The nicest strip is the **Promenade**, a treelined avenue with ornate Georgian buildings. Visit the Cheltenham Racecourse, one of England's finest steeplechase courses.

The best castle in the Cotswolds

Six miles up the A 46 from Cheltenham is **Sudeley Castle** in Winchcombe. Catherine Parr, the sixth wife of Henry VIII, and the only one to survive him, lived and is buried here. (Henry's fourth wife, Anne of Cleves, also survived him, but their marriage was annulled.)

Best places to stay

Two hotels that make ideal bases for touring the Cotswolds are the **Close at Tetbury** and the **Hotel de la Bere**, just outside Cheltenham. The Close, *tel. (44)1666-502-272*, was once the home of a 16th century wool merchant. The Hotel de la Bere, *tel. (44)1242-237-771; e-mail: delabere@coroshotels.com*, is a sprawling, grandiose 16th-century building.

The best way to get there

One of the best things about the Cotswolds is the region's proximity to London. The capital is less than two hours away by the M4 or M40 motorway.

The best place to take a bath in England

The most magnificent spa in England is, appropriately, in **Bath**. According to legend, the mineral springs at Bath were first discovered by King Bladud (the father of King Lear), who had been banished into the countryside because of his leprosy. He became a swineherd, and his pigs led him to the springs, which cured him of the disease.

Visit the Roman Baths and the Pump Room, where you can drink the bubbling hot mineral water from the fountain. The Great Bath is exposed to the sky. Next door is a museum displaying Roman and prehistoric relics. Stroll along the Royal Crescent, a sweep of 30 Georgian houses joined by one façade and fronted with Ionic columns.

England's best-preserved town

Chester, on the west coast in Cheshire County, is one of the few English towns still encircled by a medieval wall. The thick wall doubles as an attractive promenade lined with shops. Within the walls are Tudor half-timbered houses.

Founded in A.D. 60, Chester was the headquarters of the Roman XX Legion, and many Roman relics remain.

THE MOST INSPIRING REGION: YORKSHIRE

Yorkshire has inspired a number of English writers, including James Herriot and the Brontë family. Herbert Read, the poet and art critic, was a more recent Yorkshire literary light.

James Herriot Country, as Yorkshire County is known, is a patchwork of undulating pastures dotted with sheep and lined with ancient stone walls, desolate moors, rugged coastlines, and medieval towns.

The best of the Brontës

The **Brontë** family lived in Haworth, a romantic town perched precariously on a hillside, commanding superb views from its cobblestoned streets. From 11 a.m. until 5.30 p.m., April through September, you can visit the parsonage that was their home; it closes at 4.30 p.m. October through March.

The most colorful place to dine or stay in Haworth is the **Black Bull House**, *tel. (44) 1904-728-245; e-mail: blackbullhotel@bt.connect.com*. This is where Branwell Brontë obtained his supplies of opium.

The best view of the area

At **Thirsk**, a charming market town in Yorkshire, a natural ridge provides a superb hang-gliding site. Visitors are welcome to take glider rides, enjoying bird's-eye views of the area.

The best guidebook

The guidebook that offers the most insight into this region is James Herriot's *Yorkshire*. The animal lover and writer knows the region inside out—and his love of the area is evident in his writing.

The coziest place to stay

The **Black Swan Hotel**, *tel. (44) 1380-723-259; website: www.blackswanhotel. fsnet.co.uk*, is an old coaching inn on the edge of North York Moors National Park. It serves full English breakfasts, traditional teas, and traditional Sunday lunches. Try the venison, the Barnsley chops, and the puddings.

THE MOST HISTORIC CITY: YORK

In A.D. 867, the Danish Vikings vanquished York, and many of the area's street names, such as Micklegate, Bootham, and Walmgate, date from this period. After the Vikings, the Normans took possession. The city's architecture bears witness to their influence. During the sixth century, the legendary King Arthur is said to have captured York, and in the seventh century the Saxons moved in. They built a small wooden church, the original **York Minster**. (A *minster* is a church that once was a monastery.) Until the 14th century, York was strategically and economically more important than London and was the nation's capital.

In the early 1970s, it was discovered that the foundations of the York Minster were on the move; draining and underpinning were urgently required. During the work, which began in 1976, evidence of a massive Roman military fortress and Roman drainage system were discovered. The drains were in such good condition that they could be used for the necessary drainage without repair—quite impressive for something built in A.D. 71.

During the excavations, one of the workmen on the site insisted that he saw the ghosts of an entire battalion of Roman soldiers marching before him. The British workman was visibly shaken. "One of the strangest things," he said, "was that they were only visible from the knees up. You couldn't see their legs." Further excavations revealed an ancient Roman road at just about the level the soldiers' feet would have been.

The best city walk

A footpath along the top of the walls that surround York provides a pleasant three-mile saunter on a warm summer evening. You can circle the entire city on the walls, coming down the stone steps at intervals to see the sights. Modern traffic runs between these steps and their ancient gatehouses. The York Minster is visible from the walls at all times. It is a delightful contrast to the black-and-white Tudor buildings that surround it.

The best sightseeing tip

Don't take a car into York. Sights are within easy walking distance of one another, public transportation is available, and parking is a nightmare not to be contemplated.

The most esteemed chocolate maker

Just southwest of Yorkshire is a renowned chocolate maker known as **Thorntons**. Founded in 1925, Thorntons was initially famous for its distinctive toffee, but it is now equally renowned for its chocolates. Try to visit at Easter, when you can buy a chocolate egg and then wait while it's personalized with your name in icing. You can also shop for confections made of almonds, apricots, vine fruits, and the like, all of which may be carried away in one of Thornton's edible lacy-weave chocolate baskets.

The Brits' favorite holiday place

If it came to a choice between London and the Lake District, any Briton would choose the **Lake District**. An area of outstanding natural beauty, it covers the northwestern corner of England, just south of the Scottish border. It is easily accessible via the M6 Motorway, approximately a five-hour drive from London.

The Lake District is rich in literary connections. Wordsworth was born here and was visited often by Shelley and Coleridge. Robert Southey lived in Keswick for more than 40 years. And John Ruskin's name pops up everywhere, from Ruskin House Pottery in Ambleside to the cross commemorating him in the churchyard at Coniston. This is also the country of Beatrix Potter, the much-loved author of delightful children's stories. Charles Lamb vacationed in Keswick.

The best way to see the Lake District

The best way to see the Lake District is leisurely. You'll absorb more of the atmosphere by sitting beside one lake for a few hours than by racing around the largest lakes and main towns and villages. The tiny roads that weave between and over the hills will defeat anyone in a hurry. Also keep in mind that wandering sheep have the right of way here, and you'll often have to leave your car to open and close sheep gates that cross the road.

Head first for Brockhole, a country house halfway between Windermere and Ambleside on the main road. The house is an information center and has a pleasant tea room.

The World's Best Destinations

The best-kept secret in the Lake District

If you want to escape the crowds of tourists in the Lake District, head for the **Wasdale Head Inn**, *tel. (44)19467-26229; e-mail: wasdalehead inn@msn.com; website: www.wasdale.com*. This remote, secluded pub is a haven of peace set in one of Lakeland's most beautiful, unspoiled valleys. The views of Great Gable, Sca Fell, and other massive peaks are an inspiration, and nearby Wastwater is perhaps the most dramatic of the lakes. Walkers, rock climbers, and anyone interested in the great outdoors find this traditional mountain inn a real delight. And a visit to Wasdale Head will put you in good company, for Wordsworth, Coleridge, and Dickens are known to have frequented the area, and British novelist Nicholas Monsaratt bought his first glass of beer ever in the inn.

The most spectacular lake

Ullswater, which is encircled by hills and highlands rising from the water's edge, is the most spectacular of the lakes. Wordsworth immortalized the daffodils he saw here and described Ullswater as "perhaps…the happiest combination of beauty and grandeur, which any of the Lakes affords."

The best place to stay on the banks of Ullswater is the **Sharrow Bay Hotel**, *Penrith; tel. (44)17684-86301*. Proprietor Francis Coulson goes to great lengths to please his guests. A roaring fire warms the lounge, and rooms are equipped with backgammon and Scrabble boards. The views are tremendous and the food is sinfully delicious.

Mr. Coulson despises cuisine *minceur* and believes in cream with everything, so the food is very rich. Try the cream of watercress soup and, for dessert, the kiwi fruit pavlova and cream profiteroles with chocolate sauce.

The most beautiful stone circle

Just two miles east of Keswick is **Castlerigg Stone Circle**, the most beautifully situated stone circle in England. And unlike the famous Stonehenge, it is not inundated with tourists.

You can work out a number of astrological details from this circle, which is 100 feet in diameter with 38 stones in its outer ring (almost all standing in their original positions) and 10 more within.

From Castlerigg, you can see the north Lakeland hills. Three miles away is a hill called Threlkeld Knott, over which the sun rises during an equinox.

Wordsworth's favorite spot

Tiny Grasmere village is more famous for its delightful position, nestled as it is beneath Helm Crag and Nab Scar northwest of Lake Windermere, than for its amenities. Wordsworth called it "the loveliest spot that man hath ever found." He made his first home nearby at Dove Cottage. Open to the public, Dove Cottage is tiny and charming, with a museum next door.

Historian Philip Crowl says, "The management of this site is a model of graciousness combined with efficiency. Few stately homes, for all their large staffs and high entrance fees, do so well." Even the garden is a delight.

THE WORLD'S BEST GARDENS

English gardens are known worldwide for their colorful, wild abandon. Gardening is something the British do well, and the rain and mild winters, particularly in the south, provide the perfect environment for cultivating trees and plants.

Today, you don't have to be wealthy to enjoy the immense gardens of England's royal estates. Apart from financial considerations, most owners today believe that it's right to share their historic homes and gardens with the rest of us.

The most beautiful garden

Of all the gardens in England, the most beautiful is **Sissinghurst Castle Garden**, two miles northeast of Cranbrook. Created by writer Vita Sackville-West (who wrote a gardening column for the *Daily Telegraph* for years) and her husband, diplomat Sir Harold Nicolson, Sissinghurst is a series of walled gardens located between the surviving parts of an Elizabethan mansion.

The prettiest is the white garden, planted with only white flowers. Also lovely are the rose garden, with old-fashioned English roses (old-fashioned roses predate hybrids, which are what most gardens grow today), the herb garden, the yew walk, the moat walk, and the orchard. The gardens are open April through Oct. 15, Tuesday through Friday, 1 p.m. until 6:30 p.m.

The most splendid Temple gardens

The 350 acres of **Stowe**, in Buckinghamshire, are set around the great Palladian house of the Temple family, whose punning motto *Templa quam dilecta* (how splendid are the temples!) is equally splendidly realized in the grottos, columns, bridges, arches, and monuments amid the woodlands and undulating, grassy landscape. In the Augustan era of Georgian England, these classical temples were intended to evoke ancient Rome.

The Temples had dissipated their great fortune by the end of Victoria's reign and soon thereafter had to sell their Buckinghamshire estate. Today it has become one of Britain's foremost schools.

The names of the designers give the clue to Stowe's greatness: Vanbrugh, Kent, and Givvs, three of the foremost architects of the 18th century, worked on these gardens. Lancelot "Capability" Brown, the man who developed the natural look and advocated informal planning of gardens, was the Temples' head gardener from 1741. Under his visionary eye, the garden was transformed into a spectacular, classical landscape.

42

The best guides to English gardens

Historic Houses, Castles, and Gardens is an independent catalog of more than 1,400 historic properties and gardens in England that are open to the public. Included is a brief history of each, its hours, entry fees, what you'll see, and how to get to the property. Order from **DGG Historic Publications**, *World Timetable Centre, Church Street, Dunstable, Bedfordshire; tel. (44)1582-600-111.*

National Garden Scheme lists private gardens open to the public alphabetically by county. The Scheme is a charitable trust begun in 1927 as a memorial to Queen Alexandra. It now comprises more than 1,600 gardens. Proceeds are administered by the Queen's Nursing Institute. You can order the list from the **National Gardens Scheme Charitable Trust**, *57 Lower Belgrave Street, London SW1 W0LR.*

The world's largest greenhouse

Near St. Austell, in southwest England, is the world's largest greenhouse. Since it opened in April 2001, two million visitors have already visited and made the **Eden Project** one of the top three, must-see British attractions, along with the Tower of London and Madame Tussaud's.

Eden is open every day except December 24 and 25. Admission is $16 for adults with special rates for senior citizens, students, children, and families. Car parks open at 9 a.m. For details of special displays, workshops, artifacts, and audio-visual programs, contact **The Eden Project**, *tel. (44)1726-811-911; fax (44)1726-811-912; website: www.edenproject.com.*

ENGLAND'S BEST PALACES

Castle Howard, *tel. (44)1653-648-333; e-mail: house@castlehoward.co.uk; website: www.castlehoward.co.uk*, in the rugged north, is the most beautiful of England's castles. This 18th century home, 15 miles north of York, was the film site for Evelyn Waugh's Brideshead Revisited, the renowned British television series.

Actually a palace, Castle Howard was designated in 1699 for Charles Howard, third Earl of Carlisle, and is aglow with paintings by Rubens, Gainsborough, and Reynolds. Some of the furniture is by Seraton and Chippendale, and the costume galleries have displays dating from the 18th century. The grounds are extensive, with lakes, fountains, and a beautiful Temple of the Four Winds. A replica of an 18th-century rose garden has old-fashioned roses that are no longer available commercially.

Blenheim Palace, *tel. (44)1993-811-091; website: www.blenheimpalace.com*, in Oxfordshire, is a close second. Near the old town of Woodstock, it was the home of the 11th Duke of Marlborough and the birthplace of Sir Winston Churchill. The gardens and park were designed by Queen Anne's gardener, Henry Wise, and later added to by Capability Brown, an 18th-century landscape gardener who created Blenheim Lake. If you weren't told it was landscaped, you'd think it was all natural. Blenheim is open mid-March through October.

THE BEST ENGLISH CATHEDRAL

Salisbury Cathedral, the only English cathedral built from a single type of stone, can be seen for miles. Set in a grassy plain, the cathedral has the tallest spire in England, rising an outstanding 404 feet. The best way to see this immense cathedral is to take the 90-minute guided tour, which gives you a look at parts of the cathedral not generally open to the public. The tour is held at 11 a.m. and 2:30 p.m. year-round and at 6:30 p.m. during the summer.

The cloisters and **Chapter House** that adjoin the cathedral are also worth seeing. The walls of Chapter House are decorated with bas-reliefs of the Old Testament. Enjoy the open lawns of the Cathedral Close. (Novelist Henry Fielding once lived in one of the houses on the close.)

A requested, but voluntary, donation to the cathedral is asked of its visitors. Group visits can be arranged through Jam Leniston, *tel. (44)1722 555124; e-mail: jan@salcath.co.uk; website: www.salisburycathedral.org.uk/index.php.*

THE BEST ENGLISH WINE

To qualify to be called "English," a wine must be made from grapes grown in England, and some of it is very good indeed. Contrary to popular belief, you don't need long, hot Mediterranean summers to grow grapes successfully. The average English summer sun will do, as long as there isn't a late spring frost, which can kill young vine shoots.

The best English wine can be tasted at **Charles Cunningham's Woolddings Vineyard and Restaurant**, *website: www.wooldingsvineyard.co.uk*, near Whitchurch, Hampshire. A tour of the vineyard and winery is offered. At the end, a tasting of the product is included in the admission price.

THE BEST RAILWAY MUSEUM

In 1986, Britain's Great Western locomotive works at Swindon, Wiltshire, closed. But the buildings were listed Grade II and so couldn't be demolished. The former boiler works now operate as the McArthur Glen Designer Outlet Great Western—a gigantic mall containing more than 100 shops. And next door, in the former machine shop, is STEAM—the Museum of the Great Western Railway. *Websites: www.steam-museum.org.uk* and *www.mcarthurglen.com.*

THE BEST OF WALES

Wales, that poetic land to the west of England, is renowned for its mighty castles. Dozens can be visited. They perch on rocky cliffs, cling to the mountains, hide in the moors, and rise up from the sea.

Many of the finest Welsh castles were constructed by King Edward I in the 13th century. The best known and grandest Welsh castle is **Caernarfon** in the north, birthplace of Edward II, the first Prince of Wales. Enclosed by the 13th-century town walls, it is a masterpiece of medieval architecture. Prince Charles was dubbed Prince of Wales here by his mother when he turned 18. Nearby is the Roman fort **Segontium**, founded in A.D. 78.

The two best hotels in the town of Caernarfon are the **Royal**, a historic coach house, and **Black Boy Inn**, which dates back to the 14th century.

Cardiff Castle, in the Welsh capital, is the second-best castle in Wales. Built in the 11th century on the site of an old Roman camp, it was reconstructed in 1865 and given an ornate Victorian exterior. Inside, it is romantic and extravagant, especially the Arab Room and the Chaucer Room. The roof garden is colorful.

Parts of the original Roman fort on which the castle was built still exist. And you still can see the Norman keep in the northwest corner.

Last but not least is **Harlech**, an enormous castle that watches over a tiny village. Actually, you should put it first on your itinerary. Because it's not as well-preserved as Caernarfon, it's spared the crowds of tourists.

Built by Edward I in 1283, the castle was the last to yield to the Yorkists in 1468 during the War of the Roses. It is set high on a cliff and protected by a massive double doorway. One of the best views of Snowdonia Mountain is from the top of the castle wall. Nearby is the most gorgeous beach on the Welsh coast.

The best fortification in Wales

Offa's Dyke, the eighth-century earthwork created by King Offa to keep out the marauding Welsh, marks the English/Welsh border. The 1,200-year-old earthwork can best be seen from the cliffs near Llanymynech in Shropshire, six miles from Oswestry. (Llanymynech's other claim to fame is the Lion Hotel, which is half in England and half in Wales.)

If you have time, one of the best ways to see Wales is to follow the **Offa's Dyke Path**, a 176-mile path from Prestatyn, on the northern Welsh coast, to Sedbury Cliff, Chepstow. It leads from sea to sea through the Black Mountains, the Clun Forest, and the Vale of Clwyd. The prettiest part of the path is over the bare central uplands of the Clun Forest, where the remains of the Dyke are best preserved.

Another highlight is the beautiful ruin **Tintern Abbey**, the site of Wordsworth's poem of the same name. Nearby, the devil supposedly tempted the monks. The gabled ends of the 13th-century abbey church rise out of a green meadow. The slate roof of the church was destroyed after Henry VIII dissolved the monasteries in 1537. For details see *website: www.offasdyke.demon.co.uk.*

The best Welsh national park

Pembrokeshire Coast National Park is 150 astounding miles of immense beauty. It includes rocky cliffs that drop off into the sea, remote bays, caves, coves, strangely shaped rock formations, and tranquil islands. Many of the rocks along this coastline are made of lava from volcanos that erupted 600 million years ago. A marked footpath follows the coastline, passing more than 50 Iron Age fortresses, a number of Celtic churches, and Norman castles at Pembroke, Carew, Haverfordwest, Cardigan, Manorbier, and Tenby.

Visit the seaside towns nearby. Llandudno and Aberystwyth are lively, elegant resorts. Tenby and Aberaeron are quieter places with harbors and whitewashed houses. Pamper yourself at the Rock Park spa in the 19th-century spa town of Llandrindod Wells. For more information contact the **Pembrokeshire Coast National Park Development Office**, *tel. (44) 845-634-7275; e-mail: info@pembrokeshirecoast.org; website: www.pembrokeshirecoast.org.*

The highest peak in England or Wales

Mount Snowdon, in Snowdonia National Park, is the highest peak in England or Wales, at 3,560 feet. It is also the steepest and most barren mountain. A narrow-gauge railway climbs to the top. Snowdonia offers 1,000 square miles of rugged mountains and moors, lakes, and rolling green hills. The park can be visited via the Snowdon Sherpa bus service, which runs every half-hour, Monday through Thursday, July 15 through Sept. 1. You can catch the bus in Caernarfon.

The best walled town in Wales

Tenby, a 14th-century walled town, has two sandy beaches (the best is North Beach) and a lovely harbor. The town's narrow streets lead to Castle Hill, a spit of land edged by cliffs that drop to the beach. St. Catherine's Island, which has an abandoned fort, can be seen from Castle Hill.

The nicest place to stay is the **Imperial Hotel**, which uses the town wall as one of its walls. For information, stop at the Croft, above North Beach.

The best Welsh beach resort

Aberystwyth is a popular beach resort with a lively seafront promenade, pastel-colored Victorian houses, black-and-white Welsh houses, and the ruins of a castle. It is also home to the oldest university in Wales (a neo-Gothic building opened in 1877) and the center of the revival of Welsh culture. You can hear traditional Welsh music at the **Cooper's Arms**, *Northgate*

Street. Stop in at the National Library of Wales, which houses most of the surviving Welsh medieval manuscripts.

The best book browsing in Britain

Hay-on-Wye is a charming little border town with typically narrow streets and a surprising number of bookstores, the result of one man's passion for things literary. His book collection overflowed from his own huge bookstore, with shelves from cellar to attic, into the town's movie theater and dozens of smaller bookstores throughout the town. It is a monument to British eccentricity and well worth a browse.

The largest weekly market

Visit **Welshpool**, the first town over the English border, on a Monday to see the largest weekly market in Wales. Farmers have been frequenting this market for more than 500 years.

The world's oldest record store

Spillers, *tel. (44)1222-383-848*, the oldest record store in the world, was established in Cardiff in 1894. It originally specialized in phonographs, wax phonograph cylinders, and shellac phonograph discs, and today sells both vinyl and CDs.

The best island in Wales

Holyhead, off the coast of Aberystwyth, is the prettiest island in Wales, complete with palm trees, pastel-colored houses overlooking tranquil bays full of fishing boats and yachts, and fine restaurants.

THE BEST OF SCOTLAND

Scotland's capital, **Edinburgh**, lost its rank as Scotland's largest city to archrival Glasgow in the 19th century. The result has been to make Edinburgh the more attractive tourist destination (except for the Victorian buffs, who prefer Glasgow).

Edinburgh's **Royal Mile**, which runs along the spine of a hill from Holyrood to Edinburgh Castle, is the most beautiful section of the city. Parts of the stretch date back to the middle ages. Few cities in the British Isles have so well preserved a medieval quarter. The Royal Mile has survived because of the 18th-century New Town in the plains below. New Town was built to house the surplus population and to avoid demolition of the old sections.

Follow the Royal Mile beginning at the castle end. It's downhill in this direction. The castle is mostly a shrine to British militarism, complete with red-kneed and kilted Scottish guards at the entrance (the regiment changes daily) and a military museum with historic mementos of these regiments and the parade grounds where they march.

The palace, or lodging, in the castle is where Mary Queen of Scots gave birth to James I of England (also known as James VI of Scotland). The lodging was heavily restored in the last century.

The oldest building in Edinburgh, built in 1076, is the miniscule white-washed church inside the castle walls called the **Chapel of St. Margaret**. Margaret, queen of Scotland, was canonized for her holy life. (Her immediate predecessor as queen was Lady Macbeth, so she had a hard job of it.) Margaret helped Anglicize the Scots, starting with her husband, King Malcolm III.

The main street running below the castle features historic houses associated with the city's luminaries: John Knox, Robert Burns, Walter Scott, Robert Louis Stevenson. It also provides a fascinating glimpse of historic Scottish life: old shops and breweries, an old printing press, a Presbyterian cathedral, a school, a sugar refinery, and a bakery.

One of the most interesting sites along the route is the tollbooth, which was the prison setting for Sir Walter Scott's *The Heart of Midlothian*. Another is Golfers' Land, the property purchased by a 17th-century golf champion with his winnings. John Patersone, a shoemaker, began his golfing career as a caddie and later became the partner of James II.

At the bottom of the main road, just one mile from the castle, is Holyrood, a converted abbey that was home to Scottish kings. Its style was heavily influenced by the French style Charles II learned about in exile. Charles II also commissioned a series of paintings of his ancestors that graces the picture gallery. Dutch artist Jakob de Witt knew how to please his royal patron. He made all 111 forebearers of Charles II look terribly like Charles II.

Holyrood is closely associated with Mary Queen of Scots, who lived and held court here from 1561 to 1567. She married Henry, Lord Darnley in 1565 in the Chapel Royal. You can see the room where she received John Knox (who fulminated against "a monstrous regiment of women") and the room where her secretary, David Riccio, was dragged from her presence and murdered (probably by one of her husbands).

The finest hotel in Edinburgh is the **Caledonian Hilton**, *Princes Street, Edinburgh EH1 2AB; tel. (44)131-222-8888*. This grand hotel has magnificent views of the castle. Recently refurbished, the Caledonian, with 212 rooms, three dining rooms, and three bars, is a favorite among celebrities.

Britain's best festival: the Edinburgh International

Millions of people visit Edinburgh each summer for the Edinburgh International Festival, which draws prominent musicians and theater groups from around the world.

While known as one of the world's leading musical and theater festivals, the Edinburgh International Festival has a little-known sideshow. Edinburgh also provides a stage for some of the best avant-garde productions in the English language. The Fringe, as part of the festival is called, boasts more than 1,000 events and 9,000 performances, including theater, comedy, musicals, cabaret, revues, opera, mime, dance, children's shows, folk, jazz, rock/blues, poetry, and multimedia presentations.

For more information contact the festival office: *tel. (44)131-473-2001* or visit the *website: www.eif.co.uk.*

Edinburgh's ghostliest tour

Greyfriars Kirkyard has a reputation for being genuinely haunted. Thousands of 17th-century plague victims lie buried beneath the grassy slopes.

It's also the site of the Covenanters Prison. Covenanters were Scottish Presbyterians who incurred the wrath of England's Charles I. Many were put to death and then buried in Greyfriars—as was "Bloody" Mackenzie, the Scottish Advocate General of the time who ordered their imprisonment, torture, and death.

Anybody can visit the main part of Greyfriars Kirkyard during the day. However, the only way to see the Covenanters Prison and the mausoleum-lined avenue that lies beyond the prison gates is at night—with a **City of the Dead** tour. The tour begins at 9.15 p.m. at the Mercat Cross on the Royal Mile and costs $10.

While Edinburgh has lots of "ghost walks," this is the only one with Greyfriars Kirkyard on the agenda.

Scotland's top art collection

A medieval city surrounding a 13th-century cathedral, **Glasgow** houses three remarkable art collections:

The **Burrell Collection** is housed in a stunning building with glass walls through which you can see the landscape of Pollok Park. The collection includes Oriental ceramics, French tapestries, and medieval stained glass. Admission is free. For information *tel. (44)141-649-7151.*

The **Kelingrove** contains masterpieces by Lippi, Rubens, and Constable. Its pride, however, is its collection of Impressionist paintings. Works by Monet, Pissarro, Matisse, Dégas, and Van Gogh grace the walls.

The **Hunterian Museum** has paintings by Rembrandt, Stubbs, Chardin, and Whistler.

When you tire of art, take tea at the **Willow Tea Room**. Or dine at the **Ubiquitous Chip**, *12 Ashton Lane,* off Byres Road.

The **Central**, *Gordon Street; tel. (44)141-221-9680*, is the most comfortable and old-fashioned hotel in Glasgow. For more information on accommodation in the city, contact the **Greater Glasgow Tourist Board**, *Georges Square, Glasgow G1 2ER; tel. (44)141-204-4400.*

The best Scottish castle

Stirling Castle in Fife, where Mary Queen of Scots was crowned in 1543, offers magnificent views of the Grampian Mountains from its cannonades. For centuries it was Scotland's only defense against English invaders. King Robert Bruce (simply known as The Bruce) and Sir William Wallace held the castle against the English for years. In 1305, however, Wallace was betrayed to the English and hanged, drawn, and quartered in London.

For atmosphere, no hotel in Stirling beats the **Golden Lion**, *8 King Street*, which has hosted Robert Burns, members of the royal family, and movie stars.

The most authentic castle stay

There are many castles available to rent for a house party throughout Scotland. In general, the farther north and more rural you go, the more authentic they are. But to find one within easy reach of Edinburgh that doesn't have tartan drapes, reproduction suits of armor, and pine floorboards is more of a challenge. They may be genuinely 16th-century outside, but some of the travesties of conservation and restoration have to be seen to be believed.

Built in 1780, **Birkhill Castle** is the real thing—the antithesis of tourist tackiness and just 50 minutes north of Edinburgh and west of St. Andrews. Set in rolling countryside on the shores of the River Tay estuary in Fife, it is the home of the Earl and Countess of Dundee. There are 12 bedrooms and bathrooms of varying sizes and views, but each with individual charm. The atmosphere is friendly and informal, and you feel like a houseguest rather than a tourist.

Lord Dundee is an elected peer in the House of Lords and is the Hereditary Royal Banner Bearer for Scotland. The coronation banners hang proudly in the hall. Lady Dundee runs the 2,000-acre arable farm and oversees the succession of houseguests. The house is stuffed full of paintings and antiques, and the family history is worth indulging. Lady Dundee will gladly bring the pictures of their ancestors to life with details of tragic deaths, misunderstandings in love, and stories from the battlefield.

You are welcomed with a substantial afternoon tea, after which you laze about until the views of the garden can be resisted no longer. Then, geared up with borrowed wellies and two of the family dogs you set off to wander until sunset. An amble through carpets of snowdrops, woodland gardens, and the family graveyard leads eventually to a stony beach on the River Tay. Such exertion requires a couple of hours devoted to lavender-filled baths and a leisurely read before dinner. Seven o'clock and back to the drawing room for pre-dinner champagne. Dinner is a treat—soufflé, beef bourguignon, and bread and butter pudding served in a candlelit dining room with a roaring fire. After dinner, retire to the games room—complete with billiards table and an antique soccer table—with a bottle of fine port and Scottish whiskey, of course.

Taking over the whole castle is expensive. Through Loyd and Townsend-Rose, *website: www.ltr.co.uk/home*, it costs $370 per night per person—all food and drink included. A much better option is to book B&B direct with Lady Dundee, *e-mail: Siobhan@birkhillcastle.org.uk*. At $110/night per person and dinner at $50, it's a reasonable way to get the authenticity and charm of a genuine Scottish castle.

An angler's dream

The area around Loch Lomond, Stirling, the Trossachs, and the Firth of Clyde, in the heart of Scotland, offers some of the best fishing you'll find anywhere in the world. And the best spot in this region to drop your line is the western end of Loch Tay at Killin. If you are interested in fishing, this is the perfect place. Contact the **Central Scotland Anglers Association**, *53 Fernieside Crescent, Edinburgh EH12 9DQ*, or the **Scottish Anglers National Association**, *5 Kramond Glebe Road, Kramond, Lothian EH4 6ND*, for more information about the area.

The best skiing in Scotland

Where should you go for the best skiing in Scotland? The **Cairngorm** mountain range, which rises 4,084 feet and offers the most developed facilities in the country. It has the greatest range of downhill runs, as well as 17 lifts and tows. Runs vary from long, easy slopes to the black-graded West Wall, for experts only.

The most dramatic region: the Highlands

The desolate beauty of the Highlands should not blind you to its violent past. Over the centuries, the Gaelic Highlanders have suffered terrible defeats to the English, fought bloody battles among themselves, and been driven from their homes by wealthy landowners. During the Highland Clearances in the 18th century, crofters were driven from their homes by landowners who wanted to raise sheep. Those who refused to go had their houses and goods burned.

Peaceful today, the Highlands are known for their secluded glens, craggy peaks, and sparkling lochs. The country is virtually unspoiled. Route A82 leads from Glasgow into the Highlands, curving along the west bank of Loch Lomond. When the famed lake turns into a stream, you are in the Highlands. The country is wild, steep, and unfenced.

The bloodiest place in the Highlands

One of the most ruggedly beautiful places in the Highlands is **Glencoe**, the misty valley that was the scene of a brutal massacre on Feb. 13, 1692, when the MacDonald clan, which had fought for James II, was butchered by the Campbell clan, soldiers of William of Orange. The MacDonalds were stabbed to death in their beds at dawn. Their homes were burned and their cattle stolen. Nothing remains of the human inhabitants of the Glen of Weeping, as it is known today. The only residents are golden eagles and red deer.

Inverary: the prettiest Highland town

Make **Inverary**, on the peaceful shores of Loch Fyne, one of your stops in the Highlands. Meaning "at the mouth of the Aray River," Inverary has been inhabited by the Campbells of Argyll for 500 years. Its white-walled buildings are reflected in the water. Services are still held in Gaelic at the town's church, the **Episcopal Church of All Saints**, which has the world's second-heaviest ring of 10 bells, which chime every day.

Nearby **Inverary Castle**, home to the Duke and Duchess of Argyll, is open to the public. The Armony Hall, which is 95 feet high, has an impressive display of antique weapons. The family portraits were done by such famous painters as Reynolds and Raeburn. A tour of the castle takes about an hour and is a good introduction to Highland history.

Britain's highest mountain

Ben Nevis, at 4,406 feet, is the highest peak in Great Britain. Near Inverness in the Highlands, it guards Glen Nevis. The view from the summit (where the ruins of an observatory remain) seems endless. A precipice on the northeast side drops more than 1,450 feet. Combine a trip to Inverness and Ben Nevis with a look at nearby **Loch Ness**, home of the world's most famous monster.

The best place to stay near Inverness is **Culloden House Hotel**, *tel. (44) 463-790-461*, an 18th-century palace near Culloden Moor, where the final Scottish uprising was defeated in 1746. This hotel has spacious rooms, ornate trim, and beautiful antiques.

The best Highland hotel

Inverlochy Castle, *tel. (44) 1397-702-177* or toll free from USA *(1) 888-424-0106; website: www.inverlochycastlehotel.com; e-mail: info@inverlochycastlehotel.com*, near Glencoe and Ben Nevis, is the best hotel to stay in while touring the Highlands.

THE HEBRIDES: THE BEST PLACE TO ESCAPE CIVILIZATION

If you are "a mere lover of naked nature," you will be drawn to the Scottish islands as Dr. Samuel Johnson was in 1775. The **Hebrides** are the best place in Britain to escape civilization.

The most beautiful isle—Skye

The most spectacular island in the Hebrides is the Misty Isle, as **Skye** is known. Walter Scott described the Misty Isle in *The Lord of the Isles*: "The vapor which enveloped the mountain ridges obliged us by assuming a thousand shapes, varying its veils in all sorts of forms, but sometimes clearing off altogether."

Wild still and distant from population centers, the island is so far north that in June the sun never really sets. From 11 p.m. until 1 a.m. a period of twilight falls, but there is never real darkness.

Canadians, Americans, Australians, and New Zealanders of Scottish descent often look to the Isle of Skye with nostalgia. Boatloads of Skyemen were shipped, often unwillingly, to these new lands during the Highland Clearances. Traces of their habitations can be seen all over Skye—foundations of walls, weeds growing over rubble, the outlines of houses, the stones of a hearth.

A trip through Skye's jagged, cloud-enshrouded Cullins and down primitive roads to Glen Brittle leads to excellent hiking country. The Cullins are beautiful seen from across Portree Bay or from Tarskavaig, across the waters of Loch Slapin. The grandest view is from the summit of Bidean Druim nan Ramh or Sgurr a'Mhadaidh.

The **Three Chimneys Restaurant**, *tel. (44)1470-511-258; e-mail: eatandstay@threechimneys.co.uk; website: www.threechimneys.co.uk/restaurant.html*, on the Isle of Skye is an exceptional place to eat and has a world-wide following. Having won multiple awards for its cuisine, this restaurant has the best of the best.

The easiest (and most embarrassing) defeat

According to British history books, John Paul Jones was scared away from the isle of Skye by a funeral procession he mistook for an army. The American Navy captain appeared on the coast of Skye in 1779 in the Bon Homme Richard (named for Benjamin Franklin's *Poor Richard's Almanack*). He had been harrying the shipping lanes in British waters. The appearance of his gunboat caused a flurry at Dunvegan Castle, because General MacLeod was away on military service in America. But when Jones saw the funeral party bearing the body of Donald MacLeod, he thought it was the MacLeod army in full battle array. He turned and fled. (You might take this tale with a grain of salt. American history books would probably report the incident differently.)

The favorite holiday isle

The favorite holiday isle among the British is **Arran**. Fluffy Arran sheep graze on green hillsides crossed by miles of hiking trails, especially on Goatfell, the "mountain of the winds." **Brodick Castle**, once the home of the dukes of Hamilton, can be seen in Lochranza. Now a ruin, it was once the hunting lodge of Robert the Bruce, King of the Scots.

Upon arrival in Brodick, check in at Mrs. Henderson's guesthouse in time for her to serve up a true Scottish breakfast—an amazing spread of juice, oatmeal, farm-fresh eggs, bacon, broiled tomatoes, pancakes, oatcakes, toast, and coffee or tea.

The most important sight on Arran is **Holy Island**, containing the cave of St. Molaise and runic inscriptions. It lies off Lamlash Bay.

The Queen of the Hebrides

From Kennecraig, on Kintyre, a day tour crosses to the **Isle of Islay**, known as the Queen of the Hebrides. The island's fertile soil is carpeted with bright emerald fields dotted with sleek cows and ubiquitous sheep. Good roads wind over the moors past salmon-filled lochs and farmhouses snuggled amid tidy flower and vegetable gardens. Wild cliffs tower above secluded sandy bays.

Near Port Charlotte are the graves of U.S. troops who lost their lives when the *Tuscania* and *Otranto* were torpedoed in 1918.

The most thrilling three-island hop

For a thrilling three-island hop, take the tour from Oban to **Mull**, **Staffa**, and **Iona**. Bus rides on Mull are exciting enough, with single-track roads, but the trip to Staffa takes you through six-foot troughs. Huge foaming waves dash against dark columnar rocks on the island's coast. **Fingal's Cave**, a rocky formation beaten by waves, inspired Mendelssohn to compose the Hebrides Overture after his visit here in 1829. On calmer days, it is possible to disembark and explore the vast cavern.

The most sacred island

The sacred island of **Iona**, burial place of Scottish kings, is renowned as the location where Christianity was introduced to Scotland by St. Columba in A.D. 563. Abbey ruins, a reconstructed cathedral, and rugged ninth-century crosses stand silently on the buffeted shore.

The best Scottish standing stones

The islands of **Harris** and **Lewis** are famous for their Harris tweeds, but most travelers have never heard of the islands' well-preserved standing stones. Yet the prehistoric *Standing Stones of Callanish* on Lewis Island are more complete than Stonehenge in southern England and just as impressive. The best part, of course, is that they're free of Stonehenge's crowds.

THE BEST WAY TO EXPLORE THE ISLES

The **Scottish Rail Pass** can be purchased at any main rail station in Scotland; it offers unlimited travel for 15 days or seven days. The **Highlands and Islands Travelpass** can be purchased at any British rail station, or at **Hi-Line**, *Station Road, Dingwall, Ross-shire, Scotland I-V15 9GE.*

SCOTLAND'S BEST-KNOWN BATTLE SITES

The **Scottish Lowlands** were the site of Scotland's two best-known battles: **Stirling Bridge**, where William Wallace drove back the English forces in 1297, and **Bannockburn**, where Robert the Bruce was victorious against the English in 1314.

THE MOST NORDIC REGION

The **Orkney Islands**, north of mainland Scotland, belonged to the Norse from the ninth through the 16th centuries. Eventually, they became part of Scotland. The shops here sell Nordic sweaters rather than kilts. Lush and fertile, the islands, populated by birds of all species, are popular among bird watchers. The pace of life is slow and, in the summer, the days are long.

THE WORLD'S BEST SCOTCH WHISKIES

The *New York Times Magazine* recommends Macallan and Glenfarclas-Glenlivet as the best single-malt Scotch whiskies for their "sherrylike aroma" and "intense flavor," respectively. Among blends, the *New York Times Magazine* prefers Usquabach for its "peatlike aroma and hot finish." Chivas Royal Salute is hailed for its "round elegant flavor."

THE BEST OF BULGARIA

Although Eastern Europe in general is becoming an increasingly popular travel destination, the world has yet to discover Bulgaria. The traveler to Bulgaria is something of a trailblazer, charting virgin territory, as it were. For precisely this reason, Bulgaria is the perfect destination for the intrepid and adventurous explorer, not afraid to endure a bit of discomfort.

THE WORLD'S BEST MONASTERIES

Bulgaria is home to some of the world's best monasteries, many of which are located in the mountains. Some are as many as 500 years old. Although the Turks completely subjugated Bulgaria during their occupation from 1393 to 1878, outlawing Christianity and killing off the aristocracy, they sensibly hesitated to tread deep into the mountains. And it was here that Bulgarian monks built fantastic churches, painted exquisite icons, and printed Bulgarian books.

At the **Rila monastery**, for example, which is situated high in the Rila Mountains, about an hour and a half south of Sofia, the monks printed thousands of Bulgarian books on a printing press brought down the Danube from Vienna. Built in the 10th century and expanded in the early 14th century, the Rila monastery was destroyed in 1833 by fire. To rebuild the monastery, Bulgarians from all over the country contributed jewelry, money, and even belt buckles. The result is a dazzling structure that is part Byzantine fantasy, nestled in a green valley and surrounded on all sides by mountains.

The **Bachkovo monastery**, located near the Assenitsa River, is about 18 miles south of Bulgaria's second-largest city, Plovdiv. Originally governed by 50 Georgian monks, the monastery's holdings stretched as far south as Salonika in modern-day Greece. Destroyed by the Turks in the 16th century, the monastery was rebuilt. It now boasts fine frescoes and a mural depicting the ancient Greeks: Aristotle, Sophocles, and Diogenes.

Perhaps the best known of Bulgaria's monasteries is the **Transfiguration**, high above the Yantra River, about four miles from Veliko Turnovo, Bulgaria's second capital. Also destroyed during the Turkish occupation, the monastery was completely rebuilt in 1825 by the self-taught national revival architect Kolyo Ficheto.

BULGARIA'S BEST SPAS

Bulgaria boasts more than 220 mineral water springs, as well as the fabled mud from the lakes along the Black Sea coast, all believed to hold extensive curative properties. (Keep in mind that there is a tremendous difference between seaside and inland spas. The seaside spas attract thousands of foreigners, looking not only for curative treatment but also for a holiday in the sun. The inland spas, frequented mostly by Bulgarians, offer fewer amenities.)

Bulgaria's warmest and sunniest town, **Sandanski**, lies about 120 miles south of Sofia, at the foot of Pirin Mountain. The climate here is believed to have an incredible recuperative effect. The best accommodation in Sandanski is at the four-star **Sandanski Hotel**, a snow-white, seven-story building set against a background of green hills.

The spa in **Velingrad** is situated in one of the most beautiful parts of the Rhodope Mountains in southern Bulgaria. The high amounts of negative ions and oxygen released by the rich vegetation and the abundant sunshine account for the curative properties of this spa. The best place to visit nearby is the city of Plovdiv, which has a well-preserved Roman amphitheater and a neighborhood of 19th-century houses that are open as museums, art galleries, or cafés. The best accommodation in Velingrad is at the two-star **Zdravets Hotel**.

The most modern Bulgarian seaside resort, **Albena**, lies about nine miles north of Golden Sands (probably the best-known of Bulgarian seaside resorts), located on the northern part of the Bulgarian Black Sea Coast along a picturesque bay.

THE BEST SKIING IN BULGARIA

The world has yet to realize that Bulgaria offers some of the best skiing in Europe. What's more, Bulgaria's ski resorts are also the most affordable of any on the Continent. Amenities may lag behind those in Switzerland or France, especially when it comes to service, but the low cost of a package deal means you can ski much more for much less money. Add to all of this the sheer novelty of skiing in Bulgaria, which offers a natural rugged beauty you'll find nowhere else.

Bulgaria's best ski resort is **Borovets**, which lies about 43 miles south of Sofia, in the Rila Mountains. Founded in 1897 by the royal family and named after the surrounding *bor* (or pine), the resort is old and established. Snow covers the forest and slopes for an average of 100 days a year, providing excellent conditions and a long season, which stretches from late November well into May. Accommodation at Borovets ranges from a village of Finnish-built chalets to several large hotels adjacent to the slopes. **The**

Rila offers balconies facing the slopes. You can ski directly from the hotel to the chair lift. Another good place to stay is the four-star hotel, the **Samokov**.

Bulgaria's second-largest resort is **Pamporovo**, which lies about 52 miles south of Plovdiv, in the heart of the Rhodope Mountains. Today, Pamporovo offers seven downhill trails, as well as cross-country runs and six lifts. The season there runs from December through April. Stay at either the **Perelik** or the **Mourgavets**.

Bulgaria's busiest resort is **Aleko**, on Mount Vitosha. From its slopes, you have tremendous views of the city of Sofia. The resort offers two chair lifts and a gondola, as well as six trails for cross-country skiing. It is in close proximity to Sofia, so that means that you can stay in Sofia and combine sightseeing with skiing. While skiing is great at Aleko, amenities are not. You're better off staying in Sofia and traveling every day to Aleko for your skiing. The best hotels in Sofia are the **Sheraton** and the **New Otani**.

For more information on these resorts, go to *www.balkanholidays.com*.

THE BEST OF CROATIA AND SLOVENIA

Croatia has a spectacular coastline with long sandy beaches, secret coves, and dramatic cliffs. Why battle the crowds and spend a fortune to lie on the beach in Greece, when you can enjoy the same Mediterranean sun and sea for half the price in Croatia? The nations that formerly comprised Yugoslavia, particularly Croatia, Slovenia, and Montenegro, offer stunning landscapes and a rich history.

DUBROVNIK: THE PEARL OF THE ADRIATIC

Dubrovnik, Croatia's medieval showpiece city, was once a city state that rivaled Venice. Dubrovnik's history goes back over 1,300 years. Although access to its walls initially involves lots of steps and costs the equivalent of $5, do make the effort. You won't get better views of the silken Adriatic, the densely wooded Dalmatian coastline, and the distant smudge of islands.

Even at street level, it's obvious why Dubrovnik calls itself "the Pearl of the Adriatic." The drawbridge over Pile Gate leads into a marble-paved street called Stradun. Laid out before you is a treasure house of bell towers, fountains, palaces and monasteries. Steep alleyways hide cozy restaurants, bars, and hole-in-the wall boutiques.

Vehicles are banned from the medieval core, mopeds and scooters included. There's none of that annoying put-put-put noise to compete with the clanging bells or strains of classical concertos spilling out of wooden church doors. We like this car-free environment—it's refreshing to sit at outdoor cafés without breathing gas fumes or worrying about risking life and limb whenever you step off a sidewalk.

It's remarkable that anything of Dubrovnik remains. For seven months in 1991 and 1992, it was bombarded by Yugoslavian army shelling. They wreaked immense damage, but under a UNESCO reconstruction plan the city has been meticulously restored.

Europe's third-oldest synagogue

Zudioska Ulica (Jew Street), near the Ploce Gate on the second floor of a Gothic building, has a 14th-century synagogue, the third-oldest in Europe. In the early 14th century, large groups of Jews found sanctuary in Dubrovnik from persecution in Spain and Italy.

Best sunset, best swimming

The prettiest place to spend the evening in Dubrovnik is the west end of the city, near the **Fortress of St. Ivan.** Young men often gather by the Porporela jetty below the fortress, where three huge iron spikes jut out from the stone wall. To prove their manhood, they swing from one spike to the other and finally drop into the sea. According to a saying in Dubrovnik, a boy has become a man when he "passes three spikes."

THE BEST OF THE DALMATIAN COAST

Stretching from Zadar to Dubrovnik is the **Dalmatian Coast**, where the people are loud and friendly. The best beaches along this stretch are between Sibenek and Split.

The most beautiful place along the Dalmatian Coast is the island of **Hvar**, meaning sun. Listed by *Conde Nast* as one of the world's top ten most beautiful islands, Hvar is surrounded by sapphire blue seas and gets 2,700 hours of sunshine per year. This is an idyll of hidden coves, dense woodlands, and a clutch of quaint towns and villages, and because it's a long, skinny island, you're never too far from the sea. The island is famous for its lavender and wildflowers.

Hvar attracts a good-looking young crowd, which keeps the nightlife lively. The **Tvrdava Disko**, which is located in the castle, can be seen from a distance—its lights flash from its perch on a hill. From the outdoor dance floor, you have a good view of the town.

THE CROATIAN COASTLINE

Dubrovnik is certainly the best-known city on the Croatian coastline, but it is hardly the only city along this shore.

Porec, farther down the peninsula, is the most pleasant town in the region. Located near spectacular fiords, it has narrow, cobblestoned streets and a maze of red-roofed stone houses. Galleries and studios fill the medieval towers.

The area on the coast known as the Riviera is the place to stay. Spend your Riviera nights at Club No. 1, a small, chic club with surrealistic paintings, and your Riviera days sunbathing in the nude at the giant nudist complex south of Porec called FKK Koversada, located at the entrance to the Lim Fiord. Day visitors can enjoy the beach for a few dollars (though groups of men might be barred entry).

The most picturesque town along the coast is **Rovinj**, an artists' colony. This little town, which has a beautiful old church, is built into a hill. Outdoor cafés and restaurants line the harbor. Monte Bar in the Old City serves good Istrian cuisine. The Hotel Eden has an informal casino and several discos.

The best place for peace and privacy is **Rab**, a lush town shaded in ever-greens. Located south of the Istrian Peninsula, it has deserted coves where you can swim undisturbed. The residents are friendly. Spend an evening enjoying music by a live band on the terrace of the Hotel Imperial.

SLOVENIA — THE MOST GLAMOROUS BEACHES

The **Slovenian Riviera** — the area from the Italian border to the end of the Istrian Peninsula's west coast — is the most glamorous stretch along the coast. It feels like Italy.

Izola and **Piran** are the most attractive resort towns along the Slovenian Riviera — both resemble old-style Italian resorts. **Portoroz**, a more modern resort, is the most expensive.

THE WORLD'S BEST CREAM CAKES

The Slovenian town of **Bled** — just 15 miles over the Austrian border — claims to have the best cream cakes in the world. Outside almost every café, you'll see a sign depicting the traditional *kremna rezina* (two layers of butter pastry sandwiching an oversized helping of vanilla-custard and cream). This yellow and white cube has become the symbol of the town.

The pastry chefs at The Park Hotel on Lake Bled, who originally created this delicacy in 1953, are particularly renowned for their produce. From every floor in the hotel, at any time of day, the tantalizing smell of pastry wafts through the corridors. Over the last 50 years, more than eight million of these cream slices have been polished off by the hotel's guests. Many — Slovenians included — come here simply to eat cake.

We also recommend the four-star **Park Hotel**, *website: www.gp-hoteli-bled.si*, as the best place to stay in Bled. Pastries aside, the indoor swimming pool on the hotel's top floor offers magnificent views of the lake (frozen over in winter), snow-capped mountains, and the cliff-top fairytale-like Bled Castle. Rates start at $120 for a double room (buffet breakfast included). Discounts are available for children.

The Best of the Czech Republic

The **Czech Republic**, at the heart of Europe, has suffered the blows of almost every power to hit the Continent. As a result, it is rich in history and culture and filled with 40,000 monuments and 3,000 castles. Its capital, Prague, is one of the most beautiful cities in Eastern Europe, outdone only by Budapest.

This country is an outdoor-lover's paradise. The Tatra Mountains rise out of the plains to provide excellent skiing and hiking. The 1,000 lakes and ponds that dot the Czech Republic are chock-full of fish. And the deep, wildlife-filled forests attract campers, backpackers, and hunters.

The Czech Republic's most beautiful city — Prague

Prague, described by Goethe as "The most precious stone crown of the world," is one of the most beautiful cities in Eastern Europe.

The best way to see Prague is on foot. Start by climbing the 186 steps to the top of the Prasna brana (Powder Tower) in Old Town. You'll have a panoramic view of the city from the top. A remnant of the old city fortifications, it was built in 1475 and rebuilt in the 19th century.

Old Town's best treasures

Stare Mesto (Old Town) dates to 1120. Celetna Street leads from the Powder Tower through the heart of Stare Mesto. It passes the **Tyl Theater**, where Mozart's *Don Giovanni* premiered in 1787 and where scenes from the movie *Amadeus* were filmed. Then it skirts the **Church of Our Lady at Tyn**, once a center of early Protestantism. The church's twin spires dominate the skyline.

The street empties into **Staromestske namesti** (the Old Town square). A medieval astronomical clock (*orloj*) has kept time here since 1490. On the house, figures of Christ and the 12 apostles appear at two little windows above the clock face. Then the skeleton figure of Death, below, tolls the bell. Legend has it that after its completion, the designer was blinded to prevent him from ever creating such a clock again.

The **town hall**, built in 1378, stands above dungeons. Its 15th-century council chamber, decorated with the shields of Prague's medieval guilds, is still used. Novelist Franz Kafka (1883-1924) was born in the painted house next door to the town hall.

Betlemska kaple (Bethlehem Chapel), *Betlemske namesti 5*, is a reconstruction of the Gothic chapel where the reformer Jan Huss preached his revolutionary ideas from 1402 to 1415. Huss, who was burned at the stake for his views, became a symbol of freedom to the Czech people. There is a monument to Huss in the Old Town square.

The most beautiful bridge

The most beautiful bridge in Eastern Europe connects Prague's Old Town and Mala Strana (Small Town). The **Charles Bridge**, built in 1357 by Charles IV, is lined with baroque statues. The bridge is especially lovely at night, when it is illuminated.

The best of Small Town

Small Town, despite its modest name, contains many of Prague's best sights. Much here is baroque, even though the town was founded in 1257. Among other things around town, there are many things to see in the **Maostranske namesti** (Small Town square), which is dominated by **Kostel sv. Nikulase** (St. Nicholas church), a Jesuit church with a beautiful dome, a belfry, a nave, and ceiling frescoes.

Nerudova ulice (Neruda Street) is the most beautiful street in Small Town. The baroque buildings are identified by signs (a red eagle, for example), as was the custom before numbered streets were introduced.

The magnificent **Valdstejnsky Palac** (Wallenstein Palace), *Valdstejnske namesti*, built in 1624 by Italian architects for the Hapsburg's Gen. Albrecht Wallenstein, now houses the Ministry of Culture. Concerts are held here in the summer.

New Town bests

Prague's **New Town** is not really new by most standards—it was established in 1348. At its heart is **Vaclavske namesti** (King Wenceslas Square), marked by a statue of King Wenceslas and filled with shops, restaurants, and hotels. Prague's best craft shop, **Slovenska Jizba**, located on the square, sells handmade jewelry, glass porcelain, and folk art.

The **Narodni muzeum** (National Museum), also on King Wenceslas Square, behind the statue of the king, displays neo-Renaissance paintings, artifacts from Czech history, historical and archeological collections, and a famous mineral collection.

Prague's oldest pub, **U Fleku**, *Kremencova 11*, has been in existence at least since 1499. A huge place, it is filled with people singing and drinking its good dark beer.

Karlovo namesti (Charles Square), the biggest square in New Town, is named for Charles IV, who planned the city. Located in this square is the **Novomestska radnice** (town hall), which was the government center from 1398 to 1784. Antonin Dvorak's mementos are housed in the **Dvorak Museum,** *Ke Karlovu 20*, near Charles Square. During the summer, Dvorak's music is played in the sculpture garden behind the 18th-century house.

The best-preserved ghetto

Jewish merchants settled in the area north of the old town hall as early as the ninth century. As the area grew, it became a center of Jewish culture. The well-preserved Prague Ghetto is now the **State Jewish Museum**.

The **Altneushul** (Old-New Synagogue), built in 13th-century Gothic style, is the oldest surviving synagogue in Europe. Beside it is the **Old Jewish Cemetery**, which holds 12,000 graves piled in layers. Tombs date from 1439 to 1787. If you lay a pebble on a grave here, it is said your dreams will come true.

The most visited tomb is that of the 16th-century scholar **Rabbi Loew**, who created the mythical, magical being called Golem. Today, visitors place scraps of paper with wishes on them in the crack in Loew's tomb. During World War II, Jews hid their valuables in the tomb's cracks before they were transported to concentration camps.

Franz Kafka is also buried in the cemetery. When the Nazis occupied Prague, they sent Kafka's three sisters to a concentration camp, where they were killed. And they destroyed most of Kafka's letters and manuscripts. However, his diaries were overlooked and are now housed among the treasures of the State Jewish Museum.

Klausen Synagogue, *U stareho hrbitova*, has a moving collection of drawings done by Jewish children in concentration camps.

The names of 77,700 Czechoslovak Jews murdered by the Nazis are inscribed on the inside walls of nearby **Pinkas Synagogue**.

Hradcany, the royal quarter

The **Hradcany Quarter** grew up around Hradcany (Prague Castle), the former residence of the kings of Bohemia and today the seat of government. A city within a city, it holds some of Prague's best treasures.

Three walled courtyards open into each other, progressing in architectural design from medieval to the 20th century. Off the first courtyard is the former chapel, which houses the treasury. Inside are gold, crystal, and jewels.

The Hradcany also houses the **National Gallery**, which is divided into three chronological sections. The earliest and best, in the former Convent of St. George, houses the state collection of Bohemian Gothic paintings and sculpture.

The third courtyard of the castle contains the imposing **Katedrala sv. Vita** (St. Vitus' Cathedral), the biggest in Prague, and the mausoleum of Czech kings, which holds the crown jewels (including the crown of St. Wenceslas, decorated with a thorn, reputedly from Christ's crown of thorns).

Behind the Hradcany is **Golden Lane**, once the residence of alchemists. The beautiful cobblestoned street, with its small houses, great palaces, and shops, brings the Middle Ages to life.

The bookstore at Number 24 was the residence of Franz Kafka in 1917 (who lived here just after he wrote *The Trial* and before he wrote *The Castle*). Ironically, the bookstore sells no books by Kafka, who has been largely ignored by the Czechs.

Nearby is **Strahovsky Klaster** (Strahov Monastery), which houses a museum of Czech literature and beautifully preserved ancient manuscripts and Bibles from all over the world. It is one of the most impressive libraries in Europe. The **Theological Hall**, a vaulted gallery built in 1671, is lined with 17th-century bookshelves. Its white stucco ceilings are embellished with frescoes.

The **Loretta**, another monastery, was founded in 1629 by Princess Lobkowitz. It centers around a replica of the Santa Casa in Loretta, Italy. Paired half-columns and relief panels add to its beauty. Its treasury contains saints' crowns and religious objects made of gold and precious stones.

The oldest fortress

Vysehrad Fortress, believed to have been founded in the ninth century, looms above Prague from sheer cliffs facing Hradcany. The Hussites destroyed much of it—apart from the walls, all that remains are an 11th-century rotunda and the Church of St. Peter and St. Paul. Many of the Czech Republic's greatest heroes and artists are buried in Vysehrad's cemetery, including Antonin Dvorak, Karel Capek, Jan Neruda, and Bedrich Smetana.

The world's best crystal

The Czech Republic is known for its lead crystal. **Moser**, *na prikope 12, tel. (42)2-221-851*, is the best place in Prague to shop for crystal. You can order through the store's catalog, which includes patterns preferred by the world's royalty.

The best restaurants

Opera Grill is Prague's finest restaurant. An elegant establishment decorated with antique Meissen candelabra, it serves French cuisine. After dinner, brandy is served in giant crystal snifters. The restaurant is closed weekends. Make reservations in advance.

The **Zlata Praha** (Golden Prague), *tel. (420)2-248-89-914*, on the eighth floor of the Prague Inter-Continental, has a lovely view of the castle. National specialties—roast duck, sauerkraut, and dumplings—are well-prepared.

Svata Klara (St. Klara), *Prague 7, Ulice Trogskeho Zamku 9; tel. (42)2-84-12-13*, the former wine cellar of Count Vaclav Vojtech, is now a first-class *vinarna* (wine restaurant) that offers a good selection of Moravian wines. You can enjoy dinner in front of the fireplace.

The best hotels

U Tri Pstrosu (Three Ostriches), *Drazickeho namesti 12; tel. (42)2-53-61-51*, is the most charming hotel in town. Located in a 16th-century house at the Small Town end of the Charles Bridge, it has an excellent restaurant. Reservations must be made several months in advance.

Pariz, *U Obecniho domu 1; tel. (42)2-236-0820*, is an art deco hotel. Its café and restaurant are decorated with blue mosaic tile.

Hotel InterContinental, *namesti Curievyeh 43-5; tel. (42)2-231-1812*, is a quick walk from both Wenceslas Square and the Charles Bridge on the New Town side of the Vltava River.

THE BEST CASTLES

The **Czech Republic** boasts 3,000 castles, and most are worth seeing. **Hazmburk**, near Ceske Budejovice in the north, is surrounded by a 30-foot-high wall and guarded by two observation towers. (Peregrine falcons have taken up residence in one of the abandoned towers.) The ruins rise out of sheer rock and are surrounded by a valley filled with wheat fields and plum orchards. Be careful—no railings protect you from the 700-foot drop from the ruins to the valley below. You can take a day trip to this castle from Austria or Southern Germany.

Spilberk Castle, in Brno, Moravia, built in 1287 to fend off invaders, was later used by the Hapsburgs to lock up their opponents. During World War II, the Nazis also used the dungeon as a prison. Take a look at the castle's hair-raising instruments of torture. The castle has a good restaurant that serves game dishes along with Moravian wines.

The little town of **Hluboka** has a wedding cake of a chateau, gleaming white with high, crenelated towers. It is a replica of Windsor Castle in England. Brussels tapestries, fine paintings, glassware, china, antique furniture, and medieval weapons can be seen here.

THE BEST SKIING IN EASTERN EUROPE

The Czech Republic has Eastern Europe's best ski area: **Stary Smokovec**, a national park in the High Tatras with jumps, slalom runs, and long cross-country trails. You won't find the crowds and frenzy of St. Moritz here.

In addition to being the best place to ski, Stary Smokovec, which lies in the shadows of the peak called Slavkovsky, is the oldest community in the High Tatras. The first tourist buildings here were built in the late 18th century. The two best hotels in town are the Grand and the Park Hotel.

THE BEST OF FRANCE

THEY ONCE SAID, OR RATHER TOLD US, EVERY MAN HAS TWO COUNTRIES;
HIS OWN AND FRANCE. THAT MIGHT BE AMENDED NOW TO: EVERY MAN
HAS THREE COUNTRIES—HIS OWN, FRANCE, AND THE POORHOUSE.

—Ernest Hemingway, 1934

If you asked a Frenchman to name the world's most civilized country, he would surely name his homeland. Few in the world would argue. And if you asked a Frenchman to describe himself and his countrymen, he surely would assert that a Frenchman is a wine expert; a gourmet; well-versed in art, history, and literature; dressed in the latest fashion; possessing of impeccable manners; and the world's best lover. Again, few would argue.

The best cuisine, wine, and cheeses in the world come from France. High fashion begins in Paris. And the world's greatest artists and writers are drawn to the land of the Gauls.

The greatest city in the world: Paris

Paris is not only the heart of France but also one of the world's most fascinating cities. Four-star restaurants, cozy cafés, wide boulevards, colorful outdoor markets, and fascinating museums, theaters, parks, squares, monuments, and churches are found in every section of this capital city. The best way to visit Paris is to stroll—past 17th-century houses, butcher shops with whole pigs hanging in the windows, ancient churches, high-fashion boutiques, street performers, art galleries, Africans selling wooden carvings, and Gypsy beggars. The streets are filled with the smells of roasting coffee, expensive perfume, Gauloise cigarettes, crêpes, roasting chestnuts, fresh bread, diesel fuel, and the damp breeze coming from the Seine.

When you get tired, stop in a café for a comforting cup of coffee and a chance to watch the people go by. You can sit for hours. Or buy a pastry at one of the hundreds of patisseries in Paris. Your heart will soar as you bite into the flaky, creamy, or fruit-filled delight.

Paris' most famous sight

The **Eiffel Tower** is the most famous (and unarguably most touristy) Paris landmark. The view from the top is remarkable—if you don't mind waiting in an endless line to get there. Built for the Universal Exposition of 1889, it faced demolition in 1909 but was saved when the French army discovered it could be used as a radio tower.

Since its creation, the Eiffel Tower has been the site of 400 suicide leaps.

If you want to prove that you climbed the Eiffel Tower's 1,710 steps (you can cheat if you take the elevator), mail a letter from the mailbox at the top. Letters mailed here are stamped with a special Eiffel Tower postmark. At night the tower is lit up, creating a dazzling effect.

The city's most beautiful church

✗ **Notre Dame Cathedral** is stunning, especially at sunset, when the splendid stained-glass rose window glows. Druids once worshiped on this site, and the Romans had a temple here before the Christians built Notre Dame in 1163. One of the finest examples of Gothic architecture, the cathedral was used for the coronation of Napoleon. (Napoleon scandalized the world by seizing the crown from Pope Pius VII and crowning himself.)

Beneath the church are the foundations of third-century Roman structures. Take a look at the side portals of the cathedral. According to legend, they were carved by the devil after he bought the soul of ironsmith Biscornet. (The devil was unable to decorate the central portal, because that is the one the Host was carried through in procession.)

The world's best museum

✗ The **Louvre** is the greatest museum in the world. Begun in the 12th century as a palace, it has been a museum since the 18th century. A controversial glass pyramid (three stories high) by I.M. Pei now covers the new underground entrance in the main court that faces the Jardin des Tuileries. Parking arrangements, shops, cafés, and restaurants are underground.

In 1190, the Louvre was one of Philippe Auguste's fortresses. Charles V made it an official residence, and Catherine de Medici had the long gallery built. It was extended under Henry IV and Louis XIII, and the quadrangle was completed under Louis XIV. Today, the museum is divided into six extensive sections: paintings and drawings, Greek and Roman antiquities, Egyptian antiquities, Oriental antiquities, *objets d'art*, and sculpture.

The *Venus de Milo* and the *Mona Lisa* are just two of the 208,500 works of art in the Louvre. The number of masterpieces is overwhelming. So are the crowds, especially on weekends and during the summer. The best way to avoid the masses is to steer clear of the European paintings. Instead, view the collection of ancient art, located in the Cour Carree. Gigantic statues loom above you, the air is cool, and the sounds echo off the walls like long-lost voices of Greek and Egyptian gods. For information *tel. (33)1-40-20-53-17.* The museum is open daily from 9 a.m. to 6 p.m. except Tuesdays and certain public holidays. Evening openings are until 9:45 p.m. on Mondays and Wednesdays.

Paris' biggest attraction

Although it is less famous than the Eiffel Tower, the **Centre**

Beaubourg, *tel. (33)1-44-78-12-33*, is the biggest attraction in Paris. More than 25,000 visitors are drawn to this art center each day—twice as many as visit the Eiffel Tower and almost equal to the number who frequent Disneyland. The multicolored modern structure built of steel tubes, concrete, and glass houses the Musée National d'Art Moderne, which displays works by Picasso, Braque, Chagall, Leger, Brancusi, and Calder.

Officially called the Centre National d'Art et de Culture Georges Pompidou, but unofficially known as the Pompidou or the Beaubourg, this arts center also has a 40,000 volume (reference) library, a theater, a restaurant, and temporary exhibits. The library averages 11,000 visitors a day and up to 19,000 a day on weekends. Only 2,000 people are admitted at a time. Outside, street performers breathe fire, perform pantomime, and play guitars. Opening hours are daily (except Tuesdays and May 1), from 11 a.m. to 9 p.m.

The most pricey café in Paris

Café de la Paix is a famous corner café that is attached to the Intercontinental Grand Hotel. You can relax for hours over one espresso and people-watch, read, or chat with friends—but at a price. An espresso here will set you back $7.

The world's most beautiful cemetery

Père Lachaise Cemetery, located on the northeastern edge of Paris, is the most beautiful cemetery in the world. The cemetery is housed in a wooded park and is so large that the walkways are given names and maps are handed out at the entrance. The headstones are massive and highly crafted. Many famous people rest there today, including Chopin, Edith Piaf, and Oscar Wilde, but the most visited grave is that of rock star Jim Morrison.

Four favorite sights in Paris

Sacré-Coeur, a glowing white Byzantine-style church on a hill in Montmartre, can be seen from almost anywhere in Paris. On summer evenings, a cool breeze wafts across the hill. The church was begun in 1876 to celebrate the end of the Franco-Prussian War. It was completed in 1910. Its interior is decorated with mosaics and stained glass. Nearby is a hokey but entertaining pseudo-artist's quarter.

La Sainte Chapelle, located in the Palais de Justice on the boulevard du Palais, was built by St. Louis to contain the Crown of Thorns, which he purchased from the Venetians in 1238. (The Crown of Thorns was moved to Notre Dame during the French Revolution.) The Gothic chapel has 15 brilliantly colored stained-glass windows and a graceful 247-foot spire. The stained-glass windows are the oldest in Paris and among the most vivid.

The Conciergerie, around Sainte Chapelle, is where Marie Antoinette spent her last days before facing the guillotine. It is also where 1,200 less-famous prisoners were held. This fascinating place has dark, dank dungeons. The conciergerie was built by Philip the Fair in the 14th century and contains three Gothic halls in addition to the prisons.

St.-Germain-des-Prés is the oldest church in Paris, begun in A.D. 558 "in the fields" outside the walls of Paris. The steeple and tower date from 1014, when the monastery was rebuilt after attacks by the Vikings. Enlarged in the 12th century, it was once self-sufficient, housing its own bakers, butchers, law courts, and defense force. All that exists of this today, aside from the church, are street names referring to parts of the ancient abbey. The abbey precincts now form a quarter of small hotels, antique shops, bookstores, publishing houses, and l'Ecole des Beaux-Arts.

The seven best museums in Paris

Musée des Arts de la Mode, *109 rue de Rivoli, 1st*, is the most entertaining museum in Paris. The city that has set fashion for 300 years is an appropriate setting for this institution, which displays the clothing of 19th-century chambermaids as well as 20th-century celebrities.

Musée Carnavalet, *23 rue de Sevigné, 3rd*, is the most Parisian of Paris' museums. Located in the Renaissance mansion in the Marais district, Carnavelet covers the turbulent history of the city and its people from the 16th to the 19th centuries.

Musée Marmottan, *2 rue Louis Boilly, 16th*, has the most significant collection of Monet paintings in Europe. Most of the works were painted at Monet's Normandy home in Giverny. This small, private museum near the Bois de Boulogne is hidden away in what appears to be a mundane residence. Inside, it boasts 65 paintings by Money, the Wildenstein collection of medieval illuminated manuscripts, and Renaissance and Empire works. It is open on Tuesdays, when other museums are closed.

Musée d'Orsay, located in the renovated Orsay train station, is the newest in Paris. This museum of the 19th century houses many Impressionist paintings once displayed at the Jeu de Paume. The enormous vaulted glass ceiling gives a 19th-century industrial atmosphere. The exhibits include 1,500 sculptures, 2,300 paintings, 1,100 *objets d'art*, 13,000 photographs, and works by Dégas, Manet, and Rousseau.

The Picasso Museum, *5 rue de Thorigny*, in the Marais, is the best place to study Picasso. It contains an intelligent selection of the artist's work and provides a complete, carefully documented and illustrated biography. The collection charts Picasso's artistic development through the rooms of a magnificent 17th-century mansion, the Hôtel Salé.

Musée Rodin, *77 rue de Varenne, 7th*, is where the best of Rodin's work is kept. This one-man museum is housed in an imposing 18th-century residence, the Hôtel Biron, where Rodin worked and lived toward the end of his life. He presented his art as payment for rent.

Musée de Thermes (Roman baths) and the **Hôtel de Cluny**, *6 place du Paul-Painleve, 5th*, is the most beautiful museum in Paris. A combination of second-century Gallo-Roman remains and an 18th-century mansion, it is set back from the busy corner of the St. Michel and St. Germain boulevards on the Left Bank.

The Cluny, a Gothic house, once the Paris residence of the wealthy abbots of Cluny, houses one of the world's best collections of medieval art, including the exquisite unicorn tapestries. The lion represents chivalric nobility, the unicorn represents bourgeois nobility, and the lady may represent the Le Viste family from Lyons. The Roman baths were used in the third century as a vast public bathhouse.

The three most colorful quarters

The greatest pleasures in Paris are its neighborhoods, which most tourists scarcely notice as they rush from sight to sight. Take time to wander through the streets of Paris. Absorb the smells, sounds, and sights. Our favorites for wandering are the **Marais**, the **Latin Quarter**, and **Montmartre**.

The Marais

The **Marais** is vaguely bounded by the rue Beaubourg to the west, the boulevard Beaumarchais to the east, the Seine to the south, and the rues Réaumur and Bretagne to the north. Within its confines are scores of fine old town houses, many built with paved forecourts and walled gardens. You'll also find several museums; the National Archives; a half-dozen churches; the Jewish Quarter with its little bakeries, delis, and shops; and the Place des Vosges. Tour the Marais during the week, when it is possible to enter most of the buildings. Begin your walk at the St. Paul metro station.

The Marais (which means marshland) was shunned until the 13th century, when the Knights Templars (a military-religious order) built its headquarters on the rue St. Antoine, a raised highway since Roman times. In the mid-14th century, Charles V built a palace in the area today bounded by the rues St. Antoine, St. Paul, and Petite-Muse. (Some say it was originally Pute-y-Muse, or *whore's muse*.)

Place des Vosges was given its current shape in 1605, when Henri IV developed a royal square on the site of the former palace. Uniform houses were built, red-brick buildings trimmed with white stone and slate roofs.

After the court moved to Versailles, the quarter began to lose its chic inhabitants, and its popularity. By the end of the French Revolution, it was virtually abandoned. The Marais remained in a declining state until 1962, when the government named the area a historic district. Since then, the Marais has been gradually restored to grandeur.

Don't miss the **Victor Hugo House**, *6 place des Vosges*; the **Palais Soubise**, *60 rue des Francs-Bourgeois*, which contains the National Archives; the **Historical Museum of France**; and the **Hotel de Rohan**, which contains a Gobelins tapestry and the fresco Horses of Apollo by Robert le Lorrain on the wall of its former stable.

Montmartre

Renoir was among the many 19th-century artists who lived in Montmartre and loved it. When traveling in Italy in 1881 he wrote, "I feel a little lost when away from Montmartre. I am longing for my familiar surroundings and think that even the ugliest girl is preferable to the most beautiful Italian." Renoir painted *La Balançoire* sitting in a large garden, actually an abandoned park, behind the house on rue Cortot.

Traces of the artists who loved the quarter can be found throughout Montmartre. A restaurant called Mère Catherine's, looking out on the Place du Tertre, is little changed since it appeared in a painting by Utrillo. The Bonne Franquette on the corner of rues St. Rustique and des Saules once had a tea garden where Van Gogh painted La Ginguette. If you walk down rue des Saules, you'll pass a tiny vineyard and come to a bar-cabaret called Le Lapin Agile. Here artists and writers, such as Picasso and Vlaminck, kicked up their heels.

The wrought iron gate at 11 ave. Junot marks the home of Utrillo's mother, the beautiful Suzanne Valadon. A painter herself and a model for Renoir, she appears among a group of voluptuous nudes in the painting *Les Grandes Baigneuses*.

The Moulin de la Galette, a windmill in Montmartre, has been painted almost as often as the Moulin Rouge. Renoir's painting of the Moulin is well-loved. Corot painted the mill also, and Van Gogh painted it twice. The windmill survives in an altered state — it has been restored and is an architectural feature above the roofs of a new development of apartments along avenue Junot and rue Lepic.

Picasso created cubism in his studio above the *bateau-lavoir* (laundry) that once existed next to Place Emile Goudeau. This tiny space, with a bench and a fountain, is on the downward slope toward the rue des Abbesses.

The most pleasant spot in Montmartre is the vineyard at the corner of rues St. Vincent and des Saules, near the Montmartre Museum. The vines still produce a wine called *picolo*. Every autumn, more than 300 liters of wine are produced and sold, and the proceeds are given to the old age home on the *butte* (hill).

Le Quartier Latin

The **Latin Quarter**, surrounding the boulevards St. Germain and St. Michel, is a bustling student quarter with twisting little streets, street performers and street vendors, restaurants, bookstores, and throngs of people.

The Roman conquerors of ancient Gaul settled here, on the Left Bank of the Seine, 50 years before the birth of Christ. They constructed thermal baths, an arena, and a theater. What is now rue St. Jacques was the Roman road to the south.

The **University of Paris** gave the area its ambience after the departure of the Romans. One of the oldest universities in the Western world, it was established at the beginning of the 12th century. (Its rivals were Bologna, Salerno, Oxford, Cambridge, and Leipzig.) The university was started by Pierre Abèlard, who left the cloisters of Notre Dame to give lessons away from the bishop's influence. He took with him the best students and, at the foot of the Montagne Ste. Geneviève, began new courses taught by liberal masters. Rich benefactors founded colleges to house the students and classrooms. Everyone spoke only Latin; hence, the area was named the Latin Quarter.

In 1792, following the revolution, the University of Paris was discontinued. It wasn't until 1806 that the Emperor Napoleon re-established the university. It exists today pretty much as it was set up then, which is one reason its students riot and strike.

The best bus lines for sightseeing

One of the easiest ways to sightsee in Paris is by bus. And the best buses for sightseeing purposes are 24, 29, 30, 32, 38, 42, 47, 52, 58, 63, 69, 72, 73, 75, 82, 84, and 87. Use the buses for sightseeing during the off-hours, after 10 a.m. and before 5:30 p.m. In summer, when it remains light later, do your sightseeing from 7:30 p.m. until the buses stop running.

Remember, with your Carte Orange you can get off the bus, visit a museum, walk through a neighborhood, have lunch or coffee, and then get back on and finish your tour without paying any additional charges.

For information on the city's bus system, ask at the metro ticket windows.

The oddest corner of Paris

A place of great faith and pilgrimage is hidden at 140 rue du Bac, next to the department store Bon Marché. Most of the inhabitants of Paris, including those who live in the neighborhood, do not know where the high, wooden door leads. But a million-and-a-half pilgrims visit a simple chapel at the back of the court every year. It commemorates Catherine Laboure, a novice of the Sisters of St. Vincent-de-Paul.

In November 1830, Catherine swore she had a vision. In it she was instructed to have a medal cast of the image she had seen. She was told that those who wear the Miraculous Medal in faith would be blessed.

The demand for the Miraculous Medal is so great that a slot machine has been installed in the chapel. When you put in your money, the machine dispenses a medal.

An odd twist to the story behind the medal: When the body of Sister Laboure was exhumed in 1933, it was miraculously intact. Her eyes were still blue. Her limbs were still supple, as if she were sleeping. Dressed in the famous white habit of the Sisters of Charity, the body of the saint can be seen today in the rue du Bac chapel.

The most famous gallows

Paris bus number 75 takes you to an intriguing street called **la rue de la Grange-aux-Belles**. At number 53 stood the 13th-century **Gibet de Montfaucon**, one of the king's gallows. Its 16-yard arms served two purposes: to hang those condemned and to exhibit corpses (often beheaded) as examples. In 1954, while excavating for a garage at number 53, two beams believed to be from the gallows were found.

The most beautiful bridge

The **Pont Alexandre III** is the most beautiful bridge in Paris. It crosses the Seine near the Jardin des Tuileries and the Petit and Grand Palais. The view from the bridge is as beautiful as the bridge itself.

The world's finest haute couture

Paris is not only the city of fashion but also the city of haute couture. Everyone is fashion-conscious here, from eight-year-old schoolgirls to white-haired grandmothers. To make a splash, you must have an outfit specially made and custom-tailored.

Many of the world's finest couturiers are found in Paris. (A couturier, as opposed to a mere dress designer, is one who presents collections of individually made clothes twice a year.) The world's celebrities come to them looking for flair and unique style.

The top couturiers in Paris include Chanel, Christian Dior, Givenchy, Jean Patou, Yves St. Laurent, and Philippe Venet.

The largest collection of secondhand scarves

The best collection of secondhand designer scarves can be found in a tiny shop in the picturesque but hard-to-find Passage Molière that runs between rues Quincampoix and St. Martin in the 4th arrondissement, midway between the Pompidou Centre and the Forum des Halles. Thick silk scarves, mostly large squares, with hand-sewn edges, each a veritable work of art, sell for an average price of $200. Steep—unless you compare that price with what you'd pay for a Hermès or Dior scarf, new, which costs more than double that.

The best cures for homesickness

If you feel lonely in Paris and want to hear people speaking English, pop into **Shakespeare & Co.**, an English-language bookstore across the river from Notre Dame Cathedral. Writers frequent the bookstore. Poetry readings are held on Monday nights.

Also, the American Library in Paris is the oldest and largest English-language library in Europe, with more than 100,000 books and a collection of 350 periodicals. In 1928, Stephen Vincent Benét wrote *John Brown's Body* in the reading room. The library was also used by Gertrude Stein, Louis Bromfield, and Thornton Wilder. It has been an arena for debates by such formidable figures as John Kenneth Galbraith, Raymond Aron, and Charles Frankel. It survived and grew through the Great Depression, the Occupation during World War II, the Liberation of Paris in 1944, the street riots of 1968, and the energy crisis of the mid-1970s.

The best flea market

For over 100 years **Le Marché aux Puces** (flea market) has been operating every Saturday to Monday in the village of St. Ouen, just outside Paris' 18th arrondissement. The largest market in Europe, it is a maze of little booths selling everything imaginable, from fine and expensive antiques to cheap, secondhand clothing. To get there, take the metro to Porte de Champerret; take bus 85 to Gare de Luxembourg-St. Denis; or take the metro to Porte de Clignanocourt.

The best time to browse (if you can manage to wake up early enough) is from 5 a.m. to 7:30 a.m. The buyers at this hour are professionals looking for really good buys. They move fast, checking every item with an experienced eye and then buying without hesitation. Large amounts of cash are exchanged, and the goods are shipped to warehouses.

From 7:30 a.m. until 7 p.m., Le Marché aux Puces is open officially for the 200,000 visitors it receives each week.

The market began in 1890, when sanitation laws first required that used clothing and bedding likely to contain vermin not be sold in the city. The ragpickers moved out to a muddy meadow appropriately called The Plain of the Ill-Seated. They were licensed to sell only to dealers and required to clean all materials before offering them for sale.

Over the years, however, the market became fashionable and began drawing large crowds. Today, seven markets make up a large complex. There is less junk and more antiques (both good and fake).

Le Jules Vallès, a covered market, is the best place to find collector items—toys, postcards, medals, dolls, and old newspapers and magazines. **Le Marché Malik** stocks old clothes. The newest markets, **Le Marché Serpette** and **Le Marché Cambo**, specialize in art deco and period furniture, respectively.

Be careful with your money when you're shopping at **Le Marché aux Puces**, which is full of pickpockets.

The best covered markets

For the true flavor of Paris, visit one of the city's 12 covered markets, where you'll find wonderful displays of fresh fruits and vegetables, meats, cheeses, mushrooms, melons, and furred and feathered game—hare, deer, boar, wild duck, pigeon, partridge, pheasant, and quail.

The best remaining covered markets include:

- **Beauvau St. Antoine**, between rues d'Aligre and de Cotte, 12th
- **La Chapelle**, rue de l'Olive, 18th
- **Enfants Rouge**, 39 rue de Bretagne, 3rd
- **St. Didier**, corner of rues Mesnil and St. Didier, 16th
- **St. Quentin**, 85 bis blvd. Magenta, 10th
- **Ternes**, rues Lebon, Faraday, and Torricelli, 17th

The freshest food in Paris

The open-air markets sell Paris' freshest produce and meats and have the largest selection of cheeses. The supermarkets in Paris just don't compare in price or quality. Our favorite open-air market is on rue de Seine, near St. Germain-des-Pres. Other outstanding open-air markets in Paris include: **Boulevard de Charonne** (Wednesdays and Saturdays), **Carmes** (Thursdays and Saturdays), **Pere Lachaise** (Fridays and Sundays), **Port-Royal** (Tuesdays, Thursdays, and Saturdays), **Raspail** (Tuesdays and Saturdays), and **Woodrow Wilson** (Tuesdays, Thursdays, and Saturdays).

The world's best pastry shops

The best pastries in the world are made in France, where layers of cake, as light as feathers, are molded together with airy, sweet buttercream and topped with curls of fine chocolate. Pastries in France are too beautiful (and too fattening) to eat, but too delicious not to.

Within France, the most tempting *pâtisseries*, or pastry shops, are in Paris, where they adorn every corner. There are 2,300 of them!

One of the best known and most honored *pâtisseries* is **Dalloyau**, which specializes in *marrons glacé* (candied chestnuts), *mogador* (layers of chocolate cake, chocolate mousse, and raspberry confiture), and sherbet cakes. Dalloyau shops can be found at *2 Place Edmond-Rostand, 99 rue Faubourg St. Honoré, 69 rue de la Convention*, and *16 rue Linois*.

The king of pastry is **Gaston Lenôtre**, who runs Lenôtre shops throughout Paris. His 350 pastry chefs and cooks use at least 12 tons of butter and 300,000 fresh eggs each month. Lenôtre also has the best chocolates in Paris. His shops are at *44 rue du Bac, 5 rue du Havre, 44 rue d'Auteuil*, and *49 ave. Victor Hugo*.

The best ice cream in Paris

The most delicious ice cream in Paris is sold at **Berthillon**, *31 rue St. Louis-en-l'Ile*. The list of rich, homemade flavors is long; so are the lines.

The loveliest gardens in Paris

The **Jardin du Luxembourg**, in the heart of the Left Bank, is an oasis for all ages. Children romp in the park's elaborate playground, watch Punch-and-Judy shows in the outdoor theater, and sail their boats in the fountains. Adults stroll through the formal gardens and read in the sun. During the summer, palm trees line the pebble paths. In winter, they are stored in the Château de Medicis, which also houses the French Senate.

The most elaborate fountain is the **Medicis Fountain**, at the end of a long pool. Scores of statues decorate the lawns. The best are those in the Delacroix group by Dalou. Find yourself a bench and relax. But, unless you are younger than six, don't touch the grass.

The formal **Tuileries Gardens**, which lead from the Louvre to the Orangerie, are also magnificent. Colorful flowers are planted in careful formations. A pleasant day can be spent rambling through the park, from one museum to the next, stopping for a picnic in between.

The best woodland escape

Every large city needs its escape valve—even Paris. The **Bois de Boulogne** is where Parisians let off steam. You can lie on the grass in this immense wooded park (a no-no almost everywhere else in Paris). And you can hike for hours around its 2,500 acres. The Bois de Boulogne offers horseback riding, biking, rowing, and even a zoo. However, don't stay here after dark unless you want to experience Paris' seamy side. When the sun sets, streetwalkers and transvestites work the area.

The deepest tour of Paris

The creepiest but perhaps most fascinating tour of Paris takes you beneath its streets. Eighty-two feet underground is a series of endlessly branching tunnels—156 miles of them in all. They are corridors left over from when the limestone used in building the city was quarried. In 1785, these tunnels were turned into ossuaries for bones removed from graveyards. The bones of most of the victims of The Terror were transferred here.

The southern part of the city beneath Montparnasse and the northern part of the city beneath Montmartre are honeycombed with the old tunnels. It's possible to go from one end of Paris to the other by way of these passages, called les catacombes by Parisians.

The section of the catacombs directly under the Place Denfert-Rochereau is open to the public. The entrance is on the southwest side of the square. Escorted tours of the catacombs (which are not for the fainthearted) are arranged on the first and third Saturdays of each month at 2 p.m. and every Saturday during the summer. (Bring a flashlight.)

The best cafés in Paris

Cafés are an institution in Paris. Parisians use them as living rooms. (Apartments in Paris are usually tiny.) All that is required is the purchase of one cup of coffee. During the summer, tables are set outdoors. Customers soak in the sun while they watch passers-by. In the winter, cafés smell like good coffee and Gauloise cigarettes.

In the 19th century, cafés were gathering spots for artists. Modigliani, the flamboyant Italian painter, frequented the Café de la Rotonde on the boulevard Montparnasse, just around the corner from his atelier on the rue de la Grande Chaumière. He and writer Beatrice Hastings often lingered in the café smoking hashish and drinking absinthe (a potent alcohol now illegal in France). He eventually died on the steps here. The Café de la Rotonde still thrives, cheerful despite its history. You can see its red awnings.

Le Dôme in Montparnasse is decorated with old photos of bygone customers: Picasso, Bonnard, Dufy, Gauguin, and Modigliani.

Paris cafés continue to draw celebrities. Many famous faces can be seen at **La Coupole** on the boulevard Montparnasse. This café was a favorite of Gauguin and his Javanese mistress.

Three of the most famous cafés in Paris are across the street from St. Germain-des-Prés Church on the boulevard St. Germain: **Café de Flore**, **Les Deux Magots**, and **Brassérie Lipp**. All three of these cafés have attracted artists, writers, and celebrities for decades. Their notoriety, however, has made them crowded and expensive. Lipp, which is also a restaurant, has art deco décor and attracts the artistic elite. (British wine dealer Steven Spurrier is a regular.) Les Deux Magots is filled with tourists, but it is a good place to people watch. The lively Flore was Picasso's favorite.

The hottest nightlife

You'll find plenty to do in Paris, regardless of the size of your pocketbook. You can stroll free through the Latin Quarter or Beaubourg, where lively circles of spectators watch street performers. A beer in one of the little cafés won't cost much, and you can sit for hours watching the crowds. Or you can go all out and have dinner in a fine restaurant and then dance until the wee hours of the morning in a *boîte de nuit*.

The coolest clubs

Castel's, *15 rue Princesse, 6th; tel. (33)1-40-51-52-80*, is an upscale, very popular club, frequented by Paris' well-to-do. Guests are screened at the door and only the most prestigious and fashionable are permitted to enter.

Les Bains-Douches, *7 rue du Bourg-l'Abbé; tel. (33)1-48-87-01-80*, is a super-stylish club that attracts the trendiest clientele. Located in an old public bathhouse, it has a small pool. Celebrities can be seen here from time to time. Sunday night is gay night at this popular club.

The smoothest jazz joints

Le Petit Journal is a place you can go to hear excellent jazz. This club has been around for years and has featured many famous jazz talents. *Tel. (33)1-43-21-56-70.*

New Morning is another hot jazz club. Live jazz groups from all over Europe and America perform here. *Tel. (33)1-45-23-51-41.*

Le Slow Club is a wonderful place to hear great New Orleans-style jazz. It has been around for a while and standards from the 1930s and 1940s are played here. *Tel. (33)1-42-33-84-30.*

The coziest *cave*

Caveau de la Huchette, *5 rue de la Huchette; tel. (33)1-43-26-65-05*, is a *cave* wine cellar—an ultra-Parisian spot to relax and enjoy good music and wine in an atmosphere that is warm and inviting.

The best cabarets

Paris cabarets can be a lot of fun and many include dinner and drinks with the show. The **Crazy Horse** is one of Paris' most wild and entertaining cabarets. It always puts on a great show, but the late show is best. *Tel. (33)1-47-23-97-90;* e-mail: *sales@lecrazyhorseparis.com;* website: *www.lecrazyhorseparis.com.*

Cultural bests

Classical music and ballet can be found all over Paris, but the best performances are at the *Paris Opera* and the *Opera de la Bastille*. There are also many famous music halls around Paris, but if you can, catch a ballet or opera in these halls of perfection: **Paris Opera**, *8 rue Scribe 75009 Paris;* **Opera de la Bastille**, *120 rue de Lyon 75012 Paris*. For reservations *tel. (33) 892-89-90-90* or *(33)144-61-59-65*. If you are booking for ten or more *tel. (33)140-01-80-54.*

The cheapest fun

Churches in the Latin Quarter and the Marais offer free concerts. Listen for music wafting out of St. Severin or St. Julien le Pauvre around 8 p.m. The Centre Pompidou also puts on free programs: one night a ballet company, another evening a short play. Street entertainers attract crowds on the plaza outside the building. St. Merry offers concerts Saturday nights and Sunday afternoons. Contribute at the entrance.

The best restaurant in Paris

La Tour d'Argent, *tel. (33)1-43-54-23-31*, has pleased the palate of many a dignitary. Henry III learned to eat with a fork here.

Notre Dame is the backdrop of La Tour, which opened 400 years ago. A 120,000-bottle wine cellar graces this time-honored institution, where 150 employees serve 95 people.

Until the beginning of this century, the place was modest, with sawdust on its wooden floors. Frederic Delair brought it to fame in 1890, when he began serving *canard pressé*—the duck speciality of the house and still the finest dish on the menu. Each duck was engraved with a serial number. If the *maître d'hôtel* feels you are ordering something you aren't familiar with, he will explain the dish very carefully and recommend gently that you try something else.

First-class restaurants

Le Carré des Feuillants, *14 rue de Castiglione, 1st*, serves the cuisine of southwest France with a generous dash of creativity. Chef Alain Dutournier's delicacies include ravioli stuffed with foie gras and truffles.

Ramponneau, *21 ave. Marceau, 16th*, has 1920s charm. The tables are well apart, the tree-shaded terrace is delightful, the wines are excellent, and the service is perfect. The place is always full, but not with tourists.

Robouchon (formerly Jamin), *32 rue de Longchamps, 16th*, is a superb restaurant, the reputation of which is due to the finesse of chef Joel Robouchon. Enjoy the truffles, foie gras, and seafood.

Mercure Galant, *15 rue des Petits-Champs, 1st*, is a place where everything is good and the service matches the food.

Chez Pauline, *5 rue Villedo, 1st*, was handed down from father to son, and it has consistently remained first-class. It is one of the few restaurants in France where you can have a soup called Billy By that is made with cream and mussels.

L'Epi d'Or, *25 rue Jean-Jacques Rousseau, 1st*, is a relatively unknown restaurant but is very fine.

L'Oulette, *38 rue des Tournelles, 4th*, was rejuvenated by a young couple—not only the decoration but the food as well.

The best pasta

Pasta et Vino, *59 rue Dauphine, 6th*, has without a doubt the best pasta in Paris—and, unfortunately, the worst wine.

The fishiest restaurant

Charlot Ier, *128 bis blvd. de Clichy, 18th*, is closed from July 14 to Aug. 23. It's the best, but by no means the cheapest, place for good fresh fish in the city.

The World's Best Destinations

The best meals for the money

Ambassade d'Auvergne, *22 rue du Grenier St. Lazare, 3rd*, serves the most delicious Auvergnat food in town. Open Sundays and during the week until 10.30 p.m. *Tel. (33)1-42-72-31-22; e-mail: info@ambassade-auvergne.com.*

Le Babylone, *13 rue du Babylone, 7th*, is one of the best lunch buys in town. They serve traditional African and West Indian food. *Tel. (33)1-42-33-48-35.*

Kashmir, a very small Indian restaurant on the left bank, has the best Indian food in Paris at a reasonable price. You can enjoy an all-inclusive, multi-course dinner for two (including wine and dessert) for around $50.

Paris' best bistros

The best bistros in Paris are not expensive, and paying more typically means you dine with more tourists than Parisians...not that you enjoy a better meal.

Le Square Trousseau is a lively spot on the corner across from a neighborhood park in the 12th. The clientele is exuberant, the waiters are jovial, and the atmosphere playful and light. When you arrive, crusty bread and rich yellow Saint Malo butter are brought to the table.

Le Bistrot du 7ème in the elegant 7th has shockingly reasonable prices, white cloth table linens, pleasant and professional service, and perfectly prepared traditional dishes.

Le Bistrot d'Henri on a tiny but important street in the lively Odéon district, also home to the English-language Village Voice bookstore, is always teeming with diners at its (only) 32 seats. For a main course, try the *Fameux poulet de Challans à la crème,* which should be famous if it isn't already (it's the best free-range chicken in France).

La Marmotte on rue du Cherche Midi in the 6th has terracotta-colored walls and wood beams. A defender of traditional French cooking, La Marmotte attracts politicians, writers, philosophers, and journalists.

Au Petit Tonneau, not far from Le Bistrot du 7ème, is *"une cuisine de femme."* Madame Ginette Boyer, one of Paris' few female chefs, has been serving the locals for more than 20 years and is not afraid of experimenting with unusual combinations. If you like a casual French ambience, then you will feel comfortable in this almost stereotypical bistro, with its friendly female staff.

Paris' best-kept secret

Le Train Bleu is one of Paris' best-kept secrets. Most Parisians have no idea it exists. It's a restaurant on the second floor of the Gare de Lyon train station that is as much museum and art gallery as restaurant. The food, service, and ambience are excellent. The place is more than 100 years old, built for the Paris Exhibition of 1900. The artwork on the ceilings is remarkable. We recommend the duck.

The world's best cigar shop

No, it's not in Cuba—the world's best (and least expensive) cigar shop happens to be in Paris. The head bartender at the Ritz Hemingway Bar buys cigars for his customers at **Le Lotus**, *4 rue de L'Arcade; tel. (33)1-42-65-35-36.* The shop has a small American clientele, who love it for its quality Havanas. Brits cross the Channel to stock up at Le Lotus at comparatively lower prices. For example, at Le Lotus, a cabinet (box in cigar lingo) of 25 Bolivar Belicosos os Finos is 275 euro ($360). A Bolivar in a cedar-lined tube, which keeps about three months, is 15.30 euro ($20.20). Due to its good working relationship with three specialty importers, it has a fabulous range of new cigars—130 different brands for a total of 10,000 in stock. The owner, Regis Colinet, will tell you which brands are pulling and which brands are duds. He says that cigars aren't just for after dinner anymore. The chic thing in Paris these days is to enjoy the smoke during a meal specially made to marry the flavors of the food, the wine, and the cigar.

The best hotels in Paris

Hôtel des Deux Iles, *59 rue St. Louis-en-l'Ile, 4th*, is in a 17th-century bulding on the other island from the one on which Notre Dame is located. The entrance hall is filled with greenery and flowers, and the popular bar has a fireplace. Rooms are small.

Esmeralda, *4 rue St. Julien le Pauvre, 5th*, is popular with the theater crowd. Rooms are cozy with views of Notre Dame and the little park of St. Julien-le-Pauvre. Guests can use the sauna.

L'Hôtel, *13 rue des Beaux Arts*, is filled with fresh flowers and antiques. The walls are covered with fabric, and the baths are marble. A winding stair-case, marble columns, and stone floors make the entrance rather grand. Oscar Wilde died in one of the rooms.

The Royal Alma, *35 rue Jean-Goujon, 8th*, near the place d'Alma and across the street from the Seine is pleasant. This small, modern hotel has bedrooms with private bathrooms. Prices are reasonable, considering the quiet, elegant neighborhood.

The Ritz, *15 place Vendôme, 1st*, is elegant and caters to the comfort of its clients, which include many celebrities. The deluxe rooms feature Persian and Chinese carpets, but this luxury is reflected in the price—it is terribly expensive to stay at the Ritz. *Tel. (800)223-6800 (US and Canada) or (33)1-43-16-30-30; website: www.ritzparis.com.*

Plaza-Athénée, *25 ave. Montaigne, 8th*, though not as opulent as the Ritz, is more appealing. It has a 1930s ambience that is more attractive than the other super-deluxe establishments in Paris. *Tel. (33)1-800-742-6081 or (33)1-53-67-66-65.*

The best hotels for the price

Hotel d'Angleterre, *44 rue Jacob, 6th*, is a beautiful and inexpensive hotel with a lovely garden and its own classic saloon with a grand piano. *Tel. (33)1-43-59-353-45; e-mail: angleterre-champselysees@multi-micro.com; website: www.angleterre-paris-hotel.com/index.html.*

Esmeralda, *4 rue St. Julien le Pauvre, 5th*, is popular with the theater crowd and has charming rooms with views of Notre Dame and St. Julien-le-Pauvre Park. *Tel. (33)1-43-54-19-20.*

Best value bed for the night

A private, immaculately clean single room, with shower en suite—in the heart of Paris' Montmartre arts district—can be had for as little as $12 per night.

The **Ephrem** guesthouse, *tel. (33)1-53-41-89-09; fax (33)1-53-41-89-19; e-mail: pax@sacre-coeur-montmartre.com*, which is adjacent to the Basilica on Rue Du Chevalier-de-la-Barre, is a 55-room dormitory. Rooms are spartanly furnished, but comfortable and bigger than many single hotel rooms. Rooms are available to those who wish to take part in perpetual adoration and to groups on retreat, or individuals wanting time to reflect spiritually. It's up to you whether to attend mass or simply meditate peacefully as you stroll the streets in the artists' district and gaze out upon panoramic views of Paris. Singles, both men and women, and families are welcome. Most stays are three days or less.

The guesthouse is no Holiday Inn, but it's not a hostel either. If you're new to staying in convents and monasteries, don't worry, no one is monitoring your movements. However, guests are expected to adhere to a curfew. Basilica doors are locked at 10:30 p.m. All in all, small inconveniences for such an affordable and unique experience.

If you're making reservations, confirm everything precisely, in writing and well ahead of time. E-mail replies take nearly a week.

The world's best subway

The Paris subway, or metro, will take you anywhere you need to go quickly, efficiently, and cheaply. You can pick up a map of the metro system at any station and all trains are labeled with the destinations. A single ticket will take you anywhere in the city you want to go with as may transfers as you wish.

The world's most beautiful château

One side trip from Paris that you must make time for is to **Versailles**, the most magnificent of all French châteaux. The palace was created by Louis XIV and has formal gardens that cover 250 acres of land. The grounds also include 600 fountains. The king moved here to get away from the stresses of city life and during his reign, 6,000 people lived in the elaborate palace.

Be sure to see the Hall of Mirrors, the royal apartments, and the chapel. Le Grand Trianon and le Petit Trianon were smaller retreats for the royal family. Le Hameau was Marie Antoinette's little farm, where she played at being a shepherdess when she tired of the rigors of palace life.

Versailles' greatest rival

The second-best château in France is **Vaux-le-Vicomte**, an hour south of Paris. At the entrance are two enormous stone gods. Beyond the iron gates are pavilions, gardens, terraces, cascades, a statuary, and a forest. Across the moat and at the top of two grand staircases is the chateau itself, which has five floors and 80 rooms, 27 open to the public.

Nicholas Fouquet, superintendent of France's treasury and protégé of Cardinal Mazarin, dreamed up the château. He bought 12,000 acres and commissioned three artists to design the building, which was completed in 1661. Le Vau is responsible for the architecture, Le Brun for the paintings, and Le Notre for the gardens.

To celebrate the completion of the château, Fouquet made the mistake of inviting Louis XIV to feast there. Three weeks after the visit, the king had Fouquet arrested for embezzlement and imprisoned for life.

The most beautiful cathedral in France

Chartres has the most beautiful cathedral in France—and one of the finest in the world. It once drew thousands of pilgrims, who came to worship at the shrine of the Virgin. Located about 50 miles southwest of Paris, it is known for its stained-glass windows, which date from the 12th and 13th centuries. The present cathedral is the sixth built on the site.

The best French champagne

The best champagne can be found near the cathedral town of **Rheims**, within the Champagne province. The champagne cellars are often found in subterranean caves up to 13 miles long. Two of the best are **Epernay**, about 13 miles south of Rheims on N51, and **Montagne de Rheims**, near the city.

The finest church in the world

The great Gothic cathedral at **Amiens**, north of Paris, was designated the finest religious edifice in the world by UNESCO. For more information contact the **Comite Regional Du Tourisme De Picardie**, *tel. (33)3-22-22-33-66; website: www.cr-picardie.fr; email: contact@picardietourism.com.*

Europe's most expensive theme park

EuroDisney, opened in April 1992, is complete with roller coasters, castles, and miniature replicas of areas around the world. It is exactly like the other Disneys except for the prices. A one-day pass is $50 for adults and $37 for children under 12. For more information go to *www.eurodisney.com*.

LYONS: THE GASTRONOMIC CAPITAL

Although Parisians may disagree, Lyonnais are sure their city is the gastronomic capital of the world.

Sampling the fare

The best restaurant in the city of great dining is **Vettard**, *7 place Bellecour; tel. (33)4-78-42-07-59*. The house specialty is *quenelle de brochet financière* (a pike dumpling), which is incredibly light and airy. Also delicious is the sea bass in olive oil and sherry wine vinegar. The wine list includes the best regional wines at very reasonable prices. The *belle epoque décor* is pleasant, and the service is friendly. Vettard is closed Sundays and in August.

World-famous chef **Paul Bocuse's** restaurant, too, is excellent. It is located seven miles outside Lyons. Try the superb Bresse chicken and the Elysées soup, served with a flaky pastry cover.

Henry, *27 rue de la Martiniere, 69001*, has a solid reputation. It serves traditional food with inventive touches. Try the warm *salade de homard aux pusses d'épinards et au beurre de truffles* (lobster salad with spinach and truffles) and the *gâteau de ris de veau à la crème de graine de moutard* (sweetbread in a creamy mustard sauce).

Léon de Lyons, *1 rue Plény, 69001*, serves the best Lyonnais specialties. If you are adventurous, try the *Lyonnaiseries en salade* (calf's foot, lamb's trotters, cervelas sausage, brawn, blood pudding, and lentil salad). Chef Lancombe's own inventions are also delicious. Try his *pigeonneau cuit en croûte de sel* (squab cooked in salt).

The best chocolates

Before you leave Lyons, you have to stop and sample the best chocolates in the world at **Maurice Bernachon**, *42 cours Franklin-Roosevelt, 69006*. Some are sprinkled with gold leaf.

Lyons' finest hotel

The **La Cour des Loges**, *tel. (33)4-78-42-75-75*, is a Renaissance palace in the old part of Lyons that was renovated and turned into a modern hotel. It is decorated in an interesting blend of medieval, Renaissance, and modern décor. The interior courtyard, circular stairways, beamed ceilings, and terraced gardens add charm.

PEAK EXPERIENCES: THE ALPS

The Alps are the most beautiful mountains in the world. Like the Rockies, they are snow-capped and dramatically jagged. But unlike their American counterparts, their valleys and slopes are bedecked with picturesque villages. From the peaks, you can look miles down into valleys where tiny church spires are surrounded by gingerbread houses. Stone shepherds' huts offer shelter in the trees. And luxurious hotels pamper tired hikers and skiers.

While the Alps are famous for their tremendous ski slopes, you don't have to be a skier to enjoy them. They are gorgeous year-round. Wild flowers cover the mountains in the spring and summer, and during the fall the leaves turn bright yellow. Hikers, campers, fishermen, and hunters ramble the Alpine peaks long after the ski slopes have closed for the summer.

The prettiest ski resort

Les Contamines-Monjoies is one of the prettiest ski towns in the Alps, and one of the least known. This small ski area is set in a high wooded valley, not far from Chamonix. It has 62 miles of slopes and 15 miles of cross-country ski trails.

The best place to stay is **Le Gai Soleil**, *tel. (33)4-50-21-00-70*, just outside of Les Contamines-Monjoies. It has a cozy atmosphere, which meshes well with the wonderful accommodation.

(See more on skiing in France in Section 4: The World's Best Sporting Destinations.)

BRITTANY: THE MOST BEAUTIFUL COASTLINE

Brittany (Bretagne), in the west, has 600 miles of the most ruggedly beautiful coastline in France. Along it are sheltered coves, fishing villages, wide deserted beaches, dramatic cliffs, smart resorts, and lush farmland. The stone-built villages are rich in history.

The Quiberon Peninsula's rocks, caves, and reefs make its coast the most dramatic in the province. Walk to Cote Sauvage (Wild Coast) from one end to the other, stopping at the strange rock formations: Grottes du Taureau (Bull's Cave), la Fenêtre (Window), and La Vieille (Old Woman). East and south of the coast are wide beaches and fishing ports.

Brittany's greatest sight

St. Malo, a fortified island-city in Brittany that dates back to the 12th century, was bombed during WWII, but has been restored. Visit the castle (which is where you can catch the best view of St. Malo) and the Quic-en-Groigne waxworks museum.

The best seafood

Brittany has the most delicious seafood in France—sole, crabs, shrimp, oysters, and smoked salmon. Try a bottle of muscadet, the dry white wine of Brittany, or the potent hard cider.

One of the best places in the region for seafood is **Lorand-Barre**, *Damour, Ponts-Neufs*. This rustic Breton restaurant eight miles from St. Brieuc has fabulous grilled lobster and dessert crepes.

Normandy—the Riviera's coldest rival

Normandy's world-famous resorts—Deauville, Trouville, and Cabourg— are the Riviera's coldest rivals. The Gulf Stream warms these elegant towns along the Cherbourg Peninsula in summer. And they are far less crowded than their southern counterparts.

Deauville has great shopping (including branches of the leading Paris jewelers and designers), elegant hotels and restaurants, and a casino. A boardwalk runs the length of the beach.

A peaceful contrast is Honfleur, a small fishing harbor. At sunset, fishermen bring in the day's catch. A pleasant and comfortable place to stay is **Lechat**, *15 place St. Cathérine*, in the heart of the old district.

Incomparable Mont St. Michel

Mont St. Michel is an eighth-century abbey that sits atop cliffs rising from a flat island. It is said to have been built at the command of the Archangel Michael, who appeared on the spot. Guides will show you an indentation in the rock that is supposedly the archangel's footprint. The abbey contains the silver shrine of the archangel, who is supposed to have fought the devil hand-to-hand on a nearby hill. View the Escalier de Dentelle (Lacework Stairway), the Gothic buildings, and the cloister.

Mére Poulard, *Grand Rue*, has an outdoor terrace where you can dine during the tourist season and a stone fireplace where you can huddle in winter. Try the dessert omelet.

Château Country—the Loire

The **Loire Valley**, Southwest of Paris, puts Disneyland to shame. Known as Château Country, the region is filled with turreted castles. The valley's mild climate, rolling green hills, and lush pastureland attracted French nobility centuries ago. Today these châteaux, once fortresses designed to ward off invaders, are enjoyed by visitors from around the world.

The most beautiful Loire château

Chenonceaux is considered the most beautiful chateau in the Loire

Valley. Straddling the Cher River, it was embellished by eight women over a period of 450 years and has been dubbed "The Castle Women Built." It is approached by a promenade of tall trees. The interior is furnished with tapestries, statues, and portraits.

The chateau was built between 1513 and 1521 under the supervision of Catherine Briconnet, a wealthy 21-year-old heiress. After Catherine's death, Chenonceaux became the property of Henri II, who presented the castle to his mistress, Diane de Poitiers. She planted fine gardens and had a five-arch bridge built to the far bank of the Cher, where she liked to go hunting.

When King Henri died, his wife, Catherine de Medici, forced her rival out of Chenonceaux. The queen then added her own touches, including a 197-foot gallery filled with fine paintings. Catherine had elaborate, erotic parties at Chenonceaux. One party she had for the Duke of Anjou included regattas, fireworks, and satyrs chasing wood nymphs in the background. The most beautiful noblewomen in France waited on guests—topless!

The largest Loire château

Chambord is the largest of the Loire chateaux. Designed by Leonardo da Vinci for King Francois I as a pleasure palace, it is set in a 13,600-acre game reserve and surrounded by a 20-mile wall, the longest in France. The 440-room hunting lodge is laced with spires, pinnacles, gables, turrets, towers, and 365 chimneys. The palace has 74 stairways, including a double staircase constructed of twin spirals. One person can ascend while another is descending without meeting.

Where to sleep like a king

While you are in the Loire Valley, you can live like a king. The region is filled with lovely chateau-hotels that are beautiful but not expensive.

The **Domaine de Beauvois**, *tel. (33)2-47-55-50-11; email: contact@ beauvois.com; website: www.domaine-beauvois.com/francais/index.html*, dates back to the 15th century and has a beautiful, classic style. Modern amenities, such as a heated pool, tennis courts and elevators are also available.

Château de Pray, *tel. (33)2-47-57-23-67*, is a lovely château with moderate prices located two miles northeast of Amboise. It has a beautiful terrace for dining during summer.

The best of the Bordeaux wine region

The region around **Bordeaux** is known for its great red wines — Margaux, Mouton-Rothschild, and Haut-Brion. A 30-minute drive from Bordeaux will put you in the heart of the wine country. This region is full of small mansions and splendid castles, all surrounded by acres of vines.

The best wine stores in Bordeaux are **Badie**, *place Tourny;* **La Vinothèque**, *cours du XXX Juillet;* and **Vignes et Vins de France**, *4 rue des*

Bahutiers. The Maison du Vin offers maps of the wine regions and lists châteaux that receive visitors.

The prettiest wine town

St. Emilion is one of the most picturesque villages in France. The medieval town is perched on a plateau overlooking the valley of the Dordogne. While you are there, visit the 17th century hermitage, which was hollowed from rock.

Nearby is the entrance to a chapel with a strange underground shrine. It, too, was carved out of rock 900 years ago. A subterranean passage leads to catacombs containing skeletons in ancient tombs. (You must have a guide to visit the shrine.)

At the **Syndicat d'Initiative**, *place des Crénaux*, you can get a list of wine châteaux nearby. The Château Ausone produces the St. Emilion's vintage, among others.

BURGUNDY — THE MOST BOUNTIFUL

Burgundy is the most bountiful region in France. The food is sumptuous, the wine rich, and the forests filled with game. The landscape is dotted with tiny Romanesque churches, old abbeys, canals, and sleepy towns. The area is known for its medieval churches.

Bourgogne is for those who prefer to pamper themselves while slowly savoring the atmosphere, the wine, and the food. Follow the wine route through the region, sampling the vintages. Treat yourself to Burgundy's legendary casseroles, *coq au vin*, or *boeuf bourguignon*, accompanied by a bottle of local red.

Beaune is the wine capital of the region. Typical of Burgundy, Beaune has narrow cobblestoned streets and old houses with little gardens. It also has tour buses, tourists, and expensive gift shops.

Known for its fine wines, Beaune is also the center for excursions north-ward to vineyards and châteaux. Ancient cellars in town include Cave du Bourgogne, Maison Patriarche Père et Fils (a working cellar), and Maison Calvet. Nearby are the wineries around Aloxe-Corton or Nuits St. Georges. The famous Pommard vineyards are just south of the town.

To explore the greatest wine country, drive from Beaune north to Dijon on the Ouche.

Burgundy's best restaurant

L'Espérance, *tel. (33)3-86-33-39-10; e-mail: esperance@relaischateaux.fr*, is a fine restaurant in an 18th century luxury hotel. Owner and chef M. Marc Meneau is one of France's most creative and innovative chefs.

The world's best lodge

The best lodge in the world to join is the **Chevaliers du Tastevin**, which inducts new members twice a year in the Clos de Vougeot, the manor house in the midst of the Burgundy vineyards. Only wine produced from those vineyards can bear the prestigious Burgundy label.

The ceremonies begin with the entrance of the *halberdiers* (uniformed men carrying medieval weapons), who are followed by the counsels of the order in their scarlet and gold robes. Each new member, or postulant-knight, is welcomed by a witty poem recited by the grand master in French. He is then dubbed a knight by being struck three times on the shoulder with a grape-wood stick "in the name of Noah, the father of the vine; Bacchus, the god of wine; and St. Vincent, the patron of vintners."

The ceremony is followed by a dinner of six courses, each accompanied by a selected vintage—for example, meat pies with 1985 Aligoté from the Hautes-Côtes de Nuits; turbot with 1983 Puligny-Montrachet; wine-cooked eggs with 1982 Savigny-lès-Beaune; mustard chicken with 1981 Beaune Grèves; local cheeses with 1980 Latricières-Chambertin; or pear ice cream and petits fours with coffee and Marc or Prunelle from Burgundy. You may smoke only at the end of the meal.

Top places to stay

Along the wine route is the **Château d'Ige**, *tel. (34)958-227-019; website: www.circumvista.com/chateaudige.html*, a hotel in a remodeled 12th century château near Cluny. Fortified towers, ancient exposed stonework, and a spiral staircase of hewn stone give the hotel a medieval atmosphere. The castle has six rooms and serves gourmet French cuisine.

Another charming old hotel is the **Hostellerie de la Poste**, *tel. (33)3-86-34-16-19*, located off Route Nationale 6 halfway between Chablis and Dijon in Avallon. Napoleon stopped at this inn. Established in 1707, it has one of the best restaurants in France, located in old converted stables and on a cobblestoned terrace. Most of the 30 rooms have baths. The hotel is closed from December to March 11.

The Hôtel de la Poste, *5 blvd. Clemenceau*, on the site of the former ramparts, is the most popular in Beaune. A charming old place with a garden courtyard, it also has the best restaurant in town. (Try the crayfish in cream sauce or the roast quail.) The hotel is closed from November to March.

ALSACE—THE MOST GERMAN REGION

Alsatians describe themselves as *entre deux portes*, or between two gates—France and Germany. This French *département* that stretches between the Vosges Mountains and the Rhine River has been passed between France and Germany five times, and, as a result, its culture is an interesting blend of

French and German. Try the local dishes: onion pie, *choucrôute* (sauerkraut), and *charcuterie*, accompanied by a glass of the wine or beer of the region. *Kugelhupf*, a yeast-based cake, is the traditional dessert.

Strasbourg: the prettiest old town

Strasbourg is the ancient capital of the province and it contains a centuries-old center enclosed by branches of the Ill River and guarded by the Strasbourg Cathedral. The pink Gothic cathedral was begun in 1176 and completed in the 15th century.

Ancient halt-timbered buildings line the cathedral square and surrounding streets. One of the most striking is the **Maison Kammerzell**, a restaurant in a 15th-century house with elaborately carved wood trim. Wander along the rue du Bain aux Plantes to La Petite France. Four massive square towers, remnants of 14th-century ramparts, stand over the covered bridges that cross the Ill.

The best white wines

Regional wines of Alsace, unlike those of the rest of France, are labeled by grape varieties rather than by the name of the village or château. Because they don't understand this German labeling system, the French mistrust Alsatian wines. As a result, vintage Guebwiller Gewurtztraminer is the best wine bargain in France.

Along the Alsatian **Route du Vin** (Wine Road), stretching 90 miles from Marlenheim to Thann, are centuries-old towns surrounded by vineyards. Eguisheim is a 16th-century town with half-timbered houses with low door-ways. Three medieval towers guarded the town until the 15th century. Stop at the **Caveau d'Eguisheim** (dated 1603) for lunch.

Riquewihr is a pretty Alsatian town that clings to a vine-covered hill, within a circle of 16th-century walls. Cars may not enter its cobblestoned streets.

DORDOGNE — THE LEAST SPOILED AREA

This *département* in the heart of France is rural, traditional, and relatively unspoiled. But tourists are beginning to discover the area. Dordogne is known for its prehistoric cave drawings and gourmet cuisine. Deep green valleys and river gorges break up the landscape. In the Dronne Valley, walled castles top nearly every hill.

The best country cuisine

The Perigord, a historic province contained within Dordogne, is famous for its cuisine. This is a place to linger over long meals. It is more than a meal here — it's tradition. The area's truffles are famous, and its game and fish are equally delicious. Try the crayfish and the morels. Wash your meal down with a full-bodied Bergerac.

The world's finest porcelain

Limoges, the largest city in the region, is famous for its fine porcelain. Cross its Roman bridges, stroll the little streets in the old section, and visit the ancient cathedral of St. Etienne. Notice the half-timbered houses by the river. They have open spaces between the roof and the top floor, held up by wide beams. In the old days, residents dried their wash and kept food provisions in this airy space below the roof.

Tour the porcelain factories or enamel workshops. You can get a list of these from the **Tourist Information Office**, *tel. (33)5-55-34-46-87.*

The prettiest town in Dordogne

One of the most charming villages in France is **Brantôme**. Bordered on two sides by the Dronne River, it has an 18th century Benedictine abbey (now the town hall) and a good museum, the Desmoulin. Stroll along the canals past the houses and then visit the Monks' Garden.

The most spectacular town in France

Dordogne boasts medieval castles and walled cities dating back to Richard the Lion-Hearted. The most spectacular of the towns is **Rocamadour**, built into the face of a steep cliff. Narrow, cobblestoned streets climb the cliff to its summit, where the Basilica of St. Sauveur is perched along with several shrines. Pilgrims on their knees have climbed the Great Staircase to the shrine since the Middle Ages. See the Black Madonna in Notre Dame chapel.

Medieval musts

East of Le Bugue is the **Château Beynac-et-Cazenac**, a well-preserved fortress atop a cliff. The castle was destroyed and rebuilt twice: in 1189 by Sir Mercadier in the name of Richard the Lion-Hearted and in 1214 by Simon de Montfort during the Crusade against Albigensian heretics. From the ramparts of the castle, another great fortress, the Château de Castelnaud, can be seen. The restored castle was once the headquarters for Simon de Montfort.

The village of St. Cirq-La Popie sits beneath the ruins of a 1,000-year-old castle and is set in a gorgeous valley. St. Cirq is known for its woodcraft, although the art has largely disappeared.

More than 80 walled cities still stand from Perigord to the Pyrenees, including Monpazier, Domme, Lalinde, Villereal, Beaumont, and Ste. Foyla Grande.

Europe's favorite summer playground

The **French Riviera**, known as the Cote d'Azur, is Europe's favorite summer playground. It is hot, crowded, expensive, and super-trendy. The coast is 72 miles long, with 25 miles of long beaches of pebbles or sand, from Marseilles to Menton.

The most famous Riviera town is **St. Tropez**, but avoid it in July and August, when it is jam-packed. Visit in September and October, after the summer season and before the winter. Prices drop, the weather is mild and sunny, and the beaches are yours.

The coast is 72 miles long, with 25 miles of long beaches of pebble or sand, from Marseilles to Menton. From Nice to the Italian border, beaches are of gravel or rock. Between Cannes and St. Raphael, the rocks of Corniche are breathtakingly beautiful. But the best beaches are along the coast from St. Raphael to Jyeres: Cabasson, Le Lavandou, St. Clair, Cavaliere, Tahiti, Pampelone, and Salins.

The nicest town

Nice is a lovely town with old houses and wide views. Although its beach is rocky, you still can take a pleasant walk along the sea—on Promenade des Anglais. The casino is elegant. Visit the Terra Amata paleontological museum near the old harbor, located on the spot where the remains of a mammoth hunters' camp 400,000 years old was discovered.

The best Casino

In Cannes, the glamorous **Palm Beach Casino**, *tel. (33)4-97-06-36-90*, is a huge attraction. The beaches are sandy and luxury yachts line the marina. And the Palace of Festivals houses a theater, a casino, a nightclub, boutiques, and a convention center. It is the site of the famous film festival.

The best pastries and market

Gaston Lenôtre, perhaps France's best-known pastry chef, celebrated his 80th birthday this year by opening his first shop and tea salon on the Côte d'Azur. The shop, on rue d'Antibes, features more than 500 pastry specialites. Try the apple douillon and homemade ice cream. The elegant café on the first floor is an ideal place to nibble Lenôtre's stylish breakfasts or afternoon teas.

Don't visit Cannes without paying a visit to the fabulous **Marché Forville** (where the coast's top chefs come to buy their ingredients). The mushroom salesman in the left-hand aisle sometimes has white truffles and Boulangerie Paul has its own traditional bread oven. The Marché Forville is two blocks in from the Hôtel de Ville, on the rue Félix Faure.

A princely resort

Monaco is a separate tiny nation on the Riviera that attracts the world's royalty. The little kingdom is set above the sea and looks like the setting for a fairy tale. But it's far from innocent, with its casinos, decadent hotels, and beaches where the world's best bodies sun topless.

Monaco's capital, Monte Carlo, has some of the most glamorous hotels, restaurants, and casinos in Europe.

The finest hotel on the Riviera

The **Hotel de Paris** attracts jet setters, gamblers, yachtsmen, and the Grand Prix crowd. The hotel's best feature is its magnificent restaurant, **Louis XV**, *tel. (33)4-97-06-98-98; e-mail: reservation@hotel-de-paris.com; website: www.hotel-de-paris.com.*

PROVENCE: THE SWEETEST REGION

The Mediterranean region of **Provence** is a sweet land, literally and figuratively. Its air is scented by the lavender, basil, rosemary, thyme, and sage that grow in its rocky fields. Old traditions and a simple way of life survive here. This is the land of Marcel Pagnol, the beloved French writer, who wrote about his boyhood adventures in these rocky hills, olive groves, and stone houses.

Provence looks like an Impressionist painting. Villages climb the white rocks; the pines are dark green, the soil red, and the olive groves green; and lavender grows in the fields.

Framed by the sea, the Alps, the Rhone and Durance rivers, and the Italian border, Provence stretches from the medieval town of Aigues-Mortes in the west, beyond Marseille to Cassis in the east. It includes the lower Rhone Valley; the flat, windy marches of the Camargue; and the foothills of the Alps.

Best restaurant in Provence

Les Bacchaneles, *tel. (33)4-42-27-21-06*, is a small, intimate restaurant with wonderful prices. The restaurant specializes in Provençal food and offers three three-course menus.

The most beautiful walled city

Avignon is one of France's most beautiful walled cities, groaning with history. Every single building seems to tell a story of medieval murder, intrigue, or romance. It also makes an excellent base for exploring the villages of the Rhone Valley. Driving beside the Rhone River, you can see the statue of the Virgin Mary on top of the Palace des Papes, shining in solid gold, and in the distance, the arches of the Bridge of St. Benezet, better known as the Pont d'Avignon of nursery rhyme fame. But forget about dancing across the bridge. Half of it was carried away by flood waters centuries back, and it has never been rebuilt.

The **Hotel d'Europe**, *12 Place Crillon; tel. (33)4-90-14-76-76; e-mail: reservations@hotel-d-europe.fr*, is almost as ancient as its surroundings. It was built in 1580 as the private home of a Marquess, but has been a hotel since 1799. The guest list of luminaries who have stayed here is long: Napoleon Bonaparte, Pablo Picasso, Salvador Dali, Tennessee Williams, King Edward VII of England. This is one of the most elegant hotels you'll ever stay in.

The oldest houses in France

The road to the golden-hued city of Gordes leads through flat vineyards and steep hills to the **Village des Bories**. This collection of prehistoric stone buildings, or bories, dates back to 3000 B.C. The huts were used by shepherds until the 18th century. They have been restored to look as they did 4,000 years ago and are filled with old cooking implements and tools.

The best Roman ruins in France

Nîmes has the most splendid Roman arena in the country. It has been well preserved and is still used today for bull fighting. Nîmes Roman temple called Maison Caree, is also perfectly preserved.

The most fragrant town

The sweetest smelling town in Provence is **Grasse**, 10 mile from Cannes. It is the perfume capital of the world. Violet, lavender, jasmine, lily, rose, jonquil, and mimosa grow in this town. Once the favorite resort of Queen Victoria, Grasse is a picturesque old village with winding cobblestoned streets and weathered houses.

Each year the perfumeries in Grasse process more than 700 tons of roses, 600 tons of orange blossoms, and 800 tons of jasmine. You can take a tour of two perfume factories, **La Parfumerie Fragonard** and **La Parfumerie Gallimard**, which are open daily. English-speaking guides explain how the perfume is made.

THE MOST SPANISH REGION: ROUSSILLON

West of the Riviera, stretching the length of the Golfed u Lion, from the Pyrénées to the Rhone Delta, is the **Roussillon** region. Medieval walled cities, the peaks of the Pyrénées, Mediterranean resorts, and quaint villages mark this varied region. Also known as French Catalonia, Roussillon has a Spanish air. It belonged to Spain until 1659, and the people are Catalan, as are the people of Barcelona. The red and yellow Catalan flag flies over the region's capital, **Perpignan**. Some Catalans would like to see this region become autonomous.

The least spoiled coast

Traditional fishing villages still can be found along the western end of the Mediterranean coast. **Collioure** is the most charming fishing port. Matisse painted here. **Sète** also retains its original appeal.

The largest walled city

Carcassonne, Europe's largest medieval walled city, is west of Narbonne. A mighty circle of towers and battlements encircles the hilltop town. Parts of the walls were built by the Romans. In the fifth century, the Visigoths enlarged the fortress. Charlemagne laid siege to the city for five years in the ninth century. And in the 13th century it fell to Crusaders; Simon de Montfort took it over. St. Louis strengthened the fortress. It was rebuilt in the 19th century by Violet-le-Duc to conform to Victorian ideas of how a walled city should look.

The best place to stay in Carcassonne is the **Hôtel de la Cité**, *Place d'Eglise*, located in a former Episcopal palace built into the wall near Basilica of St. Nazaire. Some rooms have canopy beds, and the dining hall is beautiful. The hotel is open from April through October.

THE MOST EXOTIC REGION: BASQUE COUNTRY

The southwest of France and the northwest of Spain combine to form an exotic region known as **Basque Country**. The Basques have a common language, culture, and history identifiable as neither French nor Spanish.

The Spanish Basques, in particular, have agitated for autonomy. A separatist movement exists in France also, but it is milder. The Basque language is related to no other; it is not Indo-European. Some believe that the cavemen spoke Basque.

The mountainous region is known for its cuisine and its specialty dish, the wild dove that migrates from northern Europe to Spain in October.

The most typical town

St. Jean-Pied-de-Port, near the Spanish border, is the most typically Basque town in the region. It was fortified in the time of Louis XIV, and its narrow cobblestoned streets are guarded by a tall citadel. The typical Basque houses are stone, sturdy, half-timbered, and whitewashed with red or green trim and chalet-like stucco.

The church's clock tower tolls the hour twice, following local custom. A stone bridge crosses the Nive River to the tower. The *fronton*, or ball court, is always filled with *pelota* players. And flat, round tombstones from pre-Christian times can be seen in the graveyards. *Pelota*, or *jai alai*, is the Basque ball game, played with a hard ball and a racket. It is very fast.

The finest place to surf

Biarritz is a seaside resort on the Bay of Biscay. It has one of France's largest beaches and offers the best surfing on the French coast. A great place to stay while visiting is **Hotel du Palais**, *tel. (800)223-6800* or *(33)5-59-41-64-00*. Visit the Rocher de la Vierge for a good view of the ocean. The lower promenade, along the boulevard du Prince de Galles, leads past the foaming breakers that give the coast its name—Côte d'Argent, the Silver Coast. The lighthouse on the summit of Cap St. Martin has a splendid view.

Biarritz was made famous by the Empress Eugenie (the wife of Napoleon III), who attracted fashionable clientele to the resort. Queen Victoria and Edward VII, among others, slept in Eugenie's villa, now the Hôtel du Palais.

THE BEST OF GERMANY

GERMANY, THE DISEASED WORLD'S BATHHOUSE.

—Mark Twain

We believe Germany is the best all-round travel destination in Europe. As balanced as a fine cuckoo clock, it has something for everyone. Its old cities have museums, concert halls, and gourmet restaurants. Romantic little villages nestle beneath the snow-capped Alps. Its North Sea beaches are edged by 30-foot sand dunes and beautified with goose-pimpled, bronzed (and sometimes nude) bodies. The avant-garde lives side by side with folk culture.

BERLIN: THE MOST EXCITING CITY

Berlin has an exciting, devil-may-care atmosphere, and is one of the most exciting cities in the world to visit. Sidewalk cafés, little shops, parks, and offices exist side by side with the remains of the graffiti-covered Berlin Wall.

Berlin is a lively city. Its slogan is *"Berlin weil's Spass macht"* (Berlin because it's fun). Berlin is a fashion center, known for its chic, quality clothing. It has 5,000 restaurants, cafés, and bars situated along its *Kurfürstendamm* (Berlin's Champs-Elysées), which stay open all night.

What used to be West Berlin is more modern than its sister. There are lakes, rivers, and forests covering 35% of the city's area. Western Berlin is ablaze with neon and gleaming with chrome and glass architecture. Germany beyond the Berlin Wall was always rich in culture and perfectly preserved historical treasures—now these treasures are easily accessible to visitors.

Berlin's best museums

The **House at Checkpoint Charlie** displays many of the ingenious, homemade contraptions used by East Berliners in their attempts to cross the Berlin Wall when it stood as a barrier between East and West. The museum is located in a dilapidated tenement building at *Friedrichstrasse 44*, near the gate between East and West Berlin in the American sector. Displays include a miniature submarine created with a motor taken from a motor scooter; a low-slung sportscar that zoomed beneath the horizontal barrier at Checkpoint Charlie; a homemade bulletproof truck that crashed through the wall; and photos of a 476-foot tunnel that 57 people crawled through to the West.

Museumsinsel (Museum Island), surrounded by the Spree River and Spree Canal, is one of the world's largest and most magnificent museum complexes. It includes the Pergamon, Bode, and Altes museums, as well as the National Gallery, the Berlin Cathedral, and several ruins.

More than 600,000 people visit the **Pergamon Museum** each year, making it the most popular of the state museums. The Pergamon Altar (180 B.C. to 160 B.C.) is just one of the impressive exhibits reconstructed from the archeological collection of the Prussian court. Also on exhibit are the Gate of Miletus, a two-story Roman market gate, and a reconstruction of a street built during the reign of Nebuchandnezzar (605 B.C. to 562 B.C.). In addition to the classical collection, the Pergamon building contains the collections of the Museum of Islamic Art and the Museum of Ancient Near Eastern Art. For more information *e-mail: info@jmberlin.de; website: www.jmberlin.de*.

The **Jewish Museum** is the second most popular museum in Berlin. It opened its doors in 2001 and is a stunning piece of architecture. Summer programs are held in the gardens of the museum, including concerts and many other cultural events. Opening hours are 10 a.m. to 6 p.m. Admission is free.

The finest Opera performances

The **Deutsche Staatsoper**, *tel. (49)30-20-35-40*, hosts some of the finest opera performances in the world. It holds 1,500 people and burned down in 1843, but was rebuilt to mirror the original.

The world's largest Rembrandt collection

Gemäldegalerie displays the world's largest Rembrandt collection and is one of several museums that make up the immense Dahlem museum complex, which includes sculpture, prints, the Ethnographical Museum, the Museum of Far Eastern, Islamic, and Indian Art, and the Botanical Museum. You could spend days here.

Berlin's most famous work of art

The **Egyptian Museum**, *website: www.egyptianmuseum.gov.eg*, houses the most famous piece of art in Berlin—the painted limestone bust of beautiful Queen Nefertiti, created more that 3,300 years ago.

Germany's best park

The **Tiergarten** is Germany's most attractive park. Originally the park was the royal hunting preserve, but is now one of the world's largest urban parks. It has lakes, ponds, and a zoo, which has more species than any other zoo in the world. At its eastern edge is the Reichstag, Germany's former Parliament building, which burned down in 1933 but was rebuilt after the war. It is used for political meetings—the German Parliament now meets in

Bonn. The Brandenburg Gate at the eastern end of the Tiergarten marks the former border between East and West Berlin.

Berlin's best castle

Schloss Charlottenburg is the best example of royal Prussian architecture in Berlin. The Schloss was destroyed during World War II, but it has been restored. You can tour the castle, which is surrounded by lovely grounds and a lake, Tuesdays through Sundays, 9 a.m. until 5 p.m.

Charlottenburg houses a great porcelain collection, the museum of arts and crafts, and sumptuously decorated royal apartments, including the splendid white-and-gold rococo gallery. The Charlottenburg Mausoleum contains the tombs of King Friedrich Wilhelm III and Queen Luise.

Counterculture bests

For a taste of Berlin's counterculture, visit **Kreuzberg**, Berlin's answer to New York's East Village. Art galleries, bookstores, used-clothing shops, high-fashion boutiques, and small theaters thrive in this area. Restaurants offering every imaginable cuisine line the streets. The Berlin Wall, which is covered with colorful graffiti, is the eastern boundary of the neighborhood. A sign here reminds you that you are at the site of Gestapo torture chambers.

The heart of Kreuzberg is the Mehringhof complex, a former factory at Gneisenaustrasse 2. It is used by about 30 counterculture organizations, including theater troupes, jazz bands, political groups, a health cooperative, and a bookstore.

The most decadent shopping

Stop in at **Kaufhaus des Westens**, known locally as KaDeWe, Berlin's version of Harrods in London. Located near the Ku'damm, it has an enormous selection of clothing, as well as 450 kinds of bread, 1,000 types of sausage, and 1,000 different cheeses.

The best bargains

A much less expensive place to shop is Berlin's flea market, **Die Nolle**, open every day except Tuesday 11 a.m. until 7 p.m. It is situated in 16 old subway trains at Nollendorfplatz, a 10-minute walk from Wittenbergplatz, the square near KaDeWe. Old sewing machines, furniture, and antique dolls are some of the best buys. Stop at the little restaurant here and try a *Boulette* (hamburger without a bun). You may also hear live jazz in the streets.

The best nightlife

The **Metropol**, in a former theater building, is the largest disco in Germany and draws 3,000 Berliners a night. By the end of the night, dancers are in an elated frenzy.

Once you get past the doorman at **Sage Club**, *tel. (49)30-278-9830*, you'll face a fire-breathing dragon over the dance floor. Fortunately, finding a place to sit and talk is less of a challenge. Sage has three dance floors and a special pool area.

The **Riverboat** is an energetic nightspot, where frenetic jazz is played. The building itself is a maze of halls and booths. It is closed Sundays and Mondays.

Café Keese, *tel. (49)30-312-9111*, caters to an older crowd. It is a large dance hall and there are specific rules that have to be followed. First, women have to ask men to dance (men can ask women to dance only once an hour), and second, men are not allowed to refuse.

Top restaurants

Rockendorf's, *tel. (49)30-402-3099*, is the best restaurant in Berlin. It has one of the world's finest wine lists with a choice of over 800 select vintages. The staff is attentive, but understated.

I-Punkt has a panoramic view of Berlin from its location on the 20th floor of the Europa-Center complex. The view is spectacular at night when the city is lit up.

Ermeler Haus, *tel. (49)30-279-4028*, is located in a 16th century mansion and is a continental restaurant. The atmosphere is cozy and romantic, a perfect place for couples. Reservations are suggested.

The best hotel

The top place to stay in Berlin is **Bristol-Hotel Kempinski**, *tel. toll free (800)695-8284*. The atmosphere of this sprawling, old-fashioned hotel is warm and inviting and the staff are ready and willing to help.

Close seconds

The **Hotel Ambassador** has a heated swimming pool and colossal buffet breakfasts. The view from the rooftop is spectacular. *Tel. (49)30-21-9020; e-mail: Ambassador-Berlin@sorat-hotels.com.*

Hotel Belvedere, *tel. (49)30-826-0010*, is next to a forest and near the Havel. The hotel is a huge turn-of-the-century villa with gardens and a peaceful atmosphere. Rooms are furnished with antiques.

✳ THE BEST OF FRANKFURT

Frankfurt is the logical center for touring Germany. Frankfurt-am-Main Airport is the largest and busiest of Germany's international airports. (All major trains go beyond Frankfurt's main railroad station to the airport, allowing incoming tourists to make train connections to all parts of Germany—or Europe for that matter).

A modern, industrial city and Germany's banking and financial center, Frankfurt has a charming old section with good beer halls. The *Altstadt* (Old Town) is ringed by the *Innenstadt* (Inner Town), which developed in the 14th century.

Frankfurt's best restaurants

Weinhaus Bruckenkeller, *tel. (49)69-28-42-38*, specializes in German food served in an arched cellar with candle-lit tables and strolling musicians. The wine cellar contains over 180 German wines.

Restaurant Français, *tel. (800)223-5652* (US and Canada) or *(49)69-2-15-02*, is located in Steigenberger-Hotel Frankfurter Hof and was awarded one of Michelin's coveted stars for its delectable fare. It's a very popular place, so reservations are required.

The two finest hotels

Steigenberger-Hotel Frankfurter Hof, *tel. toll free (800)223-5652* or *(49)69-2-15-02* has been welcoming guests since 1876. Central and comfortably old-fashioned, it has two cozy bars, three amazing restaurants, and an outdoor café.

Hessischer Hof, *tel. toll free (800)223-6800* or *(49)69-7-54-00*, received four stars from Michelin for its deluxe accommodation. The restaurant is also excellent.

Frankfurt's best undiscovered hotels

The **National**, *tel. (49)69-242-6480*, is a homey, comfortable hotel with a quiet charm and affordable rooms (plus all profits from the hotel go to an orphanage). Don't be put off by the rough exterior of the hotel; the interior is cozy. Service is very friendly and many rooms have views of the neighboring park.

About seven miles outside Frankfurt is **Schlosshotel Kronberg**, *tel. toll free (800)223-6800* or *(49)61-73-70-101*, an elegant castle hotel. Built in 1888 as the residence of Kaiser Wilhelm II's mother, it became a gathering place for European royalty. After World War I, French Occupation officials took possession of the castle. After World War II, American Occupation forces used it as a club for high officers and civilians. Today, the palace is a hotel with 19th-century furnishings. The cuisine is superb and the hotel has a 250-acre golf course for guests to enjoy.

The best nightlife

Frankfurt, surprisingly for a German town, is not a big beer-drinking city. The preferred drinks are hard cider and wine. Try the cider, which is delicious, but be aware that it carries a much stronger punch than its sweet taste suggests.

Frankfurt is filled with *Weinstuben*. The **Volkswirt**, *tel. (49)69-283-419*, is popular among young professionals. It has the greatest wine selection in town.

Peter Dunker is a wine bar beneath a half-timbered building. The wine list is long, and the prices are low. **Operncafé**, *tel. (49)69-285-260*, is a trendy place where good-looking young people ogle one another before and after concerts.

Jazz is big in Frankfurt. **Der Jazzkeller**, *tel. (49)69-288-537; e-mail: info@jazzkeller.com*, features top performers. Good jazz concerts are staged Sunday mornings in the courtyard of the **Historisches Museum**, *tel. (49)69-212-7599*.

✕ HAMBURG: THE MOST WORLDLY CITY

Hamburg, an international port, is Germany's most worldly city, known for the steamy sex shows and wild discos along the Reeperbahn in Sankt Pauli. However, Hamburg also has a peaceful section. The lakes at its center are bordered by wide green avenues, opulent shops, and hotels. The best place to take in Hamburg at a glance is the tower of the baroque Michaelis Kirche.

Best museum in Hamburg

The **Museum of Hamburg**, *tel. (49)40-428-41-2360*, is a great place to research your European ancestry. If you visit Hamburg's Historic Emigration Office you can receive information on your ancestors within one to two hours.

Germany's best fish market

The best fish market in Germany is held on Sunday mornings in Hamburg. This raucous but fun affair is located by the docks in Altona and opens at 5 a.m.

Hamburg's finest dining

The best restaurant in Hamburg is the **Landhaus Scherrer**, *tel. (49)40-880-1325; e-mail: info@landhausscherrer.de*. It specializes in North German cuisine and the restaurant overlooks the Elbe. They are winners of a Michelin star and prices are reasonable.

The **Fischerhaus**, *tel. (49)40-314-053; website: www.restaurant-fischerhaus.de*, serves inexpensive but wonderful seafood. The atmosphere is plain, but the fish is not.

Hamburg's best hotel

The best hotel in Hamburg—in all of Germany, in fact—is the **Vier**

Jahreszeiten, *tel. toll free (800)223-6800* or *(49)404-3-49-40*. This elegant establishment on Lake Alster has a grand white facade rising eight stories and decorated with window boxes. Inside, you will find antique furniture, wood paneling, marble floors, brass trim, and modern facilities. All rooms have telephones, color televisions, and private bathrooms with bath, shower, bidet, bathrobes, thermometers, and toiletries.

Founded in 1897, this family-run hotel has an especially comfortable lobby, with leather armchairs, Oriental rugs, wood paneling, and a huge fireplace. Just off the lobby is a lounge with a large stone fireplace, tapestries, and views of the lake. A staff of 450 caters to the requests of guests staying in the 175 rooms. While you are here, you can have your suits mended or altered by the in-house Italian tailor.

The hotel restaurant, **Haerlin**, is also excellent. Vegetables, fruit, flowers, and poultry come straight to the restaurant from the hotel's farm on the outskirts of town. Choose a fine German wine from the hotel's 65,000-bottle cellar.

Charm for less than a fortune

Hotel Abtei, *tel. (49)40-442-905*, is a small hotel on a shady street in a quiet residential section of Hamburg. Breakfast is something you don't want to miss.

Hotel Kempinski Atlantic, *tel. toll free (800)426-3135* or *(49)40-2-88-80*, is a first-class hotel, located close to the center of town with a grand view of Lake Alster.

Hotel Prem, *tel. (49)40-24-8-34-040*, is a cozy but elegant hotel, also on Lake Alster. The rooms are spacious and always filled with fresh flowers.

BREMEN: THE MOST BEAUTIFUL CITY

Bremen is Germany's most beautiful city and its oldest port. It became a bishop's seat 1,200 years ago and in 1358 joined Hamburg and Lubekc as leading members of the Hanseatic League, an association of independent merchant towns. Bremen prides itself on its historic buildings, the oldest of which (some are over 800 years old) are grouped around the Markplatz. The Gothic city hall was built in 1405 to 1410.

The oldest building in Bremen

The massive, twin-towered **cathedral**, built in the 11th century, is the oldest building in Bremen. Its other claim to fame is the mummy in its cellar. According to legend, the body of a roofer, who fell to his death in 1450, was put in the cellar for safekeeping but forgotten. When the body was discovered many years later, it had been perfectly preserved by the cellar's dry air.

Outside the cathedral stands the famous bronze **Statue of Roland**, a famous knight of Charlemagne.

Germany's oldest inn

Der Ratskeller, west of the town hall, is one of the oldest and most traditional of Germany's inns. It is known for its huge selection of more than 500 German wines, including a 1653 Rüdesheimer.

The best fish dishes

Grashoff's Bistro, *tel. (49)421-147-40*, is a little restaurant that does not look like much, but serves the best fish dishes in the region. Reservations are recommended and the bistro is not open on Sundays.

The best ship museum in the world

Just north of Bremen in Bremerhaven (the most important fishing port in Europe) is one of the best ship museums in the world, the **Schiffahrtsmuseum**, *Columbusstrasse*, in the old section. The *Seute Deern* (Sweet Girl), a Hanseatic tall ship wrecked in 1380, is especially impressive.

Bremen's best hotels

Park Hotel, *tel. (49)421-340-80*, is Bremen's most prestigious hotel. It has spacious public rooms, a garden terrace, rooms with balconies overlooking a pond, and a fine restaurant.

The **Marriot**, *Hillmannplatz 20*, is the most convenient hotel in Bremen, just a five-minute walk from the pedestrian area. It is picturesque and located opposite a windmill.

COLOGNE: BEST CARNIVAL, BEST CHURCHES

If you like churches, you'll believe yourself at the gates of heaven when you reach **Cologne** (Köln). The number of churches marking the city's skyline is remarkable (13 in all). What's more, many of these churches are among the most beautiful in Germany. While some were damaged in World War II, most have been restored to their former beauty and are open to the public.

It's probably a good thing Cologne has so many churches, considering it is also the site of Germany's wildest carnival season. If you like a good bacchanalia, visit Cologne the week before Ash Wednesday. Carnival begins with *Weiberfastnacht*, the Women's Carnival, held on the Alter Markt. Women choose their dancing partners and dance from morning to midnight. (This custom is said to have its origins in 16th century pre-Lenten orgies.)

Cologne's beautiful churches

Cologne's famous **Gothic cathedral** is a gigantic structure that can be seen from almost any point in the city. Begun in 1248 and completed in 1880, it houses several great works of art, including the 12th-century *Shrine of the*

Three Magi, a masterpiece of the goldsmith's art created to house holy relics.

Hlg. Maria im Kapitol was the church most severely damaged during World War II, but it has been beautifully restored. Its extraordinary, carved wooden doors, with 26 reliefs illustrating the life of Christ, date back to 1050. There's also a 12th-century sculpture of the virgin on display.

Hlg. Pantaleon is a twin-towered structure with a 100-century nave and cloister. It is the oldest remaining Romanesque church in Germany.

Hlg. Aposteln is the finest example of Rhineland Romanesque architecture. Built between 1192 and 1230, it has a squat nave with ribbed vaults, a trefoil choir, and a tower.

The oldest church in Cologne is **St. Gereon**. Its walls, crypts, and pillars are from the fourth century.

When you tire of touring churches, visit **Rhine Park**. During the summer, dances and concerts are held here. Concerts begin at 4 p.m.; dancing begins at 8 p.m.

The prettiest part of Cologne is the old section, near the Rhine, where 12th-and 13th-century buildings remain.

Cologne's best restaurant

Seafood dishes and the best German wines are served at **Weinhaus im Walfisch**, *tel. (49)221-257-7879*, situated in a 350-year-old building. Reservations are recommended, and the restaurant is closed on Sundays.

The coziest hotel

The **Antik Hotel Bristol**, *tel. (49)221-120-195*, is a cozy, family-run hotel near the cathedral. Rooms on the lower floor can be noisy. The atmosphere is inviting and the rooms are decorated with carved wooden furniture.

A FAIRY-TALE LOVER'S FAVORITE: THE BLACK FOREST

A couple of hours south of Frankfurt is the **Black Forest**—the Schwarzwald. Source of scary fairytales, the Black Forest isn't as ominous as it sounds. Although place names include Hexental (Witches' Valley) and Höllental (Hell Valley), it's not all dense pine forest, but rather a patchwork of mixed woodlands, green valleys, and highlands decorated with waterfalls ...and some exceptionally pretty villages and spa towns.

If you enjoy walking or cycling you'll be in your element...and you often spy deer grazing at the forest edge. For outdoor types, the Black Forest is an all-year-round destination. During winter—invariably cold and snowy—it's a great place for cross-country skiing.

Cuckoo favorite

The woods around **Triberg** are known as the home of cuckoo birds, which cuckoo like crazy all day. Known as *cuculus canorus*, the bird is shy and rarely seen or heard anywhere else.

If you fail to spot a real cuckoo in the woods, stop at the **Heimat Museum** in Triberg, which houses the largest collection of cuckoo clocks in the world.

The oldest castle in Germany

Meersburg, an almost vertical village pitched high above a ravine, lies in the shadows of the oldest castle in Germany. Locals claim Dagobert built it in A.D. 630. Some of the walls do date back to A.D. 1000 but most of the building is from the 16th century. The entire castle was restored in 1877. The chapel and courtyard are especially worth seeing.

Across from the old castle is the ancient residence of the bishops of Constance. Stand on the terrace and enjoy the view.

Meersburg has a marvelous hotel—the stately **Hotel Bad Schachen**, which looks out over Bodensee toward Lindau. Its grand dining room serves delicious meals.

The forest's highest peak

The highest peak in the forest is **Feldberg**. Take a chair lift to the top. The village of Feldberg at the foot of the mountain was the birthplace of German skiing and is one of the oldest winter resorts in Germany.

Baden-Baden: the world's most famous spa

Baden-Baden, the world's most famous spa, is known for its curative waters. The spa was built over the ruins of the ancient Roman baths south of Heidelberg in the Black Forest. The best time to visit, if you can stand the crowds, is the last week in August, **Baden-Baden Week**, when horse races, balls, and receptions are held.

Baden-Baden's best hotels

Brenner's Park-Hotel, *tel. (49) 7221-9000*, is the best hotel in the town of Baden-Baden, and one of the best in Europe. This Edwardian hotel is a traditional part of any visit to the spa. It has large, graceful public rooms, excellent service, an indoor heated pool, a sauna, and a solarium. The hotel has views of the park and the river.

Hotel Badischer Hof, *tel. (49) 7221-9340*, U.S. and Canada *tel. toll free (800) 223-5652*, is a more affordable, family-run alternative to the rather pricey Brenner's Park-Hotel.

The coziest shelter in the forest

Romantik Parkhotel Wehrle, *tel. (49)7722-86020*, is a beautiful escape while in the Black Forest. It has a swimming pool, sauna, and an excellent restaurant known for its trout dishes

The **Bühler-Höhe Hotel**, *tel. (49)7226-55100*, is a great place to absorb the atmosphere of the forest. It is hidden behind a thick canopy of evergreens and covered with ivy. Originally a hunting lodge, it is now a fitness center.

BACCHUS' BESTS

Germany's 11 wine-growing districts, which stretch from the middle Rhine at Bonn south to the Bodensee, produce the lightest white wines in the world. These regions are filled with classic scenery—castle ruins, grand cathedrals, gabled houses, elegant spas, and enchanting little villages.

The world's best Rieslings

The Rheingau region on the right bank of the Rhine is the aristocrat of Germany's wine-producing areas. This small region, extending from Hocheim in the east to Lorch in the west, is known for the Riesling grape. Sample the wines at the local wineries for a taste of the best white wines in the world. This is also the place to buy good German wine cheaply. In addition to wine, the Rheingau is also known for its wealth of monuments, monasteries, and wine cellars, some of which date back to the time of Charlemagne.

A good place to sample the local Rieslings is the crowded but exciting town of **Rüdesheim**. The Drösselgasse, a narrow, cobblestoned alley, is lined with wine taverns and restaurants. Order a Römer (a wine goblet with a green pedestal) of the local wine and watch the crowds. Rudesheim is the site of rousing wine festivals in May and August. One of Germany's best wine museums is in Brömser Castle at the west end of town.

A fine restaurant that features wine tasting is located in the **Waldhotel Jagdschloss Niederwald**, three miles from Rüdesheim. Delicious game dishes are served in season. This castle hotel is impressive, set on a hill high above the Rhine. It is closed in winter.

The best German reds

Stuttgart is the perfect base for touring the Wurttemberg area, which follows the Neckar River south of Baden-Baden. Red wines, such as Trillinger and Limberger, can be sampled throughout Württemberg. (They are rarely exported, so this could be your only chance to enjoy them.)

Following your wine tasting, visit the old Renaissance palace or the Staatsgalerie (National Galler) in Stuttgart, the Roman baths and castle ruins in Weinsberg, or the Palace Gardens of Ludwigsburg.

The best place to sample local Württemberg wines is the **Wirtshaus zum Götzenturm**, *Allerheiligenstrasse 1*, in the medieval walled town of Heilbronn. The owner of this restaurant also runs the Beichtstuhl, a wine cellar around the corner. Both places are closed Sundays, Mondays after lunch, and in August.

The wine cellar of the Holy Roman Empire

The elegant wines of the **Rheinpfalz** region have been famous since the days of the Holy Roman Emperor Charlemagne. This area was known as the Wine Cellar of the Holy Roman Empire. The picturesque Deutsche Weinstrasse (German Wine Road) runs its length.

Detour, if you can, to nearby **Speyer** (Spier), where the town's museum houses the oldest bottle of wine in the world, dating from the third century. The best place to sample local wine is **Café Hindenburg**, *Maximilianstrasse 91*.

The oldest wine region

Fine wines are produced northwest of Rheinpfalz in the **Moselle Valley**, which has the oldest vineyards in Germany and the steepest vineyards in the world. The Moselle's vines are ancient. The Romans used the *Neumagen* wine ship in the Trier Museum to bring vines to Germany.

Markers along the Rhine describe the wines produced here: Piesporter, Wehlen, Bernkasteller, and Graach. The finest Moselle wines are Bernkasteler Doktor and Wehlener Sonnenuhr.

The most beautiful wine region

The **Ahr Valley**, Germany's northernmost wine region, is the most beautiful. Between Altenahr and Bad Neuenahr, the river forces its way in rapid, winding course between rugged slate crags. Vineyards climb steep slopes in the shadows of castle ruins. Wine villages are sandwiched by the hills.

Wine has been made here since ancient Roman times, and today the area produces Germany's best reds and bubbling whites. Try the local wines at the **Weinstube Sankt Peter** in Walporzheim or at the lively **Lochmühle** at Mayschloss. Hikers can follow the 19-mile Red Wine Trail through vineyards from Lohrsdorf to Altenahr.

The best rosés

The **Baden** region, located between Heidelberg and the Badensee, is famous for its whites and Schillerwein rosés. A giant cask holding 52,000 gallons of the region's wine is located in Heidelberg. You can try the local wines at **Perkeo**, *Hauptstrasse 75*, a large beer and wine house in Heidelberg. A more scenic place to sample the wines is on the terrace of the **Weinstube im Schloss Heidelberg**, a restaurant in a castle outside Heidelberg.

The most charming castle hotels on the Rhine

The Rhineland is a fairy-tale region, home to more than 30 medieval castles. And the best way to soak up the atmosphere here is to stay in a Rhine castle that has been turned into a hotel.

The **Klostergut Jakobsberg**, *tel. (49)6742-8080*, a monastery turned hotel, is also near the Lorelei. Built in 1157 by Kaiser Friedrick I, it is situated on a bluff overlooking the Rhine. The monastery was owned by the archbishops of Trier. In 1640, it became the property of the Jesuits, who used it as a university until the French Revolution. The monastery was later taken over by the Prussians. Today it is a hotel with modern amenities, a good restaurant, and an indoor pool.

The **Hotel Burg Reichenstein**, *tel. (49)6721-6101*, has a magnificent view of the Rhine. Its 13th-century Gothic arches and rough stonework remain. Robber-knights once watched the river from the castle's towers. Inside the castle is a museum displaying medieval weapons and armor.

Germany's best medieval castle

The best medieval castle in Germany, perhaps all Europe, is **Burg Eltz Castle**, nestled in an enchanted forest in the Rhine/Mosel region. It is the epitome of a medieval, fairy tale castle, with its graceful spires and towers. The castle remains incredibly well preserved and, due to shrewd political maneuvering, has remained in the hands of the Eltz family for more than 800 years. They still occupy part of the castle.

The best way to see this elegantly furnished castle is with a tour, included in the admission price. From the car park you take a short walk through the forest to the castle. Along the way, there is a scenic overlook where you can view the castle from a distance. Daily tours take you through many of the rooms.

THE STRANGEST HISTORY: WORMS

The city of **Worms** has a strange name and an even stranger history. It was named for a legendary giant worm with fangs and webbed feet that lived in the Rhine and demanded human sacrifices.

Worms was the fifth-century capital of the legendary Nibelungs. The tribe left the area, according to legend, after the wicked Hagen slew their hero, Siegfried, and threw their treasure into the river. A huge statue of Hagen commemorates the story. The town was destroyed in A.D. 436 by Atilla the Hun.

THE HARZ: THE MOST BEWITCHING REGION

According to legend, witches live in Germany's northernmost mountains, the Harz. They are said to fly on Walpurgis Night, the last night of

April. The residents of the area celebrate this night by dressing up as witches, demons, and devils.

However if you miss Walpurgis Night, don't despair—this region is bewitching all year round. The mountains are covered with evergreen forests, inhabited by deer, and brightened by waterfalls, ravines, and rocky streams. One of Germany's highest peaks is the Wurmberg near Braunlage in the Harz. Take a cable car to see the top.

The Harz was made famous by the celebrated German poet Heinrich Heine (1797-1856) in *Die Harzreise* (*The Harz Journey*), a cycle of poems and prose set to music by Schubert.

Bavarian bests

Bavaria, which was independent until 1918 (Munich was its capital), is the largest and most visited section of Germany. This southeastern region is touristy, but with good reason—Bavaria is beautiful. The Alps stretch along the region's southern border with Austria, offering wooded slopes, flower-filled meadows, lakes, and castles. The mountain-encircled Königsee is a gorgeous deep-blue lake surrounded by sheer alpine cliffs.

Bavaria's oddest tradition

Each year, mid-April through the end of June, Bavaria celebrates its "royal vegetable," the asparagus. "Spargel" season includes festivals and markets, an Asparagus Queen, and pick-your-own stalls along the roadsides. The grandest Spargel festival takes place in Schrobenhausen on Johannistag (St. John the Baptist's Day, June 24) to mark the official end of the season.

Munich: the most fun loving city

Munich is Germany's party town. Every season provides an excuse for a party—and in Munich, there are nine seasons: spring, summer, winter, fall, bock beer time, the opera festival, beer garden days, carnival, and Oktoberfest.

Munich's best party

If you like a good party and crowds, visit Munich during **Oktoberfest** at the end of September. Make sure you have a hotel reservation; the city never has enough room for all the revelers. If you can't find a hotel call the **Munich Tourism Office**, *tel. (49) 892-330-300; e-mail: tourismus@muenchen.de;* they may be able to help you find a homestay.

Since the first Oktoberfest in 1810, it has been celebrated every year beginning three Saturdays before the first Sunday in October and continuing for 16 days. Festivities start with a parade through the streets of Munich to the Theresienwiese. Here, after horse-drawn beer wagons arrive, the mayor taps the first of more than 700,000 kegs. Thousands quaff Bavarian brew and enjoy brass band music.

Enormous beer tents, sponsored by Germany's major breweries, are the hub of activity. Stein-serving waitresses in folk costumes weave among wooden tables. Midway rides and sideshows add to the carnival atmosphere.

The world's largest science museum

The **Deutsches Museum**, *tel. (49)89-2179-1; website: www.deutsches-museum.de*, takes up an entire island in the middle of Munich's Isar River. It's great fun for people who love gadgets. Most of the displays are interactive and lots of fun for any age. The museum is open daily from 9 a.m. to 5 p.m., and on Wednesday until 8 p.m.

Munich's top three sights

Neue Pinakothek (the new art gallery), was destroyed during World War II, rebuilt in post-war years and today is Munich's best modern art gallery. Its natural lighting sets off the paintings well. Sloping ramps lead past artworks hung in chronological order. The collection of works by 18th- and 19th-century masters is especially good—it includes works by Manet, Monet, Dégas, Cézanne, Van Gogh, Gauguin, Klimt, and Goya. The museum is closed on Mondays.

The **Schatzkammer** (Treasure House) contains the splendid treasures of Bavarian royalty: jeweled crowns and crosses, goblets, medals, swords, dishes, and jewelry. Perhaps the most beautiful object is in the third room: a statue of St. George slaying the dragon, which was made in 1590 and inlaid with precious stones.

Residenzmuseum shares a building with the Schatzkammer. Once the palace of the Wittelsbach Kings, it contains rooms from the Renaissance, baroque, and rococo periods. Damaged during World War II, it has been restored. The Ancestors Gallery houses portraits of all the Bavarian Kings.

Munich's most inviting park

When you tire of the historical sights and museums, take a walk through the **Englischer Garten**. The park has woods, brooks, and a Chinese tower-turned-beer garden that is a great place to drink huge steins of beer, eat Bavarian pretzels and Wiener schnitzel, and meet people. There is an area set aside for nude sunbathing. End your day by taking a refreshing dip in the ice-cold Isar River.

Munich's oldest church

Alte Peterskirche (Peter's Church), just off the Marienplatz near the rathaus, is often overlooked, although it's the oldest parish church in Munich. It houses a macabre relic—a gilded and bejeweled skeleton of the martyr St. Munditia (the patron saint of lonely women). Fake eyes look out of her skull, gems glitter where her teeth should be, and a jeweled coronet balances on her head of fake hair. If you climb the 277 steps to the top, you will have a spectacular view of the Alps from the Alte Peter's 300-foot tower.

The world's best Kandinsky collection

Städtische Galerie im Lenbachhaus (Municipal Gallery), has the most comprehensive collection in the world of the works of abstract painter Vassily Kandinsky. The gallery is an imitation Italian villa with a small garden.

The best place to buy folk fashions

Loden-Frey is the best place to buy German folk-style clothing in traditional fabrics. This family-run establishment has been in business since 1842. *Tel. (49)89-210-390.*

The most magnificent sight

Schloss Nymphenburg, outside of Munich, is a magnificent 17th-century palace set in a 500-acre park filled with fountains, statues, lakes, waterfalls, and a formal garden. Portraits of the 24 most beautiful women in Europe 200 years ago, commissioned by King Ludwig, hang in the south pavilion.

The darker side of Munich

Dachau Concentration Camp, now a memorial to those who died in the camp during World War II, is located outside of the city. More than 200,000 people, mainly Jews, were labeled undesirable by the Nazi's and imprisoned here between 1933 and 1945. The camp is virtually intact. Several barracks can be seen, as well as the morgue, the crematorium, and the Brausebad (where prisoners were gassed to death). Documentary films of the holocaust are shown, and photo displays are on view.

Munich's best restaurants

The best restaurant in Munich is **Die Aubergine**, *tel. (49)30-8330-7636.* The first German restaurant to receive a three-star Michelin rating, Die Aubergine serves French-influenced German nouvelle cuisine based on traditional favorites. Make reservations, as the restaurant is small.

Altes Hackerhaus, *tel. (49)89-260-5026*, is the best place for Bavarian specialities. (If you have the nerve, try the pig knuckles.)

Franziskaner und Fuchsenstuben, *tel. (49)89-231-8120*, serves delicious sausage and Leberkas, a kind of meat loaf that is made of ground beef, liver, and bacon and eaten with sweet mustard.

Traditional Bavarian food is served at **Nürnberger Bratwurstglockl**, *tel.*

(49)89-220-385, near the Dom. The décor is charming, featuring large prints, arms, and woodwork. Reservations are a must.

The best restaurant in Germany

Weichandhof, *tel. (49)89-891-1600*, is one of the most charming restaurants in Germany. Bavarian and international foods are served in the converted farmhouse. The restaurant is cozy in cold weather, with an open fireplace and a wood stove. During the summer, tables are moved outside under the apple trees. Venison is served in season. Try the Bavarian classic, *Schweinebraten mit Kartöffelknodeln* (roast pork with cracklings and potato dumplings).

The hottest nightlife

Schwabing is Munich's student district and has more than 200 restaurants and cafés, as well as myriad nightclubs and bars.

The **Park Café** is a '50s-style lounge that has some of the best new music in Munich. It is the place to go.

P-Eins is a small but good disco near the National Museum.

Steamy jazz is played at the **Domicile**, **Musicland** and **J.A.M.** in downtown Munich.

Germany's best beer cellars

Munich is famous for its beer cellars—informal halls where lots of beer is downed at long tables full of friendly people. The city has 12 historic *Bierkeller*, which serve huge steins of beer and Bavarian specialities. Sit anywhere—these are friendly places. Often an oompah band will play and patrons will sing.

The most famous beer hall is the **Hofbrauhaus**, *tel. (49)89-290-1360*. Although it is very touristy, the Hofbrauhaus is worth a visit for its friendly atmosphere. The **Donisl**, *tel. (49)89-290-8410*, is the oldest of Munich's beer halls, popular since 1715. The **Augustinerkeller**, *tel. (49)89-594-393*, is one of the oldest and nicest of the beer cellars. The restaurant attached to it, the Augustiner, is also very good.

Munich's best hotel

The **Hotel Vier Jahreszeiten Kempinski**, *tel. (49)892-1250; U.S.A. or Canada tel. (800)426-3135*, is the best hotel in Munich. A deluxe, traditional hotel with yellow stucco external walls and blue awnings, the hotel exudes Bavarian hospitality. The hotel's restaurant is excellent.

The world's best gingerbread

North of Munich is **Nuremberg**, the gingerbread capital of the world. The best time to visit is Christmas when the local bakers take advantage of the Christmas market to show off their unrivalled skills in this art.

Alpine peaks

The **Alps** stretch along Germany's southern border from the Bodensee in the west to the Waltzmann Peak near Berchtesgaden in the east. This mountain range rose from the sea about 80 million years ago. You can find fossils of sea creatures among the peaks. The beautiful lakes in the Voralpenland are remnants of the Ice Age.

(See more on skiing in the German Alps in Section 4: The World's Best Sporting Destinations.)

Germany's highest peak

The **Zugspitze**, Germany's highest peak (9,840 feet), overlooks Garmisch-Partenkirchen and is part of the Wettersteingebirge, an ancient formation of hard rock. You can take a cable car or train from Garmisch to the summit. Even when clouded over (about 35% of the time), the view is spectacular. You can see the peaks of other mountains rising above the blanket of clouds. Get a beer at the top, or just breathe in the intoxicatingly thin mountain air.

The best alpine hikes

The German Alps are crisscrossed by 9,000 hiking trails. They are well-used by the Germans, who consider *das Wandern* (walking, rambling, exploring the world) a way of life.

The most beautiful walking trail in the Alps is along Bodensee between the towns of Briedrichshafen and Lindau. The snow-capped Alps are reflected in the waters of the lake. The walk is not difficult and can be done in tennis shoes. The entire length takes about two days (longer if you stop in some of the towns along the way). For a map of the trail, stop in at the tourist office in Friedrichshafen or Lindau.

The trail from the town of Füssen to Neuschwanstein Castle is also beautiful. Fussen is a picturesque village in the shadows of the turreted castle. The trail leads past several lakes and into the shadows of the Austrian and German Alps. The walk isn't difficult.

Our third-favorite hike begins at the path leading from the Olympic Ski Stadium in Garmisch-Partenkirchen to the Graseckbahn cable car, which carries you to the Forsthaus Graseck. At the peak is an inviting little restaurant with panoramic views. From the terrace, you can pick up another trail along the spectacular Partnachklamm, a very narrow and deep gorge filled with torrents of water. You'll be thankful for the guardrails along the path, which is narrow and sometimes slippery.

Hitler's favorite hideout

The **Kehlsteinhaus** (also known as Eagle's Nest), perched on a rocky crag above the town of Berchtesgarden, was Hitler's favorite hideout. No wonder—the view from the hideaway-turned-restaurant is exhilarating. *Tel. (49) 8652-2969.*

Bavaria's looniest king

Mad King Ludwig, who ruled Bavaria from 1864 to 1886, built the most fanciful and beautiful buildings in Germany, despite (or perhaps because of) his insanity. But his magnificent creations were extremely costly, and his extravagance nearly bankrupted Bavaria. An important patron of the arts, Ludwig was a great fan of Wagner. He built the Bayreuth Opera House for the composer and lived in a fantasy world based on Wagner's operas.

Ludwig's death by drowning has raised many questions over the years. Some say his madness drove him to suicide, others say it was a fatal accident, and still others believe it was murder. Whatever the case, Ludwig died shortly after having been declared insane.

Germany's most beautiful castle

King Ludwig created Germany's most beautiful castle: **Neuschwanstein**. The turreted white castle reaches high into the sky from its perch on a cliff above a valley. Walt Disney liked it so much that he copied it for Disneyland and Disney World. It looks enchanted, with its mountain backdrop. Inside, the walls are decorated with murals of German heroic sagas. In Ludwig's bedroom, stars in the dark blue ceiling light up to look like the night sky. Ludwig lived at Neuschwanstein for 102 days before he drowned in the waters of nearby Lake Starnberg at age 40.

Guided tours take 35 minutes. You have to walk up and down 170 steps and there is no elevator provided. Open daily April to October.

Germany's smallest castle

The smallest castle in Germany also was the product of Mad King Ludwig's imagination. **Linderhof Castle**, near Garmish-Partenkirchen, is an ornate, one-man palace designed as Ludwig's personal residence. The mad king preferred to be alone and went to great lengths to maintain his privacy. He had the dining room built directly above the kitchen and installed a dining table that could be lowered into the kitchen, set by the cooks, and lifted back up to the dining room. Thus, he could be waited on at dinner without having to see the servants. Ludwig lived the longest at this castle.

Up the hill from the castle, Ludwig created a grotto. Entered by way of a hinged boulder, the artificial cave is the recreation of Venus Mountain from Wagner's Tannhäuser. Inside the grotto is an artificial lake with a waterfall and Ludwig's boat.

The world's best violins

The world's most perfect violins are crafted in **Mittenwald**, a pretty Bavarian town sporting buildings decorated with brightly colored frescoes.

The craft has been passed down through generations of local artisans, who make the instruments to order for famous musicians. The meadows, mountains, and village houses around Mittenwald are so typically Alpine that they were used as location sites for the filming of *The Sound of Music*.

DRESDEN: THE FINEST PORCELAIN

Dresden and the nearby **Meissen** are known for their fine porcelain. But Dresden is now becoming known for its newly restored buildings. During World War II, the city was fire bombed by the Allies, and 80% of it burned to the ground. It has been beautifully reconstructed. Linden trees line the banks of the Elbe River, and the city boasts some of the best museums in Germany.

Stroll along **Prager Strasse**, once one of the Dresden's most fashionable streets. It is lined with apartments and shops and embellished with fountains and benches. This street connects the new section of Dresden with the old section.

Frauenkirche (Church of Our Lady), has been left in ruins purposely as a memorial to the city's bombings.

Dresden's best

Located along the Elbe River, **Zwinger Palace**, and the portrait gallery it contains, is Dresden's drawing card. Carefully restored following the bombings of World War II, it retains much of its original structure, including a majestic courtyard where fountains play in the summer. Built as a fortress in the 18th century, it houses Raphael's *Sistine Madonna*, as well as a dozen Rembrandts, 16 Reubens, and several Tintorettos. The bells in its carillon tower are made of Dresden china.

A music lover's favorite

The **Semper Opera**, *tel. (49)351-49-11-705* or *(49)351-49-11-731; website: www.semperoper.de*, is where Wagner and von Weber conducted and Richard Strauss' operas premiered. The opera house was designed by architect Gottfried Semper and completed in 1850. After 1945, it was restored based on original drawings. The building was immortalized in a painting by the 18th-century artist Canaletto.

Dresden's best art museum

The 16th-century glass-domed **Albertinum** contains the state collection of the 19th- and 20th-century paintings, including many works by the French Impressionists. The museum's Grunes Gewodbe (Green Vault) displays works of goldsmiths and jewelers from the 15th through 18th centuries. The collection once belonged to the kings of Saxony, whose capital was Dresden. The museum is closed Thursdays.

GERMANY'S MOST BEAUTIFUL PALACE

Potsdam is home to Germany's most beautiful rococo palace, **Sanssouci**, built by Frederick the Great in imitation of the French Versailles in 1745. You must wear felt-soled slippers when you visit to protect the beautiful floors. Paintings by Rubens, Van Dyck, and Caravaggio hang in the palace galleries.

BUCHENWALD — THE BLACKEST MEMORY

Just north of Weimar is the infamous **Buchenwald Concentration Camp**, where 56,000 people died in World War II. The camp and its museum of torture and extermination devices are chilling. Even in the spring the site is so cold and bleak that you cannot imagine surviving a winter in the scanty barracks. Outside the camp there is a memorial to the victims.

HEIDELBERG: THE MOST ROMANTIC TOWN

Heidelberg is Europe's oldest university town, with students making up one-fifth of today's population of 140,000. It is also a world-leading center for medical research, as well as a technology honeypot attracting swarms of experts in such disciplines as bio-technology, environmental protection, and genetic engineering. And, for the romantics among us it offers a timeless abundance of romanticism to beguile St. Valentine himself.

The most beautiful sight

The **Heidelberg Castle**, *tel. (49)62-21-53-84-14*, is a magnificent red structure with octagonal towers and ruined belfries. From the castle, you have a panoramic view of the city's red roofs, the spire of the Heiliggeist Kirche, and the Neckar River. The castle is open from 8 a.m. to 5 p.m.

Weinstube Schloss Heidelberg, the restaurant in the middle of the castle courtyard, has marvelous food. (It is closed on Tuesdays.)

The best traditional entertainment

At the **Golden Sheep** (*Zum Guldenen Schaf* in German), you can eat and drink your way through the Bronze Age, Ancient Rome, the Middle Ages, the Renaissance, Baroque, and the Biedermeier periods, accompanied by performances on contemporaneous musical instruments. You may also be expected to conform to contemporaneous manners and customs (excluding unauthorized pillaging and ravishing, of course).

Within this 18th-century country inn, proprietor Dr. Karl Kischka has created not just an exhilarating gastronomic experience, but also a museum of musical instruments, an alchemist's kitchen, a facsimile collection of precious medieval documents, a crossbow arena, and even a 19th-century clay pigeon shooting range.

Heidelberg's best hotel

For deeply luxurious five-star opulence, you can't beat the **Hotel Europa**, (*Der Europäische Hof* in German), which has maintained an outstanding position in international tourism for no less than 130 years. In the last 40 years, it has been managed by the urbane Ernst-Friedrich von Kretschmann and his interior-designer wife Sylvia.

Walking into the Europäische feels like going back 100 years in time. Stroll the marbled corridors and fountain-lined terraces, graze its grand dining rooms, and wallow in the opulence of one of its 118 rooms and apartments, all designed by Sylvia with a nod to the Hohenzollern dynasty. European crowned heads check in to this day, most recently Sweden's King Gustav and his wife Sylvia, a native of Heidelberg, whose signature graces the glittering visitor's book. *Tel. (49)6221-515501; fax (49)6221-515555; e-mail: reservations@europaeischerhof.com; website: www.europaeischerhof.com.*

Best for youthful spirit

Cantankerous reactionaries who grumble about noisy teenagers will love this relic: the **Student Prison Museum**. From 1778 until 1914, scholars were sent here for up to three days for such common offences as drunkenness and playing tricks on officials, or for up to a month for dueling, all with time off for attending lectures. Bored young prisoners would pass the time decorating the walls, little realizing how fascinating their artwork would one day prove for innocent ticket-buying visitors.

Best souvenir—the Student's Kiss

Not only is the chocolate delicious, so too is the story behind the "Student's Kiss" label. It began in 1863 with the opening of The Café Knösel in the heart of Heidelberg. The café became a venue for the dashing young students and the young ladies of the city's once-famous finishing schools. Unfortunately, the trysts were silent because the ladies were accompanied by hawk-eyed governesses who intercepted every pass with arctic commitment. Sympathizing with their plight, the pastry chef, Fridolin Knösel, created a particularly ambrosial chocolate pastry which he dubbed the "Student's Kiss." The governesses were unable to prevent them being presented to their charges in lieu—and in anticipation—of the real thing.

Most romantic hotel restaurant

The **Hirschgasse**, *tel. (49)6221-4540; website: www.hirschgasse.de*, was built for romance and retains its fairytale charm under the ownership of Ernst and Allison Kraft. They've retrieved and installed original old lead stained glass windows and antique lamps and lovingly restored wood paneling and prints. A special feature of the Hirschgasse are the pictures of fencing student fraternities and the swords with which they carved dueling scars into their opponents' cheeks. In the rustic *Mensurstube* you can see where Count Bismark carved his name into a 200-year-old table.

Its restaurants are not just enchanting, but renowned for their regional and international cuisine. Concessions to modern hospitality include Laura Ashley-themed rooms and a hi-tech sound system that can channel music to suit your exact mood to your table.

The most romantic walk

The **Philosopher's Path** is the most romantic walk, just near the Hirschgasse. In season, it's a blaze of color from Japanese cherries, cypresses, lemons, rhododendrons, yucca trees, and more. And it has the most wonderful view of Heidelberg across the river.

THE BEST OF GREECE

HAIL, NATURE'S UTMOST BOAST! UNRIVALLED GREECE...
CLEAN SUNNY CLIMATES, BY THE BREEZY MAIN,
IONIAN OR AEGEAN, TEMPER'D KIND;
LIGHT, AIRY SOILS; A COUNTRY RICH AND GAY;
BROKE INTO HILLS WITH BALM ODOURS CROWN'D,
AND, BRIGHT WITH PURPLE HARVEST, JOYOUS VALES;
MOUNTAINS AND STREAMS, WHERE VERSE SPONTANEOUS FLOW'D;
WHENCE DEEM'D BY WONDERING MEN THE SEAT OF GODS,
AND STILL THE MOUNTAINS AND THE STREAMS OF SON;
ALL THAT BOON NATURE COULD LUXURIANT POUR
OF HIGH MATERIALS, AND MY RESTLESS ARTS
FRAME INTO FINISH'D LIFE.

—James Thomson, Liberty, 1734-1736

Greece is a breathtaking country of mountains, islands, and sea. Its special light gives a clarity to the blue sky above and the colors below—colors that include a profusion of wild flowers in early spring. When you visit Greece, forget the packaged tours. This is a do-it-yourself country that should be experienced outdoors. Camp out under Greece's stars to best experience the country. Travel light and be prepared to follow the impulse of the moment.

ATHENS: THE BIRTHPLACE OF MODERN CIVILIZATION

Athens—the birthplace of Western democracy, poetry, drama, art, and philosophy—is no longer at the center of the world it has nurtured. A decaying, polluted city, it has a Third World flavor. Nonetheless, Athens merits more than a quick visit. It has the world's largest and most remarkable collections of ancient ruins, including the ancient Parthenon and one of the world's finest archeological museums. And beyond these archeological wonders is an exciting nightlife and a unique lifestyle, part European, part Middle Eastern.

The Acropolis: the heart of ancient Athens

You shouldn't miss the **Acropolis** and the ancient city. It stands in full view on a hill above Athens, adding a majestic dignity and beauty to what otherwise would be a shabby city.

Buildings in Athens are subject to a height limit so that the **Parthenon**, the most important structure of the Acropolis, remains visible from most points in the area. Dedicated to the goddess Athena, the Acropolis was the religious center of the ancient capital. It was reconstructed in the fifth century B.C. by Pericles.

Acro means "top", and *polis* means "city." Together they mean the highest point, or citadel, of the city—which also means a stiff climb. Wear good walking shoes. It is best to visit the Acropolis at dawn or in the late afternoon, because of the play of light. In summer, midday temperatures are too intense.

To the right of the entrance to the Acropolis is the **Temple of Athena Nike**, built to commemorate the victory of the Athenians over the Persians. At the top of the hill is the beautiful Parthenon, temple of the goddess Athena. Also on the hill is the **Acropolis Museum**, which houses some of the Acropolis' statuary pieces (some older than the Parthenon) to protect them from the city's pollution. The Acropolis is open from 8 a.m. until 4:30 p.m. Tuesdays through Fridays, from 10 a.m. until 4:30 p.m. Mondays, and from 8:30 a.m. until 2:30 p.m. Saturdays and Sundays.

Just beneath the Acropolis on the southern slopes are two ancient amphitheaters. The **Theater of Dionysos**, where the first Greek tragedies were performed, dates back to the sixth century B.C. The **Odeion of Herodes Atticus**, which dates to A.D. 161, is the site for performances of theater, opera, ballet, and music during the Athens Festival held between July and September each year. The amphitheaters are open from 8:30 a.m. until 3 p.m. daily.

The ancient **agora**, or marketplace, is on the eastern slopes of the Acropolis hill, on the north end of the Plaka. Now a major archeological excavation site, this was the downtown area of the ancient city and the main crossroads for routes to other major towns, such as Piraeus. Here you will find the **Stoa of Attalus**, a trading center built in 20 B.C.; the **Roman Forum**, begun during Julius Caesar's reign; the **Kerameikos**, the ancient city cemetery; and **Hadrain's Library**, built in the second century. A museum houses artifacts found during the excavations.

The world's finest sculptures

The **National Archeological Museum** has the finest collection of sculptures in the world. Treasures include giant figures of Greek gods and men, a world-renowned collection of Greek vases, pieces of ancient Cycladic art, and magnificent frescoes from the Minoan sites of Knossos on Cyprus and Akrotiri on Santorini. The gold Mycaenean death mask here is reputed to be that of Agamemnon, the ancient Greek king of the Iliad. *Tel. (30)210-821-7717.*

Athens' main square

Syntagma Square (Constitution Square), in the heart of the business district, is Athens' main square. A favorite pastime of both visitors and native Athenians is to sit at one of the square's outdoor café tables and watch pedestrians walk by. The 3,000 chairs in the square are arranged so that they all face the sidewalk for a better view. Have a coffee, beer, or ouzo and Greek *meze* (snacks) while you watch.

The grand dame of the city's hotels, the **Grande Bretagne**, is on the north side. Watching the wealthy, famous, and sometimes outlandish-looking people step from limousines and taxicabs to be ushered into the elegant old hotel by fancy-dressed doormen is part of the fun of the long sit in the square.

Many of Athens' most important sights and monuments border Syntagma Square. The **National Parliament Building** faces the square on the east side. The changing of the palace guards takes place every hour on the hour each day. On Sundays at 11 a.m., the ritual of the *evzone*, when the guards dress in kilts, white tights, and turned-up shoes, is accompanied by a regimental brass band.

The **Benaki Museum**, to the left of the parliament building, is an old private house crammed with clothes, furniture, and photos dating from Byzantine times to the present. It is open from 8.30 a.m. to 2 p.m., and is closed on Tuesdays.

The **Byzantine Museum** is in a villa not far from the Banaki and is the best place to see Greek icons. Two rooms are replicas of Byzantine basilicas of the fifth and 11th centuries. Open Tuesday through Friday, 8 a.m., to 7 p.m. and closed on Mondays. Saturdays, and Sundays it is open from 8:30 a.m. until 3 p.m.

The **Arch of Hadrian**, located near the square in the direction of the Acropolis, was erected by the Romans in A.D. 132 to mark the boundary of the ancient city. One side of the arch bears the inscription "This is Athens, ancient city of Theseus." The other side of the arch says, "This is the city of Hadrian and not of Theseus."

The best underground museum

Syntagma Square Metro Station is almost like a small museum. When the lines were being expanded, all kinds of archeological treasures were unearthed—from mosaic floors to pre-Christian graves and hundreds of oil lamps. A number of the finds are displayed around the marble lobby of Syntagma station.

The largest Greek temple

The **Temple of Olympian Zeus** stands directly behind Hadrian's Arch and is the largest temple in Greece. It is open from 8:30 a.m. until 3 p.m. Closed on Mondays.

Best food and drink in Athens

The best guide to eating, drinking, and current events in Athens is the English-language *Athenian* magazine, which not only lists every restaurant and bar in the city but also critiques them.

The old **Xynos Taverna**, *tel. (30)210-322-1065*, serves Greek wine from the barrel and features guitar music in a wonderful and warm atmosphere.

Five Brothers, *Aiolou Street*, off the square behind Hadrian's Library, is inexpensive.

For late-night reveling, try the **Erotokritos**, *16 Lyssiou St.*, which presents musicians in national costume.

Athens' most elegant (and among the most expensive) restaurants are **G.B. Corner**, *Syntagma Square*, at the Grande Bretagne Hotel; the **Balthazar**, *27 Tsoha*; and the **Dyonissos**, *43 Roberto Galli*, a first-class restaurant across from the Acropolis.

The best fish restaurants are in Pireaus and along the coast from Glyfada to Sounion. The fish restaurants with the most atmosphere (but also the most expensive prices) are located in the yacht harbor known as Mikrolimano. In Glyfada, try the **Psaropoulos**, *2 Kalamou St.*, which has a view of the yacht marina.

Athens *ouzeries* are a dying tradition. Take the time to visit one, where you can sample Greek hors d'oeuvres and the national Greek licorice drink in the company of Greek intellectuals. Stop in at tea time or late in the evening.

Mezodopolieon are restaurants that serve only appetizers, which the Greeks call *mezes*. **Savories**, in the arcade at *10 Panepistimiou*, off Syntagma Square, is a good place to sample a selection.

Bouzoukia concentrate more on music than food. Most of these Greek-style nightclubs are located in an area along the seafront between Athens and Piraeus known as Tzitzines. Ask your hotel which clubs are in at the moment. It usually depends on the artist playing.

The best places to sleep

The **Grande Bretagne**, *tel. (30)10-33-30-000*, is located at the heart of things and is touted as one of the world's greatest hotels. It has been welcoming guests since 1862 and is a little rough around the edges today, but holds an air of 1920s splendor.

St. George Lycabettus, *tel. (30)1-729-0711*, is less expensive and has more atmosphere. Its hilltop location gives it views of the city and the sea. Its location is not convenient, but the views are spectacular.

The best escape islands

The **Agro-Saronic Islands** are the islands closest to Athens. The greenest of all Greece's archipelagos, these islands are virtually untouched. They may not have the best beaches, but their beauty and serenity is what makes them a perfect escape from the pollution of tourism.

THE BEST OF NORTHERN GREECE

Northern Greece is home of the country's tallest mountains, including the magical Mount Olympus; of the Macedonia of Alexander the Great; and of Thessaloniki, the only other city in this essentially rural nation. The farther north you go, the thicker the woods and the more Balkan the atmosphere.

Mount Athos: a misogynist's best

The large Greek Orthodox complex perched on the rocky cliffs of **Mount Athos**, at the end of the Chalkidiki Peninsula overlooking the Aegean, is one of the major wonders of the Christian world. The only self-governing monastic state in Europe, it is made up of about 20 monasteries, many of them individual walled towns.

Only adult males are allowed to visit this impressive Byzantine fortress-state. All others are considered temptations. Admission rules forbid women, children, and female animals within the complex. To this day, ships with women on board may not come within 310 miles of the shores around Mount Athos.

Mount Olympus: home of the gods

Mount Olympus is the home of the gods of Greek legend. It's easy to see why—this huge, impressive mountain looming above the clouds, which cut off its tip, captured the imagination of the ancient Greeks.

With an altitude of 9,620 feet, Olympus invites skiers in the winter (through May) and mountain climbers and hikers in the summer.

The best Greek cave

The **Petralona Cave** on the Halkidi Peninsula is 30 miles from Thessaloniki. A Neanderthal skull was found here in 1960, and the site appears to have been inhabited a half-million years ago.

The best buy on hand-woven rugs

Trikala is a small village in the mountains of northern Greece. This is where the famous shaggy Greek *flokati* rugs originated, thanks to the local sheep population and the crystal clear mountain streams that are necessary for the manufacturing process. Villagers have been handweaving the rugs, now considered an art form, for the last 700 years.

THE BEST OF CENTRAL GREECE

Most of Greece's highest mountains are in the center of the country, where all points are within a few hours of Athens.

Mount Parnassus: the best skiing

About an hour-and-a-half from Athens stands **Mount Parnassus** (8,059 feet), where Greece's most serious skiers spend their winters.

Delphi: the most sacred sight

Just a short drive down from the ski area of Mount Parnassus is one of Greece's most important and impressive ancient sacred sites, **Delphi**, where Apollo was worshiped, Greek games were held, and the famous oracle was consulted about matters of great significance by pilgrims from throughout the ancient world.

Meteora: the best monastery

More accessible than Mount Athos is the monastic complex of **Meteora**, perched on the summits of some precipitous rocks above the valley of the Pineios River, about five miles from Kalambaka. The monasteries here were built in the 14th century. In all, 33 monasteries and cells still stand, but only four are now occupied. In these are housed rare manuscripts, icons, miniatures, and ecclesiastical objects of Byzantine art.

THE PELOPONNESE: THE MOST BEAUTIFUL ISLAND

The **Peloponnese** is a lovely, wild place covered with wild flowers in spring. You will never feel you've wandered long enough among its mountains, rolling plateaus, and numerous ruins. More major archeological sites are located in the Peloponnese than anywhere else in Greece.

Among the must-see ruins are the city of **Corinth**, known for its luxury and decadence during Roman times; **Mycenae**, the main attraction, sites of some of the best archeological finds in the world; **Nafplion**, a pretty town that is the site of a Venetian fortress; **Epidaurus**, where Greek plays are performed in an ancient theater every summer; and **Olympia**, site of the ancient games.

Five miles from the site of ancient Sparta, where only a few stones are left, is the pretty Byzantine town of **Mistra**, once known as the Florence of the East. Its steep, winding streets are full of churches, old mansions, and fragrant flowers and also sport a citadel and a monastery.

The best music and drama festival

The **Summer Festival of Music and Drama at Epidaurus** is one of the world's most exciting performing-arts events. The ancient theater holds 14,000 people and its famous acoustic system enables each of them to hear the tiniest whisper from the stage.

The best hotel in Peloponnese

The **Xenia Palace**, *tel. (30) 752-289-87*, situated inside the walls of the old Venetian fort in Nafplion, is the best of the government-run hotels. Set on the bay, it has gorgeous views all the way to Mycenae.

The best eating in the Peloponnese

The fish tavernas along the waterfront in Nafplion are recommended as much for their views as for their fresh fish and wines served straight from the barrel. Roadside stands between Corinth and Nafplion sell the Blood of Hercules, the rich red wine famous here.

The most undiscovered, upscale island

The island of **Andros** remains a closely guarded secret, discovered to date only by some Scandinavian and British tourists. Most tourists on the ferry don't pay the island much attention, as they're headed, typically, to Mykonos, two islands away. Many of the streets in the capital city are paved with marble.

Two of the three museums on the island stem from the legacy of the Goulandris family, and you'll find Picassos as well as a sculpture garden. If these don't make you gasp, some of the shipping families' villas will. This northernmost of the Cyclades chain is also the greenest, with streams and even dragonflies.

The Cyclades—the most visited Greek Islands

The **Cyclades Islands** are the most visited of Greece's island groups. They offer dramatic beauty and a civilization within a civilization. The Cycladic culture was a subculture of the ancient Mediterranean civilization led first by the Minoans and then by the Mycenaens.

About 17 of the islands are suitable for vacationers. The most famous members of the group are Mykonos, Santorini, and Delos. Others often visited by tourists are Tinos, a destination for pilgrims of the Greek Orthodox faith; Los, with a dramatic setting and a town built on the side of a mountain; and lovely Paros, where you can get away from it all. The island of Kithnos has one of the best government-run Xenia hotels, situated in a renovated building dated 1840, near spas recommended for rheumatism and gynecological disorders.

Mykonos: the island for the jet set

Mykonos, a favorite spot among the jet set, has a reputation for being both wild and flashy and quaint and romantic. It is more open, vivacious, and relaxed than other Greek spots, with a philosophy of live and let live. It is a place where people are allowed and encouraged to do their own things, and where lovers of all persuasions are tolerated—and hardly even noticed. The Greek community itself is more tightly knit and warmer here than perhaps anywhere else in Greece.

Like the other islands in the chain, Mykonos is dry, with few trees, but beautiful in a dramatic way. Its whitewashed windmills are its trademark. Mykonians are almost compulsive about the spotlessness of their white houses and cobblestones, which offset nicely the beautiful colors of the potted flowers growing everywhere.

Mykonos' little houses, inns, hotels, and restaurants are hidden in a maze of tiny winding streets. It takes about a week to decipher the layout of the alleyways. Legend has it that the citizens of Mykonos purposely designed their streets in a random pattern to confound pirates.

Mykonos' beaches, by the way, particularly Paridis, Superparidis (predominantly gay), and Ilia, are covered with nude sunbathers.

Wining and dining in Mykonos

Niko's, *tel. (30)2890-24320*, just off the harbor and opposite Ta Kiouria, is the best restaurant in Mykonos, with good prices and fresh fish.

Little Venice is the most charming area to eat in, with outdoor tavernas on the water's edge looking out on a gorgeous view.

The hottest nightlife

The **Pierros Bar and Disco** on Mykonos is the place to see Greek dancing. Get here about midnight. There is a cover charge, including one drink.

Staying in Mykonos

Leto, *tel. (30)22890-22207* is the best of the in-town hotels and is located right on the harbor.

Hotel Aphroditi, *tel. (30)210-8047244* or *(30)210-8104389*, located on remote Kalafati Beach, is a beautiful place to hide away. The rooms are like bungalows, built in levels stepped up the hill along cobblestone alleyways behind the main building. Each has a balcony. In the beflowered central patio is a large warm saltwater swimming pool, just a few yards from the white sandy beach across the driveway. The Aphrodite has a small disco, a nice restaurant, and a couple of private little tavernas at the end of the beach.

The World's Best Destinations

DELOS: APOLLO'S BIRTHPLACE

An excursion you must take from Mykonos is to the tiny island of **Delos**, now an archeological park. The god Apollo was born on this sacred island. You can visit this beautiful and eerie island via tour boat from Mykonos, a half-hour away. In spring, wild flowers grow among the impressive ruins.

SANTORINI: THE BEST SUNSETS

Santorini is a volcanic island. Its town of Oia (on the northeastern tip) and Thira (the capital also known as Fira) are situated way up in the clouds, looking down on a dramatic harbor shaped like a huge cauldron. In the evening, people gather along the mountain to watch the magnificent colors of Santorini's sunset.

Ferries pull in at one of two jetties. If you are lucky, your ferry will pull in at the one just below town, giving you the opportunity to be transported to the center of town by donkey.

Akrotiri, at the southeastern tip of the island, is one of Greece's most perfect excavations of a Bronze Age town, thought by many to be the legendary lost Atlantis.

Other things to see on Santorini include churches in Thira; Oia, known for its antiques; the beaches of Kamari, Momolithos, and Perissa (black sand) on the southwest coast; the island's castles; and the active Nea Kaimeni volcano on the small island in the harbor. (Tour boats are available to take you there.)

Buses are the least expensive way to tour the island. You can also rent a car or a moped and go it on your own.

The best beds on Santorini

The **Atlantis Villas**, *tel. (30)286-71214* or *(30)286-71236*, is the nicest hotel, but the most expensive.

Hotel Villa Renos is located in downtown Thira. It is on a cliff overlooking the sea, and each room has a private balcony.

The most unusual place to stay on the island—and one of the most unusual in all Greece—is the government-renovated traditional settlement at Oia. Fifteen old Greek houses, complete with kitchens, patios, and gardens, are for rent. Oia, like Thira, is perched high on the cliffs overlooking both sides of the island.

THE BEST OF THE DODECANESE ISLANDS

Situated near the Turkish coast, the **Dodecanese Islands** have a more Turkish atmosphere than other Greek islands, because they were recently ruled by Turkey. Rhodes was a major trade hub of the ancient world.

Patmos is considered one of the most beautiful. Kalymnos offers both a busy harbor town and quiet countryside.

The best island for golfers and gamblers

Rhodes is a favorite among European tourists. It has a more sophisticated atmosphere than other Greek playgrounds. The city is located in and around the walls of the medieval **Fortress of the Knights of St. John**. There are two distinct districts: the New Town (north and west) and the Old Town below it, which is encircled by the medieval fortress walls. Wandering among the shops and restaurants inside the fortress is like visiting Disneyland. Its amusements include an evening sound-and-light show best seen from a boat off the harbor, costumed Greek dances at the summer wine festival, painting and handicraft exhibitions, an aquarium, and a small zoo.

The **Casino Rodos** in the Grand Hotel is open from 7 p.m. to 2 a.m., Mount Vasiliavias' 18-hole golf course and casino, is located at Afandou. And the archeological site of Lindos is about an hour's drive from town.

Rhodes' hottest nightlife

Kontiki, *tel. (30)241-22477*, is a houseboat restaurant/nightclub with a close-up view of the harbor. Open 8:30 a.m. to midnight.

The best places to stay

Luxury hotels with huge swimming pools are common on Rhodes. The **Grand** has great staff and is surrounded by the beautiful beach and the **Rodos Palace Hotel**, *tel. (30)241-25222*, is located just outside town and has extravagant amenities.

Patmos: the holiest island

St. John the Divine is said to have written the last book of the New Testament in a mountain cave on **Patmos**. A huge 11th-century monastery atop the rocks marks the spot.

THE BEST OF SPORADES ISLANDS

These islands, covered with pine and olive trees, are among Greece's most beautiful. Reached by plane or boat from the mainland port of Vollos, Skiathos is the major destination. Only three other of the islands receive attention from tourists: Skopelos, Ilonissos, and Skyros, all quieter versions of Skiathos.

The best places to stay

The **Skiathos Palace**, on Koukounaries beach, *tel. (1)866-LUXE-411*, is the most luxurious hotel on Skiathos—but it's a bit too perfect and not very

Greek. The government-run **Xenia**, *tel. (30)427-22042*, also on Koukounaries, has more charm if you want to stay on the beach.

Savoring Skiathos' cuisine

Skiathos' seafood restaurants offer some of Greece's best meals, prepared with more European subtlety than elsewhere. You can't go wrong at any of the outdoor *tavernas* along the harbor in town. For the best lunch, go where the local fishermen eat—it's a plain establishment, right in the middle of the row of tavernas at the bottom of the hill.

Skopelos: the least discovered

Skopelos is an unspoiled Greek gem smothered in plum trees, where traditional Greek costumes are still the everyday dress. The lack of tourists and their trappings makes this island especially inviting.

The most Turkish islands: the northeast Aegean

Less visited than others, these seven, which include Lesbos, Samos, and Chios, are the most Turkish of Greece's islands.

Lesbos: the prettiest in the group

Lesbos is a large, tree-covered island that is breathtakingly beautiful. It has a Genovese castle in the northern tower of Molyvosa and a petrified forest. The ancient castle above the lovely harbor town of Mytilani is the site of summer concerts performed by international artists each summer. The island's sardines, wine, and locally made ouzo are excellent. The best place to stay is the government-run **Xenia**, with its pool that looks out toward Turkey.

Samos: the best red wine

Dominated by 5,000-foot Mount Kerketeos, **Samos**, has been famous for centuries for its dark red wine. It was considered by the ancients to be the birthplace of Hera, Zeus' wife. The island is popular among Germans and Scandinavians.

Corfu: the most beautiful island in Greece

Northern **Corfu** is said to be the most beautiful island in Greece—which is saying something. Covered with lemon, orange, cyprus, fig, and olive groves, it is a lush place. Many of the island's beautiful villas belong to British expatriates. The main port, Kekira, is a town of Venetian elegance, more Italian than Greek. Corfu offers shops, hotels, restaurants, and nightlife.

The southern and western parts of Corfu have the most striking scenery. Eight miles south of the port is the impressive **Achilleion Palace**, once a summer residence of Kaiser Wilhelm II of Germany and now a gambling casino. Another hangout for the jet set is the **Paleokastristsa**, which is on the west coast. The north coast is the most touristy area, with several resort towns. **Kassiopi** is one of the least spoiled and most reasonable places to stay.

Corfu's best hotel

Cavalieri Corfu, an elegant Venetian mansion, was King George II's summer residence in the 1920s. It is expensive, but not the highest priced place on the island. Contact the **Sunny Greece Travel and Tourism Office** for more details, *tel. (30)210-9237-100.*

The best places to eat on Corfu

Corfu food is a combination of Greek and Italian. The island's wine is said to be among the nation's best. **Paliokastritza** is a world-renowned eating spot. After lunch, swim in this beautiful cove where Odysseus is said to have washed ashore.

Crete: the most Middle Eastern of the Islands

Crete is like a small country with its own lifestyle and culture. A huge island of more than 5,000 square miles, it really warrants a separate trip. Crete has some of the world's most impressive ruins. Rent a car to see the island.

The most important sight

The major attraction of Greece and one of the most important archeological sites of the Mediterranean world is the ancient capital of Minoan civilization, **Knossos**. If you're only in port for a day, you can sign up for tours of Knossos in Iraklion. However, the public bus, which leaves from Venizelou Square, is more economical.

Europe's most beautiful gorge

The natural wonder of the island is the **Samarian Gorge**, located in central-western Crete. It is the largest—and many think the most beautiful—gorge in Europe and a popular jaunt for hikers. Buses leave from Hania early in the morning and drop hikers off at the top. The walk down takes about five hours. The gorge exits onto a beach, where you can stop for a swim.

The best hotel

The **Elounda Beach Hotel**, *tel. (30)28410-41412*, is one of the world's best hotels. It was designed by one of Greece's great architects, Spiro Kokotas. It is on a beautiful beach, set off by lots of flowers. The adjoining Elounda Mare has bungalows with private swimming pools. This resort is outstanding, but pricey.

The best monastery stay

Panormitis Monastery on Symi Island is right on the water. Pilgrims are offered free food (haddock) with wine, as well as a place to stay at no cost. The monastery has an inn attached and during summer, rooms (called cells) are full of tourists, mostly from Greece. There are dozens of large rooms set aside for families (about $12 "donation" per family).

Visitors and overnight guests must dress appropriately—courtesy clothing may be borrowed. The complex has a pebbled courtyard, a gallery, a Byzantine Museum, and a Folklore Museum (entry is $2, covering both). Other on-site facilities include a mini-market, a taverna, a bakery, and a tiny beach.

THE BEST OF HUNGARY

Hungary is a world unto itself. While it is at the very heart of the European continent, its language, food, and music are not like those of any other European country. Its people are as unique as its culture. And the country is changing daily—even the official holidays are changing. The nicest change has been in the Hungarian attitude toward foreigners. Travelers are now made to feel completely welcome and at ease.

Hungarians, or Magyars, are descendants of fierce horsemen from the Ural Mountains, who terrorized much of Europe until the ninth century. Hungarians still speak Magyar, which is distantly related to Finnish and Estonian. Their folk music is passionate; strains of the old tunes can be heard in the works of Ferenc Liszt, Bela Bartok, and Zoltan Kodaly.

BUDAPEST: EASTERN EUROPE'S
LOVELIEST CITY

The capital of Hungary is one of the most beautiful cities in the world. Its 15th-century streets lead past Renaissance houses that hide pretty interior courtyards. At night, delicate neon signs glow from the old stone facades of the buildings. And Budapest has more museums per citizen than any other city in the world.

Budapest is made up of two sections: **Buda** and **Pest**, which are divided by the Danube River. Once two separate cities, they were united in 1873. Buda, dominated by the spires of the 13th-century Matthias Church, has medieval cobblestoned streets, centuries-old houses, and steep little stairways that climb to the castle. Pest, centered around the neo-Gothic parliament building, is the more modern business section of the city, with grand 19th-century monuments and memorials.

The best way to get to Budapest is aboard the hydrofoil that glides from Vienna down the Danube and around Czechoslovakia, reaching Budapest at sunset.

The top sights

Buda Castle, *Szent Gyorgy Ter 2*, tops Castle Hill on the Buda side. Generations of Hungarian kings were crowned at this castle, which is embellished with elaborate reliefs. Demolished during bombing raids in World War II, it has been carefully rebuilt. From the courtyard is a splendid view over the Danube. The castle houses the Historical Museum of Budapest, which contains archeological remains of Old Town and exhibits on the history of the palace, and the National Gallery.

However, the most fascinating part of the castle is underground. Labyrinths running below the castle were used to house troops and a hospital during World War I. The tunnels are now a wax museum depicting Hungary's history: the early Roman settlers, the invasion of Attila the Hun and his horsemen from Mongolia in A.D. 430, the Turkish domination of Hungary from 1526 to 1686, the Austrian rulers, and modern history.

King Charles and Matthias were crowned at **Matthias Church**, *Szentharomsag ter 2*, as were Empress Maria Theresa and Emperor Franz Josef. High Mass is celebrated every Sunday at 10 a.m., and organ concerts are held in the church on Sunday afternoons.

The **Houses of Parliament**, *Kossuth Ter*, across the Danube in Pest, are a grand replica of the Houses of Parliament in Westminster. Built 100 years ago, the neo-Gothic buildings are the seat of the Hungarian National Assembly and are used for state receptions.

Also in Pest is the **Hungarian National Museum**, *Muzeum Korut 14-16*, which features a permanent exhibit called "The History of the Hungarian People from the Magyar Conquest to 1849." One room displays a large, lavishly decorated Turkish tent, captured in 1686 when Buda was liberated from the Turkish occupation. Another room shows paintings and sculptures by Hungarian artists from the Middle Ages to the present.

Across from **Heroes Square**, where you'll see a statue commemorating Attila the Hun (a Hungarian hero, believe it or not) and Hungary's 1,000 years as a nation, is the **Museum of Fine Arts**, *Dozsa Gyorgy ut 41*. The museum has more El Grecos than any institution outside Spain, as well as three Rembrandts and major works by Goya, Raphael, Rubens, Franz Hals, Monet, Renoir, and Cézanne. (It also may have a Leonardo sculpture, depending on whether you listen to the Hungarians or the Italians.)

One of the most impressive buildings is the Italian neo-Renaissance **State Opera House**. Statues of Ferenc Liszt, Ferenc Erkel, and other renowned musicians surround the building. Inside, a visual splendor of ceiling frescoes, wall paintings and carved balustrades greets visitors. Recently restored, the State Opera House has presented continuous performances since 1884.

Another favorite area, **Vaci Utca**, attracts visitors and locals alike. In this pedestrian shopping area, large department stores and small specialty shops offer beautiful handcrafted goods. Elsewhere, workers and travelers crowd into busy cafés for *kave-spresso*, traditional *somloi galuska* (sponge cake covered with chocolate sauce and whipped cream), and delicious fruit tortes with fresh cream.

The world's best Gypsy music

Every February in Budapest, the **Gypsy Music Festival** is held. However, you can hear Gypsy music year-round at many restaurants in the city, including Feher Sandor, Lakatos Sandor, Lakatos Gyorgy, Kallai Jis Erno, and Voros Kalman. The best Gypsy music while you dine is at the restaurant called **Matyaspince**, *Marcius 15 ter 7; tel. (36)1-118-169.*

Budapest's best markets

Not far from the Matthias Cathedral, heading toward the river, a lively gypsy market is held on weekends. Gypsies in Hungary deal in secondhand goods and crafts. Among the bargains are leather clothes (jackets, skirts, and tops), embroidery (clothing and tablecloths), and jewelry. Offer to pay half the price they ask in dollars.

The **Vamhaz Indoor Food Market**, *Vamhaz Korut 1-3*, an enormous emporium of glass and iron, sells delicious sausages, salami chunks, and smoked meat, with thick slabs of bread and pickled peppers.

The best restaurants and cafés

The top restaurant in Budapest is **Gundel**, near Heroes Square in Pest, *tel. (36)18-1-321-3550*, which sets the standard for fine dining. Restaurateur George Lang serves the best of Hungarian cuisine at this inviting little restaurant. Reservations are required and formal wear is a must.

Our favorite restaurant, however, is **Alabardos**, *Orszaghaz Utca 2; tel. (36)1-156-0851*, which not only offers luxurious dining, but also is cheap. Guests are seated in a huge Gothic room with a vaulted ceiling; in the summer, you can sit at tables in the cobblestoned courtyard.

The smartest café in Budapest is **Gerbeaud**, *Vorosmarty ter 7; tel. (36)1-118-1311*, on Vaci Utca. It is also one of the best pastry shops in the city—well worth the usual wait for a table. Built in the mid-19th century, the café boasts crystal chandeliers, heavy drapes, and dark polished wood tables that provide a yesteryear ambience for enjoying some of the best pastries in Budapest.

The **Hungaria** in Buda and the **Angelika** in Pest also serve mouth-watering pastries.

Where to sleep

There are many lovely bed-and-breakfasts in Budapest. Budapest also has one of the most stunning hotels of any city in the world: the **Budapest Hilton**, *I Hess Andras ter 1-3; tel. (36)1-175-1000*, built into the ruins of a 13th-century abbey on top of a hill in Buda. It is next to Matthias Church and has views of the city and the river.

The **Duna-Intercontinental**, *Apaczai cfere jano utca 4; tel. (36)1-117-5122*, the **Atrium-Hyatt**, *Roosevelt ter 2; tel. (36)1-138-3000*, and the **Forum**, *Apaczai* *cfere janos utca 12-14; tel. (36)1-117-8088*, are beautifully designed palaces all on the Pest side of the Danube. The Duna, within walking distance of the main shopping district, has river views. The Atrium has a glass-covered central court, through which glass-sided elevators soar. The Forum, a four-rather than five-star hotel, is within easy walking distance of downtown.

Also on the Pest side, the **Grand Hotel Corvinus Kempinkski**, *Erzsbet 7-8; tel. (36)1-266-1000*, is a five-star hotel within walking distance of Vaci Utca, an exclusive shopping area.

Budapest's incomparable spa hotel, the **Hotel Gellert**, *Szent Gellert Ter 1; tel. (36)1-185-2200*, is famous for its spring-fed baths. The radioactive pools are located in mosaic-decorated art deco halls with ornate balconies, massive columns, and skylights.

Bacchus' best

Every September, the Budapest castle district is transformed into a wine-lover's dreamland during the **Budapest International Wine Festival**. Top winemakers from across the country share their best vintages in anticipation of the upcoming harvest, while chefs prepare tasty feasts, cheese masters provide rare cheeses, and violins passionately wail as folk dancers whirl around in colorful costumes.

Visitors to the festival can choose from hundreds of Hungarian and international wines and personally meet the top winemakers, who are always happy to talk about their products. Since this is a small community, there's a good chance that the person pouring your glass of wine played some role in producing it.

Along with wine tastings, the festival offers art exhibitions, dinners, concerts, and an auction. A wine competition is simulated, at which guest judges taste award-winning wines to see how their opinions compare with those of the professionals. Anyone interested in the scholarly side of Hungary's wine tradition can attend lectures. After five decades of Communist policy, mass production, neglect, and under-funding, Hungarian viniculture is being brought back to life by the new generation of wine artisans.

The wine festival is an ideal place for tasting these changes. And when you discover your favorite Hungarian wines, be sure to buy a few extra bottles for your suitcase, because you probably won't find many of these wines again outside of Hungary.

Bests beyond Budapest

It is now easier than ever before for the Western traveler to venture beyond Budapest. Hungary is filled with delightful towns and little-known historic sights outside its capital city. **Szentendre**, on the right bank of the Danube, dates from the 1300s. Cobblestoned streets lead to an ancient main square in the inner town, where you'll find shops and market stalls selling embroidered linens, distinctive china and crystal, leather goods, and souvenirs.

Visegrad is another must-see. The Romans occupied Hungary for centuries. In the fourth century, they built a *castrum*, or fortress. A monastery was added in the 11th century. Visegrad, the country's first fortress and watchtower, commands magnificent views of green countryside and the Danube.

To the south is **Pecs**, one of Hungary's oldest cities. A Celtic settlement in the third century, Pecs has become a sophisticated university town. Its main claim to fame is a former Turkish mosque, built in 1580 and since converted into a Catholic church. Pecs also boasts a television tower. You can take an elevator to the top to view the surrounding countryside, a fabulously ornate cathedral, and remarkably well-preserved fourth-century Christian burial chambers, adorned with wall paintings much in the style of the Roman catacombs.

HUNGARY'S BEST WINES

If you do not go anywhere else in Hungary, you must not miss **Eger**, the country's best wine region. It is a delightful city, rich in history, with yet another castle and the most delectable wines on earth. Visit the tiny wine cellars bored into the hillside for a leisurely wine tasting. A nearby *csarda* offers magnificent food at incredible prices.

HUNGARY'S VERSAILLES

Not far from Budapest, in Fertod, is **Esterhazy Palace**, the 18th-century home of Prince Nicholaus Esterhazy the Magnificent, who ruled at the height of the Hapsburg monarchy. Joseph Haydn was concertmaster here.

The palace, which was looted by Soviet troops during World War II, has been restored recently and is open to visitors. Nicholas modeled the palace after Versailles, which he had visited on a diplomatic trip.

HUNGARY'S LARGEST CATHEDRAL

Esztergom, a town on a narrow side channel of the Danube, contains the largest cathedral in Hungary, built between 1822 and 1856. However, the 19th-century marble cathedral pales in comparison with the Primate's art collection in the attached museum. The Renaissance chapel adjoining the cathedral houses a 13th-century gold cross, upon which Hungarian kings took their oaths. Marcus Aurelius wrote *Reflections* in this town, which was once an important Roman outpost. It was the seat of the Magyar kings in the 12th and 13th centuries and the center of the Hungarian Catholic Church.

CENTRAL EUROPE'S LARGEST LAKE

Hungary's **Lake Balaton**, Central Europe's largest lake, is 48 miles long and 36 feet deep in some places. It is known for its sandy beaches, its warm water (you can swim here from spring through late fall), its resort hotels, and its fine fishing (for 42 kinds of fish). The tastiest of the fish caught here is the giant pike-perch (*fogas*).

Lake Balaton served as a line of defense against the Turks for centuries. The remains of border castles can be seen in Tihany, Nagyvazsony, Szigliget, and Fonyod.

The most popular resorts are on the south shore of the lake, where the water is warmer and the beaches have a softer grade of sand. The north shore is relatively undiscovered and a good place to get away from the crowds; however, the water is colder and the beaches aren't as nice.

Siofok, the largest town on the southern shore, is also the most crowded. The **Hotel Balaton**, *Petofi Setany 9; tel. (36)84-10-655*, is the best place to stay, with reasonable prices.

Other good places to stay in Siofok are the **Europa**, *Petofi Setany 15; tel. (36)84-13-411*; the **Hotel Lido**, *tel. (34)84-10-633*; and the **Hungaria**, *Petofi Setany 13; tel. (36)84-10-677*.

The best restaurant on the lake is just outside Siofok. **Menes Csarda**, *15 Apaczai Csere J., Szantodpuszta; tel. (36)84-170-803*, serves spicy food cooked according to local custom. The restaurant is housed in a restored stable and is decorated with antique art.

The healthiest place along the lake is the small spa town of **Balatonfured**, on the northern shore. It has 11 medicinal springs that are supposed to be good for the heart and the nerves. This hilly old town is covered with twisting streets. At its center is **Gyogy Ter** (Spa Square), where the waters of volcanic springs bubble under a pavilion.

The most charming hotel in Balatonfured is the old-fashioned **Arany Csillag** (Golden Star), *tel. (36)84-40-323*, a four-story hotel in a small grove of trees. It doesn't have a view of the lake or private baths, but the rooms are airy and clean.

Also in Balatonfured are three one-star hotels: **Annabella**, *Beloiannisz utca 25; tel. (36)86-42-222*; **Margareta**, *Szechenyi utca 29; tel. (36)86-43-824*; and the **Marina**, *Szechnyi utca 26; tel. (36)86-43-644*.

Nearby Zichy Castle hosts the annual **August Horse Show**. This is the best place to observe top riders and horses—Hungary is famous for its equestrian traditions. And riders for this famous horse show dress in medieval costumes. For more information contact **IBUSZ**, *1 Parker Plaza, Fort Lee, NJ 07024.*

You can bathe in a warm-water lake surrounded by rose-colored Egyptian lotus plants in **Heviz**, a town near Lake Balaton. Fed by a thermal spring, Heviz Lake has a temperature that varies from 82 to 100 degrees Fahrenheit. The mud from the bottom of the lake is also therapeutic; it is dried and exported for mud packs. Cemeteries dating back to Roman times have been found along the lake.

THE BEST OF IRELAND

The good-natured Irish people are a joy to spend time with, so make sure you visit the people of Ireland as well as the Irish countryside. Don't miss the most pleasant occupation in Ireland: sitting in a pub, sipping a pint of Guinness, and chatting.

The best way to tour Ireland's emerald countryside, charming villages, and ancient ruins is to circle around its coast, traveling from Dublin to Wicklow, Wexford, Waterford, Cork, Killarney, and finally Limerick. Venture inland to Kilkenny. Then go to the region the English never conquered: the Burren, Galway, Mayo, and Sligo.

The best ways to explore Dublin

The most pleasant way to visit Dublin is to follow the lines of an old song: "Have coffee in Dublin at 11 and walk in Stephen's Green, and you'll be in heaven." Actually, have tea—it's usually better than the coffee. Later, spend time shopping along bustling Grafton, Anne, and Duke streets.

If you are in a hurry, use the **Dublin Trail**. Well posted, it leads past the city's major sights.

Another good way to explore Dublin is to follow in the footsteps of James Joyce. The house where Joyce was born, 41 Brighton Square W., in the agreeable suburb of Rathgar, is marked with a plaque. **Mulligan's**, *Poolbeg Street*, a pub Joyce frequented in his student days, has a special aura, especially in the back parlor, where Joyce often sat and wrote. Joyce once lived at Martello Tower Museum, at Sandycove, as did his characters in Ulysses.

Also look for the homes of other famous Dubliners: Shelley lived at 1 Grafton Street; Sheridan lived at 79 Grafton Street; and George Bernard Shaw was born at 33 Synge Street.

Dublin's greatest treasure

The jewel in Dublin's crown is *The Book of Kells*. More than 1,000 years old, it is the most intricate illuminated manuscript in the Western world. The manuscript is kept at **Trinity College**.

Ireland's best stout

The **Guinness Brewery** at St. James' Gate on the banks of the Liffey in Dublin produces Ireland's rich and frothy national drink, the brown stout found on tap in every pub. Guinness Storehouse is open from 9.30 a.m. to 5 p.m. seven days a week. The interactive tour takes you through the brewing process, the history of Guinness, and ends in the Gravity Bar, where you get to enjoy a pint of the famous "black stuff" while enjoying 360-degree views of Dublin city.

The oldest pub in Ireland

The **Brazen Head**, *Bridge Street*, Dublin, is the oldest pub in Ireland, dating back to the 12th century. It is five minutes away from the antique shops on Francis Street, and it's a perfect break from your shopping. The Guinness here is superb; the brewery is only a stone's throw away, and the smell of hops stays with you for hours after you've moved on.

The pubs with the most atmosphere

Dublin boasts more than 600 pubs, but if you want atmosphere, head to the **Palace Bar**, *Fleet Street*, or the **Long Hall**, *South George's Street*. Both have authentic stained-glass partitions, wood paneling, and collections of Victorian prints. But smokers beware—smoking is now illegal in pubs and restaurants throughout Ireland.

Dublin's best sights

Dublin Castle, restored after a bombing, has handsome state apartments that are open to the public. Castle upon castle has been built on this site. The earliest construction was Celtic. The Vikings later improved upon this; then, in the 13th-century King John of England built a fortress on the site. The British ruled Ireland from this stronghold for 400 years.

The **General Post Office**, *O'Connell Street*, was the scene of the 1916 Easter uprising, the major step along Ireland's road to independence. You can read the declaration of Irish independence on the walls. After they proclaimed the free Republic here, the Irish Volunteers were bombed by a British gunboat docked in the River Liffey. Those who surrendered were hanged.

The **National Museum**, *Kildare Street*, has a collection of Irish antiquities from the Stone Age through the War for Independence. It is open daily.

The **National Gallery** has a fine collection of old masters, including works by Rembrandt, Caravaggio, Monet, and Picasso. It also houses a collection of works by Jack B. Yeats, Ireland's most important 20th century artist; and the National Portrait Gallery.

Dublin's creepiest experience

Centuries-old bodies lie perfectly preserved in the dry crypt of **St. Michan's Church** on Church Street. The 17th-century church was built on the site of a 10th-century Viking church. Perhaps because of its dryness, the crypt has remarkable preservation qualities. You can actually touch an eight-foot Crusader. It is said to be good luck to shake the hand of one of the corpses here. The crypt is open weekdays and Saturday mornings.

The best park

Phoenix Park in Dublin is the largest public park in Western Europe and the largest enclosed city park in the world. The official residence of the Irish president is here, as well as the residence of the American ambassador. The 1,760-acre park includes a racetrack, a soccer field, sports grounds, flower gardens, a herd of fallow deer, a lake, and a monument to Wellington, as well as Dublin Zoo.

Dublin's most picturesque bridge

Peer into the Liffey from the wrought iron **Ha'penny Bridge**, named after the toll once charged for crossing the river. Its southern end brings you through Merchant's Quay into the cobblestoned alleyways of Temple Bar. This is Dublin's "left bank," teeming with secondhand bookshops, bars, and cafés.

The best escape from Dublin

If, by some amazing chance, the weather is hot while you are in Dublin, visit the famous seaside resort **Bray**. It is about 15 miles south of Dublin City, adjacent to the town of Dun Laoghaire (pronounced Dunleary) in County Dublin.

Dublin's best nightlife

The best spots in Dublin are the pubs, with their evenings of Guinness, ballads, and poetry. Busiest from 9 p.m. onward, most pubs open at 11 a.m. and close around midnight. Some of the most famous pubs include **The Brazen Head**, **The Abbey Tavern**, and **Slattery's Pub**.

The world's best pub crawl

Every summer, the infamous "Dublin Literary Pub Crawl" staggers off at 7 p.m. every Monday through Thursday. First pints are downed at **The Bailey** on Duke Street, where the owners still display Michael Collins' revolver. Also on Duke Street, try **Davy Byrne's Pub**, where Leopold Bloom fictionally dined on Gorgonzola and Burgundy.

The best Dublin market

For local color head for the **Moore Street Market**, off O'Connell Street. Although you won't meet Molly Malone with her wheelbarrow, you will be able to shop for everything from socks to strawberries, sold out of battered old prams. The language is just as colorful as the people.

The best place to buy antiques

Go to **The Liberties**, the oldest section of the city and the address of its best antique shops. Start at one end of Francis Street and continue to the other. You'll pass a dozen or more quality antique shops. Don't be fooled by their small fronts. The shops stretch back a block or more.

The best seafood restaurant

King Sitric, *East Pier, Howth*, offers the best seafood in or around Dublin. It is a popular, small restaurant overlooking the harbor at Howth, well worth the 30-minute drive out of the city.

Dublin's finest hotel

The **Shelbourne Hotel**, *tel. (353) 1-663-4500; website: www.shelbourne.ie*, which graces St. Stephen's Green, is a Victorian hotel where the Irish Constitution was drafted. Inside the hotel's turreted red-brick façade are ultramodern rooms. Don't miss the sumptuous afternoon tea at the Shelbourne. **Jury's Hotel**, *tel. (353) 1-660-5000*, is also a good hotel in Dublin, as well as many other parts of Ireland.

IRELAND'S GREENEST COUNTY

County Wicklow, which is known as the Garden of Ireland, is the greenest of Ireland's counties. **Enniskerry**, one of Ireland's prettiest villages, is here. Located in a wooded hollow and surrounded by hills, the village is famous for Powerscourt, one of Ireland's great estates. The ruins of a Georgian mansion are surrounded by 14,000 acres of grounds, including the 400-foot Powerscourt Waterfall.

Wicklow's other highlight is **Glendalough**, a deep valley in the Wicklow Mountains. In the sixth century, St. Kevin took refuge in this peaceful glen between two lakes. However, his refuge didn't remain secret. His disciples followed him and founded a monastery and a famous center of learning here. View the remains of a medieval round tower, as well as buildings from the ninth through 13th centuries. This is a good region for hikers; nature trails head through the valley.

Waterford: The world's best crystal

Waterford is a fine old harbor city and an important shipping port, and is best known for producing some of the finest hand-cut crystal in the world. The Waterford Crystal Plant, which you can tour, is about two miles from the city center on the right-hand side of N25, the main road between Waterford and Cork. Craftsmen make about 90,000 pieces of crystal a week. 70% goes to the United States.

Lismore—Ireland's tidiest town

Lismore, in west County Waterford (about 45 miles from Waterford city) was voted Ireland's tidiest town in 2004. The town is nestled in the Blackwater River Valley among rolling, wooded hills. It grew around a monastery founded by St. Carthage in A.D. 636.

Lismore Heritage Center, located in the former courthouse, is a must for those who wish to experience the rich history of the town and its surroundings. Here, the story of Lismore is creatively interpreted by Brother Declan, one of the followers of St. Carthage, and the voice of Niall Toibin, one of Ireland's finest actors and entertainers.

St. Carthage's Cathedral stands on the site of a church built in 1207. Gravestones from monastic times suggest that this site was a place of worship from the time of St. Carthage.

The loveliest gardens

The typical Irish "soft day," of gentle drizzle and intermittent sunshine, makes for ideal growing conditions. **Lismore Castle** is the best place to see the flowers grow. The castle itself, which is the Irish residence of the Duke and Duchess of Devonshire, is not open to the public, but the castle gardens are. Some of the gardens here are 800 years old. You can enjoy them May through September.

The best antique shopping

Rody Keighery's auction house, just off the quay, is the best place in Waterford to shop for antiques. This country hides antique treasures at bargain prices. In Waterford, Rody's inventory turns over regularly, and his prices are often half what you would pay in the United States for comparable pieces.

Waterford's best restaurant

Coast Townhouse & Restaurant, *Upper Branch Road, Tramore, Co. Waterford; tel. (353)51-393-646*, is the best restaurant in Waterford. It is located in a three-story Victorian property in the coastal village of Tramore, 15 minutes drive from Waterford city. The restaurant's emphasis is on the best of local seafood. A juxtaposition of old and new creates a soothing and comfortable atmosphere.

The best pubs

The best Trad (traditional Irish music) sessions are at **Kitty Kieran's**, *40 Barrack Street*. Most weeknights they have a jam session; sometimes it's Trad and sometimes it's "Mad." During these latter sessions you are as likely to hear Bob Marley as your favorite Trad songs.

Geoff's, *8 John Street*, has little nooks and corners with names familiar to regulars—the Protestants Corner, the Catholics Corner, and the Queen's Chair—that provide a certain intimacy despite its large area.

Downes, *8 Thomas Street*, has been owned by the same family since Henry Downes founded it as a distillery and pub in 1797. The pub is large and rarely crowded, except on Saturday nights when it's a popular local hangout. Don't come expecting to meet tourists, but do taste Downes No. 9, the blended whiskey that has been made and served at Downes since its founding.

If your tastes run toward tourist hotspots, visit **T & H Doolans**, *George's Street*. They feature crowd-pleasing Irish music every night of the week. There's plenty of singing, and you are sure to hear classics like *The Irish Rover* or *Wild Colonial Boy*. The place always has a lively crowd and good atmosphere.

CORK: THE BEST IRISH MARKET

County Cork's capital, **Cork**, houses the fascinating **English Market**, a vast covered arcade on Prince's Street that was built in 1788. Here you can soak up a bit of local color and enjoy the unmistakable Cork accent. Home-grown produce is sold at the **President's Restaurant**, *Longueville House, Mallow; tel. (353)22-47156*, which is nearby on a 500-acre estate. Reservations are required.

Cork's biggest bell

Be sure to climb the pepperpot steeple of **Shandon Church** and ring its bells. Using numbered cards you can even regale the "rebel" city with your own eight-belled version of *Waltzing Matilda*.

Cork's best country restaurant

For country house ambience (including a heated swimming pool), try **Ballymaloe House**. Twenty miles from Cork City and only two from the coast, Ballymaloe is run by Ivan and Myrtle Allen. Produce for the award-winning restaurant comes from the home farm; other members of the Allen family run the Ballymaloe Cookery School, arguably the most prestigious in Ireland. For more information visit *www.ballymaloe.com*.

The blarniest sight

Outside Cork City is **Blarney Castle**, where kissing the **Blarney Stone** is said to give the gift of eloquence or the gift of the gab as it is known locally. Doing so is practically an acrobatic feat. You must lie on your back over a sheer drop and stretch to kiss the stone. The legend is that the Lord of Blarney Castle, McCarthy, flabbergasted Queen Elizabeth with his eloquent excuses for having attacked England. She finally dropped the charges against him, calling his excuses "blarney."

The yacht crowd's favorite

Kinsale, about 20 minutes drive from Cork city, is an international yachting center overflowing with gourmet restaurants. The *Lusitania* was torpedoed off its coast by a German submarine in 1915. This was also the site of the 1602 Battle of Kinsale, during which the northern chieftains were defeated by the English, establishing English domination of Ireland. The heavy, woolen Kinsale cloak is a popular purchase.

The best wildlife

Fota, *Carrigtwohill, Co. Cork*, is Ireland's best wildlife park. Fota is home to free-ranging monkeys, zebras, giraffes, ostriches, flamingos, emus, bison, cheetahs, red pandas, and kangaroos, wandering freely over 70 acres. The park is open March through October. Admission is 9.50 euro ($12) for adults, 6 euro ($7) for children.

Ennis—the best base for exploring

The town of **Ennis** in County Clare is the best base for exploring the west of Ireland, from which so many Americans stem. The old market town has escaped relatively unscathed from the tourist flow, even though Shannon Airport is close by.

The main street in Ennis boasts antique shops selling genuine (if pricey) antiques. But the town's gem is its monastery—the most evocative in Ireland. This roofless, weed-covered ruin's tottering Gothic walls exactly fit Shakespeare's phrase, "bare, ruined choirs."

Bunratty House, built in 1846, is worth a visit. (Skip the fake feast in its cellar.) The house gives you an idea of how Irish nobility lived. The folk park behind the elegant house shows how lesser Irishmen survived.

The **Old Ground**, *O'Connell Street*, is the most charming place to stay in Ennis. Rooms are well-equipped. The restaurant at the Old Ground is splendid and serves Irish specialties, including Dublin Bay prawns (shrimp), mutton chops with kidneys, and apple pie.

Ireland's most spectacular cliffs

The **Cliffs of Moher**, a few miles north of Ennis, are the most spectacular in Ireland, perhaps in all Europe. The 700-foot black cliffs face the constant onslaught of the Atlantic.

Ireland's loveliest lakes

The town of **Killarney** offers a dreamlike setting of lush green hills and deep blue lakes. Spend time enjoying the town, but concentrate on the surrounding Lower, Middle, and Upper lakes. At their banks, ferns and mosses grow in the shade of oak, birch, holly, and ash trees. Much of this lake district lies within the 11,000-acre Bourne Vincent Memorial Park.

The Aran Islands—time's greatest foe

The **Aran Islands** are fascinating, if barely habitable. Gaelic language and traditions survive on these three islands 35 miles from the mainland. The islanders grow potatoes in a mixture of sand and seaweed and fish in wicker-framed, hide-covered *curraughs*, or boats.

Dun Aengus, an Iron Age fortress built on a cliff on the island of **Inishmore**, has 18-foot-thick walls. The prettiest islands are the two smallest, **Inishman**, which is known for its traditional music and dancing, and **Inisheer**. In good weather, boat service is available regularly to most of the islands. The closest point on the mainland is Doolin, where you can catch a boat to Inisheer. Boats also run daily from Galway to Kilronan on Inishmore.

The best horseback riding

The **Connemara Trail**, which winds its way along the coast of Ireland's County Galway, passes through rugged mountains and along deserted beaches. Beginning near the sea in Barna, the trail goes from village to village and mountain to mountain, leading you eventually to the Atlantic Ocean on the beaches near Clifden.

Biggest horse fair, smallest ponies

Held annually in County Galway, the **Great Fair of Ballinasloe** is Ireland's oldest and biggest horse fair. For the first week of October, Ballinasloe's Fair Green heaves with horseflesh. Many deals are done with a spit and a handshake.

Ireland's smallest ponies are found in the wilderness of **Connemara**. Clifden, the color-washed capital of this mountainous region, hosts the annual Connemara pony show during the third week in August.

The most delicious oysters

For some of the best oysters in all Ireland, visit **Paddy Burke's Oyster Tavern**, *Clainbridge; tel. (353)93-962-26*. Oysters are sold by the dozen, or you can sit down for a good meal. To preserve the taste of the sea, you should hold the shell horizontally. With nothing more than perhaps a squeeze of lemon for flavoring, squash the oyster with your tongue, savor its flavor, and then gulp the liquid from the shell.

Yeats' favorite land

The dramatic countryside of **Sligo** is where the poet William Butler Yeats spent his childhood summers. He asked to be buried in Drumcliff Churchyard, five miles from Sligo proper. The area around Sligo claims one of the largest concentrations of prehistoric graves and monuments in Western Europe. Most are neither fenced off nor mentioned in tourist brochures. You must find them by word-of-mouth.

"A pearl, a gem, a jewel in the crown of mother Ireland"

Well, that's how **Hargadons** on Sligo town's O'Connell Street modestly describes itself. Even the atmosphere in this peculiar drinking den is intoxicating. Needless to say, it serves memorable Guinness. But there's more to Hargadons than fine brew—just look around; you'll see a potbellied stove, huge glittering mirrors, open turf fires, and customers who can talk the hind leg off any proverbial donkey. Don't miss it.

DONEGAL: THE BEST TWEED

"You'll wear out two suit linings," the Irish brag, "before you'll wear out a Donegal tweed." The county of **Donegal**, in northwest Ireland, sells some of the best tweed in the world. Magee's Tweed Shop in Donegal town is a good place to begin your search.

Also try the peninsula just west of Donegal town. Take the road to Glencolumbkille and stop in **Mount Charles** (pronounced Charless) at the Tweed Shop. Owen Gillespie and his sister Mary, proprietors of the shop, are both knowledgeable about tweed and tailoring. Their parents owned the shop before them. Spend some time here looking through the selection of herringbone, houndstooth, and Harris tweeds. If you buy any tweed during your visit, be sure it is labeled "Genuine Donegal Hand-Woven Tweed. Pure New Wool."

The toughest pilgrimage

In the bare blue hills of County Donegal, the **Lough Derg** pilgrimage is a trip to purgatory. Every year, from June 1 through Aug. 15, pilgrims spend three days on Station Island, site of St. Patrick's purgatory, depriving themselves of food, sleep, and all physical comforts. The cost to join in is not much, but make sure you know what you're letting yourself in for. The penitential exercises include dragging your bare feet over the jagged remains of monastic cells. It is an excruciating experience.

Ireland's most beautiful ruin

In the northern midlands of Ireland, south of Athlone in County Offaly, is the haunting ruin of **Clonmacnoise**, a flourishing monastic settlement more than 1,000 years ago. Still here are ruins of an abbey founded in A.D. 541 by St. Kieran, the Seven Churches of Clonmacnoise, a castle, a bishop's palace, and two round towers where townspeople watched for invading Vikings in search of Celtic gold. Celtic crosses from the time when Ireland was the Island of Saints and Scholars also stand here still.

The best riverboat cruising

Winding past Clonmacnoise and cutting through the bogs like a broad silver ribbon is the magnificent River Shannon. It's the perfect place for fishing, bird-watching, or simply lazing on a summer afternoon. The river is navigable for 120 of its 220 miles to the sea, and cruising is a popular activity. For more information on expeditions down the river, contact **Emerald Star**, *tel. (353)1-782-0234.*

The holiest mountain

Ireland's holiest mountain is **Croagh Patrick** in County Mayo. More than 2,500 feet high, it was from here that St. Patrick reputedly banished all snakes from the island. Each Garland Sunday, the last Sunday in July, 60,000 pilgrims clamber to the summit.

The stoniest wilderness

Stark, strange, and almost brutal to the eye, dotted with megalithic tombs and disappearing loughs, County Clare's Burren region seems an unlikely place for a flower show. The landscape is lunar: a vast gray sea of rock stretching for mile upon mile. But look closer—hidden in limestone crevices are orchids, vivid blue gentians, and a profusion of other rare wild flowers. It's a real botanist's paradise.

The strangest festival

If you're looking for romance, head for **Lisdoonvarna** on the southern edge of the Burren, where men are men and women are scarce. Each September, this small spa town hosts a matchmaking festival that boosts the population from 700 to 7,000. And although the matchmaking business isn't as serious as in days gone by, the ballrooms of romance still fill with dancers until dawn.

The best hostel

Ireland's best hostel is the **Valley House Holiday Hostel and Pub** on Achill Island, off the coast of Mayo. The island, about 14 miles across and 19 miles long, is Ireland's largest and only bridged island—you can drive there. Achill has several blue flag beaches, white or golden, plenty of restaurants, and pubs to wet your whistle. The locals are friendly characters.

The hostel itself is situated in a huge white manor more than 110 years old. Its bedrooms range from new, comfortable bunks to bouncy twins. The hostel also offers two nicely decorated private rooms, as well as a lawn for tent campers.

Ireland's best accommodation: the castle hotel

The best places to stay in Ireland are the country's castle hotels. Scores of these delightful, historic places dot the countryside.

The finest in all Ireland is **Ashford Castle**, *tel. (353)92-46003*, in Co. Mayo. The original castle was built here in 1228. In the 16th century, the troops of Queen Elizabeth battled in the area and stormed through the castle, which later became an English fortress. In the 18th century, a French château was incorporated into the old complex. Nearby are several ancient abbeys, churches, and points of archeological interest. Note the 20-foot fireplace and the fine woodwork.

THE BEST OF THE ISLE OF MAN

The politically independent **Isle of Man**, located halfway between Ireland and England and only 20 miles south of Scotland, is one of Europe's hidden bests. It is one of the best banking havens in the world. Europe's best ice cream is created here. Manx kippers are world famous, and Man has been noted by the World Health Organization for its high-quality lamb and beef. The fishing here is terrific. And some of Britain's prettiest walking trails flank the isle's shores.

The Isle of Man, covering a mere 343 square miles, is probably the least-known country in Europe. Still a member of the British Commonwealth, the Isle of Man has been ruled by Ireland, Wales, Norway, Scotland, and England. Though it is part of the British Isles, it is not part of the United Kingdom. The island has its own representative assembly and courts.

The world's oldest legislature

The **Tynwald**, as the Manx legislature is called, is more than a thousand years old and has the longest continuous history of any legislature in the world. Tynwald derives from the Norse word *tingvollr*, meaning assembly field.

The **Royal Chapel of St. John the Baptist**, in the town of St. John's, is on the field where the open-air Tynwald Ceremony of the Norsemen began 1,000 years ago. Each year on July 5 (or the Monday after, if the fifth falls on a weekend), the Tynwald assembles at the chapel to sign new laws. Any Manx citizen may present a petition on this occasion.

Man's strangest sight

The Isle of Man's strangest monument in stone is a modern tower in **Corrin's Folly** overlooking Peel Bay. It was built by a man who wanted to be on his feet when Judgment Day arrived. He left instructions to have his glass-lidded coffin stood on its end in front of the tower window. The rest of the family was buried below.

Man's best fishing

Sports fishermen adore the Isle of Man because of its variety of fishing: surf casting, river fishing, and deep-sea fishing.

Sea fishermen can cast their lines for skate, mackerel, and tope from spring through late summer; pollack (the local name is *calig*), conger, dog-fish, plaice (a flat fish that is a bottom eater), coalfish, bass, and mullet from June through October; and whiting, brill, monkfish, and flounder in the fall.

The best place for surf casting is the **Point of Ayre**, where you can fish at any tide. The best time, however, is low tide.

Sea-angling boat services are available from Douglas. Freshwater fishing in the Isle of Man is for salmon, sea trout, brown trout, and rainbow trout, primarily in the rivers that flow through the Manx national glens. The main run of salmon and sea trout starts in late summer.

For information on fishing and licenses, contact the offices of the **Isle of Man Board of Agriculture and Fisheries**, *Government Offices, Douglas*.

Man's best walking trails

The best walking trail is the **Millennium Way**, established in 1979 to commemorate the millennium of the Tynwald. It follows the Regia Via, or Royal Way, one of the earliest recorded highways. In medieval times, it was used by the king and his attendants traveling to the Tynwald from Ramsey. Clearly marked, the Millennium Way is approximately 21-miles-long and can be walked by an experienced hiker in a full day.

The Way starts approximately one mile from Ramsey Town Square on the main road to Kirk Michael at the foot of Sky Hill. It ends in Castletown at Castle Rushen, the site of the fortification built by the Noresemen to guard the south of the island.

The world's largest waterwheel

Laxey has the largest waterwheel in the world, with a diameter of 72 feet, six inches; a circumference of 217 feet, and a top speed of two revolutions per minute. Built in 1854, it was christened the Lady Isabella after the wife of the lieutenant governor. Originally, it was used to pump water out of the lead mines.

The world's best ice cream

Manx ice cream is the best in the world. This prize-winning concoction is the creamiest and richest we have ever tasted. Visit the **Manx Ice Factory**, *tel. (44)45-4244*.

The Isle's best coffee shop and restaurant

The best place for a light meal and a great cup of coffee is **Harris's**. It is both elegant and extremely comfortable.

The best restaurant on the Isle of Man is **Boncompre's**, located in the Admiral House Hotel, *tel. (44)1624-629551*. The continental cuisine is excellent and the atmosphere is sophisticated.

Hotels with the most charm

Admiral House Hotel, *tel. (44)1624-629551*, is not ostentatious, elegant, or expensive. It has a warm and comforting atmosphere, which is emphasized by its inviting library.

The Grand Island Hotel, *tel. (44)1904-620033*, is situated along the coast of Ramsey. It offers a health spa and an 18-hole golf course.

The Grosvenor Hotel, *tel. (44)1624-834124*, this is one of the best hotels on the island for the money.

The Ascot Hotel, *tel. (44)1624-661512*, is a great economical choice. It offers a good bed and a great breakfast.

THE BEST OF ITALY

FOR ALL THOSE CIRCUMSTANCES THAT RENDER THAT CLASSICAL COUNTRY
ILLUSTRIOUS, THE SEAT OF GREAT MEN—THE THEATER OF THE MOST
DISTINGUISHED ACTIONS—THE EXCLUSIVE FIELD IN WHICH THE ELEGANT
AND AGREEABLE ARTS HAVE LOVED TO RANGE—WHAT COUNTRY CAN
BE COMPARED TO ITALY?

—*Arthur Young, 1792*

The Italians live alongside the world's greatest art the way the rest of the world lives next door to tacky neon signs and billboards. Where else but Italy would an insignificant-looking neighborhood church contain paintings by Botticelli? What city but Rome would go about its business amid the ruins of once-great buildings built by ancestors who ruled the then-known world? What people except Italians can be so surrounded by the greatest vestiges of Western civilization—yet so unpretentious?

ROME: THE WORLD'S MOST CELEBRATED CITY

Rome has been the world's most celebrated city for more than two millennia. Before Christ was born, Romans watched gladiators fight lions in the Coliseum. For 1,500 years, Rome has been the center of Christianity. Five centuries ago, Michelangelo painted the Sistine Chapel here. Today, Rome is one of the biggest tourist attractions in the world.

The most important sights

The **Coliseum** is the greatest architectural remnant of ancient Rome. Shaped like an oval bowl, it was built by Titus and used for monthlong spectacles, including battles between animals and gladiators. Christians were fed to the lions here, according to legend. The structure is well-preserved. Today it is inhabited by hundreds of cats, whose eyes glow from dark archways.

The **Roman Forum** was the chief public square and a center of government in ancient Rome. Only a few ruins remain. The **Pantheon** is the architectural and civic symbol of the city. The **Piazza di Spagna** (Spanish Steps) is filled with vendors, tourists, artists, street musicians, and Romans on their lunch break—and it truly shows the spirit of Rome. All of these sights are must-sees when visiting Rome and will show the true ambience of the city and the people that live there.

The world's second smallest country

✗Vatican City, the world's second-smallest country, occupies one square mile within the city of Rome. It is headquarters of the Roman Catholic Church and has its own post office and postage stamps, printing press and newspaper, currency, railway, and radio station. It is governed by the Pope and protected by Swiss Guards, whose colorful blue and gold uniforms were designed by Michelangelo.

The Vatican museums have the most impressive art collections in the world. The ✗Sistine Chapel is one of the great marvels of the Renaissance. The frescoed ceiling was painted by Michelangelo and has recently been restored. Some art critics view the cleaning as a desecration; others applaud it. Judge for yourself. A pedestrian walkway leads through the many museums to the Sistine Chapel, which covers an area of more than 40,000 square yards. En route, keep an eye out for the four rooms painted by Raphael and his assistants in the 16th century, as well as the little Chapel of Nicholas V, with frescoes by Fra Angelico.

✗St. Peter's Basilica in the Vatican reveals both the grandeur of the Papacy and the impact of Catholicism. When 300,000 people gather together to hear the pope's blessing, you understand his power. The basilica was built by Constantine in A.D. 350 on the site where St. Peter was martyred and then buried. Parts of the original building still exist, underground in the crypt. A cupola designed by Michelangelo crowns the church. Be sure to dress modestly when you visit St. Peter's—shorts are forbidden, and women may not wear dresses without sleeves or with hems above the knee. Many travelers are barred from St. Peter's because of improper clothing.

If you would like a papal audience or to attend a special ceremony in St. Peter's, apply in writing to **Prefettura della Casa Pontifica**, *00120 Citta del Vaticano*. When the pope is in Rome, public audiences are held each Wednesday at 11 a.m.

On the edge of the Vatican is an ancient fortress, **Castel Sant' Angelo**, built in A.D. 135 as a mausoleum for the Emperor Hadrian. The sixth-century chapel on top of the mausoleum was built to commemorate an angel who appeared to announce the end of the plague. Corner towers and bastions were added in the 15th and 16th centuries. Pope Clement VII lived in the castle in 1527. The fortress is connected to the Vatican by a long passageway.

Rome's best park

In the northern section of Rome is the city's most remarkable park— **Villa Borghese**. The gardens around the former estate of Cardinal Scipione Borghese were designed in the 17th century. Rome's zoo is here, as well as two museums housed in the cardinal's palace. The main entrance is at Piazzale Flaminio, just outside the Porta del Popolp. You can also get here by walking up the Spanish Steps and following via Trinita dei Monti to the left until you can see all seven hills of Rome.

The most macabre sight

The mass of skulls in the church of **Santa Maria della Concezione dei Capuccini** is the most macabre sight in Rome. Monks at this church maintain a crypt that contains more than 4,000 skulls and bones of past Capuchin monks. Two of the five chapels contain floors of earth brought from Palestine. On Nov. 2 (All Soul's Day), the crypt is brightly lit, making it even more gruesome.

Rome's best kept travel secret: the Aventine

One of Rome's fabled seven hills, the Aventine, is rarely traveled by tourists. Mons Aventius, as it was known in ancient times, was developed by Caesar's contemporaries into a dignified district of majestic temples, fashionable homes, and plush gardens. The rich vegetation and serene setting that attracted the Romans both remain, untouched by the pollution and crowding of the rest of the city. The Aventine's main attraction however, is its many striking churches.

Near the temple to Diana, seven centuries-old churches remain. The most ancient, **Santa Prisca**, was the residence of a Jewish couple, Prisca and Aquila, who allowed Saint Paul and others to worship in their home after their own conversion to Catholicism. The earliest Christians also worshiped at another fourth-century residence nearby, now **Santa Sabina**. Along the same street is **Sant'Alessio**, named for the son of a prominent Roman senator who fled the city to avoid an arranged marriage. He returned two decades later, a beggar, to die beneath the front stairwell of his parents' home.

The oldest café in Rome

Antico Caffè Greco is one of the oldest cafés in the world. Founded on July 24, 1760, it has been frequented by artists, celebrities, and politicians, including composer Hector Berlioz, Mark Twain (in fact, a statue of Twain decorates the café), Hans Christian Andersen, James Fenimore Cooper, Sir Walter Scott, Henry James, Lord Alfred Tennyson, Richard Wagner, Benjamin Franklin, Henrik Ibsen, Goethe, Schopenhauer, Orson Welles, Federico Fellini, Stalin, and Adolf Hitler. The café was declared a national monument by the Italian government in 1953. Homemade ice cream is served, as well as the best cappuccino in Rome.

Rome's most beautiful bridge

The **Fabricio Bridge**, known to Romans as the Bridge of Four Heads, connects Tiber Island, in the middle of the Tiber River, to the rest of Rome. A pillar in the middle of the bridge is carved with four faces representing the four builders of the structure, beheaded for not finishing it by the day promised. Tiber Island has been occupied since 292 B.C., when a temple was built in honor of Aesculapius, the Greek god of health.

The most remarkable fountain

The **Fountain of Rivers**, completed in 1651 by Gian Lorenzo Bernini, is the most beautiful fountain in the city. Located in the heart of Rome's picturesque Piazza Navona, it is a mass of rockwork and grottos. The four colossal figures that create the fountain's four corners represent the Danube, Ganges, Nile, and Plate rivers.

The best places to buy red lingerie

Every December, Romans buy new red lingerie to wear when they usher in the New Year. As a result, the city is home to many shops that specialize in red underwear. For the finest lingerie in Rome (red and otherwise), visit the via Frattina area. Try **Vanita**, *via Frattina 70*, which has beautiful lace slips, hand-embroidered silk items, and a good selection of beachwear. Lacier, more tantalizing creations can be found at **Tusseda**, *via Frattina 25*.

The world's most beautiful crèches

During the Christmas season, Rome is decorated with crèches rather than lights and Santas. The three most beautiful are on the Spanish Steps, in the Piazza Navona, and in St. Peter's Square. The oldest crèche is in the **Church of S. Maria Maggiore**, the most beloved crèche is at **S. Maria d'Aracoeli**, and the **Cosma e Damiano** houses an 18th-century Neapolitan masterpiece, which is on display all year.

The best midnight Mass

The most beautiful Christmas midnight Mass in the world is at **St. Peter's Basilica**. The pope celebrates the Mass with the assistance of dozens of cardinals. The Choir of the Sistine Chapel sings, and the Vatican ushers, known as San Pietrini, turn on hundreds of lights. You can write in advance for tickets to Christmas midnight Mass. Contact the **Prefettura della Casa Pontifica**, *Citta del Vaticano, 00120*.

Rome's best hotel

The **Hassler**, *tel. (39)6-69-9340*, which crowns the Spanish Steps, has the best view and the best service. The rooms on the fifth floor have little balconies with tables and chairs and views of the Spanish Steps. If you prefer quiet (the steps can be noisy), the most peaceful rooms are in the back, overlooking the courtyard. To make a reservation from the U.S., contact the **Leading Hotels of the World**, *tel. (800)223-6800*.

Italy's most prestigious wine

Just a short drive from Rome is a 14th-century castle overlooking the fertile valleys of Ombrone, Orcia, and Asso. Called **Montalcino**, it is surrounded by a medieval stone wall that boasts the ruins of 19 defense towers. But more than medieval artifacts, Montalcino is home to the most prestigious of all Italian wines, the legendary **Brunellow di Montalcino**.

THE BEST PRESERVED ROMAN RUINS IN THE WORLD

Ostia Antica boasts the best-preserved Roman ruins in the world, as well as a beautifully preserved fortress and a borgo with history spanning from the fourth to the 15th century. Situated four miles from the Fiumicino airport, it is accessible by car, bus, or by train via Rome.

On arrival in this small town, you'll be welcomed by the imposing view of the Rocca di Giulio II. The fortress was built during the papacy of Giulio II and served as a major defense point for the city of Rome—it was strategically situated on a bend of the river Tiber. A walk around the borgo, away from the cars and the chaos, is a good way to start your tour of town. And the fortress itself is worth a visit, giving you a feeling for what life as a soldier must have been like back in those days.

In 1557, the river changed its course and the fortress lost its importance. It was used for a while as a prison, but soon ceased to have any appeal to rulers and enemies alike.

The small town and surroundings went into decay and became marsh. In the 19th century, a small group of farmers from Romagna was called in by the Pope to drain the area. Today's town is the result of the hard work of those 500 men.

Although still uncertain, the origins of Ostia have been traced back to the 7th century B.C. The ruins are so well preserved that the amphitheater still stages shows from opera to Roman tragedy and Shakespeare (in Italian).

You can spend hours marveling at the mosaics, thermal baths, and imposing structures of the temples. It costs $5 to take a look around the ruins, with concessions for pensioners and students. You can get back to Rome easily, too, by train, car, or ferry.

FLORENCE—THE MOST BEAUTIFUL CITY

Florence is the most beautiful city in this country of lovely places. Ringed by hills, its streets are lined with red-tiled houses. Graceful domes rise from curving, narrow, cobblestoned streets. The ochre-colored walls of the ancient buildings are decorated with weathered gargoyles and faded coats of arms. Within Florence is some of the greatest artwork in the world. For three centuries, from Giotto to Michelangelo, Florence was the center of the art world. Paintings and frescoes by the great Renaissance masters decorate even the most mundane churches.

The world's finest Renaissance art

The immense **Uffizi Museum** has the world's greatest collection of Renaissance art, including paintings by Giotto, Raphael, Titian, and Botticelli. The museum also has a room of modern art. Be sure to see restored *Doni Tondo* by Michelangelo and Botticelli's *Birth of Venus*. The most impressive room holds Botticelli's *Primavera, Birth of Venus, Madonna della Melagrana*, and *Pallas and the Centaur*.

The best-kept secret in Florence

The **Vasari corridoio** is a long, covered, secret passage built by Vasari in 1565 for Cosimo I de Medici. It links the Uffizi with the Pitti Palace, now one of Florence's great picture galleries but then Cosimo's residence. It crosses the Arno with the Ponte Vecchi and passes through the Church of Santa Felicita, another Vasai masterpiece, where the Medicis attended chapel.

The largest dome in Christendom

Il Duomo, one of the world's largest cathedrals, is topped with the largest dome in Christendom. Its marble walls are striped with alternating colors. For this reason, it has been called the Cathedral in Pajamas. Built in 1296 by Brunelleschi, its vast walls are decorated with frescoes illustrating Dante's *Divine Comedy* and works by Ucello. Climb up into the dome for a terrific view of Florence.

The Gates of Paradise

The **Baptistery**, an octagonal building in Piazza del Duomo dedicated to St. John the Baptist, is famous for its three sets of gilded bronze doors. Michelangelo called the east door facing the cathedral the "Gates of Paradise." Begun in 1425 by Ghilberti, they weren't completed until 1452, when the artist was 74. They are made up of 10 panels that illustrate the Old Testament. On the Feast of St. John (June 24), the relics of the saint are displayed in the Baptistery, and candles are lit in his honor

The most important sights in Florence

Pitti Palace, a huge structure built by Renaissance banker Luca Pitti, is now divided into five museums, including the Palatine Picture Gallery, where works by Titian, Raphael, and Rubens are displayed. The Silver Museum houses Lorenzo de Medici's vases.

Santa Croce, a striped-marble church, has frescoes by Giotto. The most elegant church in Florence, it contains tombs and monuments to Michelangelo, Galileo, Machiavelli, and Dante. Go through the sacristy into the Leather School started by the monks about 40 years ago.

Accademia is where the original of Michelangelo's magnificent *David*

stands. You'll want to see this, of course, but be prepared to stand in incredibly long lines. The worst days to visit are Sunday and Tuesday; the best times are 8 a.m. and noon, when the lines are shortest.

Bargello, the national museum, was once a fortress that served as a prison. In centuries past, men were thrown out of the tower for their misdeeds. Today, the building contains the best of Florentine sculpture. Several early Michelangelos are housed here, including his first unfinished *David* and his statue of Bacchus. Upstairs are Giambologna's bronze animals created for a Medici garden grotto. This museum doesn't draw the crowds it merits.

The **Basilica of San Lorenzo** and the **Palazzo Medici** were built by the Medici family north of the Duomo. Brunelleschi began work on the church in 1419, incorporating the coat of arms of the Medicis in the design. Conatello's sculpture fills the church, and Filippo Lippi designed the altarpiece. The Medici Chapel, adjacent to the basilica, can be reached only from outside. Actually a mausoleum, the chapel has two sections: the Princes' Chapel, which contains the tombs of six Medici grand dukes, and the New Sacristy (Sagrestia Nuova), built by Michelangelo.

Santa Maria Novella is a grand church with splendid frescoes by Ghirlandaio and Filippino Lippi. They are best seen on a sunny day; the chapels are dark. The wealthy merchants of Florence had special chapels built in their honor in this church. Alberti contains Chirlandaio's most important frescoes, which his student, Michelangelo, helped to create. The cloister of the church is colored with Uccello's frescoes.

Florence's best bridge

Ponte Vecchio, a bridge dating back to Roman times, is lined with goldsmith shops and street musicians. Butchers and tanners originally plied their trades on this bridge, but they were ousted by the Medici family in favor of the more seemly goldsmiths. During World War II, the commander in charge of the German army's retreat refused to blow up the bridge. Instead, he destroyed the buildings at its base so the rubble would block the span.

The prettiest Florentine church

San Miniato al Monte, one of the oldest churches in Florence, has an inlaid marble façade with 13th-century mosaics. Inside, the pavement is patterned with astrological signs, lions, and doves. The church contains superb Della Robbia terracottas. You can hear a Gregorian chant at San Miniato al Monte daily starting at 4:45 p.m.

The best dining

Our favorite restaurant in Florence is the **Enoteca Pinchiorri**, *tel. (39)55-24-27-57; website: www.enotecapinchiorri.com*, Located in the 15th-century Ciofi-Iacometti Palace, it has a pleasant courtyard for dining and serves nouvelle cuisine. Reservations are required, which can be made through their website.

The best nightlife

The two best nightclubs in Florence are **Manila**, *tel. (39)55-894-121*, and **Tenax**, *tel. (39)55-373-050*. Manila is avant garde and decorated with elaborate graffiti. The crowd is ultrasophisticated. Tenax is in an enormous old warehouse on two floors. The clientele here is also very fashionable.

The best ice cream in Florence

Vivoli's, *tel. (39)55-292-334*, behind Santa Croce Square, is one of the best places in the world to buy ice cream. The lines are long, but the choice of flavors is great and the ice cream is out-of-this-world.

The best convent stay

Villa Agape in the hills above Florence is a 17th-century villa with perfectly manicured gardens. The nuns prepare true Tuscan fare and pamper their guests. Dinner can match any you would have at the top restaurants in Florence.

The rooms are furnished with antique furniture (some have air conditioning) but the bathrooms are modern. A night's bed and breakfast will set you back $60.

After roaming through the busy streets of Florence from museum to museum, returning to Villa Agape at the end of the day is a welcome retreat. But night owls beware: the Villa has an 11 p.m. curfew.

The best antiques fair in Italy

The city of **Arezzo** is home to one of the best antique fairs in Italy. On the first Sunday of every month and the preceding Saturday, Arezzo's old town streets are closed to traffic and transformed into a great outdoor bazaar/antique fair for both professional and amateur shoppers. Here you can find antiques, collectibles, new articles, or just old cool stuff from all over the world. Artwork, ceramics, apparel, accessories, jewelry, lighting, furniture, collectors' stamps, maps, nutcrackers, dentistry and medical instruments, terracotta vases, planters… You could spend hours here; there are hundreds of stands.

Buyer beware, of course. Some stands sell not-so-authentic antiques at steep prices. You can, however, find good-quality items at good prices. Bargaining hint: If the item is still available at the end of the day, you ought to be able to negotiate a bigger discount.

Arezzo is a charming city strategically located 30 minutes from Florence and accessible by railway or car—it's on the main railway line between Rome/Florence and Milan. If you are driving from Northern Italy, Arezzo is 30 minutes south of Florence on the A1 autostrada (freeway).

THE MOST MAGICAL CITY: VENICE

Venice, a city made up of 118 islets held together by a maze of 150 narrow canals and 400 lacy bridges, has a magical air. The interlocking waterways are plied by graceful wooden gondolas. Domed churches look over the shadowed pedestrian streets, where throngs of people (but no cars) roam.

Venetians took refuge in their watery home after centuries of invasions by the likes of Attila the Hun, the Goths, and the Vandals. In A.D. 687, they elected a president, called a doge. He was the first in a line of 117 doges, each reigning for life, that ended in 1797.

The five most important sights

The heart of Venice is the **Piazza San Marco**, which is dominated by the beautiful basilica on one side and the Doge's Palace on the other. This huge square attracts flocks of pigeons as well as tourists.

Once the doge's private chapel, the **The Basilica of San Marco** is now open to the public. Built in the ninth century to house the body of St. Mark's body, the basilica houses the saint's tomb, paintings by Titian, and the Pala d'Oro, a huge panel behind the altar bedecked with rubies, emeralds, sapphires, pearls, topazes, amethysts, and cloisonné figures, all set in gold. The basilica also has Byzantine treasures. These artifacts and the saint's body were the booty of the fourth Crusade, taken from Constantinople by Doge Enrico Dandolo.

The **Palaxxon Ducale** (Doge's Palace) is an ornate structure on the water with carved figures symbolizing the trades. On one side are the Quattro Mori, four Moorish warriors embracing one another. Inside are the doges' apartments, the senate chamber, and the Room of the Council of Ten, which is covered with beautiful paintings. The sinister box outside is intended to receive denunciations of traitors or criminals.

The **Bridge of Sighs** passes between the Doge's Palace and the prison where Casanova was once held. The covered bridge is so named because condemned prisoners sighed as they were led across it to their deaths. They were allowed one last look at Venice from the bridge before their executions.

The **Grand Canal** has been called the finest street in the world. It is lined with 200 marble-covered palaces built between the 12th and 18th centuries. Wagner died in the Palazzo Vendramin-Calergi, now the Municipal Casino. Lord Byron lived in the Palazzo Mocenigo. Gold leaf was used to coat the balls protruding on the façade of the Ca'D'Oro on the right bank. Its pointed arches were influenced by Islam. A good way to see these palazzos is to take a boat ride along the two-mile length of the canal. Take vaporetto (water bus) 1 or 4.

The **Galleria dell'Accademia** (Gallery of Fine Arts) houses paintings by

Giorgione, Bellini, Tiepolo, Titian, and Canaletto. Admission is free except Sunday.

The Lido—the most fashionable Adriatic resort

Venice is protected from the rage of the Adriatic Sea by a beautiful sand spit called the **Lido**. A fashionable resort, the Lido draws visitors from around the world to its sandy beaches, elegant hotels, and swank casino. To get there, take vaporetto lines 1 and 2 from Venice across the Lagoon.

Before you go to the Lido, read *Death in Venice* by Thomas Mann. And (if you can afford it) stay at the legendary **Grand Hotel des Bains**, *Lungomare Marconi 17*, where Mann's character, Hans Aschenbach, spent his days. Rooms are expensive.

The romantic islands of the Lagoon

The **Lagoon** is filled with romantic little islands that can be reached by vaporetto. (Boat 12 leaves from the Fondamenta Nuove, near Campo dei Gesuiti, for Murano, Burano, and Torcello.) Burano and Torcello have especially inviting beaches, fishing villages, and small art museums. Murano is famous for its glassmaking.

Burano Island, actually four tiny islets connected by bridges, is a half-hour water-bus ride from the mainland. Everything here is miniature—the canals and bridges are tiny, and the colorfully painted houses look as if they were built for dwarfs. Burano has its own leaning tower, the bell tower of the **Church of San Martino**, *Piazza Baldassare Galuppi*.

However, the island is best known for its lace making. Wherever you go on Burano, you will see old ladies knitting lace and selling it from outdoor tables. You can buy handmade lace doilies, lace tablecloths, lace mats, hankies, baby bibs, and collars. The **Consorzio Merletti di Burano** (lace museum), *Piazza Galuppi*, is open daily.

Murano Island has dozens of workshops where you can watch glass being blown. The **Museo Vetrario**, *Fondamenta Giustinian*, along the main canal, has an immense collection of glass from Roman times to the present. It is closed Wednesdays.

San Francesco del Deserto is a tiny, cypress-covered island inhabited by Franciscan monks. According to legend, St. Francis of Assisi was shipwrecked here in 1220. His wooden staff, which he stuck in the ground, turned into a tree, part of which still can be seen. Gardens and lawns surround the cloister and church. Peacocks and bantams wander the grounds freely.

A surprisingly pleasant island is Venice's cemetery, **San Michele**, which is filled with shade trees, flower gardens, and leaf-covered paths. Ornate tombs and mausoleums are surrounded by gardens and terraces. The ferry-boat to San Michele is free on Sundays. The entrance is through the cloister of the island's 15th-century church.

The island of **San Lazzaro** has been the site of an Armenian monastery for 200 years. A priest dressed in a black cassock and sporting a heavy beard will give you a two-hour tour of the cloister, which contains an Egyptian mummy, Armenian paintings, ivories from the Orient, and the room where Lord Byron lived in 1816, when he decided to learn Armenian. One of the rooms contains a collection of rare illuminated manuscripts.

The greatest opera house

Gran Teatro La Fenice, *tel. (39)41-521-0161*, is one of the greatest opera houses in the world. The 18th-century décor is graceful, with chandeliers, plush armchairs, box seats, mirrored corridors, parquet floors, and a grand staircase with marble columns. The acoustics are flawless. You cannot make reservations for an opera by telephone; you must visit the box office in person between 9:30 a.m. and 12:30 p.m. or one hour before an evening performance.

The most fantastic hotel in Europe

Venice has the most fantastic hotel in Europe, the luxurious **Hotel Cipriani** on Giudecca Island. A polished motorboat fetches guests at the Piazza San Marco. Rooms have private, flower-bedecked terraces that gaze out over the water. Excellent seafood is prepared in the dining room. The Cipriani has Venice's only tennis courts and its largest swimming pool. To make reservations in the United States, contact **Leading Hotels of the World**, *tel. (800)223-6800*.

The best Venetian restaurants

Antica Trattoria Orsetta, is the best place to go for authentic Venetian cuisine. The restaurant is hidden in the back streets of Venice and is very difficult to find. **Harry's Bar**, *tel. (39)41-523-6797*, has two Michelin stars and was one of Hemingway's favorites. Only a few minutes from the piazzetta on the Piazza San Marco, it has been owned and run by the Cipriani family for 60 years.

Europe's largest maze

The largest and most complicated maze in Europe is in **Stra**, 18 miles south of Venice. Here, the odds are a zillion to one that you will get lost. **Il Labirinto**, as it is known in Italy, is part of the stately gardens of the Villa Pisani. This life-size puzzle is one-third the size of a football field and has four miles of paths lined with tall, thick hedges. If you get lost, the caretaker will rescue you. He can reach the tower at the center of the maze in three minutes.

The most colorful day-trip

The **Isle of Burano** is a short boat ride from Venice, but a world apart. The Isle is off the beaten path and the most colorful setting you will ever see—every house is painted a bright and different color. The restaurants offer the most wonderful, fresh seafood in the area, and you can eat at your own pace. There are wonderful little shops in which to browse, and the school of Venetian lace is located within walking distance.

MANTUA: VENICE WITHOUT THE CROWDS

Mantua has the charm of Venice without the crowds. The River Mincio wraps around the ducal city like a cloak and threads its way through the city via little canals. Graceful bridges cross the winding waterways. Once the seat of one of the most brilliant courts of Europe, today it is one of the best-preserved medieval cities in Italy.

Mantua feels medieval; it has no modern industry and no highrise buildings. The **Ducal Palace**, built in the Middle Ages, is actually three interconnected buildings. The palace has 500 rooms, seven gardens, and eight courtyards. Frescoes by Pisanello, depicting episodes from chivalric tales, hang in the Hall of Dukes. Painted in 1440, they were rediscovered in 1969 under two coats of plaster. In Camera degli Sposi (bridal chamber), built in 1474, hang Andrea Mantegna's frescoes of the Gonzaga family.

The **Church of Sant' Andrea** has a coffered ceiling and grandiose arches more reminiscent of the Pantheon than a Christian church. This is a good place to get a feeling for the time when the Pagan and Christian worlds met. The **Palazzo Te** was a pleasure palace for Federico, the favorite son of Mantua's great lady, Isabella d'Este. This palace is filled with artwork depicting early times.

When you tire of sightseeing, enjoy Mantua's delicious egg pasta at **Il Cigno**, *tel. (39)376-327-101*.

Two comfortable hotels in Mantua are the **San Lorenzo**, *tel. (39)376-327-153*, and the **Hotel Rechigi**, *tel. (39)376-320-781*.

NAPLES: THE MOST ITALIAN CITY

Tourists shy away from **Naples**, because of its reputation for crime—although the crime situation here is actually no worse than in New York and other major cities. Because of its rather undeserved bad reputation, Naples is truly an Italian city—free of crowds of gaping foreigners.

A huge, hilly town in the shadows of Mount Vesuvius, Naples is cooled by the breezes of the Gulf of Naples. The city's waterfront is lined with booths where you can stop for a cool drink.

Neapolitans have a lugubrious interest in the macabre. In the **Cappella**

Sansevero, for example, is the 16th-century corpse of a family servant mysteriously preserved by the alchemy of the Duke of Sansevero. Thousands of capillaries can be seen through the skin of the body. The chapel, which is hidden on a small side street off Piazza San Domenico Maggiore, also holds an uncanny effigy of the body of Christ covered in diaphanous veils carved by the sculptor Sammartino.

The most important sight

The cathedral in Naples is dedicated to San Gennaro. It was built in the 13th century on the site of a previous basilica dedicated to Santa Stefania. The original basilica was built on the foundations of a Roman temple dedicated to Apollo.

Within the cathedral are an ancient round baptistery, the Byzantine basilica of Santa Restituta, and the 17th-century chapel, which holds San Gennaro's head and blood. The blood has liquefied from its crystalized state the first Sunday in May and on Sept. 19 nearly every year since the Middle Ages. If the blood does not liquefy, it is believed that a disaster will happen. (Great importance is placed on San Gennaro in Naples. When Mount Vesuvius acts up, for instance, the saint's image is taken to the mountain as a pacifier.)

The world's best antiquities

Il Museo Archeologico Nazionale in Naples houses one of the most important collections of Greek and Roman antiquities in the world, including many of the treasures excavated from Pompeii and Herculaneum. Among these treasures are the *Young Satyr*, a graceful figure carrying a wine casket, and the famous statues of Apollo and Diana, which once stood at Pompeii's Temple of Apollo. You can't miss the *Farnese Bull*, the largest surviving sculpture from antiquity, carved out of a single block of marble.

Naples' best Renaissance museum

Outside Naples is the **Capodimonte Museum and Picture Gallery**, which houses one of Italy's best collections of paintings from the 14th, 15th, and 16th centuries. Located in an 18th-century palace in the hills northeast of the city and surrounded by a park, it contains works by Bellini, Botticelli, Correggio, and Titian. Capodimonte is also a famous brand of porcelain.

Nightlife at its hottest

Naples nightlife can be found in and around vias Caracciono and Partenope, commonly referred to as the **Margellina Quarter**. Within walking distance is the **San Carlo Theater**, renowned for classical music and dance. Information on the performances here can be obtained at the box office, which is open 10 a.m. to 1 p.m., and 4:30 p.m. to 6:30 p.m. every day except Mondays. To obtain more information visit *www.teatrosancarlo.it*.

The best ways to thwart thieves

Pickpockets are common in Naples, and they make their living off tourists. Don't drape your purse over your shoulder. Thieves on motorbikes grab bags as they zoom past, often dragging the person along with the bag. Thieves generally work in pairs. They pull up to people carrying shoulder bags or camera bags. One thug hops off the bike, grabs the loot, and hops back on, and the pair then speed away.

Avoid carrying a wallet in your back pocket. Leave all jewelry—including watches—in your hotel. It's best to carry limited amounts of cash and your passport and credit cards in the inside pocket of your pants.

When driving, never put anything in the back window of the car. Traffic in Naples is dense, and thieves often break rear windows of cars stuck in traffic jams. And don't leave things in parked cars—not even in the trunks. Most rental cars in Italy have Milan tags, and thieves know to look for them around hotels, restaurants, and museums.

The most delicious fare

Avellinese da Peppino, *via Silvio Spaventa 31-35*, is a friendly place with cheap but good seafood. Try the pesce frigole, a mixture of crayfish, octopus, squid, mussels, and clams. Italian singers serenade you as you dine.

La Cantinella, *tel. (39)81-40-48-84*, is a favorite among Neapolitans. The clams and mussels cooked with garlic, parsley, and tomato and served with linguine are exquisite. This restaurant is closed on Sundays.

La Fazenda, *tel. (39)80-769-7420*, serves the best Neapolitan dishes, including home-raised chickens. This rustic restaurant has spectacular views of the bay and is decorated with a profusion of flowers. It is closed Sundays and for two weeks in August.

Il Gallo Nero, *tel. (39)7-42-343-454; e-mail: info@ilgallonero.it*, is in an antique-filled 19th-century villa. Dine on the terrace, where you'll have a splendid view of Mergellina. The fresh fish is terrific.

Sleeping beautifully

The most luxurious hotels in Naples are the Excelsior and the Vesuvio. The **Excelsior**, *tel. (39)81-76-40-111*, has terraced seaside rooms with views of the Castel dell'Ovo and the bay. The restaurant is good. Rooms are rather old-fashioned and sparsely furnished.

The **Vesuvio**, *tel. (39)81-41-70-44*, faces the port of Santa Lucia and has a variety of rooms ranging in style from antique to modern. It has air conditioning and a garage.

The strangest sight: the door to the Underworld

Near Naples is one of the strangest sights in Italy—the cave said to have been the door to the Underworld of ancient mythology. Very few people visit the **Grotta della Sibilla**, as it is known.

In the *Aeneid*, the Roman poet Virgil described the cave:

> "A deep, deep cave there was, its mouth enormously gaping
> Shingly, protected by the dark lake and the forest gloom:
> Above it, no winged creatures could ever wing their way
> With fuming up from its black throat to the vault of heaven:
> Wherefore the Greeks called it Avernus, the Birdless Place."

Alessandro, the elderly guide who has given tours and told the tale of the cave for the past 50 years, begins his tour at the entrance of Lago di Avernus.

According to the guide, Lago di Avernus was once a volcanic flat with bubbling mud and sulfur fumes that rose into the sky. Because the fumes were poisonous, birds flying over would die and fall into the inferno. (*Avernus* means no birds in Latin.) This description matches Virgil's. When Mount Vesuvius erupted, the volcanic action stopped here, and the crater filled with water. The eruption cut off the tunnel leading to the Underworld.

The guided tour takes about an hour. While no set admission is charged, most visitors tip Signor Alessandro at least one euro. Open Friday, Saturday, and Sunday 9 a.m. to 5 p.m. and weekdays 11 a.m. to 3 p.m.

To get to the cave from the via Domitiana in Naples, turn left after the Olivetti factory toward Archo Felice. At the intersection, turn right onto via Miliscola, which goes along the waterfront toward Baia. Go about one mile, past a newsstand, the Lido di Napoli, and the Sibilla Restaurant. A sign points right toward a bumpy road that takes you to a brick wall on your left marked with a white painted sign indicating Grotta della Sibilla.

Volcanic bests

Mount Vesuvius, 15 miles southeast of Naples, can be seen from the city on a clear day. It last erupted in 1944, and it averages one eruption every 35 years. You can take a chair lift up to the top, or you can drive part way and then walk. Take the Ercolano exit from the Autostrada, then drive nine miles up a zig-zagging path across a sort of moonscape. The oval crater, when you finally get there, is 2,000 feet wide and 525 feet deep. Wisps of smoke rise from the top. If you say your name, Vesuvius will echo it back.

Pompeii and Herculaneum: the world's best ruins

Pompeii and **Herculaneum**, once bedroom suburbs of Roman Naples, were destroyed when Mount Vesuvius erupted in A.D. 79. Today, the ruins are preserved in volcanic ash illustrations of everyday life nearly 2,000 years ago. Explore the shops, baths, and houses of ordinary Roman families.

While Pompeii is packed with tourists, Herculaneum is not. What's more, Herculaneum is closer to Naples and is better preserved than Pompeii. Known as *Ercolano* in Italian, Herculaneum once had 5,000 inhabitants. Much of the town remains unexcavated beneath the modern town of Resina. However, among the ruins that have been excavated you'll see cakes in ovens, eggs in cupboards, chicken bones on kitchen tables, fishnets and hooks on a line, and graffiti on bathroom walls. One of the houses has a small cross, the oldest evidence of Christianity in the Roman Empire. The baths are the most interesting sights. You can see cold, warm, and hot water baths, a gym, and a swimming pool. The skeletons of bath attendants have been preserved intact in the men's cloakroom.

The best-preserved Greek temples

The best-preserved Greek Doric temples stand by the sea in **Paestum**, ancient Poseidonia, not far from Naples. The three major temples are along the ancient via Sacra. The basilica, which is dedicated to Hera, is the oldest, dating back to the sixth century B.C. Next to the basilica is the Temple of Neptune (450 B.C.), one of the most beautiful Doric temples in the world. See the frescoes of a diver and a dinner party, the earliest surviving Greek paintings, in the museum across the street from the ruins.

CAPRI: ITALY'S MOST BEAUTIFUL ISLAND

Capri is a beautiful but crowded island that can be reached by hydrofoil from Naples, Sorrento, or Pozzuoli. After the boat ride, relax and have a pleasant lunch on the terrace of the Hotel Belvedere Tre Re, on the harbor. Take a funicular from the harbor up to the town of Capri. The best view is from the top of Mount Solaro, where an old monastery stands. To get there, take a bus to Anacapri and then a chair lift to the summit.

The blue grotto sea caves are lovely, but touristy. Visit the pagan shrine of the Martomania Cave. Roman Emperor Tiberius built 12 villas on the island to honor the 12 Roman deities. You can best sense his might around Villa Jovis, his headquarters for a decade.

Hotels on the island book up fast, so reservations are a must. One of the most romantic is **Scalanitella**, *via Tragara 8; tel. (39)81-837-0633*, in the town of Capri. A staff member meets visitors upon arrival and leads them along the narrow streets to the little hotel. Cut into a steep and rocky hill, Scalanitella has a Moorish air. Its glistening marble lobby, winding corridors, classical paintings and busts, carved doors, floor-to-ceiling windows, outdoor garden, and little luxuries create a delightful atmosphere. Its pool is one of the best in Capri. The hotel is open Easter through October.

The **Quisiana and Grand Hotel**, *via Camerelle 2; tel. (39)81-837-0788*, attracts the jet set with large suites, wide arcades, and an ocean view. **Hotel Luna**, *tel. (39)81-837-0433*, combines old-fashioned style with modern conveniences.

Good food is served at **La Sceriffa**, *via Acquaviva 29; tel. (39)81-837-7953*. **La Pigna**, *via Lo Palazzo 30; tel. (39)81-837-0280*, is another good bet.

THE BEST OF THE ITALIAN RIVIERA

The **Italian Riviera**, which stretches from the French border to Tuscany, is less expensive than the French Riviera and just as pretty. It lies within the prosperous northern region of **Liguria**, which has its own lingo and culture. The heart of Liguria is Genoa, a thriving seaport and a good place to stay if you find coastal resorts too pricey. North of Genoa is the Riviera di Levante (Coast of the Rising Sun). Below and to the east is the Riviera de Ponente (Coast of the Setting Sun).

During July and August, rooms are almost impossible to come by. The best time to visit is spring or fall, when the weather is warm and hotel rooms are vacant.

The oldest resort on the Riviera

San Remo, the oldest resort on the Riviera, is overcrowded and over-built. But it has a casino and a yacht basin, and the hotels are affordable despite their Edwardian elegance. The tourist office is helpful if you can't find a room.

Where the *crème de la crème* rises

Italy's crème de la crème surfaces in **Portofino** during the summer. Very private and romantic, Portofino is one of the most photographed places in the world. Its remarkably deep natural harbor attracts yachtsmen from all over the world. Hike out to the lighthouse following the footpath marked "al faro" for a spectacular view of the coastline.

Hotel Splendido, *via le Baratta 13; tel. (39)185-269-551*, is Portofino's most luxurious hotel. It is perched in a spectacular setting above the yacht harbor, set into a cliff. It has an old-fashioned charm despite its modern swimming pool on the terrace.

The Riviera's most charming town

From the docks at the coastal town of Camogli, you can take a boat to **San Fruttoso**, the most charming town on the coast. This tiny fishing village on the Portofino Peninsula is accessible only by sea. It is surrounded by pines, olive trees, and oaks that lead down to the sea. Walk through the cloisters and corridors of the Benedictine Abbey of San Fruttoso di Capo di Monte, which consists of a 13th-century palace, 11th-century church, and a Romanesque cloister.

Camogli has one of the best hotels along the coast, **Cenobio dei Dogi**, *via Cuneo 34, 16032 Camogli; tel. (39)185-770-041*, set in a manor house on the beach. Once the seat of the bishops of Genoa, this manor has lovely grounds, a beach, a swimming pool, tennis courts, facilities for the handicapped, and central heat.

Cinque Terre: the least crowded

At the southern end of the coast is one of the least crowded, most picturesque areas. The mountains, woods, vineyards, and hilltop villages of the Cinque Terre cover 15 miles of coastline. The area's five villages—Monterosso, Vernazza, Corniglia, Manarola, and Riomaggiore—are perched on the rocky coast north of La Spezia. The rare local wine is worth a taste; it is called Sciacchetra.

Monterosso is the largest and most crowded town. But it has a beautiful beach at the southern end of the cove. You can rent boats here. Climb the hill to the Convento dei Cappuccini, which houses Van Dyck's Crucifixion. After the strenuous climb, relax at Gigante, Monterosso's best restaurant.

Hiking trails lead from Monterosso to Cinque Terre's quainter towns. A one-and-a-half-hour hike along a goat path leads through vineyards and olive groves to **Vernazza**. Another hiking trail leads to **Corniglia**, which has a long, pebbly beach.

If you're up to another hour's walk, follow the trail along the jagged coast to **Manarola**, the most beautiful of the Cinque Terre towns. Here, yellow houses balance on cliffs, and artists and writers seek their muses.

THE ALPS AT THEIR CHEAPEST

The **Dolomites** (Italian Alps) are just as beautiful as their French and Austrian counterparts, but visiting them is far less expensive. The skiing is almost as good as it is to the north, and the hiking can be even better.

Valle d'Aosta is just over the border from France. You can take a cable car to the Italian side from Chamonix, France. The panoramic view from the cable car is beautiful—and a bit scary if you fear heights at all.

Alto Badia, 50 miles south of the Brenner Pass through the Dolomites into Austria, is made up of little Tyrolean villages. This region has the beautiful scenery of Austria, but it also has lower prices, summer skiing, and good Italian restaurants. The best-known and largest among the hamlets is Corvara. Less crowded are Colfosco, La Villa, Pedraces, and San Cassiano.

(See more on skiing in the Italian Alps in Section 4: The World's Best Sporting Destinations.)

The best hiking

The Dolomites, which are crisscrossed by trails, also boast some of the world's best hiking. Bring hiking boots, a windbreaker, a sweater, socks, and gloves. The best time to hike is in August and September, when the snow has melted completely. Don't hike in April or May unless you are an expert. The melting snow causes avalanches.

Pedraces, near the Austrian border, is one of the best places for hiking. For one of the most scenic routes, take a chair lift to the foot of the Croce Mountains and then follow Trail 7.

The **National Park of Abruzzi**, near escasseroli, is another beautiful place to hike. The trails, which are named for animals, wander through a forest of pine trees blanketed with snow.

La Pieja, *Opi; tel. (39)863-910-756*, a few miles from Pescasseroli, is one of the best places to stay in the region.

The best base for exploring

Aosta is the best base for exploring the Italian peaks. Near mountain trails and several old castles, it has Roman ruins dating from the time of the Emperor Augustus, including a Roman theater, two Roman gates, the Porta Praetoria, and the Arco di Augusto.

The cloister of the medieval **Church of St. Urdus** dates back to A.D. 1000. St. Ursus, responsible for the first conversions to Christianity in the valley, is buried in a crypt below the altar. Modern history can be contemplated at the **Istituto Storico della Resistenza della Valle d'Aosta**, *Xavier de Maistre 22; tel. (39)165-40-846*, which documents the Italian resistance during World War II.

Make hotel reservations early if you plan to be in Aosta in July or August or during the Christmas or Easter season. A good place to stay is **Mancuso**, *via Voison 32; tel. (39)165-34-526*. This family-run hotel is clean and has inviting rooms. The hotel restaurant is good and inexpensive.

Italy's most beautiful national park

The **Gran Paradiso National Park** in the Valle d'Aosta is 363 square miles of protected area set aside for wildlife. The park has breathtaking scenery, wild flowers, and hiking trails. **Cogne** is the best base for exploring the park. You can get there from Aosta by bus. From Cogne, walk to Vanontey and then take Trail 2, which climbs to Rifugio V. Sella. The view from the refuge is mind-boggling. Stop to eat or spend the night before setting out on the six-hour trek to Eau Rousse in Valsavaranche. Again, the views are incredible.

Sleeping like royalty in the Italian Alps

A number of old castles have been made into hotels in the mountains of Italy. **Schloss Rundegg**, *tel. (39)473-34-364*, is an old castle nestled in the mountains of southern Tyrol. The square towers date back to the 12th century. The main structure dates to 1580. Public rooms have grand staircases, vaulted ceilings, and arches. Private rooms are furnished with antiques. A pool, sauna, solarium, and massage center are open to guests.

THE BEST OF THE ITALIAN LAKE DISTRICT

Italy's Lake Country has steeply rolling hills and a Mediterranean touch. Olive groves and palm trees surround the warm waters.

The largest and clearest lake

Lake Garda is the largest, clearest, and most visited of the Italian lakes. It is surrounded by Mediterranean scenery—rugged, tawny hills dotted with olive and lemon groves and long, shuttered farmhouses. Desenzano, one of the lake's major and most crowded towns, lies on the Venice-Milan train line. From there, it is easy to get to other lake towns by bus or boat. **Torbole**, at the far end of Lake Garda, is the windsurfing capital of Europe because of the steady breezes that blow across the lake.

Europe's deepest lake

Lake Como is Europe's deepest lake. Sadly, it is too polluted for swimming near the main towns of Como and Bellagio. Como is worldly, wealthy, and refined. Its *duomo* is one of the most famous churches in Italy. Built between 1457 and 1485, it has a lovely rose window and houses Bernardino Luini's *Adoration of the Magi*.

The artists' favorite

Bellagio, the Lake District's art center, invites artists to spend a month or more there developing works in progress. Located at the point where Lake Como intersects with Lake Lecco, it has narrow streets and ancient buildings. The beach is next to Villa Serbelloni in the center of town.

The music inspiring waters

The litany of composers who've been inspired by the tranquil waters of Lake Como is staggering. It was here that Verdi wrote *La Traviata*, Bellini penned *Norma*, Rossini wrote *Tancred*, and Franz Liszt composed his *Dante Sonata*. As the American writer Henry James declared, being at Lake Como is like "wallowing in a libretto." Bellagio, Menaggio, Cadennabia, Tremezzo, Lenno…even the names of the villages sound melodious.

The most entertaining restaurant

The most entertaining restaurant in the Lake District is on an island in the middle of Lake Como. To get there, you must take a ferry, but it is well worth the trip. When you arrive at **Locanda dell'Isola Comacina**, *tel. (39)344-55-083*, introduce yourself to the owner, Benvenuto Puricelli. He will show you to your table and the food will start coming. You do not choose from a menu—a vast selection of fresh meat, fish, and vegetables are simply brought to your table. As a finale, Benvenuto turns out the lights and puts a torch to an alcoholic concoction. Then, as the liquor burns, he ladles the brew into the air in fiery garlands while reciting the history of the island. (According to legend, a curse was laid on the island in the 12th century.)

Europe's finest resort hotel

Villa d'Este, *tel. (39)31-511-471; website: www.villadeste.it*, in Cernobbion on Lake Como, is one of Europe's finest resort hotels. Located in a 15th-century villa begun by Cardinal Gallio, it was later used as a palace by an Empress of Russia, a Princess of Wales, and other members of royalty. In 1873 it became a hotel. It is beautifully furnished and offers concerts, dances, tennis, golf, riding, swimming, water sports, and boating.

The gem of the lakes

Floating in the middle of peaceful **Lago d'Orta** is emerald-green **San Giulio Island**, the little-known gem of the lakes. According to legend, St. Julius (San Giulio) ventured to the forested island in the latter half of the fourth century to rid it of an infestation of snakes and dragons. The island, which is 330 yards long and 175 yards across, hides an age-old settlement and an assembly of Romanesque art treasures. Only one family and the 22 nuns who maintain the island's towering convent live here year-round.

On Wednesday mornings, while mist is still rising off the lake, nuns cross the lake in small fishing boats, as their predecessors did, to attend the weekly open-air market in Orta.

Each year in July, when the population of San Giulio Island reaches 300, townsfolk gather in the main square to sing popular island songs. This ancient tradition is believed to date back to the time of St. Julius, when early Christians gathered in front of the island's basilica to sing hymns.

On Sundays in September, San Giulio sponsors concerts that combine classical and regional folk music. But the island's most colorful festival is Jan. 31, St. Julius Day. From midnight until later into the following evening, there are fireworks, music, and dancing.

On San Giulio, among the elegant villas, terraces, clusters of rich green trees, and fragrant flower gardens of the summer, are some of the finest examples of Romanesque art in all Italy. The Romanesque basilica has undergone several renovations. Its history can be traced to the 11th century, but islanders will tell you that it goes back nearly 700 years earlier, to the time of St. Julius.

Inside the basilica is a remarkable collection of frescoes from the 15th century, most by local painters. The masterpiece of the basilica is a 12th-century Pulpit of the Comacine Masters. Gorgeously ornamented with the symbols of the four Evangelists and splendid animals, the polychrome wooden bas-reliefs are supported by marble columns. The bells of the basilica ring on Sunday morning and can be heard for miles around.

The island's only restaurant is the **Ristorante San Giulio**, where succulent regional specialties, such as *minestrone alla Milanese* and *costoletta* (a veal dish), are served, along with a fine selection of sparkling white and red wines.

The island has no hotels. Stay at one of the hotels in nearby Orta; contact the tourist office, *tel. (39)22-90-354*, for assistance.

UMBRIA: THE BEST OF THE HEARTLAND

Undulating **Umbria** is Italy's heartland, stretching between Rome and Florence. This hilly, forested countryside is dotted with Renaissance architectural gems, ancient farmhouses, vineyards, olive groves, and orchards. Umbria's medieval cities perch on hilltops and hang from mountainsides. St. Francis was born in Umbria, and he left his mark throughout the region.

Umbria's strangest sight

The small town of **Bomarzo** is known for the fascinating but creepy garden at the Villa of Orsini. In the late 15th century, Prince Vicino Orsini created these landscaped gardens, which are dotted with bizarre sculptures. Known as Il Sacro Bosco (the Sacred Wood) or the Parco dei Mostri (Park of Monsters), it is filled with statues of half-human, half-animal monsters.

The most beautiful Umbrian town

Orvieto, perched on an enormous rock, is the most beautiful town in the region. It is known for its *duomo*, built in 1229, which has a golden, mosaic-decorated front that glitters when it reflects the sun. Pope Nicholas IV commissioned the *duomo* to commemorate a miracle. According to Church lore, drops of blood appeared on the Host consecrated by a Bohemian priest who had doubted the Doctrine of Transubstantiation (the belief that during the sacrament of communion the bread actually becomes the body of Christ and the wine His blood). The blood-stained chalice cloth is kept in the cathedral and carried through town during the feast of Corpus Christi and again on Easter Sunday. The *duomo* has opaque alabaster windows, a rose window designed by Andrea Orcagna, and frescoes begun by Fra Angelico.

The best place to stay in Orvieto is three miles outside town in La Badia. The **Hotel La Badia**, *La Badia, Orvieto Scalo 05019; tel. (30)763-90-359*, a former abbey that dates back to the 1100s, has comfortable rooms with private baths and a first-class restaurant that features produce from the abbey's own farm. This beautiful complex has a swimming pool and tennis courts, as well as a church of Romanesque-Lombard style and a 12-sided tower. The buildings contain frescoes from the 12th, 13th, and 14th centuries. In the 15th century, the abbey was a retreat for cardinals. It has been in the hands of the family of Count Giuseppe Fiumi for the past century.

Perugia: a historical treasure house

Perugia is a town of historic treasures. The most fascinating sight is the via **Bagliona Sotternea**, an underground street filled with the ruins of the 15th-century houses. Visit the 13th-century **Fontana Maggiore** and stroll along the palace-lined **Corso Vanucci**. The town's **Collegio del Cambio** was frescoed by Perugino and his helpers, one of whom may have been Raphael, in the early 16th century. Upstairs is the **National Gallery**.

Perugia's best hotel is **La Rosetta**, *Piazza d'Italia 19; tel. (39)75-20841*. Located at the top of the Corso Vannucci, near the main sights, it is friendly and efficient, and the food is delicious. Rooms at the back are quieter.

Umbria's most inviting hotel

Torgiano, a walled town complete with towers, boasts the splendid **Baglioni Palace**, which houses a wine museum founded by the local producers of Chardonnay.

Another reason to stop in Torgiano is the **Hotel Le Tre Vaselle**, *tel. (39)75-988-0447*. Housed in a 300-year-old villa, it has 16th-century wooden doors, thick walls, and hand-hewn ceiling beams and arches. It is a peaceful place on a side street, with spacious bedrooms and views of the countryside. Rooms are decorated with textiles and flowers, and Umbrian specialties are served in the dining room. Try artichoke risotto sage-and-onion bread tarts baked in a wood oven and the traditional Umbrian wafer made in 16th-century molds and flavored with anise. The hotel is often used for conferences of oenologists (wine experts), because it is owned by the Lungarotti Wine Company.

IN THE FOOTSTEPS OF ST. FRANCIS

Traces of peace-loving St. Francis are evident throughout **Assisi**, an ethereal mountainside town with medieval houses. Just outside Assisi is the **Basilica Santa Maria**, which includes the fourth-century Chapel of Porziuncola, used by St. Francis and his followers.

St. Francis is buried in the **Basilica of San Francesco**—his remains are kept in the structure's 19th-century crypt. Giotto painted 28 scenes from the life of the saint here. Black-robed pilgrims flock to the basilica from the countryside year-round.

The corpse of St. Clare is exposed and can be viewed in its crystal casket in the crypt of the **Basilica of Santa Chiara**, across town.

Outside Assisi, visit the **Convent of St. Damian**, where St. Francis received his holy orders. See the crucifix that supposedly spoke to St. Francis and the rooms where St. Clare lived, worked, and fought off marauders. Go on to the Eremo delle Carceri, a minute church hollowed out of rock by St. Francis and his followers in a nearby wood.

Hotel Fontebella, *tel. (39) 75-812-882*, is located in a 17th-century palazzo in the center of town. Most rooms have a balcony with a view of the city. Guests can play cards and drink cocktails in the comfortable sitting room. The hotel restaurant, Il Frantoio, is expensive.

THE BEST OF BOLOGNA

"La grassa, la dotta, la rossa"—fat, red, and brainy. Not the most flattering of descriptions, but that's how Bolognese proudly define their city.

Fat, because it's one of the world's leading gastronomic centers; brainy, as home of the world's oldest university, founded in 1088, and as the cradle of such inventions as Marconi's radio; and red, for the dominant terracotta and russet hues of its handsome buildings threaded by its 35 miles of ochre-shaded arcades.

Fat could also refer to the shape of the wallet needed to enjoy much of the best of Bologna. It's a major commercial hub, boasting Europe's fifth-largest exhibition center and hosting major international fairs and conventions such as the **Future Film Festival**, *website: www.futurefilmfestival.org*.

The best hotel—the Grand Hotel Baglioni

On arrival, you will be ushered into the 124-room **Grand Hotel Baglioni**, *tel. (39) 51-225-445; website: www.baglionihotels.com*, by two gloved doormen, greeted by a concierge, and, having trekked to the end of the hall, welcomed by a small platoon of svelte receptionists. En route, the white pillars and marble floors dazzle, the antique furniture glows and the décor takes the breath away. You are in the footsteps of the global glitterati. The VIP guest book is crammed with grateful messages from concert artistes like Rostropovich and Muti, sporting legends like Pelé, and such show business stars as Liza Minnelli, Bob Dylan, and Diana Ross, and friends and family of the great Pavarotti who has a home nearby. The accommodation is fabulous too—canopied beds, ornate furnishings, 18th-century paintings and elaborate chandeliers.

The best place for people watching

The **Piazze Maggiore** is one of Italy's most imposing sights—a wide pedestrianized square flanked by massive palaces: the Palazzo Comunale, the Palazzo Podesta, and the Basilica di San Petronio. People come here to sit in one of the sprawling cafés and watch everyone else teem. Sitting not far away is Neptune, a bronze statue complete with bubbly mermaids.

Apparently, before its designer, Giambologna, began work on it back in the 1500s, he sought permission from the pope to expose a great deal of the sensual *Il Gigante's* abundant flesh. The pope is said to have replied "For Bologna, it's okay."

The best arts and crafts

Bologna's intriguing backstreets are full of treasures for the specialist, hobbyist, and connoisseur. Interested in buying or restoring a violin? Then drop in on Bruno Liutaio's, website: *www.brunostefonini.it*, in the via del Belle Arti. To watch iron being wrought into extraordinary shapes, drop in on Pierluigi Prata's ironworks in via Caldarese. And for exquisite collections of antique and modern art, there's the charming Galleria Caldarese in via Caldarese.

Bologna's most impressive towers

Bologna is not short on towers, but there are none more impressive than **Torre Asinelli**, whose 498 wooden steps wind upward for 330 feet to a breathtaking view. At its side is the 160-foot-high **Torre Garisenda**, with a Pisa-rivaling tilt. The towers are nicely situated near to the Palazzo dei Congressi, which is itself linked to the Municipal Gallery of Modern Art.

The best restaurant

For a relaxed but professional atmosphere, you can't beat the **Pappagallo**, built on the foundations of a 13th-century palace. Manager Leopoldo Monari supervises classical Bolognese dishes, including Pappagallo's own home-made tortellini. Try the gamberoni served with black rice and asparagus tips. If you prefer meat, another speciality is Costola di Vitello alla Bologna, a scintillating blend of marinated veal, ham, and parmesan with zuchinni.

THE BEST OF TUSCANY

Tuscany has historic towns, fashionable beach resorts, and a leading spa favored by the Italian *bene* (elite). The region that gave us Michelangelo and Leonardo da Vinci continues its artistic traditions, creating marble sculpture and fine gold and leather crafts. Yet it is seldom crowded with tourists.

The oldest Tuscan town

Drive up into the hills above Florence to visit **Fiesole**, one of the 12 great towns of ancient Eturia. Long before there was a Florence, this little town sat above the Arno Valley. In 283 B.C., Etruscan Fiesole was conquered by the Romans, who left behind an amphitheater built in 80 B.C. Classical plays are presented in the restored ruins.

An ochre-colored path leads from the Piazza Mino to the San Francesco Monastery in Fiesole. From the path, you can enjoy one of the best views of Florence. The cloister of the Gothic monastery is filled with Chinese art from the era of Marco Polo.

The town's *duomo*, built in A.D. 1000, has gray Corinthian columns and Romanesque arches. Paintings by Fra Angelico and Fra Filippo Lippi are displayed at the Museo Bandini.

The best place to dine in Fiesole is the **Hotel Aurora**, *Piazza Mino, 50014 Fiesole; tel. (39)55-59-100*. It has a charming garden and great views, as well as inexpensive Tuscan fare.

Villa San Michele, *via Doccia, 4 Fiesole, 50014 Florence; tel. (39)55-59-451*, is a deluxe hotel in a former Franciscan monastery. Monks' cells have been converted into lavishly decorated bedrooms and suites. Michelangelo is supposed to have designed the building.

The best wine-making estate

Not far from Florence, just off Superstrada 67, is the winemaking **Artimino Estate**, with its 740 acres of vineyards, olive groves, and gardens. In the late 16th century, the villa was commissioned by Grand Duke Ferdinand I to house his court. It became known as La Ferdinanda.

An excellent restaurant, **Biagio Pignatta**, is located on the estate's grounds. It offers Tuscan dishes and the eight wines grown on the estate according to age-old traditions. Wood-burning ovens braise the meats to perfection. The *scaloppina ai carciofi* (veal and artichokes), *bistecca alla Fiorentina* (charcoal-broiled beefsteak), and *faraona alla brace* (broiled guinea hen) are superb. The restaurant is closed on Mondays and Thursdays.

Hotel Paggeria Medicea, *tel. (39)55-87-18-081*, adjacent to the villa, has 37 rooms with wood beams and enormous fireplaces, as well as 20th-century conveniences, such as telephones, televisions, and refrigerated bars. The hotel is in a 17th-century building formerly called Il Corridoio (the Hallway), because it once separated the court residence from the servants' quarters.

The prettiest Tuscan town

Lucca, a small city enclosed within vast ramparts, is the prettiest town in Tuscany. The 12th-century town is beautifully preserved and maintained. Delightfully cool and shaded green walkways follow the massive 16th-century brick and turf walls that surround the town. The curious towers here are typical of Tuscan towns. In the Middle Ages, most patrician houses were dominated by very high and slender towers often crowned with ilex trees. After exploring Lucca's historic churches, wander through the narrow streets, which are filled with boutiques.

Lucca's grand **Romanesque cathedral** is filled with artistic treasures.

Jacopo della Quercia designed the tomb of Ilaria del Carretto, wife of the Lord of Lucca in the early 15th century. A strangely lifelike statue of Ilaria reclines on top of the tomb. Other treasures include Tintoretto's *Last Supper* and Ghirlandaio's *Madonna and Saints*. A life-sized statue of Christ that drifted ashore at the nearby town of Luni is kept in a round chapel in the north nave. Every Sept. 13, the statue is carried through town in memory of the day it miraculously appeared. The façade of the cathedral is carved with religious allegories and fantastic animals. Nicola Pisano's *Deposition* and *Nativity* are above the door on the right.

Inside the **Church of San Michel** is a painting of saints Sebastian, Roch, Jerome, and Helen by Fra Filippo Lippi.

The **Church of San Frediano** houses the mummy of Santa Zita. On April 26, the townspeople place the body in the middle of the church and stroke and kiss its withered limbs.

The best restaurant in town is the **Buca di Sant'Antonio**, *via della Cervia 3, Lucca 55100; tel. (39)583-55881*. Kid roasted on a spit is a specialty. Try the local wine, Rosso delle Colline Lucchesi.

Lucca has a shortage of hotels. Of the nine small hotels here, the most comfortable and convenient is the **Albergo Universo**, *Piazza Puccini, Lucca 55100; tel. (39)583-491-543*.

The best-preserved Tuscan town

San Gimignano, with its noble towers, is one of the best-preserved medieval towns in Italy. Unfortunately, tourists flock to this 14th-century gem, crowding the streets. It's difficult to imagine where they all stay—only three hotels are located within the town walls. During the fall, the town is filled with hunters. (Hunting is good in the surrounding hills.)

Fourteen of the 72 towers that once protected this town still stand. At one time, all 72 spires crowded around the main square that surrounds the 13th-century *cisterna* (well). The small square is curiously paved with bricks laid on their narrow sides in a herringbone pattern.

The best hotel in San Gimignan is **La Cisterna**, *tel. (39)577-940-328*, located in the main square. It is an elegant, comfortable, well-run place with an excellent restaurant, **La Terrazza**. Sit on the terrace to watch the lights blink on in farmhouses and peaceful villages as night falls over the valley.

Tuscany's crown jewel: Siena

The jewel in Tuscany's crown is **Siena**, a beautifully preserved town with wide-open spaces and ancient palaces. It is known for its university, its musical academy, and the annual Palio (a centuries-old horse race). Siena's cathedral, a striped marble structure, reaches high into the sky.

The 14th-century walls that surround Siena were used during World War II to prevent retreating German troops from passing through the city.

When the ancient portals were shut, the 20th-century tanks couldn't get through!

Siena's most beautiful square is the **Piazza del Campo**, which is bordered by the city's magnificent palaces and the 13th-century Palazzo Pubblico (city hall), which houses the town museum. Built of brick, the city hall is a fine specimen of pointed Gothic architecture. The slim, elegant, 334-foot tower (Torre del Mangia) soars high over the city. Its shadow moves across the brick paving as the day progresses. The Sienese Museum is a good introduction to Siena.

In the evening, join the Sienese in their stroll along the *passeggiata*, or promenade, along the curving Banchi di Sopra. The *passeggiata* leads through the banking district. Notice the Monte dei Paschiu di Siena, a bank housed in the 14th-century Palazzo Salimbeni. The bank was founded in 1472 and is still in business. Nearby is Palazzo Tolomei, the oldest private palace in Siena, now home to the Cassa di Risparmio di Firenze, another bank.

The most beautiful Sienese artwork is on display at the **Pinacoteca**, which contains Byzantine paintings and works by Simone Martini.

The most exciting time to visit

The most exciting time to visit Siena is during the **Palio**, which is held July 2 and Aug. 16 each year. This bareback three-lap horse race around the shell-shaped Piazza del Campo is one of the most genuine and fascinating of all Italian spectacles. It lasts 90 seconds but generates feuds that continue for decades.

The Palio is a competition between 10 of Siena's 17 *contrade*, or districts. During the days preceding the race, the people of Siena revert to the venality of the Middle Ages. Bribery, meddling, and skullduggery are not only permitted but also encouraged. *Contrade* captains are expected to indulge in intrigue as part of their efforts to outdo their rivals.

The Palio has roots in the Middle Ages, when Siena was an independent republic. At that time, the 17 *contrade* were separate military societies, each defended by its own military forces. Life in Siena in the Middle Ages was not easy. Homes were small, cold, badly ventilated, and had little light. The streets were narrow and murky and bristled with the threat of ambush. The walls that surrounded the city and those of the high buildings along the streets were blackened by smoke. The danger of epidemic was great, as was the possibility of dying by the sword or dagger. In light of all this, it is no wonder the people looked for escape. The Compagnie Popolari were organized to help provide distraction. These companies, each from a different section of the city, were intended to keep the people happy and free from worries (and thoughts of revolt, no doubt) by initiating games. One of the games the Compagnie Popolari initiated was the Palio.

The best hotels and restaurants

The **Park Hotel**, *tel. (39)577-44-803*, is the best place to stay in Siena. Located in a 15th-century villa, it has modern amenities, such as air conditioning, a heated swimming pool, and central heating. Terraces, gardens, and vineyards surround the villa. Situated on Marciano Hill, it has good views.

Pisa: Tuscany's most famous sight

Pisa, which is famous for its leaning tower, has lesser-known sights that are also worth seeing: the cathedral, the baptistery, and the Campo Santo. The *duomo* is fronted by white columns that support five tapered arcades. Winged angels peer out from the corners, and mysterious inscriptions can be found on the walls. Inside are Corinthian columns and striped walls. Art in the cathedral includes an ivory Madonna by Giovanni Pisano, Andrea del Sarto's *Sant'Agnese Mourning*, and Giovanni del Biondo's *Flight From Egypt* and *Presentation at the Temple*.

The **baptistry** has gables, arches, and stained-glass windows. A white shaft of light shines through the baptistry dome onto the floor. Sounds echo eerily in the dome.

The **Campo Santo** is a walled cemetery filled with earth brought back from Calvary by the Crusaders. The cemetery walls are covered with terrifying medieval frescoes: *The Triumph of Death*, *The Last Judgement*, and *Hell*. The last is a picture of snakes, skewered corpses, and demons punishing sinners.

SICILY: ITALY AT ITS MOST EXOTIC

Sicily, an island at the southern tip of Italy, is a land unto itself. In ancient times, Sicily was part of Greece. Later, it became part of the Roman Empire. After the fall of Rome, northern tribes, Saracens, Byzantines, Normans, French, and Spanish invaded it, each group leaving its mark on the island's culture. Sicily didn't become part of Italy until 1860.

Sicily's climate is more like that of northern Africa than that of Europe. So the best time to visit is in the spring or fall. (It is blisteringly hot in the summer.)

The best-preserved relics

Some of the best-preserved relics of ancient Greece are scattered across Sicily. Taormina's amphitheater is spectacular, with Mount Etna smoking behind it. The temple in Segesta (a town in western Sicily) is set on a lonely hill facing a huge amphitheater. In Agrigenta, the temples to Juno, Concordia, and Hercules are awe-inspiring. Visit Messina, founded by the Greeks in the eighth century, and Siracusa, which has archeological evidence of the ancient Greeks and Romans.

Europe's highest active volcano

Europe's highest active volcano is in Sicily. **Mount Etna** rises 9,840 feet. Don't take the organized tour of Mount Etna—it is a terrible disappointment. The trip takes all day, and you will see nothing but dirt and rocks. The group never goes near the crater.

The least-changed towns

The smaller hill towns in Sicily are some of the least modern in Italy. Donkeys and mules rather than cars and trucks carry loads. Women carry water from wells in jars on their heads. Each morning, a goat herder follows his goats into town. He milks the goats at each door, delivering fresh milk to the residents. Plumbing in some towns is nonexistent, and water is scarce.

Sicily's most charming resort

Taormina is the most charming resort town in Sicily. Set on a ridge with a spectacular view of the bay, its greatest sight is the Greek Theater carved out of the hillside, which is still used for productions during the summer theater festivals. Palazzo Vorvaia, the site of Sicily's parliament in the 14th century, is on the Piazza Vittorio Emanuele. Enjoy a glass of wine and a view of the bay from one of the many cafés along the Piazza 9 Aprile.

The best way to get to Sicily

The most beautiful way to get to Sicily is by ferry or hydrofoil from the southern tip of the mainland at Reggio di Calabria or Villa San Giovanni across the Strait of Messina. The crossing is long and often tough, but always lovely. Boats also connect with Naples, Livorno, Genoa, and Cagliari. You can also fly to Palermo and Catania from major Italian cities.

Sicilian cuisine—Italy's most colorful

Sicily is known for its exotic and colorful dishes, which have a slightly Arabic flavor. One typical dish of the region is *pasta con le sarde*, in which pine nuts and currants lend a Middle Eastern touch to *bucatini* (thick, hollow spaghetti) in a sauce of fresh sardines and wild fennel. The combination of pine nuts and currants is common. Eggplant and sun-ripened fresh tomatoes are also commonly used.

La Scuderia, *viale del Fante 9; tel. (39)91-520-323*, one of the best restaurants in Palermo, serves sophisticated Sicilian cooking. It is expensive by Sicilian standards.

Trattoria Primavera, *Piazza Bologni 2; tel. (39)91-329-408*, also in Palermo, has simple food and low prices. It is closed Fridays.

The best place to sleep in Sicily

Palermo's luxury hotel is the **Grand Hotel Villa Igiea**, *tel. (39)91-543-*

744. Designed to look like a castle, this hotel is right on the sea. It has lovely flower gardens with palm trees and the ruins of an ancient temple. A swimming pool, tennis courts, an elevator and a bar add to the amenities of the Grand. All rooms have baths. You can have a car sent to pick you up at the train station.

Villa San Michele, *tel. (39) 942-24-327*, in Taormina is inexpensive. The food is lavish. Ask the staff to pack you a picnic lunch, then walk down the steep hill to spend a day at the beach.

UNCONQUERED SARDINIA, THE WILDEST REGION

Sardinia is the least-tamed region in Italy. It is still the land of the *banditti*, family clans, and blood feuds. It has produced such rebels as Antonio Gramsci, theorist and founder of the Italian Communist Party.

Today, Sardinia attracts movie stars and royalty. Prince Karim bought 35 miles of coastline and established the most luxurious resort in Italy: the Costa Smeralda.

Despite an onslaught of foreign tourists and developers, Sardinia is beautiful—hilly and occasionally tropical. The coast has granite cliffs and long, sandy beaches. The water is the cleanest in the Mediterranean. What's more, Sardinia has fascinating Roman ruins at Nora and Tharros, as well as prehistoric stone towers called *nuraghi*.

Beautiful sights of Sardinia

Very little of Sardinia has been built upon. Most new residential developments have been carefully planned, and there is little that is unsightly. Planning regulations ensure the coastline remains unspoiled. Developers can't build within 330 yards of the sea, and all paintwork must be in natural earthy or ocean colors.

Cagliari, the best bet

Cagliari, on the southern coast, has inexpensive hotels and a charming medieval district called the Castello. Narrow streets and tall towers cover the hills rising out of the harbor. This friendly town is near the nuraghi ruins at Barumini and the sandy beaches of the Costa del Sud. Pink flamingos inhabit the lagoons outside town. The tourist office in Piazza Matteotti can help you find a room.

Cagliari has good seafood restaurants. **Dal Corso**, *viale Regina Margherita 28; tel. (39) 70-66-43-18*, serves fresh lobster, eel, shrimp, and fish.

Trattoria Gennargentu, *via Sardegna 60; tel. (39) 70-65-82-47*, serves enormous plates of lasagne, shish kebab, and squid. The trattoria is comfortable, has plenty of local atmosphere, and serves a good house wine.

A good, cheap place to stay in Cagliari is **Locanda Firenze**, *Corso Vittorio Emanuele 50; tel. (39) 70-65-36-78*. It has clean, pleasant rooms, and the management speaks English. The hotel, which is on the third floor, has no elevator.

Sardinia's oldest city

Nora, a small city near Cagliari, is the oldest city in Sardinia. Settled by Phoenicians, who left the ruins of their temple behind, it became a bustling Roman town before it died about A.D. 500. The Roman roads and theater are well-preserved, and the ruins are being excavated. Climb to the Spanish watchtower for tremendous views of the sea, which breaks on either side of the isthmus.

Sardinia's unique ruins

Don't leave Sardinia without examining its *nuraghi*—ancient stone towers found only in this part of Italy. They were once used as tombs, temples, or forts of refuge. The **Nuraghi of Su Nuraxi** in Barumini, near Cagliari, are the best-preserved in Sardinia. Set on a hill, they are the remains of an ancient village. The huge blocks of stone were designed primarily for defense. The huge central tower dates back to about 1300 B.C. The Nuraghi of Su Nuraxi can be visited every day except Mondays.

The town of **Sassari** has the best Sardinian museum, the **Museo Givanni Antonio Sanna**, *via Roma 64*. See reconstructed nuraghi, Sardinian paintings and costumes, Roman statues and mosaics, and an ethnographic section where Sardinian music is played. Open 9 a.m. until 2 p.m. Tuesdays through Saturdays and 9 a.m. until 1 p.m. Sundays.

Two good, inexpensive hotels in Sassari are **Albergo Gallura**, *Vicolo San Leonardo 9; tel. (39) 79-238-713*, and **Albergo Guisy**, *Piazza Sant'Antonio 21; tel. (39) 79-233-327*. The first is well-run and located in the center of town. The second is very comfortable and located at the far end of Corso Vittorio Emanuele.

The best Roman ruins

Near Sassari, **Porto Torres** occupies the site of the Roman town **Turris Libisonis**. Remains of the Roman settlement, including a circular marble altar and the baths of the Palace of the Barbarian King (Palazzo di Re Barbaro), can be seen next to the train station. Seven arches of an ancient Roman bridge span the River Turritano. The Church of San Gavino is one of Sardinia's most notable monuments. Built in the 11th century, it has 28 columns and a wooden truss ceiling.

Sardinia's most beautiful city

Alghero, the most beautiful and best-preserved city in Sardinia, has a Spanish flavor. Sardinia was united with Aragon in 1325, and the Spaniards left their mark on Alghero, which looks somewhat like Barcelona. Alleys are covered with arches, and some restaurants serve *paella*. Starting at the Bastione della Maddalena in the port, walk around the ramparts and the 16th-century Spanish towers to enjoy the view of the shimmering sea.

Outside Alghero are two beaches with clean, clear water—**Spiaggia di San Giovanni** and **Spiaggia di Maria Pia**. Both are crowded. A short boat trip away is the **Grotto di Nettuno**, which puts Capri's Blue Grotto to shame. The large underwater cavern can be visited by boats that leave from docks in front of Bastione della Maddalena.

One of the best restaurants in **Alghero is Il Pavone**, *Piazza Sulis 3/4; tel. (39) 79-97-95-84*. This family-run restaurant serves excellent soups, antipastos, risottos, and seafood. It is closed Wednesdays and from Dec. 20 through Jan. 20. Reservations are a good idea.

THE BEST OF MONTENEGRO

Montenegro (Black Mountain) is a small republic in the heart of the Mediterranean, divided from Italy by the Adriatic Sea. It follows the Adriatic Sea for 200 miles, from Kotor south to Albania. The scenery is dramatic, varying from high mountains to flat meadows to coastline beaches. The drive down the old Post Road (now the coastal highway) to Dubrovnik is especially beautiful.

Herceg Novi, in the north, is the oldest town along the coast. It was founded 600 years ago by Tvrtko, the first Bosnian King. The old part of town has ramparts and towers that contrast sharply with the new villas and hotels. Herceg Novi is known as the rainiest spot in Europe. The Topla is a good place to stay.

The area around Risan is filled with bays and waterfalls. It is said that Illyrian Queen Teuta, after valiantly trying to fight off the invading Romans in 228 B.C., drowned herself here rather than surrender.

PLITVICE LAKES: NATURE AT ITS BEST

UNESCO has classified the **Plitvice Lakes National Park**, halfway between Zagreb and the coast, as one of the unique natural wonders of the world. Here, 16 magnificent blue-green lakes merge one into the other in a chain of waterfalls that rushes into the Korona River. The highest waterfall is 247 feet. The lakes are surrounded by walking paths, deep forests, beaches, and hotels.

The best hotel in the area is the **Hotel Jezero**, perched in the mountains overlooking the largest of the lakes, Kozjak. The hotel has a large indoor pool, and two ski lifts are located only a mile away.

SKADAR LAKE: THE MOST SUPERLATIVE

A list of superlatives describes **Skadar Lake** in the Zetsko-skadarska valley: the last habitat of pelicans in Europe, the biggest bird reservation in Europe, one of the last freshwater marshes at the Mediterranean, and the largest lake in the Balkans. Some parts of the lake bottom are below sea level.

The numerous islands dotted around the lake are interesting not only as bird paradises but also for their cultural and historical monuments. **Starcevo Islet**, for example, has a restored church from the 14th century, a renovated tavern, and the tomb of Bozidar Vukovic-Podgoricanin, the printer of the first Cyrillic books.

THE DEEPEST CANYON IN EUROPE

The **Tara River** canyon in the Durmitor National Park is the deepest canyon in Europe. The furious Tara River rises in the mountain range in the northern part of the country and for centuries has been hollowing out the soft limestone, creating a 50-mile-long canyon. In some places the canyon is almost a mile deep. Its banks are covered with forest.

THE MOST ATMOSPHERIC RESTAURANT

Kod Miska, *tel. (381)69-022-868*, in Ulcinj, is built on a wooden raft on the river Bojana. The restaurant is famous for its food as well as its atmosphere. The surrounding scenery is reminiscent of the Amazon jungle. Fish is a specialty here and the prices are moderate.

SVETI STEFAN: THE MOST EXCLUSIVE RESORT

Off the coast of Montenegro is the island of **Sveti Stefan** (St. Stephen), a 15th-century fishing village that became an exclusive resort in 1960. The original fishermen's cottages have been preserved intact, but the interiors have been renovated in luxury. Flower gardens add color to the stone surroundings. The Duke of Bedford came here on his honeymoon; Adlai Stevenson, Kirk Douglas, and Princess Margaret also have been among the resort's guests.

THE BEST OF POLAND

Poland doesn't have the tourist amenities of Western Europe—or even the amenities of Hungary or the Czech Republic—but it does have the Polish people. Self-effacing and fun loving, they are among the warmest people in all Europe. If you get lost in Poland, a Pole is likely to take you out for dinner and drinks before he points you in the right direction.

Nature, too, welcomes visitors to Poland. The country's 12 natural parks and 500 wildlife preserves contain animals that have already disappeared in other parts of Europe—bison, chamois, bear, moose, and tarpan (small horses). And Poland's 325-mile Baltic seacoast is lined with long, sandy beaches.

WARSAW: WORST DESTRUCTION, BEST RESTORATION

Warsaw has had the bloodiest history of any Polish city. Hitler ordered that not one stone be left standing in the city following the 63-day Warsaw Uprising against the Nazis. As a result, more than 200,000 people were killed and the city was razed. Between 1940 and 1945, a total of 750,000 of the city's residents died.

The Nazis weren't the first to demolish Warsaw. In the 17th century, the city was razed by the Swedes. It was sacked again in the 18th century. In 1795, Warsaw was given to Prussia. Napoleon took the city in 1806. And the Russians claimed it in 1813.

Although most of Warsaw's old buildings and monuments have been destroyed, many have been beautifully rebuilt. The Old Town section was reconstructed after the war according to prints and old family photographs. It looks much as it did before, with narrow houses, winding streets, and Gothic churches. The district is closed to all traffic except horse-drawn buggies.

At the heart of Old Town is **Market Square**, surrounded by recreated baroque houses, shops, and cafés filled with flowers. The **Negro House**, Number 36 on the square, was once a center of the slave trade. It is marked by a bust of a black man. It is now the home of the **Warsaw Historical Museum**, where chamber music concerts are held on Tuesdays. The oldest house on the square is the **House of the Mazovian Dukes**, or St. Anne's House, at Number 31. It has the greatest number of Gothic details.

The **Royal Castle**, blown up during the war, is the most beautiful in Poland. Built between the 14th and 18th centuries, it was restored after

World War II. It can be seen from Zamkowsky Square along with **King Sigismund's Column**, a symbol of Warsaw. The slender column was the first monument rebuilt after the war. Originally built in 1644, it honors King Sigismund III, who made Warsaw his capital in the late 16th century.

The old walls surrounding the city and a 16th-century tower called the **Barbican** also have been reconstructed. You can see fragments of the old defensive walls along Kamienne Schodki Street. They are defended by the statue of Syrena, a mermaid with a raised sword. According to legend, the mermaid rose out of the Vistula River and told two children playing on the banks to found the city. Their names were Wars and Szawa, hence the Polish name for the city: Warszawa.

The most frightening sights

The horrors of World War II are evident throughout Warsaw. The most frightening reminder is **Pawiak Prison Museum**, *Ulica Dzielna 24.26*, where 35,000 Poles were executed and 65,000 imprisoned.

The walled Jewish ghetto called **Muranow** was flattened by the Nazis. Today, Spartan modern apartments stand in its place. The Monument to the Heroes of the Ghetto stands on a small square at the intersection of Zamenhofa and Anielewicza streets, once the heart of the ghetto. It is a slab of dark granite with a bronze bas-relief.

The **Jewish Historical Institute**, *Swierczewskiego 79*, has exhibits of the ghetto uprising. The **Mausoleum to Struggle and Martyrdom**, *Armii Wojska Polskiego Street*, is located at the former gestapo headquarters and prison.

A less obvious memorial to the war is a manhole cover at the intersection of Dluga and Miodawa streets. Here, 5,300 insurgents left the sewer canal through which they escaped from Old Town during the Warsaw Uprising in September 1944. The horrors of their journey through Warsaw's sewers are graphically depicted in Wajda's film *Canal*.

Poland's prettiest palace

Lazienki Palace and Park is among the most beautiful places in the world. In 1766 King Stanislas Poniatowski bought the neoclassical castle, which stood on an island in the middle of a lake, and had it enlarged and remodeled. The grounds also contain the Myslewicki Palace, the White Cottage, an old orangery, a baroque bathhouse, and a theater by the swan-filled lake, complete with artificial ruins.

The Polish Versailles

Wilanow Palace and Park, called Warsaw's Versailles, was built in the late 17th century by King Jan III Sobieski. The building is crowned with parapets, and the façade is carved with deities symbolizing the virtues of the royal family. Inside is the gallery of Polish portraiture and the world's first poster museum.

Warsaw's most famous residents

Stop by the often-overlooked **Maria Sklodowska Curie Museum**, *Ulica Freta 16*. Madam Curie was born here. The scientist was twice awarded the Nobel Prize for her discoveries of the radioactive elements polonium and radium.

Another little-known treasure is the house where **Chopin** was born in 1810. Set in a park in Zelazowa Wola, 33 miles west of Warsaw, the ivy-covered cottage is now a museum. A black Steinway grand piano stands in the corner of the music room. A 19th-century upright grand, which looks something like a harp, stands in another room. Framed musical compositions hang on the walls along with poems Chopin wrote as a boy for his parents. During the summer, Chopin concerts are held here on Sundays.

CRACOW: THE ONLY UNSCATHED POLISH CITY

Cracow is Poland's city of kings and intellectuals. It was the country's capital from 1039 to 1596. Cracow is also the only Polish city that escaped demolition during World War II. The city is dominated by **Wawel Hill**, with its fortified castle and Gothic cathedral. UNESCO described the castle, now a museum, as one of the most beautiful in the world. Poland's kings lived here until 1609, when the royal court moved to Warsaw. Even after the move, Polish kings continued to be crowned here.

Wawel Castle looks like a movie set, with gargoyles hanging from walls, elaborately carved doorways, columns, and brightly painted roof tiles. The castle museum contains the "Szczerbiec," a 13th-century sword used in coronation ceremonies, and the world's largest collection of tapestries—356 in all. The 71 rooms of the castle are richly decorated—one is covered entirely in embossed, hand-painted Spanish leather.

The **Czartaryski Palace** has a collection of tapestries, pottery, weapons, and paintings by old masters, including da Vinci and Rembrandt.

The **cathedral** on Wawel Hill contains the elaborate tomb of St. Stanislaus, Poland's patron. Lovely 15th-century frescoes decorate the cathedral's **Chapel of the Holy Cross**. **Sigismund Chapel**, an 11th-century crypt, contains red marble tombs of royalty, bishops, and national heroes.

Mariacki (the Church of the Virgin Mary) is famous for its bugler. Seven-hundred years ago, a bugler in the church tower was sounding an alarm when he was stopped mid-toot by a Tartar's arrow. Today, a bugle sounds every hour on the hour. The call is cut off suddenly, just as it was centuries ago.

The church is also famous for its 500-year-old altarpiece with life-size figures in gold raiment depicting the assumption of the Virgin Mary.

You enter the Old City via the **Florian Gate**, which is next to a round fort called the Barbican, with walls 10 feet thick and pierced by 130 peepholes. Pedestrians can climb medieval staircases here and view the gargoyles. This area is the site of one of the world's oldest universities, **Jagiellonia University**, which was founded in 1364 and counts Copernicus among its alumni.

All streets in the Old City lead to **Rynek Glowny** (the main marketplace). Once the largest municipal square in Europe, it is the site of political rallies, festivals, and public performances. Hundreds of pigeons share the square with crowds of people.

Oldest new market

Nowy Targ, which means New Market, is a town of 10,000 in the foothills of the Carpathian Mountains. The market was new in the 15th century and has operated continuously ever since. Now open every Thursday, the market attracts buyers and sellers from all over Poland. Beginning at the break of day, the market is like a carnival, and fascinates as long as you watch.

CZESTOCHOWA, A MECCA

Every year on Assumption Day (Aug. 15), hundreds of thousands of pilgrims come to the drab little town of **Czestochowa** on the Warta River to pay homage to a portrait of the Madonna, said to have been painted by St. Luke. The Madonna's cheeks are marred by two slashes that, according to legend, were made by an enraged Tartar who felt the painting getting heavier and heavier as he tried to steal it.

The portrait is kept in a huge monastery called **Jasna Gora** (Hill of Light), founded in 1382 by Paulist monks. Swedish armies were halted here in 1655 and driven out of Poland.

CENTRAL EUROPE'S LAST PRIMEVAL FOREST

Bialowieza National Park, the last primeval forest in Central Europe, covers 480 square miles, half in Poland, half in the Soviet Union. A thick wall of 1,000-year-old oaks, pines, and spruce trees, it is home to Europe's only wild bison, as well as moose, lynx, wild tarpan, bears, foxes, deer, and wild boars. You can explore the forest on four-hour excursions in a horse-drawn carriage.

THE BEST OF PORTUGAL

I AM VERY HAPPY HERE, BECAUSE I LOVES ORANGES, AND TALK BAD
LATIN TO THE MONKS, WHO UNDERSTAND IT AS IT IS LIKE THEIR OWN.
AND I GOES INTO SOCIETY (WITH MY POCKET PISTOLS), AND I SWIMS IN
THE TAQUS ALL ACROSS AT ONCE, AND I RIDES ON AN ASS OR A MULE
AND SWEARS PORTUGUESE.

—*Lord Byron, 1809*

As beautiful and historic as neighboring Spain, Portugal is far cheaper and less developed. Don't make the mistake of most foreigners and visit only Lisbon. Portugal has much to offer outside this capital city, including quaint old villages surrounded by rolling hills, Moorish cities, long sandy beaches, and mountain vistas.

Portuguese culture has been influenced by the Moors, Catholicism, and seafaring history. The Portuguese sing the fado, a heart-rending, wailing sort of blues. Their unique cuisine includes *bacalhau*, a dried codfish served a different way every day of the year. Portugal has its own sweet wines, port and Madeira. And the Portuguese have a version of the bullfight gentler than that in Spain. Portuguese matadors wrestle the bull but never kill the animal. At the end of a bullfight, the bull is enticed out of the ring by a cow.

Portugal's cultural center: Lisbon

The capital of Portugal is studded with ancient Moorish quarters and bordered by lovely beaches. Its National Museum of Ancient Art houses one of Europe's best collections. Outside Lisbon are palaces that rival the chateaux of the Loire in France. And at the heart of the city are winding streets that pass medieval churches and inviting cafés.

Built on a series of hills, **Lisbon** has 17 overlooks, called *miradouros*, that offer side views of the city. The best is at the Castelo de Sao Jorge, built in the fifth century by the Visigoths and later used as a Moorish stronghold. Another panoramic view is from the top of the statue of Cristo Rei, or Christ the King (a smaller replica of the one in Rio de Janeiro), located on the opposite side of the Tagus River from the city. To get there, cross the Ponte 25 do Abril.

The must-sees of Lisbon

Lisbon's most beautiful landmark is the **Basilica de Estrela**, *Largo da Estrela*. Queen Maria I promised God she would build the basilica if he granted her a son. God kept His part of the bargain, and the basilica was built in the late 18th century of luminous pale marble and topped with an enormous stone dome. Maria's tomb is inside. Look for the life-size manger scene carved by Machado de Castro.

The **Se** (cathedral), *Largo de Se*, is downtown's most imposing structure. It was once a fortress and has battlements, two towers, and massive walls. Behind the austere façade are Gothic cloisters and a burial chapel.

Igreja de São Roque is a Jesuit church with an ornate chapel called Sao Joao Baptista, which is lavishly decorated with amethyst, agate, marble and entire columns of Chilean lapis lazuli.

The **Gulbenkian Museum**, *ave. de Berna 45*, houses the huge collection of French furniture, Oriental carpets, and great paintings of the eccentric millionaire Calouste Gulbenkian, as well as Beauvais tapestries.

The **Museu de Etnologia**, *avenida Ilha da Madeira*, has one of the finest collections of African art in the world.

Museu National de Arte Antigua, *rua das Janelas Verdes 9*, contains one of Portugal's greatest treasures, the polyptych of the *Adoration of St. Vincent*, painted by Nuno Goncalves between 1460 and 1470. The six-panel work surrounds a statue of St. Vincent, patron saint of Portugal.

Igreja da Madre de Deus has Europe's best display of antique tiles, called *azulejos*, which line the 16th-century crypt.

Belém: an island of bests

Belém, an island in the middle of the Tagus, west of downtown Lisbon, is surrounded by museums and monuments. The Torre de Belem, a five-story tower, is the most outstanding landmark. Built between 1515 and 1521, cannons on this Gothic structure protected the Tagus for centuries. A statue of *Our Lady of Safe Homecoming* on the tower's peak welcomes sailors home from sea.

In 1502, the profits of the spice trade were used to build the magnificent **Mosteiro dos Jeronimos**, a celebration of Vasco da Gama and other Portuguese explorers. This was de Gama's point of return after finding the sea route to India. He is buried in this church, which is backed by a decorative cloister with columns, arches, fountains, and cool stone benches. In front is the **Monument to the Navigators**—erected in 1960 in the shape of a ship's prow.

Belém is also home to the **Museum of Folk Art**, the **National Coach Museum**, and the **Naval Museum**, which houses beautifully restored ships, as well as early airplanes. (The Naval Museum has spurred much controversy because it spoils the view from the Torre de Belém.)

Lisbon's oldest quarter, the Alfama

The only neighborhood in Lisbon not destroyed by the great earthquake on All Saints' Day, 1755, is the **Alfalma**, whose tiny medieval streets twist and turn between rows of shops and old houses. Forty-foot tidal waves and fires that burned for a week followed the violent earthquake, which struck while most of the city's residents were in church. At least 60,000 people died. Voltaire wrote about it in *Candide*.

The Alfama existed before the Visigoths arrived in the fifth century. It clusters beneath the Castelo São Jorge on one of Lisbon's tallest hills. The cobblestoned streets are so narrow that in some places you must walk single file. Wrought-iron lamps light the streets. Canaries and geraniums brighten the balconies. Laundry waves from lines strung above the streets. Tiles portraying the Virgin Mary, St. Anthony, and St. Martial decorate buildings, some of which date back to the Moors or the Middle Ages.

Walking along **Beco do Mexias**, you pass dozens of tiny shops and come to a doorway that leads to a large fountain where local women do their laundry. Also explore **rua da Regueira**, which is lined with restaurants and shops, and **Patio das Flores**, a little square with houses faced in tile.

Lisbon's most colorful market

Begin your day in Lisbon wandering through the fish market at the foot of the Alfama. Weathered fishermen bring in their catches here, and *varinhas*, or fishwives, march about with baskets of fish on their heads. The *varinhas* wear black skirts with aprons and go barefoot in the summer, gold hoops dangling from their ears.

Portugal's liveliest country market

If you're in Lisbon on the first Sunday of the month, take a detour to the country fair at **Vila Nogueria de Azeitao**, 21 miles south of the city. Portugal's liveliest and largest marketplace, the Azeitao offers everything from livestock and household furnishings to clothing and food. If you miss the fair at Azeitão, the nearby villages of Pinhal, novo, Coina, and Moita have fairs on successive Sundays. Prices at these fairs are lower than those in city stores. Haggling is expected.

The best dishes

Lisbon is famous for its seafood, and the Alfama and the Bairro Alto are the best places to dine on the local *camaroes* (shrimp), *langosta* (lobster), *pesca espada* (swordfish), *salmonete* (red mullet), *linguado* (sole), and *bacalhau*, as well as the ubiquitous *sardinas grilhadas* (fresh grilled sardines), which are delicious. If you see *carne de porco com ameijoas* or *ameijoas na cataplana* on a menu, order it. These are uniquely south Portuguese combinations of pork and sausage with clams.

Drink *Sumol* (lemon or orange soda), Sagres *cerveja* (beer), or local wine, Dão or Vinho Verde. Most of the gin and whiskey in Portugal is faked.

Fado: Portugal's saddest music

Fado, which means *fate*, is as important to Portugal as flamenco is to Spain—although it is more intense and somber. The best fado is played in the Alfama, the Mouraria (another neighborhood with Moorish traditions), the Bairro A lot (the old section), and the Madragoa (the fisherman's quarter). Fado songs range over many octaves, almost always in a minor key, and are usually sung by women dressed from head to toe in melancholy black and carrying red roses. Male fado singers or guitar accompanists wear black monks' robes.

Some of the songs date back to the 13th century; others are influenced by Portugal's Moorish past (and sound atonal) or by Portugal's seafaring tradition (and are reminiscent of sea chanties). Most are about unrequited love.

The places to hear the best Fado

Recommended Fado restaurants include **Adega do Machado**, *tel. (351)1-342-87-13;* **Adega Mesquit**, *tel. (351)1-346-20-77;* **Lisboa a Noite**, *tel. (351)1-346-85-57;* and **O Faia**, *tel. (351)1-342-67-42.* You must make reservations to hear Fado, and you should go after a late dinner; most shows don't start before 10 p.m.

The hottest nightlife

There are many discos in Lisbon, each with its own character and charm. Included are three of our favorites: **Alcatara Mar**, *R. da Cozinha Economica, Alcantara;* **Benzina**, *Travessa teixeira junior, Alacantara;* **Incognito**, *Rua dos Poiais de Sao Bento.* These discos play all kinds of music, including rap, hip-hop, jungle, cool-jazz, funk, and rock 'n' roll.

The cheapest fun

If you're trying to save money, you still can spend a pleasant evening in Lisbon—by strolling through the old sections. You'll find plenty of free entertainment. Student choral groups dressed in caps and gowns sing traditional college melodies to the accompaniment of Spanish and Portuguese guitars.

Lisbon's best hotels

The most luxurious hotel in Lisbon is the **Ritz**, *tel. (351)1-213-83-2020* or *(800)332-3442 in the U.S.*, set on a hill overlooking Parque Eduardo VII. Rooms at the Ritz are decorated in silks, satins and suedes. For something less known, try the **Principe Real**, *tel. (351)1-34-60-116*, a tiny hotel tucked away in the Barrio Alto.

The least expensive places to stay are off of the avenida de Liberdade. **Hotel Jorge V**, *rua Silveira 3; tel. (351)1-35-62-525*, has clean, modern rooms and elevators. A good budget hotel in the old city, near the river is **Hotel Duas Nações**, *tel. (351)1-34-60-71-01.*

The best side trips from Lisbon

Queluz, Portugal's version of the Palace of Versailles, is not far from Lisbon. The 18th-century pink rococo palace is filled with Portuguese Empire antiques and surrounded by ornamental gardens. The palace kitchen, Cozinha Velha, is now a famous restaurant.

Cabo Espichel, a windy cape jutting into the Atlantic, is an ancient pilgrimage center. Explore the ruins of the 17th-century baroque church, **Nossa Senhora do Cabo** (Our Lady of the Cape), as well as the arcaded outbuildings that once housed pilgrims. Go around the church to the edge of the cliff, which drops 350 feet into the ocean.

Estoril is a beach resort 13 miles west of the city with a casino that is open from 3 p.m. to 3 a.m. You can take a train to Estoril from Lisbon's Cais do Sodre station. You must show a passport to get into the casino, and men must wear suit coats. The **Hotel Palacio**, *rua do Parque; tel. (351)1-468-0400*, is a gracious old hotel in Estoril near the beach with gardens, a swimming pool, and excellent service.

Nearby is a fishing village that has been turned into a sophisticated resort, **Cascais**. A fine sandy beach lines its beautiful bay. Cascais has had an elegant air since 1870, when the court first moved here for the summer. A royal palace was constructed in the former citadel and is still used by the head of state. **Dois Mil e Um** (2001), Cascais' famous disco, offers British and American rock and a good sound system.

Just outside Cascais is one of the strangest sights on the coast—the **Boca do Inferno** (Jaws of Hell). This great hole, formed by the force of the ocean entering under a rock arch, roars when waves crash into it.

Praia do Guincho, five miles west of Cascais, is a long, sandy beach with dunes. Its massive headland is the westernmost point in Europe. It is famous for good fishing and surfing (but beware the undertow).

Setubal is a busy fishing port with 16th- and 17th-century churches and a medieval fortress. Inside the walls of the town's castle, São Filipe, is the attractive **Pousada de São Filipe**, *tel. (351)65-523-844*. Built in 1590, the fortress is 600 feet above the harbor and has many towers and massive battlements. It is entered via a dark, sweeping stone staircase. Underground tunnels and prison cells are now used as wine cellars and storage areas. The chapel is completely tiled.

Just north of Setubal is **Pousada do Castelo de Palmela**, *Castelo de Palmela, 2950 Palmela; tel. (351)1-23-51-226*, a beautiful castle hotel.

SINTRA— THE MOST ROMANTIC TOWN

Sintra is the breathtaking mountain resort made famous by the poet Byron, who wrote, "The village of Sintra is the most beautiful, perhaps, in the world." For centuries, Sintra was favored as a summer refuge by

Portuguese royalty. It's a 45-minute train ride from Rossio Station in Lisbon.

Once a mountain stronghold of the Moors, Sintra is dominated by a seventh-century Moorish castle. Situated 1,400 feet above sea level, it has crenelated walls and battlements that extend along rocky cliffs. From the walls, you have a view of the cliffs and the sea.

The most romantic sight in Sintra is the **Pena Palace**, a towering pseudo-medieval palace built in the 19th century. From the windows are views of the coast, the cliffs, and the sea. The palace's 500-acre park, which you enter by crossing a drawbridge, has 400 kinds of trees and plants.

EUROPE'S SUNNIEST SPOT — THE ALGARVE

Spanning 200 miles of Portugal's southern coast, from Sagres in the west to the Spanish border in the east, the **Algarve** is Europe's sunniest site, with 300 sunny days per year. During the summer, temperatures range from 68 to 86 degrees Fahrenheit. The hottest days are tempered by refreshing breezes off the Atlantic. Spring and fall have warm weather just right for swimming.

Separated from the rest of Portugal by a spine of mountains, the Algarve was once considered a separate kingdom. The Phoenicians, Greeks, Carthaginians, and Romans all traded here before the Moors took over and ruled for 500 years. The Algarve was the last province taken from the Moors by Portuguese kings, and many towns still more closely resemble the villages of North Africa than those of Europe.

Albufeira—the hottest town

Albufeira, a Moorish town, has the most beautiful bodies and the hottest nightlife in the region. **Sir Harry's Bar**, an English-style pub on the main square, draws revelers of all ages. But the real action is along rua Candido dos Reis, a cobblestoned pedestrian street that leads from the beach to the plaza. In the evening, the outdoor cafés, the restaurants, and the bars along here are filled. The two most popular bars are **Fastnet**, which is big with the British, and **Twist**, a Scandinavian and German hangout.

The discos in Albufeira get going after midnight. **Sylvia's** is the best, filled with Scandinavians on the prowl and handsome night owls. Across the street is **7 1/2**, which is almost as exciting.

A good, inexpensive place to stay here is the **Hotel Rocamar**, *tel. (351)28-954-02-80.*

Nature's best show: sea caves and rock formations

Between Albufeira and Portimao, near the cliffside village of Praia do Carvoeiro, nature provides one of its most beautiful spectacles. Drive to the **Nossa Senhora da Encarnaçâo**, a chapel at the summit of a steep hill east of Praia do Carvoeiro. Climb down 134 steps through oddly shaped red rocks to see the gaping holes leading into the sea caves, which are engulfed every few minutes by waves. The sights here are simply breathtaking. A path leads to a bluff from which you have a clear view of the entrance to an underwater sea cave.

The **Caves of Cape Carvoeiro** are best seen by boat, which you can do during high season. Ask for information at the tourist office in Praia do Carvoeiro or in Portimâo harbor.

Lagos: the saddest past and the sandiest beaches

Ten miles west of Portimao is the town of **Lagos**, once a center of the African slave trade. The **Praca da Republica** is the site of the first slave trade market established in Europe. Sections of Roman walls remain in the old quarter of Lagos, and you can walk along the walls of the old fortress that guards the harbor. The 18th-century baroque Chapel of St. Antonio is known for its ornate gilded woodcarvings.

South of town is Ponta da Piedad, a headland with fine beaches connected by natural rock tunnels. The scenery is striking—the rocks are a reddish color that contrasts with the green of the sea. The boulders have been carved into strange shapes by pounding waves. Hire a boat to take you to the offshore grottos.

SAGRES: THE END OF THE WORLD

Sagres, the most southwesterly point in Europe, is guarded by the fortress of **Prince Henry the Navigator**. His famous navigational device, the **Compass Rose**, is laid out in the stone.

Prince Henry founded his navigation school here at the beginning of the 15th century. It also was here that he planned his expeditions into Africa and west into the unknown.

Before the great explorations began, sailors believed that **Cabo de São Vicente** (Cape St. Vincent), near Sagres, was the end of the world. The place is marked by a famous lighthouse. Waves crash ferociously on the rocks 250 feet below the lighthouse. If you're going to walk here, bring a windbreaker. Or buy one of the handsome handmade sweaters the women of Sagres are famous for knitting.

Pousada do Infante, *Sagres; tel. (351)82-64222*, has views of the coast and the lighthouse on the promontory of Cape St. Vincent. Delicious soups are served in the dining room, including *crème de espinafres* (spinach cream soup) and *sopa do mar* (fish soup). The fish is always fresh and well-cooked, and the wine list is extensive.

THE BEST WILDLIFE

Monção is a good base for exploring the **Peneda-Geres National Park**. The National Forest Department can arrange guided trips through the mountainous 170,000-acre park, where wild horses, stags, and boars roam and where you can spot milestones along the ancient Roman Way. For more information, stop at the tourist office in Monção.

The **Pousada de São Bento**, *Canicada 4850; tel. (351)53-647-190*, is a good place to stay if you want to explore the park. A modern hotel with dizzying views of the Minho Valley, it is cozy in the winter, with the atmosphere of a hunting lodge. It has high ceilings, massive rafters, and large picture windows overlooking the mountains. The swimming pool and tennis courts are inviting in warm weather.

OPORTO — THE PORT WINE CAPITAL

Originally a Roman settlement, **Oporto** has many old palaces, convents, and churches. (The cathedral is famous for its gilded wood altars and grand organ.) However, Oporto's true fame comes from port wine. If you wander along the banks of the River Douro, you will see rabelos, or barges, bringing the distinctive port wine grapes down from the vineyards.

The area upriver from Oporto is the only place in the world that grows grapes for port, and Oporto is the only place where it is made. You can try port wine and the local Vinho Verde at any restaurant or café in the city. Also, you can visit the **Port Wine Institute**, *tel. (351)2-200-2522; website: www.ivp.pt.*

Vila Nova de Gaia, on the south bank of the Douro, opposite Oporto, is the center of the port wine trade. You can sample port at the wine bodegas here and learn how it is matured for at least 25 years before being sold.

PORTUGAL'S SADDEST LOVE STORY

The **Santa Maria Monastery** in the town of Alcobaça is the final resting place of the ill-fated lovers **Dom Pedro** and **Ines de Castro**. When Prince Dom Pedro married his beautiful mistress Ines de Castro, his father, King Alfonso IV of Portugal, was so outraged by the unequal union that he had Ines assassinated in 1355. When he succeeded to the throne, Dom Pedro got his revenge. He dressed the body of Ines in royal attire and forced the noblemen who had killed her to pay homage by kissing her decomposed hand. The lovers are positioned in their ornate tombs so that they will face each other on Judgment Day.

Constructed by Cistercian monks in 1178, the kitchen in the monastery was built above a trout stream so the cooks could have fresh water and fish.

THE OLDEST UNIVERSITY TOWN

Coimbra, where Princess Ines was murdered, is one of the oldest medieval university towns in Europe. The city's streets are dotted with students wearing traditional black capes. A steep cobblestoned street leads to the university courtyard, where you can join a tour of the old university buildings, including the Manueline Chapel, with its ornate door and 17th-century *azulejos*, and the library, with its carved and varnished wood embellishments.

THE VENICE OF PORTUGAL

Aveiro, at the northernmost tip of the Costa de Prata, claims to be the Venice of Portugal. It is surrounded by salt flats, beaches, and lagoons and dominated by the Central Canal. Gaily-painted *moliceiros* (boats reminiscent of Venice's gondolas) move through the waters gathering algae to be used as fertilizer.

A good hotel in Aveiro is the **Arcada Hotel**, *tel. (351)23-442-30-01*.

BUÇACO: THE MOST BEAUTIFUL FOREST

Buçaco National Park, which has 700 species of trees from around the world, has been considered a holy place for centuries. Benedictine monks built the hermitage here in the sixth century. In 1622, Pope Gregory XV forbade women to enter the oak and pine forest. And the Barefoot Carmelite monks began the arboretum here in 1628.

In 1810, **Buçaco Mountain** was the site of a battle between the combined British and Portuguese forces under Wellington and the French. (Wellington's forces won.) The Portuguese government took over in 1834 and expanded the arboretum. Today, the park covers 250 acres of woodland.

In the center of the park is the royal hunting lodge built by Carlos I (1888-1907). Today it is the **Palace Hotel**, *tel. (351)31-930-101*, an incredibly ornate luxury hotel.

PORTUGAL'S MOST SPECTACULAR MONASTERY

Portugal's most spectacular monastery is in **Batalha**. King João vowed to the Virgin Mary that he would build a monastery if she helped him defeat the Castillians. The king's army was indeed victorious against the Castillian army in the Battle of Aljubarrota on Aug. 14, 1385, ensuring Portugal's independence for the next 200 years.

The monastery does justice to the victory, with flying buttresses, turrets, a mass of gables, columns, and elaborate tracery. King João and his wife

Philippa of Lancaster are buried here along with their children, including Prince Henry the Navigator.

The **Pousada do Mestre A. Domingues**, *tel. (351) 44-96260*, next to the monastery and named after the architect of King Joao, is a comfortable place to stay. The dining room serves excellent seafood, especially the clams and the shrimp.

THE PRETTIEST PORTUGUESE TOWN

Obidos, one of the best-preserved medieval fortified towns on the Iberian Peninsula, has a feminine look, with tiny whitewashed houses and flower-lined streets. The 12th-century **Obidos Castle** dominates the city. **St. Mary's Church**, where King Alfonso V married his eight-year-old cousin Isabella in 1444, is tiled with blue *azulejos*. The octagonal Senhor da Pedra Church has a remarkable second-century stone cross.

The **Pousada do Castelo**, *rua Direita; tel. (351) 62-959-105*, housed within the castle walls, is furnished with antiques and has excellent cuisine and extensive wine cellars. Because it has only six rooms, early reservations are recommended.

The **Estalagem do Convento**, *rua Dom Joao de Ornelas, Obidos. 2510-074 Óbidos; tel. (351) 262-959-214*, is a medieval hotel in Obidos furnished with tables and chairs from the days of the knights and Crusaders. This is a novel place to stay the night, with little rooms and cobblestoned courtyards.

MIRACULOUS FÁTIMA

The village of **Fátima**, where Catholics believe the Virgin Mary appeared to three shepherd children in 1917, is a major shrine and place of pilgrimage. Special ceremonies are held on the 13th day of each month between May and October. Make reservations well in advance if you plan to visit Fátima during that time—throngs descend upon the town.

PORTUGAL'S ODDEST DANCE

The mountain town of **Miranda do Douro**, perched on a ravine just across the River Douro from Spain, is famous for its *pauliteiros*, who perform a traditional sword dance each year on the Feast of St. Barbara (the third Sunday in August). Dancers carry sticks representing swords and wear kilts, embroidered shirts, and black hats covered with ribbons and flowers. They move in an ancient pattern to the sounds of tambourines and bagpipes. Another regional remnant of bygone eras is *Mirandes*, a Latin slang that the locals speak among themselves.

The **Pousada de Santa Catarina**, *tel. (351) 73-42255*, balanced on the edge of a rocky gorge, has lovely views of the River Douro. Occasionally you'll see a golden eagle. The food, cooked over a wood fire, is good. Try the *guisado de polvo a transmontana*, or octopus ragout.

ÉVORA — THE MOST ROMAN

Évora, one of the oldest towns on the Iberian Peninsula, has the best Roman ruins in Portugal. Originally a Roman settlement, the town was later inhabited by the Visigoths. Under the Moors, it became a major trade and agricultural center. And during Portugal's heyday in the 15th and 16th centuries, Évora's university was a magnet for the best scholars and writers of the time. Now a public high school, the old university's great hall is covered with 17th-century tiles.

The Roman **Temple of Diana**, dating from the second century, is well-preserved. Before it was excavated in 1870, it was used as a slaughterhouse. The 1975 bloodless revolution was planned beneath its Corinthian columns.

Notice Evora's quaint street designations — streets bear the names of a countess's tailor, a cardinal's nurse, the lisping man, and the unshaven man. And take a look at the macabre **Igreja de São Francisco**, *Praca 28 de Maio*. It contains a chapel built of 50,000 monks' bones. The Franciscans thought this a good way to encourage meditation upon the transitory nature of life. Above the entrance is a warning, *"Nos ossos que aqui estamos pelos vossos esperamos"* — which means "The bones here are waiting for yours."

Evora's **Pousada dos Loios**, *Largo Conde de Vila Flor; tel. (351)66-24051*, is one of the best in the country. It faces the Temple of Diana and is located in what was the St. Eligius Monastery, consecrated in 1491. The cloisters have been glassed in to form a dining room, which has a vaulted ceiling, horseshoe arches, and a marble font. The bedrooms are converted monastic cells. One of the suites has a baroque antechamber.

PORTUGAL'S POTTERY TOWN

Estreméoz has been an artistic center since the 16th century. It is famous for its Alentejo pottery, sold in the main square on Saturdays. Typical wares include narrow-mouthed jars called *barris* and wide-mouthed jars called *bilhas*. Local artists also create clay figurines of people and animals. Local crafts are displayed at the Rural Museum on the main square.

MADEIRA: THE MOST FRUITFUL ISLAND

About 600 miles off the coast of Morocco lies **Madeira**, a garden paradise that belongs to Portugal. The lush, semitropical volcanic island was discovered by Portuguese explorers in 1419 and soon became a regular port of call for seafarers. Ships coming from the New World and Asia stopped here and left behind specimens of exotic plants, which islanders grew in rich volcanic soil with great success. The result is an island abounding in tropical fruits, vegetables, and flowers. Madeira's mild temperature ranges from 60 degrees Fahrenheit in winter to 72 degrees Fahrenheit in summer.

The best footin'

The best way to see the interior of the island is to walk along the *levadas*, or footpaths, which follow ancient Madeiran irrigation channels carrying water from high up in the mountains down through the terraced farms to the fields and villages below. The paths are graded one to four, from easiest to most difficult.

For the most difficult walks, you need more than hiking boots—you also need a good head for heights. On one side of the foot-wide paths is the irrigation stream, which may be running 18 gallons per minute, while on the other is a vertical precipice hundreds of feet high. The natives, often carrying high bundles on their heads, scurry fearlessly up the paths.

A map of all canal walking paths is available form the **Direcção Regional de Turismo**.

Portugal's best thrill

If you're brave enough, make time during your visit to Madeira to take an exhilarating ride in a little wicker fruit cart with steel blades from Monte downhill to Funchal, the island's capital. You use levers to control the wooden carts as they roll like bumper cars down the hill. Once used for practical purposes, such as transporting fruits and vegetables, today the carts are used purely as amusement rides. To arrange a ride, visit the **tourist office**, *ave. Arriga 18; tel. (351)91-29057*.

Bacchus' favorite—Madeira

After such an exploit, you will probably need a drink. Try the island's fortified sweet wine, called **Madeira**. According to legend, when early settlers reached Madeira (which means wood), they burned off the thick forests in a fire that raged for seven years. When vines were planted in the resulting soil, the grapes acquired their characteristic smoky flavor.

During the days of the American Revolution, Madeira could be imported to Colonial America in non-British ships, which made it the drink of independence. It was the favorite tipple of the early American revolutionaries.

Tour the wine bodegas in Funchal to see how Madeira is processed and stored. At the end of the visit, you can sample the stuff.

Funchal's best sights

Funchal's most famous sights, its **botanical gardens**, are brightly colored year-round. Against the natural beauty of these gardens, the works of man fade. The churches in Funchal range from the 15th-century **Capela de Santa Catarina** (in the Manueline style, a Portuguese version of Gothic characterized by nautical-inspired stone carving) to the **Se** (cathedral), with its carved-wood and gilded altars. Church paintings in Funchal and throughout the island show a strong Flemish influence. The **Palace of the Conde de Carvalhal** is now the town hall.

The island's early houses with black stone trim are made of the volcanic rock of Madeira. The customhouse in the harbor (Alfandega) is an often-overlooked site; especially noteworthy are the second-floor carved and painted ceiling and the 17th-century illuminated Bible, on which captains had to swear they had nothing to declare.

The world's second-highest sea cliff

Cabo Girão, on Madeira, is the world's second-highest sea cliff. This promontory has extraordinary views. Go at sunset. (The highest sea cliff in the world is the north coast of East Molokai Island, Hawaii.)

Madeira's best festival

One of the best times to visit Madeira is June, during the **Ribeira Brava Festival of St. Peter**. In celebration of the patron saint of fishermen, residents join in solemn processions, which are followed by dances, including the traditional sword dance.

Madeira's best eats

Good restaurants near Funchal include **A Seta**, which serves barbecued beef and chicken on sword skewers hung from the ceiling, along with mounds of fresh-baked bread and pitchers of red wine.

A Gruta is a particularly inviting outdoor café, where you can sit for hours sipping ice-cold Mateus. The fish is fresh, the bread crusty and warm. Costumed folk dancers sometimes perform.

In the fishing village of **Camara de Lobos**, perched on a rugged cliff, is the **Restaurant Coral**. From the windows, you can see brightly painted fishing boats bobbing in the water and children mending fishing nets along the jagged coastline.

The most gracious hotel

Reid's, *tel. (351)91-23001*, is Madeira's most gracious resort hotel. Set on a cliff overlooking the sea, it has a British colonial flavor. It is surrounded by tropical foliage and flowers and has a private beach, tennis courts, two pools, and boat rentals.

Portugal's best accommodation: the *pousada*

The 25 *pousadas* throughout Portugal offer historic accommodation and fine food. They are housed in converted medieval castles or convents in areas of great natural beauty. For more information, contact **Enatur**, *tel. (353)1-848-1221.*

THE BEST OF ROMANIA

Romania is a land for romantics. More Gypsies live here than anywhere else in the world. Romanians claim to be descendants of a lost Roman legion. The Roman poet Ovid was exiled here, on a lagoon north of Constanta. And Vlad the Impaler—the man behind the myth of Dracula—led his bloody life in Transylvania.

BUCHAREST: THE PARIS OF EASTERN EUROPE

Thousands of years ago, a little Stone Age settlement was established on the trade route that crossed the forest-covered Romanian plains. Today, that settlement is Bucharest, the capital of Romania, and the trade route is the chain of grand boulevards that earned the city the title of the "Paris of Eastern Europe."

The boulevards—N. Balcescu, 1848, Magheru, and Ana Ipatescu—are lined with restaurants and brasseries. Along their southern stretch is the **Princely Palace**, which is surrounded by the trading quarter called **Lipscani**, where narrow medieval streets wind past little shops. The palace, which is now the **National Art Museum**, *Stirbei Voda St NR1*, was inhabited by the notorious Vlad in the 14th century.

The most beautiful hotel in Bucharest is the **Hanul Manuc**. The Russian-Turkish Peace Treaty of 1812 was signed here. **Stavropoleos**, a nearby church built in 1724, has superb wood and stone carvings.

Calea Victoriei, Bucharest's most famous street, passes many of the city's major sights. Starting at the **Operetta Theater**, *Piata Natiunile Unite*, it leads north past Stavropoleos Church to the History Museum of Romania in the former post office. The museum displays the 42-pound golden Hen with Golden Chickens, a fifth-century treasure made of 12 gold pieces.

Like Paris, Bucharest has a triumphal arch. Built in 1922 to celebrate the Allies' victory in World War I, it is located on the wide avenue of Soseaua Kiseleff.

BUCHAREST'S BEST RESTAURANTS

Capsa, *16 Edgar Quintet St.*, is the traditional meeting place for Bucharest's artists. It offers a choice of local or continental cuisine and excellent desserts.

Pescarus, *Aviatorilor Boulevard*, located along the Herastrau Park, serves international cuisine on a terrace overlooking a lake in the park.

The **Casa Lido**, *3 Magheru Blvd.*, is another restaurant worth visiting; it has a reputation for fine food.

BUCHAREST'S BEST HOTELS

The deluxe hotel **Bucuresti**, *tel. (40-0)14-21-77*, in the center of town has 800 rooms, two restaurants, two swimming pools, a sauna, and a gym.

The **Athenee Palace**, *Strada Episcopiei 1-3; tel. (40)14-08-99*, a prewar grand dame, has a slightly faded grandeur. It has two restaurants, a pastry shop, and very affordable prices.

DRACULA'S CASTLE

While in Brasov, make a day-trip to the town of Poiana Brasov (Sunny Glade) to see **Bran Castle**, the legendary home of Count Dracula. It is actually the home of the Prince of Wallachia, who repelled a Turkish invasion by impaling hundreds of his countrymen on tall stakes and lining the route of the enemy's march. The Turks, frightened by the brutal display, avoided the region. In truth, the Prince stayed at this castle only occasionally.

THE BEST OF
SCANDINAVIA

Summer, when the sun hardly sets over Scandinavia, is the best time to visit this northern land. After months of darkness, Scandinavians come out of hibernation to celebrate the golden months of June and July with parties that would go on until dawn—except dawn never comes.

Scandinavia—for our purposes Denmark, Norway, Sweden, and Finland—has both cosmopolitan cities and the most enormous wilderness area in Europe. Lapland, which crosses Norway, Sweden, and Finland, is a stunning region with glittering glaciers and bright blue skies. Lapps herd their reindeer across the tundra as they have for centuries. The region's parks offer well-marked trails and huts, where hikers can sleep in comfort.

DENMARK: THE MOST ACCESSIBLE COUNTRY

The southernmost of the Scandinavian countries has a romantic land-scape crisscrossed by waterways and dotted with thatched-roof houses. It is easy to imagine the trolls, werewolves, and sorcerers of Danish legend; Hans Christian Andersen was inspired by these legends to write his famous fairy tales.

The most accessible of the Scandinavian countries, **Denmark** is the only one attached to mainland Europe. North of Germany and south of Sweden and Norway, Denmark is made up of the Jutland Peninsula, which shares a border with Germany, and two major islands, Zealand and Funen. Altogether, the Danish islands number 480. Most are uninhabited.

The best way to meet the Danes

Through the **Meet the Danes** program, you can spend an evening in a Danish home in any of eight cities: Århus, Aalborg, Esbjerg. Fredericia, Lønstrup, Odense, Roskilde, or Skive. Local tourist offices can arrange the visit if you give them 24 hours notice. For more information, contact the **Danish Tourist Board**, *tel. (212) 949-2333.*

Copenhagen: the best fun

Copenhagen (København), on the east coast of the island of Zealand, is a city dedicated to entertainment. What other capital city revolves around an amusement park (**Tivoli Gardens**)? Merrymaking Danes of all ages scream with fear and excitement aboard Tivoli's rides. (The best is Det Flyvende Taeppe, or the Flying Carpet.) The famous Ferris wheel has a far-reaching view.

Built in 1843 on 20 acres in the heart of Copenhagen, Tivoli is more than just an amusement park. It has gardens, lakes, theaters, dance halls, games, bars, and scores of restaurants to suit every budget. At night it is illuminated by 100,000 colored lights, and you can enjoy vaudeville acts, concerts, music, and dancing.

Strøget: the best stroll in Denmark

The longest pedestrian thoroughfare in the world, the **Strøget** (Strolling Place) meanders through the heart of Copenhagen. This mile-long stretch is lined with cafés, banks, department stores, and boutiques selling everything from cheap T-shirts to fine Icelandic sweaters and expensive watches. The most elegant shops are clustered at the eastern end. The **Sweater Market**, *Frederiksberggade 15*, sells hand-knit designer sweaters.

The Strøget is actually an area made up of five streets: Frederiksberggade, Nygade, Vimmelskaftet, Amagertorv, and Ostergade. It is between the city's two main squares: Raadhuspladsen and Kongens-Nytorv. All this is made more confusing by the fact that "the Strøget" isn't marked as such on city maps.

The world's largest porcelain factory

The **Royal Copenhagen**, the largest porcelain factory in the world, has a shop on the Stroget at 6 Amagertorv. It is housed in a 16th-century Dutch Renaissance building and offers a fine collection of all four brand names of china. The Royal Copenhagen has been working at its craft for more than two centuries, producing elegant, hand-painted dinnerware and figurines.

The best amber and silver shopping

The best place on the Strøget to shop for amber and silver is the **Danish Silver Shop**, *2 Frederiksberggade*, which offers unique and elegant Scandinavian jewelry. Small amber heart-shaped pendants and solid amber necklaces are half the price charged in other countries.

The two best museums

Copenhagen has 40 public museums and galleries, most within easy walking distance of the Strøget. The largest is the **Nationalmusseet** (National Museum), which has the best display of Viking artifacts in the world. It is behind the Christiansborg Palace, where Parliament meets.

Nearby is **Ny Carlsberg Glypotek**, which has extensive collections of Roman, Etruscan, and Egyptian art, as well as a respectable number of Impressionist paintings. Its arboretum is a tranquil place where you can sit beneath immense trees and listen to a Gregorian chant.

A beer lover's best

If you love beer and don't mind crowds, visit the **Carlsberg** and **Tuborg** breweries. The tours and beer are free, and it's always a good time—especially after a few tastes.

Copenhagen's two castles

Rosenborg, *Oster Voldgade 4A*, a 17th-century castle, houses the crown jewels and the royal treasures of the Danes. **Amalieborg Castle**, *Amalieborg Square*, is the residence of the royal family. Witness the changing of the guard daily at noon.

Capital nightlife

Copenhagen is a chic city with a nightlife that is sure to satisfy any traveler; the only problem is keeping up with all there is to do in the capital city. Two of the most popular nightclubs are **Rust**, *Guldbergsgade 8*, and **Vega**, *Enghavevej 40*. If a nightclub is not exactly your pace, there are plenty of other good night spots to choose from; visit *www.visitcopenhagen.dk*.

The cheapest way to go

The major problem with Copenhagen is that it is expensive. The best way to cut costs is by buying the **Copenhagen Card**, available from the **tourist office**, *22 H.C. Andersen Blvd.*, train stations, Copenhagen's hotels, and travel agents. The card gives you free entry into museums, free bus and train travel, plus discounts on many of the city's attractions.

The best eating

Krog's Fiskerestaurant, *tel. (45)3-315-89-15*, across the canal from Christiansborg, is the best seafood restaurant. For Danish and French cuisine, try **Kommandanten**, *tel. (45)3-312-09-90; website: www.kommandanten. dk*. For Danish cooking with inspiration from abroad, try **Restaurant Thorvaldsen**, *tel. (45)3-332-04-00; website: www.thorvaldsens-hus.dk*.

The best hotels

D'Angleterre, *tel. (45)3-312-0095*, is the oldest and most fashionable hotel in Copenhagen, located at the far end of the walking street, Strøget. The hotel also houses a good French restaurant and a popular nightclub. The **Scandinavia**, *tel. (45)3-396-50-50*, is a large, ultramodern skyscraper hotel run by SAS (the Scandinavian airline). This hotel caters to those preferring Scandinavian modern over Scandinavian provincial. The **Savoy Hotel**, *tel. (45)3-326-75-00*, is a very old, but modernized hotel that has retained its Old World charm. Here, style and service with a smile are still the order of the day.

Roskilde: the first capital

The ancient city of **Rosklide**, west of Copenhagen, was the capital of Denmark until 1445. It is also the site of the first Danish church, built in A.D. 960. Members of Denmark's royalty are buried in marble and alabaster tombs in the 12th-century cathedral (known as the Westminster Abbey of Denmark), including Harald the Bluetooth, a 10th-century king; Margarethe, once queen of Scandinavia; and Christian X, the Danish king during World War II who wore a yellow star to demonstrate his sympathy for the Jews.

The **Vikingskibshallen** (Viking Ship Museum) at Havnen displays five Viking ships painstakingly pieced together from hundreds of pieces of wreckage. An amazingly well-preserved seagoing cargo ship from A.D. 1000 sits in the main hall.

Lindenborg Kro, *Holbaekvej 90*, just outside Roskilde, is one of the most pleasant inns in Denmark. The original inn, built 300 years ago, burned in 1967, but a new one was built on the site.

Denmark's best castles

If you see only one castle in your lifetime, it should be **Frederiksborg**. This 17th-century treasure trove in Hillerød is surrounded by a moat and has an ornate, gilded chapel with a rare 1610 Compenius organ. Here, Danish kings were crowned. The castle houses the most important national history museum. Every square foot is covered with art and antiques, including four-poster beds, ebony cabinets, coats of arms, and tapestries.

Kronborg Castle at Elsinore is the bleak and imposing castle where Shakespeare set *Hamlet*. It has secret passages and turrets, exactly as you would imagine. Built in 1574 and restored in 1629, it now houses the Danish Maritime Museum.

Nyborg Castle, on the island of Funen, is the oldest royal castle still standing in Scandinavia and is believed to have been built in the 12th century. Until the 15th century, the moated castle guarded one of the most strategic spots in the country. Be sure to see the knight's hall and the old danehof, which was used by the medieval parliament, an uneasy alliance between noblemen and clergy. Nyborg can be reached by ferry from Zealand.

Egeskov, near Odense, is the best-preserved moated castle in Europe. A Renaissance structure with magnificent gardens, it was built in 1554 on oak pillars in the middle of a small lake. Legend tells of a maiden who bore an illegitimate child to the young nobleman of the castle and was locked in one of the castle towers from 1559 to 1604. The landscaped gardens are open to the public every day. But the castle itself is a private home and can only be visited during chamber music concerts held during the summer.

Denmark's best bike route

The **Haervejen** (pronounced Hairvine), a marked bike trail, follows an ancient military road along Denmark's spine. It leads through the center of Jutland past *menhirs* (large monumental stones erected by prehistoric Danes), barrows (mounds of earth or stones over burial sites), rune stones etched with characters from the ancient Scandinavian alphabet, and churches built by the first Danish Christians.

The trail runs 170 miles from Viborg in central Jutland to the Eider River in Germany. For centuries, it was the only road connecting Scandinavia with continental Europe. For more information, contact the **Danish Tourist Board**, *website: www.dt.dk*, or the local tourist board in Svendborg, *tel. (45)62-22-25-33*.

A kids' best

Families traveling through Copenhagen should set aside at least one day to visit Denmark's unique theme park, **Legoland**. Specially trained Lego artists used more than 33 million Lego blocks to create 25 acres of colorful fantasy land. Most of the exhibits, displaying historical sights and events from all over the world, are scaled down to one-twentieth of the real-life size. For more information on Legoland, *tel. (45)75-33-13-33; website: www.lego.com*.

The two prettiest Baltic islands

Ærø, a tiny island in the Baltic, is the best place to get a glimpse of the traditional Danish seafaring life. A five-hour trip from Copenhagen by train and then ferry, it is one of many Danish islands in the archipelago north of the German coast.

Brightly painted little fishing villages fringe this 22-mile-long island. Its picturesque beaches are occasionally dotted with nude sunbathers. Inland, thatched-roof farmhouses break the rolling hills. The villages are tiny, but they usually have hotels and bakeries.

Ærøskøbing, on Ærø, is Denmark's most carefully preserved medieval village, dating from the 13th century. Its narrow cobblestoned streets are lined with gingerbread houses roofed with round tiles and painted blue or red. They were once the homes of Ærø's sea captains.

Bornholm, a Danish island between Sweden and Poland, has the world's finest-grained sand and is known for its grandfather clocks and smoked herring. The island's towns balance on sloping rocks. The ruins of a 13th-century castle can be explored at Hammershus Slot. And half-timbered houses and ancient round churches, once used as protection against pirates and enemy armies, still stand here. The greatest round church is in Ølsker. Built in 1150, the structure is literally round.

The best natural sight on the island is at **Rø**, a 72-foot rock formation filled with columns, caves, and crevices. Its name means Sacred Thing.

The most beautiful beach is in Dueodde on the south coast, where the sand is incredibly fine, dunes rise 45 feet, and there is a 145-foot lighthouse. If you tire of the sea, explore Bornholm's forest, Almindingen, the third-largest in Denmark.

The bluest light in Scandinavia

Skagen, a harbor village at the top of the Jutland Peninsula, was discovered by a group of painters in the middle of the 19th century who were drawn here by the unique play of light in this area of Scandinavia. As one Skagen painter said, "Where two seas meet, the light can't help but be the bluest in creation."

For the cheapest meals in Skagen, go around the red tackle houses to the opposite side. This is where the Danes purchase their seafood, and anything you get here will be good.

NORWAY: THE MOST RUGGED

Norway, with the second-lowest population density in Europe, is the most rugged Scandinavian country. It has deep-gouged, sharp mountains rising from the jagged coastlines and frigid glaciers glittering beneath the midnight sun. Grass-thatched houses occupy little patches of land on steep hillsides. This is a country that challenges the sportsman, with superb skiing, hiking, sailing, orienteering, hunting, and mountain climbing.

Oslo: the world's most forested capital

Oslo, the capital of Norway, is the most heavily forested capital in the world—encompassing farms as well as nightclubs. The 175-square-mile city was founded in the 11th century by Viking King Oslo. Because it was completely destroyed by fire in 1824, little medieval architecture remains. The finest residences that survived are along Raadhusgate.

Oslo's most dramatic sight

Akershus Castle, the ancient protector of the city, looms from atop a cliff that juts out into the eastern half of the harbor. The well-preserved medieval structure (built in 1300 by King Haakon V Magnusson) was an impregnable fortress and royal residence for several hundred years. Although it has suffered through nine battles, it was never conquered and eventually was transformed into a Renaissance palace by Danish-Norwegian King Christian IV.

Today, the castle is used by the government for state occasions. The bastions offer tremendous views of Oslo. Inside, some of the works of Expressionist painter Edvard Munch are on display.

Scandinavia's oldest church

The oldest church in Scandinavia, **Gamle Aker Kirke**, *Akersbakken 26*, is still in use after 890 years. Daily services are held May 15 through Sept. 10, and Sunday services are held year-round (at 11 a.m.). You can visit the church with an appointment Tuesday's and Thursdays. The tour is free.

Top sights

Next to Akershus Castle is the **Norsk Hjemmefrontmuseum**, Norway's Resistance museum, which documents World War II and Norway's resistance to the Nazi's.

Domkeirken (Oslo's cathedral), *Stortorvet*, built between 1694 and 1699, has its original altarpiece and pulpit. The stained-glass windows were created by the Norwegian artist Emanuel Vigeland (the younger brother of Norway's most famous sculptor Gustav Vigeland). The bronze doors and ceiling decorations are also impressive, and the cathedral's organ rises five floors. Sunday services are at 11 a.m. and 7:30 p.m.

Raadhused, Oslo's city hall, completed in 1950, was embellished in a collective effort by Norway's greatest artists and designers. Inside are more than 2,000 square yards of bold, colorful murals, including Munch's *Life*. The walls are a rainbow of colorful stones and woods.

Norway's most memorable sculptures are at **Frognerparken**, a 75-acre park devoted to the works of Gustav Vigeland. In 1921, the city gave the sculptor free rein in the park. The result: a 1,150-piece collection of huge, writhing nude figures illustrating the human struggle. The works were once the subject of much controversy.

The best of the Vikings

Three Viking burial ships excavated on the shores of the Oslo fiord, the clay from which had preserved them since A.D. 800 and A.D. 900, are kept at the **Vikingsskiphuset** (Viking Ship House), *Huk Aveny 35; tel. (47)2-21-35-280*, on the Bygdøy Peninsula. The most spectacular is the *Oseberg*, a 64-foot dragon ship with animals carved on its prow. It is believed to have been the burial ship of Harald Fairhair's grandmother and her slave, who were buried in it along with 15 horses, an ox, four dogs, and some artifacts.

The greatest Norwegian adventure

The balsa-log raft *Kon Tiki*, on which Norwegian scientist Thor Heyerdahl sailed 5,000 miles in 1947, is kept at the **Kon Tiki Museum** on the Bygdøy Peninsula. The *Kon Tiki*, designed according to specifications for early Peruvian boats, sailed from Callao, Peru to Raroia, Polynesia to prove that pre-Inca Indians could have crossed from South America to populate Polynesia.

The museum also houses the papyrus *Ra II*, in which Heyerdahl crossed the Atlantic from North Africa to Barbados in 1970, and artifacts from his voyage to Easter Island.

A close-up view of folk life

Over 100 historic buildings from all over Norway have been transported to the **Norsk Folkemuseum** (Norwegian Folk Museum), a 35-acre area on the Bygdoy Peninsula. Sights there include *Taulandstua*, one of the oldest wooden dwellings in the country; a hand-built wooden stave church that dates back to 1200; historic log cabins; Lapp artifacts; and a reconstruction of the last apartment of Norwegian playwright Henrik Ibsen.

The highest lookout in Scandinavia

For a dizzying view, climb to the lookout tower at **Tryvannstaarnet**. To get there, take the Holmenkollen subway near the National Theater in Oslo to the end of the line, Voksenkollenn. From there, it's a 15-minute walk uphill to Tryvannstaarnet, the highest lookout in Scandinavia.

Another 20-minute walk down the hill leads to the Holmenkollen ski jump, one of the most famous in the world and the site of Olympic competitions in 1952. At the base of the jump is the **Ski Museum**, which displays 2,500-year-old ski equipment and equipment used on polar explorations.

Holmenkollen has the widest network of ski trails in the world (more than 1,300 miles of them, many with floodlights to allow nighttime skiing.) The best skiers in the world gather for **Holmenkollen Ski Festival** each winter to compete in downhill, slalom, cross-country, and ski jumping competitions, drawing thousands of spectators.

The best way to make friends

The **Know the Norwegians** program, sponsored by the **Oslo Travel Association**, *Raadhusgate 19*, and the Lions Club allows you to visit local English-speaking families. Invitations are not arranged during July and August when most Norwegians take a three-week summer holiday.

Eating well

Norwegian cuisine consists primarily of fish. The smoked salmon (*røklaks*) and mackerel (*røkmakrel*) are delicious. However, the meat, especially during fall hunting season, is equally good — try a reindeer or moose steak. The Norwegian *koldtbord* is a buffet that includes everything from herring to roast beef. In Sweden, it's known as a *smørgasbord*.

The best seafood restaurant in Oslo is **La Mer**, *Pilestradet 31; tel. (47)2-20-34-45*. It is open every day except Sunday after 4 p.m.

Mølla, *Sagveien 19; tel. (47)2-37-54-50*, a fish and game restaurant in an old textile mill on the banks of Akerselva River, was the setting for Oskar Braaten's novels about factory workers at the beginning of the century. It is open daily except Sunday after 3 p.m. Reservations are necessary.

Étoile, *Karl Johans Gate 31; tel. (47)2-42-93-90*, on the top floor of the Grand Hotel, has a beautiful view and serves savory French and Norwegian food. It is open daily from noon until midnight.

Tostrupkjelleren, *Karl Johans Gate 25; tel. (47)2-42-14-70*, is a basement restaurant popular with politicians, journalists, and business people.

Noberto, *Majorstuveien 36; tel. (47)2-46-02-02*, specializes in nouvelle cuisine and is a pleasant respite from traditional Norwegian dishes, although some find its basement locale a distraction.

Oslo nights

Oslo doesn't have enough hotels to house all its visitors, so make reservations well in advance, especially if you are visiting during the summer.

The **Holmenkollen Park Hotel Rica**, *Kongeveien 26, Holmenkollasen; tel. (47)2-29-22-000*, has cozy albeit tiny rooms with views of the city. The public salon has a huge fireplace, and the exceptionally attractive restaurant serves Norwegian specialties.

The **Scandinavia**, *Holbergs Gate 30; tel. (47)2-21-13-000*, is Norway's largest hotel. Very centrally located near the royal palace, its rooms have views of the city and the fiord. It has a pool, five restaurants, and several bars.

The **Hotel Continental**, *Stortingsgaten 24-26, 0161 Oslo 1; tel. (47)2-28-24-000*, has been owned by the same family for generations. It enjoys an excellent reputation as one of the best hotels in Scandinavia.

Many consider **The Grand Hotel**, *Karl Johans Gate 31; tel. (47)2-32-12-000*, Oslo's most prestigious hotel. It has spacious rooms, character suites (if you have the money, stay in its Tower Suite, one of the finest anywhere), and charming eateries. Esther Williams stayed here, as did Diana Ross, and Miles Davis.

The best sights outside Oslo

Fredrikstad, a fortified town with ramparts, a drawbridge, and a moat, has a flourishing artists' colony. The cobblestoned streets are lined with 18th-century houses and artisans' workshops. You can take an hour-long guided tour of the workshops weekdays between 9 a.m. and 3 p.m. Outside town is the 17th-century Kingsten Fort, which has secret passages and dungeons.

Tonsberg, Norway's oldest town (founded in A.D. 870), is where Norwegian kings were once crowned. The **Vestfold Folk Museum** at the town's entrance contains relics of the once-mighty whaling industry and of Viking chieftains. A trip to Tonsberg can be combined with a trip to **Sandefjord**, once a great whaling town. This summer resort is just two hours by express train from Oslo. Old whalers work as guides in the **Whaling Museum**, relating stories about the whaling days and explaining the sights.

A 13th-century Norwegian stave church is located in **Heddal**, southwest of Oslo. Only 32 of these tiered timber churches with their pointy shingled roofs are still standing.

The **Brakanes Hotel**, *N-5730*, at Hardanger Fjord in *Ulvik, tel. (47)5-52-61-05*, gives you an incredible view of the fiords.

Bergen: a music lover's best

If you like Grieg's music, you'll love **Bergen**. The city's native son left traces wherever he went. And you can hear his music at the ultramodern **Grieg Hall**, which seats 1,420.

Grieg's music is also played during the international arts festival held in Bergen during the last week in May. (The festival also features opera, ballet, and folklore.) Details are available from the **Festival Office**, *Grieghallen, Lars Hilles Gate 3A; tel. (47)5-230-010*.

Climb up to **Troldhaugen**, the summer villa of the composer in Hop, outside Bergen. The Victorian house contains Grieg's Steinway grand piano (which is used for concerts given at the house during the annual festival). The composer created many of his best works in the cottage on the estate. Grieg and his wife are buried in a cliff grotto here.

Bergen was the seat of the Viking kingdom of Norway until the 14th century and was a member of the Hanseatic League, which linked free towns in northern Germany and adjacent countries for trade and protection. Most of ancient Bergen was destroyed by a fire in 1702. A row of Hanseatic timbered houses, rebuilt along the waterfront after the fire, is all that remains. This area, called **Bryggen**, houses the **Hanseatic Museum**, which illustrates commercial life in Bergen hundreds of years ago.

The oldest building in Bergen, dating back to the 12th century, is a Romanesque church called **St. Mary's**. The baroque pulpit, donated by Hanseatic merchants, is covered with carved figures symbolizing the Virtues. Visit during one of the free organ concerts held at 8 p.m. on Thursday evenings in the summer.

The **Fantoft Stave Church**, built in 1150, is covered with both pagan and Christian designs—serpents, dragons, and crosses. It was built to withstand the winter wind and has overlapping roofs and interlocking gables.

THE BEST OF SWEDEN

Progressive, wealthy **Sweden**, the fourth-largest nation in Europe, is sparsely inhabited. This California-sized country is made up of wheat plains, pine forests, thatched and timbered villages, cosmopolitan cities, historic islands, mountains, waterfalls, 95,000 lakes, and miles of rugged coastline. Best of all, its capital, Stockholm, is the least-traveled and least-crowded of all European capitals.

Stockholm: Mother Nature's favorite

While **Stockholm** has museums and fine old buildings, the city's real attractions are natural: the waterways, the beaches, the parks, and the 24,000 little islands of the archipelago that lead to the Baltic Sea (most of them uninhabited). The city is built on 14 islands in Lake Malaren and, believe it or not, the waterways are clean enough for swimming.

The heart of the city

Founded 700 years ago, Stockholm's roots are visible in the twisting streets of the medieval Old Town, **Gamla Stan**. At the heart of the area is the **Stortorget** (the old marketplace), surrounded by little streets lined with thick-walled, crooked buildings, as well as boutiques, galleries, and inexpensive restaurants.

Top sights

To the east of Gamla Stan is **Djurgården** (Deer Park), a lake-encircled forested park. Stockholm's great estates and gardens are located here, as is the Royal Flagship *Wasa*, a man-of-war that sank 20 minutes into its maiden voyage in 1628.

Skansen, an open-air museum on Djurgarden, displays more than 150 18th- and 19th-century buildings from all over Scandinavia, including windmills, manor houses, workshops, and a complete town quarter. At the old workshops, you can see how early printing, silversmithing, glassblowing, and leather making were done. During the summer, chamber music concerts are held at the Skogaholm manor house. At night you can dance in the outdoor pavilion.

The **Nordiska Museet** (Nordic Museum), also on Djurgården, is the world's best museum on Scandinavian life, with tools, clothing, and furnishings illustrating life from the 1500s to today.

The **Nationalmuseet** (National Museum), at the tip of a peninsula on Sodra Blasieholmshamnen, has works by Rembrandt and Rubens and a rare collection of Russian icons, most from the 1400s. Room 45 features the works of Rembrandt, including *Portrait of an Old Man* and *Portrait of an Old Woman*.

Stadshuset (the city hall), on the island of Kungsholmen, designed by Ragnar Ostberg, is one of the finest examples of modern architecture in Europe. The poet Yeats said of the building, "No architectural work comparable to it has been accomplished since the Italian cities felt the excitement of the Renaissance." Completed in 1923, the city hall is dominated by a lofty tower topped with three crowns, the symbol of the defunct Scandinavian Union. Its Golden Hall is decorated with 19 million pieces of pure gold mosaic. Banquets following the Nobel Peace Prize ceremony are held here. Climb the tower for a view of Stockholm's islands and waterways.

Drottningholm Palace, on Queen's Island in Lake Malaren, is the French-style, 17th-century palace of the royal family, surrounded by fountains and parks. The **Drottningholm Court Theater**, the best-preserved 18th-century theater in the world, is located on the palace grounds. Each summer, operas and ballets are staged with full 18th-century rigalia. For reservations, contact the theater, *P.O. Box 27050, S-10251, Stockholm*.

The **Moderna Museet** (Museum of Modern Art), on the island of Skeepsholmen, has works by Andy Warhol, Salvador Dali, Picasso, Braque, and Leger.

The best nights out

If you're interested in meeting someone of the opposite sex, the place to go in Stockholm is the **Café Opera**, located in the same buildings as the national opera across from the Grand Hotel and directly across the bridge from the royal palace. The Café Opera has a dance floor, a bar, and a casino, where men toss away thousands of kroner playing roulette while some of the most beautiful unattached females in the world dance with one another or sit lingering over drinks.

For a different kind of fun, stop by **Grona Lund's Tivoli** (not to be confused with Tivoli in Copenhagen). Enjoy the amusements and go up to the top of the revolving tower for a wide view of Stockholm. Tivoli is open April to September from 2 p.m. to midnight. **Jump In**, a disco in the park, attracts a lively crowd and is open from 8 p.m. to midnight.

Stockholm's best hotels

Nobel Peace Prize winners usually stay at Stockholm's finest, the **Grand Hotel**, *Sodra Blasieholmshamnen 8; tel. (46)8-221-020*. It is the best hotel in Sweden and one of the best in the world. The staff is intelligent, thoughtful, and prompt. This luxurious, expensive establishment faces the royal palace and has two restaurants and a bar. Ask for a room facing the water.

Runners-up to the Grand are the **Sergel Plaza**, *Brunkebergstorg 9; tel. (46)85-17-26-300*, the **Royal Viking**, *Vasagatan 1; tel. (46)81-41-000*, and the **Malardrottningen**, *Riddarholmen; tel. (46)8-54-51-87-80*, across from the Old City.

The **Diplomat**, *Strandvagen 7C; tel. (46)8-6635-800*, at the edge of the diplomatic quarter, is a small, sophisticated, expensive hotel furnished with antiques. It has a cocktail bar and an elegant teahouse.

Lady Hamilton, *Storkyrkobrinken 5, 2-111 40; tel. (46)8-234-680*, in the old town of Stockholm, has rooms furnished with nautical antiques. Nearby church bells mark every quarter hour, but you get used to them after a couple of nights.

If you are looking for a bargain that's full of charm, try **Hotel Anno 1647**, *Mariagrand 3, on the Island of Sodermalm; tel. (46)8-6440-480*. The old brick building that dates (surprise!) to 1647 was originally the home of a tailor who achieved a senior position in his guild. It has a fine view of Gamla Stan.

Best restaurant, best wine cellar

The Swedes like to eat, which is why Stockholm has so many first-class resturants.

Ulriksdals Wärdshus, *Erlichstals Slottspark 1; tel. (46)8-85-08-15*, located on the grounds of a royal park a few miles outside Stockholm, has a sweeping view of gardens stretching down to the water. This might have been the setting for the movie *Elvira Madigan*. The current owner, Lauri Nilsson, is the ninth restaurateur to have run an establishment on this spot.

Nilsson has the best—and best engineered—wine cellar in Scandinavia. Press a button, and things happen. A tour takes you from one automated passage to another and finally into the inner sanctum, a kind of bacchanalian boardroom, where Sweden's most posh wine-tasting club gathers to chew bread and spit Mouton Rothschild into crystal bowls. At the center of the room is the pièce de résistance, a high-tech wine spittoon that seems to be a combination of a pagan baptismal and some cruel machine you would find in a dentist's office. The queen of Sweden comes here to taste champagne.

The food at **Ulriksdals Wärdshus** is superb. Chef Carl-Heinz Krucken specializes in preparing a butterfly of chopped avocado with Swedish caviar and chopped onions. For the main course, try the noisettes of reindeer with raisin and green peppercorn sauce. The cloudberry mousse dessert is delicious.

The best side trips from Stockholm

Sigtuna, founded at the beginning of the 11th century on the shores of Lake Malaren, is Sweden's oldest town, containing remnants of Vikings and early Christians. Low-timbered buildings line Storagatan. Sweden's first cathedral, St. Peter's, is here, along with the 13th-century Monastery of St. Maria.

Uppsala, Sweden's major university town, has a famous 15th-century cathedral and a 16th-century castle. The first Swedish university was founded here in 1477. (The university at Uppsala remains a well-respected institution.)

Walpurgis Eve, April 30, is the best time to visit Uppsala. Alumni and students wearing white caps celebrate the rebirth of spring and the death of winter with a torchlight parade and festivities until dawn. Thousands gather to join in hymns to celebrate the arrival of spring and to hear speeches about the end of winter.

Walpurgis Eve, according to folklore, is when witches ride. It is the night before the birthday of St. Walpurgis, the medieval protectress against magic.

Gamla Uppsala (the old quarter of Uppsala), two miles north of Uppsala, was once a sacred grove, where animals and people were sacrificed to Norse gods. The Viking burial grounds date back to the sixth century. Nearby, on the site of an old pagan temple, is a 12th-century church. An open-air museum illustrating the life of peasants is open June through August.

While you're in the area, visit **Odinsborg**, an old wooden inn where you can drink mead from silver-tipped ornamental oxhorns—as the Vikings once did centuries ago. Waitresses wear Viking breastplates over provincial dresses, old murals adorn the walls, the corner fireplace has copper kettles, and the main room is decorated with crude furniture.

Midsummer magic at its best

Darlarna Province in the heart of Sweden has preserved the rites of Midsummer (with a Christian touch, these days) as they were celebrated centuries ago. On **Midsummer Eve**, young people race through forests gathering birch boughs and wild flowers for the maypole. Once the pole is raised, villagers dance around it until dawn, weaving long ribbons that hang from the top.

In the morning, the townspeople go to church in rowboats decorated with greenery. A young girl will dream of her beloved on Midsummer Night if she places a bouquet containing seven wild flowers under her pillow. And if she looks into a reflecting pool on Midsummer Day, the next man she sees will be her loved one. The morning dew supposedly cures all ills.

The most colorful Midsummer celebrations are in the villages around Lake Siljan: Rattvik, Leksand, and Tallberg. In Siljansnas, a church boat race is held on Midsummer Day. In Hjortnas, traditional dancing takes place on the jetty the Saturday night following Midsummer.

Two simple but comfortable hotels in the region are the **Hotel Langbers**, *79303 Tallberg; tel. (46)247-50290*, and the **Romantik Hotel Tallbergsgarden**, *79303 Tallberg; tel. (46)247-50850*.

The world's oldest cross-country ski race

The town of **Mora**, about four-and-a-half hours north of Stockholm by car, is a peaceful place that comes alive suddenly once a year on the first Sunday in March. This is the day of the **Vasalöppet**, the world's biggest and oldest cross-country ski race. As many as 12,000 cross-country skiers race along the course, fueled by the blueberry soup, lime juice, and Swedish meatballs offered by spectators. If you are brave, a good skier, and in good condition, enter the race. For application forms, contact **Vasalöppet**, *Vasagatan 19, S-79200 Mora, Sweden; tel. (46)250-16000*. Arrangements can also be made through major travel agencies.

The rest of the year, you can cross-country ski more peacefully. Exquisite trails run along the frozen rivers and fields. Situated on the shores of Lake Siljan, Mora guarantees snow in the winter. It is about as far north as Anchorage.

The **Mora Hotel**, *tel. (46)250-117-50*, is the best place to stay. Room rates include dinner and breakfast. The hotel has a swimming pool, a sauna, a solarium, and a good restaurant called Terrassen.

Visby: the most medieval town

A massive, two-mile wall and 44 towers protect Sweden's best-preserved medieval town, **Visby**, on the country's largest island, Gotland. Punctuating its skyline are 100 churches, 91 of which were built before 1350. Known as the City of Roses, Visby is filled with the sweet-smelling flowers. Nearby are beautiful sand beaches that are remarkable for their marine stacks—piles of oddly shaped rocks sculpted by wind and water.

FINLAND: THE LEAST SPOILED SCANDINAVIAN COUNTRY

Finland is an unspoiled land with the cleanest air in Europe. Its historic towns and cities are simple, elegant, and brightly colored, and its countryside is covered with virgin forests and 62,000 freshwater lakes. Although the population is less than five million, this is the fifth-largest nation in Europe. The lengthy coastline is marked by coves and framed by 20,000 small islands. During the summer, Finland basks in perpetual sunshine.

Finns are known as great sailors and great magicians. Their language is not related to other Nordic tongues, except Lapp. The Finno-Ugric language family is more similar to Hungarian, Turkish, Estonian, and even Eskimo than to Swedish, Norwegian, or Danish. However, Finland has a Swedish-speaking minority, and most Finns have studied English.

Helsinki: where east meets west

The capital of Finland is located halfway between Russia and Sweden and shows signs of both Eastern and Western influences. It has been ruled by both over the centuries. The skyline is marked by the domes of the Lutheran cathedral and a Russian Orthodox Church.

A light-colored city built of white granite and surrounded by water on three sides, Helsinki is carefully laid out, with 240 parks and scores of modern buildings, such as the Temppeliaukion Church—an underground church blasted from solid rock and decorated with purple wood and copper.

The city's most imposing sight

The approach to Helsinki by sea is guarded by the 18th-century **Suomenlinna Fortress.** You can walk the fortress' old ramparts, visit its gardens, and have lunch in its open-air cafés.

A bit of the East

In front of the cathedral is **Senaatintori** (Senate Square), which is so reminiscent of Leningrad that many movies set in that city have been shot here, including *Reds*. The square even holds a statue of Czar Alexander II, a Russian ruler of Finland who is fondly remembered for allowing the Finns some independence. Also on the square is the oldest building in the city: the Sederholm residence, built in 1755.

The best picture of Finnish history

Finnish history is long and involved. A good place to begin absorbing it is the **Suomen Kansallismuseo** (National Museum), which has relics of the seafaring life of Viking times and the migration of the Finnish people northward 1,300 years ago. Located in a 22-year-old wooden building on Mannerheimintie, the city's main artery, the museum was designed by Eeno Saarinen. Opposite the museum is the ultramodern cultural center **Finlandia Hall**.

The world's best fur bargains

Furs are well-made and inexpensive in Finland, the world's biggest seller of farmed furs. Furriers there say you can easily buy a coat and pay for your trip to Finland for what it would cost to buy a similar coat in the United States, for example. Mink coats start at about $5,000; mink jackets at $2,000. In Helsinki, the best places to look are along the Pohjoisesplanadi and Etelaesplanadi, the northern and southern ends of the city's main shopping street, and in the shops at Station Tunnel and Hakaniemi Market Hall.

A sacred tradition: the sauna

Don't miss the chance to enjoy a Finnish sauna, a 2,000-year-old tradition that will make you feel euphoric. You take a sauna in a wood-lined room with layers of benches that climb toward the ceiling (the hottest are at the top). A stove heats the room to about 200 degrees Fahrenheit, and water is thrown on a layer of stones in the stove to produce steam.

Finns consider the oldest saunas the best. Built by early Finno-Ugric tribes, they are log cabins with earth floors, a pile of rocks above a fire, and no chimney.

Most saunas are built by the water—not surprising considering Finland has 188,000 lakes. Country saunas are stoked for hours, until the stones of the hearth are red-hot and the log walls have absorbed the heat and reflect it back.

If you're lucky, you'll be invited to take a sauna at the house of a native, which is a sign of hospitality. Because a sauna involves certain rules of etiquette, you should imitate your host. Allow him to create the first *loyly*, or vapor, by pouring water on the stove. Always ask other bathers if they are ready for a new cloud of steam before taking it upon yourself to create one.

If you're on your own (nearly every hotel has a sauna), take off your clothes and sweat. Then brush yourself lightly with birch branches. When you've had enough, dive into the frigid waters of a lake, roll around in the snow, or take a cold shower. (If you have a heart condition, you should skip the last step.) The ritual can be repeated three or four times. After the sauna, soap the perspiration off your body.

Don't take a sauna for at least one hour after a meal, and don't drink alcohol before a sauna—it strains the heart. Remove all jewelry, including rings and pierced earrings, because metal gets hot and can burn you.

The best saunas in Helsinki are at the Palace Hotel, the Kalastajatorppa, and the Hesperia. You don't have to be a guest, but you must book in advance.

The best—and most affordable—restaurant

The most delightful restaurant in Helsinki, composed of a wine cellar, a coffeehouse, and several dining rooms, is **Kappeli**, *Etela Esplanadi 1*. Housed in a glassed-in pavilion on the edge of a park, Kappeli is always crowded with local Bohemians chatting over coffee and enjoying the view. Wander around until a table opens up.

The best Russian restaurant in Finland

Saslik, *Neitsytpolku 12; tel. (358)0-170-544*, is a little crowded but very cozy. The *zakuski*, assorted appetizers for two, include several smoked, cured, and fresh varieties of fish, caviar with sour cream, meats, cheeses, and vegetables. An order of *zakuski* can be a meal in itself. For dessert, try the homemade Samarkand ice cream.

The best hotel in Finland

The **Hotel Strand Inter-Continental**, *John Stenbergin ranta 4, 00530 Helsinki*, overlooks the harbor of Helsinki and is ideally located next to the exciting Old City. The Botanical Gardens and the market square are also nearby. But more than a prime location, the Strand offers outstanding service and comfort as well as a popular sauna on the top floor. To make a reservation from the United States, *call (800)332-4246*.

The best side trips

One of Finland's greatest surviving castles is the citadel at **Hämeenlinna**. Built over a long period of time and used for many purposes, including a prison, it displays a collection of Finnish art. Composer Jan Sibelius was born in this town; his house is a museum displaying his violin, his family's piano, and photos. One of the town's centuries-old wooden buildings houses a historical museum.

Operas are staged in the courtyard of **Olvinlinna Castle** in Savonlinna each July by the Finnish National Opera. Begun in 1475, the castle stands on a small island in a passage connecting two large lakes. You can stop by the festival **ticket office**, *Puistokatu 3; tel. (358)57-244-84*, about 4 p.m. on the day of the performance to see if tickets are available.

The largest church in the world is in **Kerimaki**, near Savonlinna. The 150-year-old church seats 3,600 people. Strange, considering the town's population is 2,900. According to legend, the builders were tipsy when they began working on the church. They misread centimeters as inches, making the structure two-and-a-half times the size planned by the architect.

LAPLAND: EUROPE'S LAST WILDERNESS

Lapland, where the tundra never completely thaws and the winter darkness is broken only by the glimmering aurora borealis, stretches across the northern halves of Norway, Sweden, and Finland. This is Europe's last true wilderness, suffering long, cold, dark winters. During the summer, however, it is eerily beautiful under the Midnight Sun, reflected by glaciers, waterfalls, rivers, lakes, and mountains. For six weeks in June and July, the sun never sets.

A nomadic group, the Lapps (who call themselves Sami), lives on this land. They herd reindeer for a living and retain old traditions long forgotten elsewhere in Scandinavia. Some Lapps still wear traditional costume of blue felt with contrasting bands of red, yellow, and green, often decorated with embroidery. Men wear the "caps of four winds," with four floppy points. Women wear red felt bonnets with flaps over the ears.

Try the Lapp specialties: *poro* (reindeer meat), *lohi* (salmon), and *siika* (whitefish). Also taste the local liqueurs and desserts made from Arctic cloudberries.

The northernmost point in Europe

Nordkapp, Norway's North Cape, is the northernmost point in Europe, the place where the sun doesn't sink below the horizon for half of May and all of June. This mountain plateau rises 1,000 feet out of the ocean—a bleak but beautiful black cliff. In August, when the sun dips below the horizon for a few minutes, the sky is lit by the Northern Lights, a rainbow of spectacular colors. Even though most people come in July to see the Midnight Sun, August is still the best time to visit. The North Cape is snowbound until early June.

Nordkapp is on Mageröy, an island about 15 miles north of **Honningsvaag**, the northernmost village in the world. During the summer, a Lapp camp with reindeer herds is usually set up at Nordmannset, a little more than a mile outside Honningsvaag.

The northernmost hotel in this northernmost region is the **Sas**, *tel. (47)84-72331*, in Honningsvaag. A modern place, it has great views. Make reservations in advance.

The best of Finnmark

Several towns bring civilizations of a sort to **Finnmark** (Norwegian Lapland). **Tromsø** is the best base for trappers, whalers, sealers, and polar explorers. (It is also home to Greenpeace, the international volunteer organization that crusades for the environment.)

The **Arctic Church**, one of the most impressive pieces of modern architecture in the world, is in Tromsø. Built across the longest suspension bridge in Scandinavia (1,100 yards), it is shaped like an iceberg and made of aluminum that reflects the Midnight Sun.

The best way to visit the Lapps

The town of **Alta** in Finnmark is the best base for excursions into Lapp country. Most Lapps live on the tundra south of here. In Masi, about 44 miles from Alta on the main road to Finland, they wear traditional costumes, although many have taken up a modern way of life.

During the winter, the Lapps live inland. In May and June, they migrate to the coast as they have for centuries, herding thousands of reindeer across rivers and fiords—a spectacular sight. Colorful reindeer roundups usually take place between September and February.

The **Alta Gjestestue**, *tel. (46)864-35-336*, in Alta is an inviting guesthouse.

The best of Norrland

Norrland, the Swedish word for Swedish Lapland, covers half the area of Sweden. One-quarter of the country is north of the Arctic Circle, and about 10,000 Lapps live here. It is easier to reach than you might imagine. Trains come here from Stockholm. Postal buses continue even farther north and connect with smaller villages and settlements. You can fly to the airports at Umeå, Luleå, and Kiruna. Or you can drive there on Road E4.

Arvidsjaur is modern but has an old Lappish center, with well-preserved, cone-shaped huts. Reindeer are rounded up here in June and July. Pine forests surround the town.

Norrbotten is a Lapp trading and cultural center. A market is held here the first week of February, when traditional Lapp handicrafts (delicately carved wooden utensils, silver jewelry, and colorful and elaborate woven fabrics) are sold.

Kvikkjokk is the gateway to Sarek National Park, the largest wilderness in Europe. There are no roads or trails in the park.

The best hiking trails

Svenska Turistföreningen (the Swedish Touring Club), *tel. (46)8-46-32100; website: www.stfturist.se*, maintains hotels and marked hiking routes for hundreds of miles through Swedish Lapland. About 80 cabins are available with beds and bedding, cooking utensils, and firewood. The cabins can be used for one or two nights only.

Swedish hikers prefer the **Kungsleden,** or Royal Trail, the longest marked trail in the world, leading from the resort of Abisko to Jakkvik, a total of 210 miles. Cabins are spaced a day apart along the trail, which follows the old nomadic paths of the Lapps.

The National Swedish Environmental Protection Board owns several basins in **Padjelanta National Park.** The mountain's park is known for its unusual flora and many lakes.

The best of Finnish Lapland

Finnish Lapland, the largest and most northerly of Finland's provinces, occupies one-third the area of Finland and lies almost entirely above the Arctic Circle. It adjoins the Lapland districts in neighboring Norway and Sweden, but the landscape contrasts sharply. Some parts are barren, while others are covered by vast forests of pine and spruce and watered by rushing rivers. There are only about four people per square mile.

About 3,500 Sami, or Lapps, live in the northernmost parishes: Utsjoki, Enontekiö, Inari, and Sodankylö. Until the seventh century, Lapps inhabited all of Finland. After the arrival of the Finns from the Volga, they retreated to the north, where they continue their traditional ways.

Finland's best hiking

In the summer, hiking expeditions are led through Lapland by experienced guides. Don't attempt an independent excursion unless you really know what you're doing. And bring the right equipment—boots; protective, warm clothing; and maps, which can be obtained from the **Map Center,** *Karttakeskus, Pasilan Virastokeskus, Opastinsilta 12, 00520 Helsinki.*

A marked 49-mile hiking trail called **Karhunkierros** (the Bear's Ring) runs near Kuusamo, about 124 miles from Oulu, just south of the polar circle. You don't need a guide to follow the clearly marked trail, which passes the most dramatic scenery in the area. You can spend the night free in huts along the trail. However, in July and August, it is a good idea to carry a tent in case the huts are full. Bring food and mosquito repellent as well. Traveling the entire circle takes four to six days. (Shorter trails are also marked.)

The best base for exploring Lapland

Rovaniemi, the capital of Lapland, is a good base for explorations. This modern town five miles south of the Arctic Circle is easy to reach by train or plane from Helsinki. **Lapin Matkailu**, *Maakuntakatu 10, 96100 Rovaniemi, tel. (358)60-346052*, has a reservation service.

The best adventure: Lapland in the winter

If you like romping in the snow, you'll love Lapland in the winter. Days and nights are spent cross-country skiing, taking reindeer rides, and whizzing across the powder in snowmobiles. Light from the stars and moon reflects off the snow, providing enough visibility for these activities 24 hours a day.

The terrain makes for some of the finest cross-country skiing in the world. Competitive skiers come here from around the world to train. Lapland offers a vast network of maintained ski tracks. Seasoned skiers can book a cabin in one of the fell regions and take on the unmarked country-side. Caution! If you are going out into the wilderness, hire a guide. This is a wild, isolated, and frozen netherworld, and you could easily become lost forever. Arrange guides through the **Finnish Tourist Board**, *655 Third Ave., New York, NY 10017; tel. (212)370-5540.*

A reindeer safari is a great way to discover the land. On a guided trip, you are given a sled (a canoe-shaped contraption of wood planks) and a reindeer. The reindeer wears a harness, which is attached to the sled with a colorful braid. Tucked into blankets, you control the critter with a single rope.

A reindeer safari can last from 20 minutes to an entire week—it's up to you. The longer excursions are definitely for the hardy—you sleep in a tent or cabin and eat reindeer meat (which can be tough) cooked over an open fire.

To explore Lapland at a faster pace, take a snowmobile safari. You wear enormous Arctic overalls, sled shoes, gloves, and a hat. The cold, dry air is exhilarating as you fly through the forests and across the frozen lakes.

THE BEST OF SPAIN

I WOULD SOONER BE A FOREIGNER IN SPAIN THAN IN MOST COUNTRIES.
HOW EASY IT IS TO MAKE FRIENDS IN SPAIN!...I DEFY ANYONE TO BE
THROWN AS I WAS AMONG THE SPANISH WORKING CLASS AND NOT
BE STRUCK BY THEIR ESSENTIAL DECENCY; ABOVE ALL,
THEIR STRAIGHTFORWARDNESS AND GENEROSITY.
—*George Orwell*, Homage to Catalonia

Spain is the most exotic West European nation. Although it is linked to the European continent at the French border, in many ways it feels more like North Africa. Not until the reign of Ferdinand and Isabella in the 15th century did Spain become part of Europe culturally. But when it did finally join hands with Europe, it became a great power, colonizing much of the world.

No longer mighty, Spain still has Roman ruins, Moorish fortresses, and early Christian cathedrals. The landscape is ruggedly beautiful, the traditions colorful, and the art collections among the greatest in the world. A tour of Spain will lead you from Madrid's gigantic Prado Museum, which rivals the Louvre as the best museum in the world, to the rich and elaborate Alhambra, idyllic sandy beaches, and quaint fishing villages.

MADRID: SPAIN'S MOST COSMOPOLITAN CITY

Madrid is a cosmopolitan city with museums, elegant restaurants, and trendy discos. It is worth visiting, despite its pollution problem. Situated more than 10,000 feet above sea level, Madrid is filled with trucks and cars spewing hydrocarbons unhindered by any anti-pollution devices.

The most picturesque quarter

The most picturesque section of Madrid is the labyrinth of narrow streets between **Puerta del Sol** and the **Royal Palace**. Each street has a sign depicting an activity that distinguished it in the past. For instance, Pasadizo del Panecillo has a picture of friars distributing bread to the poor. The best way to explore is on foot. You will find Velazquez's grand statue of Philip IV in the center of the Plaza de Oriente, east of the Royal Palace.

Have a glass of sangria in the vast and uniform old main square of Madrid, the **Plaza Mayor**, near the Royal Palace. You will be surrounded by 17th-century buildings with balconies and arches. Descend the stairway at the southwest corner of the plaza to an area filled with lively bars.

El Prado: the Louvre's greatest rival

✶**El Prado**, in the Plaza Canovas del Castillo, is Madrid's number-one attraction. One of the greatest museums in the world, it holds the cream of the collections of Spanish monarchs from the 16th through 19th centuries, including works by Velazquez, Goya, Murillo, El Greco, Breughal, Rubens, and Durer. The best time to visit the Prado is in the late afternoon, when the sun adds light to the somewhat dim interior.

The most remarkable work at the Prado is *Las Meninas* (Maids in Waiting), painted by Velazquez in 1656. This is a painting of the artist painting an unknown subject, probably the royal couple, who are reflected in a mirror behind him. He appears to be painting the viewer, however, because of his direct, straightforward gaze. The artist is surrounded by the royal entourage—the little infants, *las meninas*, or ladies-in-waiting, dwarves, and a dog.

The black Goyas, so called because of their dark backgrounds and tragic themes, are housed in a special gallery within the Prado. The Spanish resistance to Napoleon (1808 to 1814) is their theme.

On the ground floor is a special section with tapestries designed by Goya for the Escorial (see below) and his *Disasters of War* etchings, inspired by his experiences during the war agains Napoleon.

Opposite the Prado is the new Thyssen-Bornemiszka museum, which houses the collection of the German family formerly housed in Villa Favorita in Lugaro, as well as overflow from the Prado.

Madrid's most impressive palace

El Palacio Real (the Royal Palace) is a baroque structure created under Charles III in 1764. About 50 of the 2,800 rooms are open to the public. They are filled with chandeliers, floral-patterned wallpaper, and colorful rugs. In one room the walls and ceilings are covered with 400 panels of painted porcelain. One of the strangest sights in the palace is what appears to be a doll in a glass case in the private Royal Chapel. Actually, these are the bones of St. Felix, a Christian martyr, wrapped in wax and silk and made to look like a small person. The figure was a gift from the pope to Queen Isabella II.

The **Royal Library**, housed in the Palace holds more than 300,000 books, including 15th-century books, rare manuscripts, and Queen Isabella's prayer book.

You still can see bullet holes and other signs of the bloody Civil War of 1936-1938 in the tapestries, frescoes, and furniture at the Palacio Real. The victorious Franco regime decided to keep these as reminders of the war (but you won't find this information listed in guidebooks).

Madrid's best market

El Rastro, the flea market that starts at the Plaza Mayor and spills down Madrid's streets on Sunday, is a shopper's mecca. Vendors sell fine cotton shirts from India, Moroccan belts of brass and leather, leather bags, alabaster pots, and bootleg tapes of U.S. musicians, semiprecious stones, fossils, and antiques.

Throughout the flea market are gypsies who have a talent for spotting unwary tourists. They will pull you aside and offer you watches, jewelry, and electronic equipment at prices that are too good to be true. Be careful. These watchcases are often empty or filled with cheap materials. The jewelry is fake, and the electronic equipment usually doesn't work. But if they offer you leather goods, you may get a bargain. Look at the items carefully. If they interest you, offer the seller a tenth of the asking price. Haggle!

The best jogging

Parque del Retiro is a great place to take an early morning jog. Part of the park is designed to look like the pattern on a blue willow plate. Avoid the places designated *"Zona de perros en libertad"* (Zone of dogs in freedom)! You can also rent a rowboat or have a picnic.

The best bull in town

While bullfights may seem barbaric to animal lovers, the Spanish believe the odds between man and bull are even. They see bullfights as a match between man and the untamed elements. The Spanish sense of fair play in a bullfight can be gruesome to the uninitiated.

Bullfights can be seen nearly every Sunday and Thursday from Easter through October at **Las Ventas**, *Plaza de Toros Monumental*. Tickets can be purchased at the door. Shows usually start at 5 p.m. or 7 p.m. (Make sure you buy tickets for the shaded side of the ring, even though they are more expensive.)

Tapas—the world's best snacks

Madrileños don't eat dinner until very late—after 10 p.m. It is impossible to order dinner before 8 p.m. The solution is a little snack called a *tapa*. Madrileños, too, get hungry around 6 p.m., so they nibble on tapas (sardines, squid, octopus, olives, fried potatoes, sausage, shrimp, almonds, and any number of other delicious concoctions) with a glass of sherry or sangria in a tapas bar.

The most popular tapas are those made from *chorizo* (a Spanish sausage). The best are those that have been aged in a farmer's well and then cooked to kill the bacterial growth. Foreigners, however, should be careful with such local tapas. Build up a tolerance slowly for these new foods and their unusual bacterial elements. (Severe disorders have been reported by people who have overindulged in exotic fare on unacclimated stomachs.)

A small version of a tapa, a *pincho*, is usually served free with the first drink in any of Madrid's tapas bars, known as *mesones* and *tabernas*. The custom is to have only one drink per taberna and then move on to the next one. Many of the tabernas are located around the Plaza Mayor. Two classics are the **Meson de la Tortilla** and the **Meson del Champiñon**, on Cava de San Miguel.

Europe's disco capital

Spain's capital has more discos than anywhere else in Europe. They don't get going until midnight. The music tends to be about five years behind what's playing in London and New York.

If you enjoy dancing, you will have no problem finding your niche in one of the many nightclubs in Madrid.

The finest flamenco

Flamenco dancing has evolved into a unique art form in Madrid. Dinner nightclubs, such as the **Café de Chinitas**, *tel. (34)1-248-5135*, have superb shows. Flamenco nightclubs can be expensive, however. Often you can watch a show free just by roaming the streets around the Plaza Mayor. Keep your eyes open; you might see an impromptu dance by an Andalusian Gypsy troupe. A good place to see flamenco dancers is the pedestrian street off Calle Serrano outside the Casa Inglese department store.

Spain's most luxurious hotel

Hotel Ritz, *Plaza de Lealtad 5; tel. (34)91-701-6767*, is unrivaled for luxury. The late King Alfonso XIII's favorite hotel was built in 1910 to regal standards of luxury. Over the years, the hotel became a bit worn around the edges. It was restored in 1984 when a British hotel chain took over. All the old luxuries are still there (Limoges china, handwoven carpets, silverware) and some new ones have been added, such as individual temperature control for each room. The bathrooms at the Ritz are magnificent. Large bouquets of gladioli or exotic birds of paradise give color to the muted greens and grays of the rooms.

When you stay at the Ritz, you are served a breakfast of fresh croissants, Seville marmalade, and hot tea or coffee, served on immaculate white tablecloths with a little vase of pink carnations, shiny starched napkins, and polished silver.

Twice a day, the splendid bowl of fruit on your dressing table is replenished. It is accompanied by a knife, fork, napkin, and finger bowl in which geranium petals float.

The Ritz is in a splendid location, too. The Prado museums and shops are within walking distance.

A night at the Ritz isn't cheap, but you're paying for exquisite service and handsome surroundings. **Leading Hotels of the World**, *tel. (800)223-6800*, can make arrangements in the U.S.

The closest competition

Although topping the Ritz is impossible, Villa Magna and Miguel Angel come closest. Both are expensive luxury hotels with beautiful décor and first-class service.

Villa Magna, *Paseo de la Castellana 22; tel. (in the U.S.) (800)223-1234*, is quiet, despite its central locale. The hotel's garden is gorgeous, set beneath the balconied, nine-story structure. Rooms are large, with bathrooms, individual thermostats, and huge, comfortable chairs. The hotel is decorated with marble, glass, and stainless steel. The bar is cozy. The hotel also has an elegant lounge, a hairdresser, a sauna, and a shopping area.

Miguel Angel, *Miguel Angel 31; tel. (34)9-14-28-1999*, looks like an ice palace. Enormous chandeliers hang from the ceilings, and the balustrades are crystal. Silk spreads cover the beds, and plush carpet cushions the foot. Perhaps the nicest aspect of the hotel, however, is its marvelous indoor pool surrounded by white furniture.

The best luxury hotel without the high price

Undoubtedly the best place to stay in Madrid if you want to avoid the exorbitant price at the Ritz is the **Palace Hotel**, *tel. (in the U.S.) (800)228-3000*. You will still be pampered, but the rooms here cost about half as much as the rooms at the Ritz.

Sweet nights at sweet prices

Alcalá, *Alcalá 66; tel. (34)1-435-10-60*, is one of our favorites. Near the Retiro Park, it is cozy, with a circular hearth. Rooms are air-conditioned, and dual-glaze windows keep out the sounds of traffic. Full-length mirrors and walnut-paneled walls grace the bedrooms. The hotel restaurant is very good also, serving Basque specialties.

Spain's best restaurant

Zalacaín, *Alvarez de Baena 4; tel. (34)1-561-59-35*, with its 15 cooks, is one of the finest restaurants in Europe. Michelin was so impressed that it gave the elegant restaurant three stars. The food is imaginative and delicious. The restaurant is closed Saturday afternoons, Sundays, Holy Week, and in August.

Spain's restaurant capital

Madrid has become a restaurant capital in recent years. Hundreds of fine restaurants have opened, serving good regional dishes as well as seafood and international cuisine.

The best Castillian cuisine is served at **Casa Botín**, *Cuchilleros 17; tel. (34)1-266-42-17*, and **Posada de la Villa**, *Cava Baja 9; tel. (34)1-266-18-60*, both in Old Madrid. Castillian cuisine is known generally for its use of garlic, onions, and olive oil. Try the roast baby lamb and suckling pig. Both restaurants are more than 200 years old. The restaurants are closed for dinner on Sundays.

Casa Lucio, *Cava Baja 35; tel. (34)1-265-32-52*, is one of Madrid's oldest restaurants. Despite its unpretentious service and surroundings, this cozy establishment has attracted the king and the prime minister of Spain. It is closed Saturday afternoons and in August.

Cabo Mayor, *Juan Hurtado de Mendoza 11; tel. (34)1-250-87-76*, is elegant. One of its best dishes is *ensalada de rape y almejas*, paper-thin slices of raw monkfish and whole clams marinated in lemon, oil, and fennel. The salmon and corn salad is also good. The restaurant is closed Sundays and from Aug. 15 through Sept. 2.

El Amparo, *Callejon de Puigcerda 18, corner of Jorge Juan; tel. (34)1-431-64-56*, in the exclusive residential neighborhood known as Barrio de Salamanca, serves the unique cuisine of chef Ramon Ramirez, French and Basque. The house wines are exceptional and fairly priced. The restaurant is closed Saturday afternoons, Sundays, Holy Week, and in August.

Horcher, *6 Alfonso XII; tel. (34)1-522-07-31*, one of the most elegant restaurants in Madrid, serves unusual game dishes. The restaurant is closed Sundays.

Jockey, *Amador de los Rios 6; tel. (34)1-319-10-03*, is a fine restaurant that serves Spanish and French dishes.

The Spanish passion: paella

Paella—a delicious concoction of rice with seafood and spices—is a national passion in Spain. It is generally served in huge, heavy black skillets and comes in two varieties: *valenciana* has chicken, sausage, and seafood; *mariscos* has only seafood.

The place for *paella* in Madrid is **El Pescador**, *José Ortega y Gasset 75; tel. (34)91-40-21-290*, an informal restaurant in Old Madrid near the Puerta del Sol. Long communal tables are shared by diners, who serve themselves paella from large pots. If you stop by in midafternoon, you will see fishermen with weathered faces peeling freshly caught seafood for the evening's *paella*.

The best way to get around

The best way to get around Madrid is the city's fast and efficient subway. Buy your tickets at booths and machines in the stations for less than a dollar a ride. Tickets are inserted into electronic turnstiles that let you enter the system. Don't throw away your ticket—you'll need it to get back out again. The subway is open from 6:30 a.m. to 1 a.m.

Spain's most intimidating edifice

El Escorial, on a mountain northwest of Madrid, is a 16th-century monastery-palace. It was the home of Phillip II, who commissioned the Armada to try to conquer England—they failed. A giant, gloomy building with hundreds of rooms and thousands of windows, it is full of history, art, and rare manuscripts. Almost all of Spain's royalty is entombed here, as well as a number of saints, in a cavernous, black-marble room.

Trains to the palace leave 20 times a day from the Atocha station in Madrid. A bus takes visitors from the station to the palace.

Spain's best medieval walled town

Avila, Spain's most beautiful walled town, is just 90 minutes from Madrid. Perched on a crest and enclosed within massive 38-foot-high walls, Avila is the highest provincial capital in Spain. Six archways lead into this austere and intimidating town, and 90 towers keep watch over the area. It was also the town of St. Teresa, the 16th-century mystic and reformer.

The town has a handful of main tourist sights: the cathedral, the Convent of St. Teresa, and the Basilica of St. Vincent. Visit these first and then explore the streets at random. The best view is from the town walls on the edge of Avila's *parador*, or government-run hotel. Go through the parador's garden and climb the flight of stairs to the wall. You will see the River Adaja, the road to Salamanca, and the endless plain. A tourist information office is located opposite the cathedral on the main plaza.

TOLEDO: THE RICHEST HISTORY

Toledo, a city rich in history, is an hour's drive from Madrid. In the words of Gerald Brennan in *2* (1950), "Like Fez, it reeks of the Middle Ages; like Lhasa, of monks."

Lording over the city is a fortress called the **Alcazar**. El Cid, the Lord Champion of the 11th century, whose courageous deeds were described in Spain's epic poem, lived here. Destroyed during the Spanish Civil War, the Alcazar has been reconstructed. It houses a museum of the Spanish Civil War.

Ferdinand and Isabella built a cathedral at the heart of Toledo in the 15th century and filled it with art, sanctuaries, and chapels. For a great view of the city and a small adventure, climb the cathedral's tower and examine its 18th-century bell, which is still in use.

El Greco left his mark on Toledo as well. His famous painting *The Burial of the Conde de Orgaz* is housed in Iglesia Santo Tome (St. Thomas Church) at Angel Santo Tome. The **El Greco House and Museum** (Casa y Museo del Greco), *Paseo del Transito*, contains paintings and memorabilia of the 16th-century artist.

A 14th-century synagogue called El Transito is down the street from El

Greco's house. It was once a house of worship for Jews in Toledo. During the Inquisition, it became a church, and its members were forced either to convert to Christianity or flee the country. A museum containing Sephardic religious articles is located in part of the synagogue.

Don't buy any tourist knicknacks in Toledo. Prices here are almost twice as high as elsewhere in Spain. The merchants stalk gullible foreigners.

The best view of this dramatic city is from the **Circunvalación**, a road that runs parallel to the Rio Tajo.

The best sword shopping

Don't leave Toledo without purchasing one of the city's world-famous swords or steel blades. For a good selection, visit **Fabrica Bermejo**, near the Santiago church beyond the Visagro gates, or **Fabrica Garido**, next to the city's bullring. **Real Fabrica de Armas**, about three miles from town on Highway N0401, is another good shop.

The best places to stay

Outside Toledo is a highly recommended *parador*. **El Parador Nacional Conde de Orgaz**, *Cerro del Emperador; tel. (34)25-22-18-50*, is one of the most beautiful in Spain. The two-story hotel has a sweeping view of Toledo. Its restaurant serves Castilian cuisine and international fare. Rooms are air-conditioned, and guests can use the hotel's pool.

Another good place to stay is the **Hostal del Cardenal**, *Paseo de Recaredo 24; tel. (34)25-22-49-00*. Built in the 18th century as a summer palace for Cardinal Lorenzana, this is a quiet place to stay.

The best times to visit

The best times to visit Toledo are during the city's festivals: the **Olive Festival**, held at Mora de Toledo on the last Sunday in April; the pilgrimage to the shrine of **La Virgen del Valle**, held on May 1; the **Feast of San Isidoro** at Talavera de la Reina, May 15th to 18th; the annual fair in August that salutes **La Virgen del Sagrario**; and the fiesta known as the **Rosa del Azafran**, held on the last Sunday in October at Consuegra.

BARCELONA: THE MOST EUROPEAN CITY

Flower-filled **Barcelona** is sociable, stimulating, and the most European Spanish city. Residents love their town. To them, Barcelona's ancient hegemony over the Mediterranean is only temporarily in eclipse.

The city's Catalan culture is in full swing—street signs, maps, museum labels, and conversations are in the distinctive Catalan language.

Adding to Barcelona's charms are low-priced hotels, restaurants, and transportation.

The most interesting quarter

The **Gothic Quarter** (Barrion Gotico), at Barcelona's heart, is filled with shops, bars, nightclubs, and 14th-century buildings. Roman, Gothic, and medieval walls still stand. Wander around—you probably will chance upon crumbling classical arches and statuary.

The barrio's handsome Gothic cathedral is worth a visit, even if you stop in only to see the white geese in the cloister gardens. Interesting contrasts to the medieval buildings are the street lamps, which were designed by Antonio Gaudi, an innovative architect associated with the art nouveau movement. This quarter is a great shopping area, especially if you're looking for trendy clothes and unusual art.

Barcelona's most entertaining avenues

The first thing to do in Barcelona is stroll along **Las Ramblas**. These wide avenues go from the Diagonal (a wide avenue that cuts diagonally across the center of Barcelona) to the Columbus monument at the harbor. (Although the contiguous segments of Las Ramblas have their own names—Rambla Dels Estudis, Rambla de Sant Josep—they are known collectively as Las Ramblas.)

On Las Ramblas near Placa de Catalunya is Orator's Corner, where men gather to discuss the issues of the day. You'll also find the grand opera house, ornate churches, and elegant cafés, as well as Barcelona's intriguing seedy side on Las Ramblas.

This exotic stretch is the place to shop for everything from colorful tropical birds and flowers to postcards showing Barcelona's lewd and kinky nightlife. A little street called Riera Alta, between Las Ramblas and Calle Ronda San Antonio, hides a wine shop called Bodega. A little old man runs this dark place lined from floor to ceiling with bottles. If you ask for a sample, he will give you a squirt from a wine skin, or *bota*. He squeezes the *bota*, creating an arc of wine in the air, which you must artfully capture in your wide-open mouth. After dark, a parade of colorfully dressed transvestites joins families and tourists strolling along Las Ramblas near the Diagonal.

One note: Be careful when walking along Las Ramblas—about 30 purse snatchings a day take place here. Don't carry anything valuable with you if you go through the seedy Barrio Chino at the lower end of Las Ramblas.

Spain's most magnificent opera house

About halfway down Las Ramblas on the right is the **Gran Téâtre del Liceu**, *tel. (34)3-318-91-22*, where the Barcelona opera is held. This is where Casals first bowed his cello and Caballe hit her first incredible high C. Opened in 1847, it is unassuming on the outside, but inside is one of the most beautiful opera houses in all Europe.

Toulouse-Lautrec's favorite brew

An adventure to try in Barcelona is drinking *absenta*, or absinthe, a potent liquor that is illegal in most countries but perfectly legal in Spain. *Absenta* has given a number of writers and artists their inspiration (and probably rotted their brains), including Toulouse-Lautrec.

This licorice-flavored wood alcohol (not to be confused with milder Pernod) is sold at the beautiful Antique Bar on San Pau, near Jeronimo, in the Barrio Chino. The bar is old and ornate and has a sign that reads "Prohibited to Sing."

Limit yourself to two shots of *absenta*, at the most. After three, you won't know where you are or what you're doing there! (And you don't want this to happen when you're in the shady Barrio Chino.)

The best of Picasso

Museo de Picasso, *Calle Montcada near the Barrion Gotico*, has one of the world's most comprehensive collections of Picasso's works, starting from his childhood and continuing through his entire life. Few people take advantage of the free guided tour, available in English, so you rarely have to wait and often can have the guide to yourself.

The most expensive walls in the world

Such artists as Picasso and Utrillo frequented **Los 4 Gatos** (The 4 Cats) café in Barcelona. At one time, their paintings hung on the walls there. (They decorated the café when the owner allowed them to use the premises to stage an art show.) This may mean that, at today's prices, these walls were the most expensively covered in the world.

Gaudi's greatest works

Walking around Barcelona, you can't miss the strangely beautiful works of **Antonio Gaudi**. The luxury apartment buildings on and around the Paseo de Gracia were designed by the architect. They are distinguished by their asymmetrical shapes and unusual colors.

Templo de la Sagrada Familia is Gaudi's never-completed but extraordinary church. Its stonework resembling an enormous dribbled-sand castle, the structure towers above the Plaça de la Sagrada Familia. Climb the tiny, twisting and turning, steep stairs in the church towers to enjoy the view from the top.

Work continues to complete the church whenever a bit of money is collected. (Many Gothic cathedrals took centuries to build, too.)

Gaudi died on the street here. He stepped off the curb into the road to look at his work and was hit by a car.

Park Guëll, north of the city, was also created by the imaginative artist and is full of wild, beautiful, and sometimes decaying sculptures and objects.

The benches and walls are studded with pieces of pottery and glass, and caves are hollowed out of a hill.

Barcelona's tip-top displays

Barcelona lies in the shadows of an intriguing hill, **Montjuïc**, which is topped with the remains of the 1929 World's Fair. It is a pleasant place to visit—during the day. Don't stroll around by yourself, however, as the park attracts its share of strange characters.

The walk to the top of Montjuïc is long and strenuous (but enjoyable if you are in good shape). If you don't feel up to the hike, take the funicular on weekends and holidays from the Parallel metro station or bus 61, 101, or 201.

The most beautiful of the World's Fair pavilions is a starkly modern structure designed by Mies van der Rohe. Reconstructed last year in celebration of the 100th anniversary of the architect's birth, it was the first of its kind, with chrome, glass, reflecting walls, and an exterior that played an important part in the interior design of the building. Van der Rohe designed the building for the German exhibit, using green marble and golden onyx in the construction. Inside, scarlet velvet curtains sweep across glass walls. White-kid covered chairs once served as thrones. George Kolbe's statue *Morning*, a classical nude, is reflected in the interior pool. The pavilion is open during daylight hours; entry is free.

Pueblo Español, also designed as a pavilion for the 1929 World's Fair, is still in operation. Typical buildings from all over Spain were reproduced in this village, designed as a miniature view of Spain. Houses are of stone, stucco, or intricately laid brick, topped with Spanish tiles and embellished with elaborate balconies. Typical woodcarvings, metalwork, pottery, glass, leather, and crafts are sold in the village's 35 shops.

Museo d'Art de Catalunya, at the summit of Montjuïc, specializes in Catalan Gothic religious art. The mosaics, frescoes, and artifacts come from isolated churches and hermitages in the Pyrenees. The museum is open Tuesdays through Sundays from 9 a.m. to 2 p.m.

The **Miró Museum** features the work of Joan Miró, whose paintings were inspired by the art and landscape of Catalonia. His painted-bronze sculptures are displayed on the museum balconies, and his stark, late paintings are in alcoves overlooking the courtyard. Perhaps his best work is *Self Portrait*, begun in 1937 and completed in 1960. He drew himself from a reflection in a convex mirror, creating an enlarged, distorted image. His eyes are star-like. The Miró Museum and Contemporary Art Center is open Tuesdays through Saturdays from 11 a.m. until 8 p.m., Sundays and holidays from 11 a.m. until 2:30 p.m.

Barcelona's best nightlife

As in Madrid, nightlife begins well after midnight here. Then it rolls on full-steam until sunrise. Hundreds of bars and nightclubs are located all over the city.

The trendiest nightclub right now is the zany **Otto Zutz**, *Lincoln 15*, where you'll see Barcelona's most beautiful and fashionable. The latest music is played, and the décor is ultramodern.

Barcelona's jet-setters can be found at **Up and Down**, *Numancia and Diagonal*.

Two popular bars are **Network**, *Avenida Diagonal 616*, and **Vaticano,** which was opened by a Catholic priest and plays good music. On the north side of Las Ramblas is the **Born**, named after a huge market surrounded by tiny streets filled with bars, *coctelerias*, and *xampanyerias*, where local wines and champagne are drunk in vast quantities.

Barcelona's best restaurant

The best restaurant in Barcelona is **Neichel**, *tel. (34)3-203-84-08*. Michelin awarded this restaurant two stars. Try the duck paté, the lamb, or the veal in truffle sauce. Reservations are essential. Closed Sundays, bank holidays, Holy Week, Christmas, and August.

The finest fish

Barcelona is known for its fish restaurants, where specialties are made with seafood fresh out of the Mediterranean.

The section of Barcelona between the port and the beach, called Barcelonaeta, has several traditional fish restaurants. One of the best is **Cal Pinxo**, *Final Calle Maestranza*, which also serves a good—and cheap—house wine.

The best places to sleep

The best hotel in Barcelona is the **Ritz**, *tel. (800)223-6800*. One of the four original Ritz hotels founded by Caesar Ritz, it has been restored to its 19th-century opulence. Rooms are large, all with private bathrooms, and the atmosphere is elegant. But the real drawing card is the efficient, friendly staff.

Another grand hotel is the **Avenida Palace**, *Gran Via 605-607; tel. (34)3-301-96-00*. Less formal than the Ritz, it has comparable service. The lobby is lovely, with gleaming brass, marble, and wood. Rooms have air conditioning, wood furniture, and white chenille bedspreads. However, the dining is mediocre, and the bar is boring.

The **Hotel Colón**, *tel. (800)845-0636*, is relatively inexpensive, but charming. You couldn't find a more scenic location—it faces Barcelona's ancient cathedral in the Gothic Quarter. Despite its medieval surroundings, it offers air conditioning and private bathrooms. The best rooms are on the sixth floor. They have terraces with views of the cathedral and the streets below. Prints and gilded mirrors hang on the walls above velvet chairs.

Hotel Calderón, *tel. (34)9-3301-0000*, has a rooftop swimming pool with a panoramic view and air-conditioned bedrooms with televisions and private bathrooms.

Bests outside Barcelona

A **Benedictine monastery** whose Marian shrine has attracted pilgrims for more than 700 years is located in the Montserrat Mountains 38 miles northwest of Barcelona. The Black Madonna (La Morena)—a 12th-century statue of the Virgin Mary—is the focus of the pilgrims' journey.

SEVILLE'S GREATEST PLEASURES

Seville is a city of simple pleasures: warm sunshine, brightly colored flowers, an expressive river, fragrant orange groves, rustling palm trees, ancient buildings, and shining white houses with patios, flat roofs, and shuttered windows.

In a sense, Seville is the essence of Spain. It has typically ornate and colorful architecture and warm and friendly people. Located on the left bank of the Guadalquivir River, the city is sunny but surrounded by marshland and swamps.

Seville's history is colorful. The Romans conquered the city in 205 B.C. (when it was known as Hispalis), and it became so Romanized that it produced several Roman emperors, including Trajan and Hadrian. Under the Moors it became splendid and the subject of poetry. During the reconquest of Spain, it was the capital. It became the headquarters of trade with the New World in the 16th century. Cervantes spent his youth here, and his famous *Don Quixote* was created in a Sevillian prison.

The old quarters of the city, with narrow winding streets and tiny squares, were built in medieval times in a way intended to provide the best shelter from the heat of the Andalusian summers. The twists and turns of the narrow streets lead to surprises and unexpected views. The houses in the old part of the city have white lime-washed fronts and lots of flowering plants on the balconies.

Spain's most graceful bullfights

Even if you're squeamish, you should see a bullfight in Seville, which is famous for its bullfighters. The Sevillian school of bullfighting teaches a graceful style. Andalusian bulls are bred for the fight and show their stuff in the handsome Maestranza bullring.

Seville's top sight

The most outstanding monument in Seville is the **Giralda**. Built on Roman foundations as a minaret in 1184, it is adorned with four huge gilded-bronze apples. In the 1500s, a belfry with 25 bells was added, as well as the enormous statue representing faith, which serves as a weather vane.

The world's third-largest church

Seville's cathedral was built on the site of one of Spain's largest mosques, partly destroyed in the 15th century. It is the third-largest Christian church in the world. The Gothic structure has five spacious aisles, and the main chapel is decorated with a magnificent wrought-iron screen. The tombs of King Alfonso X (the Wise) and his mother, Beatrice of Swabia, are here, as well as an urn containing the remains of King Ferdinand.

Many people visit the cathedral without realizing they can also visit the crypt below, which contains the royal coffins of King Pedro the Cruel and Dona Maria de Padilla. The cathedral also contains jewels, vestments, and the sword of King Ferdinand. The Sacristy of the Chalices has paintings by Murillo, Zurbaran, and Goya. Before leaving the cathedral, see the Patio de los Naranjos (Orange Court) and the Christopher Columbus Library. The former was originally the *shan*, or courtyard, of the Mosque. The library contains manuscripts by the discoverer of America.

Best Mudejar architecture

The façade of the old **Alcazar** is one of the finest examples of Medejar art in Spain. (Mudejars were ex-Muslims who remained after the Reconquest.) It was built on the ruins of King Almontamid's palace. After the conquest of Seville, Ferdinand and Isabella and their successors also lived here. Among the remains is the Patio del Yeso.

The Alcazar as it is today was built by King Pedro the Cruel. Moorish master masons, Sevillian craftsmen, and Toledan decorators took part in creating this building.

The prettiest palace

Casa de Pilatos, or Pilots' House, a typical 15th-century Andalusian mansion, was built as a reproduction of the Praetorium in Jerusalem. The patio, with a graceful fountain and two ornamental statues of Minerva, is one of the most beautiful examples of Spanish Renaissance art in Seville.

Seville's best museum

The **Museum of Fine Arts**, located in a monastery, displays Spanish primitives, a magnificent El Greco, and nearly 50 Murillos.

GRANADA, THE MOST ROMANTIC CITY

Granada is one of those romantic towns that makes you feel like you're living a legend or lost in a movie set. It is most famous for its beautiful Moorish palaces and gardens, collectively called the **Alhambra.**

The palace is delicate, with multi-colored ceilings carved with stars. Arched windows look out over the water, and private patios open off bathing rooms. The Patio de la Ria and the upper garden are exquisite. The gardens have intricate waterworks, with channels of water that run alongside the steps. Elaborate fountains dance amid the flowering trees.

Patio de los Leones and the adjoining rooms were the heart of the private apartments of the ruler. Light, filtering through the patio, bathes the rooms and glimmers on the patio's fountains and water channels.

Washington Irving wrote *Tales From the Alhambra* from his apartment on the Lindaraja patio, which looks out on tall cypress trees and a gently gurgling fountain.

The **Alcazaba** was the guardian of the Alhambra. Its watchtower (Torre de la Vela) is the outstanding feature. In moments of danger, bells rang an alarm. Ferdinand and Isabella flew the banner of Castile from the tower when they took Granada on Jan. 2, 1492. From the tower you can see the entire city and the Alhambra.

The ugliest sight in the Alhambra

Charles V decided to plop a huge marble Renaissance palace into the middle of the Alhambra. His imperial majesty felt the Moors' remains were not majestic enough, so he built his monumental palace (now a museum).

The most passionate dancing

Outside Granada at **Sacromonte**, the summit of Mount Albaicin, are famous Gypsy caves, where, to the beating of hands and the sounds of guitars, Gypsies dance the *zambra*, a colorful and passionate dance. The caves sound primitive, but they are warm in the winter, cool in the summer, and often elaborately decorated.

A word of warning: you may be asked for handouts and pickpockets are common.

SALAMANCA: SPAIN'S INTELLECTUAL CENTER

Salamanca is the Oxford or Cambridge of Spain—colored greatly by the country's centralization and religious conformity. **The University of Salamanca**, the oldest in Spain, was founded at the end of the 15th century, almost at the same time as the Spanish Inquisition, by Cardinal Cisneros, adviser to the monarchs who financed Columbus. The campus is now split between the seminary and the secular university—but many figures on the lay side dress in Roman collars, soutanes, monkish habits, wimples, and coifs.

Perhaps the most telling clue to the way the Renaissance was viewed as both a threat and an opportunity is the large sign at the entrance to the university library, threatening with excommunication those who read books without getting permission from the bishop. All the 16th-century bookshelves lock—and this is not in an effort to stop book thieves!

Near the library is the splendid chapel, which has a painted Renaissance ceiling and is now used for ceremonial occasions. The university buildings are mostly 17th to 19th century, built in tiers around central courtyards. You can visit lecture halls if you enter without disturbing the classes.

Apart from the university, the city also boasts not one but two cathedrals, built partly on top of each other in the local pinkish granite. The older cathedral holds a beautiful retable and the polychrome shrine of Bishop Anaya—both masterpieces.

As is normal in a college town, Salamanca has plenty of cheap eats and cheap digs. If you can't get into the *parador*, do not despair. We have tried the **Alfonso X**, *Tor 64; tel. (34)23-21-44-01*, in Old Town, and it is quite delightful—an international-level hotel built into an old townhouse.

Good eating includes the Michelin-starred **Chez Victor**, *Espoz y Mina 26; tel. (34)23-21-31-23*, which features cockles in *noilly prat* on homemade noodles and *isla flotante* (floating island). Chez Victor is closed in August (when the university closes), Sunday nights, and Mondays.

VALLADOLID, A BEST FOR HISTORY AND ARCHITECTURE BUFFS

A busy provincial capital in the heart of the Meseta Central, **Valladolid** has medieval churches, university buildings, and traces of Spain's greatest writers and artists. The view of the city as you arrive from the highway is memorable—the cathedral, the university buildings, and church spires.

Valladolid's two literary giants

Valladolid produced two famous Spanish literary figures: Zorrilla and Cervantes. The house where poet **Jose Zorrilla** was born, on Calle Fray Luis de Granada, is a small whitewashed building that contains his letters, manuscripts, and death mask.

The house of **Miguel de Cervantes** (author of *Don Quixote*), on Calle Miguel Iscar, has been converted into a museum and a public library. The room that Cervantes used as a study is filled with maps and has a painting of the Battle of Lepanto. One of the writer's manuscripts is exhibited, and the furnishings, carpet, and tapestries were his. Two of his works were written here, *El Licenciado Vidriera* and *El Coloquio de los Perros*.

The most important sights

The **College of San Gregorio** is one of the marvels of pre-Renaissance art. It houses the National Sculpture Museum and contains the finest and most valuable carved figures from the Castile.

Igesia de San Pablo, next door, was originally a Dominican monastery built in the 15th century. Inside are two exquisite small doorways and a vaulted ceiling.

La Séo cathedral is quite impressive. Begun by the medieval architect Juan de Hererra (who also built the Monastery of El Escorial), it was continued in the 18th century but never completed. The interior is sober and grand, with 32 pillars. Next door is a Diocesan Museum, which contains fine images and jewelry.

Spain's castle country

A great number of castles were built outside Valladolid for its defense. **La Mota**, in Medina del Campo, is one of the most beautiful castles in Spain. Built in the 13th century, it was later home to Ferdinand and Isabella. Over the years it imprisoned Hernando Pizarro, Rodrigo Calderón (the favorite of Philip II), and César Borgia.

Seven miles outside Valladolid stands **Simancas**, originally a bishop's see. It was a Moorish castle until the 11th century, when the Christians reconquered it, it was granted town status in the year A.D. 927.

Simincas' cylindrical towers and walls are well-preserved. The inner part of the castle is used as the General Archives of the Kingdom. In its 52 rooms and halls are more than 30 million documents.

Farther down the Douro River is **Penafiel Castle**, a fabulous 14th-century structure that looks down over a historic village. Built in the 10th century, it looks like a huge ship, with 12 buttresses and an interior tower 27 yards high.

SPAIN'S MOST PICTURESQUE CITY — CUENCA

Cuenca is famous for its ancient hanging houses that jut out over a 600-foot gorge. These *casas colgadas*, as they are called, went unoccupied for 200 years before the government restored them. They date from the 14th century, when they were summer residences of kings and queens. Today, they are national monuments.

One of the houses is now a restaurant that serves delicious trout caught from the Huecar River and crayfish from the Jucar River. From the restaurant's balcony, you can look down into the gorge and watch swallows swooping from cliff to cliff.

Climb the steep, stony streets to the cobblestoned main square with its wrougt-iron window grills. Relax in one of the cafés over a glass of *resoli*, the local liqueur made of pure alcohol, coffee, sugar, orange peel, and cinnamon.

A light flickers in the town's lower gate every night in memory of the victory of King Alfonso over the Moors. According to legend, King Alfonso got his troops through the gate by dressing two soldiers in sheepskin and having them slay the gatekeeper. Alfonso's troops then opened the gates and conquered the town without shedding any Spanish blood. A festival is held Sept. 20 to 22 every year in celebration of the victory.

The town is prettiest at night when it is lit by hundreds of lights that cast odd shadows on the crooked buildings and winding streets.

MÉRIDA: THE BEST ROMAN RUINS
OUTSIDE ROME

Mérida, founded in 25 B.C. as a rest home for retired Roman legionnaires (it was then known as Colonis Emerita August), has the most impressive Roman ruins outside Rome itself. While it was on the main Roman road in antiquity, Merida today is a backwater. It is on a road that goes to the Portuguese border, on a river that you can navigate all the way to the sea at Ayamonte—if you have reason to do so.

Mérida's Roman sights include a multitier bridge over the Guadiana River, which carries both traffic and drinking water. The city's monumental aqueduct system, built in granite blocks striped with red clay bricks, is Roman and partially still in use. The city had both a Roman theater (for plays and performances of music for the legionnaires) and a Roman amphitheater (for sports events). The Romans were just like modern soldiers—the sports theater is four times as large as the cultural theater.

The theater was built into the slope of a hill, with seats in a horseshoe shape facing the stage. The stage was made of brick and decorated with marble pillars and columns two huge stories high. Statues of the Roman gods are visible between the pillars and the wall. Here and there are little doorways cut into the brick, through which entrances and exits were made. In the middle is a two-story doorway used for spectacular *effects* (deus ex machina, for example). Behind the façade you can see the actors' dressing rooms, built into the brick structure. You enter the theater (as you do the Coliseum in Rome) through arched stairways.

The huge amphitheater held 40,000 spectators. On the hillside where both structures stand were Roman notables' houses. The mosaics, paintings, and statuary from these houses can be seen in the Museo Arqueologico. (You pay only one admission price to view the lot.) The bas-reliefs in the museum include depictions of a lute player and of a tavern keeper drawing wine from a barrel.

As if being a major Roman center were not enough, Mérida also was a power center under the Moors. The Moorish fortress by the Guadiana is graced by a lovely colonnaded walk, created of ocher and cream stucco with marble pillars. Even more impressive is the *aljibe*, a set of staircases leading to a bath fed water from a river. Despite the Muslim prohibition against alcohol, the frieze on the entrance to the *aljibe* is decorated with bunches of grapes.

The Romans' greatest engineering feat

The Roman **aqueduct** in Segovia is the most powerful example of Roman engineering and architecture in Spain. After centuries of use, it still carries water from the River Frio to the town. Running across the center of Segovia, it has 118 arches and rises 96 feet. It was built in the time of Trajan of uncemented limestone blocks.

Segovia is a beautiful walled town on a rocky ledge above the Eresma River. A 14th-century alcazar (with 19th-century modifications) dominates the town. But the late Gothic cathedral, which dates from the 16th century, vies for attention.

Just south of Segovia is the bridge described by Hemingway in *For Whom the Bell Tolls*.

THE MOORS' MOST BEAUTIFUL CITY: CÓRDOBA

Córdoba was the capital of Muslim Spain in the eighth century and one of the major cities of the Muslim world. It once had 500,000 inhabitants and 300 mosques; today 255,000 live here, and most of the mosques are gone.

La Mezquita: a Moorish masterpiece

The city's most amazing monument is **La Mezquita**, a masterpiece of Moorish-Spanish architecture topped by a beautiful cupola and boasting an Eastern wall studded with priceless mosaics. Construction of the mosque, which was built on the site of a Visigothic cathedral, was begun in the middle of the eighth century at the orders of Abd-er-Rahman I. Elements of the early cathedral were incorporated into the mosque. Later in the eighth century, Muslims and Christians shared the building, which was also used as a cathedral.

Walk through the Door of Forgiveness into the Orange Tree Patio, an enchanting place with fountains and orange trees. Beyond the patio is a forest of columns—alabaster, jasper, and marble—topped by horseshoe arches. The columns came from North Africa, where they were taken from Roman, Visigothic, and Phonecian ruins.

Christians transformed the mosque into an enormous cathedral after they conquered Cordoba in 1236. But they never really got rid of its Moorish look and feel. The interior is vast, large enough to hold hundreds of Muslims facing east. The ceilings are low, with rounded arches. Striped columns hold up the ceiling. Baroque chapels embellish the edges of the cathedral, trying desperately to make it look Christian. In front of the western wall of La Mezquita is the Episcopal Palace, the residence of the Visigothic governors and later the caliph's alcazar.

The most inviting corners

Outside La Mezquita is **Cordoba's Old Quarter**, which is filled with inviting nooks and crannies. Look for good buys in filigree silver and Cordoba leather in the quarter's little shops.

The **Jewish Quarter** (Juderia), northwest of the Moorish structure, has a 14th-century synagogue, located on Calle Judios. Around the corner, on Calle Averroes and Calle Judios, is a patio where you can watch flamenco dancers.

Glance into Cordoba's patios. You will see white-lime walls draped with trailing plants and embellished with wrought-iron balconies. In the center are wells, marble columns, and fountains surrounded by flowers.

PAMPLONA: THE ULTIMATE MACHISMO

Each July in **Pamplona**, the ultimate display of *machismo* takes place. The townsmen pit their lives against hundreds of bulls set loose in the streets and herded toward the bullring. To display their courage, the men run before the bulls, often injuring themselves.

Festivities begin when a rocket is fired from the town hall. The streets fill with people who stare in amazement as the race begins. The celebration was made famous by Ernest Hemingway in *The Sun Also Rises*.

All this festivity is in the name of the town's patron saint, San Fermin, a bishop and martyr from Pamplona. Buried in Amiens, France, his body mysteriously disappeared. The body was miraculously found six centuries later, and legend says that, although it was midwinter, the trees burst into leaf.

THE COSTA DEL SOL:
A PEOPLE-WATCHING PARADISE

The **Costa del Sol** is the best place in Spain for partygoers, extroverts, and people watchers. However, it's the worst place to go if you are looking for a charming getaway. The Costa del Sol is for you only if you thrive on the excitement of crowds and nightlife. It's overdeveloped and overcrowded. Between Malaga and Algeciras are the most crowded resorts—Torremolinos, Fuengirola, and Marbella. Every imaginable language is spoken.

Marbella: the chicest resort

The chicest town on the coast is **Marbella**—it is also the most expensive. Movie stars and oil sheikhs keep prices high. Puerto Banus has a marina that houses yachts from all over the world. Nueva Andalucia, a community within Marbella, has a fancy casino and chic nightclubs. This is nightlife at its best.

Torremolinos: the busiest resort

Torremolinos, once a quiet fishing village, is now the busiest resort on the coast. Germans seem to love Torremolinos, flocking there by the hundreds. Highrise hotels and condominiums line the beaches, and restaurants, nightclubs, and boutiques line the streets. The place is packed with tourists all summer long.

El Torcal—the strangest landscape

When you tire of the beaches, take a trip inland to **El Torcal**, a plain covered with fantastically shaped boulders. The softest parts of the park's limestone rocks have dissolved over the years, leaving the oddly shaped hard sections of rock. You will think you're on the moon.

THE COSTA BRAVA—THE MOST BEAUTIFUL COAST

Spaniards who would rather relax on a secluded beach than gaze at masses of bodies head for the **Costa Brava**, which stretches from Blanes to the French border. The wild coast is known for its ferocious, rugged beauty. Pines fringe the rocky cliffs that drop to the fine, sandy beaches. Little towns are sheltered by the coast's protective coves.

Phoenicians, Greeks, Romans, and Arabs all have taken refuge in the Costa Brava's harbors. Ruins left by these early invaders dot the coast, as do fortified villages from the days of pirate invasions. You'll find Phonecian ruins at Rosas, Greek in Ampurias, and a Moorish fortress at Tossa del Mar.

Gerona is the best town for exploring the coast. It is filled with dungeons and ramparts, medieval walls and paintings. The old quarter is dominated by the majestic cathedral, built in the 17th century above Roman ruins. St. Felix Church, next to the cathedral, contains Roman sarcophagi.

The most popular resort

Tossa de Mar, a shiny white town by the sea, is the most popular resort along the Catalan coast. It has an old quarter (that predates even Roman civilization) and a Moorish alcazar, as well as walls that were built in the 12th century.

El Codolar beach, behind Vila Vella, and Playa Llorell beach are the least crowded.

Dalí's favorite town

The Costa Brava attracts artists and writers. **Salvador Dalí**, born nearby, was one of the first major artists to live here—at Port Lligot, Cadaques, near the French border. You can visit his estate, which is marked by gigantic egg-shaped ornaments and has a whimsical garden.

Cadaques is a purely Catalan fishing village where white houses contrast with a dark mountain backdrop. Tourists haven't yet flooded this tranquil town. Mediterranean cooking is served at **Es Baluard**, *Riba Nemesio Llorens 2; tel. (34)72-25-81-83*, a favorite among local artists. The restaurant is closed Oct. 15 to Dec. 15.

Make hotel reservations in Cadaques in advance. The few hotels book up fast. One good place to stay is the **Playa Sol**, *Playa Pianch 5; tel. (34)72-25-81-00*. It has a pool and tennis courts and is reasonably priced. The hotel is closed in January and February.

SPAIN'S LOVELIEST CATHEDRAL

The largest city in Cantabria is frequently overlooked by travelers, who stick primarily to the coast. **Léon** was the center of the Spanish movement led by El Cid to oust the Moors, as well as one of the great cities along the pilgrim route to Santiago de Campostella.

As you might expect from a city with such important religious traditions, Leon has a splendid cathedral. But you'll be surprised at just how splendid it is. The stained-glass windows here are second only to those of Chartres in France. Because the cathedral was built before the art of using flying buttresses had been mastered, the way the light plays into the Léon cathedral is even more dramatic, being at ground level. The windows are predominantly red and gold (as you might expect in Spain), rather than mostly blue as in Chartres.

In addition to the windows, Léon's cathedral has a beautiful Romanesque cloister with fountains, gardens, and a rood screen by an unknown master, depicting the deposition of the body of Christ.

Léon is the center of the Gallego region, where the people speak a dialect of Spanish closer to Portuguese than Castilian. Leon is not close enough to the sea to provide good fresh fish, and gastronomically it is pretty disappointing.

The best hotel is the **San Marcos**, *Plaza San Marcos; tel. (34)87-23-73-00*, built into the remains of a magnificent 16th-century monastery. This is a rare free-enterprise hotel—most monastery hotels are *paradors*.

Santiago de Compostela — Spain's Pilgrimage Center

All the roads in northwest Spain (and many roads in France) lead to **Santiago de Capostela**, the greatest pilgrimage center on the Iberian Peninsula. During the Middle Ages, this town was the destination of pilgrims from all over Europe, who came to worship at the tomb of St. James (Santiago), housed in the 11th-century cathedral. Santiago was as important a pilgrimage destination as Rome or Jerusalem.

According to legend, the Apostle James came to this part of Spain to bring Christianity. He landed at Padron on an estuary of the Ulla River. After his death, his remains are said to have been brought back to Spain, where they were lost during invasions by Barbarians and Moors. In the ninth century, a star is said to have appeared marking the point where St. James' remains were buried. They were then taken to Santiago and placed in the cathedral.

Another tale says St. James appeared during a battle against the Moors in A.D. 844, dressed in armor and carrying a white standard with a red cross on it. He fought off the infidels and became known as Matamore, or Slayer of Moors. Later, the saint is said to have fled the Moors by swimming across a river. When he emerged on the other side, he was covered with seashells. For this reason, pilgrims wear cockleshells to show they have been to Santiago de Compostella.

Even if you aren't a pilgrim, Santiago is worth visiting. It is especially beautiful at sunset, when its church spires, hospitals, monasteries, and palaces glint with the sun on their roofs.

The town's Romanesque cathedral and Old Town, where ancient houses and little shops fill the streets, are worth exploring.

The best place to stay in Santiago de Compostela (perhaps the best place to stay in all Spain) is **Los Reyes Catolicos**, *Plaza de Espana 1; tel. (34)81-58-22-00*. Built in the 16th century by Ferdinand and Isabella as a hospice for pilgrims, the parador is in the form of a cross, with an interior square and four patios. Bedrooms have high ceilings and ornate furniture.

San Sebastian: Basque-ing with the Best

Beautiful **San Sebastian**, bordered by the Urumea River, Bahia de la Concha, and three hills, is where Europe's wealthiest vacationers play during the summer. Drive to the top of Mount Urgall for a long vista of the bay and the sea. An even better view of the city, the bay, and the sea can be seen three miles west of the city at Mount Igueldo.

San Sebastian is known for its Basque cooking with Spanish and French touches and its original use of seafood.

The best restaurant in San Sebastian is **Arzak**, *Alto de Miracruz 21; tel. (34)43-27-84-65*. Chef Juan Mari Arzak won Spain's National Gastronomy Prize for his river crabs with truffles and lobster sauce, his apple pudding with strawberry cream, and his mousse. Arzak specializes in nouvelle Basque cuisine. The restaurant is closed in June and November and on Sunday nights and Mondays during the winter.

San Sebastian's best hotels

The two most elegant hotels in town are **De Londres y de Inglaterra**, *tel. (34)943-440-770*, and **Costa Vasca**, *tel. (34)943-211-011*.

GALICIA — THE FISHERMEN'S FAVORITE

Galicia, the westernmost coast of Spain, is a land of fishermen and damp, green landscapes. It has changed little over the centuries and has yet to draw hordes of tourists, probably because of its damp weather. The coastline is beautiful—a great place for romantic walks.

Vigo, the main fishing port

Vigo is the main fishing port of Galicia. Hemingway described this town as "a pasteboard village, cobble-streeted, white and orange plastered, set up on one side of a big, almost land-locked harbor."

Vigo lies at the end of a swampy river valley. Sheltered bays and quiet inlets surrounding the town produce the shellfish for which Galicia is famous, as well as sardines, tuna, and hake. During the winter, the port is battered by winter gales.

Snug little bars and restaurants can be found on the steep, winding streets of Vigo. Fishermen drink the local wine, *ribeiro*, and chat among themselves in Gallego, the local Spanish dialect, similar to Portuguese. Early in the morning, Vigo bustles. Fisherwomen wearing clogs push cartloads of fish to market.

White sandy beaches called Samil and America stretch south of Vigo. A road, lined by vines that produce *ribeiro*, hugs the shoreline, dipping into tiny hamlets and climbing the hills. Narrow one-lane bridges cross muddy creeks.

THE CANARY ISLANDS: ATLANTIS REGAINED

Scattered off the bulge of West Africa, Spain's 13 **Canary Islands** are blessed with 360 days of sunshine. Only on record-breaking days does the temperature dip below 65 degrees Fahrenheit. As a result of this year-round springlike climate, farmers in the Canaries can harvest four crops a year. The Canaries have markets filled with an incredible variety of fruits and vegetables.

According to legend, the islands are all that remain of the lost city of Atlantis. Roman discoverers named the islands Canaria, from *canus*, after the wild dogs that lived there.

Tenerife, the largest Canary

Tenerife, which covers 1,231 square miles, is the largest Canary. Through the center of the island runs Mount Teide, the highest peak in all Spain, at 12,192 feet.

Throngs of Europeans come here from cold Scandinavia, Germany, and Britain. They romp among the sand dunes and fill the hotels and restaurants all seasons of the year. The burgeoning growth of discos, bars, and multi-sorted highrises, along with planeloads of tourists, makes south Tenerife another Costa del Sol. However, the pace of growth is being checked as building requirements become more stringent.

Cosmopolitan Santa Cruz

The most cosmopolitan city in the Canaries is **Santa Cruz**, on Tenerife, the largest port in Spain. The capital city of 200,000 looks for all the world like San Francisco, located at the foot of a gentle slope. It has attractive stores, great restaurants, museums, art galleries, theaters, and even a symphony orchestra.

Shopping in Santa Cruz is a special joy. Because the town is a duty-free port, items can be purchased for prices lower than in their countries of origin. Chinese silks, pearls from Japan, watches, designer clothes, and photographic equipment are some of the best bargains.

Puerto la Cruz, the prettiest town

On the northwest coast, toward Buena Vista, is the small city of **Puerto de la Cruz.** Built on a rocky coast, it has a 600-acre man-made lake and a chain of natural pools that are terrific for swimming. Yellow and red hibiscus, trailing pink geraniums, 30-foot-tall poinsettias, and other tropical greenery surround the pools, and fountains shoot 20 feet into the air. However, the ocean has no beach.

Perhaps the most entertaining thing about Puerto de la Cruz is its underwater nightclub, where you can sip your drink and look through the water to the stars.

Stroll along the town's pedestrian street to the best ice cream parlor in the Canaries (if not Spain). It has more than 40 flavors and just as many fresh toppings. Imagine cinnamon ice cream smothered in fresh mango and blueberries!

The best times in Tenerife

The two best times to visit Tenerife are July, when a two-week fiesta attracts people from all over Europe, and February, for Carnival.

The island's best hotel

Tenerife's most attractive hotel is **Semiramis**, *tel. (34)922-37-32-00*, an imaginatively designed structure overlooking the ocean.

The best of Gran Canaria

Gran Canaria is a mountainous island with banana trees, coffee groves, sugarcane, and almond trees. Along the southern coast, from the tourist-ridden Playa San Agustin to the more quiet and chic Puerto Mogan, is an unbroken chain of serious sunbathers, windsurfers, campers, and other winter refugees from all over Europe.

Las Palmas, the capital of this 922-square-mile island, is a duty-free port and a shopper's paradise. Although it's difficult to imagine wearing a fur coat in this warm climate, they are a tremendous bargain in the Canaries, where they are available from 30% to 50% less than in European shops. A good shop is **Voula Mitsakiu**, *Luis Morote 28.*

The most gorgeous resort area in the Canaries is **Maspalomas Oasis**, *tel. (34)28-76-01-70.* It has long, sandy beaches, lagoons, graceful sand dunes, and enormous palm trees swaying in the breeze.

The Oasis Maspalomas shopping center has boutiques, restaurants, bars, banks, car rentals, and book and trinket stalls. Moroccans and other Africans enthusiastically greet you with their wares: camel-skin bags complete with desert aroma, stuffed coiled cobras, and carved ebony elephants. Bikini bottoms are relatively inexpensive, and the selection includes bright colors as well as leopard and zebra prints. But forget about finding matching tops. Topless is the *moda de la playa.*

The most charming village on the island is **Mogan**, a fishing village that rises from the sea on its natural wall of crags and burned earth. Tanned people chat in a half-dozen languages on the streets here. A village artist portrays flamenco dancers on the outside of his house. And the valley is brightened by flowering almond trees and tropical fruits.

Unsurpassable meals

Gran Canaria is a paradise for food lovers. Most restaurants serve delicious meals in gigantic portions for incredibly low prices. This holds true whether you dine in a tiny shack or an elegant restaurant.

Choose from a variety of fresh meats and fish, including *chulletas de cordero* (thick, juicy, grilled pork chops); *solomillo pimentas* (steak smothered with roasted sweet peppers); *tuna casuela* (home-style tuna steaks baked with garlic, onions, and red and green peppers); and local fish, such as *salmonetta* (red mullet) and sole, all prepared with fresh parsley and garlic. Tiny island-grown potatoes called *papas arrugadas* are steamed with sea salt and served with a spicy dipping sauce (*mojo picon*) made of chopped chili peppers, garlic, and oil. A good wine is the velvety Lanzarote.

Our favorite restaurant on the island is the rooftop **Restaurante Rio** in the town of Puerto Rico. Try the **langosta Americana**—grilled rock lobster with mayonnaise. A Latin band plays, and after your meal you can dance until dawn.

Sleeping in the lap of luxury

Maspalomas Oasis, *tel. (34)928-14-04-18*, is a huge resort complex with a nightclub, a golf course, horseback riding, tennis, and a health club. It's popular and expensive.

Tamarindos, *tel. (34)928-77-40-90*, is a sophisticated hotel with two swimming pools and a nice beach. A full buffet is set up next to one of the pools. A disco and several bars keep the atmosphere friendly.

THE BEST OF THE BALEARIC ISLANDS

The **Balearic Islands** peek sleepily out of the Mediterranean. Europeans love the islands for their perfect summer weather, easygoing inhabitants, and lovely beaches. Mallorca, Menorca, Ibiza, Formentera, and scores of rocky islets make up the Balearics, which lie 100 miles southeast of Barcelona. The trip from Barcelona can be made in 25 minutes by air or in nine hours by boat.

The islands have changed a great deal since the days when Mallorcans stoned George Sand for wearing pants. You will see artists and jet setters, punk rockers and tourists, as well as old women in traditional black.

Mallorca—a jet-set getaway

Mallorca offers craggy mountains, Roman temples, and unspoiled beaches.

The biggest Balearic island with the starkest contrasts, Mallorca has office buildings and windmills, highways, and ancient villages. Although tourists sunbathe topless, the natives wear traditional costumes. And children inherit thousand-year-old olive trees when family farms get passed down.

About half the island's residents live in Mallorca's capital, Palma de Mallorca. Here, visit the cathedral, Santa Maria, which boasts one of the world's biggest stained-glass windows. Construction of the cathedral began in 1230 and continued for 300 years.

The prettiest town in Mallorca

The most peaceful town in the Balearics is **Deya**, on the northwest coast. It is a haven for artists and writers who yearn for the romance of the sea, yet despair of spending too much time alone with blank paper or canvas. Robert Graves, who wrote *I Claudius*, lived here for years.

A road leads two miles from town through goat fields and over terraces built by the Moors to a beautiful beach. Princess Diana used to vacation here—but it isn't expensive. The aspiring painter can rent a small cliffside dwelling for very little.

Mallorca's best hotel

The island's most beautiful hotel is **La Residencia,** *tel. (800)225-4255.* The place holds less than 100 people. There isn't even a reception desk—just a low table in the lobby. The hotel is composed of two huge stone farmhouses, dating back from the 16th and 19th centuries, respectively.

THE BEST OF IBIZA

The cobblestoned streets of **Ibiza**, decorated with rainbows of flowers, wind through bright white buildings that lead to the sea. Orange and lemon trees climb terraces to sturdy farmhouses on hilltops. A grove of fig and almond trees curtains sandy beaches. In the evening, lovers stroll to Vedra, the Magic Rock, which reflects the moonlight and is washed gently by the sea.

This island off Spain's east coast has been inhabited by Phoenicians, Greeks, Carthaginians, and Romans. Centuries of invasions by Vandals, Byzantines, and Arabs led to the construction of an enormous fortress here. But the forbidding citadel isn't enough to keep the tourists away.

Now is the time to see Ibiza. Despite efforts to enforce zoning restrictions, houses and apartment buildings are going up at a rate that bodes ill for people who like the island's secluded beaches. Already, hotels line some of the island's most languid beach strips. Ancient olive groves are being razed for golf courses. And the visitor's appetites for nightlife have made clubs and bars materialize in out-of-the-way places.

Of course, all this modernizing has its good points (depending on your point of view). Ibiza was the pioneer of nude beaches in Spain, and Agua Blanca beach is an excellent place to get a full-body tan. Cabo Falcon also has a good nude beach called El Cavallet.

Comida San Juan is the best and one of the cheapest restaurants in Ibiza. Local patrons swear by it. **La Marina** is also good and cheaper.

THE MOST SPANISH TIME TO VISIT SPAIN: HOLY WEEK

The ritual religion of medieval times is resurrected each year in Spain during Holy Week. Candlelight processions mourning the death of Christ file silently through the old quarters of Spain's cities and towns. Statues depicting the life of Christ are carried through the streets. In some areas, residents don the attire of Biblical times and re-enact the life of Jesus.

The biggest Holy Week celebrations are in **Seville**. More than 50 orders of priests and laymen march in procession following an ancient route from the Plaza de la Campana along winding Sierpes Street, past the town hall, and through the Gothic cathedral. They end up in front of the Giralda and the baroque Bishop's Palace. *Pasos* (platforms of wood and silver) carry statues of the Virgin. They are covered with carnations and rock gently on the shoulders of the bearers to the rhythm of *saetas*, short and fervent prayers or hymns.

Not all the ritual is serious. The **Burial of the Sardine** is a nighttime tradition in Murcia that marks the end of Lent. It includes 25 carriages, each with an accompanying group of merrymakers, bands, and *hachoneros*, or men who carry bras. Little toys are thrown to the spectators from the carriages. At the end of the festival, a huge papier-mâché sardina is burned at the old bridge in Puento Viejo, and fireworks are set off.

The Burial of the Sardine dates back to the 19th century, when university students, who could afford to eat nothing but sardines, would bury some to celebrate their graduation.

SPAIN'S BEST WINES

Spanish wines rival French wines and are half the price of their Gallic counterparts. Spain's champagnes are darn good too.

Of the Rioja wines, the two best are **Marques de Murrieta** and **Marques de Riscal**. And the rare **Castillo Ygay Reserva**, made four times a century, is incomparable. The Riscal clarets are delicious; the best of the Riscal reds is the 1922.

Vega Sicilia, which is aged for 10 years, is the best of the Penedes wines (1966 is the best year). Torres is the best brand; the best Torres is the Gran Coronas Black Label.

Spanish sherry too is world-famous, yet underpriced. **Barbadillo's Sanlucar Manzanilla** is the elegant before-dinner drink in Spain. The best-selling dry sherry in the world is **Tio Pepe**.

THE BEST OF SWITZERLAND

EXQUISITE POSTAL SERVICE. NO BOTHERSOME DEMONSTRATIONS, NO SPITEFUL STRIKES. ALPINE BUTTERFLIES. FABULOUS SUNSETS— JUST WEST OF MY WINDOW, SPANGLING THE LAKE, SPLITTING THE CRIMSON SUN! ALSO, THE PLEASANT SURPRISE OF A METAPHORICAL SUNSET IN CHARMING SURROUNDINGS.

—Vladimir Nabokov

Mountainous Switzerland is at the peak of Europe. Its mountains are threatening, yet nurturing, encompassing fruitful farms, lakeside resorts, and picturesque old towns. The Rhine, the Rhone, and the Inn rivers originate in Swiss mountain glaciers. The Swiss Alps challenge the world's best mountain climbers, skiers, and hikers. The famous Matterhorn rises above Zermatt, and the Berner Oberland mountain range guards Interlaken. Davos and St. Moritz sit snugly in their Alpine valley.

ZURICH: BEST FINANCIERS, BEST FUN

Zurich, a prosperous banking town, is a two-sided coin. A seat of the Reformation in Switzerland, it later became a center for Dadaism. While it is the home of staid bankers, its German-speaking people also have a vile, witty side that is evident during the city's festivals. During **Sechselauten** (Zurich's spring festival, held toward the end of April), for example, Zurich's bankers don costumes and celebrate the end of winter by burning a huge straw dummy named the Böögg.

Zurich has hosted writers as well as financiers. Joyce, Mann, Brecht, and Kleist all lived here at various times during their careers.

The cleanest street in the world

The Bahnhofstrasse, Zurich's main artery, is the cleanest street in the world. James Joyce once said, "Zurich is so clean that should you spill your soup on the Bahnofstrasses, you could eat it up with a spoon." The avenue does have its dirty laundry, however. Some of the most powerful bankers in the world, the gnomes of Zurich, work here.

273

Zurich's top sights

On the left bank of the Limmat River is the **Fraumunster**, *Stadthaus-quaistrasse*, an austere Gothic cathedral enlivened with stained-glass windows by Marc Chagall and Augusto Guacometti.

The *Altstadt* (Old Town), on the right bank of the Limmat River, is a maze of steep cobblestoned streets lined with cafés, sex shops, and night-clubs. A series of 17th- and 18th-century arcaded guildhalls line the Limmatquai and surrounding streets. Inside, the guildhalls are decorated with ornate friezes and ceilings. Most are now restaurants, so you can enjoy lunch as well as the surroundings.

Above it all is Zurich's massive cathedral, the **Grossmünster**. The Romanesque cathedral was the center of the Reformation. Here, Ulrick Zwingli preached against the sale of indulgences, common at that time in the Roman Catholic Church.

Zurich's **Schweizerishches Landesmuseum** (Museum of Swiss History), *Museumstrasse 2*, behind the railroad station, displays prehistoric artifacts, medieval and Renaissance art, and the richly carved furniture of an old peasant civilization.

The **Kunsthaus** (Fine Arts Museum), *Heimplatz 1*, northwest of the opera house, has paintings, sculptures, and graphic art from the Middle Ages to today. The museum has a strong collection of 19th- and 20th-century works by Monet, Munch, Giacometti, Rodin, and Chagall. The Kunsthaus is a large open gallery that is not divided by floors, walls, or stairs.

The **Rietberg Museum**, *Gablerstrasse 15*, in the former Wesendonck Villa on the western shore of Lake Zurich, houses Europe's best collection of non-European art. Most of the collection was donated by Baron von der Heydt. Works are mainly Indian, Southeast Asian, Chinese, Japanese, and African. Richard Wagner was often a guest at this enchanting villa, and his love affair with the hostess inspired him to compose *Tristan* and *Isolde*. A private park surrounds the museum.

Zurich's coziest café

When you tire of sightseeing, stop at the **Café Schober**, *Napfgasse 4*, which serves a scrumptious chocolate cake. Students and businessmen alike enjoy the atmosphere (although the two generations ignore each other here).

The best nightlife

Most of Zurich's nightlife centers around the **Niederdorfstrasse** and the **Limmatquai**, where you'll find bars, clubs, and street musicians. The night-clubs in Zurich are expensive, mineral water being only slightly less expensive than a beer. If you are on a budget, stick to the cafés and bars.

Top three restaurants

The best dining in the area is at the restaurant that's just a 20-minute drive from the heart of the city. **Bienengarten**, *Regensbergstrasse 9; tel. (41)1-853-12-17*, is in an old, half-timbered house. Chef and owner Karl Gut spares no effort to make his dishes exceptional. The eight-course meal must be ordered a day in advance.

The restaurant at the Dolder Grand Hotel, **La Rotonde**, *Kurhausstrasse 65; tel. (41)1-269-38-70*, is also superb. The restaurant features traditional French cooking of premier quality. The *éminçe de filet de veau à la Zurichoise* (finely sliced milk-fed veal in a white wine and parsley sauce) is one of the many delicious dishes here.

Les Vacances-Chez Max, *Seestrasse 53; tel. (41)1-391-88-77*, on Lake Zurich, is famous for its luxurious décor and first-class food and service. The menu includes *soupe de homard glacee* and *salade de foie gras aux truffes tiedes*. The restaurant is closed for lunch Sunday and Monday.

Kronenhalle, *Rämistrasse 4; tel. (41)1-251-6669*, which was frequented by James Joyce, is more famous for what is on the walls than what is on the tables. The walls are decorated with works of Braque, Miro, Giacometti, and Leger. You can sit at one of the wide tables designed by Giacometti and enjoy the art while eating a rather overpriced meal. Service is perfect—most of the staff have been here for years.

Kronenhalle has become an institution in Zurich, revered by locals, who favor it as a spot for after-theater and after-work refreshments.

Zeughauskeller, *Bahnhofstrasse 28a* and *In Gassen 17; tel. (41)1-211-26-90*, a huge restaurant with outdoor dining during the summer, is the best place for traditional Swiss dishes, including potato salad (17 tons of potato salad are sold here every year) and suckling pig. It also has a good selection of local wines. An authentic Zurich guildhouse restaurant, it is cheaper than most Zurich eateries and is popular among business people from neighboring banks.

Au Premier, on the upper floor of the main railroad station, *Bahnhofplatz 15; tel. (41)1-211-15-10*, is an inexpensive restaurant that offers a wide selection of Swiss wines. You can order exactly the amount of wine you want, in carafes of two, three, or five deciliters (called decis). Local dishes, such as *Kalbsbratwurst*, are offered, as well as fancier fare, such as veal sweetbreads with sherry vinegar or veal steak with morels.

Zurich's best desserts

When you crave something sweet, stop by the **Confiserie Sprungli**, *Am Paradeplatz 15; tel. (41)1-211-0795*. The biggest chocolate maker in Switzerland, it serves delicious fresh white truffles. The chocolate is made with fresh Swiss milk and cream. You can get lunch here, too.

The best hotel in Zurich—and one of the best in the world

The **Baur au Lac**, *Talstrasse 1; tel. (41)1-220-50-20*, was named the best hotel in the world by *Travel & Leisure* magazine and received a Pomme d'Or for its elegance from travel writer William Chamberlayne. Built in 1830, it is not a glitzy palace but a four-story masterpiece of elegance located on the edge of the Zurchsee, not far from the center of town. The Baur au Lac's restaurant, the **Grill Room**, is one of the best in Zurich.

When you stay at the Baur au Lac, you will be in prestigious company. The hotel's guest book has included the King of Sweden, Kaiser Wilhelm II, and Margaret Thatcher. The hotel was built by Johannes Baur, who began life as a baker's apprentice. (Baur's son founded the Hotel School of Lausanne, alumni of which include Charles Ritz and other hotel magnates.)

Bests outside Zurich

Winterthur, a town north of Zurich that dates back to Roman times, is known for its art collections. Oskar Reinhart, an arts patron who died in 1965, left his comprehensive art collection to the town. His collection is divided between the **Oskar Reinhart Foundation**, *Stadthausstrasse 6*, and the **Oskar Reinhart Collection Am Romerholz**, *Haldenstrasse 95*. Works by Swiss, Austrian, and German painters from the 18th through the 20th centuries can be seen at the Oskar Reinhart Foundation. The Oskar Reinhart Collection, which is housed in the collector's former house, has paintings covering five centuries, including some of Picasso's paintings from his Blue Period. The collection of 19th-century works by Corot, Delacroix, Courbet, Manet, Renoir, and Cezanne is comprehensive.

Winterthur also has a good **Fine Arts Museum**, which displays works of the 16th century, the local schools of the 17th and 18th centuries, and the Swiss and German painters of the 19th and 20th centuries. It also has paintings of the French schools and sculptures by Rodin, Maillol, Haller, and Marini. A private collection of clocks is displayed in the center of town, at the *Rathaus*.

Four miles outside Winterthur is **Kyburg Castle**, a feudal castle built in the 10th and 11th centuries and passed from the counts of Kyburg to the Hapsburgs. Since 1917, the castle has belonged to the canton of Zurich. It has a collection of furniture and arms and a panoramic view of the surrounding countryside. The castle is open 9 a.m. until noon and 1 p.m. until 5 p.m. (4 p.m. in the winter). It is closed Mondays.

GENEVA: THE PLACE TO WATCH MODERN HISTORY UNFOLD

Geneva, a French-speaking city on shimmering Lac Leman (Lake Geneva), is an international center and the home base of some 200 organizations. This is the best place in Europe to grasp the magnitude of modern history as it unfolds.

The European headquarters of the United Nations is housed in the **Palais des Nations**, *14 ave. de la Paix, Pregny Gateway*. Built in 1936 as the seat of the League of Nations, the Palais des Nations is situated in the Parc des l'Ariana. Marble of various hues was donated by U.N. member countries to create the Salle des Pas Perdus, which leads into the Assembly Room, where U.N. meetings are held. The walls of the Council Chamber, where the most important conferences are held, are decorated with huge frescoes illustrating the achievements of mankind. From the terrace you have a panoramic view of Geneva, the lake, and Mont Blanc. Guided tours of the palace are conducted 9 a.m. until noon and 2 p.m. until 4:45 p.m. (5:15 p.m. in the summer) every day except during conferences and the Christmas and New Year holidays.

Not far from the Palais des Nations are the **World Health Organization**, the **International Red Cross**, and the **International Labor Office**. Group visits can be arranged by special request.

The world's tallest fountain

In the center of Lake Geneva is the tallest fountain in the world, the **Jet d'Eau**, which spouts 476 feet. The fountain is striking, backed by the Swiss Alps. For a good view, walk out onto the Quai du Mont Blanc, near the bridge.

The best of vieille ville

Most of Geneva's monuments are in Old Town, called here *vieille ville*. The most prominent is **St. Peter's Cathedral**. Built between the 12th and 13th centuries, it was partly rebuilt in the 15th century and has an 18th-century neo-Grecian doorway. The cathedral is huge, but the décor is plain.

St. Peter's has been a Protestant church since 1536, when it became a center of the Reformation. You can see Calvin's seat in the north aisle. And the tomb of the Duc de Rohan, who headed the Reformed Church in France at the time of Louis XIII, is in the first chapel on the south side of the chancel.

The flamboyant Gothic chapel in St. Peter's is more elaborate than the rest of the church. It was built by Cardinal de Brogny in the 15th century and was restored in the 19th century.

Climb the 145 stairs to the north tower of the cathedral. From the top, you have a view of the Jura Mountains, Geneva, the lake, and the Alps.

The **Reformation Monument** was built against a 16th-century rampart of *vieille ville*, in what today is a park. At the center of the 100-yard wall are statues of the four Genevan Reformers: Calvin, Knox, Farel, and de Bèze. The monument was built in 1917 and includes texts that recall the origins of the Reformed Church.

Geneva's **Hôtel de Ville** (town hall), parts of which date back to the 15th century, has an old courtyard with cobblestoned ramp once used to carry litters to the upper floor. The Geneva Convention (the first convention of the Red Cross) was signed in the Alabama Room on Aug. 22, 1864.

The oldest house in Geneva is the **Maison Tavel**, *6 rue du Puits-St. Pierre*, near the cathedral. The first written record of the house is in 1303, but it was built long before then. The Museum of Old Geneva, which has a display of historic engravings, is located here.

Lac Leman—the deepest Alpine lake

Lac Leman—the deepest of the Alpine Lakes (1,000 feet), is 45 miles long, 7.5 miles wide at its widest point, and covers 143,323 acres. The best cruise of Lake Geneva is the "Tour of the Upper Lake," which lasts 12 hours. Official timetables and rates are posted at landing stages throughout Geneva, including Quai du Mont Blan, Jardin Anglais, and Eaux vives, opposite the Parc de la Grange.

Chillon, the most poetic castle

Chillon Castle, perched on a rocky island at the opposite end of the lake from Geneva, inspired the poet Byron to write the lyrical poem "The Prisoner of Chillion."

Prior François Bonivard was imprisoned in the castle dungeon for four years for trying to introduce the Reformation to Geneva. The Duke of Savoy, an ardent Catholic, had him chained to one of the pillars. If you visit the dungeon, take a close look at that pillar and the floor around it—you can see the prisoner's footprints traced in the rock. Byron carved his name on the third pillar in Bonivard's cell in 1816.

The fortress was built in the ninth century, but it took on its present-day appearance when it was expanded by the bishops of Sion and embellished by the counts of Savoy from 1150 to the mid-13th century. To get to the castle, you cross a moat on the 18th-century bridge that replaced a drawbridge.

The Great Hall has an imposing 15th-century fireplace, a large collection of pewter, and 13th-century Savoyard furniture. The Banquet Hall's timber ceiling is shaped like an inverted ship's hull. From the keep, you have a view of Montreux, Lake Geneva, and the Alps.

The best of the French

Parc des Eaux-Vives, *tel. (41)22-735-41-40*, is the most famous French restaurant in Geneva. Located in the park of the same name, Eaux-Vives has splendid views and good classic cuisine. The service is always good, and the wine list is the best in Switzerland. The restaurant is closed Monday and Tuesday, April through October.

La Perle du Lac, *128 rue de Lausanne; tel. (41)22-731-79-35*, across the lake, is another superb French restaurant with a view of Mont Blanc. Servings are generous, but the prices are high. The restaurant is closed Monday and Dec. 20 through Feb. 15. (You may want to try the brasserie next door, which serves the same fare from the same kitchen at one-third the price!)

One of the best restaurants in Geneva is the often underestimated **Béarn**, *4 Quai de la Poste; tel. (41)22-21-00-28*. The *rable de lapereau aux basilic et petites legumes* (rabbit fillets served with liver and kidneys and young vegetables) is superb. Bankers lunch here on the *repas d'affaires*, which changes daily. The market's seasonal fare (fish and game) is presented, uncooked, on a trolley. The restaurant is closed Saturday for lunch, Sunday, and July 15 through Aug. 15.

Geneva's best hotel

Hotel Le Richemond, *Jardin Brunswick; tel. (41)22-7157-000*, is one of the best hotels in the world. Run by the Armleder family, this imposing, seven-story building has 120 bedrooms that accommodate your every need. The hotel has two fine restaurants, and the wine cellar contains 80,000 bottles.

Adolphe-Rodolphe Armleder founded the Richemond in the 1870s. What makes staying at the hotel so special are the elegant little touches, such as finding your ties hung in order of color and your clothes perfectly folded. Hotel Richemond has served writers Colette and Antoine de St. Exupery, as well as Russian delegations of the 1930s and the Chinese delegations of the 1950s.

BERNE — THE LOVELIEST CITY

Switzerland's capital, **Berne**, is one of the best-preserved medieval cities in Europe. It is filled with turreted buildings and has more fountains per capita than any other city on the Continent. The Alps surround the city, which is divided twice by the Aare River.

Established in 1191 by the duke of Zähringen, Berne was originally a hunting ground. The duke and his cronies decided that the town should be named after the first animal caught on a particular hunt. The unfortunate beast was a bear (*Bär* in German), so the town was called *Bärn* (Berne is a corruption). A bear appears on the city's coat of arms, and for centuries mascot bears have been kept in the *Bärengraben*, or bear pits.

The best way to explore Berne is to get a map from the tourist office and follow its walking tour along arcaded, cobblestoned roads and through little squares with fountains past all Berne's major sights.

Berne's five top (and topless) sights

St. Vincent Cathedral is an impressive Gothic Church with 16th-century statues depicting the Last Judgment. You'll have an incredible view of Berne and the Alps if you climb the 254 steps to the 330-foot tower.

The **Kunstmuseum** (Art Museum), *Hodlerstrasse 8-12*, has the world's largest Paul Klee collection. (Klee was a native of Berne.) Works by Modigliani and Picasso also are featured.

The **Bernisches Historisches Museum** (Historical Museum), *Helvetiaplatz 5*, displays booty from the Burgundian wars, including the tapestries and embroideries of Charles the Bold, Duke of Burgundy. The museum also has replicas of rural Swiss rooms and objects dating back to the Stone Age.

Zeitglockenturm, the city's medieval clock tower, rings several times a day to the delight of audiences. Mechanical bears, clowns, and kings perform at four minutes before every hour.

One of the most popular sights in Berne is the city's beach, lined with topless sunbathers. These free-spirited sun worshippers caused a good deal of controversy when they first disrobed (probably because the beach is right beneath Parliament's windows).

GIMMELWALD—THE MOST PICTURESQUE SWISS TOWN

Gimmelwald, a sleepy little town in the mountains near Interlaken, looks like something straight out of *Heidi*. You'll hear cowbells here and see farmers in lederhosen. Cars aren't allowed in Gimmelwald, which explains why it is so peaceful.

To get to Gimmelwald, take the Lauterbrunnen-Grutschalp funicular from Interlaken to Murren, where you'll find several good hotels. You have to hike the rest of the way from Murren.

Once in Gimmelwald, take the cable car to the summit of the Schilthorn, where you can dine in a revolving restaurant with a view across the valley to the German border. This was the setting for a James Bond movie.

ALPINE WILDERNESS AT ITS BEST

The **Swiss National Park** is the best place to enjoy a view of the Alps as God made them, untouched by the hand of man. The Swiss obviously want to keep it this way—fires, camping, pets, and mountain climbing are prohibited, and visitors may not leave designated trails. If you want to sleep in the park, you must stay in one of the designated lodges.

These rules may seem restrictive, but the results are a wonder. The 40,000-acre park is filled with wild valleys of woods and broken by torrential creeks. You'll see deer, ibex, camois, and marmots—but you won't see any trash dumps or unsightly trailer parks.

Walks through the park are organized at the Tourist Center, Zernez; *tel.*

(41)82-8-13-00. They are offered from the middle of June through the middle of October. The Sierra Club publishes a little book by William Reifsnyder called *Footloose in the Swiss Alps* that describes the park's trails and accommodations in detail and is updated every few years.

THE VALAIS — SWITZERLAND'S BEST VALLEY

The canton of Valais, situated in the heart of the Alps, is encircled by more than 50 peaks, all more than 13,000 feet high. To the north are the **Bernese Alps**, and to the south rise the **Alpes Valaisannes**. For centuries, the small town of Brig, capital of the Valais, has been a center of trade with Italy, but it is perhaps best known for three other characteristics: its hospitality (a huge and colorful sign decorated with a mountain fräuline welcomes you in German and French as you enter downtown); its Stockalper Castle, Switzerland's largest private residence, built between 1658 and 1678; and its position as the starting point for the beautiful Simplon Pass to the south.

And the Valais does not end in Brig. The **Rhone** continues from here, traveling northeast to a number of tiny towns that give you a true feeling of the area. Make a point of stopping in **Reckingen** to see its 18th-century Baroque church, perhaps the most beautiful building in the Valais. Also travel to **Crans-Montana**, which is actually two towns, **Crans-sur-Sierre** and **Montana**. Although it is perhaps the most touristy place in the entire valley, it is a skier's haven, attracting jet-setters from all over the world.

In the summer, the Valais is green and growing, with acres of terraced vineyards and fruit trees. Wander along the ancient aqueducts and canals, known as *bisses*. For a complete map of all the walking trails in the Valais, contact the **Swiss Hiking Association**, *Im Hirsalm 49, 4125 Rienen*.

The most affordable places to stay in the Valais

Unfortunately, the Valais region is as expensive as the rest of Switzerland, but there are ways to cut corners and still enjoy the scenery and sights. One way to cut costs is to stay in a *simmer-frei* instead of a hotel. These are similar to bed-and-breakfasts and are very affordable. In the mountains, stay in *cabanes*. These Alpine huts are scattered throughout the Valais. Some are open only to members of climbing clubs, but others are open to everyone.

For specifics on where to stay in the Valais, contact the local tourist offices: **Brig**, *tel. (41)28-23-19-01*; **Montana**, *tel. (41)27-41-30-41*; and **Crans-sur-Sierre**, *tel. (41)27-41-21-32*.

Switzerland's prettiest ski resort: Zermatt

Zermatt may be the most desirable piece of real estate in the world. It is a small, automobile-free village with a picture-postcard tangle of stately hotels. The Matterhorn dominates the town, which has very good skiing. But in season, the queues for the ski lifts are daunting. The hotels and restaurants, too, are crowded.

Zermatt's winter lifts reach as high as 11,500 feet, offering some of Europe's highest slopes and a whopping vertical drop of 6,300 feet. Zermatt's summer skiing is also Europe's best. The most popular run is down to Cervinia on the Italian side, which any strong intermediate skier can do in a morning.

Zermatt is also the best place in Europe for heli-skiing. The best hotels are the **Mont Cervin** (French for Matterhorn), which has an indoor pool, a sauna, and day-care facilities, and the **Zermatter Hof**, a modern hotel with a swimming pool, saunas, and a fitness center. Both are expensive.

Hotel Alex, *tel. (41)28-67-17-26*, run by former Matterhorn guide Alex Perren and his wife Gisela, is the center of social life in the winter. Facilities include an indoor swimming pool and indoor squash and tennis courts.

The **Hotel-Garni Metropol**, *tel. (41)28-67-32-31*, in the center of town on the banks of the Vispa River, has fabulous views. The Taugwalder family, which runs the hotel, recently bought a meadow opposite the hotel so that the views won't be spoiled. Each room has a private bathroom and a balcony facing the Matterhorn. The best are on the south side of the hotel.

Outside Zermatt, in Villars sur Ollon, is the first-class **Panorama Hotel**, *tel. (41)25-36-21-11.*

For more information on lodging and attractions in Zermatt go to *www.switzerlandtourism.com.*

Matterhorn: the most daunting peak

The killer Alp, as the **Matterhorn** is known, was scaled for the first time July 14, 1865. Four men were killed in the process. A young British illustrator named Edward Whymper arranged the climb. He, three British friends, a guide from Chamonix, and two guides from Zermatt first reached the peak.

On the return journey, one of the men slipped, dragging three of his fellow climbers with him to their deaths, 4,000 feet below. After the fall, Whymper and his two Swiss guides, the Taugwalders, father and son, reported seeing two crosses shining in a great arc of clouds in the sky.

The Matterhorn (14,688 feet) is intimidating, but you don't have to be an experienced mountain climber to scale its sides. You can climb the daunting mountain with the help of a Zermatt guide. It takes three to five days to take the easiest trails. Information on hiking the Matterhorn is available at the **Mountaineering Office**, *tel. (41)28-67-34-56*, near the tourist office.

THE BEST SWISS TRAIN RIDES

A more comfortable and relaxing way to climb the Alps is aboard the **Glacier Express**, which runs from Zermatt to St. Moritz. This train leisurely crosses 291 bridges, passes through 91 tunnels, spans the valleys of the Rhone and Rhine rivers, stops in typical mountain villages, heads into the wild, barren Gotthard region, and then climbs the 6,706-foot Oberalp Pass. The grand finale of the trip is a series of spectacular loops and tunnels that ends at St. Moritz.

THE MOST SPECTACULAR VIEWS OF THE ALPS

The most spectacular view of the Alps—indeed one of the most incredible mountain views in the world—is from **Kleine Scheidegg**, a peak near Interlaken. Take a train from Interlaken to Grindelwald and then another train to Kleine Scheidegg—or even higher to Mannlichen.

Kleine Scheidegg has a lodge and an outdoor restaurant, where you can watch mountain climbers dangling in the distance. You can hike back to Interlaken through the Lauterbrunnen Valley if you have the energy. Or you can take a train from Wengen to the valley floor.

THE PEARL OF THE SWISS LAKES

The pearl of Swiss lakeside resorts is **Montreux**, with its six-mile promenade lined with palm trees and tropical flowers on the shores of Lake Geneva. The climate here is the mildest on the north side of the Alps and produces fig trees, almond trees, cypresses, magnolias, and bay trees.

Montreux is famous for its international music festivals, especially the jazz festival in July, the International Choral Recitals the week after Easter, and the Musical September concerts.

Eden au Lac, *11 rue du Theatre; tel. (41)21-963-55-51*, a turn-of-the-century hotel on the lake in Montreux, is the best place to stay. Lunch is served in the hotel garden, right on the lake.

La Rotisserie de Chateau, *1844 Villeneuve; tel. (41)21-960-20-09*, a towered 17th-century building at the foot of a mountain, was once the residence of the Bouvier family (related to the House of Savoy). Wood-beamed ceilings and other antique touches, as well as the outside terrace, add charm to the rotisserie. The famous Castle of Chillon is nearby. The restaurant is closed Monday and Tuesday.

The best local specialties are served at **La Vieille Ferme**, *tel. (41)21-964-64-65*, a rustic restaurant outside town in Montreux-Chailly. The raclette is good, as is the country music. The restaurant is closed Mondays.

THE BEST OF LAUSANNE

Lausanne, another resort on Lake Geneva, is a French-speaking city and a university center. Its universities date back to the 16th century, but its students keep the atmosphere young. Excavations in Lausanne have uncovered Neolithic skeletons and a section of a Roman road where the Geneva-Lausanne highway now comes into town.

The best place to begin exploring Lausanne is **Place de la Palud**, in Old Town. This square is bordered by the Renaissance façade of the town hall and centered around the 16th-century Fountain of Justice.

Behind the fountain is an unusual covered staircase that leads to the town's 12th-century cathedral, one of the finest Gothic buildings in Switzerland. It shelters one of the last night watches in the world, whose duty is to call out the hour during the night. The south door of the cathedral, known as the Door of the Apostles, is covered with 13th-century sculptures. A 700-year-old rose window illustrates the elements, seasons, months, and signs of the zodiac. Climb the 232 steps to the top of the tower for a view of Lake Geneva and the Alps.

Switzerland's best restaurant

Lausanne boasts the best restaurant in Switzerland (and most of Europe): **Girardet**, *tel. (41)21-634-0505*. The chef does amazing things with fish and fresh produce. He is precise, yet inventive. Leave room for the chocolate soufflé. Make reservations far in advance.

Lausanne's most romantic hotel

The most romantic place to stay in the region is **Château d'Ouchy**, *tel. (41)21-26-74-51*. This 12th-century stronghold of the bishops of Lausanne is on Lake Geneva. It was the site of the Louis de Savoie Treaty in 1300 and became a government customhouse in the 1700s. A hotel was built around the castle in 1884, and the Lausanne Peace Treaty was signed here in 1923. The Salle des Chevaliers hasn't changed in 800 years. The hotel offers dancing, tennis, and excursions.

SWITZERLAND'S MOST BEAUTIFUL WATERFALLS

Near Interlaken, in the village of Lauterbrunnen, is the **Staubbach Waterfall**, which plunges 1,000 feet and then dissolves into a fine spray. Lord Byron described the falls as the "tail of the pale horse ridden by Death in the Apocalypse."

Not far away are the **Trummelback Falls**, which leap and boil, forcing their way through a series of eroded potholes.

THE BEST OF THE COMMONWEALTH OF INDEPENDENT STATES

"A riddle wrapped in a mystery inside an enigma." Those are the words that Winston Churchill used to describe the Soviet Union more than 60 years ago. And they are as appropriate today as they were when Churchill first spoke them.

MOSCOW'S BEST SITES

The first thing you must see in Moscow is a ballet at the **Bolshoi Theatre**, *tel. (7)095-250-73-17*. The second thing you must do while in Moscow is attend a traditional Russian banquet at the **Rossiya Hotel**, *tel. (7)812-329-39-25*. The banquet includes all the caviar and smoked salmon you can eat and all the champagne and vodka you can drink and the cost is cheap. But you have to know the right people—or be willing to offer a bribe to get in.

The **Arbat** has become Moscow's Speaker's Corner. Here you can enjoy the local street artists' scathing political cartoons and listen to the speakers, who rant and rave about anything that happens to be on their minds.

Also visit the country's largest department store, **GUM**, on Red Square. GUM boasts an elegant turn-of-the-century interior, comprising three parallel arcades centered on a fountain and overlooked by galleries. Light floods in through the building's glass roof and souvenir stands; foreign stores and designer boutiques fill the arcades.

The best eats

Shesh-Besh, *tel. (7)95-241-6542*, has a pleasant serving staff with an incredibly comfortable atmosphere, including quiet music playing in the background. Everyone can enjoy the cuisine, even vegetarians.

White Swan, *tel. (7)95-928-6000*, has been described as a small piece of Venice. In this restaurant choose a table by the window so you can enjoy the fabulous view of the pond, while enjoying outstanding European cuisine.

Samovar, *tel. (7)95-921-4688*, is a restaurant that mixes the new with traditional recipes. The atmosphere is welcoming and very charming. It specializes in Russian cuisine and is a great place to go to get the best meal for your money.

Tzarskaya Trapeza, *tel. (7)95-298-1327*, specializes in real Russian cuisine. This restaurant oozes Russian culture even in the décor. Could get a little pricey, but you should go for the unforgettable experience of a real Russian meal.

The best place in the world to buy an original work of art

The best values in Moscow, by far, are in art. Be the first on your block (or in your city) to own an original Russian painting. It will cost you just a few dollars—and there's the chance that it will be worth a small fortune one day. Arbat Street, closed to all but pedestrian traffic, is lined with shops and street vendors selling these original pieces of art, as well as souvenirs, clocks, books, linen, and ice cream.

THE BEST OF BELORUSSIA

Belarus is home to **Minsk**, a surprisingly attractive town (although it has the reputation of being one of the ugliest cities in the world). The avenues are wide and tree lined and a river flows through the town. Many of the public buildings are grand and well-designed. There is a pleasant walkway along the riverbanks (though it is littered by chunks of concrete that have fallen from nearby buildings). There is even a historic section that has been restored and preserved.

The best sites

Walk around the Old Town and along the river; you'll pass the city's hotels and art galleries. Also visit the house where Lee Harvey Oswald lived, the site of the first Communist meeting, and the city's monuments, scattered around town.

An interesting market is the **Storazhovsky Renok**. Here you can find fresh vegetables, fruits, bread, and other good food. There's also a lively pet and livestock market here.

THE MOST REMOTE REGIONS

Few Westerners have ever seen the remote peaks of the Central Asian Tien Shan and Pamir mountains. Travel here is still highly restricted.

The snow-peaked mountains of the **Tein Shan** (Heavenly) mountain range rise out of the hot and arid Central Asian steppelands to heights of 11,500 feet and 13,125 feet, extending into China in the east and the Himalayas in the south. Everlasting glaciers, green valleys, emerald lakes, rapid rivers, and ancient towns and cities are hidden in the mountains' valleys.

The Sairam Valley—the best gateway

The mountain valley of **Sairam**, at 5,580 feet, boasts a dry climate, crystal clear water, unusual rock formations, and birch and juniper woods. It acts as a gateway to the mountains in general. The mountains of Sairam are formed of limestone and basalt. The northern and western slopes are precipitous; the southern ones are more gradual and easily accessible.

The best practice climb

Among the most challenging climbs you can make is up **Mount Lenin**. At 23,400 feet, it is one of the highest peaks in this part of the world. It is a good place to practice before tackling the Karakorum or the Himalayas.

The best way to see the mountains

The best way to see the Tien Shan and Pamir mountains is with **ALTEX**, *Alma-Atinsky Prospekt, P.B. 22, 486011, Chimkent, Kazahkstan*, an organization specializing in hiking, rafting, and horseback riding programs in the CIS. Every package includes airfare, ground transportation, accommodation, and meals. The trips emphasize the people of the region, and accommodation is generally in the national Kazakh yurtas. The group is based in **Chimkent**, the regional center of southern **Kazahkstan**, one of the crossroads of the ancient silk caravan routes.

The best way to see the Soviet Far East

The Soviet Far East has been off limits to Western visitors since the 1930s, but no longer. You can visit this frontier land as a passenger on the **TransSiberian Express**. For more information contact **Intourist**, *tel. (7)95-753-000-3; e-mail: info@intourist.ru; website: www.orientexpress.ru/siberia.htm.*

THE BEST OF CHINA

CHINA? THERE LIES A SLEEPING GIANT. LET HIM SLEEP! FOR WHEN HE
WAKES, HE WILL MOVE THE WORLD.

—Napoleon

The People's Republic of China, the largest country in the world, is as big as all the countries in Europe combined. Its civilization flourished when the Occident was struggling its way out of the Dark Ages. It has the world's tallest mountains, the Himalayas, and it controls the world's highest city, Lhasa, in Tibet.

Although 92% of China's population is made up of Han people, the remaining 8% contains nearly 105 million members of minority groups. Tibetans, in their land of monasteries above the clouds, consider the Dalai Lama the head of the Buddhist religion; Mongolian horsemen roam the Gobi Desert; Chinese Muslims (Hui) live in the north; the Miao and Dai people in the south are related to the hill tribes of Southeast Asia.

THE BEST OF BEIJING

Beijing (Peking), one of the oldest cities in the world, has been the capital of China for 700 years. People have been living in this area for the last 50,000 years. Peking man, a fossil found in 1918 in a village southwest of Beijing, is one of the oldest relics of early man yet found.

Situated at the end of the route followed by camel caravans for centuries, Beijing is the site of many cities that have come and gone. Kublai Khan built his palace here and called the city Ta-tu (Great Capital). The northern part of the city has remnants of the old Mongol town visited by Marco Polo.

Beijing houses are some of the greatest man-made wonders of the world. The Emperor's Forbidden City in the heart of Beijing and the Great Wall on the outskirts of the city are the most notable attractions.

The Forbidden City

The **Forbidden City**, where the emperor of China once lived, is no longer barred to common man. Hundreds pass through the palace museum every day, gaping at the royal opulence. Surrounded by red brick walls and guarded by tile-roofed towers, the palace was built by Ming Emperor Yung Lo in the early 15th century and covers nearly 250 acres. For five centuries, China was ruled from here by the emperor, who was considered the son of heaven. His every wish was granted. His meals were prepared by 5,000 to

6,000 cooks, and concubines, eunuchs, court favorites, and entertainers were kept here.

Surrounded by 35-foot walls and a wide moat, the city contains six palaces, all roofed in yellow tile, and many gardens and pavilions. See the apartments of the emperor, the empress dowager, and the concubines; the halls of Supreme Harmony, Perfect Harmony, and the Preservation of Harmony; the temples; the libraries; and the art collection. Altogether, the rooms number 9,000.

The best way to prepare yourself for touring the palace is to see Bernardo Bertolucci's film *The Last Emperor*, which tells the sad story of China's last ruler who was, as a child, virtually imprisoned in the palace.

The world's largest public square

Tiananmen Square (the Square of Heavenly Peace), where Mao Zedong proclaimed the People's Republic of China in 1949, is the largest public square in the world, covering 100 acres and capable of holding one million people. As they have for centuries, the Chinese people come to hear government proclamations and to rally and demonstrate.

Ironically, thousands of students demonstrating here, in the Square of Heavenly Peace, were killed in 1989.

The square is bounded to the west by the Great Hall of the People, which contains a 328-foot-long marble hall and reception rooms where diplomatic meetings are held; to the east by the Museum of Chinese History and the Museum of the Chinese Revolution; to the north by the Tiananmen Gate to the Imperial City, built in 1417 and hung with a portrait of Mao Zedong; and to the south by the Quianmen gate, built in the 15th century. In the center is the 120-foot Monument to the People's Heroes, an obelisk depicting scenes from the revolution and inscribed with quotations by Mao Zedong and Zha En Lai.

Kite flying in the square is a popular pastime and a good way to meet locals. You can buy a colorful Chinese kite in any Friendship Store (government stores for tourists)—an exotic souvenir, unless it gets tangled in the gates to the Imperial Palace.

The most beautiful temple

The blue **Tiantan** (Temple of Heaven), built in the 15th century, is the finest example of Chinese architecture. Actually a complex of buildings, the temple is surrounded by a walled park. The most beautiful building in the complex is the Qi Nian Dian (Hall of Prayer for Good Harvest), set on three marble terraces, each with a 36-foot balustrade, connected to one another by eight flights of stairs. Supported by 28 columns and topped by 50,000 glazed blue tiles, the 123-foot hall was built of wood with no nails. Blue-roofed pavilions flank the temple.

Nearby is the **Huan Qiu Tan** (Round Altar), where each year for centuries on Dec. 20 (the day before the winter solstice), the emperor made a mysterious animal sacrifice that determined the destiny of the whole nation. The altar is made up of three terraces, each surrounded by a white marble balustrade with 360 pillars.

Beijing's best park

The most famous of Beijing's many parks is **Beihai**, or North Lake. The park has pagodas, formal gardens, and three lakes. Created in A.D. 300, the park is the best-preserved ancient garden in China. Young people row on the lakes and whisper sweet nothings on the shores. Closed during the Cultural Revolution, the park reopened in the 1980s.

In the middle of Beihai is an island called **Qionghua**, which is crowned by a Tibetan-style white dagoba (a shrine for sacred relics) built in 1651 to commemorate the visit of the Dalai Lama. The lovely **Zhichu Qiao** (Bridge of Perfect Wisdom) leads to the island.

The Empress Dowager's favorite place

Yiheyuan (the Summer Palace) on the outskirts of Beijing was the extravagant summer retreat of the infamous Empress Dowager Ci Xi. Located in the Haidian district and surrounded by a walled 692-acre park, the palace was built in 1888 to replace an older and supposedly more beautiful palace that was destroyed by British and French troops in 1860. (All that remains of the original are a marble arch, pillars, and a wall.) The existing palace, too, was burned by Western troops, during the Boxer Rebellion in 1900, but it was restored a few years later.

Stroll along the **Long Corridor**, bordering the lake and exquisitely painted with scenes from Chinese mythology. Visit the royal apartments, which contain jewel-encrusted furniture and beautiful works of art. Climb Longevity Hill, at the heart of the palace.

The best undiscovered sights

The **Gulou** (Drum Tower), near Shichahai Lake in northern Beijing, is a 15th-century structure in brick and wood, so named because a drum was beaten here to summon officials to audiences with the emperor. For some unknown reason, it is seldom visited by tourists.

Just 100 yards behind is the **Zhonglou** (Bell Tower), similar in design, built about 1745. The night watch announced the hour from here until 1924.

Between the two towers is a charming maze of residential streets that feel like they belong more in a small village than a large city. The stone houses here are tightly packed, topped with tiled roofs, and entered through doors that are thick, old, and decorated with iron. Clay walls surround courtyards that are broken by doors at irregular intervals. The area is safe at any hour, but you may get lost and have trouble finding someone who speaks English and can set you back on the right trail.

Another neighborhood worth exploring is a tangle of streets off **Wangfujing**, one of the main shopping streets, where Manchu nobility once lived. The formidable Empress Dowager Ci Xi was raised in one of the mansions on Xila Hatung. Another landmark in the neighborhood is the **East Church**, built in 1666 by the Jesuits. Pao Fa Hatung is lined with remnants of the **Fa Hua Si Temple** (Temple of Buddha's Glory), built in the 15th century. You can see the original walls, entry gates, and a small antechamber. The rest is gone.

The Great Wall

Forty-six miles from Beijing is the **Great Wall**. It stretches nearly 4,000 miles through the hills of northern China. It is the only man-made structure visible from the moon. Construction on most of the wall began in 403 B.C. and continued until 206 B.C. Thousands of men, many of whom were political prisoners, carried stones and dirt that make up the gigantic defense. Some of their bodies are buried inside. Once 6,000 miles long, much of it has been destroyed.

The section most visited is at **Badaling**, northwest of Beijing, which was constructed during the Ming dynasty (1368 to 1644). You can walk along the top—it is 18 feet wide and 21 feet tall. Look through the slots in the wall along the top and imagine the terrible battles that once raged against the barbarians from the north. Special trains and buses connect Beijing and the Great Wall.

To avoid all the tourists who gather at Badaling, go a bit farther afield to **Mutianyu**, where a restored section of the wall opened in the 1980s. A great fort with 22 watchtowers was built along this stretch. From the top, you'll have a view of the surrounding mountain slopes, forests, and the town of Mutianyu. To get to Mutianyu, hire a car or take the Dongzhimen Long Distance Bus Line. (Tickets must be purchased one day in advance.)

The Ming Tombs

On the way to the Great Wall are the **Ming Tombs**, where 13 of the 16 Ming emperors chose to be buried. **Shisanling**, the peaceful valley where the tombs are located, was chosen by the rulers because the winds and the water level ensured that only good spirits wandered the area.

The road to the tombs, known as the **Sacred Way**, is lined with 24 immense statues: 12 animals, real and mythical, and 12 mandarins in ceremonial dress. One of the Qing emperors is said to have wanted to take the statues to line the road to his own tomb. He abandoned the plan after dreaming that the statues are forever loyal to the Ming dynasty and that if he should move them an evil wind would blow across the capital.

Only two of the tombs have been excavated, those of Chang Ling and Ding Ling. The best-preserved and largest tomb is that of Chang Ling (the burial name for Yong Le), who died in 1424. It is entered through a red gate that opens into a courtyard. Another gate leads into a second courtyard, where the marble **Ling En Dian** (Hall of Eminent Favors) is supported by 32 giant tree columns. To get to the sepulcher, you must continue into a third courtyard.

The tomb of Ding Ling (the burial name for Emperor Wan Li) was the first to be excavated. A deep marble vault four stories underground contains the coffins of Ding and two of his wives, who were buried here in 1620. A bronze lion and gigantic marble doors guard the tomb. Inside are three coffins and 26 chests filled with jewelry.

Beijing's best restaurants

Fang Shan (Imitation Imperial), *tel. (89)10-6401-1879*, is the restaurant in Beihai Park. The goal of the chefs, who are said to have studied with the last empress' chefs, is to recreate dishes served to the royal families of the past. The restaurant is set on the shores of North Lake. It can be difficult to get reservations.

On the grounds of the Summer Palace, on Longevity Hill overlooking Kunming Lake, is **Ting Li Guan** (Listening to the Orioles Pavilion) restaurant, *tel. (89)6288-1608*. This restaurant features dumplings, velvet chicken, and other northern dishes. The **Sick Duck**, *13 Shuaifuyuan* (one block off Wangfujing), takes its name from a nearby hospital, not from the condition of its poultry. It is comfortable and close to the Beijing Hotel.

Beijing's best hotels

The **Beijing Hotel**, *33 East Chang'an Avenue and Wangfujing Street; tel. (86)1-513-7766*, takes the honorable first position. It was once the only good place in Beijing, and it's still the most exclusive. Foreigners cannot book rooms directly—you must go through an influential Chinese contact. Rooms are modern and spacious, many with color televisions, radios, and refrigerators. Some have balconies with views of the Forbidden City.

Xiang Shan (the Fragrant Hills), *Xiangshan Park, Haidian District; tel. (86)1-256-5544*, a 40-minute drive outside town and halfway to the Great Wall, was designed by the famous Chinese-American architect I.M. Pei. Jackie Kennedy was one of the hotel's first guests.

A grand, white fortress of a place, Xiang Shan has beautifully landscaped gardens and skillfully lit rooms. Double beds (an unusual feature in Chinese hotels), an outdoor swimming pool, and a health club are special features. While the Fragrant Hills is not conveniently located if you want to visit Beijing every day, it is surrounded by lovely countryside and situated near little-known shrines and monuments. For this reason, it may be the best place to stay on your *second* trip to Beijing.

    Zhu Yuan (Bamboo Garden Hotel), *24 Xiaoshiqiao, Jiugulou Street; tel. (86)1-444-661*, in an attractive residential neighborhood in the northern section of the city, has bamboo gardens, rookeries, air conditioning, and color televisions. It is near the Drum Tower and was once home to Kang Sheng, one of the Gang of Four.

    The **Holiday Inn Lido Beijing**, *Jichang and Jiang Tai roads; tel. (86)1-500-6688*, is Beijing's version of an American resort hotel. It has a bowling alley, restaurants and lounges, a health club, a swimming pool, and rooms with air conditioning, private bathrooms, color televisions, and direct-dial telephones. While it is comfortable, the Lido is outside town on the road to the airport.

    The **Shangri-La Hotel**, *29 Zizhuyuan Road; tel. (86)1-841-2211*, is another Western-style luxury hotel. It has an extensive health center with a pool, a sauna, a solarium, a squash court, and tennis courts. The business center is also well-developed, with meeting facilities of up to 1,000.

THE BEST OF GUANGZHOU

    Still known to most English-speaking people as Canton, **Guangzhou** is a popular point of entry for foreign tourists visiting China—it is only three hours from Hong Kong by train. (By the way, you can buy lovely silk Chinese scarves on the Guangzhou train from Hong Kong for half-nothing.)

    Unlike the rest of China, which stayed free of outside influence until well into the 19th century, Guangzhou began dealing with foreign traders in A.D. 714. Thus, a foreigner has never been much of a rarity here. Besides Shenzhen, China's Special Economic Zone, Guangzhou is the most capitalist (and Western-influenced) city in China.

    Early on, the Chinese government thought it best to canton the barbarians, as foreign traders were known, so they wouldn't corrupt the rest of the kingdom—hence, the name Canton. Arab, Portuguese, English, French, and American traders who sailed up the Pearl River were isolated and cantoned in their own areas. After their victory in the First Opium War, the Europeans were given an island in the Pearl River off Canton's waterfront, called Shamian. French and Victorian buildings still can be seen here.

    Another result of foreign influence: Guangzhou has one of China's largest Muslim communities and the nation's oldest mosque, dating from A.D. 627.

    This city remains a trading capital, and the mixture of local and foreign influences is as exotic today as it must have been to residents and traders of the Middle Ages.

Top sights

    Zhenhailou (Tower Overlooking the Sea) is a five-story red pagoda built in 1380 on the highest hill in Yuexiu Park, originally a temple. Today it is the Guangzhou Historical Museum—fitting, considering the pagoda's involvement in Guangzhou's history. It served as a watchtower during the Opium War, when it was seized by French and British troops, and again during the 1911 revolution.

If you climb all the way to the top of the tower, you will be rewarded with a cup of green tea and a view of the park and the city. The museum's exhibits are displayed in chronological order from prehistoric times to the modern day.

The graceful Five Goats Statue, a reminder of Guangzhou's mythical beginnings, is also in Yuexiu Park. According to legend, the city was founded by five gods bearing stalks of rice who rode to earth on five goats, the rice symbolizing a promise that the city would never go hungry. (That promise wasn't kept.) Guangzhou is still known as Yangcheng, or Goat City.

Cultural Park, near the Pearl River, covers 20 acres and includes an aquarium, an opera house, a concert hall, seven exhibition halls, three television screens for the public, two open-air theaters, a roller-skating rink, a teahouse, a Ping-Pong area, and flower gardens.

Chen Clan Academy, a 19th-century compound, is one of the world's best examples of late imperial southern Chinese architecture. The roof and walls are decorated with terracotta sculptures, and the windows, doors, columns, and roof beams are carved. This family-run school of Confucian studies was built around an ancestral temple where you can still see an altar and a shrine.

At the Chen Clan Academy, you can buy bottles, decorated inside with Shantou paintings, a characteristic art form of southern China. These tiny glass bottles, about three inches high, are elegant and antique in style. Pictures are drawn within the bottles, which have pea-sized mouths. Fine scenery, all sorts of characters, flowers, birds, insects, and fish are painted on the inside surface. Golden patterns on the outside surfaces of the bottles enhance their beauty. These bottles are appreciable art treasures, seldom seen except in museums.

China's largest garden

The largest garden in China, the **South China Botanical Gardens**, is found just northeast of Guangzhou. Covering 750 lush acres, it boasts one of the best botanical collections anywhere in the world. For more information *tel. (212)382-3725.*

The oldest mosque and the best cathedral

Foreign visitors brought foreign religions to Guangzhou and, as a result, the city has two buildings that may seem out of place in a country with a Buddhist past and a Communist present. On Zhongshan Road, near the intersection with Haizhu Road, is the **Huaisheng Mosque**, the oldest in China. It was built in A.D. 627 by an uncle of the prophet Mohammed, who is said to have brought the first Koran to China. It is now the mosque of China's largest Muslim community, which is estimated at 4,000. On the Yide Road, near the popular Renmin Daxia Hotel, is a Gothic-style cathedral that was designed by the French architect Guillemin and built in 1860. During the Cultural Revolution, this building was used as a warehouse; however, it was renovated and reconstructed in 1979 and now holds regular Sunday services.

The best shopping

International traders still flock to Guangzhou for the **Chinese Export Commodities Fair**, held October 15th to October 30th and April 15th to April 30th, in the big exhibition hall near the Dong Fang Hotel.

If you are interested in more modest retail purchases, wander along Renmin Road, home of the Nanfang department store complex, the biggest in the city. Number eight is a well-stocked poster store, number 14 is a tea shop, number 20 is a housewares store, and number 60 is a barbershop that brings a bit of the American West to Southeast Asia. You can unearth fine antiques on Hongshu Road, in an antiques warehouse that has just about anything you could want.

While shopping, stop for a snack in the most popular dumpling shop in town, the **Nanfang**, *number 35*.

China's best food

Guangzhou's cuisine is the best in China and the best-known in the West, where Cantonese restaurants are common. However, exported Cantonese cuisine is not the real thing. In Canton, the ingredients are exotic, including snake, dog, frogs, and rats. The people of Guangzhou have an expression that explains, "The things flying in the sky, except the planes, can be eaten. The things on the ground with four legs, except the tables, can be eaten."

If you're feeling adventurous enough to try monkey brain, try **She Canguan**, *41 Jianglan Lu*. Guangzhou's most palatable contribution to the world is dim sum or dyan syin, a Chinese brunch that consists of a long series of small courses, served over one to two hours. Most of the dishes are different varieties of dumplings filled with pork, seafood, or vegetables.

Banxi, *tel. (86)20-8181-5718*, is Guangzhou's biggest and best dim sum restaurant. Yuyuan, tel. (86)10-6502-5985, is also good. Try the chicken steamed in Maotai and the crab paste dumplings. If you prefer atmosphere, eat at **Nanyuan**, *120 Qianjin Road;* it offers dining in a splendid garden.

The best hotels

The **White Swan Hotel**, *tel. (86)20-8188-6968*, was China's first five-star hotel. Rooms are decorated in jade-colored silk and filled with walnut furniture. The hotel opened in early 1983 and quickly distinguished itself with its many guest services (including a 24-hour laundry), its 30 dining rooms, its trilingual staff, and its astounding variety of fitness activities. The hotel offers its guest services of a tiny but strong Chinese masseuse, who will give you a great acupressure massage, including walking on your back.

The lobby is one of the most beautiful anywhere. And the hotel has reasonably priced shops selling Chinese silk rugs, hand-painted screens, gigantic carved jade boats, and silk paintings. The building is situated on Shamian Island in the Pearl River, where a legendary hero is said to have been spirited away by a white swan. Free shuttle service is available to the hotel from the train station.

The most romantic temporary address in Guangzhou is the **Dong Fang Hotel**, *120 Liuhua Road; tel. (86)20-669-900*—not so much for its appearance, which is strictly Soviet revival, but for its inhabitants. Journalists, consular personnel, and powerful international businessmen have stayed in the rooms here. The dining room serves everything from Wiener schnitzel to Indian curries, from Japanese tempura to American apple pie.

Two of China's most luxurious hotels are outside Guangzhou, on the slopes of Baiyun (White Cloud Mountain): the **Shanzhuang** and the **Shuangxi**. Guests stay in large villas with sunken baths, private gardens, and lovely sitting rooms. Chinese government officials and high-ranking foreigners are among the guests.

The best side trips from Guangzhou

Nine miles from Guangzhou is **Bai Yun Shan**, which rises 1,400 feet and has a panoramic view of the city, the countryside, and the river. At the top are teahouses and pavilions, where you can recover from the six-hour climb. Don't stray from marked paths—the government doesn't want Americans getting too close to the nearby defense installations.

China's best mineral springs are in **Conghua**, 50 miles north of Guangzhou. The eight springs are about 104 degrees Fahrenheit and are said to cure chronic ailments. They are worth visiting, even if you feel fine, just for the views—they are surrounded by mountains, lichee orchards, plum trees, and bamboo groves.

Zixingyan (Seven Star Crags) is a series of natural rock towers connected by arched bridges and little pathways. Five small lakes and several caves lie in the shadow of traditional pavilions, which provide shelter. You can get to Zixingyan by bus or taxi in three hours.

SHANGHAI: CHINA'S LARGEST CITY

Shanghai was the most powerful city in China before the Communists took over in 1949. Merely a fishing village in the 17th century, it gained its wealth from trades as a treaty port opened by the Europeans during the Opium Wars. Controlled by the British from 1842 until 1949, Shanghai still has a western air and has been compared to New York and Rome. Before the Chinese Revolution, it had a lively stock market and great wealth.

Today, Shanghai is one of the largest cities in the world—and, with more than 15,000 coal-burning factories, the most polluted. Until a few years ago, it was considered China's most important city economically. Covering 2,344 square miles, metropolitan Shanghai remains China's most cosmopolitan city.

The prettiest neighborhood

Shanghai's most charming corner is **Old Town**, the Chinese ghetto during the British occupation. Between Jinling, Renmin, and Zhonghua roads are narrow streets, thatched huts, tiny shops, and outdoor markets with piles of fresh produce. In the northeast section of Old Town is a bazaar where you can buy beautifully carved walking sticks and traditional Chinese handicrafts. A little farther north are the Temple of the Town Gods and the Garden of the Purple Clouds of Autumn. Be careful; it's easy to get lost in this maze.

Forget the fancy restaurants and eat in the area's little food shops. (But don't drink the water.) Chinese lunchtime fare is cheap and fun to eat.

The best opium dens and brothels

Until 1949, the area west of People's Park, off Fuzhou Road, was the heart of Shanghai's world-famous red-light district known as **Blood Alley**. Before it was cleared out, it was inhabited by thousands of opium addicts and prostitutes. Liberation Lane alone, then known as Meet-With-Happiness Lane, has 34 brothels worked by more than 1,000 women. From 1949 until 1954, the brothels and opium dens were closed, the prostitutes given new work and new identities, and the addicts detoxified.

Yu Yuan: the happiest garden

At the heart of the Old Town is **Yu Yuan Garden** (Garden of Happiness), built in 1577 by a city official as a peaceful retreat for his ageing father. It includes more than 30 halls and pavilions, all with charming names: Pavilion for Paying Reverence to Weaving, Fairyland of Happiness, Tower for Observing Waves, and Tower for Appreciating the Moon. A tall, white brick wall topped with stone dragons divides the garden into three separate areas. Each section is designed to create the illusion of space and depth via artificial hills, ponds, bridges, and miniature gardens. A small lake at the center of the garden is crossed by zigzag bridges and bordered by teahouses and pavilions. The scene inspired the famous Blue Willow china pattern.

When you tire of the crowds in Yu Yuan Garden, take a break at **Wuxing Ting** (Five Star Pavilion), a teahouse just opposite the garden.

The World's Best Destinations

The Temple of the Town Gods

Not far from Yu Yuan is **Cheng Huang Miao** (Temple of the Town Gods), devoted, as its name implies, to the ancient town gods. Once, every Chinese town had such a temple. This is one of the few that remain. Behind the temple is a garden with a lake, pavilions, and artificial hills. Qiu Xia Pu (the Garden of the Purple Clouds of Autumn) was laid out during the Ming dynasty.

The liveliest promenade

The most delightful place to stroll in Shanghai is **Wai Tan** (the Bund), the area around Zhongshan Park, Zhongshan Road, and the Wiusong River, near the Old Town. The park is green with shade trees and decorated with rock and flower gardens. During the British occupation, the Chinese were forbidden to be in this area. The tall buildings that line the Bund once housed international banks and corporations; now they house the Bank of China and government offices.

Evening is the best time to stroll along the Bund, when city lights reflect in the water. If you are energetic, come here in the morning and join the locals in their daily Tai Chi Quan exercises.

China's best art collection

The three stories of the **Shanghai Museum**, *tel. (86)29-523-6688* or *toll free (1)800-840-9555*, house the finest art collection in China. The first floor has bronzes from the Shang and Western Zhou dynasties (1523 B.C. until 771 B.C.). The most interesting objects are the instruments of torture. The second floor has ceramics from the Neolithic era to the present, including life-size terracotta statues of warriors and a horse from Emperor Qin Shi Huangdi's tomb in Xi'an. Scrolls from the Tang, Song, Yuan, Ming, and Quing dynasties are kept on the third floor, where good reproductions are sold.

The best Buddhas

The **Jade Buddha Temple**, in northwest Shanghai, has two statues of Buddha, each carved out of a single piece of white jade. Monks brought them to China from Burma in 1890. Several other statues fill the halls of the temple. Twenty-four monks still live here.

The oldest and biggest temple

Shanghai's oldest and largest temple is **Longhua**, in the southern suburbs. Built before A.D. 687, it has four main halls, drum and bell towers, and a seven-story pagoda next door. The best time to see the temple and pagoda is early spring, when the peach trees blossom.

The best entertainment

The **Shanghai Acrobatic Theatre**, *tel. (86)6327-7182*, presents skilled and exciting shows every day except Tuesday. You should see this impressive show, but realize that it is a production intended entirely for tourists and part of every package tour in the city.

The best undiscovered entertainment

The best place to people-watch and listen to great jazz is at the nightclub in the **Peace Hotel**, *tel. (86)21-632-1688*. The band members play as if they have been playing together forever. The music is good and atmosphere unbeatable. You can get the band to play your favorite tunes all night—just buy them a carton of Marlboro cigarettes.

The most exotic foods

Food is sold helter-skelter on the streets of Shanghai. Shortly before New Year's Day, the sidewalks are piled with carcasses of pigs ready for the butcher. The below-freezing temperatures keep the meat from spoiling. On New Year's Day, men sell pancakes cooked over barrel stoves in the streets and set out chickens in cages or baskets of eggs.

Snake is a specialty. Customers choose their favorite snakes from squirming masses on the snakemongers' tabletops. Restaurants devoted exclusively to this delicacy are located throughout Shanghai.

The best Shanghai cuisine

Lao Fandian (Old Restaurant), *tel. (86)6328-2782*, is a local café serving typical Shanghai food and a good lunch stop after a morning in the Old City. It's beside the parking lot at the entrance to the Old City shopping area.

Meilongzhen, *tel. (86)6253-5353*, is a well-established spot for Shanghai and Sichuan cuisine, located in the 1930s Communist Party Headquarters.

Gongdelin, *tel. (86)6327-0218*, is a veteran vegetarian (Buddhist) restaurant with a long history of artistic and savory dishes.

Laozhengxing Restaurant, *tel. (86)6511-2145*, meaning Old Prosperity, is a small, well-respected place famous for its turtle, crab, and fish.

The best hotels

The **Heping (Peace) Hotel**, *tel. (86)21-632-1688*, is part of the last of the metropolitan life Shanghai used to have. The hotel rooms have high ceilings and are spacious 1930s-style suites that even have attached servant rooms.

Another aging hotel is the **JinJiang**, *tel. (86)6258-2582*. It is in a group of mansions surrounded by a wall in the French Quarter. The grounds are beautifully landscaped, with a feeling of sophistication.

The **Shanghai Mansions Hotel**, *tel. (86)21-632-46-260*, has average rooms, but its suites are breathtaking. Some come with a private balcony and a grand piano and the view from the rooftop terrace is picturesque.

Hua Ting Sheraton, *tel. (86)21-6439-1000*, offers modern luxury and superior service.

Shenzhen—the most open door in China

Shenzhen, the coastal region just across the border from Hong Kong, is China's most successful economic experiment. The Special Economic Zone, as it is known, is rapidly becoming a thriving metropolis.

The best miniature recreation of a place

Shenzhen is home to one of the best sites in China: **Splendid Miniature China**, a huge park where all of China is laid out in miniature. It displays models of the best of China, including the Imperial Palace in Beijing (China's largest), Zhaozhou Bridge in Hebei (the most ancient stone arch bridge), the Ancient Star Observatory in Beijing (the oldest astronomical observatory), the Great Wall, and the terracotta soldiers and horses near Xi'an.

In most any other country in the world, we would tell you to shy away from a splendid miniature recreation of a place. Tourist trap, we'd warn. But China is a special case. Travel here is so difficult and slowgoing that most travelers would never be able to see everything this ancient country has to offer.

For more information contact **China Travel Service Ltd.**, *21st Floor, CTS House, 78-83 Connaught Road, Central, Hong Kong; tel. (852)853-3888*, or the **Shenzhen Splendid China Development Company Ltd.**, *Overseas Chinese Town, Shenzhen Special Economic Zone, People's Republic of China*.

Shenzhen's best hotel

As Shenzhen struggles to transform itself into a modern metropolis, beautiful hotels are springing up where chicken coops and rice paddies stood only a few years ago. One of the finest is the **Forum**, *tel. (1)800-359-4827*. It has seven restaurants and very comfortable rooms, with 24-hour room service.

Hangzhou: the best silks and embroideries

Hangzhou, which lies on the startlingly beautiful Xi Hu (West Lake), is known for its silks, embroideries, tea, and gourmet restaurants. You can watch silk being made at the Hangzhou Silk Dyeing and Printing Mill, where nearly 5,000 workers produce silk by reeling fibers off silkworm cocoons, and then print designs on the finished fabric. Mulberry trees, where silkworms' cocoons are found, grow in profusion in the surrounding countryside.

Longjing (Dragon Well) tea is picked and dried at the **West Lake People's Commune**, where you can watch the work or try your hand at tea-leaf picking.

Four islands with pavilions and temples float in West Lake. The largest and most beautiful is **Gu Shan** (Solitary Hill) in the northwest. The second largest, **Three Pools Mirroring the Moon**, is beautiful on moonlit nights, when the pagodas along the water, lit with candles and sealed with thin paper, look like moons on the water.

SUZHOU, THE VENICE OF CHINA

With its maze of canals bordered by small whitewashed houses and weeping willows, **Suzhou**, is the most romantic town in China. China's most famous romantic novel is set here, *The Dream of the Red Chamber*. Gnarled sycamore branches bend low over the town's narrow cobblestoned streets, where high walls shield private gardens.

Suzhou's other claims to fame are its gardens—150 in all. The two loveliest are **Zhuozhengyuan** (the Humble Administrator's Garden) and **Liuyuan** (the Tarrying Garden). Both have elements of traditional Chinese gardens: pavilions, ponds, bridges, rock sculptures, and temples. They are two of China's four nationally protected gardens (the other two being the Summer Palace in Beijing and the Imperial Mountain Resort in Changde).

Most of Suzhou's shops are grouped close together in the downtown area. One of the best places to shop is the Friendship Store, which caters exclusively to foreigners. Here you find a large and varied selection of silk (Suzhou is known for the quality of its silk), dry goods, and clothing. Collectors will drool over the extensive selection of unusual Chinese antiques. Local handicrafts also are featured, including fragrant sandalwood fans and double-faced embroidery.

GUILIN AND THE LI RIVER: BEAUTY DEFINED

The sharp peaks so often depicted on the Chinese scrolls exist in Guilin, know for its majestic natural beauty. Set in the Karst Hills of southern China, Guilin has shrouded limestone peaks and subterranean caverns.

You can visit some of the spectacular caves in the hills around Guilin. Reed Flute Cave in the northwest suburbs was once a refuge for villagers escaping enemy armies and bandits. Inside is a grotto, **Shuijinggong** (Crystal Palace), that holds 1,000 people.

A Stone Age matriarchal people lived in **Zengpiyan Cave**, where 14 human skeletons have been found, as well as skeletons of elephants, boar, and deer. The cave is open to visitors.

Seven Star Park contains six caves. The most famous **Long Lin** (the Dragon Refuge Cave), has walls carved with ancient inscriptions.

The best river cruise

The best way to see this region is to take a cruise on the **Li River**. As you float downriver, look for Elephant Trunk Hill, Old Man Mountain, Folded Brocade Hill, and Crescent Moon Hill. You'll be able to recognize each by its name.

You will pass lush tropical scenery—fruit trees, bamboo groves, sugarcane, and rice paddies—as well as a 1,300-year-old banyan tree.

Boats leave at 7:30 a.m. or 8:30 a.m., depending on the season, and sail for five hours, docking for a time at the small village called Yangdi, at the base of two mountains. This is a good place to shop. Local peasants meet the boat, anxious to sell their produce and handicrafts, at bargain prices.

For more information on Li River boat cruises stop by the **Tourist Office**, *14 Ronghu Bei Road, Guilin.*

XI'AN: ONCE THE WORLD'S LARGEST CITY

Once the largest city in the world, Xi'an, in north central China, is filled with archeological wonders. The most famous is the tomb of China's first emperor, Qui Shi Huangdi, which is guarded by 8,000 life-size terracotta soldiers.

Chang An, as the city was known in ancient times, was the capital of 11 dynasties, and the hills to the north of the city are filled with ancient tombs. Qin Shi Huang Di, who completed the Great Wall in the third century B.C., chose Xi'an as his capital. Under the Tang dynasty, from the seventh through the 10th centuries, it became the largest city in the world, with a population of about one million.

Today, the masses are returning to Xi'an, this time as tourists. In fact, more foreign visitors are appearing in the city than at any time since the eighth century.

While Xi'an is an industrial city congested with throngs of bicyclists, remnants of the city's loftier past remain. A medieval city wall can be seen in places. Two pagodas, Big Wild Goose and Small Wild Goose, watch over the city from a distance. (The view from the top of Big Wild Goose takes in the city and the green fields beyond.) And the city museum has the Forest of Steles, 1,000 standing stone tablets inscribed with ancient poems, essays, and images.

Xi'an has a large Muslim population and a functioning Great Mosque. This, too, is a remnant of the city's past, when trade routes from all over the world led here. The best day to see the mosque is Friday, when about 2,000 Chinese Muslims arrive to pray in the splendid Ming dynasty prayer hall.

The best collection of ancient artifacts

The **Shaanxi Provincial Museum**, in a former Confucian temple in the south of the city, has the best collection of ancient artifacts in China. It is made up of three main buildings and three annexes and can hold 4,000 separate exhibitions. The Forest of Steles—1,000 standing stone tablets inscribed with ancient poems, essays, and images—is the museum's most important display. Also important is the stone menagerie—a collection of gigantic statues of real and imaginary animals that once guarded royal tombs.

Xi'an top sights

At the center of Xi'an is a Ming dynasty bell tower that provides a convenient vantage point when scouting out street routes. Within sight is Xi'an's drum tower (inside is the city's best antique shop), marking the city's Hui, or Chinese Muslim, neighborhood. The aquiline features and bearded faces of the men here bear witness to their Arab ancestry. Arab and Persian merchants and mercenaries came to Chang An during the Tang dynasty (A.D. 618 to A.D. 907). The men of this neighborhood often congregate on the tranquil grounds of the Chinese-style mosque.

Throughout old Xi'an are many small shops offering handmade products. Follow the hammer taps to the tinsmith. Simple enamelware, army canteens, straw hats, oilcloth umbrellas, and chopsticks are some of the souvenirs you can buy here. Roast chicken is sold by Hui street peddlers, whose lamplit stands dot the street corners in the evenings.

Stop at the **Hua Xing Hot Springs**, outside town, where, according to a local joke, Chiang Kai-Shek left his dentures when running from the Chinese Red army. (He was arrested here in 1936.) The lush oasis was popular with the Chinese emperors, who bathed in the hot springs with their concubines and built a number of palaces in the area. After the court moved from Xi'an, the palaces were turned into a Taoist monastery.

Today, some of the buildings are used as a spa. The springs, discovered 2,800 years ago, have a temperature of 110 degrees Fahrenheit and are said to be curative.

The **Xing Jiao Temple**, located southeast of Xi'an, is the burial site of the Tang dynasty monk, the patron saint of the Silk Route. Xuan Zhuang traveled to India and back in A.D. 627 on a quest for Buddhist scriptures.

China's greatest archeological find

The 8,000 life-sized terracotta warriors found in Lingtong County, 20 miles east of Xi'an, are the 20th century's most exciting archeological find. In 1974, a group of well diggers accidentally unearthed the ancient figures, which stood guard at the tomb of Emperor Qin Shi Huangdi for 2,000 years.

The first emperor of China, Qin Shi Huangdi united warring states and completed the Great Wall, as protection against northern barbarians. His tomb is divided into three vaults. The first contains the infantry, each statue with an individualized face. The second and third contain an additional 2,000 figures of men, horses, and chariots. The emperor himself is buried a distance away, hidden in a maze of corridors and gates.

The emperor began to build the army of life-sized soldiers when he came to power at age 13. Over a period of 36 years, Qin conscripted three-quarters of a million countrymen to build 6,000 figures and ordered the statues to guard his tomb. (The model soldiers acted as substitutes for real soldiers, who in earlier times would have been buried with their emperor.)

The figures have stood for centuries 20 feet underground in an area the size of a football field. Most are lined up in marching positions as they would have been on a military campaign, while others are being pulled in chariots by teams of horses. The painted soldiers are modeled after Qin's live honor guard and carry real swords, spears, and crossbows, set to be triggered by invaders. Despite the decoys and booby traps, however, looters raided Qin's tomb four years after his death.

The best food and spirits

Sichuan Restaurant, *Jiefang Lu, near the train station; tel. (86)29-714-863*, is Xi'an's most inviting restaurant. No less than 125 varieties of *jiaozi* (Chinese ravioli) are served here, with names such as Buddha's Claw and Make Money. Try the local liquor with your dinner, a pale spirit with the unappetizing name *Kueihua Chen Chew* (yellow osmanthus thick wine). This sweet but potent brew has a way of obliterating your memory.

De Fa Zhang Jiaozi Shop specializes in dumpling feasts. The restaurant has numerous feasts to choose from, all delicately sweet and rich.

China's best hotel

The **Golden Flower Hotel**, *8 Chang'le Road W., Xi'an, Shaanxi; tel. (86)29-323-2981*, offers rooms that are vast by present-day standards in China, well-lit, tastefully decorated, and equipped with two queen-sized beds. The staff is impeccable and speaks English.

Facilities at the Golden Flower include secretarial and translation services, money changing, and a gift shop. The hotel runs tours and a fleet of taxis, and the concierge can negotiate restaurant reservations, prices, and menus. The local restaurant offers Sichuan and Shaanxi food.

THE MOST EXOTIC DESTINATION: THE SILK ROUTE

The legendary **Silk Route** is far from silken. Ancient caravans following the route braved trackless deserts, towering mountains, and staggering distances to barter with foreign merchants or to spread new religions. Although some of the terrain is paved today, it remains a difficult passage. However, the payoff for undertaking the trip is great: the stark beauty of the land-scape; the friendly, freedom-loving Uygurs; the colorful bazaars; and the incomparable religious art.

This 3,720-mile network of routes has spanned Eurasia since the second century B.C. Beginning at China's ancient capital Chang An (moder Xi'an), it snakes to Kashgar in western China and then splits. The main route climbs the Himalayas and continues west to Samarkand (the southern part of what used to be the Soviet Union), Persia (now Iran), and Rome. One alternate route dips down to Pakistan.

The Chinese leg of the route is probably all you'll have the time and for-titude to travel. Guided tours are practical for those with limited tolerance or language skills.

Buddhist bests

Twenty miles from Lanzhou are the **Bilingsi Buddhist Caves**, which are definitely worth visiting. China International Travel Service (CITS) arranges inexpensive tours to the caves. Buddhist monks dug the caves into the face of a 180- foot cliff about 1,500 years ago. They are full of Buddhist statues, sculptures, and murals. From here, the Silk Route crosses the Wei River Valley into the arid province of Gansu, where it flanks the Great Wall for 700 miles. Eventually, it comes to **Jiayuguan**, a fortress built by Ming dynasty rulers in 1372 as their western outpost.

Northwest of Jiayuaguan are the **Thousand Buddha Grottoes** at Dunhuang, an oasis stuck in the middle of the Gansu Desert. In the old days, this dusty little place was a vital staging post for camel caravans going east and west—here the northern and southern branches of the Silk Route met. Only 40 of the 500 cave temples are open to the public. Each enshrines superb paintings and sculptures that were commissioned over a period of 1,500 years by rich and pious pilgrims and merchants as gestures of thanks for a safe journey on the Silk Route. Bring a flashlight to see the details of the works.

The best of the desert

The **Taklmakan Desert**, which the route follows on the southern border, translates from Uygur to mean "Once you go in, you never get out." The desert is haunted not by the specters that the ancients feared but by the sounds of underground nuclear testing. A long, parched trip via bus and train will lead you out of the desert and into Turpan, a cultural oasis where grape arbors shade courtyards.

The friendliest people

Descendants of the Uygurs make up the region's largest—and friendliest —ethnic group (besides the Han Chinese). Their language is Turkish, their religion Islam. Cool evenings, when the people are outdoors, are the best times to meet the Uygurs. Invitations to their adobe huts are not unusual.

The best of the past

Nearby ruins of two ancient Silk Route cities still have recognizable streets, town walls, and buildings. **Gaochang**, the larger of the two cities, was the capital of the Uygur kingdom in the ninth century. It once hosted Marco Polo and is a vast and slightly terrifying place.

Jiaohe, perched above a riverbed, was a Chinese garrison until it came under local control. Its main road is still clearly visible.

Join with other travelers and hire a minibus to take you to the ruined cities.

The Silk Route's best guesthouse

The best place to stay in Turpan is the **Turpan Guesthouse**, *Qingnian Road*, not the garish Tour group hotel up the road. The guesthouse is one of the great joys of the Silk Route. Plan to stay several days. Relax on the vine-covered verandas, sipping cool beer, snacking on grapes, and contemplating the pat splendors of the Silk Route.

China's least desirable digs

The **Turpan Depression**, which surrounds the town of Turpan, has been called one of the strangest places on earth. It lies nearly 500 feet below sea level and can get so hot in the summer that people live in the underground cellars of their homes. An underground irrigation channel was built 2,000 years ago to bring melted snow from the Tian Shan Mountains in the north (hence the profusion of well-watered melon and grape crops in the middle of the desert).

Ugliest city, loveliest carpets

A few hours beyond Turpan is **Ürümqi**, one of the ugliest, most polluted cities in China. One thing saves this industrial city—it has the country's best carpet market. To find it, go to the **Hua Qiao Hotel** (popular with overseas Chinese), *51 S. Xinhua Road; tel. (86)991-70530*, head toward the city center, and turn into the fourth lane on the right. At the end is a bustling little market with noodle restaurants, kebab stalls, teahouses, clothes shops, and a magnificent array of carpets.

The best of Switzerland in the desert

Once you have visited the market, head out of town toward **Heaven Lake**, a bit of Switzerland halfway up Bogda Shan (the Mountain of God). The trip takes four hours.

Deep Blue Heaven Lake is surrounded by pine forests and snow-capped peaks. The Kazakhs, herders, and horsemen (not to be confused with Russian Cossacks) set up their yurts (dome tents) in the cool meadows here during the summer.

If you can't face returning to Ürümqi, you can rent a yurt from a Kazakh nomad. Or you can stay at the Heavenly Lake Hotel, on the shore of the lake.

The best horsing around

While in Ürümqi, you may be invited to see the *boz kashi*, a contest of horsemanship. Riders must carry a headless goat or lamb from one end of the field to another. Because this spectacle appears to lack either a referee or rules, it's best to view it from a safe perch.

China's westernmost city

From Ürümqi, you can fly to **Kashgar**, China's westernmost city and the end of the Chinese portion of the Silk Route. (If you continue on from here, you will end up in Pakistan.) But taking the three- or four-day trip in the company of Uygurs, Mongols, Tibetans, and Han Chinese better duplicates Silk Route sojourns of long ago. The buses make frequent stops that give you a chance to sample the area's plentiful melons.

They say Kashgar is farther from the sea then any other town on earth. When you get there, you'll believe it. The streets are narrow and dusty, lined with adobe houses. This is one of the most important cities on the Silk Route; it is at the borders of Russia, Afghanistan, India, and Pakistan. When Marco Polo passed through Kashgar, he called it "the starting point from which many merchants set out to market their wares all over the world."

One thing above all must be seen in Kashgar: the **Sunday Market**. When you plan your trip, make sure you will be in town on a Sunday. Hundreds of thousands of people (mostly Uygurs) swarm to an area on the outskirts of town, where they buy and sell everything you can imagine—and much you can't. The most exciting part of the market is where the Kazakh horsemen test-ride horses in an enclosure full of donkeys, sheep, goats, cows, and camels.

Near the market is **Id Kah Mosque**, one of the largest in China. Built in 1442, it dominates the old town and draws thousands of worshipers every Friday. If you aren't in town on a Sunday, many of the goods available at the market can also be purchased at the bazaar near the Id Kah Square.

When you tire, relax over a meal at the **Tian Nan Restaurant**, tucked behind the hotel of the same name, 300 yards east of the imposing Mao statue. The food is excellent (which is evidenced by the number of Han Chinese who crowd the restaurant.)

The best hotel in Kashgar is the **Kashgar Guesthouse**, *tel. (86)998-222-*

2368, on the eastern side of town. It is comfortable, but a bit far from the center of things.

The **Seman Hotel**, *Seman Lu; tel. (86)998-282-2060*, is more central. Its old wing was once Kashgar's Russian Consulate. Little seems to have been repaired since the Russians left in 1949, but the dilapidated rooms are rather charming. They have the biggest and best bathtubs you'll find within 1,000 miles! What's more, you'll be provided with plenty of hot water.

Hong Kong is the best place to arrange a trip along the Silk Route.

Dali — China's newest vacation spot

Dali is one of the most popular new destinations in Yunnan province. It is a handsome historical city in a spectacular setting. Look one way and you can see the snow-capped Cangshan (White-Haired Mountain), look the other way and you see the blue Erhai (Ear Lake). Between the mountain and the water are well-irrigated green fields dotted with villages.

The majority of Dali's natives — about 80% — are of Bai nationality. For hundreds of years, they formed a kingdom independent from China that flourished until conquered by Kublai Khan in 1253. A stone tablet commemorates the event.

The Bai people are extremely friendly and will greet you constantly with "Hi." Women wear traditional colorful clothing, including ornately decorated backpacks for carrying small children.

When Chinese emperors moved the provincial capital to Kunming, Dali sank into oblivion. Because of this, the town is well-preserved, with narrow cobblestoned streets and old buildings of wood, plaster, and stone. A short walk takes you down the main street from one Ming dynasty gate to the other. The gates have been impressively rebuilt, but most of the wall that surrounds Dali is now little more than earthworks with rice planted on the top.

You can buy colorful clothing at the marketplaces in and around Dali. The largest is held every Monday at Shain, on the north side of the lake, about 18 miles from Dali. In addition to pigs, seed, and farming tools, you can buy coins, handkerchiefs, and fabrics. Tailors in Dali can stitch up clothing to order.

Beyond the wall, two competing entrepreneurs rent out bikes. The bikes are crude one-speeds, and the roads are very bumpy.

Finagle a boat ride across the lake and watch the fishermen with their nets. Hike up the mountains, where many old temples are still in use. To relax your tired muscles, get a vigorous massage at Dali's public bathhouse.

Food in Dali is cheap and good. The **Peace Café** caters to travelers. The **Garden Café**, a family restaurant, serves locals as well as visitors. Late at night, three generations of the owner's family gather in the back room to eat, squabble, watch television, and make a lot of noise.

April is the best time to visit Dali, when the town holds its **Third Month Fair**, an annual festival that dates back 1,000 years. People come from miles around for their once-a-year trip to town.

Getting to Dali involves a nine-hour bus ride from Kunming, the capital of Yunnan province. Flights to Kunming depart from Hong Kong, Beijing, Guangzhou, Shanghai, and Rangoon.

XISHUANGBABBA: TROPICAL CHINA

The southernmost region of China's Yunnan province, **Xiashuangbanna**, is more like Thailand than China. Bordering Burma and Laos, this is a lush, tropical land with hillside tea and rubber plantations, markets full of exotic fruit, and coconut-palm-shaded villages where women dress in brilliantly colored sarongs.

The liveliest time to visit is during the **New Year Water Splashing Festival** (mid-April). Festivities in Jinghong, the capital, include dragon-boat races on the Mekong River, Dai music and dancing, bamboo rockets, and a riot of water splashing. If you plan to visit during the festival, make reservations far in advance. Both flights from Kinming to Jinghong and accommodation become scarce.

A better time to visit is off-season, when you can enjoy the tranquil countryside and the gentle ways of the attractive Dai people (one of Yunnan's largest and most prosperous minority groups).

Jinghong is a small, sleepy town of broad streets bordered by palm trees. Buddhist monks in saffron robes bicycle slowly along the streets, while Dai women carrying pretty parasols congregate in the open markets. If you are lucky, one of the Dai will present you with a sticky cake of glutinous rice wrapped in palm leaves, a common sweet snack in Xishuangbanna.

About 35 miles west of Jinghong lies **Menghai**, one of the great tea regions of China and home of the most famous temple site in the province: the **Octagonal Pagoda**. This tiny gem of intricate architecture was built in the 17th century.

Far to the south, five miles from the Burmese border, lies **Damenglong**, a village with a 13th-century white pagoda and a lively Sunday market. Here you can see a panoply of other minority people, who come to trade with the local Dai: Lahu women in brightly colored bodices; Bulang with colored tufts of wool for earrings; and women of the Hani and Aini tribes (who are similar to Thailand's Akha people) bedecked in breastplates and headdresses of silver and metal coins, embroidered black leggings, belts of cowrie shells, and short black miniskirts that have an alarming tendency to fall off.

Another market is held at **Menghan**, southwest of Jinghon, which you can get to by slow boat on the brown Mekong River. It's a one-hour trip downstream, with stops to pick up villagers. Women can be seen on the river's edge panning for grains of gold.

The life of the Dai in these villages is slow and traditional. They live along the northern shore of Menghan's Virtuous Dragon Lake in large wooden houses built on stilts. You can see men making bamboo baskets and girls weaving cloth. In the Buddhist temple, boy monks learn their sacred texts. Chickens and pigs roam the dusty village paths, and buffalo plow the fields. Inside the thatched-roof wood and bamboo houses, gold-toothed Dai women prepare banquets: purple rice, spiced zucchini, sesame beef, and fried bumblebees.

The easiest way to reach Xishuangbanna is to fly from Kunming to Simao (75 minutes) and then take a bus or taxi the 100 miles to Jinghong. You'll pass spectacular scenery, including rice plains, hillsides of tea and rubber, and dense jungles.

HAINAN, THE RED HAWAII

Hainan Island off the coast of China is slated to become the Hawaii of the Far East. The island is off the southernmost part of China, not far from Vietnam, and is nearly as big as Taiwan. Recently, it was made a separate province. (It had been part of Guangdong.)

Despite its coconut groves and pristine golden beaches, the island has a few problems. Telephones are unpredictable. Until recently the only airstrip on its south coast was a military field, although a new airstrip has been opened. Passengers are ferried in venerable Russian planes. Sanya, slated to be the tourist center, has only 500 hotel rooms, none with a private bath.

LHASA: THE WORLD'S HIGHEST CAPITAL

Lhasa, Tibet, at 12,087 feet above sea level, is the world's highest capital. Set in royal blue skies above the clouds, tourists are given oxygen bags when they arrive. The city is closed to individual travelers, but is open to group travel.

The former seat of the Dalai Lama, the head of Tibetan Buddhism, Lhasa is filled with palaces and temples. Behind these grandiose man-made monuments are towering snow-covered mountains that make the Rockies seem mundane.

The **Potala**, where the Dalai Lama lived until he was ousted by the Communists in 1959, is an enormous 17th-century edifice that dominates the entire valley. The 13-story, 1,000-room palace is a museum today. Inside are gigantic, bejeweled Buddhas, murals illustrating Buddhist legends, and solid gold crypts containing the remains of former Dalai Lamas. The 10,000 chapels are decorated with human skulls and thighbones. Beneath the palace are torture chambers, where criminals and dissidents were kept in dungeons or stung to death by scorpions.

The **Deprung Monastery**, which is about three miles outside Lhasa, is where lesser religious leaders lived. The stone building, constructed in 1416 and set precariously against a mountainside, was once the largest cloister in the world. Although thousands of monks once lived here, the monastery is now inhabited by 300.

The **Jokhang Temple** houses two enormous gold and bejeweled Buddhas. Built 1,300 years ago, it is still visited by pilgrims who can be seen prostrate in front of the temple at dawn and dusk. Beautiful from the outside, the temple is smelly inside, because of the fermented butter burned by monks as part of their religious ceremonies.

One of the best bazaars in all China takes place around the outside. Pilgrims from across Tibet congregate in the Barkhor and walk around it clockwise, praying, shopping, and socializing as they move along. A fantastic variety of goods is sold in the Barkhor, including prayer wheels, silver inlay boxes, and Tibetan musical instruments. Be prepared to bargain fiercely.

The best hotel in Lhasa is the **Holiday Inn**, *93 W. Bejing Road; tel. (86)3-22221*. Rooms are air-conditioned and equipped with televisions, telephones, and oxygen tanks. Prices are relatively high, as all supplies must be transported by truck for miles up the mountain.

THE BEST WAY TO TRAVEL

If you have the time, the most pleasant way to travel through China is by boat. Several boat routes allow you to make the circuit of the major Chinese cities. One goes from Guangzhou to Wuzhou, a small town en route to Guilin, in 20 hours.

Everyone on these boat trips gets his own berth, either in an upper with a window view of the Pearl River or on a lower-level berth with easier access. No one sits in the aisles. Thick mats and quilts are provided in the dormitory-like setting. You'll enjoy lovely views and great people-watching opportunities.

THE BEST OF HONG KONG

Hong Kong, the pearl of the Orient, is the most dynamic city in the world. It is a thriving financial center, a shopper's paradise, and a gourmet's delight. Everyone works in this city, where fortunes are made and lost overnight and almost anything can be bought—at a bargain price.

A British Crown Colony until 1997, Hong Kong is a unique mixture of British and Chinese cultures and a gateway between worlds: Eastern and Western, ancient and modern, communist and capitalist, poor and wealthy.

Hong Kong has more people per square mile than any other spot on earth. And most of its six million people are crammed into tall buildings in an area just a few miles wide and long. However, despite its claustrophobic urban crowds, Hong Kong has more open space than cities half its size. And you can travel easily from the city to the rural countryside, where the dramatic terrain is inspiring.

The best view of Hong Kong

One of the world's greatest views is that of **Hong Kong Harbor** from **Victoria Peak**. Guarded by a tall fortress of mountains, behind which looms the awakening giant China, Hong Kong Harbor is alive with ships and boats from every corner of the earth. Rimmed by skyscrapers, the harbor is dotted with picturesque Chinese junks, hydrofoils, Russian cargo ships, big navy vessels, and the tiny sampans of those who make their livings from the sea. Some of these boats carry people who have never stepped foot on land.

Out in the water beyond the traffic jams of the central harbor rises a large emerald mountain called **Lantau Island**. And if you look hard or climb very high, you'll see 236 other such islands floating in the South China Sea.

You can either take the trolley up Victoria Peak or, if your legs are up to it, make the trek on foot. The mile-long Governor's Walk takes you through jungle-like growth around the top of the mountain.

The best of everything Chinese

For anything Chinese, shop at one of the **Chinese Arts & Crafts stores**, which you'll find throughout Kowloon and Central. (One is located at the Star House by the ferry terminal in Tsimshatsui.) Don't be put off by the department store atmosphere. You can't bargain here, but you'll find many high-quality Chinese goods, including art, crafts, jewelry, clothing, carpets, furniture, porcelain, silk, furs, leather, watches, cosmetics, shoes, cameras, electric appliances, and Chinese medicines. Chinese-style dresses, made in Western proportions, are a particularly good deal.

The best-known street market

The most famous of Hong Kong's many street markets is the **Stanley Market**, on the south side of the island. Stanley is an old fishing village with a large expatriate community. Silk dresses, sunglasses, fresh fruits, rattan furniture, porcelain ware, shoes, and luggage are all available for incredible bargain prices.

Antique bests

Shop for antiques on **Hollywood Road**, about two streets up from Queen's Road Central. This picturesque area has the atmosphere of a Chinese city from the 1930s. Follow the road around the hill to the old Cat Street quarter, where you can browse through the **Cat Street Galleries**, *Lok Ku Road*. Antique porcelain, traditional Chinese furniture, wall scrolls, old

Chinese photographs, jade, ivory, carved woods, vases, and other curiosities fill the crowded stalls. Remember, though, that it is illegal to bring even small amounts of ivory into the United States.

The world's most famous jade market

The **Jade Market**, located under Kansu Street in the Yau Ma Tei section of Kowloon, is the heart of the world's jade trade. You'll recognize the big-time dealers—they're the Chinese with newspapers covering their hands. They bargain by tapping each other's hands beneath the papers, which keeps competitors from seeing what the bids are. You're not likely to get a bargain here unless you know a lot about jade.

The best Buddhas

The **Temple of Ten Thousand Buddhas** actually contains about 12,800 of the statues. **Yuet Kai**, the gold plated monk on exhibit, is actually a mummy, sealed in gold leaf and serenely dressed in his saffron robe. Also look for the scarlet Buddha, a bright red statue of the philosopher. The temple is near the train station at Shatin.

The busiest Buddhist temple

Wong Tai Sin Temple, Hong Kong's busiest Buddhist temple, is perhaps the best choice for foreigners interested in having their fortunes told. You have a choice of 150 fortune-tellers, whose booths are lined up in a winding concrete alley like dominoes. Some speak English, but you'll mostly have to depend on a translator.

The place for bird lovers

Birds are an important part of Chinese life. And **Bird Street**, a small alley in Kowloon, is where the Chinese buy their feathered friends. Hundreds of them— whistling, singing, talking, screaming—are on sale, along with elaborate bamboo cages and live insects (bird food). The street's name is Hong Lok Street. It is a few blocks west of the intersection of Argyle Street and Nathan Road.

Nightlife in Hong Kong

There are three districts in Hong Kong that are famous for their entertainment spots. The first is **Central** where most expatriates and trendy locals go to after work, especially in the areas of Lan Kwai Fong. The second is **Wan Chai**, which includes nearby Causeway Bay with its many bars and discos that open till dawn. The third is **Tsim Tsa Tsui** in Kowloon where there is a distinct difference between bars exclusively for locals and those that appeal more to tourists.

The most tranquil escapes

If you're looking for relief from the hectic city, retreat to Hong Kong's quiet coves, beaches, and small villages. You can reach them by ferry from the city center. Lantau, Lamma, and Cheung Chau Islands have beautiful beaches and seafood restaurants. Lamma is the best getaway spot—it has no cars or motorcycles, and its villages have no more than a few hundred inhabitants. It is known as Hong Kong's Stone Age Island.

The best restaurants

Felix, *tel. (852)2315-3188*, is ridiculously expensive but one of the best places to eat in town. Located on the top floor of the Peninsula hotel in Kowloon, the restaurant commands an incredible view of Hong Kong harbor and the city's incredible skyline.

The best afternoon tea

The **Verandah**, *tel. (852)2812-2722*, is like a step back to colonial times. The waiters wear gloves and ceiling fans twirl lazily overhead. Try the eggs benedict topped with caviar.

The world's best Chinese food

The best Chinese cooks fled to Hong Kong in 1949. The finest Cantonese restaurant is the **Yung Kee**, *tel. (852)2522-1624*, with three floors crammed full of tables. The *congee* (rice soup) is the best in Hong Kong.

Hong Kong is full of *dai pai dongs* (outdoor noodle stalls). Look for the most crowded and you shouldn't have to worry about hygiene safety. One of the best is **Temple Noodles** in Shek O Village. The owners speak English.

The world's oldest eggs

The oldest eggs in the world are served in Hong Kong. *Pay daan*, known as 1,000- or 100-year-old eggs, are actually only about three months old. *Pay daan* are buried in dung, and their whites turn to a clear, gel-like substance. Despite their odd name and dirty appearance, many find them quite good.

Hong Kong's best seafood

The freshest seafood dinner in Hong Kong can be had at **Lei Yue Mun**, a fishing village on a tiny peninsula in east Kowloon. You take a ferry to an enclave of fish stalls, where you can wander among hundreds of tanks and tile pools filled with fish, crabs, multicolored lobsters, prawns, eels, scallops, and myriad other live sea animals. Watch your dinner flop on the floor as you bargain with vendors; then make your way to one of the 20 restaurants around the market, where you can have your seafood cooked to order for a reasonable charge.

The most romantic dining

Dining afloat is one of Hong Kong's most novel gastronomic experiences. You can have a meal on one of the big floating restaurants in Aberdeen or on board a tiny sampan in a makeshift restaurant with room for six to eight people. Sampans are for rent at the Causeway Bay Typhoon Shelter. They will pull alongside the dock to cook your meal, serve your drinks, and even serenade you. All this is not cheap, of course.

The best hotels

Service is what sets hotels in the Orient apart from those in the rest of the world—and the service in Hong Kong is unsurpassed anywhere.

The **Peninsula**, *tel. (852)2722-4170*, is a unique establishment reminiscent of the best days of the British Empire.

The **Inter-Continental**, *tel. toll-free (800)90-8855; tel. (852)2721-1211*, is an expensive and luxurious hotel with a commanding view of the harbor.

The **Mandarin**, *tel. (852)2895-9288*, is an elegant, well run hotel in a superb location right in the heart of the business district.

The **Salisbury YMCA**, *tel. (852)2736-0922*, is the best place to stay for the money and location. YMCA offers attractive, air-conditioned rooms with all necessary amenities.

A quiet retreat

If you are looking for a reasonably priced place to stay, away from the tourists and crowds of Central Hong Kong, make a reservation at the **Trappist Monastery Retreat House**. You receive a simple, but comfortable room looking onto a beautiful garden. No radios are permitted in the retreat house, though, which is operated by Trappist monks, and lights are turned out at 10 p.m.

The world's cheapest transportation

The **Star Ferry** is the best way to cross Hong Kong's harbor. It is one of the cheapest and most scenic journeys in the world. In the eight minutes it takes to go from Central to Tsimshatsui, you'll experience the essence of Hong Kong. Twilight is the best time to take the trip.

The best way to see Hong Kong

The best way to see Hong Kong is on foot. Driving is too hectic. Besides, Hong Kong is so compact and so efficiently laid out that you'll have no trouble traveling around the city. Public transportation is the best way to explore the surrounding countryside.

After you go through customs at Kai Tak Airport, pick up a free Hong Kong Tourist Association (HKTA) map at one of the stands outside the customs area. The street names are in English and Chinese, and the map indicates hotels, office buildings, markets, and important sights.

The **Mass Transit Railway** (MTR) is fast, efficient, clean, and cheap. If you are planning on using the railway frequently, buy a Common Stored Value ticket. Tourist tickets are also available.

MACAU: ASIA'S OLDEST EUROPEAN COLONY

Macau is one of the last remnants of the 16th century Portuguese Empire, renowned for its gourmet food, exotic setting, and outrageous gambling. Officially a Portuguese territory until it reverted to China in 1999, Macau has a tangible sense of history preserved in its beautiful colonial buildings.

For centuries, it was a place where smugglers, pirates, prostitutes, drug lords, sailors, and flesh merchants made their home. Today, Macau is a refuge from the hustle and bustle of Hong Kong. However, Macau, too, has an exciting nightlife, with a flavor all its own.

The best gambling tables in Asia—and the ugliest hotel in the world

Macau is famous for its casinos. The biggest is the **Casino de Lisboa** in the Lisboa Hotel. The Lisboa is probably the ugliest hotel in the world, designed to look like a roulette wheel, which it wears like a crown on its head. The **Macau Palace**, known as the Floating Casino, is a more exotic place to gamble. This red and gilded Chinese boat is moored on the inner harbor of Avenida de Almeida Riveiro.

Games include both those familiar to Westerners, such as blackjack, and Chinese games, such as *dai-siu* and keno. Slot machines are known locally as "hungry tigers."

The oldest shrine

The **A Ma Temple** is the territory's oldest temple, built before the Portuguese came to Macau. According to legend, A Ma, the goddess of fishermen, was the sole survivor of a fishing boat caught in a severe storm.

The temple is a series of shrines built at various levels on the Barra hill-side and linked by winding paths and steps. The shrine has a mysterious religious atmosphere, with its painted rocks, prayer sticks, tiny shrines, and statue-filled pavilions. Keep a close eye on your purse or wallet. Beggars congregate here, and signs warn against pickpockets.

The best place to get away from it all

Take a day trip to visit Macau's two outlying islands, **Taipa** and **Colonne**. These quiet retreats offer tree-shaded lanes, wide sandy beaches, small Chinese villages and lush forests. Both islands are easily accessible, connected by a causeway to Macau City.

Macau's best hike

The **Rua da Praia Grande** is a lovely promenade alongside the South China Sea—a great place to stroll at night. Along the elegant walk you'll see the pink Government House, a typical example of colonial Portuguese architecture. There are also benches where you can rest beneath huge banyan trees.

If you are feeling adventurous and fit, follow one of the steep paths leading up to the lighthouse. Birds, frogs, and dogs will greet you as you climb the hill. At the top, you'll have a bird's-eye view of the city, with its bright lights and neon far below.

Macau's best restaurant

The best restaurant in Macau, if not all of Asia, is **Pinocchio's**, *4 Rua do Sol, Taipa Island; tel. (853)827-128*. This garden restaurant off the village of Taipa's main street draws crowds from Hong Kong on weekends. Try the superb roast quail, chili crab, prawns, roast suckling pig, and baby lamb.

Macau's oldest restaurant

Fat Siu Lau, *64 Rua da Felicidade; tel. (853)573-580*, which opened in 1903, is the oldest restaurant in Macau. It serves excellent Macanese cuisine—an exotic mixture of Chinese and Portuguese food and wines. The fresh seafood dishes are exceptionally good.

The best times to go

The best times to visit Macau are spring and fall. Unless you want to visit this island when it is jam-packed with people, avoid the Chinese New Year and the November Grand Prix. For more information contact the **Department of Tourism**, *11 Largo do Senado; tel. (853)315566*.

THE BEST OF INDIA

THIS IS INDEED INDIA! THE LAND OF DREAMS AND ROMANCE, OF FABULOUS
WEALTH AND FABULOUS POVERTY, OF SPLENDOUR AND RAGS, OF PALACES
AND HOVELS, OF FAMINE AND PESTILENCE, OF GENIIES AND GIANTS AND
ALADDIN LAMPS, OF TIGERS AND ELEPHANTS, THE COBRA AND THE JUNGLE,
THE COUNTRY OF A HUNDRED NATIONS AND A HUNDRED TONGUES,
OF A THOUSAND RELIGIONS AND TWO MILLION GODS, CRADLE OF THE
HUMAN RACE, BIRTHPLACE OF HUMAN SPEECH, MOTHER OF HISTORY,
GRANDMOTHER OF LEGEND, GREAT-GRANDMOTHER OF TRADITION.
                                                    —*Mark Twain, 1897*

India is an exotic, ancient, multicolored land. The size, variety, and
grandeur of this country make it a feast for visitors. Every region is
different. The bordering Himalayas contain the highest peaks in the world,
including Mount Everest. The Ganges Plain is one of the world's greatest
stretches of flat land—as well as one of the world's most densely populated
regions. There are towns dating back to 3000 B.C. and mosques that draw
pilgrims by the thousands. The country's diverse population shares the land
with elephants, tigers, camels, and millions of sacred cows.

The religions of India are as varied as its climate. You'll find Hindus,
Muslims, Sikhs, Buddhists, Jainists, Jews, Christians, Zoroastrians, and
former headhunters. The different groups are lively and colorful, each with
its own festivals, dances, culture, and cuisine. Each has left its artistic mark
on India—ancient, elaborately carved temples are located throughout
the country.

We will explore India counterclockwise, beginning with Delhi and
moving southwest toward Mumbai (Bombay), southeast to Madras, northeast to Calcutta, and finally to the farthest corners of India for a look at the
continent's least-known regions.

DELHI, THE OLDEST INDIAN CITY

When Bombay and Madras were mere trading posts, **Delhi** was the capital of a 500-year-old empire. India was ruled from Delhi by various Hindu
dynasties, then the Moguls, and finally the British. And it was here that
India was granted its independence.

Eight cities have flourished where Delhi is today. And each of the city's
former rulers has made significant architectural contributions.

Today, Delhi is divided into two cities: Old Delhi, once the Mogul capital, which is filled with ancient forts, temples, and monuments; and New Delhi, the present capital, which has wide boulevards, modern office buildings, parks, and hotels.

Tour Delhi from south to north, because growth has moved steadily northward. Bring a sweater if you plan to travel during the winter months, when temperatures drop to 40 degrees Fahrenheit.

The Seventh Wonder of Hindustan

Ten miles south of Delhi is **Qutb Minar**, a 234-foot victory tower known as the Seventh Wonder of Hindustan. One of the earliest monuments of the Afghan period in India, and built in pre-Muslim Delhi, it has stood for 800 years. You can climb the 11th-century tower via a spiral staircase.

At the foot of the tower lies the **Quwwat-ul-Islam Mosque**. The first mosque built in India, it was erected in the 12th century on the foundations of a Hindu temple. The mosque contains the **Iron Pillar**, which has remained rust-free for more than 1,500 years.

Delhi's top sights

East of Qutb Minar is the fortress of the first Tughlaq king. A seven-mile, inwardly sloping wall guards the tombs of the founder of Tughlaqabad and his son. The fortress has a panoramic view of the surrounding countryside.

Following the road back toward Delhi you'll come to the **mausoleum of Emperor Humayun**, erected in the 16th century. This was the precursor of the Taj Mahal, and it features rose-colored sandstone walls inlaid with white marble and surrounded by gardens. Opposite the tomb is a place of pilgrimage, the **shrine of Nizam-ud-din**, which encloses a mosque covered with a fine Byzantine dome.

A few minutes away is the **Purana Qila**, a fort standing on the site of Indraprastha, a mythological Delhi of prehistoric times. The present fort, built in the 16th century, frames one end of the two-mile vista leading to the Presidential Palace.

Pass through the **War Memorial Arch** honoring Indian soldiers who died in World War I. This leads to the fabulous **Rajpath**, the broadest avenue of Delhi, lined with government buildings. **Parliament House** is a huge circular structure with an open colonnade. The **Presidential Palace**, built in this century, has 340 rooms and covers 330 acres.

The strange **Jantar Mantar Observatory**, *Parliament Street, Tolstoy Marg*, was built in 1725 by Maharaja Singh II of Jaipur to view the sun, moon, and stars. Every year on the March 21st and Sept. 21st equinoxes, the sun shines through a slit in the wall.

Jama Masjid, India's largest Mosque, has three white marble domes and two 134-foot minarets. Typical of Mogul architecture, its 450-square-foot courtyard is paved with marble.

Facing the mosque is the **Red Fort**, the finest example of Mogul architecture, built in 1648 behind red sandstone walls. Once the imperial palace of Emperor Shah Jahan (1627-1657), today it houses the Museum of Archeology. It is open to the public during daylight hours.

Rajghat (Shrine of Mahatma Gandhi), southeast of the Red Fort, is where Gandhi was cremated in 1948 following his assassination. A black marble slab in the garden is inscribed with the leader's last words, "Oh, God."

The best zoo in India

Delhi Zoological Park, next to Purana Qila on Mathura Road, is a home to rare white tigers. Magnificent gardens brighten the park, which has an especially extensive collection of birds. The zoo is open until 6 p.m.

India's most colorful festival

Try to time your visit to Delhi to coincide with **Ram Lila**, when gigantic effigies of Ravana and his minions are burned on the last day of the 10-day **Dusseha Festival** to symbolize the destruction of evil. According to Hindu mythology, the evil Ravana kidnapped the wife of the good Lord Rama. Commemorating the story of Lord Rama, Ram Lila is one of the biggest events in Delhi.

Dussehra usually falls in October and includes colorful dramas and dances reenacting the stories of gods and demons.

The best dancing

The **Bhangra Dance** of the Punjab, a community dance marked by its energy and hilarity, can be seen in Delhi. Men dance in a line on one side, wearing brightly colored turbans, vests, and pants, while women dance on the other.

The best hotels in Delhi

The **Ashok**, *tel. (91) 848-827-5839*, is a modern hotel with a pool, miniature golf facilities, gardens, tennis courts, an art gallery, and an open-air theater that features performances by a highly rated contemporary Indian dance company.

The **Imperial**, *website: www.theimperialindia.com*, at the edge of town is surrounded by a palm garden. Rooms are large, with private bathrooms and air conditioning.

Oberoi Maidens, *tel. (91) 11-397-5464*, is a gracious old hotel with colonial-style bedrooms and private baths, a swimming pool, tennis courts, and gardens.

THE TAJ MAHAL—ONE OF THE WORLD'S GREATEST WONDERS

South of Delhi, in the town of Agra, is the **Taj Mahal**, one of the world's greatest wonders. Built in white marble by Emperor Shah Jehan as a mausoleum for his queen, Mumtaz Mahal, it is most beautiful at sunset and under moonlight.

Twenty-two years went into the construction of this palace, which was completed in 1652. Beautiful formal gardens and a reflecting pool lead to the arched entrance. An enormous dome, accompanied by two smaller domes, tops the structure, and four minarets mark the corners. It is said that the architect's right hand was cut off upon completion of the Taj Mahal so that he could not duplicate his creation.

RAJASTHAN: INDIA AT ITS MOST TRADITIONAL

Southwest of Delhi is a desert land broken up occasionally by jungle. Here are some of the most ornate temples in India. **Rajasthan**, which translates as *Abode of Kings*, is the home of the Rajputs, an ancient people whose mythology includes tales of chivalry and romance. You can recognize Rajputs by their colorful clothing: the men wear pink and yellow turbans, and the women wear full skirts and half-bodices and wrap themselves in long mantles.

Jaipur: the rosiest spot in India

The buildings of **Jaipur**, the capital of Rajasthan, are made of rose-colored stone. The city was founded in 1727 by the brilliant Maharaja Jai Sing II, who built an observatory with a remarkably accurate 90-foot gnomon (an object whose shadow serves to indicate time), which housed exotic animals, including peacocks, elephants, buffalo, and camels.

The most beautiful building in Jaipur is the **City Palace**, which is now a museum housing rare manuscripts, arms, and paintings. The loveliest structure within the palace walls is the lofty **Chandra Mahal**, a seven-story building with a view of the city. While there, wander through the **Man Singh II Museum**. Also visit the **Jantra Observatory**, constructed in 1718.

Next to the palace are the **Jai Niwas Gardens**, filled with fountains, statues, and artificial lakes where well-fed crocodiles swim.

Hawa Mahal, or Palace of the Winds, *Siredori Bazaar*, with its delicate overhanging balconies and perforated windows placed one above the other in a symmetrical pattern, is another important landmark in Jaipur. Although it looks like a palace, it is actually a façade behind which women of the court would watch processions secretly.

Guarding the city from the hills above is **Naharagarh**, or Tiger Fort. You can get there from the Amber palace by jeep or rickshaw.

Amber: a little-known treasure

The 17th-century palace at *Amber* stands high above a lake, its towers and domes reaching to the sky. An arched gateway leads into the courtyard, where a broad flight of stairs climbs to the royal apartments. Inside are Persian mosaic walls, filigreed doors, fountains, aqueducts, and high ceilings covered with mirrors. Beneath the palace are vaults said to contain the treasures of Jaipur.

You can visit the palace astride an elephant. Musicians play as you make the slow climb to the palace apartments.

Mount Abu—India's most beautiful sunset

While **Mount Abu** is most famous as an archeological and religious landmark, you should come here for another reason as well: to see the sunset. From **Sunset Point** you can see much of Rajasthan illuminated by the pink glow of the setting sun.

Mount Abu, which is due south from Jaipur, was originally a center of the cult of Siva. The Jains (a Hindu sect that abhors the killing of animals) still make pilgrimages to this mountain, which is known in Hindu legend as the son of the Himalayas. Between Abu's peaks are five Jain shrines, the most beautiful of which was built of pure white marble by Vimal Shah in the 11th century. Inside, marble elephants carrying statues of Vimal Shah and his family climb from the pavilion to the domed porch, which is intricately carved and supported by eight sculptured columns.

Udaipur: India's most romantic city

Udaipur, known as the City of Dreams, is the most romantic city in India. Founded in the 16th-century by Maharana Udai Singh, supposedly a descendent of Sri Ram (the hero of the Ramayana epic), Udaipur is bastioned by a wall and five spiked gates. Inside the walls are whitewashed houses painted with murals.

The ruler of the city, known as the Maharana, or Sun of the Hindus, lives in a sparkling palace surrounded by a lake. Amber, jade, and colored glass sparkle on the palace pinnacles. Inside are ivory doors, marble balconies, stained-glass windows, and mirrored walls. You can visit every day, 9:30 a.m. until 4:30 p.m.

Udaipur's second most beautiful sight, after the palace, is **Sahelion-ki-Bari Park**, one of the best examples of Hindu landscaping. The park is filled with ornamental pools, fountains with water spouting from elephant trunks and bird beaks, and black stone monuments.

How to travel like a maharaja

Maharaja's Palace on Wheels, a reincarnation of the elegant train that once carried maharajas and viceroys, is the most pleasant way to travel through Rajasthan. The plush cars have been restored, and each coach is equipped with individual sleeping cabins, bathrooms, a kitchen, and an attendant dressed in traditional Rajasthani clothing. The train has two dining cars and a library/bar.

The trip takes eight days and seven nights and includes stops at Jaipur, Udaipur, Jaisalmer, Jodphur, the Taj Mahal, and the bird sanctuary at Bharatpur. The train leaves from Delhi Cantt Station every Wednesday at 10:45 p.m.

For more information, contact the **tourist office**, *30 Rockefeller Plaza, Room 15, North Mezzanine, New York, NY 10020*, or **Tours of Distinction**, *Central Reservations, Rajasthan Tourism, Chandralok Building, 36 Janpath, New Delhi.*

THE BEST OF AHMEDABAD

Founded in 1411, Ahmedabad was once considered the finest city in India. Of the many Muslim monuments there, the finest is Ahmed Shah's Masjid Mosque, which contains his colored marble tomb, 250 massive pillars, carvings, and inscriptions. The shah's queens lie in ornate tombs across the street.

Another Muslim architectural feat is the Haibat Khan Mosque, built in the 16th century by the Rani, one of the two wives of Mahmud Begara, after her son was executed for "misbehavior."

Also see the stone carving of a slave of Ahmed Shah in the **Mosque of Sidi Sayvid** and the **Mausoleum of Shah Alam at Batwa**.

The **Sun Temple of Modhera**, 60 miles northwest of Ahmedabad is the best of the many temples built by the Solanki kings of Anhilwad Patan. The grandeur of this temple is enhanced by its wide steps and pillared porch. The shrine was designed so that the image of Surya (the sun god) can be illuminated by the rising sun and the equinoxes.

KASHMIR: INDIA'S MOST BEAUTIFUL REGION

North of Delhi, wedged between China and Pakistan, is the most beautiful region in India, the **Vale of Kashmir**. At 5,200 feet, it is circled by mountains (the Himalayas to the southwest, the Karakorams to the north). It feels as if it is cut off from the rest of the world. Snowcapped peaks appear to float above the clouds. Houseboats and lotus leaves bob in spring-fed lakes. The fair-skinned residents look surprisingly European, despite their vales and nose rings.

Mogul emperors (descendants of Genghis Khan) were partial to Kashmir and built lavish palaces and gardens in the valley. In the colonial days, this was one of the few places in India where Europeans were not allowed to build. (They resorted to living in houseboats instead of houses.) For centuries, caravans from China and elsewhere passed through Kashmir on their way to the southern reaches of India, giving it an international flavor.

The best time to visit Kashmir is around April or May when the spring flowers are in bloom. But every time of year has its charms. The leaves turn scarlet in the fall, and the fields are lush during the summer. Winter brings deep snows and good skiing conditions.

Srinagar, the capital of Kashmir

Srinagar, the capital of Kashmir, has flowering rooftops (the roofs are made of earth, which bursts into bloom in the spring). Painted shutters and dyed-wool doors brighten the brown houses that line the river. Houseboats with canopied roofs sail the river toward the Dal and Nagin lakes, where they anchor. The men wear fur caps, the women veils to cover their hair. Turbaned old men smoke hookahs on the sidewalks.

Srinagar's most important landmark is a small temple to Siva at the peak of a 1,000-foot hill, which can be climbed by steep stone steps. The view from the top encompasses the town, the river Jhelum, and Dal Lake.

The best places to stay

The **Broadway**, *tel. (91)194-75621*, in Srinagar, has a swimming pool and a good restaurant.

The **Palace Hotel**, *tel. (91)194-71241*, overlooks the lake. A 100-acre terraced garden surrounds the hotel. There is a golf course on the property, and the hotel restaurant and bar are recommended.

Shahenshah, *Boulevard Road; tel. (91)194-71345*, is a reasonably priced hotel in Srinagar with a pool, a garden, and a good restaurant.

Garden paradises, beautiful lakes

The Dal and Nagin lakes are bordered by two beautiful gardens: the **Shalimar Bagh** (Garden of Love), which was designed 400 years ago by one of the Great Moguls for his queen; and the **Nishat Bagh** (Garden of Pleasure), which has terraces of flowers and avenues of cascades.

Lake Manasbal, also in this area, is covered with lotus blossoms. **Lake Wular** is the largest lake in the region.

The holiest spot

In the mountains above the Liddar Valley is the sacred cave of **Amarnath**, reached by steps cut into the rock by pilgrims. Situated at 13,000 feet, the cave is surrounded by snow and ice most of the year. The night of the full moon in the month of Sravan (July or August) is considered the luckiest time to visit.

India's best skiing

Kashmir has beautiful, pristine ski slopes but its facilities, including the number of lifts and T-bars and the selection of rental equipment, are limited, which can be frustrating to good skiers. The conditions are improving, however, and, for the more adventurous skier, Kashmir offers heli-skiing.

Contact the Institute of Skiing and Mountaineering in Gulmarg or ask your hotel for more information. The **Hotel Highland Parks** offers ski packages during the winter months.

THE BEST OF MUMBAI

Mumbai, formerly known as Bombay, is India's most prosperous and cosmopolitan city, an industrial metropolis, and one of Asia's busiest seaports. Despite its industry, Mumbai is also a beautiful city, backed by mountains and hugging the Arabian Sea. Hilly islands dot the harbor.

The best introduction to Bombay is a cruise along **Marine Drive**, also known as the Queen's Necklace. Tracing the coastline, it is the city's main boulevard and offers views of the sea and the Mumbai skyline.

Wander Mumbai's intriguing neighborhoods on foot. Venture beyond the Colaba market—a village of the Kolis, one of the original fishing tribes of the region. Old traditions are maintained here, and the women dress in colorful saris and flowers.

Chowpatty Beach, with its statue of Tilak, a great political leader of this century, is the political center of Mumbai. This meeting place by the sea is always crowded with people fishing, playing, and eating at food stalls. The entertainment here is free: yogis buried in the sand, soapbox orators, fishermen hauling in their nets. The fortunetellers here are said to be disconcertingly good.

Not far from the beach is **Mani Bhavan** (the Mahatma Gandhi Memorial), which has photographs of the master of passive resistance, along with books he wrote.

The **Prince of Wales** in Fort Bombay has a good collection of Nepalese and Tibetan art, as well as 18th-century miniatures, jade, crystal, and china. It is open every day except Monday, 10 a.m. until 6:30 p.m. March through June, and 10 a.m. until 5:30 p.m. July through February.

The **Hanging Gardens**, where you can find respite from the noise of the city, have a beautiful view of the city. Here you can walk among bushes cut to resemble elephants, monkeys, cows, oxen, or giraffes.

The greenery on the left as you go beyond the gardens is part of the Parsee Towers of Silence, where locals dispose of their dead. The area is concealed by a park, which is surrounded by a high wall. Bodies are carried to the top of towers, where they are left to be devoured by vultures. The Parsee originally came from the city of Pars in Peria, 1,300 years ago. Today their descendants are a key part of the fabric of life in Bombay.

In Byculla, an old residential area, is **Veermata Jijabai Bhonsel Udyan** (the Victoria Gardens), a park full of trees and plants. The park also includes the city zoo, the Victoria and Albert Museum, and a gigantic statue of an elephant that once guarded the Elephanta Caves outside Bombay. Visit the park between dawn and dusk but, if you want to see the zoo or the museum, make sure you arrive before 6 p.m. Tuesday through Saturday you can rent a boat or ride an elephant or camel from 8 a.m. until 9:30 a.m. and 4 p.m. until 5:30 p.m. Compared with the noise and crowds of most of Mumbai, this is a peaceful place to escape for a while.

Juhu Beach, 12 miles northwest of Mumbai, is the best place to cool off after wandering through the city. To get to the lake, you cross **Mahim Creek**, a fishing village with ancient boats. After your swim, you can watch the performing monkeys.

Best buys in Mumbai

Mumbai's shops display beautiful pure silk saris for $10 to $100 and silver earrings for around $20. Bargain for the best prices.

The city's two most colorful markets are the **Mahatma Jyotiba Phule Market** and the **Thieves Market**, near Mohammed Ali Road. The first is a good place to buy fruits and vegetables, cotton, animals, and flowers. It is also a good place to take photos. Thieves Market is a junk-lovers delight, offering everything from old car parts to fine antiques. Both markets are open from early morning until late evening.

The best time to visit

The best time to visit Mumbai is during **Gansh Chaturthi**, a festival that glorifies Ganesh, the god of good omens. Hindus worship images of the deity, which are later sunk in a lake. A spectacular procession follows. The festival is usually held in September.

The best place to stay and eat

The best restaurant, which is also the best hotel, is the **Taj Mahal Hotel**, *tel. (91)22-5665-3366*, a five star establishment that has an Indian restaurant with probably the best curry in Mumbai. There are also French and Chinese dishes, but the Indian food surpasses them by far. The hotel has rooms that, while decorated with antiques, are pleasantly modern at the same time.

The Elephanta Caves—the most important site outside Mumbai

The most important side-trip from Mumbai is to the island of **Elephanta**, six miles across the harbor, where five cave temples have been excavated.

No one knows who carved the temples, which were created between the 5th and 6th centuries.

The caves contain beautiful, life-size sculptures of Hindu gods. The most impressive is a 15-foot sculpture of three-headed Mahesamurti, a trinity made up of the gods Siva, Brahma, and Vishnu. Outside the main cave is an enormous columned veranda, approached by steps and sculptured elephants. To best appreciate the subtleties of the religious statues and carvings here, read up on Hindu mythology before your trip. Bring a flashlight if you want to see anything.

The holiest village

Mahabaleshwar, a tiny village on a hill south of Mumbai was once considered so holy that Englishmen were not allowed on any part of the hill. Five streams of water representing the sources of the five holy rivers flow through the Krishnabai Temple. They combine and travel through a sculpture of a cow's mouth into two cisterns where Hindus take holy baths. Mahashivaratri, a festival of Siva held in February or March, brings throngs of pilgrims.

Climb to nearby **Pratapgarh Fort**, built in 1656, for a view that extends all the way to the coast. On the western side of the fort, a precipice drops 2,000 feet to the Konkan plain below. Prisoners once met their deaths here.

The **Frederick Hotel**, *Bombay-Goa Road*, is the nicest in town, with private bathrooms, tennis courts, and a golf course.

LITTLE PORTUGAL: GOA

South of Mumbai is **Goa**, a Portuguese colony from 1510 to 1961. It has a mixture of local and Portuguese charms and some of the most beautiful ocean and river beaches in India. In addition to all this, Goa has perfect weather (except during monsoon season, June through September). Whitewashed houses and Catholic churches give Goa a European look. Traders first traveled to Goa seeking spices.

St. Francis Xavier came here in 1540 and converted many of the people to Catholicism. Although he died in China, his body was returned to Goa. His embalmed remains lie in a silver, gem-encrusted casket in the **Basilica of Bom Jesus** in Panaji. Once every 10 years the saint's body is displayed. If you look closely, you will notice that his big toes are missing—they were bitten off by religious fanatics. His arm, too, is gone—it was sent to the pope. Built in 1593, the basilica is Goa's primary example of Portuguese architecture.

Nearby is the magnificent, all-white *sé* (cathedral), noted for its five bells. Its Golden Bell is the largest of its kind in the world. A small chapel in the back of the cathedral contains a crucifix on which a vision of Christ is said to have appeared in 1919.

The World's Best Destinations

Goa's delights are physical as well as spiritual. The silvery beaches along the Malabar Coast are incomparable. The best are near Panaji, the capital. **Dona Paula** is the most chic. Across the Mandovi River from Panaji is the spectacular **Calangute Beach**. **Colva Beach**, on the south coast near Margao, is also beautiful. At some of Goa's beaches, the swimming is spoiled by fierce undertows. Ask around before you test your strength against the sea.

The best place to stay if you are a beach lover is the **Dodge Holiday Village**, *Candolim Bardez*, run by the Taj Group, on Calangute Beach. You can sleep in a cottage near the sea, use the sports facilities, and lounge in hammocks on the beach, as well as visit nearby restaurants and bars.

THE WORLD'S OLDEST BUDDHIST SCULPTURES

The Buddhist caves of **Ajanta** were carved into the face of a 259-foot rock cliff 2,000-years ago and contain the oldest Buddhist art in the world. Frescoes cover the walls, ceilings, and pillars of the 25 monasteries and temples here.

The **Ellora Caves** form another fantastic complex of Buddhist, Jain, and Hindu temples carved side by side from rock. The 34 elaborately carved and frescoed caves were constructed between A.D. 600 and A.D. 1200. The Hindu temple Kailasa is the most beautiful, with enormous pillars, painted ceilings, and grand statues. It took 100 years to quarry the three million cubic feet of rock here.

Aurangabad is the best base for visiting the caves. Stay at the **Rama International Hotel**, *R-3 Chikalthana*. The staff is efficient and the manager personally meets guests at the airport.

Daily flights run between Bombay and Delhi via Aurangabad. By train, you can get to Aurangabad aboard the Punjab Mail and the Panchavati Express from Mumbai to Manmad. Daily bus service connects Aurangabad with Ellora, Ajanta, and Jalgaon.

Bus tours to the Ellora Caves from Aurangabad are conducted by the Maharashtra Tourism Development Corporation. Tour guides will pick you up at Aurangabad Railway Station at 9 a.m. and return you there at 6:30 p.m.

The Maharashtra Tourism Development Corporation also provides four-day excursions to Ajanta-Ellora-Aurangabad from Mumbai. Buses leave daily.

THE MOST SACRED JAIN HILL

Shatrunjaya (the Place of Victory), a hill by the river of the same name, is the most sacred of five hills considered holy by the Jains. It is covered by 863 temples. You must remove all leather before you will be permitted to climb the hill. To see the temple jewels or to take photos, you must ask permission from the Munimji, Anandji Kalyanji Trust, in Palitana. Your hotel can give you the daily viewing times for the jewels and help you get permission to take pictures. The temples are closed in the monsoon season (the summer months) and after dark.

The best place to stay while visiting the hill is the nearby town of **Palitana**, due south of Ahmedabad in the province of Gujarat. **Hotel Sumeru**, *Station Road*, is pleasant, with a pretty garden and good vegetarian food.

THE BEST LION VIEWING

The **Gir Forest**, on the coast of the Arabian Sea in Gujarat, is the last stronghold of the Asiatic lion. The best time to see the king of beasts is during the hot months, from March through May, when they frequently congregate around the water hole, but the forest is open to the public from December until June.

To make arrangements to visit the forest, contact the **Regional Manager**, *Gir Tourism Development Corporation, Rang Mahal, Diwan Chowk, Junegadh*. Gir Tourism Development Corporation offers two-day trips, which include transportation (by jeep), binoculars, guides, and accommodation.

MOST SPLENDID ANCIENT RUINS

The empty shell of a once-courtly kingdom of Malwa sits atop a plateau in Mandu, Northeast of Mumbai. Known centuries ago by the Muslims as the City of Joy, today it is a ghost town. Raj Bhoja first noticed the charms of the location, which is cut off from the world below, and built a retreat here in the 10th century. The Muslims took over in the 13th century and expanded the city until it covered eight square miles, the whole surrounded by massive walls.

The oldest monument is the mosque, which is to the right as you enter the grand Delhi Gate. The most beautiful is the tomb of Hoshang Shah, a white marble structure with a great dome and four turrets. The buildings are divided into three main groups: the Royal Enclave, the Village Group, and the Reva Kund Group.

You can stay overnight at the modern **Travellers' Lodge**, which has eight rooms with attached bathrooms. It is located on the main road on the way to the Village Group. The **Taveli Mahal**, once the royal stables, is located closer to the fort.

THE LEAST-KNOWN BUDDHIST CAVES

A drive through the jungle from Mandu brings you to **Bagh**, where sixth-century Buddhist caves rival those at Ajanta (but they're not as crowded). Sadly, the beautiful wall paintings have been somewhat damaged over time.

The river Bagmati flows in front of the humid sandstone caves. The foliage has been cut back to prevent sneak attacks by pythons and tigers.

Only four of the nine caves have survived. Hewn from solid rock, each has a veranda, a large central hall, gloomy monks' cells, and a prayer hall. The second cave has a maze of passageways and hidden chambers. It contains larger-than-life sculptures of the Buddha and his disciples and paintings of animals and flowers. The most beautiful paintings are in the fourth cave, Rang Mahal, which on its veranda has a mural of life-size figures.

Sanchi—the best Buddhist art

Northeast of the Bagh Caves, near Bohpal, is **Sanchi**, the world's most important center of Buddhist art. Emperor Asoka built his most beautiful monuments here on a hilltop overlooking the forest. (The emperor's son, Mahendra, left Sanchi for Sri Lanka, where he worked to spread the influence of Buddhism.) After the decline of Buddhism in India, the town lay forgotten until 1818, when it was rediscovered. Restoration was begun in 1912 by Sir John Marshall. Of the eight stupas (sacred mounds) originally built on the hill, only three remain.

What catches the eye first in Sanchi is the **Great Stupa**, a 106-foot second-century round burial mound with elaborately decorated gateways. A fence with four ornate gates surrounds it. The bas-reliefs on the yellow stone gates are the most beautiful early Buddhist works of art that exist today. Don't expect to understand the elaborate religious illustrations—one archeologist published three enormous volumes on Sanchi.

The **Travellers' Lodge** is a pleasant little inn near the caves with eight air-conditioned rooms and a restaurant.

INDIA'S GREATEST MAN

If you head south from Sanchi through the jungles, you will come to the tiny town of Sevagram, where Mahatma Gandhi established his *ashram* (retreat) in 1933 and began putting his doctrines into practice. The Hindu leader established a self-sufficient community, with a dairy, a tannery, and cloth weaving. He refused to acknowledge the caste system, with its untouchables and "unclean" occupations. His simple hut is preserved exactly as he left it. At the Nai Talimi Sangh School in Sevagram, students continue to follow Gandhi's way of life, growing their own food and weaving their own cloth.

The best place to stay (if you share Gandhi's values of simplicity and modesty) is the guesthouse at the ashram, where food is served communally. If you prefer creature comforts, stay at **Mt. Hotel**, *Commercial Road, Nagpur*, 50 miles away. (Nagpur is known for its fragrant orange groves.)

MADRAS — THE MOST TRADITIONAL CITY

The state of Tamil Nadu, at India's southern tip, is more traditional than the rest of the country. Because it is so far south, this region was untouched by the many invaders who once assailed the north. Founded by the Dravidians more than 5,000 years ago, Tamil is the home of India's oldest sculptures.

The capital of the region, **Madras**, is as colorful as the cotton cloth it is famous for producing. The fourth largest city in India, it sprawls across 68 square miles.

The best place to stay

In Madras, the best place to stay is the **Taj Coromandel**, *tel. (91)44-2827-2827*, a modern building with both Indian and Chinese restaurants. It also has an excellent coffee shop.

The best sights

Fort St. George, built in 1640 by the British, is the best sight to see in Madras. It is also a perfect place to begin a tour of Madras. Twenty-foot walls loom over the city, which acts as the government center of Tamil Nadu. Inside is **St. Mary's Church**, the oldest Anglican Church in Asia, built in 1680. The Fort Museum contains memorabilia of the East India Company, as well as costumes, coins, and china.

Madras National Art Gallery houses the famous 10th-century bronze statue of a dancing Nataraja-Siva and rare Mogul, Rajput, and South Indian paintings.

Next-door is the **Government Museum**, which has the best bronze collection in India, as well as rare second-century Buddhist sculptures.

Madras Snake Park and Conservation Center in the beautiful **Guindy Deer Park** is home to cobras, pythons, and other exotic reptiles. The surrounding Deer Park shelters black buck and spotted deer.

Traditions say that the apostle Thomas (Doubting Thomas) came to Madras as a missionary and was martyred on St. Thomas Mount in A.D. 78. The **Cathedral of St. Thome**—the first Christian church in India—is a Gothic structure built on the site of the chapel said to have held the remains of St. Thomas.

Kapaliswarar Temple, dedicated to Lord Kapaliswarar (Siva), was built by the Dravidians. It was destroyed in 1566 during a war but rebuilt 300 years ago. Its gopura (pyramid-shaped entrance) marks the city's horizon.

Madras is home to the world headquarters of the **Theosophical Society**, an international organization promoting the interplay of religion, science, and philosophy. The banyan tree in the garden of the society's building is the oldest in India, shading 40,000 square feet.

The best dancing

Madras is the best place to see the classic **Bharata Natya** dance, in which dancers exhibit perfect control over every muscle in their bodies. (They can actually move their necks while keeping their heads motionless.) Originally a temple dance, this is the most ancient dance form in India, and it is performed to the accompaniment of musical instruments and singing.

The beauty of the Bharata Natya lies in the grace of its symmetrical patterns and in the emotions portrayed by the elaborate gestures and facial expressions of the dancers. Check the local newspapers—*The Hindi* and *Indian Express*—for show listings. You can watch Indian dancing every night during tourist season in the Mysore Room of the Taj Coramandel. (During the summer, performances are often canceled.)

Madras' most important side trips

The ancient city of **Mahabalipuram** has the world's largest bas-relief, *Penance of Bhaghirata*, an 80- by 20-foot work in stone. The city's other claim to fame is its group of seven pagodas, which look like flat-topped pyramids and are guarded by statues of an elephant, a lion, and a bull. The walls of the pagodas are illustrated with images from Hindu mythology.

Mahabalipuram was once the main harbor of the Pallava empire, which died out about 1,200 years ago. Hindu sculpture can be found in the cave temples carved from the rock here. When you tire of the ancient works of art, relax on Mahabalipuram's gorgeous beach.

Kanchipuram, the capital of the ancient Pallava empire, has 1,000 temples and 124 shrines. It is an important place of pilgrimage for Hindus. The **Kailasanatha Temple**, believed to be 1,200 years old, contains excellent seventh- and eighth-century paintings. Smaller but prettier is the **Varadarajaswamy Temple**. The best Hindu murals, which illustrate various wars, are in the Vaikunthanatha Perumal Temple.

One of the oldest cities in the south, **Kumbakonam**, on the banks of the Cauvery River, has 18 temples decorated with lively Hindu sculptures. Once every 12 years pilgrims invade the city for the bathing festival.

A half-hour away is **Thanjavur**, lying at the foot of India's greatest temple, **Brihadiswara**, whose tower rises more than 200 feet. The tower's dome rests on an 80-ton block of granite brought in from a village four miles away.

Forty miles south of Madras is the breathtaking ninth-century **Temple of Nataraja** at Chidambaram. Two of the temple's four granite gopuras are covered with sculptures illustrating the 108 positions of Natya Sastra, the Indian science of dancing. No one knows how the granite was brought to the temple, for there is no granite for 50 miles around.

INDIA'S MOST ELEGANT HILL STATION

Ootacamund, renamed Udhagamandalam (but still affectionately known as Ooty), is a small, elegant hill station in Nilgris, the famed Blue Mountains of southern India. Situated 8,000 feet above sea level, Ooty appealed to the royalty and the wealthy of many cultures. English is the major tongue here, and Ooty feels for all the world like a Victorian town in the heart of England.

The best way to reach Ooty is to rent a car and driver and travel through the Mudamalai jungle along the intricate hairpin turns that wind through parrot- and monkey-crowded bamboo jungles. It is a dramatic surprise to make the last turn and find yourself in a bit of England. Ooty's flowers are celebrated throughout India. Garden clubs present a floral spectacle each May, mingling familiar English varieties with exotic blooms.

Less than 50 miles away is a large wild-animal sanctuary. Not far from the hill station, entire families of monkeys scamper about, panhandling from passersby, running off with fruit from trees or market stalls, and gazing at humans as intently as the humans stare at them. Now and then you'll catch a glimpse of an elephant, and you'll see birds everywhere. An excellent and inexpensive place to stay is the **Savoy Hotel**. Faded but still elegant in its full Victorian regalia, the Savoy is a treasure. Its gardens are famous throughout India.

ORISSA: INDIA IN A NUTSHELL

For a capsule view of India, visit the state of **Orissa**, on the Bay of Bengal. You can explore mountains, jungles, valleys, plains, tribal villages, coconut groves, and 250 miles of beach in this area of 60,000 square miles.

The recorded history of Orissa begins in 260 B.C., when the edicts of the Emperor Asoka were carved in rock in Dhauli, five miles from Bhubaneswar, the capital. The peak of Orissan civilization was reached between the 4th and 13th centuries, when thousands of temples and monuments were built. The British took over in 1803.

The Adivasi, a tribal group in Orissa, are descendants of the inhabitants of Orissa before the Aryan invasion 3,000 years ago. Over the centuries they have been pushed into the heart of Orissa, the least fertile section of the state. Now they are protected by the government.

Orissa's main sights

Bhubaneshwar is a picturesque town with a myriad of temples, some dating back to 300 B.C. They are covered with spirals, turrets, decorations, and sculptures depicting good and evil, morality and immorality. The **Great Lingaraj Temple**, built in A.D. 1000, is the finest Hindu temple in India, with a tower that can be seen for miles. Outside town are Udayagiri and

Khandagari hills, where caves were carved by Jain monks as far back as the first century B.C.

Konarak (the Black Pagoda), outside Bhubaneswar, is one of the most beautiful sights in India. More than 1,000 workers took 12 years to build the 100-foot-high temple. Dedicated to the sun, the 13th-century Konarak rests on a base of 24 wheels pulled by seven horses. The roof is topped by a three-tiered spire. The entire temple is covered with carvings and sculptures.

Puri, a site of Hindu pilgrimages, is one of the four holiest places in India. Hindus believe that if you stay here for three days and three nights, you will attain eternal life. The enormous **Jagannath Temple**, dedicated to the Lord of the Universe, was built in the 12th century. While non-Hindus are not allowed to enter the structure, you can get inside the 20-foot temple walls from atop the neighboring Raghunandan Library.

The most colorful (and most crowded) time to visit Puri is June, during the **Rath Yatra Festival**, when the image of Lord Jagannath is taken from its temple and carried in a canopied car by thousands of pilgrims to Gundicha Mandir, the god's Garden House.

Puri is also a great place to shop. If you know how to bargain, you can get good buys on statues, toys, and shoes.

The place to stay in Puri is the **South Eastern Railway Hotel**, *Chakratirtha Road*, which is near the beautiful but polluted beach.

INCREDIBLE CALCUTTA

Calcutta is incredible—a huge and growing industrial metropolis inhabited by the Bengalis, an emotional and artistic people who produce many of the best books, dramas, and films in India. The city is a convenient base for exploring the Himalayas, Sikh temples, and the temples of Orissa and Bhutan. No one can claim to really know India without visiting Calcutta.

If you arrive in Calcutta by train, you will see families camping on the platforms of Howrah Station, water vendors, newsboys, rice peddlers, tea-serving waiters, running children, and shouting porters.

When you leave the station and cross the **Howrah Bridge**, you will encounter cars, bicycles, cows, rickshaws, oxcarts, trucks, and crowds of people. Below the bridge, on the banks of the Hooghly River, live Calcutta's masseurs and barbers.

Calcutta's best sights

On the other side of the Howrah Bridge (the third-largest single-span bridge in the world) is **Old Calcutta**, the core of the city, which grew out of three tiny villages: Sutanati, Govindpur, and Kalikata (Anglicized as Calcutta). Kalikata was once a sacred spot with two temples. Aside from the temples, however, the area is unsavory.

Victorian Calcutta sprang up around **Fort William**, built in 1780. At the south end of Maidan Park, in front of the fort, is **Victoria Memorial**, completed in 1921 and filled with relics of British rule.

North of **Dalhousie Square** (now called B.B.D. Bagh) and surrounded by busy bazaar streets is the **Nakhoda Mosque**, which holds up to 10,000 people.

The **Indian Museum**, *Chowringhee Road*, is the oldest in India and one of the most comprehensive in the Orient. Its archeology section is the largest in Asia and one of the most important in the world, with a large representative collection of antiquities illustrating the cultural history of India from prehistoric times to the Muslim period. The museum also has a fine collection of coins, gems, and jewelry. It is open 10 a.m. until 4 p.m.

Parasnath Jain Temple, *Badris Temple Street*, built by the court jeweler in 1867, glitters with crystals and precious stones. A French crystal chandelier hangs above the gleaming mosaic-tile floor. The temple lamp has burned continuously for 112 years. A landscaped garden surrounds the structure. You can visit the temple 6 a.m. until noon and 3 p.m. until 7 p.m.

Calcutta has a fabulous zoo with white Bengal tigers, monkeys, reptiles, and white peacocks, among other exotic beasts and birds.

The **Botanical Gardens** cover 273 acres with mahogany trees, Royal Cuban palms, an orchid house, and other exotic flora. Its crown jewel is its banyan tree, the largest in the world, with a circumference of 1,000 feet. The garden was established in 1786 by the East India Company.

In the evening, stroll along **The Maidan**, a two-mile stretch of green lawn bedecked with statues of Indian heroes. When the sun sets, the locals use this as a rendezvous point. If you feel lucky, try out the Maidan Racetrack.

Calcutta's finest hotel

Calcutta's best hotel is the **Oberoi Grand**, *tel. (91)848-827-5839*, which is centrally located and has rooms with beautiful private baths and refrigerators. Guests may use the swimming pool, health club, in-house astrologer, and disco. The hotel has four restaurants and a shopping arcade.

The most sacred river

The **Ganges River**, considered sacred by the Hindus, is believed to originate in the hair of the god Siva. Regardless of its origins, the water is indeed pure, running downhill from the Himalayas.

Hindus believe that washing in the Ganges washes away sin. The holiest place to bathe is **Allahabad**, where the Ganges and the Yamuna (or Jumna) rivers meet. This is also considered a good spot to scatter the ashes of loved ones.

The **Magh Mela**, India's biggest religious bathing ceremony, is held at Allahabad in the spring. During the festival, pilgrims stay in tents along the river, holy men lie on thorns and give sermons, barbers shave the heads of those who intend to bathe in the river, and women throw rose petals and marigolds into the water.

If you decide to join the pilgrims in their holy bath, you can't just walk into the water—the river has no beaches. You must take a boat to the middle and dive in from there.

The bathing festival is largest every 12th year, when millions convene to celebrate the Kumbh Mela, the most important religious ceremony.

The area's best hotels are the **Yatrik**, *33 Sadar Patel Marg*, and **Barnetts**, *14 Mahatma Gandhi Marg*.

DARJEELING: FOR THE MOST DARING

The train ride to **Darjeeling** is spectacular and dizzying. The 52-mile trip begins at New Jalpaiguri, near Gagdogra, which is a 55-minute flight from Calcutta, and takes about six hours. For the first few miles, the train rushes through dense jungle. Then the steep climb begins. The train chugs through lush tea plantations, clinging to the mountainsides. When it passes through the center of Kurseong, children jump the running boards and make faces at passengers.

From there the train climbs to Ghoom, 8,000 feet, to the site of a Tibetan monastery. Monks here worship a 15-foot image of the Coming Buddha and fly prayer flags.

Darjeeling, which lies four miles farther north and about 1,000 feet lower, has absolutely amazing views of the Himalayas. **Kanchenjunga Mountain** is especially awe-inspiring; the Hindus believe it is the god Siva lying down.

Darjeeling is built on a series of steps. At the top are hotels, cafés, and shops. Halfway up are smaller hotels, Indian restaurants, and more shops. The people of Darjeeling live at the bottom. Nepalese, Tibetans, and Lepchas, in their colorful tribal costumes, crowd the bazaars and markets. Women wear nose ornaments and huge necklaces.

At the center of the town is **Observatory Hill**, where the Mahakala Cave is located. The view is beautiful. Also visit the **Lloyd Botanical Gardens**, which are devoted to the flowers of the Himalayas, and the **Bhutia Busty Tibetan** and the **Aloobari**, two Buddhist monasteries.

Darjeeling also boasts the smallest and highest **racetrack** in the world, where ponies run the course three times before finishing a race. Seven miles from Darjeeling is **Tiger Hill**, from which you can see Mount Everest on clear days. The best time to see the mountain is at sunrise, when the white mountain peaks turn rose-colored.

You can learn to mountain climb in 40 days at the **Himalayan Mountaineering Institute**, *Jawahar Road West*, in Darjeeling. The instructor climbed Mount Everest with Sir Edmund Hillary in 1953. The institute has a museum that displays climbing equipment. It is open 8:30 a.m. until 1 p.m. and 2 p.m. until 4:30 p.m.

INDIA'S MOST EXOTIC AREAS

India's most exotic and remote areas are **Assam** and **Nagaland**, located in the extreme northeast corner of the country. Some years ago they were off-limits to foreigners, which makes these two locations all the more fascinating. They are inhabited by little-known tribes, some of which were headhunters only a generation ago. This is a paradise for wildlife enthusiasts, hunters, and fishermen. The region has incredible waterfalls, high peaks, and wild rivers.

The **Kaziranga Wild Life Sanctuary** is the best place for big-game hunting in India, if not the whole world. Because the grass here is 16 feet high, the only way to see the sanctuary is astride an elephant. The reserve protects several species of deer, birds, wild boars, jackals, buffaloes, elephants, and tigers.

Note that, for Nagaland at least, you will need a *Restricted Area Permit*. Contact your travel agent for details on obtaining one.

THE BEST TRAVEL PLANNING

India is immense, so it is important to plan your trip carefully. Bombay, Delhi, Calcutta, and Madras are the best places to begin your travels.

Most travelers to India *must* have a visa. There are five different Indian consular offices in the United States; each issues its own application form and requirements may vary. For further information, visit *website: www.traveldocs.com.*

Foreign visitors receive special assistance and concessions in India. Booking information sections for foreigners, which are located in railway stations and the major offices of Indian Airlines, enable you to avoid the usual long waiting lines and can greatly reduce costs of transportation throughout India. In states where alcohol is banned, foreigners can apply for a liquor permit. The Indian government is anxious to promote tourism.

Keep in mind that certain parts of India, which are politically sensitive or strategic, are designated by the government as "restricted" or "protected" areas. Foreign tourists can enter them only with special permits from the Foreigners' Regional Registration Offices (in Mumbai, Calcutta, Delhi, and Madras).

You also need a permit if you plan to stay more than 30 days in the Andaman Islands. This can be obtained through local travel agents in Calcutta or directly from the **Home Ministry**, *North Block, New Delhi.*

Western Kashmir is not a recommended destination for travelers, and some areas of the Andamans are restricted. Check at your local consulate or in New Delhi for current restrictions. To visit Bhutan, you need a permit from the Bhutan Government.

You can visit Sikkim for four days with a permit issued by the **Deputy Secretary Ministry of Home Affairs**, *North Block, New Delhi*. It takes about six to eight weeks to process the permit, so make your plans well in advance.

Permits are also required to photograph railway stations or trains.

THE BEST TIME TO GO

The best time to go to India is between November and the end of March. This avoids the rainy season and the severe heat of October and April in northern India and the hill stations of southern India. It's wise to plan your travels around the weather. Making your way through India demands tremendous energy; trying to make your way through India during the rainy season or in severe heat can be miserable.

THE BEST OF INDONESIA

Indonesia is a nation teeming with 160 million people and more than 9,000 islands. Although now mainly Muslim, these islands have a rich history of Buddhism and Hinduism, which can be seen in the ruins of ancient temples and cities scattered among the lush tropical landscape. Its capital, **Jakarta**, located on the main island of Java, is the least attractive of all the cities in Indonesia; its only real claim to fame is that it has more monuments in the city proper than any other city in the world. Once you've escaped Jakarta, you'll discover that Indonesia offers some of the most beautiful scenery in the world.

The best island to visit—Bali

No other island in the archipelago can compare with Bali. Bali has everything: stunning beaches, ancient temples, and an active volcano. The best beach is **Nusa Dua**. See it, but don't stop there. Explore the island's lush interior and its temples. The best base for this is the village of **Ubud**. Ubud, discovered by Dutch artists in the 1920s, is still home to a thriving colony of Indonesian artists and wood sculptors, each with an individual style.

If your pocket book can handle it, stay at the ultra-exclusive **Amandari Resort**. If it can't, stay at one of the area's many good guesthouses. You can hire a cab to drive you around the surrounding countryside. It's cheaper to negotiate a rate with the driver for an entire afternoon or day than to pay for individual trips. Just tell the driver to show you the temple and the volcano; it will be money well-spent.

The world's biggest Buddhist monument

Java's ancient city of **Jogykarta** is home to the world's largest Buddhist monument, the circular ruin of Borobodur. The stone friezes that circle the monument tell the life story of Buddha and his search for enlightenment. Legend has it that originally only the initiated were permitted to view the higher levels, as they are said to contain the key to a happy life.

The best place to stay is the **Hotel Ambarukmo Palace**, *Jalan Laksda Adisucipto*.

THE BEST OF ISRAEL

The Land of Milk and Honey holds a special place in history. A professor at the Hebrew University once wrote a study comparing Israel to a newborn child that has emerged from a centuries-old womb. Israel is a 20th-century country built on a 4,000-year-old prophecy; even the modern high-rise buildings carry a history of conflict.

A war-torn desert nation, bordered by four seas, the promised land has dozens of uncrowded beaches and a fertile Mediterranean coast that rivals the French Riviera. The country's three largest cities offer nightlife and historical landmarks.

The national *aliyya* (settlement) programs attest to Israeli concern for growth and building; however, this dedication has not come without problems. Israel is bordered to the north by Lebanon and to the east by Jordan, its enemies since the country was established in 1948.

Israel is small — about the size of Rhode Island — but it offers a diversity of terrain, weather, and people. You can ski the slopes of Mount Hermon, swim in the Mediterranean, and hike in the desert all in the course of one day. Yemenite, American, South African, Ethiopian, and Moroccan Israelis mingle with one another and with one million Arab Israeli citizens.

JERUSALEM, THE ETERNAL CAPITAL

Israel is best visited in two trips: one to see **Jerusalem** and one to see the rest of the country.

The capital city has been the center of both conflict and faith for 3,000 years. Divided by Israel and neighboring Jordan for 20 years, the city was reunited after the 1967 war.

It is the largest city in Israel. Expansion and construction mark the New City; inside Old Jerusalem, heavy industry is banned and archeological research continues.

Jerusalem's heart: the Old City

The 40-foot-high crenelated wall encircling the Old City is surrounded by a belt of grass and bushes. Most of Jerusalem's sights are inside this wall, which has eight gates. **Golden Gate** is thought to lie over the Closed Gate of the First Temple, the entrance through which the Jewish Messiah is expected to pass. **Jaffa Gate** is the most convenient entrance to the New City and houses a helpful tourist center. At **Damascus Gate** you can buy a ticket to ascend the rampart onto the top of the wall, where you'll have a view of the entire Old City.

Among the Old City's attractions are the Dome of the Rock (Mosque of Omar), the Church of the Holy Sepulcher, and the Via Dolorosa (Way of the Cross). The **Dome of the Rock**, an ornate shrine standing on Temple Mount, is usually filled with Muslims facing Mecca and praying. Inside is the rock from which Mohammed is said to have ascended to heaven. The **Church of the Holy Sepulcher** contains the tomb where Christ was laid to rest after the crucifixion, as well as the tomb of Joseph of Arimathea.

The **Via Dolorosa** is the path along which Jesus walked from the court of Pilate to the hill of Golgotha. You can retrace His steps; the 14 stations, or places of devotion, where Jesus rested along the way, are marked. Not far away is the **Coenaculum**, the room of the Last Supper, and to the east stands the Garden of Gethsemane, where Christ prayed the night before his crucifixion.

The **Wailing Wall**, the western wall (and sole remains) of the Second Temple, is the holiest structure in Judaism. Jews have gathered here for centuries to pray and bemoan the temple's destruction. If you write a prayer on a scrap of paper and slip it between the stones of the wall, it is said God will hear you more quickly. Jewish boys' bar mitzvahs are held here nearly every day. And at night, floodlights cast shadows on the ancient stones, and you can hear old men murmuring in prayer.

The nearby **Mount of Olives** has a famous Jewish cemetery, and the Greek Orthodox Church there houses the **Tomb of the Virgin Mary**. According to Christian tradition, the mount was the site of Jesus' Ascension; according to Jewish tradition, the Mount of Olives is where the Messiah will resurrect the dead. At dawn, **Temple Mount** has a golden glow.

Near the Old City walls is **Mount Zion**, the site of King David's tomb. (It's a bare room.)

More interesting is **Hezekiah's Tunnel**, built about 1000 B.C. so water could be brought in when the city was under siege. Begin at the **Gihon Spring** and slosh through the tunnel all the way to the **Pool of Shiloah**.

The **Museum of the Potential Holocaust**, *31 Usishkin St.*, on the Mount of Remembrance, displays contemporary anti-Semitic works from such groups as the American Nazi Party and the Klu Klux Klan. The museum is open Sunday through Thursday 9 a.m. until 5 p.m. and Friday 9 a.m. until 2 p.m.

The Hadassah Hebrew University Medical Center and its synagogue are decorated with stained-glass windows designed and painted by Marc Chagall.

The best of the New City

The first thing to see in the New City is the **Knesset**, Israel's parliament, which is decorated with mosaics by Chagall. You can catch a lively debate (in Hebrew) when the Knesset is in session Sunday and Thursday, 8:30 a.m. until 2:30 p.m. Be sure to bring your passport, and expect to be searched thoroughly when you enter.

Two blocks away is the **Yad Vashem**, a monument honoring the six million Jews killed in World War II. The photos and documents trace Hitler's rise and focus on those who fought back, particularly the Warsaw Ghetto.

Walk through the picturesque **Yemenite Moshe Quarter**, which has been renovated into residential and artists' neighborhoods. The nearby village of En Karem is the birthplace of John the Baptist. Take note of the beautiful Church of St. John, with its soaring tower.

The **Rockefeller Museum**, *Suleiman and Jericho roads*, displays Middle Eastern artwork from the last two millennia. The Billy Rose Sculpture Garden contains works by Picasso and Degas, as well as Israeli artists. It is open 10 a.m. until 5 p.m. Sunday through Thursday and 9 a.m. until 2 p.m. Friday. The **Israel Museum**, *Rehov Ruppin*, which incorporates the Bezalel Museum, has a large collection of Jewish folk and ceremonial art. Main areas devoted to archeology, Judaica, and Israeli painting mix with major exhibits from abroad. The Dead Sea scrolls are displayed here, at the Shrine of the Book. The museum is open Sunday, Monday, Wednesday, and Thursday, 10 a.m. until 5 p.m., Tuesday, 4 p.m. until 10 p.m., and Friday and Saturday, 10 a.m. until 2 p.m. Take bus 9, 17, or 24.

The best entertainment

While in Jerusalem, try to attend a performance of the Israeli Philharmonic, which stages winter concerts at **Binyanei Haoma**, *Yafo Street*, or the popular Jerusalem Dance Company. A less-known dance troupe is Kol U'Demama (Sound and Silence), an art-dance ensemble with both hearing and deaf dancers. It is the only group of its kind in the world. The Cahanna Ticket Agency can provide tickets to most cultural events.

The most festive times to visit

In the summer, musicians, dancers, and actors from around the globe converge on Jerusalem for the **Israel Festival of Music and Drama**. The holiday of Simchat Torah, which usually falls in early October, is marked by **Hakafot** ceremonies—which consist of singing, dancing, and parading the Torah through the streets. In Jerusalem, Hakafot festivities take place in the Liberty Bell Garden area, located on Recham HaMelekh (King David) Street. (The Liberty Bell was set up to fete the U.S. Bicentennial.)

Christmas and Hanukkah are special times in Jerusalem. Christmas is marked by a weeklong festival of choral music called the **Liturgica**, and Hanukkah begins with a public candle-lighting ceremony at the Western Wall. The largest Christmas tree in the city is set up and lit at the West Jerusalem Y.M.C.A. Eastern Orthodox Christmas celebrations include a parade with bagpipers. On Dec. 24 at 12:30 p.m., people gather at Jaffa Gate for the Procession of the Latin Patriarch, commemorating the journey of the Three Wise Men. Anyone can join the procession, which winds its way from the Old City to Bethlehem, about seven miles south. Once in Bethlehem, choirs accompany the priest into St. Catherine's Church for High Mass. If you're thinking of spending Christmas in the holiest of cities, make reservations months in advance.

Jerusalem's best bargains

The **Arab bazaar** in the Old City offers Jerusalem's best bargains. (Haggling is the rule.) Throw rugs and Bedouin-style dresses are among the most popular items. A good buy for a dress is $25. You can get a *keffiyah* (Arab head scarf) for about $4.

The best jewelry shop in Jerusalem is **Tarshish**, *18 King David St.*, where you can buy intricate Yemenite jewelry. Tarshish is open until 5 p.m. every day except Friday and is located right across from the King David Hotel. For handcrafted jewelry made with malachite and Israeli glass, go to the jeweler/artisan Uri Ramot; he, along with other jewelers and weavers, displays his goods along the **Khutsot Hayotser** (Arts and Crafts Lane) just outside the Jaffa Gate.

The best dining

For Mideastern cuisine, go to the **Caravan**, located about a half-mile before the entrance to Bethlehem along the road from Jerusalem. Chef Abu-Isaac's succulent *mezze* (appetizers), cubed shashlik, and lamb kabobs stuffed with onions are delicious and inexpensive. Don't try making reservations; the restaurant has no telephone.

The **National Palace Restaurant**, in the National Palace Hotel, is another good place to get an Arabian meal. Ask your waiter what he recommends—this is considered proper. Order a selection of *mezze*—you'll be served a plate of appetizers ranging from olives to brain salad (it's good). The shish kebab and the grilled mutton marinated in yogurt are delicious. Before your meal, try a glass of arrack, an anise-flavored brandy mixed with water and ice.

Caty's Restaurant, *16 Rivlin St.*, popular with the smart set, has first-class French food plus some North African specialties. Brooke Shields has eaten here.

Ticho House, *9 Haravkook St.*, part of the Israel Museum, is a pleasant café in the former home of artist Anna Ticho, whose works are on display. The villa has a Persian garden and a collection of Hanukkah lamps. The kitchen is kosher and serves good crêpes, soups, and salads.

Shemesh on Ben Yahudah Street, is an elegant eatery decorated with figurines of the sun (which is the literal translation of *shemesh*). The stuffed veggies and various kabobs, as well as the *mezzes* (the best is the hummus with tahini) are excellent. And the prices are moderate.

In Jerusalem, a restaurant doesn't have to be expensive to be good. The **Shulchan Restaurant**, *2 Kikar Remaz*, across from the train station at the Khan Theater, serves quiches, salads, and hearty soups by the fireplace.

Middle Eastern food sold by street vendors is even cheaper. You can fill up on *felafel*, *mezze*, and *fuul* (beans).

Premier hotels

The city's premier hotel is the **King David**, *23 King David St.*, famous for its celebrity guests. Considered one of the classic hotels of the Middle East, the King David has more than 250 rooms, air conditioning, tennis courts, a pool, and a sauna. Make reservations far in advance.

The **American Colony Hotel**, *Naplus Road, P.O. Box 19215*, once the home of a Turkish Pasha, is a luxurious hotel walled off from the hectic streets of Jerusalem. Rooms have gold and blue ceilings, antique Arab and Turkish furnishings, and modern bathrooms. Archeological finds are displayed in the lobby. The garden and the swimming pool are inviting. Ask for a room in the old building; the new building is not as interesting.

Overlooking the Old City is the **King Solomon Sheraton**, *32 King David St.*, near the YMCA, with more than 100 rooms and great service.

Less expensive is the **Windmill**, *3 Mendele St.*, a peaceful hotel with air-conditioned rooms.

Babylonian nightlife

For a good time in Jerusalem, go to **Herod's Bar**, *28 King David St.*, near the YMCA, which has a young crowd and, occasionally, belly dancing. The **Jerusalem Khan**, *David Remez Square*, is an entertaining nightclub. It's open 9:30 p.m. until midnight every night. The **Taverna** is another good club with a floor show, and the cellar bar at the American Colony Hotel has good jazz bands.

Most of the city closes down on Friday afternoons (Friday is the Muslim Sabbath, and Jewish shopkeepers must begin to prepare for their Sabbath), but you can catch an earful of jazz on Fridays at 1:30 p.m. at the **Pergod Theater**, *94 Bezalel St.* And the **Tourist Bureau** conducts synagogue tours on Friday afternoon.

For more information, contact the **Jerusalem Tourist Information Center**, *24 King George St.*

The best side trips

Outside Jerusalem is the intercultural village **Neve Shalom** (Oasis for Peace), an experiment in peaceful coexistence among Arabs, Christians, and Jews, which has received several Ford Foundation grants. Visit Neve

Shalom's School for Peace and the educational center for intergroup relations. Few tourists know about the village.

A visit to **Hebron** is a good day-trip (if the West Bank is quiet). Egged (a cooperative bus company) buses 34, 440, and 443 (which you can catch at the Jerusalem Central Bus Station) will take you to Hebron's main square, outside the Cave of Machpelah, where the three patriarchs—Abraham, Isaac, and Jacob—are buried with their wives (except Rachel). This is a major shrine for Jews and Muslims. The large, fortresslike synagogue above the cave opens to a long hallway. On the right is the tomb of Jacob and Leah. Across the courtyard is a tomb covered with calligraphy commemorating Abraham and Sarah. The Machpelah is closed to non-Muslims on Friday.

BETHLEHEM: CHRISTIANITY'S BIRTHPLACE

Bethlehem, the birthplace of Jesus and King David, is only seven miles south of Jerusalem. This town of 25,000 is so touristy that post offices stay open on Christmas Day so tourists can mail postcards. On the road from Jerusalem is the Garden Tomb, where, according to the Gospels, Christ was buried.

The frenetic heart of Bethlehem is crowded **Manger Square**. On the east side of the square is the imposing **Church of the Nativity** (the oldest church in Israel, built by Constantine in A.D. 326), which you enter through a low doorway designed to stop visitors on horseback. Twelve pillars decorated with images of the apostles hold up the oak ceiling. Armenian, Greek, and Franciscan priests take care of the church. Descend into the cave beneath, where Jesus was born. The manger is holy to both Christians and Muslims.

Other important sights are the **Milk Grotto**, where the Virgin Mary is said to have dropped milk when nursing the baby Jesus, miraculously turning the cavern rocks white; **Rachel's tomb**, a small domed shrine built in 1860 and visited by Muslims, Jews, and Christians; and **Shepherds' Field**, just outside town off Shepherds' Street, believed to be the place where shepherds were told by angels that Christ had been born.

The colorful *souk* (market) is crowded, but worth a trip just to visit **Barakat Antiques**, *4648 King David St.;* this is the finest antique shop in Israel.

The **Casa Nova Inn**, *10 Casa Nova St.*, just east of Manger Square, is a newly renovated pilgrims' inn. Rates include not only a Continental breakfast but also a five-course afternoon dinner and a late supper. This is by far the best place to stay in Bethlehem; not only is it cheap, but it is also undiscovered and free of tourists.

TEL AVIV: ISRAEL'S BUSIEST CITY

Tel Aviv is Israel's bustling metropolis, the fastest growing city on the Mediterranean coast. Most countries have their embassies here. Established in 1909 as a suburb of ancient Jaffa, Tel Aviv has become a second capital. It is situated conveniently, only an hour's drive from both Haifa and Jerusalem.

Tel Aviv's top museums

Tel Aviv Museum, next to the Municipal Central Library at *27 King Saul St.*, houses a comprehensive collection of art, a sculpture garden, and a children's wing. The museum is open Sunday, Monday, Wednesday, and Thursday, 10 a.m. until 5 p.m.; Tuesday, 9 a.m. until 1 p.m. and 4 p.m. until 10 p.m.; Friday, 10 a.m. until 2 p.m.; and Saturday, 7 p.m. until 11 p.m.

Diaspora Museum, *Beit Hatefutzot,* on the campus of Tel Aviv University, uses films, computers, and audiovisual displays to trace the history of the Jewish people and the birth of Israel. It's open Sunday, Monday, Tuesday, and Thursday, 10 a.m. until 5 p.m., and Wednesday, 10 a.m. until 7 p.m.

The **Eretz Museum** (Museum of the Land), *Ramat Aviv*, displays glass, coins, ceramics, and other archeological finds. It is open Sunday through Thursday, 9 a.m. until 2 p.m., Tuesday, 4 a.m. until 7 p.m., and Saturday, 10 a.m. until 2 p.m.

Israel's Miami Beach

Tel Aviv's seafront smacks of Miami Beach. It is lined with tourist hotels, outdoor cafés, shops, and restaurants, especially in **Kikar Namir** (Namir Square).

Tel Aviv's best park

Yarkon Park, an urban oasis in the northern part of the city, can be reached by Egged buses 1, 4, and 5. During the daylight hours, you can rent a rowboat on the Ha Yarkon River; contact **Irgun HaYarkon**.

Israel's best nightlife

Tel Aviv's discos are the best in the country. Try **Colosseum**, *Kikar Atarim*, where you can dance until 4 a.m.

Music and theater flourish in Tel Aviv. The 3,000-seat **Mann Auditorium** is the home of the world-famous Israeli Philharmonic, which gives 180 concerts a year, often with such acclaimed Israeli-born musicians as Itzhak Perlman and Pinchas Zuckerman. Habimah, the famous repertory group, and the Cameri Theater offer first-class productions of classical and contemporary drama. The ticket office is on *Ibngzirol Street;* purchase tickets as far in advance as possible.

The most delicious dining

The best restaurants in Tel Aviv can be found along the old port. **Restaurant Yamit**, *18 Kikar Kedumim*, has an outdoor terrace with a view of the sea and serves good drinks. It is open from 10 a.m. until midnight. A good place for Yemenite food is the **Zion Restaurant**, *28 Peduyim St.*, which is open 11:30 a.m. until midnight. Dizengoff Street cafés remain open on the Sabbath. Especially recommended is **Cherry's**, *145 Ben Yehuda St.*, which is open from 7 a.m. until 2 a.m. and serves breakfast, lunch, and dinner. For a great meal on Saturday, visit the **Taj Mahal**, *12 Kikar Kedumim*; it is open for lunch from noon until 3 p.m. and for dinner from 7 p.m. until midnight.

The best hotels

Considered by many to be the best hotel in Israel, the **Tel Aviv Sheraton**, *115 Hayarkon St.*, has spacious, air-conditioned rooms, restaurants, discos, and shops. It is within walking distance of the beach and Dizengoff Street shops.

Others argue that the **Dan Hotel**, *99 Hayarkon St.*, is the best in Israel. On the beach close to the city, it is one of the oldest hotels in Tel Aviv.

More modestly priced accommodation is available at the **Hotel Tamar**, *8 Gnessin St.* Slightly better and cheaper still is **Hotel HaGalil**, *23 Bayit Josef.* This hotel, near Souk HaCarmel, offers rooms with private balconies.

The **Greenhouse**, *201 Dizengoff St.*, is the best hostel in Tel Aviv; it offers dorms, double rooms, and private apartments with showers. Call in advance; availability is limited. **Immanuel House Christian Hospice**, *Jaffa*, is a quiet, friendly place built by Peter Ustinov's father. It also has a dorm room, singles, and doubles. Plan ahead in the busy season.

JAFFA: AN OFFBEAT BEST

Jaffa, the Biblical port town, is now part of Tel Aviv. Its winding lanes are filled with shops, restaurants, and nightclubs. The reconstructed Old City houses an artists' colony, private and public art galleries, and studios. Shops and boutiques here remain open until midnight. The flea market off Aleystion Street is where everyone ends up; it is as colorful as it is inexpensive.

Old Jaffa, with its intimate restaurants and romantic cafés, is a splendid counterpoint to the dangerous and rocky coastline on its border. **Toutoune**, *1 Simpat Mazel Bagitn*, is an outstanding restaurant that serves excellent French cuisine on the roof of an old Turkish house. It is rivaled only by **Via Maris**, *6 Kikar Kdumim*, where you can sit on a vine-covered terrace and enjoy delicious seafood and a view of the floodlit town. Both restaurants open for dinner around 6 p.m. and serve until midnight.

Jaffa comes alive at night, especially on Hayarkon Street near the old port and in the new cafés and restaurants around city hall.

ASHKELON: DEFYING FATE

Located on the Mediterranean coast 30 miles south of Tel Aviv, **Ashkelon** is a flourishing port city—despite the Biblical prophecy that "Gaza shall be deserted, and Ashkelon shall become desolation" (Zephaniah 2:4). In response to the prophecy, the center of town is named Zephaniah Square.

Ashkelon, associated with Samson and his battles with the Philistines, is one of the three famous Philistine city-states. The seaside National Antiquities Park here has ancient ruins, including pillars and walls dating back to Canaanite times. The most extensive ruins are Roman, and the haphazard collection of columns, statues, and capitals is highlighted by the Boulouterion, the third-century square filled with marble statues of Atlas, Nike, and Isis.

Ashkelon is big on tennis. Its tennis center has 17 courts, and the Ashkelon Tennis Tournament plays to a crowd of 2,000. For more information, contact the **Ashkelon Tourist Center**.

THE WORLD'S BEST SPA: THE DEAD SEA

The greatest natural wonder of Israel is one of the healthiest as well. At 1,312 feet below sea level, the Dead Sea region is the lowest point on earth. As a result, it has one of the driest climates in the world, and its pure and pollen-free air is especially good for those with allergies or respiratory problems. (People with skin disorders also come here for the therapeutic ultraviolet rays.) Because this region has the highest atmospheric pressure on earth (which reduces the danger of sunburn), it is one of the most relaxing places to sunbathe—and it has more than 300 cloudless days a year.

The main wonder is the sea itself, with 10 times as much salt as any ocean in the world. The surface of the calm brown water is periodically broken by the green-white salt mounds. It is considered the only sea in which you cannot drown, because the salt-laden water makes you float like a cork. Don't try to swim if you have cuts—the salt will irritate them.

The shores of the sea are lined with resorts and historic sites—few tourists realize just how lively the Dead Sea is.

Mezad Zohar, near Jericho on the Dead Sea coast, is an ancient stronghold surrounded by fantastic rock formations. Natural freshwater bathing pools mark green oases.

Ein Gedi, about 11 miles north of Masada, is the oasis where David hid from King Saul. Now a kibbutz facing the Dead Sea, it contains waterfalls, a nature reserve, hot springs, and an archeological site.

A revitalizing visit to the Dead Sea spa is a must. Spend a week at the five-star **Moriah Dead Sea Spa Hotel**, enjoying Dead Sea hydrotherapy and treatment in pools and mud. When you are fed up with the brackish water, you can swim in fresh water (indoors or out) or use the hotel's various sports facilities. Rates will vary depending on the package and the season.

If you're going to the Dead Sea, also visit **Arad**. Located a half-hour from the Dead Sea, but 3,500 feet higher, Arad sits on a plateau overlooking an ancient Roman fort. This Biblical city, renovated in the 1960s, is a mixture of old and new. The nearby Tel Arad excavations include a temple dating back to King Solomon and a fortress that was rebuilt six times before Julius Caesar was born.

The best Dead Sea digs

The best areas to stay in while visiting the Dead Sea are En Boqeq and Arad. The **Margoa Arad**, *Moav Street, P.O. Box 20*, has a nightclub, a cinema hall, and a private pool.

The two outstanding hotels in En Boqeq are **Ein Bokek**, which has a pool, a nightclub, and tennis courts, and the **Moriah Gardens Hotel**, a four-star hotel with an outdoor pool, an indoor seawater pool, a private beach, and a famous spa fed by waters of the Zohar Hot Springs.

The **Ein Gedi kibbutz** has a reasonably priced guesthouse. The 92 rooms have televisions and radios and the price includes two meals.

For more information on hotels in the area of the Dead Sea, contact the **Arad Tourist Information Office**; it is open 9 a.m. until 5 p.m.

MASADA — THE MOST DRAMATIC

Masada, the famous hilltop fortress built by King Herod, is one of Israel's most important sights. Commanding a view of the pink mountains of Moab, Masada was the last stronghold of the Jews when Rome invaded the country. In 73 B.C., after three years of fighting, the Romans finally broke through Masada's defenses only to find that the 960 rebels had committed mass suicide rather than surrender to slavery. Built on a cliff that drops 1,300 feet, Masada is dramatic in both history and appearance.

The peak can be reached either by foot (follow the Snake Path) or by cable cars, which run every 15 minutes from the eastern side of the mountain. The bathhouses, storehouses, water cisterns, and Herod's three-tiered palace have been restored. See the mosaics in the lavish palace halls; the world's largest collection of first-century Roman and Jewish coins; the world's oldest synagogue; and the Mikvot, the world's oldest extant ritual immersion baths, predating baptism by 100 years.

JERICHO — THE WORLD'S OLDEST CITY

Jericho, the world's oldest city, was a walled community as early as 7000 B.C. According to the Old Testament, Joshua toppled Jericho's walls with trumpet blasts. Since then, the city has been rebuilt and destroyed several times. Lush scenery surrounds this oasis. Explore the many levels of the ruins and the remains of the magnificent palaces.

HAIFA — THE PRETTIEST CITY

Although **Haifa** is heavily industrialized, it is one of the most beautiful cities in Israel. The nation's third-largest city and main port, it has been compared to San Francisco. Hugging a beautiful bay on the Mediterranean, it encompasses the hilly suburb of Mount Carmel.

Israel's biggest museum

The **Haifa Museum Complex**, *26 Shabatai Levi St.*, is one of the largest in Israel, with three separate exhibits: Israeli modern art, ancient art, and Jewish folklore and ethnology. Visit 10 a.m. until 5 p.m. Tuesday through Thursday. Also visit the **Haifa Illegal Immigration and Naval Museum**, *204 Derech Allenby*. It illustrates the history of Jewish migration to Palestine when it was under British mandate. (Although the British outlawed further migration, Israelis managed to smuggle their relatives in for another 20 years.) The museum is open 9 a.m. until 4 p.m. Sunday through Thursday, 9 a.m. until noon Friday and Saturday.

Highest tech in the Middle East

The **Technion** (Israel Institute of Technology), *Neve Sha'anan*, is the university that makes Israel the most technologically advanced nation in the Middle East. Covering 300 acres and including 50 buildings, it has a panoramic view of the city, the bay, and, on clear days, Lebanon. Students from all over the world can be seen strolling the campus lawns. Stop by the Coler-California Visitor Center on campus, where a robot welcomes you and a free film is shown about the technological discoveries made here.

The world's most internationally minded religion

Haifa is the world center of **Baha'i**, a religion that broke away from Islamic mysticism in the 19th century. The Baha'i believe in the unity of all religions and advocate an international language and government.

Few travelers visit the beautiful gold-domed **Baha'i Shrine and Gardens**, halfway up Mount Carmel. (You can get there via Bus 23 from Hanevi'im Street.) The Bab, the herald of the primary Baha'i prophet, Bahaullah, is buried in the shrine. (Bahaullah is buried a few miles north of Haifa in Akko.) You must remove your shoes to enter the shrine. The gardens are filled with statues of animals and graceful cypress trees. You can visit 9 a.m. until noon.

The **Baha'i International Archives** and the **Baha'i Universal House of**

Justice are also located in Haifa. The archives were modeled after the Parthenon, and the House of Justice is noted for its 58 marble columns and its hanging gardens. Unfortunately, neither attraction is open to tourists.

Israel's largest national park

Mount Carmel, the site of Elijah's confrontation with the priests of Ba'al, is the site of Israel's largest national park, with 25,000 acres of eucalyptus and cypress forests, picnic areas, and a restaurant. At the peak of the mountain are hanging gardens. Beautiful homes cling to the slopes. Mount Carmel also has some of Haifa's best hotels. Climb the mountain just before sunset, when the sun is a flaming red ball, dipping below the horizon.

The best restaurants

Haifa's speciality is seafood. The two best places to enjoy it are downtown: **Neptune**, *19 Pinhas Margolin St.*, and **Misabag**.

The best place for a traditional home-style Jewish meal is **Shmulik & Dany**, *7 Habankim St.* This popular establishment papers its walls with rave reviews and fine paintings. Try the roast duck, the house specialty.

Peer, *1 Atlit St.*, is a good Arabic restaurant open for breakfast, lunch, and dinner.

The best place for European food is **Bankers Tavern**, *2 Habankim St.*

Haifa's best hotels

Haifa's best hotel is the five-star **Dan Carmel**, *85-87 Sderot Hanassai*, with the most luxurious rooms and the best view of Haifa Bay in the city.

Almost as good and less expensive is **Yaarot Hacarmel Rest House**, *Mount Carmel.*

Nof, *101 Sederot Han Nasi, Carmel*, has a panoramic view and luxurious rooms. The restaurant serves excellent kosher food.

Another good hotel in Carmel is the **Shulamit**, *15 Kiryat Sefer St.*

Highlights near Haifa

Ten miles south of Haifa is En Hod, a famous artists' colony that is open to the public. It is situated on Atlit Beach, where a castle juts up from the water. This was the site of the Crusaders' last stand before they were expelled from the Holy Land.

Nahariyya, a half-hour north of Akko (Acre), is an old-fashioned village where horse-drawn carriages are still the mode of transportation. This friendly town is a popular Israeli honeymoon resort. A small stream flows through the center of town into a wide beach, where legend has it that man first learned to make glass. Sailors made a huge bonfire on the sand, so powerful and hot that it turned part of the beach into glass.

Caesarea—built to rival Baghdad

South of Haifa is **Caesarea**, built by King Herod in the first century B.C. to rival Baghdad. Once the port could hold an entire Roman fleet. Today, it is an impressive recreation center, with horseback riding, swimming, and one of the few 18-hole golf courses in Israel. Concerts, both classical and rock, are held in the Roman amphitheater.

The extensive historical remains in Caesarea include a Roman hippodrome, part of the Roman harbor and aqueducts, and the remains of a Crusader town, walls, and moat. Archeological digs continue constantly in Caesarea.

The beach in Caesarea is pleasant. The famous Sharon Coast runs from Caesarea down to Tel Aviv—this is where the lilies of Sharon bloom in the sand during the fall.

If you stay in Caesarea, your best bet is the **Dan Caesarea Golf Hotel**, which has three restaurants, a pool, tennis courts, a sauna, and a Turkish bath. The beach and shops are nearby.

GALILEE — PASTORAL PERFECTION

Galilee, in northeast Israel, is a green region dotted with small cities and world-famous historical sites. It borders the **Sea of Galilee**, which is also called Lake Kinneret (which translates as violin-shaped harp), because of its shape.

Greatest knowledge, best baths

Tiberias is the largest city on the shore and a good base from which to tour the area. This holy city, full of synagogues and churches, was founded 2,000 years ago in honor of the purity of Caesar Tiberias (who turned out to be an extremely decadent ruler). For 200 years after the fall of Jerusalem, it acted as the center of Jewish learning, and it was here that the books of Jewish law, the Mishnah and the Gamorah, were written.

Tiberias is also a winter resort, where foreigners and natives have traveled for hundreds of years to enjoy the therapeutic hot springs. After you've wandered through the city's bazaars, shops, and monuments, a visit to the health resort Hamme Teverya will limber up your aching muscles.

The best restaurant in Tiberias is the little-known **Lido**. Located right on the water, it serves delicious Near Eastern food. Try the grilled St. Peter fish.

You won't find much in the way of nightlife in Tiberias. Across the Dead Sea, however, the En Gev Music Festival is held every year during Passover.

In the footsteps of Jesus

Outside the city are numerous landmarks easily reached by bicycle, taxi, bus, or boat. **Capernaum** (Kefar Nahum) was the site of Jesus' first miraculous cures, as well as where He found His first disciples. Nearby is the **Mount of Beatitudes**, where Jesus delivered the Sermon on the Mount. **Qursi**, on the opposite side of the lake, has the remains of a beautiful church and monastery built on the site where Jesus drove the devils out of a possessed man and into a herd of swine.

Tabgha, traditional site of the miracle of loaves and fishes, has an ornate church with a Byzantine mosaic floor. And in nearby **Hittim** is the Nebi Shueib, the Druze holy place. Jethro, the father-in-law of Moses, is buried here.

Near the sea is **Kafr Kanna**, with its impressive Fransiscan and Greek churches. Have a glass of wine here; this is where Jesus performed His first miracle, changing water into wine.

To complete your religious/historical tour of Galilee, visit **Nazareth**, just to the south. The childhood home of Jesus is filled with shrines, including Mary's Well, the Church of St. Joseph, and the Basilica of the Annunciation. Completed in 1966, the basilica is an ornate shrine to which almost every church in the world contributed. And just southeast of Nazareth is an archeological site that shouldn't be missed. **Bet Shean** is the oldest of the old. Towering above the excavation site is a tell, a mound composed of the remains of successive settlements. The one at Bet Shean consists of 18 cities superimposed one atop the other, attesting to more than 5,000 years of continuous occupation from roughly the fourth millennium B.C. to the early Arab period (in the seventh century).

Safed—mysticism and magic

Take a short trip north to the intriguing hillside town of **Safed** (Zefat), one of the Four Holy Cities of Israel. Jewish refugees expelled from Spain took refuge in this town, which clings to the steep slope of Mount Canaan, in 1492, and Safed became a center for the study of Cabala—Jewish mysticism and magic. (Cabala is so arcane that men may not study it until they are 35 years old and married.)

Six of Safed's old synagogues are named after the city's most learned rabbis of Cabala. The most famous of these is the **Ha'Ari Synagogue**, traditionally guarded by the ghost of Rabbi Luria. (Luria developed a branch of mysticism in the 16th century now known as Lurianic Cabala. The people of Safed named him Ha'Ari, or the Lion.)

Explore the Synagogue Quarter on foot—the streets are too narrow for automobiles. Safed was the site of the first printing press in Israel in 1563. The former Arab Quarter houses a thriving artist's colony, where, among the winding lanes, dozens of painters and artisans work in the sunshine as it glares off the white stone. Most artists open their studios daily to visitors.

Safed's Rimon Inn, off the standard tourist route in the Artists' Quarter, has secluded rooms with spectacular views.

For information about walking tours, contact the **Safed Tourist Information Center**, *50 Jerusalem St.*

The best horsing-around in Galilee

Kfar Hittin Ranch, *Ms. Shadmot Dvora, Galil Hatchton 15240*, a member of the Israel Camping Union, offers a horseback-riding tour of Galilee. You follow a trail that leads to a lookout on Ginossar Hill, an ancient synagogue near Zukei Arbel, the Ginossar Valley, and through a riverbed to the Sea of Galilee. You'll have a breathtaking view of the Jordan River.

The best food and lodging

The most elegant restaurant in the city is **La Coquille**. It is expensive but luxurious. Located on the North Beach near the Gala Eilat, it offers the finest French food on the Red Sea. It is open 7 p.m. until 1 a.m.

Two good seafood restaurants are **La Bohème**, *Coral Beach*, which is open for lunch and dinner, and the **Last Refuge**, *Hof Aimog Jetty on Coral Beach*, which is only open for dinner.

The best hotel is the **Sonesta Suites Hotel**, *Haraba Road*, with a tennis court, a pool, and a private beach.

The **Red Sea Sport Hotel**, *Coral Beach*, is an excellent little hotel with a pool.

Hazor—Israel's biggest archeological site

Hazor, about 10 miles north of the Sea of Galilee, is the biggest excavated archeological site in Israel. The original city, which served as the capital of Biblical Canaan, dates back to 2500 B.C. Centuries after Joshua and the Israelites leveled the city, Solomon rebuilt it. The excavations at Hazor span 4,000 years of history and 22 cities layered one atop the other.

The Hykssos (Hittite) fortress, palaces, tablets, and chariot remains on display show the cruelty of the Hittites, who led the way in using chariots and became the world's first conquerors.

THE BEST OF JAPAN

A CASE MIGHT BE MADE FOR JAPAN AS PANDORA'S BOX.
—John Gunther, Inside Asia, *1939*

Japan is at once the best-known yet least-understood countries in Asia, a unique combination of Eastern and Western cultures. The Japanese go to great lengths to provide Western travelers with American-style hotels and modern amenities; yet, the Westerner may be excluded from a geisha club or a traditional Japanese inn. In the space of a few miles, you can race with the dizzying traffic of Tokyo's Ginza district and then revel in the silence of a remote Buddhist temple.

An ancient country, Japan is also the most modern nation in Asia. It is at once tranquil and chaotic, trend setting and traditional. Young people wearing the latest fashions share sidewalks with elderly people in ancient costumes. Japanese businessmen taking the international market by storm also take time to meditate in centuries-old temples.

THE BEST OF TOKYO

Japan's capital and largest city is one of the most expensive cities in the world. Tokyo is not known for its beauty. Indeed, the central districts are an architectural study in neon and chrome. But the city has hidden temples and flower gardens that preserve the serene, traditional side of Japanese culture.

The metropolis of Tokyo sprawls to the horizon, covering 800 square miles and comprising 26 cities, six towns, nine villages, and several islands. Curiously, this industrial city also has 20,679 farmers.

The best ways to travel

The subway system in Tokyo is excellent. Its routes are color-coded, and most stations are marked in Roman letters. The bus network is efficient as well, but information is printed only in Japanese. Taxis are luxurious, many with television sets and doors that open and close by remote control.

Despite all this, walking is the best way to see Tokyo. Even at night, the streets in this virtually crime-free city are safe. However, many of the streets are not named, and buildings aren't always numbered, so it is easy to get lost. If you do get lost, you're in luck as long as it's a weekday between 9 a.m. and 5 p.m. or Saturday between 9 a.m. and noon. During those times, you can stop by a police box and call the **Tokyo Information Center**, *tel. (81)33-503-2911.* A member of the English-speaking staff will be able to help you.

The number-one sight

At the heart of Tokyo is the **Imperial Palace**, a 28-acre retreat surrounded by a moat filled with swans. The palace stands on the site of Edo Castle, built in the 15th century by Lord Dokan Ota. From the 1500s to 1868, when it was the residence of the Tokugawa shoguns, it covered 608 acres and was defended by a 10-mile wall with 111 gates, 20 turrets, and 30 bridges. The city of Tokyo grew around the edifice, which has been destroyed and rebuilt several times.

Behind the palace walls there is a silkworm farm, rice paddies, and a mulberry field. Visitors can enter the palace only twice a year: on January 1 and on the emperor's birthday.

You can visit the **Imperial Palace East Garden** every day except Monday and Friday from 9 a.m. to 3 p.m. You'll think you are in the shoguns' Japan, not a modern city. Still standing are four gates that once led into ancient Edo Castle. The Kitakibashimon, the entrance to the castle tower, is the most imposing, its stone bulwarks reflected in the deepest part of the moat.

The **Kitanomaru Koen** and **Chidorigafuchi Suijo Koen** parks are open to the public year-round. The Kitanomaru Koen Park contains the National Museum of Modern Art; the Crafts Gallery, located in the former headquarters of the Old Imperial Palace Guard; the Science and Technology Museum, and the Nippon Budokan (built for the 1964 Olympics), a concert hall that looks like a Buddhist temple but hosts performances by such rock stars as Rod Stewart.

The Imperial Palace is encircled by a 4.6-mile bike trail. Five hundred free bikes are available at the police station in the Imperial Palace Plaza if you'd like to make the *tour du palais*. Or you can join the locals in a jog around the palace's perimeter. The Imperial Hotel provides its guests with complimentary running gear and shoes for this purpose.

For the best view of the palace and its gardens, have lunch or dinner in the 10th-floor restaurant at the nearby Palace Hotel. Another good view is from the 36th floor of the Kasumigaseki Building, southwest of the palace. On a clear day, you can see all the way to Mount Fuji.

The loveliest shrines and temples

Beyond the palace grounds and up a hill is the **Yasukuni shrine**, *3-1-1 Kudan Kita, Dhiyoda-ku*, dedicated to the souls of those who have fought and died for Japan. Surrounded by park-like grounds, its entrance is marked by a huge, yoked wooden gateway called a *torii*. Walk through the mazelike shrine, with its many pillars. Toss some coins in the box by the door, clap your hands to awaken the spirits within, and say a prayer. Flocks of doves seem somehow symbolic. Inside the shrine is a museum containing war memorabilia.

The **Askakusa Kannon temple**, at the heart of the Asakusa neighborhood, is dedicated to Kannon, the Buddhist goddess of compassion. According to legend, the temple was built in A.D. 628 by three fishermen who had discovered a statue of the goddess in their fishing net. It is marked by a 10-foot red paper lantern that weighs 220 pounds. An enormous incense vat sends sweet-smelling smoke into the air from the courtyard in front of the temple. When cupped in one palm and patted on the body, the smoke is said to cure ailments. The flock of doves that fly around the temple are considered sacred messengers of Kannon. Many of Tokyo's temples hold annual festivals, but the one held here May 16th to 18th is the largest in the city.

The **Hie shrine**, *2-10-5 Nagata-cho*, is dedicated to Oyamakuni, the money god, who grants fertility and good relationships and wards off evil. The best time to visit the shrine is every other Juen (odd years), during the Sanno-sai Festival, when miniature shrines are carried through the neighborhood.

The **Meji shrine**, *Shibuya-ku*, is one of the most popular Shinto shrines in Tokyo. Founded in 1920, it is dedicated to the Emperor Meiji (1868-1912), who ended the 600-year rule of the shoguns and opened Japan to the West. The shrine is surrounded by a 180-acre garden, and before it stands Japan's largest *torii*. The shrine's best feature is its iris garden, which bursts into color in June and July. Horsemen wearing samurai costumes compete in the yearly archery contest held here.

The **Sengakuji temple**, *Takanawa*, is the burial site of the 47 samurai of Asano Naganoni, Lord of Ako. They died for their master after avenging his death. Naganoni had made the mistake of drawing his sword when the court chamberlain insulted him. As punishment, he was forced to commit suicide. His faithful samurai then cut off the head of the chamberlain, for which they too had to commit suicide. Their story is re-enacted in the Kabukin play *Chushingura*. The faithful still come to lament the death of the samurai by lighting joss sticks on stone memorials in the temple gardens.

Tokyo's best park

On weekends, Tokyo residents flock to busy **Ueno Park**. Weekdays are less crowded. Try to visit during the Cherry Blossom Festival, from late March through mid-April, when the trees are breathtaking.

The **Ueno zoo** is worth visiting, if only for its pandas. Also visit the **Shitamachi History Museum**, at the far end of the park, featuring everyday objects donated by Tokyo residents.

Japan's best baseball (*besuboru*)

One of the most popular destinations in Tokyo is in the Korakuen district, southwest of Ueno Park: the **Korakuen baseball stadium**. With two baseball leagues and 12 teams, the Japanese are passionate *besuboru* (baseball) fans, and the stadium is often sold out through the entire season. (The Japanese baseball season is roughly equal to ours.)

The best theater in Japan

There are three traditional forms of theater in Japan; they are Kabuki, Noh, and Bunraku, all of which can be seen at their finest in Tokyo. The **National Theater of Japan**, *tel. (81) 3-3230-3000*, is the best Kabuki and Bunraku. It was designed based on centuries-old Kabuki theaters.

Kabuki plays have fantastic plots, elaborate costumes, a lot of action, and singing. All parts are played by men, and performances go on for hours. (You don't have to sit through an entire performance. It is acceptable to leave or arrive in the middle.) Musicians are seated on stage, and stagehands wearing black hoods bring actors their props during performances.

The largest Kabuki theater in Tokyo is **Kabukiza**, in the Ginza. (However, as mentioned above, the best place to see Kabuki is at the National Theater because performances are translated and explained via earphones.)

Bunraku—puppet versions of Kabuki—are heroic tales of samurai enacted by life-size puppets. A small theater in the National Theater is designed especially for Bunraku.

Noh plays, which date back to the 12th century, are highly stylized and symbolic dramas. The stage is bare except for a backdrop showing a huge tree. Actors wear masks and speak in falsetto voices. The best places to see Noh plays are small Noh theaters, including **Ginza Nohgakudo**, *6-5-15 Ginza, Chuo-ku; tel. (81) 33-571-0197* (for performances every even-numbered month); the **National Noh Theater**, *4-18-1 Sendagoya, Shibuya-ku;* (for performances every Wednesday at 1 p.m. and every third Friday at 6 p.m.); **Kanze Nohgakudo**, *1-16-4 Shoto, Shibuya-ku; tel. (81) 33-469-5241* (for performances on the first Sunday of every month at 11 a.m. and the second Thursday on even-numbered months at 5 p.m.); and **Hosho Nohgakudo**, *1-5-9 Hongo, Bunkyo-ku; tel. (81) 33-811-4843* (for performances every second Sunday and every third Saturday at 1 p.m., except in July and August, and on Wednesday in odd-numbered months at 6 p.m.).

The best flower arranging

Ikebana, the Japanese art of flower arrangement, follows strict aesthetic and philosophical principles. Flowers are placed to symbolize heaven above, earth below, and man in the middle. Ikebana was developed in the eighth century, when it was practiced at the Imperial Court. Today, the art can be seen in every temple and many households throughout Japan. The **Ohara School of Ikebana**, *7-17 Minami-Aoyama, 4-chome, Minato-ku; tel. (81) 33-499-1200*, offers a two-hour course in traditional Japanese flower arranging, Monday through Friday mornings.

Tea ceremony secrets

The Japanese make even the English look careless when it comes to making tea. O-cha (green tea) is served ceremoniously on important occasions, at the beginning of conversations, at temples, and at the end of meals. The many details of the ceremony have been carefully preserved throughout the centuries. Tea is served without sugar in small cups without handles as participants sit silently in a circle. The tea is ground into a fine powder and then, after steeping, whisked until it foams. The cups are held and contemplated before the tea is sipped. Every movement has symbolic significance.

You can see tea ceremonies at a number of hotels in the city, including the **Imperial Hotel**, *1-1-1, Uchisaiwaicho, Chiyoda-ku; tel. (81)33-504-1111;* **Hotel Okura**, *2-10-4, Toranomon, Minato-ku; tel. (81)33-582-0111;* and **Hotel New Otani**, *4-1, Kioicho, Chiyoda-ku; tel. (81)33-265-1111.*

Super sumo

The best place to witness sumo is the Ryogoko district in northeast Tokyo, home to more than 30 stables for the immense wrestlers who wander the streets dressed in kimonos and topknots. You can watch them competing (wearing slightly less) at the sumo stadium called New Kokugikan.

Sumo tournaments take place in mid-January, mid-May, and mid-September. If you can't make it to the tournaments, have your hotel call a stable to ask permission for you to watch a morning practice session. Two stables to try are **Kasugano-beya** or **Takasago-beya**.

Bathing at its best

Japanese *onsens* (hot springs), *osento* (public baths), or *ofuros* (at home) are the best way in the world to bathe. In Japan, a bath is not just a bath. It is a ceremony. Tokyo has 1,865 public *sento* (bathhouses)—which indicates the importance of the bath to the Japanese. Natural hot springs feed 16 of the baths. You can enjoy one, but you must follow the rules.

Shoes are left in lockers by the front door, and clothes are exchanged for small towels with which you attempt to cover yourself as you walk to the communal bath. Men and women bathe separately. Before climbing into the steaming water, wash yourself with soap and water using your little towel. Remember to rinse thoroughly. Once you are clean, climb into the *furo* (tub) and soak.

You can also try a mountain *rotenburo* (hot spring outdoors), set in visually stunning locations. Or take your bath as the Japanese do before a mid-evening meal. Wear the crisp pure cotton *yukata* with traditional decorations, navy on white background, and relax on the tatami mats. It is pure pleasure.

The best restaurants

The best place to get eel is at **Chikuyo Tei**, *tel. (81)3-3542-0787*. You sit on the floor on *tatami* mats and enjoy the small teahouse atmosphere.

Chinzanso, *tel. (81)3-3943-1101*, is an enormous restaurant set in a magnificent garden. The food and atmosphere are delightful.

Asia's most dangerous food

If your culinary curiosity is stronger than your common sense, try *fugu* (poisonous blowfish), considered the greatest Japanese delicacy. The meat is fine, but the innards are deadly. (About 30 Japanese per year die from eating fugu.) The fish is served as *fugusashi* (raw flakes eaten with a soy, orange, and chive sauce), *birezake* (sun-dried fins dipped in hot sake), and *fuguchiri* (fugu soup). You should eat it only during a month with an R in it (as with oysters), and only when prepared by a licensed fugu cook.

Sake at its best

Tokyo has a number of *nomiya* (sake houses), where you can sample this peculiar Japanese brew. **Sasashu**, *tel. (81)3971-9363*, is the best, serving little goodies along with the warm white wine. **Chichibu Nishiki**, *tel. (81)3541-4777*, is the most attractive sake house, a historic building filled with antiques.

Tokyo's best (and most traditional) hotels

The best accommodation in Japan is at *ryokan*, a traditional Japanese inn. They are virtually unchanged since the times of the samurai, with translucent paper windows, sliding doors, mat floors, alcoves, polished wood, and intricate gardens. (They do, however, have electricity, running water, and modern toilets.)

When you arrive at a *ryokan*, you are greeted at the entrance (where you leave your shoes), then escorted to your room, served tea, and given a freshly laundered cotton kimono. The rooms are furnished with tatami mats and cushions. Sliding-glass walls usually overlook Japanese gardens. After the ritual bath in a sunken wooden tub, dinner is served in your room by a maid in a kimono, who later prepares your futon bed.

Ryokans in Tokyo vary widely. **Fukudaya**, *tel. (81)3-3467-5833*, is expensive, but has a wonderful atmosphere and great service.

Tokiwa Ryokan Shinkan, *tel. (81)154-24-1777*, is less expensive and has great amenities and good service.

A slightly cheaper but less intimate version of the ryokan is the *minshuku*. These inns are frequented primarily by vacationing Japanese. You are not always given a kimono or served your meals in your room, but they are cheaper than the ryokan. For reservations, contact the **Japan Minskuku**

Center, *tel. (81)3-3216-6556, e-mail: info@koyado.net* or the **Japan Minskuku Association**, *tel. (81)3-3364-1855*.

Tokyo's finest Western-style hotels

Hotel Okura, *tel. (81)3-3582-0111*, next to the American Embassy, offers both Western-and Japanese-style suites. The hotel is elaborately decorated and has all needed and wanted amenities.

Imperial Hotel, *tel. (81)3-3504-1111*, is next door to the Imperial Palace, overlooking its grounds and Hibiya Park.

Keio Plaza, *tel. (81)65-6235-2498*, was the first highrise in Tokyo and has magnificent views.

Gajoen Kanko, *tel. (81)3-3491-4111*, is an old-fashioned hotel with ornate doors and 1940s décor.

The **Hyatt**, *tel. toll free (1)888-591-1234*, overlooks Shinjuku Central Park and has views of Mount Fuji.

The best places for romance—with a twist

Just outside of Tokyo are **rabu hoteru** (love hotels), where you can choose from rooms with exotic themes: water beds that look like space shuttles, revolving roulette-wheel beds, or beds built into copies of the Sphinx. Most rooms have mirror ceilings and large television screens.

Although the tourist boards are not likely to give you the names of specific love hotels, they are not hard to find—they are everywhere. They resemble American motels. And their garages are designed with curtains, in order to hide visitors' cars and protect their privacy.

The best of Tokyo nightlife

Tokyo's liveliest nightlife is in the Roppongi district, where clubs stay open until 6 a.m. Wandering the maze of streets, you'll find everything from intimate jazz cafés to huge hostess clubs. The nightclub hostess, although often clad in a kimono, is not to be confused with the geisha, who presides only at private parties, usually to entertain businessmen.

Geishas undergo intensive training in the arts of dance, music, and song. They serve at parties as entertainers, waitresses, and witty conversationalists. Hostesses, on the other hand, are employed by nightclubs to pour sake, provide conversation, and sometimes serve as dance partners. Neither a geisha nor a hostess is a prostitute.

Maniac Love, *tel. (81)3-3406-1166*, is known for its techno, garage, and ambient music. If you love to dance, then this is your place.

Shinkukan Soul is an upbeat reggae/mix club. They play an eclectic mix of music.

328, *tel. (81)3-3401-4968*, plays all genres of music and is often crowded because of its reputation for fun.

Cave, *tel. (81)3-3780-0715*, has great DJs, but it is rather small.

The seediest side

The seedy side of Tokyo's nightlife is in the **Shinjuku district**. The streets here are crammed with neon signs for X-rated movie theaters, brothels, often called Turkish baths, and little local bars, where *mama-san* will serve you cheap *mizuwari* (watered-down whiskey).

These local bars are also the places to experience *karaoke*. Well-whiskied customers with microphones and accompanying tape recordings entertain the bar with their favorite love songs. Talent is of little consideration in these late-night shows. What counts is volume. (*Karaoke* has been forbidden in many residential areas.)

Yoshiwara, known as the Turkish massage district, is Tokyo's lust-ridden den of iniquity.

MOUNT FUJI: THE WORLD'S BEST SUNRISE

Those who have seen the sun rise from the top of **Fuji-san** (Mount Fuji) claim it is a mind-altering experience. Mount Fuji, which the Japanese consider a goddess, hides its dazzling beauty in a cloak of clouds most days. When the cloak is lifted, the 12,390-foot peak glitters white. You can climb the mountain only from the end of June through the beginning of September. Six trails lead to the top.

A short train or bus ride from Tokyo brings you to **Fuji-Hakone-Izu National Park**. Although the climb takes four to six hours, most of the trails are easy to hike, and the view is spectacular. Fellow trekkers, who sport everything from the latest fashions to the long white robes of religious pilgrims, are interesting additions to the view.

You can spend the night in communal stone huts along the way and wake up in time to see the sunrise. Or you can begin hiking at night and reach the peak above the clouds just as the rising sun illuminates the sky. Wear sturdy shoes or boots and bring along warm, waterproof clothing and a flashlight. It is windy at the summit.

KYOTO: JAPAN'S MOST BEAUTIFUL CITY

For more than 1,000 years, **Kyoto** was the political, cultural, and religious capital of Japan, and the city's heritage is still evident in its 1,600 temples, 200 shrines, and well-preserved traditions of architecture and craftsmanship. After trying to make your way through Tokyo, you'll find Kyoto's gridlike street plan a pleasure. Kyoto, about three hours from Tokyo, merits a visit of several days. The city's treasures are many.

Kyoto's most important sights

The **Imperial Palace** and its 220-acre park are the city's central attractions. Built by Emperor Kammu in A.D. 794, it has been destroyed several times by fire, but the existing building follows the original design. To visit the palace, you must get a pass at least 20 minutes and sometimes up to two weeks in advance. Register for a pass at the **Imperial Household Agency**, *tel. (81) 75-211-1215*. Bring your passport.

The **Heian shrine**, with its impressive torii gate, was built to commemorate the 1100th anniversary of Kyoto's founding. The shrine itself is a replica, 12 times reduced, of the original Chinese-style Imperial Palace, set in Kyoto's most beautiful gardens. In the spring, you can walk among weeping cherry trees and azaleas; in the fall, chrysanthemum displays decorate the stepping stone pond. The shrine is a favorite spot for weddings, and often you will catch a glimpse of a bride and her party, all dressed in kimonos.

Kinkaku-ji (Temple of the Golden Pavilion), in the northwest corner of the city, is Kyoto's prettiest temple. Surrounded by a lake, its exterior walls are gilded. The existing temple is a reconstruction of the original one. Trees shade the structure, and you can see the mountains in the distance.

Southwest of Kinkaku-ji is **Ryoanji** (Temple of the Peaceful Dragon), founded in 1473. Its famous stone garden is simple yet thought-provoking. Stones are raked in Zen patterns (the sea, the desert, or the mountains) that are said to aid meditation.

The **Kyoto National Museum**, *tel. (81) 75-541-1151 (outside Japan)* or *(81) 75-541-1151 (inside Japan)*, houses an impressive collection of Chinese paintings from the Ming and Ch'ing dynasties, as well as treasures from Buddhist temples and Shinto shrines.

The **Toji temple**, which is five stories and 183 feet high, has the tallest pagoda in Japan. The temple's stone house, built of wood without using nails, houses an unrivaled collection of art treasures.

Nijo Castle, situated on 70 acres and surrounded by stone walls and a moat, was owned by the first shogun of the Tokugawa family. Of the palace's five buildings, don't miss the Ohiramai and its Great Hall, decorated with paintings by Tanyu Kano. Corridors in the Imperial Messenger's chamber are constructed so that anyone stepping on the floor will trigger a sound resembling the song of the Japanese bush warbler, warning guards of approaching intruders. The shogun's apartments, in the fifth building, contain hidden chambers, where samurai guarded their master out of sight of palace guests.

Sanjusangendo (Temple of 33 Niches), a few blocks east of Kyoto Station, is a national treasure. It is so named because the facade is divided into 33 niches, one for each of the goddess Kannon's 33 personifications. The goddess is embodied here in a 10-foot statue, the *Thousand-Armed Kannon*.

Saiho-ji (Moss Temple), founded in 1339, is an incredible green. Its pond is shaped like the Chinese character for *heart and mind*.

The **Katsura Villa** is widely admired as the crowning achievement of Japanese architecture. It is silent, austere, and perfectly balanced.

The **Shugakuin**, a villa in the foothills of Mount Hiei, has three large stepped gardens. Both the Katsura Villa and the Shugakuin can be visited by permission of the Imperial Household Agency.

The craft quarter

Kyoto's old **Nishijin** district is the place to buy famous Nishijin silk brocade, which is still hand-woven. You can hear the sounds of silk looms along the narrow back streets. Displays of the district's handwork can be seen at the **Nishijin Textile Museum**, *Omiya Imadegawa, Kamigyo-ku*.

Another Kyoto specialty is Kiyomizuware pottery, produced by a 16th-century technique. Kiyomizuware is sold everywhere in Kyoto, but a concentration of particularly good shops is located along Teapot Lane near the Kiyomizu temple.

A good place to watch a variety of craftsmen at work on damascene metalware, wood-block prints, dolls, and porcelain is the **Kyoto Handicraft Center**, *Kumano Jinja Higashi, Sakyo-ku*. You'll also see painters, weavers, and goldsmiths here. The restaurant on the top floor has a good view of the city.

Yuzen cloth, decorated by using a special 300-year-old dyeing process, is another Kyoto specialty. To achieve its perfect color, the cloth must be washed in the cold running waters of the Kamo River. Walk along the river between the Nijo-dori and Shijo-dori bridges for a good view of this activity.

The world's best knives

Aritsugu, *Gokomachi Nishi-iru, Nishikikoji-dori, Nakagyo-ku*, in the heart of the market district in central Kyoto, has been supplying Japan with swords and knives since 1560. Fujiwara Aritsugu, who began the family business, was the sword maker to the imperial household and supplied feudal warriors with their weapons.

Today, cooking knives, which are direct descendants of the original Aritsugu swords, form the core of the business. The assortment is bewildering: the *deba-bocho*, for slicing through fish, meat, and bones; the *usuba* and the *nakiri*, for chopping and slicing vegetables; knives with rosewood or black synthetic composition handles; and knives banded with buffalo horn to help prevent cracking.

Kyoto's best restaurants

Kyoto's restaurants tend to be smaller, more old-fashioned, and more intimate than those in Tokyo.

Sagano, *tel. (81)847-382-8980*, which offers 10 kinds of tofu dishes, is unknown to non-Kyoto residents. Dinner is served overlooking the lush garden. This restaurant is particularly cozy in the rain.

Another excellent tofu restaurant is **Okutan**, *tel. (81)75-771-8709*, where you are served by kimono-clad waitresses. Order the *yudofu* or the *shijin-age* for deliciously prepared Zen-style vegetables. The restaurant is open 10:30 p.m. until 7 p.m. except Thursdays.

Junidanya, *tel. (81)75-561-0213*, is also small and intimate. If you can't read the Japanese menu, they have one in English.

Good places to look for a restaurant are the English-language *Kyoto Restaurant Guide*, published by the Kyoto Restaurant Association, and the *Kyoto Gourmet Guide*.

Japan's best hotel

The **Tawaraya Ryokan**, on a quiet back street in Kyoto, *tel. (81)75-211-5566*, is a Japanese paradise. Dim and cozy, it has rooms that are booked year-round. You must remove your shoes at the door, where you are welcomed with a warm washcloth, tea, and a *yukata*, a light cotton version of a kimono. (Your street clothes are packed neatly away.)

Bedrooms at the Tawaraya open onto a wooden platform overlooking the garden. Guests sit on *zabuton*, square cushions placed on the tatami mats that cover the floor. The bathroom looks out onto its own garden. All utilitarian items, such as televisions, telephones, and tea-making sets, are hidden. There are no room keys, and futons are kept in the closets. You are served eight-course dinners on a lacquered table. You must make reservations at least two months in advance.

The top Western-style hotels

The most luxurious hotel is the **Takaragaike Prince Hotel**, *tel. (81)75-712-1111*, in the northern suburbs.

Other good western-style hotels are the **Miyako**, *tel. (81)75-661-7111*, and the **International Kyoto**, *tel. (81)75-222-1111*.

Three hotels with both Western-style and Japanese-style rooms are the **Kyoto Royal**, *tel. (81)75-223-1234*; the **Fujita**, *tel. (81)75-222-1511*; and the **Kyoto**, *tel. (81)75-211-5111*.

The hottest nightlife

Gion district is the place to be. All the best theaters are located here. Gion is also the best place to attend a geisha party. Make arrangements through your hotel or travel agent. Settle on the price beforehand—these are usually costly evenings.

Gion Corner, *tel. (81)75-561-1119*, was established by the Kyoto Visiting Club. Classes here teach various aspects of Japanese traditional arts. In two evening shows, demonstrations are given of the tea ceremony, flower arrangement, Bunraku puppet plays, *kyomai* (Kyoto-style dance), court music, and *koto* music, which is played on a 13-string instrument.

Nihon Seibukan, *60 Shimogawa izumikawa-cho, Sakyo-ku; tel. (81)75-701-3121*, is an exercise hall for karate, kendo, and judo. Geisha dances are performed during April and May at the **Pontocho Kaburenjo** (Kamogawa Dance), *Pontocho-dori 3 jo, lower level, Nakagyo-ku; tel. (81)75-2212025;* the **Kitano Kaikan** (Kitano Dance), *Shinsei-cho; tel. (81)75-461-0148;* and the **Gionkobu Kaburenjo** (Cherry Blossom Dance), *Hanamikoji Gion; tel. (81)75-541-3391.*

✗OSAKA: BESTS BENEATH THE GRIME

Osaka, the industrial center of Japan, seems an ugly city at first glance. But if you look behind the city's utilitarian façade, you will discover its traditional temples and shrines, secluded in their gardens; a mighty castle; and two good museums.

Visit the 10th-century **Temmangu shrine** on July 24th and 25th when the annual Tenjin Festival is held. On these nights, the normally solemn shrine to Tenjin, the god of learning, is transformed, as lantern-lit boats sail down Osaka's canals accompanied by a fireworks display.

The 16th-century **Osaka Castle** was built by the warlord Hideyoshi, who ordered huge stones for its construction, some of which are still in place. One of the stones, called Higo-ishi, is 47 feet long and more than 19 feet high.

Tennoji Park, in the southern part of the city, contains a zoo, botanical gardens, the Shitennoji temple, and the Keitakuen, one of the best examples of a Japanese strolling garden.

Two excellent museums of Chinese and Japanese art are the **Fujita Art Museum,** *tel. (81)6-6351-0582* and the **Masaki Museum of Art,** *tel. (81)725-21-6000.*

Tree-lined **Mido-suji** is Osaka's best street for strolling and window-shopping, but for serious shopping you are better off in one of the city's shopping districts or arcades. An underground labyrinth of stores is located in Kita, near Umeda Station. Shinsai-Bashi-Suji is another well-known shopping street. Also visit the shopping arcade between Shinsai-Bashi-Suji and Ebisu-Bashi-Suji.

Osaka's best restaurants

Benkay, *Hotel Nikko Osaka; tel. (81)6-6244-1111.* If you appreciate Japanese-style red snapper (*tai*), which is served with stewed plums (*ume*), Benkay is the place to go. Sea urchin, squid, and prawns are also on the menu here; tempura and sushi are popular as well. The restaurant uses traditional blond-wood paneling, and there's a sushi bar on one side. Jacket and tie are required.

Chambord, *Rihga Royal Hotel; tel. (81)6-6448-1121*. This restaurant specializes in French cuisine. From its perch on the 29th floor of the Rihga Royal Hotel, the restaurant has a panoramic view of Osaka's lights and river activities. There's a pianist providing gentle background music, which makes this one of Osaka's most romantic dinner spots. Reservations are essential.

Fuguhisa, *tel. (81)6-6972-5029*. Expect a warm and hearty welcome at this no-nonsense little restaurant that specializes in *fugu ryori*, the blowfish delicacy for which Osaka is famous.

The best accommodation

Two deluxe hotels in Osaka are the **Royal Hotel**, *tel. (81)6-6448-1121*, and the **Miyako Hotel Osaka**, *tel. (81)6-6773-1111*. Both hotels have great service and wonderful amenities.

The liveliest entertainment

Kokuritsu Bunraku Gekujo (National Puppet Theatre), *tel. (81)6-6212-1122*, is considered the original home of the 300-year-old art of puppeteering. The best Bunraku shows in Japan are presented here. Bunraku is not just for children, but for all ages.

Kabuki performances are given in the five-story **Shin-Kabukiza**, *tel. (81)6-631-2222*, in the southern part of the city. The Takarazuka all-girl revue, Japan's most famous all-girl opera, performs at the Grand Theater in Takarazuka City, 40 minutes by train from Osaka.

The best bars and nightclubs can be found in Sonezaki Shinchi in Kita, near the Umeda arcade.

✴HIROSHIMA: THE WORLD'S MOST SOBERING CITY

Hiroshima, the place where the first atomic bomb was dropped in 1945, is a sobering site. Heiwa O-dori (Peace Boulevard) leads to the **Hiroshima ✴ Peace Memorial Museum**, *tel. (81)82-241-4004*, south of Peace Park. The center features the Peace Tower and a museum of objects left after the explosion, as well as photographs of the bombed city and its victims.

The Industrial Promotion Hall, the building believed to have been directly below the center of the blast, is also located here. It has been left standing, gutted from the explosion, as a reminder of the bomb. On August 6, the day of the bombing, Hiroshima holds its annual Peace Festival in the Peace Memorial Park.

You can reach the city of Hiroshima, set on a bay of the Inland Sea, by a two-hour bullet train ride. The stretch between Okayama and Hiroshima (when traveling from Osaka or Kyoto) is considered the most beautiful train ride in Japan.

The best place for singles

A worthwhile excursion from Hiroshima is to the island of Miyajima to see the Shinto shrine **Itsukushima**, known among the Japanese as one of Japan's three great sights. (The other two are Amanohashidate and Matsushima.) The island is dedicated to a Shinto goddess who, according to legend, is extremely jealous. For this reason, married couples might want to think twice about visiting the shrine. Singles can take the train or bus from Hiroshima to Miyajimaguchi, where a ferry will take them to the island. Offshore stands the red painted *torii*, the gate of the Shinto shrine.

The shrine itself and its smaller galleries are on stilts above the water — when the tide is high, both the shrine and the torii appear to be floating on the water. The sight is most spectacular in April, when the cherry blossoms are out, and in the fall, when the maples turn glowing red. These are also the most crowded times.

For an incredible view of Hiroshima surrounded by mountains and the Inland Sea, take the ropeway from Momiji-dani Park behind the Itsukushima shrine to the highest peak on the island, Mount Misen. From this height, you also can see the ninth-century Gumonjido temple.

Hiroshima's best hotels

Hiroshima Kokusai, *3-13 Tate-Machi, Naku-Ku; tel. (81)82-248-2323*, and the **Hiroshima River Side**, *7-14 Kaminoboicho, Naku-Ku; tel. (81)82-227-1111* are good Western-style hotels. The best *ryokan* is **Minakiso**, *1-7 Mitaki-ocho, Nishuhi-ku; tel. (81)82-237-1402*.

✴NAGOYA: JAPAN'S BEST PEARLS

Japan's best pearl farms are in **Nagoya**, between Tokyo and Kyoto. You can get from Tokyo to Nagoya Station in just two hours on the super-express trains on the Shinkansen line. The station is the commercial center of the city, with stores and restaurants located in the network of under-ground passageways that connect to neighboring buildings

The heart of the pearl industry is just south of Nagoya in Ago Bay and five other bays off Ise-shima National Park. To learn about the process of pearl cultivation, visit Toba, where pearls are developed, harvested, and prepared for sale. *Ama* (women divers), ranging in age from adolescence to their early 40s and dressed in white cotton bodysuits, face masks, and caps, collect the oysters, making six or seven dives an hour to depths of up to 100 feet. The oysters are then seeded and suspended in cages from bamboo rafts. More than 200 million pearls each year are harvested after about six months, sorted, and polished.

Ama demonstrate their diving methods at the Toba Aquarium and on Irukajima, also in Toba bay. Nearby Pearl Island has a model pearl farm that you also can visit.

Nagoya's two most important sights are its castle and the Atsuta shrine. Nagoya Castle is topped by a famous pair of golden dolphins and boasts a five-story inner tower.

The Atsuta shrine is considered one of the most important Shinto shrines in Japan, housing the Kusanagi-no-Tsurugi (Grass-mowing Sword), one of the nation's Three Sacred Treasures. (The other two are the Sacred Jewels at the Imperial Palace in Tokyo and the Sacred Mirror of Ise Grand Shrines.) Nagoya also claims to have one of the largest zoos in the Orient, in Higashiyama Park.

Nagoya's best Western-style hotels are the **Meitetsu Grand**, *1-2-4 Meieki, Nakamura-Ku, Nagoya; tel. (81)52-582-2211;* **Nagoya Castle**, *3-19 Hinokuchicho, Nischi-Ku; tel. (81)52-521-2121;* **Nagoya Kanko**, *1-9-30 Nishiki, Naka-Ku; tel. (81)52-231-7711;* and **Nagoya Miyako**, *4-9-10 Meieki, Nakamura-Ku; tel. (81)52-571-3211.*

Japan's strangest festival

Japan's strangest festival is the **Konomiya Naked Festival**, held every January 13 in Inasawa City, near Nagoya. This festival, first held in A.D. 780 to ward off the plague, is still thought to drive out devils. Each year one man is chosen to act as a divinity that takes on the sins of others and purges them. The divine man appears naked before the crowd of also naked men at the Owari Okunitama shrine and exorcises spectators' demons. The male worshipers surge forward to touch the holy man and transfer their sins to him.

The best fishing and parasols

The most colorful fishing spectacle in Japan takes place in **Gifu**, 30 minutes by train north of Nagoya. From mid-May to mid-October, cormorant are fished at night along the Nagoya River. Boats are hung with fire baskets to attract *ayu*, a kind of river smelt. The fishermen then command large tame birds, tied to long leashes, to dive in and retrieve the fish from the illuminated river.

Gifu is also famous because it contains one of the few remaining *bangasa*, or Japanese parasol factories, where you can watch paper and silk dancing parasols being made and individually painted. If you buy one, the factory will ship it home for you.

Kyushu: Japan's best seaside resort

Kyushu, the southernmost of Japan's islands, is a popular summer resort for Japanese vacationers. Because few Western visitors make their way here, it is a good place to sample Japanese culture as well as sandy beaches. Stay in a *ryokan* in one of the remote towns in the area and explore the secluded coves at your leisure.

Kitakyushu, the largest on the island, is a good place to find a hotel and make travel arrangements. The island's nicest drive is from Kitakyushu to Fukuoka, which takes you along the coast and through Genkai-Quasi National Park. En route are oddly shaped rock formations and pine groves that dot the white sand beaches.

At the southernmost tip of the island is **Ibusuki**, a popular seaside resort. The **Ibusuki Kanko Hotel**, *tel. (81)993-222-131*, a Western-style hotel facing north to Mount Sakurajima, is a good place to stay. A good place to eat and also to stay is the **Ibusuki Royal Hotel**, *tel. (81)993-232-211*.

Ibusuki's seawall is lined with small *ryokan*. The beaches cover underwater hot springs, and in certain spots attendants will dig holes so you can immerse yourself from toe to chin in warm sand.

The best of *Fukuoka's* many parks is **Ohori**, a large open parkland surrounding a tidewater lake formed from the moat of an old castle. Bridges link the surrounding park with smaller island parks in the lake. In the background is a forest with remnants of the stone walls of Fukuoka Castle.

NAGASAKI: JAPAN'S FIRST OPEN DOOR

Curving around the mouth of the Urakami River, **Nagasaki** is considered Japan's first open door. This was the first major port of trade with the Portuguese and Dutch in the 16th century. European influences are still visible in the city's old forts, brick buildings, and cobblestone streets.

Nagasaki was also the first place in Japan to accept Christianity. However, in the 16th and 17th centuries, the Christian communities here were forced underground. Monuments to martyred Christians can be found throughout the city. The most impressive is the **Oura Catholic Church**, built in 1865 to commemorate 26 Christians who were crucified here in the 16th century. The church is the oldest example of ecclesiastical Gothic architecture in Japan.

Glover Mansion is the house where Madame Butterfly (from the opera of the same name) waited for her lover's return. Set on a hilltop, the house has a panoramic view over the harbor.

Nagasaki is also known as the second city on which the Americans dropped the atomic bomb. Peace Park and the Atom Bomb Museum are monuments to the horror.

Good Western hotels in Nagasaki are the **Nagasaki Grand**, *5-3 Manzai-Machi, Nagasaki; tel. (81)958-231-234;* **New Nagasaki**, *tel. (81)958-266-161;* and **Nagasaki Tokyu**, *1-18 Minamiyamate-Machi; tel. (81)958-251-501.*

Suwa-so, on a hillside overlooking the city, is a ryokan visited by Japan's royal family.

Nagasaki's most threatening volcano

A short ride by bus or ferry from Nagasaki brings you to the active volcano **Mount Aso** in Aso National Park. A toll road leads most of the way up the side of the volcano. You can reach the rim by foot or ropeway, unless volcanologists have closed the area. Standing at the rim, you will see white smoke and gases spurting from the bottom of the crater and feel the ground rumbling.

HOKKAIDO'S MINORITY

Hokkaido is known as the home of the **Ainu**, a fast-disappearing people originally from Honshu who have been forced north into the mountains. The Ainu are Caucasians, who unlike other Japanese, have light skin and hairy bodies. The men often have thick beards, and the women have blue tattoos around their mouths. The best place to see their huts and their ritual worship is a small colony in **Asahikawa**, Hokkaido's second-largest city. You can also visit a display village in **Shiraoi**, near Noboribetse Spa on the south coast.

KARUIZAWA: THE BEST MOUNTAIN RESORT

Karuizawa, two hours north of Tokyo, is the mountain escape of which Japan's powerful elite take advantage. They come here to play tennis or golf, to horseback ride, and to sail on the lakes. Since the future emperor Akihito met and married the untitled Michiko Shoda at the Karuizawa Kai tennis club in the late 1950s, Karuizawa has been seen by many as a fairy-tale town where anything is possible—even falling in love with a prince.

The countryside is embellished with waterfalls and streams dotted with elegant villas. In the summertime, classical music concerts are staged outdoors.

Generally, the hotels in Karuizawa have great restaurants. The Karuizawa Prince complex holds about 13 restaurants, including an informal Japanese grill and an excellent French restaurant where diners eat overlooking a pond while being entertained by a harpist. The Suehiro (a steak house) is a favorite, as is the Akasaka Hanten, a Chinese restaurant with a pleasant garden.

The elegant **Karuizawa Prince**, *Karuizawa, Karuizawa-machi, Kitasaku-gun, Nagano Prefecture 389-01; tel. (81)267-46-1111*, offers three types of accommodation: the original hotel, log cabins, and a fancy annex overlooking a pond and golf course.

Hoshimo Onsen Hotel, *2148 Oaza Nagakura, Karuizawa-machi, Kitasaku-gun; tel. (81)267-45-5121*, has hot springs as well as comfortable rooms.

Tsuruya Ryokan, *678 Kyu-Karuizawa, Karuizawa-machi, Kitasaku-gun,*

Nagano Prefecture 389-01; tel. (81)263-93-2331, is a cozy little Japanese inn.

Asia's most alluring women

Geishas are highly talented entertainers, well versed in all traditional arts of Japan. They are not prostitutes. They are good conversationalists who serve food and drinks and provide high-caliber singing and dancing. Geisha parties, often organized by Japanese businessmen, feature pretty entertainers dressed in kimonos, elevated clogs, white face makeup, and elaborate hairdos. Generally these parties are for men, but women can be included.

The Asasaka district in Tokyo has a concentration of exclusive houses where geishas perform. Company presidents and others who can afford the high prices frequent these places.

You can see young apprentice geishas, called *maiko*, near Gion Corner and Ponto-cho in Kyoto. The young women appear at 6 p.m., dressed in colorful costumes, and shuffle in tiny steps from their residences to their places of work.

THE BEST OF
SOUTHEAST ASIA

✳THAILAND—THE MOST EXOTIC
ORIENTAL COUNTRY

Thailand can rightly claim to be the most exotic Oriental country. Unlike many of its neighbors, it has never been colonized. Nevertheless, Thailand has always been open to foreign influences. Its king plays the jazz clarinet, many of its royals were educated in England and Switzerland, and wealthier Thais speak English.

This openness and friendliness toward foreigners makes Thailand an ideal vacation spot. The Thai people are so friendly and polite that they make you feel right at home. Moreover, Thailand is cheap; it's possible to find accommodation here for as little as $10 a night. (When reading through this section, be aware that many hotels in this part of the world add a service charge and taxes to the prices quoted. Be sure to inquire about these additional charges when making reservations to avoid an unpleasant surprise when the bill comes.)

✳BANGKOK—THE MOST SOPHISTICATED CITY

Bangkok, Thailand's largest city is a mix of beauty, crowds, sophistication, and sin. It is, at once, polluted and congested downtown—and quiet and serene in its outlying corners.

Bangkok's best attractions

Bangkok has more than 400 temples; you can't help but run into them wherever you go. And they are all worth seeing. The most famous include **Wat Pho**, the oldest and largest in Bangkok; **Wat Phra Kaeo**, the Temple of the Emerald Buddha in the Grand Palace; and **Wat Arun**, situated by the Chao Phraya River. Wat Arun is open daily, 8 a.m. until 4:30 p.m.

Bangkok's **Floating Market** is also a must-even though it has become tourist-trodden in the last several years. You can arrange a tour from the Oriental Hotel's pier, departing about 7a.m., for 300 baht ($12.50). Another good—and lesser-known—floating market is at **Khlong Damnoen Saduak**, about 65 miles west of Bangkok. Tours can be arranged from all major hotels. In addition to a floating-market tour, arrange a *klong* (canal tour); for details, ask at any pier in the vicinity of the Oriental Hotel.

Thailand's royal barges

For centuries, visitors have marveled at the sight of Bangkok's royal river barges. Unfortunately, Royal Barge Processions, a breathtaking tradition for many years, are rare today. The last major procession honored the bicentennial of Bangkok in 1982, and it will likely be years before the royal barges ply the waters of the Chao Phraya River again.

But you can still see them on display at the **Royal Barge Museum**, on Klong Bangkok Noi near the Phra Pinkloa Bridge and Arun Amarin Road. The museum and its barges, all restored and reconstructed, are housed in a cavernous shed. The best way to get to there is by river taxi or as part of a general canal trip. The shed is open daily, 8.30 a.m. until 4.30 p.m.

The most slithery farm

The **Bangkok Snake Farm**, *tel. (66)2-252-0161-4*, at the Thai Red Cross Society, is by far Thailand's most interesting farm. This is where cobras, kraits, spotted vipers, and other poisonous snakes are fed and milked for their venom. Milking snakes is not an exciting process. The snake's mouth is simply forced open, and the venom squirts out into a small Petri dish. However, it is not meant to be a form of entertainment. It is part of a life-saving process. The Queen Saovabh Memorial Institute, the scientific division of the Thai Red Cross Society, provides snake-bite serum for much of the world.

What follows the milking process is very exciting. When its show-time, the handlers use long poles to remove the snakes form the pits and place them on the ground. The audience sits only a few feet away, but several feet off the ground, and watches as the handler encourage the snakes to hiss and slither, display their hoods, and strike and spit venom. Although it's all done very casually, rest assured that the handlers don't take their jobs lightly—one recently lost his life.

The best market in Southeast Asia

Be sure to visit the Chatukak weekend market. Take a hotel car to the market and ask the driver to wait, as taxis can be difficult to find.

Haggle ferociously over the prices and realize that not all of the antiques are real. Don't buy the pirated videotapes; they will not play on Western-format televisions.

The most luxurious places to stay

The **Oriental**, *tel. (66)2-236-0400*, has been called the best hotel in the world, a haunt of millionaires and beautiful women. Although lately showing signs of decay, it remains a traditional and beautiful place to stay.

The Oriental is also known for its Thai Cooking School, which conducts classes year-round, Monday through Friday, 9 a.m. until noon. The five-day course includes accommodation at the hotel, all classes, materials, and two meals daily.

Close runners-up are the **Regent**, *155 Rajdamri Road; tel. (66)2-251-6127*, and the **Sukhothai**, *13/3 S. Sathorn Road; tel. (66)2-287-0222.*

The **Dusit Thani**, *946 Rama IV Road; tel. (66)2-236-0450*, located only minutes from Bangkok's famous Patpong (bar) district, is also a good place to stay. It is less expensive than other luxury-class hotels in the city.

The best bargain hotel

The **Nana Hotel**, *4 Soi Nana Tai, Sukhumvit Road; tel. (66)2-252-0121*, is a good—and attractive—budget hotel.

The oldest settlement

Chiang Mai is the hill capital of northern Thailand, home to a million people. Founded in 1296, it is one of the oldest continually inhabited settlements in Thailand. It was at one time an independent kingdom, surrounded by a moat and fortified gates. The best way to get to Chiang Mai from Bangkok is by air; a round-trip flight is $100.

Chiang Mai's greatest attraction

Wat Phra That Doi Suthep, a temple high on a mountain peak, and **Phuping Palace**, the summer residence of the royal family, are two beautiful and ancient monuments that alone make the visit to Chiang Mai worthwhile.

The best place to shop

The best place to shop in the city is the **Night Market**, just off Thapae Road. It's also the cheapest: Cassette tapes, for example, go for 25 baht ($1). Also available at bargain prices are rugs, clothes, and leather goods. This is also the place to buy a pair of boots made out of chicken skin, should your tastes run in that direction, as well as silver and Burmese lacquer and handcrafts.

The best pastime

From Chiang Mai, you can arrange to go elephant trekking. Avoid the big, touristy elephant camp; instead, ask a tuk-tuk or taxi driver to take you to one of the smaller camps, farther up the hills (about 45 minutes outside the city). It will be the adventure of your life.

The driver sits on the elephant's head, and usually two people share the seat strapped across the animal's back. The elephant can go anywhere; they can cross streams on tiny stepping stones with the grace and balance of gymnasts. As they step down, you are tilted at a 90 degree angle to the ground. The motion may make you feel sick at first, but soon your body will become accustomed to it.

The second-best pastime

In a spectacular setting at the foot of the famous Doi Suthep Mountain, just 10 minutes from the center of the city, sits the **Lanna Golf Club**. The course is moderately difficult, with more than 20 lakes and water hazards and with elevated greens planted with Bermuda grass.

The best place to stay

Stay at the **Chiang Mai Orchid**, *100-102 Huay Kaew Road; tel. (66)53-222-099*, a lovely, first-class establishment.

The best place to buy silk in Thailand

Although Jim Thompson's silk shops are the best-known in Thailand—with good reason—they are also the most expensive. (They are easily located all over the major Thai cities.) If you're looking for a bargain, try one of the city's smaller shops. Although the quality is not as good, the prices are much cheaper.

We recommend **Shinawatra Parnich**, *72 Chiangmai-Sankumpaeng Road; tel. (66)53-331-187*, and **Shinawatra Thaisilk**, *145/1-2 Chiangmai-Sankumpaeng Road; tel. (66)53-331-172*.

Asia's hottest resort

If you're male, single, and tired of Bangkok's Patpong, there's no better place to vacation than Thailand's Pattaya Beach. The nightlife is wilder than the wildest London, New York, or Hong Kong has to offer.

For centuries Pattaya was a sleepy fishing village astride the invasion routes across the Gulf of Siam. According to local lore, the legendary Thai King Taskin's soldiers once put ashore here on their way to conquer what is now southern Thailand. Two hundred years later, Pattaya was a favorite destination for American GIs on leave from Vietnam. Today, it is a mecca for sun worshippers and sybarites from all across Asia and Europe.

THE PHILIPPINES—THE FRIENDLIEST NATION

The Philippines has always been known for the friendliness of its people, who speak 67 different dialects. This has not changed in recent years, despite the turmoil the country has suffered.

And the country is certainly as beautiful as ever. Made up of about 7,100 island paradises stretching toward China and Japan in the north and Malaysia and Singapore in the south, the Philippines offers a combination of exciting cosmopolitan cities, white-sand beaches, and achingly blue waters.

Manila's best sites

Manila, the capital of the Philippines, is a hustling, bustling international city on the island of Luzon and a good base for excursions to the surrounding countryside. The city is within two hours of beautiful resorts and beaches. See the **Pagsanjan Falls**, about an hour outside Manila, where you can take a scenic boat tour of the rapids along 330-foot-high falls. Also visit the **Hidden Valley Springs**, a series of mineral springs in Alaminos, Laguna, that are buried in a 295-foot crater and surrounded by lush vegetation.

Other attractions near Manila include the **Malacañang Palace**, by the Pasig River; **Coconut Palace**, which was built, in part, using coconut trees and is the national symbol of life and abundance; **Makati**, the financial center of the country; and the **San Agustin Church** in Intramuros, the oldest church in Manila.

The best place to stay in Manila

The **Manila Hotel**, *Rizal Park, P.O Box 307; tel. (63)2-527-0011 or (800)44-UTELL in the United States*, is a luxury hotel in a good location. The staff is attentive.

The best hotel outside Manila

The best place to stay in Laguna, just outside Manila, is the **Villa Escudero**, *P.O. Box 4, San Pablo*, which offers exceptional service, atmosphere, and comfort. This coconut plantation, less than two hours by road from the capital city, gives you a glimpse of typical village life. Even if you can't stay the night, take time to visit the grounds.

The summer capital of the Philippines

The cool, mountainous region of **Baguio City**, located in the province of Benguet, offers a break from the city crowds. Only three or four hours from Manila by car, or 50 minutes by jet, Baguio City is becoming increasingly popular among travelers, who appreciate the region's incredible views and cool climate.

The best place to stay in the city is the **Bagula Park Hotel**, *Harrison Road, Baguio City*. Also recommended are the **Vacation Hotel**, *tel. (63)74-442-4545*, and the **Safari Lodge**, *tel. (63)74-442-2419*, both of which face the Baguio Botanical Gardens on the Leonard Wood Road.

The most attractive city in the South

Cebu City, the "Queen city of the South," is a beautiful and graceful city, located on the island of Cebu in the Visayas, south of Manila. It is the oldest city in the Philippines founded by the Spaniards. Ferdinand Magellan, who landed on its shores in 1521, fell in love with the place and eventually died there. He planted Magellan's Cross, which is now more than 460 years old and still standing. It is the symbol of the Rajah Humabon and his queen's acceptance of Christianity.

The most festive time to visit Cebu City is during its festival of Sinulog, a weeklong religious celebration held every January.

The best of the oldest in Cebu

The image of **Santo Niño de Cebu** is the oldest relic in the country; it was given to Queen Juana by Magellan in 1521. The **Basilica Minore del Santo Niño**, built in 1565, is the oldest church in the Philippines and was built on the site where the image was found.

The oldest street in the country, **Colon Street**, is also in Cebu. Located in Cebu's Chinatown, in the center of the city, it was built by the Spanish soldiers.

The Philippines' last frontier

The best place in the Philippines to enjoy water sports is on the island of **Palawan**, 70 minutes by plane southwest of Manila. This island is known as the Philippines' last frontier, a paradise for sailors, sunbathers, deep-sea divers, and fishermen.

The island is surrounded by coral reefs, and the waters are filled with fish. Manta rays are common. New marine species have been discovered in the waters off the exclusive El Nido Resort on the island's northern shore.

The best seafood

The best seafood on the island is served at the **French Café Puarto**, *277 Rizal Ave.*

The best place for water sports

The upscale **El Nido Resort**, *Miniloc Island, El Nido*, is the place on Palawan for deep-sea diving. Designed to resemble a native village, this resort was named for the birds' nest (*nido*) found on the surrounding cliffs.

El Nido is several hours by car from the airport at Puerto Princesa. You can hire a jeepney at the airport to take you out to the resort. The best way to get there, however, is to charter a plane from Manila. Charter flights are offered by **Ten Knots Philippines Inc.**, *Ground Floor, Makati Stock Exchange Building, Ayala Avenue, Makati, Metro Manila.*

Another good spot for water sports is the area around Port Barton, which is peppered with beach resorts. We recommend **Mantaray Resort**, *Capsalay Island, Port Barton.*

The best time to visit

The best time to visit the Philippines is between December and May, especially April or May. The rest of the year is typhoon season.

LAOS — THE MOST SERENE

It's hard to get to **Laos**, and one you're there, it's hard to get around. Only recently have Americans been able to travel here at all. But it is worth the effort. What you'll remember most about Laos is its serenity: There are no hawkers on the streets; in fact, there are no vehicles on the streets — at least no four-wheeled vehicles. Instead, the streets of Laos are given over to bicycles and tuk-tuks.

Laos' largest town—the best set for a spaghetti Western

In 1963, UPI war photographer Tim Page described Vientiane, Laos' ancient capital, as resembling "a set for a spaghetti Western or a Graham Greene thriller." Forty-odd years later, nothing has changed.

The best restaurant in Vientiane

The best place to eat in Vientiane is the **Nam Phu Restaurant**, behind the Lan-Xang Hotel. This French-style Laotian restaurant is famous for its venison steak and Bulgarian red wine. Reservations are recommended, as this reasonably priced restaurant is always crowded with visiting diplomats, who have few other options.

Asia's most beautiful temples

Laos is notable for possessing the most beautiful Buddhist temples in Southeast Asia — temples that have not fallen to explosives, tourism, or redevelopment, as have most of those in Burma, Vietnam, Cambodia, China, and Hong Kong.

Twice daily, weather and inclination permitting, Laos Aviation flies from Vientiane to Luang Prabang, Laos' most beautiful town and the site of **Wat Xiengthong**, one of the most impressive temples in all of Southeast Asia, with its courtyard filled with bougainvillea and its location on the Mekong River.

The best place to arrange your trip

The best place to arrange a trip to Laos is Bangkok, where several tour operators specialize in tours to this remote country. **Diethelm Travel**, *Kian Gwan Building II, 140/1 Wireless Road; tel. (662)255-9150; fax (662) 256-0248*, one of the city's largest and best known, has a reputation for getting you there — usually on schedule — with the least amount of inconvenience. It is possible to book directly with Diethelm Travel or through **Siam Exclusive Tours**, *Building One, Seventh Floor, 99 Wireless Road*.

The most economical ride

Although daily flights are scheduled in and out of Laos, it's far less expensive and far more adventurous to take the overnight train from

Bangkok to Nong Khai in northern Thailand on the Thai/Laotian border. An express train departs Bangkok Railway Station at 8:30 p.m. and arrives in Nong Khai at 7:30 the next morning. Save the picturesque daytime ride for the trip home, as the border closes at 5 p.m., and you can't take a day train to Nong Khai from Bangkok and return in the same day.

PALAU, THE MOST UNDISCOVERED IN THE PACIFIC

In the far western Pacific, about 800 miles southwest of Guam and 500 miles east of the Philippines, the 36-mile long, 15-mile wide, reef-encircled archipelago known as **Palau** remains largely the secret of the world-class scuba divers and marine experts, who count it among the wonders of the world.

About 9,000 Palauans live on Koror, capital of the not-quite-independent Republic of Palau. It boasts 18 miles of paved road, nearly 200 taxis, a speed limit of 25 miles per hour, and no passing. The longest stretch of road wanders eight miles from Palau International Airport to the Palau Pacific Resort. Life on the islands of Kayangel and Angaur, which mark the northern and southernmost tips of the archipelago respectively, revolves around fishing along the reef or in the lagoon and the cultivation of taro, tapioca, coconuts, and bananas.

The jewels of Palau

The pièce de résistance of Palau is the group of 200 Rock Islands, scattered in strings between Koror and Peleiu. Found nowhere else in the world, these jungle-covered knobs of solid coral and limestone, undercut at tide level because of the water-soluble limestone, look from a distance like so many green mushrooms floating on a turquoise sea. The islands fringed by white sand are ideal for picnicking or snorkeling.

The best places to stay

Stay at the deluxe **Palau Pacific Resort**, *tel. (680) 488-2600*, or the somewhat worn **Nikko Hotel**, which commands breathtaking views of the Rock Islands. The restaurant at the Nikko Hotel offers international foods and seafood specialities daily, 6:30 a.m. until 10 p.m.

The best bargain accommodation

The best buy in town is the DW Motel, run by a friendly Palauan named Dave Williams and his family. Close to downtown Koror and within walking distance of the central business district, the DW offers large and airy rooms with air conditioning and refrigerators.

The best restaurants

Take at least one meal at the **Fuji Restaurant**, located downtown next to the West Plaza Hotel. The Fuji serves seafood, local specialities, and international dishes Monday through Saturday, 6 p.m. to 10 p.m.

The **Carp Restaurant** near the government fish dock serves Japanese-style dishes, in addition to crab and lobster varieties, Monday through Saturday 11 a.m. until 9 p.m. and Sunday 9 a.m. until noon.

The **Pirates Cove**, otherwise known as the Royal Belau Yacht Club, at the fish dock, welcomes all. It serves an international selection of foods, seafood, and pizza specialities and is open daily 9 a.m. until 2 p.m. and 4 p.m. to 11 p.m.

MYANMAR — A DESTINATION FOR THE MOST ADVENTUROUS

Myanmar is becoming a more accessible destination for the adventurous traveler. It is not a journey to be taken lightly, but an adventure suitable only for the strong of body and spirit. Nonetheless, it is worth the effort it takes to get there. Those who see it invariably describe it as one of the few places left in the world where you can get a feel for what Asia "used to be like."

The busiest city

Yangon (formally Rangoon), Myanmar's capital, is a gray city of prewar buildings, faded grandeur, and wide streets cluttered with lampposts, loiterers, and round-fendered cars. Street vendors sell cold drinks made of sugarcane and water, dipping the gray-green liquid from big glass tanks. (Don't be tempted.)

The best attractions

The glowing **Sule Pagoda** in the center of town is an impressive spectacle at night. But it pales in comparison with the 2,500-year-old **Shwedagon Pagoda**. High on a hill, the Shwedagon is reached either by elevator or by a breathless climb up an enormous stairway lined with hawkers and souvenir vendors. At the top is a Disneyland-like arena of jeweled spires, gold-plated domes, and gilded statues. People mill about in their bare feet trying to sell flowers, fortunes, and medical advice.

The Strand—Myanmar's oasis

Yangon's **Strand Hotel**, *92 Strand Road*, is considered the best hotel in all Myanmar. It is a white-pillared relic from the days of British rule. The ceilings are high, the stairways wide and polished, and the elevator an ornate, wrought-iron cage. In the dining room, waiters in white jackets serve mutton and potatoes from dented silver platters. In the hotel bar, a pianist plays Henry Mancini while sparrows nest in the light fixtures. It is an oasis.

The most historic city

Mandalay is a sprawling, walled city of historic monasteries, bridges, moats, and, of course, more pagodas. Men in sarongs pedal trishaws through the dusty streets. It isn't a beautiful city, but it is a good jumping-off point for excursions along the Irrawaddy River.

The best ruins

Pagan is one of the wonders of Asia, a sprawling landscape littered with thousands of ancient ruins. During the Golden Age of Pagan, in the 11th century, riches were spent on pagodas, shrines, and temples. It is believed that these buildings numbered 13,000 when Kublai Khan sacked the place in 1287. A major earthquake in 1975 caused more damage, but most of the important structures have since been restored.

The ancient city of Pagan is now deserted except for a tiny village. Surrounding the village are the remains of the ancient temples. If you join the other travelers here, moving from one temple to another on foot or rented bicycle, you'll have the opportunity to glimpse dark, cold rooms filled with marble Buddhas and terracotta tiles.

The best resort in Myanmar

The **Candacraig Hotel**, *East Ridge Road*, in Maymyo, is a 19th-century hill station that used to serve as the officers' residence of the Bombay-Burma Trading Company. Its restaurant serves English food.

The best ways to travel to and through Myanmar

The best way to travel Myanmar is, as always, through Bangkok, where a number of small agents, most with family contacts in Myanmar, specialize in arranging travel to this hard-to-reach country.

While independent travel is possible, the amount of time you will be allowed to travel alone varies according to the whims of the government. Nonetheless, it is well worth the trouble to, if possible, avoid the travel agencies and go it alone.

Make your airfare arrangements with **Thai International**, which flies from Bangkok to Myanmar three times a week. Pay for an upgrade to business class on the return flight; the unlimited champagne on this one-hour trip will seem like heaven after roughing it in Myanmar.

All international flights are with Myanmar Airways, known for the poor condition of its planes and its frequent fatal crashes. But you don't have any choice if you want to cover long distances.

Myanmar Airways offers daily flights between Yangon and all other cities open to travelers (which, right now, include Bago, Bagan, Mandalay, Taunggyi, Mawlamyine, Sittwe, Pathein, Pyi, and Pyin Oo Lwin). The alternative is to travel by train, but train travel in Myanmar is time-consuming and sometimes unreliable. It is not possible to rent a car on your own, but day-trips can be arranged with a car and driver. In some areas, you can travel by bus, boat, or horse and buggy (not a tourist treat, but the primary means of local transportation).

SINGAPORE — THE CLOCKWORK CITY

Singapore is an exciting, pulsating place, very cosmopolitan, very well-run, and incredibly clean. In fact, you can be fined $2 for spitting on the sidewalk. But gone are the days of sprawling British colonial homes. Today, the 225-square-mile island is sparsely dotted with these vestiges of a more relaxed, distinctive past, and the 2.6 million people living here are discovering that space is precious. Modern Singapore is a city of highrise structures.

Colonial Singapore is north of the Singapore River. **Empress Place** is decorated with the statue of Sir Stamford Raffles (the Brit who founded Singapore and made it the trading port that it is today), overlooking the river where the explorer first stepped onto the island.

The newly restored **Raffles Hotel**, *1 Beach Road*, is a must, a symbol of colonial Singapore. Have a Singapore Sling on the terrace (touristy, but fun). Chinatown is an interesting area to explore, full of mosques and temples.

The best places to stay

The 90 year-old **Goodwood Park**, *22 Scotts Road*, is known for its true Singaporean service and its elegant rooms. Its 13-acre site near the Orchard Road shopping district is convenient.

Another good place to stay is the more reasonably priced **Carlton Hotel**, *76 Bras Basah Road* at the corner of Victoria Street. The décor is beautiful, the service good.

The best custom-made clothing

Singapore is also the best place for custom-made clothing. Here, prices are cheaper, the selection of fabrics is greater (you'll find an especially wide selection of cottons, silks, and polyester fabrics), and the workmanship is at least as good as that of anyplace else in the world. And there is certainly no shortage of tailors. (Allow four to five days for a custom-made suit.)

Justmen in the Tanglin Shopping Center is a good place for men's tailoring.

New Guinea — the second largest island in the world

New Guinea, the second largest island in the world (Greenland is the largest), looks in profile like a bird taking flight. The head of the bird, a place the Dutch named Vogelkop (bird's head), is now called Irian Jaye and is part of Indonesia. The other end of the island is Papua New Guinea. Either end of the island makes a perfect destination. But overall, the eastern half, the "bird's tail" has the most to offer. Myriad islands litter the Bismarck Sea off the north coast. And there are mountains, some snow-covered, some with valleys so remote that the life they contain has not changed noticeably since the Stone-Age. Mighty rivers, such as the Fly and the Sepik, coil their way through lowland jungles to the sea in this land that is home to 700 languages and many cultures.

One of the world's greatest adventures

If you're looking for an adventure, you couldn't do better than to set off from Port Moresby, the capital of Papua New Guinea, and fly to Milne Bay, the bird's tail, 250 miles to the east. From there, you can negotiate the coastline all the way from the fabled Trobriands to the upper reaches of the Sepik River.

You can make the journey in two ways. You can either hunt down locally run trading vessels, take a flight with Air Niugini, and ride a bus from Lae to Madang. Or, if sailing on tiny, Spartan vessels and being jolted around on dusty buses doesn't appeal to you, consider the *Melanesian Explorer*, an expeditionary ship that begins its voyages off the northeast coast and heads south after a few days through the D'Entrecasteaux Islands — tiny green places with talcum-white beaches. The journey eventually ends 200 miles upriver, where you can take a plane to the highlands town of Mount Hagan, from which it is another hour by plane back to Port Moresby.

For information on the *Melanesian Explorer* and the newer *Melanesian Discoverer*, contact the **Melanesian Tourist Services Pty. Ltd.**, *P.O. Box 707, Madang*, or *302 W. Grand Ave., Suite 10B, El Segundo, CA 90245.*

Malaysia — the most bountiful country

Malaysia is known for its extreme beauty, including gorgeous beaches and spectacular mountains. Although it does not have the history of other countries in Southeast Asia, it is one of the most developed and prosperous nations in this part of the world. Kuala Lumpur, the capital (complete with luxury hotels and skyscrapers), is a pleasant stopover from your explorations in other parts of the country. It is a modern city, but colonial-era buildings are evident everywhere.

The most rustic place to eat in Kuala Lumpur

The **Coliseum Café**, *98-100 Jalan Tuanku Abdul Rahman, Kuala Lumpur*, has seen it all since 1921: The Japanese occupation in World War II, the communist uprising popularized in *The War of the Running Dogs*, Malaysian Independence, and, more recently, the burgeoning of the Malaysian economy and the attendant influx of fast-food joints and yuppie bars.

The run-down whitewashed shop/house dates back to its colonial origins when then-owner, Mr. Wong, set the place up. It's now in the hands of the third generation, with his granddaughter, Jo Wong, in charge.

Inside the glass-paneled doors, emblazoned with gold Wild West-style saloon lettering, little has changed. The décor consists of largely bare walls that run up to the high ceilings, kitschy red and green glass light fittings, and whirring ceiling fans. Open daily from 8 a.m. to 10 p.m., the café's 16 or so tables are usually full of locals noisily tucking into a mix of Chinese, Malay, or Indian specialties…or indulging in chicken, sausages, or fish. But the reason most still come to the Coliseum are for its steaks—mouth-watering.

Fifty ringgit ($13) per head is more than enough for a steak and a Tiger Beer. If you just want to drink, a bar to the left will take care of you—the same bar which hosted late-night sing-alongs around the piano for hard-drinking rubber planters who used to pile their weapons on the counter, and has God-knows-what other stories to tell. For that is the real beauty of the Coliseum—its rustic walls seem to speak to you.

The best three excursions from Kuala Lumpur

While in Kuala Lumper, you should take three day-trips. First, visit **Malacca** (Melaka), 93 miles south of the capital city. This splendid old port city on the infamous, formerly pirate-infested Straits of Malacca, boasting a rich Portuguese, Dutch, English, Chinese, and Malaysian heritage, is a fertile shopping ground for antique enthusiasts. To visit, rent a car and driver in Kuala Lumpur or join one of the day tours that depart from all the major hotels. The journey itself, through plantation after plantation of rubber trees and oil palms, is worth the trip.

A shorter but equally rewarding journey takes you to the limestone **Batu Caves**, a Hindu pilgrimage center notable for its swarms of bats, whose guano adds to the eerie mystical atmosphere inside the caves. Frequent and inexpensive minibuses from Kuala Lumpur take travelers to the Batu Caves. Or you can hire a car and driver.

Another must is the island of **Penang**, which lies off the east coast of the Malasian peninsula. It is the oldest British settlement in Malaysia. Georgetown, its major town, is a compact, attractive city, known for its good food. From here, you have easy access to the rest of the island and its beautiful beaches, rubber-tree plantations, and forests (filled with monkeys and bananas).

The most romantic colonial-style hotel

Penang's **Eastern & Oriental Hotel**, *10 Farquhar St., Penang*, at the waterfront end of Jalan Penang, is unreservedly Malaysia's most romantic colonial-style hotel, a vestige of the former British rule. Even if you're staying in more modest accommodation, stop by the Eastern and Oriental for a gin and tonic on the terrace.

THE BEST OF AFRICA

The best travel tips

Before you begin your travels through Africa, prepare yourself for an astonishing level of corruption. (The local term for bribes is *dash*.)

A word about currencies… Many West African countries use the CFA franc (connected to the French Franc); Nigeria uses the naira (N); and South Africa uses the rand (calculated at both a commercial and a financial rate). Airports are usually good places to exchange your money.

THE WORLD'S BEST SAFARIS

East Africa, one of the last strongholds of the lion, the elephant, the gorilla, and other exotic beasts, is the best place in the world to go on safari. Enormous national parks where the great beasts roam freely, uninhibited by the progress of mankind, have been established throughout the region.

Kenya and **Tanzania** are the best countries for viewing wildlife; they offer comfortable accommodation and have mild climates with warm, sunny days and cool nights. Hunting is now banned in Kenya and many other African countries, where the typical safari has been replaced with a viewing safari. Plan your adventure for July through March to avoid the rainy season.

Zambia and **Zimbabwe** are also good safari destinations; they are less known by Westerners and therefore less spoiled. Zambia is the only country where walking safaris are still common. And Zimbabwe is one of the few African countries where hunting safaris are still permitted.

Your first step in planning a safari should be to read up on the subject. Michael Tomkinson has written an excellent guide called *Kenya, A Holiday Guide*, available from Ernest Benn Ltd. in London.

The most accessible game park is **Masai Mara**, on the border between Kenya and Tanzania, in the **Rift Valley**. It has the largest diversity of game—rolling hills dotted with herds of elephants, antelopes, baboons, and lions. Masai tribes people, who wear beautiful colored cloth garments, also inhabit the area.

The **Ngorongoro Crater** and **Serengeti Plain** are part of the **Ngorongoro Conservation Area**, a 3,200-square-mile tract of Masai land. Together, these two areas have the largest concentration of game in the world.

✷KENYA: THE MOST INVITING COUNTRY

Kenya's 225,000 square miles of mountains, plains, and coastline provide an extraordinary variety of terrain. This country is beautiful and—once you have arrived—inexpensive. Kenya is perhaps the most inviting country in Africa—it is English-speaking, politically stable, and easily accessible.

Not only valued for its beauty, the land includes some of the most fertile tropical soil in the world. Although famous for its large exportation of coffee and tea, Kenya is also one of the world's leading horticultural countries. Germany and the Netherlands are among the biggest customers for its carnations and many varieties of roses. Fruits and vegetables flourish as well.

In Kenya, you can experience both the sophistication of the big city and the savage excitement of the bush country. The population of this nation defies generalization, composed of British colonial descendents, black Muslims with a Middle Eastern culture, Luo and Kikuyu farmers, Somali nomads and tall, inscrutable Masai warriors. The majority of the population is now Christian—but this general category comprises extreme Pentecostalism and a mélange of Christianity with indigenous religions as well as traditional Roman Catholicism and Episcopalianism.

Before a Kenyan football team will play a game, a witch doctor must be hired to set up nail fetishes around the goalposts to stop the opposing team from scoring any goals. In 1987, Kenyan courts were hearing a case involving a widow's suit against her brothers-in-law, who wanted to bury her late husband according to tribal ritual. Had his brothers-in-law buried him under the Luo ritual, the dead man's property would have gone to the tribe—and not his family. Even among modern city families, the Kikuyu custom of female circumcision (excision of the woman's clitoris) is tolerated, although not supported, by the government.

Swahili, the official language of Kenya, combines African grammar with Arabic words. Because it is the language of trade, you will hear it in the markets and on the streets of Kenya. However, English is spoken by government officials, bankers, and international businessmen.

The best place to view the heavens

Because of its location across the equator, Kenya is one of the best places in the world to stargaze. The cloudless deserts and high, isolated Mount Kenya also contribute. Being on the equator means that every constellation in the sky is visible every night of the year. They simply change positions. What was on the western horizon at sunrise is on the eastern horizon 12 hours later, along with the sun. Mount Kenya and Lake Turkana in the northern Kenya are the best viewing sites.

Africa's metropolis: Nairobi ✗

"Nairobi is the Paris of the East African coast" said Negley Farsoin in

Behind God's Back (1940). The towers of the city shine in the hot noon sun and stand guard in the cool cascades of bougainvillea (a genus of South American climbing shrub), clumps of carnations, and banks of orchids. Residents harmonize with this tropical gaiety in brightly printed and tie-dyed garments.

Kenya's best museum

The **National Museum of Nairobi**, on Museum Hill off Uhuru Highway, has the world's foremost collection of fossils of human evolution. The museum houses many archeological discoveries of the late Dr. Richard Leakey, as well as 184 watercolor paintings by Joy Adamson, author of *Born Free*. Children can enjoy a special "please touch" exhibit. The museum is open daily 9:30 a.m. until 6 p.m.

Snake Park, across the street from the National Museum, is also of interest to nature enthusiasts, containing more than 200 species of snakes.

Kenya's best art gallery

Paintings, sculptures, batiks, and photos by the best artists in Kenya and other African countries can be seen at **Gallery Watatu**, *Lonrho House, Standard Street; tel. (254)2-228737*. The gallery displays and sells works Monday through Friday, 9 a.m. until 5 p.m., and Saturday, 9 a.m. until 12.30 p.m.

The best animal viewing

A visit to the Animal Orphanage in **Nairobi National Park** five miles outside town is a good way to prepare for a wilderness safari. The orphanage is most famous for its lion and leopard cubs, which are as endearing as kittens—as long as they are tiny.

The best way to send a message

At the **Thorn Tree Message Center** in Nairobi, you can leave a free message for anyone anywhere in the world. By the sidewalk café at the **New Stanley Hotel**, *Kimathi Street and Kenyatta Avenue; tel. (254)2-33233*, is a thorn tree with bulletin boards affixed on four sides. You can fill out blank message forms with personal messages, advertisements, or announcements.

The most exotic meals

Food is a bargain in Nairobi. Foods of all nationalities are served, as well as local specialities, such as *ugali*, a corn and bean dish, and *ino*, a mixture of seeds. The best place to try traditional Kenyan foods is **African Heritage Ltd.**, *Kenyatta Avenue and Muindi Mbingu Street*. Among specialities served in the rear garden are grilled whole tilapia fish, roast lamb, and beef kabobs with salad.

The best restaurant in town is the **Carnivore**, *Langata Road*, where the speciality is—you guessed it—meat. You can try an unlimited amount of exotic skewered meats, anything from antelope to zebra.

The **Mount Kenya Safari Club**, *P.O. Box 35, Nairobi*, where a meal of pan-fried Nile perch, potatoes, and salad costs 176 Kenyan shillings ($2.30), is the most elegant place to dine.

Good Indian curry, made with African ingredients, can be found in restaurants throughout Kenya. Many of the Indians, imported by British colonialists as administrators, were Muslims, which is why the curries are made with beef (which Hindus are not allowed to eat). Try Kenya colonial curry (which will probably be cooked by an African rather than an Indian, because many Indians emigrated to England after Kenya gained its independence). Curry is usually served with a proliferation of accompaniments: chutneys and fried and roasted breads as in India; bananas, coconuts, mangoes, and other fruits, very hot red pepper sauce; peanuts; and even soy sauce.

Nairobi's best beds

Nairobi's best hotel is a remnant of the colonial cays called the **Norfolk**, *Harry Thuku Road, P.O. Box 40064*. It is Kenya's answer to the famous Singapore Raffles Hotel, with individual bungalows in a tropical formal garden.

Another good place to stay—if you can arrange an invitation—is the private **Muthaiga Club**, where members can arrange accommodation for their friends.

The **Hotel InterContinental**, *Uhuru Highway, P.O. Box 30353, City Hall Way*, and **Mount Kenya Safari Club** are also good bets. If you can stand the name, the **Hotel Comfy** is very reasonably priced.

The least expensive place to stay is the **Hotel Ambassadeur**, *Moi Avenue, P.O. Box 30399; tel. (254)2-336-803*. The hotel boasts a fine Indian restaurant called **Safeer**.

The best revolution

The revolving restaurant at the top of the **Kenyatta Conference Center** (the highest building in Nairobi) has a spectacular view of the city, particularly at sunset.

The best java

Kenya produces the best coffee in the world and is one of the world's leading exporters of Arabica coffee. The **Coffee Board of Kenya**, *Mama Ngina Street*, serves the most tempting coffee in town, as well as light snacks. A snack of coffee, *mandazi* (fried dough), and *samosa* (meat pie in the Indian fashion as interpreted by Kenyan cooks) is only 6.4 Kenyan shillings (nine cents).

The World's Best Destinations

Coffee was first introduced to Kenya by the French Holy Ghost Fathers (who liked a good cup of coffee) in the 1890s. It was developed in the region of north of Nairobi. African farmers were forbidden to grow coffee until 1954. It is now Kenya's main export crop (which causes problems when the coffee crop fails). The berries are handpicked twice a year.

The second leading export crop is tea—another crop Africans were forbidden to grow. Today the region around Limuru supports more than 100,000 African smallholders, who grow enough tea to make Kenya the third-largest producer in the world, after India and Sri Lanka.

The country's best dancers

The best places to watch tribal dancing in Kenya are the country's *bomas*, miniature replicas of Kenya's 40 tribal villages, located seven miles outside Nairobi, on Langata Road. They are also good places to shop for woodcarvings.

A bird watcher's best

Lake Nakuru Park, 100 miles northwest of Nairobi, is the habitat of more species of birds than all the British Isles; it is also home to millions of pink flamingos. The best accommodation here is at the **Lake Nakuru Lodge**, *P.O. Box 561*.

Lake Naivasha is also an excellent place for bird watching. More than 340 species can be spotted near this beautifully situated lake. Dominated by the shadow of Mount Logonot, an extinct volcano, Lake Naivasha also provides water sports and hiking opportunities. Joy Adamson wrote her best-selling novel *Born Free* here.

Accommodation is available at the **Lake Naivasha Hotel**, *South Lake Road, P.O. Box 15*, which is a collection of cottages on the lakeshore, each with a private veranda overlooking the water.

World-class craftsmanship

Kenya has become one of the leading exporters of handicrafts, including soapstone, stone and woodcarvings, and sisal baskets (popularly know as *kiondos*). Woodcarvings, however, top the list. Wamunyu, a small township about 60 miles east of Nairobi, is the birthplace of this growing industry. It began with Mutisya Munge in the early 1840s and today over half of Wamunyu's population of 20,000 are wood-carvers.

You can visit woodcarving studios in Wamunyu, Mombasa, and Nairobi, where you watch rows of men effortlessly creating exquisite statues. Visitors can buy items at wholesale prices.

Mombasa: gateway to the coast

Mombasa, gateway to the coast, is Kenya's second-largest city, combining African, Indian, and Arab cultures. Its narrow side streets, impassable by car, are lined with Indian temples, bazaars, and houses decorated with intricately carved wood doors. Curry scents the air, and the Muslim women are veiled in black buibuis.

While in Mombasa, stay at the **Castle** in Old Town or the **Outrigger** by the yacht club. To make reservations, contact **Alliance Hotels**, *College House, University Way, P.O. Box 49839, Nairobi*.

The best way to get to the beach

Although it is possible to fly to Mombasa via Kenya Airways, old-timers prefer to take the overnight train from Nairobi. This train offers a good meal, a private sleeper, and a porter who wakes you up at 6:30 a.m. with a delicious cup of locally grown tea or coffee.

Malindi: the best modern beach resort

Malindi, an island 74 miles north of Mombasa, is known for its modern hotels, lively nightclubs, and ocean sports, including big-game fishing, sailing, water-skiing, skin and scuba diving, and underwater photography. It also has a half-dozen nature preserves; the Malindi Marine National Park, where you can see technicolor fish, the moray eel, and octopi; and Gedi, the ruin of an abandoned Islamic settlement in a thick tropical forest inland.

The best hotel on Malindi is **Lawford's**, *P.O. Box 20, Malindi*, which offers two restaurants and two swimming pools.

The best way to get to Malindi is by plane — taxis are expensive, and buses are slow.

The least-developed islands

From Malindi, you can take a boat to the barely developed and sparsely inhabited out islands of **Manda**, **Kuwayuu**, and **Pate**. Pate Town can be reached only if the tide is right. Faza and Siyu, also on Pate Island, are more accessible.

The best-preserved Swahili town

The island of **Lamu** is a perfectly preserved 18th-century Swahili town, where men and women still wear the traditional dress — women are veiled and men wear *kofia* (white embroidered caps).

Don't expect to tour Lamu by car. The only car in town is reserved for use by the island's government representative. The best way to travel is by *dhow* (handmade sailboats).

The islanders are obviously Islamic. There are outdoor Koran schools and 29 mosques. Don't try to photograph the island residents; it is a violation of the Orthodox Muslim religious injunction against graven images.

The World's Best Destinations

Africa's deepest valley

The **Rift Valley**, a geological fault that originates in Syria and runs to South Africa, is best seen in Kenya. Sheer cliffs several thousand feet high-rise above the valley floor, which is 50 miles wide in places. Changes in climate and topography when one descends the valley slopes are abrupt. Coffee plantations are everywhere. Large herds of relatively tame animals graze along the valley edges.

Kenya's best watering holes

Comfortable (even luxurious) lodges have been built near many of the country's watering holes. If you don't think you're up to a safari, opt for a holiday at one of these lodges. Instead of roughing it in the wilds, you'll be relaxing, while elephants, lions, hippos, and monkeys come up to you. All you need is a pair of binoculars.

The best watering hole is Kilaguni, 200 miles south of Nairobi in the giant Tsavo National Park. Animals can be viewed day and night, game drives and walks around Mzima Springs are available, and camping facilities are available for true adventurers. **Kilaguni Lodge**, *P.O. Box 30471*, has a swimming pool, safari vehicles, and a restaurant and bar overlooking the watering hole.

The most famous of the watering holes is Kenya's original, **Treetops**, *c/o Block Hotels, P.O. Box 47557*, 80 miles north of Nairobi in the Aberdares Mountains. You climb (slowly) to cedar huts where you are welcomed by servants, who spoil you, and by baboons, which pester you if you don't keep the windows shut. As night falls, wild animals visit the water hole below the lodge; the scene is periodically floodlit. Treetops is the most expensive watering hole lodge in Kenya.

The Ark, *P.O. Box 449*, Nyeri, near Treetops, is comparable in amenities to its more famous counterpart—but it's slightly less expensive, at 3,616 Kenyan shillings ($47.50) a night, including full board. In addition, many argue that the game viewing is better at The Ark than at Treetops; a tunnel leads you to a hide right next to the watering hole.

Africa's most spectacular peaks

Kenya is home to the two most spectacular mountain peaks in Africa: **Mount Kilimanjaro** and **Mount Kenya** (known as Nyandarua among the Kikuyu). The eternal snows of these equatorial peaks seem like the stuff of legend even after you climb them. Mount Kilimanjaro can be climbed from the Tanzanian side of the border or the Kenyan.

A five-day trip from the base to the peak, Mount Kilimanjaro is the most challenging. The **Uhuru Park** (20,000 feet) can give climbers quite a rush of success. Tourist agencies in Tanzania will organize a climb of the mountain. No climbing is allowed during the rainy season in April and May.

In the language of the Masai, who live in its shadow, Kilimanjaro means *White Mountain*. The Masai climb only to an altitude of 10,000 feet, where the air gets thin. It's another 9,340 feet from there to the top. It can be done, thanks to an easy trail, encouraging Tanzanian guides, and comfortable Norwegian huts.

The standard hike to the top takes five days, from the park entrance at 6,000 feet, the first day's hike is along a gently rising trail for three to four hours until you reach Mandara Hut. Tropical forest animals inhabit this lower altitude.

After five to seven hours of walking, you come to Horombo Hut at 12,000 feet. It has one notable difference from the first hut: the view of the snow-capped Kibo Peak above and the ocean of clouds washing the base of the mountains below.

The third day demands a climb to 14,000 feet over a stream marked "Last Water" and across wind-blown dusty terrain. It takes another three hours to climb to 15,600 feet, where the cold, dark, and uncomfortable Kibo Hut awaits you.

By tradition, you must reach the mountaintop in time to see the sunrise. So at 1 a.m. you will be awakened to trudge to Uhuru Peak. You will feel nauseous, lethargic, and sore. But when you see the sunrise from the mountain's peak, it will all seem worthwhile.

Mount Kenya, a snow-covered peak on the equator, is more scenic and easier to climb than Mount Kilimanjaro, due to the lower altitude. (It's 17,000 feet high.) Both are volcanos, but unlike the case with its southern neighbour, Mount Kenya's fires have long been extinct. The two highest peaks—Batian at 17,058 and Nelion at 17,022 feet—are named after 19th-century Kenyan medicine men. They stand like huge black tombstones and are the domain of technical climbers of rock and ice. The average climber takes an easier route to Mount Lenana at 16,355 feet.

From the entrance gate at 9,500 feet, another 5,000-foot ascent brings you to the hut at Met Station Lodge, where a troop of Sykes monkeys entertains.

Before passing the tree line the next morning, you might be able to see black and white Colobus monkeys flinging themselves madly through the trees overhead. At an area called the Vertical Bog, from 11,000 to 13,000 feet, the serpentine trail is covered with soggy peat and leads eventually to the foot of the glacier.

You sleep in the Kami Hut, made of corrugated iron, until 4 a.m., when you begin the trek across ice-coated boulders, using flashlights to light the way. A guide is essential to chop steps with an ice-ax. By dawn, you will reach the top.

Hikes of Mount Kenya must be arranged through **Naro Moru River Lodge**, *P.O. Box 18, Naro Moru.* You can rent any equipment you will need at the lodge.

TANZANIA: THE BEST OF THE WILD

Tanzania is Kenya's southern neighbor. This country is the result of the fusion of the offshore island of Zanzibar, once an Arab stronghold, and the mainland (called Tanganyika in colonial days), inhabited by the Bantu and other African ethnic groups. The political unrest this fusion created was complicated by the country's adoption of Ujamaa, a form of socialism promoted by President Julius Nyerere. Tanzania is still suffering economic woes from its turbulent past; the country is desperately poor, hungry for tourism, and cheap.

Because it is so inexpensive (guides can be hired for 375 Tanzanian shillings, or $1.25, a day), Tanzania is beginning to draw tourists to its enormous game parks. Tanzania is really where the wild things are. The famous **Serengeti Plain**, where you can witness the spring wildlife migration every year, has the largest concentration of game in the world.

Seronera Wildlife Lodge, *P.O. Box 3100, Arusha*, in the center of the park, has an airstrip and a swimming pool carved from natural rock. **Lobo Wildlife Lodge**, *P.O. Box 3100, Arusha*, is an entire building carved from natural rock.

One of the undiscovered wonders of Tanzania is **Selous**, the largest game reserve in the world. This unspoiled, undeveloped wilderness is populated by more than one million animals, including Africa's greatest elephant and lion populations. Animals are less visible to visitors in this park, though, due to the immense area of the reserve.

Luxury accommodation is offered in Selous at **Mbuyu Safari Camp**, *Bushtrekker Safaris, P.O. Box 5380, Dar es Salaam*, a hotel constructed around a baobab tree.

Be cautious when visiting **Dar es Salaam**, Tanzania's capital. It is a city rife with criminals who prey on tourists. And before you enter Tanzania, ask government officials for exact information on how much currency you must exchange. The rules are complicated and strict. The black market exchange rate in Tanzania is much higher than the official rate.

ZIMBABWE: BEST HUNTING, BEST WATERFALL

Zimbabwe, formally Rhodesia, is the best place to go on a hunting safari (for which a hunting license is required). However, peaceable safaris are also offered. **Victoria Falls**, located on the border with Zambia, is over a mile wide. The **Zambezi River** falls 300 feet here, creating a spray visible for miles. Spectacular rainbows arc over the cliffs.

American passport holders theoretically do not require visas to enter Zimbabwe, but there have been instances when travelers on their own have been stopped and imprisoned in Harare, the capital, for not having a visa. Traveling with a group tour is advisable.

Rwanda: the best place to observe gorillas

Perched high in the Rift Valley Mountains west of Tanzania, tiny land-locked **Rwanda** is the best place in the world to see mountain gorillas. To visit the heart of gorilla country, you must hike through dense bamboo forests to an altitude of 10,000 feet. Professional guides lead small groups and carry rifles in case you meet wild buffalo, elephants, stray leopards, or poachers.

The hour-long trek begins easily, ascending through fields of flowers and potatoes before you enter the forest, where the trail becomes steep, narrow, and slippery. Just when you're out of breath, the path ambles across flat mountain meadows—but not for long before making another jungle climb.

It takes a while to find the gorillas. They roam over a wide area and move more easily than humans through the dense vegetation—their physiques are better suited to bending and swinging than ours.

When the guide sights a troop of gorillas, he motions to hurry forward quietly. You can hear the gorillas snorting and cracking the vegetation beneath them. The guide makes low vocalizations to assure the gorillas' leader of friendliness before deciding if the great apes seem willing to allow visitors. If they are, you can crouch silently within feet of the primates for about 60 minutes. You are warned not to stare at the 500-pound creatures; they interpret this as a sign of aggression. In the unlikely event of an attack, the best defense is no defense—just lie flat.

The best ways to get there

Direct flights from Belgium, France, and Kenya are available to **Kigali**, the capital of Rwanda. There, you can rent a car or take an inexpensive but crowded bus to the gorillas' habitat, **Virunga Volcanoes National Park**. The most picturesque town to stay in is **Gisenyi**, which is on Lake Kivu, an hour's drive from the park.

To minimize disturbance to the gorillas' habitat, tour groups are restricted to six people. Tours must be booked in advance through the Rwandan Office of Tourism and National Parks in Kigali, and there is a 10- to 20-day waiting list.

Bring your own food, water, and camping equipment from Kigali.

With fewer than 250 of these gorillas in the wild, they are listed as an endangered species. Because gorillas are susceptible to human diseases, a visitor with even a bad cold may not be allowed to visit the troop. Children under 15 may not participate.

The World's Best Destinations

✴ UGANDA: BIRTHPLACE OF THE NILE

Uganda's tourism industry is still in its infancy. Nonetheless, Uganda is worth visiting for two reasons. First, it is cheap. Second, its people are hospitable.

Fifty miles from **Kampala**, Uganda's capital, lies Lake Victoria, the largest lake in Africa and the second-largest lake in the world. Here you can witness the beginning of the Nile's long journey to the Mediterranean Sea.

About 150 miles downriver, **Kabalega National Park** is home to not only hippos, crocodiles, and other aquatic life but also the famed **Murchison Falls**. Here, the great river is crammed through a 20-foot fissure in the rocks and led down a 1,000-foot drop.

While in Kampala, visit Kabaka's Palace and Kasubi's Tomb. These are where the royal chiefs of the Buganda tribes were interred. There is also a traditional marketplace where you can purchase traditional Ugandan goods.

The **Nile Hotel Complex** in Kampala is the best place to stay in Uganda. It has parklike grounds with tennis courts, swimming pools, and restaurants.

THE SEYCHELLES: PARADISE FOUND

Some say the **Seychelles**—an island country 1,000 miles east of Kenya in the Indian Ocean—was once the Garden of Eden. Because of its government's strict environmental guidelines, some of its islands are among the least spoiled on earth. Tall palms line these sandy beaches that stretch along the pale-blue Indian Ocean. The people are an exotic mixture of African, Arab, French, British, Indian, and Chinese.

Ninety percent of all Seychellese live on the island of **Mahé**. The high mountain peaks at **Morne Seychellois National Park**, in the center of the island, offer views of the other islands.

Authors Somerset Maugham, Ian Fleming, Alec Waugh, and Noel Coward have been lured by the beauty of the islands. Most of them stayed at the **Northolme Hotel**, *Mahé, Glacis, P.O. Box 333*. The original hotel building is no longer in use, but guests can visit it and see the rooms labeled with names of former guests. Today's visitors are housed in a new building patterned in the old style and equipped with modern conveniences. The Northolme also has a French and Creole restaurant.

Another hotel on Mahé is the **Coral Beach**, *Beau Vallon Beach*.

The second-largest island of the Seychelles, **Praslin**, is home to the rare black bulbul parrot and the Coco-de-mer palm, which produces a large double coconut shaped somewhat like a woman's derrière and is said to have special fertility powers. **Vallée de Mai** on Praslin is the best place to glimpse rare birds and see the Coco-de-mer, and **Anse Lazio** is the Seychelles' most spectacular beach. **Baie des Chevaliers** is more secluded and can be reached by boat or airplane.

The best place to stay on Praslin is **Maison des Palmes**, a guesthouse on Grande Anse Beach with individual cottages that have private baths and terraces. A twin room is 410 rupees ($78) a night, including breakfast.

The forests of **Silhouette Island** contain plants and animals found nowhere else in the world. And the island's beaches are ideal for swimming and snorkeling. The 250 islanders raise cattle, goats, coconuts, sugarcane, cinnamon, vanilla, and fruit. There are no roads, only paths. The island has a superb hotel, the **Silhouette Island Lodge**, *P.O. Box 608, Victoria*, which has thatched bungalows.

The most picturesque and expensive of the Seychelles is the coral **Denis Island**, only 30 minutes by plane from Mah. You can stay in thatched cottages by the sea at **Denis Island Lodge**, *P.O. Box 404, Denis Island*. Creole food is served at the buffet.

The least developed of the inhabited Seychelles is **La Digue**, with no cars but plenty of bicycles. Enormous boulders and tall palms line the surf. And 30 pairs of rare paradise flycatchers live in the Indian almond trees. If you like to snorkel or scuba dive, contact **Gregoire's Watersports**, *Gregoire's Island Lodge, La Digue*. You can stay at **Gregoire's Island Lodge**, *Anse Reunion, LaDigue*, on the beach.

Cousin, Bird, and Aride islands draw flocks of rare birds. More than a million sooty terns nest on Bird Island from May to November every year. The endangered bush warbler lives on Cousin. Aride is home to the world's largest colonies of lesser noddy and roseate terns.

Bird Island Lodge, *P.O. Box 404*, has cottages with private baths and terraces, and prices include English breakfast, Creole lunch, and European dinner.

✳ SOUTH AFRICA: A WORLD OF CONTRASTS

South Africa is opening up as a whole new paradise for international travelers. The country is a land of contrasts. **Johannesburg**, its capital, is its industrial, financial, and cultural center. The nouveau riche (and many foreigners) have settled here in droves. But this is hardly the essence of South Africa. Each direction you travel will reveal a different and beautiful landscape, and another culture. From the rocky expanses and beautiful beaches of the west coast to the subtropical forests of the east coast, South Africa is teeming with energy and beauty. And once you get there, you'll find that travel in general is very affordable.

The best beds

The best accommodation in the country is organized through **Bed 'N Breakfast**, *Eighth Avenue, Melville 2092, P.O. Box 91309; tel. (482)22067*. It operates a network of bed-and-breakfasts, through which South Africans offer their own homes to travelers.

Cape Town: South Africa's oldest city

With Table Mountain as its backdrop, Cape Town is not only South Africa's oldest city but also its most beautiful. In fact, it is boasted as one of the most beautiful cities in the world. Its diverse architecture reflects the city's Victorian background, as well as its 20th-century influences.

South Africa's oldest—and best—museum

The **South African Museum**, *Government Laan Road*, is South Africa's oldest museum. It features an extensive natural history collection of mammals, reptiles, birds, fish, and insects. The whale gallery, life-size Bushman models, and planetarium are also worth a look.

World-renowned wineries

The wineries east of Cape Town are world-renowned. If you're a connoisseur of the fruit of the vine, you'll want to make time to visit this region while in South Africa. Stay the night at the **Lanzerac Estate**, *P.O. Box 4, Stellenbosch 7600*, an original Dutch homestead. Rooms are furnished with original Cape antiques.

The most challenging maze

Larger than the legendary maze at Britain's Hampton Court, the garden maze in Cape Town at **Three Anchors Bay** offers some of the world's most challenging hedges.

South Africa's smallest province

Although **Natal** is South Africa's smallest province, it offers beautiful countryside, as well as bustling city life. **Durban**, Natal's capital, is known for its Golden Mile, where five-star hotels and diverse restaurants abound. You'll also find an abundance of nightclubs, discos, or concert halls, theaters, and galleries—something for everyone.

The best way to experience Zulu life

Just north of Durban is **Eshowe**, where three Zulu *kraals* accommodate visitors in authentic beehive huts, giving you the chance to experience first-hand the lifestyle, rites, and rituals of tribal life. Also visit the **Zululand Historical Museum** (at Fort Nonquai).

The most plants

If plants are your fancy, the Cape Peninsula is the place for you. It has more indigenous plant species per square meter than anyplace else on earth. The **National Botanic Gardens of Kirstenbosch**, on the eastern slopes of **Table Mountain**, is a prime viewing location.

Africa's largest game preserve

Along the northeastern border (adjacent to Mozambique) lies **Kruger National Park**, Africa's largest game preserve. The 12,000 square miles of land is home to more species of wildlife, birds, and plants than any other park in Africa. The park is less than four hours by car from Johannesburg; local flights are also available, to get you there more quickly.

The best adventure

The newest nature thrill available in South Africa is underwater shark watching. Four shark spotters at one time can spend three hours in sturdy cages, watching the great whites circling in search of prey. Contact **Exotic Drive Tours**, *45 Rosmead Ave., Kenilworth, Cape Town 7700.*

The best ways to see South Africa

If you're looking for flexibility and independence, the best way to see South Africa is from the driver's seat of a rented motor home. This makes a lot of sense, especially because camping space is often easier to book than cottages at national parks throughout the country. One of the best companies is **CI Leisure Rentals**, *P.O. Box 137, Pinetown 3600*, with offices in Johannesburg, Cape Town, and Durban.

Another adventurous way to see South Africa is on board the world's most luxurious steam train, *Rovos*. You can spend four days and three nights exploring the former gold-rush country of the eastern Transvaal.

MADAGASCAR: HOME OF THE RING-TAILED LEMUR

Madagascar, off the southeastern coast of Africa in the Indian Ocean, is the fourth-largest island in the world. It is also one of the least visited, famous primarily for its large lemur population.

The capital of Madagascar, **Antananarivo** (known locally as Tana), is a good place to start your exploration. This charming little city offers hundreds of tiny shops and the Zuma marketplace. Every Friday, this giant market overflows with people looking for bargains in leather, jewelry, and other local goods. Pickpockets and muggers roam the streets, so keep your belongings close.

Also venture over to **Nosy Be Island**, off the northwest coast of Madagascar. Coffee, vanilla, and ilang-ilang trees (their oil is used to make perfumes and soaps) are grown here. Stay at the **Andilana Beach Hotel**.

The best lemur watching

If you came to Madagascar looking for the infamous ring-tailed lemurs, visit the **Berenty Lemur Reserve** in Fort Dauphin. Large, clean guesthouses are available on the grounds, and lemurs run rampant. The furry little creatures here are so tame they take food right from your hand.

The best beds

You can find clean, convenient accommodation on Madagascar. The **Hotel Select**, *avenue 18 de juin;* **Hotel Terminus**, *ave. de la Liberation 2;* and the **Bridge Hotel**, *avenue Marguerite Barbier*, are all good places to stay.

The **Acropole**, *11 ave. Lenine*, has quality rooms and a restaurant that serves good Malagasy and French food. The **Hotel Colbert**, *rue Prince Ratsimamanga*, has air-conditioned rooms and a restaurant and casino.

The best travel tips

Because of its tropical setting, Madagascar does experience a lengthy rainy season (November through March). Avoid visiting during this period, when inland travel becomes difficult. The local buses and taxis are suitable methods of getting around the island, but avoid the *proper* buses (which hold about 30 people, not very comfortably). They tend to be slow and do not handle the unsurfaced roads well.

The island trains are inexpensive and faster than buses, but you must make reservations in advance. They run daily except Sunday.

SENEGAL: A FRENCH HOLIDAY FAVORITE

Senegal is a paradise of European sunseekers, who make up the majority of visitors to this West African country. Americans have yet to discover Senegal, although it is the African country geographically closest to the United States, a mere six-and-a-half-hour flight from New York. The Senegalese government is working to attract more American visitors by expanding the denationalized tourist industry.

Senegal offers 350 miles of beach, two national game parks (open seasonally), a bird reserve, sailing, and fishing — as well as history and a pleasant climate (relatively speaking — remember, this is West Africa). Because it juts out into the Atlantic, pleasant breezes waft through the country, and the heat is less unpleasant than in neighboring countries.

The Senegalese Dance Troupe is world-acclaimed, and the local handicrafts are beautiful: precious jewelry crafted by hand, printed and woven fabrics, and snakeskin and crocodile leather goods.

The three negative aspects of this African country are the panhandlers, the dangerous ocean currents, and the unpleasant creatures of the surf, including sharks and jellyfish.

Dakar: the best Paris of Africa

Several cities claim to be the "Paris of Africa," but **Dakar** best fits the description. Good restaurants and outdoor cafés can be found throughout the French-speaking capital. The architecture shows signs of French influences, including wrought-iron balconies and little courtyards. But mosques also punctuate the cityscape, and little dirt streets weave between the grand boulevards.

The best of Senegalese art

The best place to see the art of Senegal is the **Musée d'Art Nègre-Africain** (African Art Museum), *Place Tascher*. The entire first floor of this museum is devoted to Senegalese culture, displaying clothing, furniture, jewels, costumes, and instruments. The museum is open Tuesday through Sunday 8 a.m. until noon and 2 p.m. until 6 p.m.

Local galleries also exhibit the works of contemporary Senegalese artists. The best is **Galerie 39**, *avenue Pompidou*, which displays paintings, drawings, and textile work.

The most important monuments

Dakar's two great architectural monuments are its cathedral and the Grand Mosque. The **cathedral**, *Boulevard de la Republique and avenue du Président Lamine Gueye*, is one of the finest examples of Senegalese architecture. The **Grand Mosque**, *Allée Coursin*, built in 1964, is one of the largest mosques in Africa. (You must be content to view it from outside, because visitors are not permitted to enter.)

The best digs in Dakar

Novotel Dakar, *avenue Sarraut, B.P. 2973*, which belongs to the French Novotel chain, boasts two restaurants, two bars, a swimming pool, and tennis courts.

La Croix du Sud, *20 ave. Albert Sarraut*, has a view of the flower market.

Dakar's best cuisine

Senegalese food tends to be spicy, often garnished with *sauce piment* (hot pepper sauce). Most entrées consist of rice combined with meats and sauces. French cuisine is also available in Dakar. Because alcohol is forbidden to Muslims, only non-alcoholic beverages—mostly teas—are served in restaurants.

La Région du Fleuve, located near the Foreign Ministry and operated by a Frenchwoman and her African husband, is decorated with African masks and textiles and serves African fare. Meals are inexpensive. The restaurant is closed Wednesdays.

La Croix du Sud, *20 ave. Albert Sarraut*, is an elegant but expensive French restaurant. All produce for the meals is imported from France. The restaurant is closed Sundays.

The best entertainment in Dakar

The Senegalese National Theater Company and the Mudra Dance Group, in addition to many other groups, appear at the **Sorano** (the National Theater), *Daniel Sorano Building, boulevard de la République.*

The darkest history

Just 20 minutes from Dakar is the **Island of Gorée**, once the most important transit center for slave traders, who bought Africans for shipment to America. It was from this appalling place that hundreds of thousands of shackled prisoners were loaded onto ships for the so-called Middle Crossing. The first crossing carried rum from the American colonies to Africa to pay for black gold; the final crossing was of sugar to New England to make the rum. A small museum on the island has chilling displays of shackles, chains, and other unpleasant instruments of the trade.

The best seashells

The **Island of Fadiouth**, 60 miles from Dakar, is so covered with seashells that the populace uses them as building material. Everything here is made of shells: a cemetery, a church, granaries built on stilts. Natives follow a traditional, self-sufficient, African lifestyle, making their own cloth and growing their food. You can reach the island from the mainland region of Joal via the wooden bridge or in a *pirogue* (a wooden canoe).

The best place to view game

Basse Casamance, a 12,350-acre game park near Ziguinchor in southeast Senegal, has thick forests inhabited by 52 species of mammals and 172 species of birds. You can visit on guided boat or car tours. A limited number of guests can spend the night in the park at Impluvium Lodge, where light meals and drinks are served.

The best bird sanctuary

One of the most important bird sanctuaries in the world is the 25,000-acre **Djoudj Park**, in the Saloum Delta, where you can see 180 species, including pelicans, herons, flamingos, and egrets. You can observe from a mirador without scaring the birds away.

Mauritanian Blue People camp on the edge of the park from time to time, providing a rare opportunity to see these Berbers.

You, too, can camp here, in a hut in the Campement de Djoudj.

The best duck hunting

Less benevolent bird watchers prefer **Maka Diama** (150 miles north of Dakar), a paradise for duck hunters, who from Dec. 15 to April 15 are licensed to shoot here. In addition to ducks, bags include fancolin, guinea fowl, hare, and quail.

TOGO: A MICROCOSM OF AFRICA

Togo, a small west coast country, is sub-Saharan Africa in miniature, with plains alive with game, plantations fertile with crops of cocoa and coffee, and mud-brick villages where the old traditions remain unchanged.

Originally a German protectorate, and then a French colony, Togo is now an independent country. **Lomé**, the capital, offers a wide choice of restaurants, while the coast boasts idyllic beaches.

In Lomé, women hold powerful economic and political positions, and every village has a women's union. The powerful Nana Benz—made up of matronly merchants—wields considerable force in the politics of this country (and has overthrown at least one government). The women sell everything imaginable in the marketplace—from a fully equipped Mercedes Benz to a pair of plastic slippers. Many of the older Nana Benz members are illiterate—but they can calculate their margins and execute foreign-exchange transactions in their heads. Although the language of Togo is officially French, the people also can converse in Pidgin English.

Where to go in Togo

The best way to get a taste of the native life in Togo is to visit **Le Grand Marché** in the center of Lomé, where the smell of roasting meats and tangy spices permeates the air and tie-dyed caftans and printed pagnes are sold. These colorful swaths of cloth are used to make the dresses, shirts, and headdresses worn by West Africans, but they also can be used as unique tablecloths, draperies, or sheets back home. (The textiles are on the second floor of the market.)

For an in-depth look at Togo's culture, visit the **National Museum**, housed in the headquarters of Togo's only political party, the Rassemblement du Peuple Togolais (R.P.T.), a building decorated with reliefs sculpted by a leading Togolese artist. Museum exhibits include shells (which were formerly used as currency), pottery, musical instruments, and ceremonial relics. The museum is open Monday through Friday 8 a.m. until noon and 3 p.m. until 5 p.m. Admission is free.

The **Odef Craft Center** attracts the best of the area's traditional woodcarvers. The center also has a selection of macrame, batik, fiber, and clay works.

The best place to settle a score

Voodoo is practiced in **Bé**, a residential area on the east side of Lomé. At **Bé Market**, near the Hotel de la Paix, you can buy unusual charms—bones, little figurines, skulls—from both pagans and Muslims. The charms are said to bring success or money, to defeat a rival in love, or to attract a lover.

Togo's most interesting village

Deep in the **Tamberma Valley** live the Tamberma people, who continue a lifestyle unchanged by the passage of time. Famous for their masonry, they live in cool tata dwellings constructed by hand from clay and wood. The houses are situated in a compound that is surrounded by a circle of conical towers connected by a wall. The towers are used primarily to store grain.

The Tamberma spend most of their time outdoors on patios—they even do their cooking outdoors. They wear little clothing and smoke long pipes. The women are marked by scars in intricate patterns; they are tattooed when they are eight days old to protect against miscarriages and stillbirths.

The best hotels in Togo

The best hotel in Togo is the **Hotel de 2 Fevrier Sofitel**, *B.P. 131, Lomé*, which rivals any posh American hotel. The 36 stories of this glass building include two restaurants, two bars, a nightclub, and a casino.

Hotel Sarakawa, *B.P. 2232*, is a favorite of the French, a five-star hotel with restaurants, a disco, and recreational facilities.

Less expensive is the **Hotel Le Benin**. This hotel is Togo's training ground for restaurant personnel—the dining room serves fine cuisine for low prices.

NIGERIA: THE MOST POPULATED AFRICAN COUNTRY

Don't spend much time in Nigeria's capital, **Lagos**. It is an appalling place. Built on a lagoon, the city has a mushrooming population, but it lacks the infrastructure to deal with it. Roads, sewage, garbage collection, and water are all becoming problems. The results are a perpetual traffic jam and generally unpleasant conditions. Telephones seldom work, and electricity is erratic. Most of the Westerners in Lagos are diplomats and businessmen, who leave for the country as quickly and as often as they can.

In the days of high oil prices, Lagos was the most expensive city in Africa; now it is cheap—the one point in its favor. Cars and airplane tickets, however, have become more expensive. (This is helping to lessen the congestion on the highways and at the airport.) Another thing in Lagos' favor is its restaurants, which are good—and cheap. Recommended restaurants are **Chez Antoine**, *61 Broad St., Tabriz*, which serves French and Lebanese cuisine but is closed Sunday, and **Club Bagatelle**, *208/212 Broad St.*, which serves Indian and Middle Eastern cuisine.

The **Federal Palace Hotel**, *Victoria Island*, is the best place to stay in town. It has a good restaurant/nightclub, the Atlantic, which serves Italian food.

But you shouldn't let Lagos spoil your opinion of all Nigeria. The country has much more attractive cities, notably Ife, Ibadan, Jos, Onitsha, and Kano. And a new capital is being built in Abuja, which is roughly the geographic center of the country.

Kano: the best place to explore Islamic history

In the Old City of **Kano**, an oasis on the edge of the Sahara Desert, you can step back into the Islamic past. A mud wall inscribed with Islamic scriptures and Hausa engravings here is believed to protect the faithful from intrusion from the outside world. Livestock wander freely through the streets, along with men and women in flowing, Islamic robes and head-dresses. Camel caravans of the nomadic Tuareg, dressed in immaculate sheaths and tall turbans, roam the streets.

Men in pastel *baba riga* robes and women in drab wrapper dresses trot freely with goats and lambs along winding footpaths in a maze of mud huts. The only modern addition to the Old City is the heavily guarded electric gate built into the mud wall surrounding the centuries-old Emir's Palace.

The towering 40-foot Nassarawa Kofar mud gate connects the Old City with Kano's hastily constructed replica of a Western commercial center, where business is transacted but aesthetics are forgotten.

Climb to the top of the Dalan or Goren Dutse hills for a view of the city skyline against the Sahara desert.

The drawbacks

Kano has been the center of much of the political turmoil that has wracked Nigeria since it became an independent country. From this city, Muslims waged holy wars against rival groups for control of the country, which has the largest population in Black Africa.

Perhaps this history explains the terrible delays and red tape at Kano's international airport. Soldiers toting submachine guns guard the hangarlike terminal, where a sea of scuffling, sweating bodies crashes against two tiny immigration desks. One correspondent reported waiting six hours to get out of the airport after landing. She finally had to pay a bribe to get through.

Water is scarce and must be boiled, strained, and purified. Sometimes, running water is not available.

The best Hausa food

If you enjoy sampling unfamiliar foods, try the local *sire* or *souya*, sold every evening at dozens of food stands all over town. Watch at dusk for small flaming fires where chunks of meat, tomato, onion, and pepper roast on skewers.

You can enjoy authentic tribal food at restaurants throughout Kano. Try the **Akesan Restaurant** and restaurants in the Ikeja, at the Usman Memorial, and in the international hotels. Prices are generally expensive, but the meals are worth it.

Hotels: smaller is better

The cost of a hotel room in Kano is usually not worth the price. The major hotels are no better than any of the smaller hotels in town (except that they usually have recreational facilities), and they are twice the price. All hotels are subject to water, electricity, and food shortages, but the smaller hotels are cleaner and offer more courteous service.

The two best hotels in Kano are the **Daula**, *150 Murtala Muhammed Way, PM Bay*, and the **Central**, *State Road*. The key to getting a room at a hotel is often a small bribe, not a confirmed reservation.

The best side trips

If you want to shake the dust of Kano off your shoes for a few days, visit one of the three ultramodern spa resorts an hour south of the city. The **Baguada** and **Tiga Lake** resorts and the **Rock Castle Hotel** offer iced drinks under the palms.

Or take a trip to **Daura**, a town two hours north of Kano, where the nomadic desert culture that once dominated the Sahara continues unchanged.

Kano is an excellent base for safaris. The **Yankari Game Reserve** is a four-hour drive due south in the state of Bauchi. East of Yankari is the **Jos zoo**. Both nature reserves offer safaris that take you to see thousands of native species.

Yoruba: best markets, best art

Yoruba cities, such as **Ibadan**, which is as large as Lagos but much nicer, are the African cities most welcoming to tourists. Ibadan boasts the best market in Nigeria, called Dugbe, and has a large Lebanese population made up of Middle Easterners who came to Africa to trade and stayed to open restaurants.

Benin City, the Yoruba capital, boasts the best market for souvenirs in Nigeria. Its other claim to fame is **Oba's Palace**, which is difficult to get into—you must apply for permission in advance. (An *oba* is a Yoruba ruler.)

Far more accessible is the public **Ife Palace complex**, another former home of a Yoruba ruler. Ife is the center of a flourishing art colony, where printmakers have adapted skills once used on cloth to produce gorgeous woodcuts.

Top travel tips

Nigeria doesn't have to be the bureaucratic nightmare it is often reported to be. You just have to be prepared. Before arriving at the international airport in Lagos, make sure you have a visa, a passport, a yellow fever vaccination certificate, and a return ticket. You will have to pay a minimal airport tax when you leave.

The Côte d'Ivoire: the richest African country

The **Côte d'Ivoire** has the highest standard of living in sub-Saharan Africa and is one of the continent's most politically stable nations. Originally a French colony, the Cote d'Ivoire (the government refuses to answer to the English name, Ivory Coast) is now an independent democratic republic (although it retains a strong French influence).

In the Côte d'Ivoire, you can examine Ashanti and Senoufu art at the National Museum, observe wild animals at West Africa's largest game reserve, and bathe in the sun and water of the African Riviera. The country also boasts Africa's only ice-skating rink.

Africa's most European city

In **Abidjan**, capital of the Côte d'Ivoire, splendid African ladies dress in brightly colored long dresses and head wraps and carry baguettes fresh from the bakery—on their heads. This metropolis is reminiscent of European cities. Unfortunately, the beauty of the city has been diminished by recent downtown development. But beautiful sites remain along the lagoon, by the seashore, and in the suburbs.

Musée National, *boulevard Nangui-Abrogoua*, houses more than 20,000 works of art, including jewelry, statues, ritual costumes, and furniture. It is open Tuesday through Sunday 9 a.m. until noon and 3 p.m. until 6 p.m.

Marché Sénégalais, *boulevard de la République*, and Marché de Cocody sell art and handicrafts imported from all areas of Africa. Both are open every day. The **Treichville Market** is a treat for veteran shoppers who know how to bargain. The second floor of the market, which is open daily 7 a.m. until 2 p.m., features special regional textiles.

A forest reserve called **Banc National Park** is just within the city limits. Its 7,500 acres are scored with trails that lead past exotic—and labeled—flora.

The best local dishes

Most Ivorian cuisine is based on the plantain, which looks like a banana but isn't, and the yam, which looks like a sweet potato but isn't. From both, the Ivorians make a stew called *foutou*, a mush covered in a nut or palm-seed sauce. *Aloco*, fried plantains, is another specialty. Drink specialties are *bandji*, made with palm extract, and *lemonroudji*, a concoction of lemon and ginger. Meat and fish are usually fresh and grilled on outdoor barbecues. Try fresh fruit for dessert.

The best African restaurants are in the Treichville section of Abidjan. For good meat and fish, try **Kedjenou**. For Ivorian-style cuisine, try the Marquis restaurants: **Le Senat** and **La Bache Bleue**, both in Marcory in Abidjan.

The best native dances

A troupe of 35 dancers performs the ritual dances of the Côte d'Ivoire at **Le Wafou**, *Boulevard de Marseille*, an expensive cabaret on the lagoon. Dinner is served here also.

The best places to stay in Abidjan

Hôtel Ivoire, *08 B.P. 001, Abidjan 01, boulevard de la Corniche, Cocody*, is an immense luxury hotel that houses 14 boutiques, five restaurants, five bars, a supermarket, a cinema, a concert hall, sports facilities, a casino, a man-made lake, and the only ice-skating rink in Black Africa.

Le Forum Golf Intercontinental, *boulevard Lagunaire, La Riviera, Cocody, 08 B.P. 18*, on the banks of the lagoon, has a nightclub, a pool, a restaurant, and, of course, golf facilities.

The best place to view wildlife

Comoe National Park, 440 miles north of Abidjan—a comfortable distance only by air—is a government wildlife reserve where you can see buffalo, antelope, wild boar, baboons, and a very few lions. The reserve is open December through May. Food and drink are available here, but they are expensive.

The best place to stay is the **Gomoe Safari Lodge Hotel**, which has a restaurant, a bar, a pool, and organized excursions. Traditional dances are performed on the premises.

The best place to buy textiles

A modern textile center is located in the provincial town of **Bouaké**, 235 miles from Abidjan. Here, the area's oldest textile factory, **Ets. Gonfreville**, manufactures cotton goods. **Solinci**, a lingerie factory, is also located in town. Both are open to the public on Thursday. But you can buy seconds any day of the week from the factories at the **Bouaké Market**. Look the goods over carefully, but usually they have been rejected only for minor flaws. Among the goodies are household linens.

In Bouake, stay at the **Hôtel du Centre**, *B.P. 54*. Although the hotel's rooms are simple and plain, its location is excellent; next to the hotel is the Artisan's Center, where you can buy leather crafts, cane furniture, ivory sculpture, jewelry, and Baoulé masks. (The Baoulé are a traditional carving tribe whose work is less known than that of peoples elsewhere in Africa.) Traditional masks are used in initiation ceremonies and to ward off misfortune.

Sierra Leone—the best of the British in West Africa

If sightseeing isn't really your cup of tea, visit West Africa's former British colony, Sierra Leone. This country has no outstanding attractions, but it does offer beautiful tropical scenery, a dry climate, and a friendly population, made up of 18 different ethnic groups. Perhaps the best part (at least if you're a foreign visitor) is that Sierra Leone has one of the unhealthiest economies in West Africa, so your foreign currency will go a long way.

Although English is the official language of Sierra Leone, a form of English called Krio, enriched by several West African languages, is more widely spoken.

Freetown: the heart of Sierra Leone

Freetown, the capital of Sierra Leone, offers the best opportunities for accommodation and dining in this quiet country. And its peninsula is the only place along the West African coast where mountains rise near the sea, providing beautiful views. It's also one of the few areas where the water is safe for swimming.

The best beds in Freetown

The **City Hotel**, *Lightfoot Boston Street*, is a run-down, chaotic hotel built in the 1920s. Once an architectural gem, the City Hotel remains intriguing for fans of author Graham Greene. Greene wrote *The Heart of the Matter* in a room at this hotel during World War II.

The renovated **YMCA**, *32 Fort St.*, is the best of all the YMCAs in West Africa. You have use of a library, a TV room, and a fully equipped kitchen. There are only six rooms, so be sure to make reservations.

If your priority is the beach, stay at the **Cape Sierra**, *P.O. Box 54*, just off the water.

The best place to try African cuisine

If you're in the mood for ethnic food, and a lot of it, try **Provilac**, *Congo Cross Road*.

Every Wednesday at lunch, Provilac serves an all-Sierra Leone buffet. The best dishes include potato-leaves sauce, okra sauce, palm oil stew, groundnut stew, and pepper soup.

Freetown bests

Across the street from the City Hotel is the city's major landmark, the **Cotton Tree**, more than 500 years old. Next to the Cotton Tree is the **Sierra Leone National Museum**.

A must for hikers is the half-hour climb to **Leicester Peak**. The highest point in Freetown (1,952 feet), this mountain offers a spectacular view of the bay area and the peninsula.

The most popular beach in Sierra Leone is the **River No. 2 Beach**, 45 minutes south of Freetown. Many consider it one of the most beautiful beaches on the entire West African coast.

The Best of North Africa

North Africa is a mixture of civilizations: the pharaohs of Egypt, whose history dates back to the beginning of time; the exotic Moroccans, whose intriguing culture mystifies Westerners to this day; and the elusive Algerians, who live in a land yet to be discovered—trapped in time.

The best of Egypt

For 4,000 years, the pharaohs of Egypt reigned over a civilization with a stability and technology that have yet to be duplicated. Recently, a team of Japanese engineers tried to build a pyramid just 35 feet high using the ancient Egyptian methods. They couldn't finish it. Thus, the pyramids of Egypt are eternal reminders of the lost wisdom of a great civilization.

A few days among the tombs and temples of Egypt will convince you that the pharaohs had something we have now lost. But a few days among the guides and the multitudes of poor asking for *baksheesh* (tips) may also convince you that what the pharaohs succeeded in building was merely a nation of the greatest tourist attractions known to man.

While Egypt is largely a desert nation, most of its people live on the water—along the banks of the Nile, by the Red Sea, or on the Mediterranean. So one of the best ways to see this country is by boat. One of the geographic peculiarities of this land is that the southern half of it is known as Upper Egypt; the northern half is Lower Egypt.

Cairo: the greatest paradox

Founded in the 10th century by invading Muslims, this noisy, crowded city thriving in the shadow of the pyramids is one of the most intriguing capitals in the world. Cairo's mixture of poverty and riches exemplifies the paradox of the Middle East, which is made up of nations straddling the Third World and the Western world. Minarets rise imperiously from 10th-century mosques, cars hurtle recklessly down narrow streets, poor families live in the graveyards of wealthy relatives, and merchants crowd the bazaars selling Arabian Night perfume and "genuine" Pharaonic scarabs.

Metropolitan Cairo, jam-packed with one-quarter of Egypt's population, is split by the Nile into two districts: Cairo on the east bank and Giza (a suburb on the edge of the Giza Plateau) on the west. In between are two small islands: Zamalek and Roda. Zamalek (also called Gezira) lies across from the northern, more upscale New City, with its Tahrir Square—Cairo's downtown—and its Islamic section and tourist bazaar of Khan el-Khalili. Roda is parallel to the southern, squalid Old Cairo, which includes the Coptic neighborhood bordered by the Fatimid Wall built in 1087.

The best view of Cairo

Most people come to Cairo to see the pyramids; in the process, they often miss the city itself. The best place to get your bearings is atop the 600-foot **Cairo Tower** in Zohria Garden on Zamalek. The view from the observation deck stretches to the pyramids. (Skip the mediocre restaurant.)

Cairo's two best museums

Two museums on the island provide insight into modern Egypt: the **Mukhtar Museum** shows the works of Mahmud Mukhtar, the father of modern Egyptian sculpture, and the **Gezira Museum** displays rare paintings, sculptures, and Islamic and Coptic artifacts.

The most fashionable neighborhood

Walk around the fashionable neighborhood of **Heliopolis** in the New City, where Egyptian President Mubarak lives. Buildings mix Western and Islamic architecture. Notice the Palace of Prince Husayn, the arcades on Abbas Boulevard, and the Palace of Empain, a copy of a Hindu temple with an electronically controlled tower that rotates to follow the path of the sun.

In search of the *Arabian Nights*

Islamic Cairo, with its magic lanterns and flying carpets even better than those of Baghdad, has preserved the atmosphere of the *Arabian Nights*. It takes several mornings of walking to really see the area. Visit some of the 500 mosques here—remember that not all of them are open to non-Muslims and that you won't be allowed to enter any mosque until after prayer.

When visiting a mosque, dress conservatively and don't draw attention to yourself; women should cover their heads. You must remove your shoes at the door. (Give the man who watches them 25 piastres, or four cents.) Anyone who opens special doors or explains things in detail also should be tipped. Some mosques charge an admission in Egyptian pounds.

The world's oldest university

Cairo's most famous mosque is certainly the **Al-Azhar Mosque**, on the corner of Al-Azhar and Al-Muizz streets. Built in A.D. 972, it was the world's first university, and today it serves more than 90,000 Muslim students. Restored in bits and pieces, the mihrab in the center aisle is from the 10th century. You can take photographs here, as in any mosque, as long as you don't focus on any one person.

The holiest mosque

Across the street from Al-Azhar Mosque is **Sayiddna al-Husayn**, Cairo's most venerated Muslim shrine. It is closed to non-Muslims, but you can examine the finely decorated exterior walls. Inside rests the head of al-Husayn, grandson of the prophet Muhammad (transported to Cairo in a green silk bag from Iraq).

Westernization has hit even Sayiddna al-Husayn. Just inside the door is a green neon light reading "Allah."

The Citadel

South of the Al-Azhar is the **Citadel**, a monolithic complex that dominates Cairo's skyline. Built in the late 12th century by Salah al-Din on the Mokattam hill range, it has a strategic view of the capital.

The 19th-century ruler Muhammad Ali added a mosque to the Citadel, one of the great features of Cairo. The silver domes and marble and alabaster decorations are rivaled only by the building's vast interior.

The Citadel houses the Mostafa Kamel Museum and the Military Museum.

Cairo's oldest mosque

Southwest of Salah al-Din Square is the city's oldest mosque: **Ibn Tulun**, *Calen el-Salikban Street*. It was built in A.D. 879 by Ibn Tulun, who seceded from the Islamic Empire and built himself the largest mosque in Egypt, decorating it with sweeping contours and intricate inscriptions. The mosque's courtyard covers almost seven acres, and the building's lacy stuccowork surrounds inscriptions from the Koran. Climb the external staircase to the top of the tower, from which you have a view of the city and the pyramids to the west. You can visit Ibn Tulun from 8 a.m. until 6 p.m.

The most beautiful windows

The mausoleum complex of **Qalaun**, *Gonar al-Qaid Street*, in northern Sharia al-Muizz, is famous for the colors in its stained-glass windows. During the times of the Crusades, Egypt was the world's center of glasswork, and the incredible craftsmanship of these windows set a standard for all Islamic tombs and Gothic churches in Europe.

The best Islamic art

The **Museum of Islamic Art**, off Ahmad Maher Square at the corner of Port Said and Muhammed Ali streets, is an overlooked treasure. This museum houses a little of everything, from Persian carpets to Islamic glassware to Kufic script woodcarvings. Because most visitors to Egypt dwell on Pharaonic art, the Museum of Islamic Art is rarely crowded. The exhibits are arranged by craft, so it's easy to trace stylistic developments over time, giving yourself a mini-art history course. Don't miss the Koran engravings. The museum is open Saturdays through Thursdays, 9 a.m. until 4 p.m.

Giza: the most tranquil district

Giza Square, in the heart of Cairo's Giza district on the west bank, marks the beginning of Pyramids Road. Cross Al-Gamaa Bridge to get to the Al-Urman Botanical Garden and the Cairo zoo. To the north is Dokki, Giza's fashionable residential neighborhood, which contains several embassies and two good museums.

The **Museum of Modern Art**, *18 Ismail Abu'l-Futuh St.*, exhibits postwar Egyptian art and has an excellent sculpture garden. The **Agricultural Museum**, at the western end of the 6th of October Bridge, contains the only remaining mummified bull.

The best of Old Cairo

South of Tahrir Square is **Old Cairo**, which surrounds the old Roman fort Babylon outside Fatimid Wall. You'll find evidence of Greco-Roman culture and early Christianity throughout the quarter. From the time of the last pharaoh to the first mosque, Egypt was part of the Greco-Roman world and Christianity, which in Egypt emerged as the Coptic Church.

The world's finest Coptic art

The **Coptic Museum**, built on the site of the Roman fort in Qasr al-Shama, has the finest Coptic art collection in the world. The buildings, courtyards, and gardens of the museum tell the story of early Christianity from the third through the seventh centuries. See the intricately woven robes and curtains for which the Copts were renowned. The museum is open Saturdays through Thursdays, 9 a.m until 4 p.m.

The most beautiful Coptic church

In front of the Coptic Museum are the remains of the fort that took invading Muslims seven months to overpower. The **Church of al-Muallaqa** was built atop the gate of the fort, giving it the name the Hanging Church. Also known as the Church of St. Mary, this is the most beautiful of Cairo's Coptic churches. The pointed arches and carved relief are interesting changes from the Gothic style commonly associated with Christian churches.

Climb the 24 stairs to see the interior. The famous pulpit stands on 13 slender columns (symbolic of the 12 apostles and Jesus, with the black column representing Judas).

Unlike in mosques, baksheesh is not paid in churches. Photographs are prohibited.

The three most charming churches

North of al-Muallaqa, on Mari Girgis Street, is the **Church of Mari Girgis** (St. George), noted for its fine stained-glass windows. To the left of the church is a staircase descending into an old alley, at the end of which is the elegant **Church of Abu Serga**. The crypt below is supposed to be where Joseph, Mary, and baby Jesus stayed during their flight to Egypt. (The crypt is now flooded and closed to the public.)

To the right of Abu Serga is the **Church of St. Barbara**, an ornate structure with striped-marble steps. According to legend, the order was given to destroy one church and restore the other, but the caliph's architect couldn't decide which to destroy. He paced back and forth between the two buildings until he died of exhaustion—so the caliph restored both churches.

Egypt's oldest synagogue

Near the Church of St. Barbara is the **Ben Ezra Synagogue**, the oldest in Egypt. The interior is beautifully decorated, and the custodian is a humorous, talkative fellow. You can follow the steps to the spot where the pharaoh's daughter is said to have found the infant Moses.

The Cities of the Dead

The vast and forbidding **Cities of the Dead**, where thousands live in and around graveyards, are to the northeast and south of the Citadel. The poor use parts of mausoleums as their homes and parts of tombs as clotheslines or soccer goals.

Wealthy citizens are buried in the northern cemetery, and their graves are marked with elaborate tombs. Especially fine is the tomb of Umm Ahuk. The many-ribbed dome caps an ancient pointed archway.

The most impressive monument in the southern cemetery is the mausoleum of **Imam Al-Shafi'i**, *Imam Al-Shafi'i Street*. Built in 1211, the mausoleum contains an 800-year-old carved cenotaph. The nearby tomb of Shagarat al-Durr was built for Shagarat, the Muslim queen who poisoned two husbands and her son to remain in power. The mausoleum is decorated with Kufic carvings and a mihrab with Byzantine glass mosaics.

Egypt's most important museum

The **Egyptian Museum**, like the British National Museum and the Smithsonian, exhibits an entire culture on several carpeted floors. Located in Tahrir Square just down the road from the enormous Ramses Hilton, the Egyptian Museum (commonly called the Cairo Museum) is the world's unrivaled warehouse of Pharaonic art. More than 100,000 pieces are crammed together with little order; the most exquisite are not always highlighted. The famous mummy room has been closed for religious reasons; however, the museum has enough ankhs, scarabs, and statues to fill several days of exploring.

The second floor houses the treasures found in Tutankhamon's tomb, the only one that escaped plundering, because of its hidden location. When viewing the incredible gold statues, alabaster lamps, and general ostentation, remember that Tutankhamon died young and his treasure was comparatively small.

The Cairo Museum is always crowded but less so when the tour groups break for lunch. It is open daily 9 a.m. until 4 p.m. Cameras are prohibited.

The most colorful markets

In Cairo, you can buy not only an aphrodisiac but also an anti-aphrodisiac, made from baby crocodiles. The two Arabic phrases you'll want to know when shopping are *Bikam hadha?* (How much does this cost?) and *Hatha Kathir* (That's too expensive). The main shopping areas are **Zamalek**, **Dokki** (in Giza), and **Heliopolis** (northeast of the New City).

Khan el-Khalili is the largest bazaar in Egypt, with hundreds of shops grouped by trade: gold merchants, silversmiths, and spice sellers. The 14th-century courtyards buzz with the sounds of haggling. You will find the best buys on *galabiyyas*, full-length cotton robes worn by Egyptian men, and local crafts. **Nassar Brothers**, *Khan Al Khalily Street*, is the best place for precious and semiprecious stones.

Every Friday morning, a camel market is held in **Imbaba** (on Zamalek Island). Traders sell and swap hundreds of Sudanese camels, horses, sheep, and goats, as well as food, wagons, jeans, and baskets. (You can buy a camel for about 1500 Egyptian pounds, or $260.) The sights and smells are strong: you may witness a camel giving birth or a goat being butchered and skinned for immediate barbecue. Remember to bargain. And don't pet the camels—they spit and bite.

The **Bab Zuwayla** district of Old Cairo teems with people and livestock. Peddlers transport their goods by bicycle and truck and on foot. Saffron, cumin, coriander, and hibiscus perfume the air. Along the Street of the Tentmaker, men sit cross-legged, plying their needles in the traditional art of applique stitchery. Also to be found are food, silk carpets, gold jewelry, clothing, ceramics, baskets, and two fez factories. Bab Zuwayla is more commercialized than **Khan el Khalili**, which is across the street, but just as colorful.

Finally, you can't leave Cairo without purchasing a *cartouche*, the quintessential Egyptian souvenir. These Pharaonic 18-karat gold pendants are personalized with your name or initials translated phonetically into hieroglyphics. Prices are $70 to $180. The best place to shop for a cartouche is **Ohnig of Cairo** in the **Egyptian Museum**.

Cairo's best cuisine

In a city where butchers slap flies off pieces of meat to show them to customers, only certain restaurants can be trusted. However, if you're willing to

The World's Best Destinations

venture beyond the hotel restaurants, you will find that the food in Cairo is exotic and inexpensive. Typical Egyptian dishes include *mulokhiya*, a gelatinous soup made with a spinachlike herb; *fool*, a big brown bean; *feteer*, which resembles pizza; *taboula*, ground wheat and parsley salad; and *kofta*, tiny grilled meatballs.

Andrea, *59 Mariouthia St.*, an outdoor farm restaurant near the pyramids, serves delicious grilled chicken and some of the best *mazza* (a collection of appetizers) in Cairo.

Nearby **Felfela Village**, *off Pyramids Avenue*, offers fine Egyptian cuisine and occasional folklore shows.

Abu Shakra, *69 Kasr el-Nil St.*, specializes in shish kebab and *kofta*.

A full-course Egyptian meal is best at **Aladin**, *26 Sherif St.*, in the Cairo Sheraton, a watering hole popular among foreign journalists. Kebabs, barbecues, and *om ali*—a spicy bread pudding—are tasty and filling.

The best seafood restaurant in Cairo is **Hag Mohammed el-Samak**, *Abdel-Aziz Street*, across from the Omar Effendi department store. The grilled fish is good at this restaurant, which is decorated with art deco furnishings.

The most romantic meals in Cairo are served on Nile boats. The food is a little more expensive, but the atmosphere is worth it. The two best floating restaurants are **Scarabee**, *16 July 26th St., Azakabia*, opposite the Shepheards Hotel, and the **Pharaoh Hotel**, *12 Lotfi Hassouna St., Dukki*. Both have floor shows and large crowds, so make reservations.

The most recommended hotels

Maintaining its reputation as the best hotel in Cairo is the **Nile Hilton**, *Tahrir Square*. Across the street from the Egyptian Museum, it is well-run and elegant. It has luxurious rooms and the best pool in the city.

Located at the northern tip of Roda Island, the **Meridien Hotel**, *Corniche El-Nil*, is quieter but also first-class. All rooms have Nile views.

Nearby is the world-famous **Shepheard's Hotel**, *Corniche El Nil*, which has developed a reputation as a hideaway for international spies.

The **Club Med**, *Em Manial Palace, Kasr Mohommed Aly*, in nearby Mena, is outstanding.

Good hotels need not all be five-star. The **President Hotel**, *22 Taha Hussein Street*, in the residential section of Zamalek, is spacious and clean. The rooftop restaurant has an extensive wine cellar.

The best nightlife

At night, when the temperature drops, Cairo's nightlife gets hot. Discos are crowded, especially on Thursday nights. The popular ones include **After Eight**, *6 Kasr El Nil St.* and **Rasputin**, *Green Pyramids Hotel, Helmiat Alahram Street*. The **Atlas Hotel**, *2 Mohamed Roushdi St.*, has good rock'n'roll music. **Al-Capo**, *22 Taha Husayn St.*, is a great place for live music. **Al-Sokkareya**,

Abd'l-Hamid Badawy Street, Heliopolis, has singers and musicians, a penny arcade and fortune-tellers, good drinks, and the popular *sheesha* (water pipe), all in an Egyptian garden.

Surprisingly, nightlife in Cairo can be liveliest during Ramadan, a month-long holiday during which devout Muslims fast from sunrise to sunset. After dark, however, they indulge in large meals and take to the streets around al-Azhar and the Nile, where you'll find street theater performances, magic shows, and noisy crowds.

The Nile Hilton, Marriott, and Sheraton hotels have casinos, where gambling takes place in American currency.

If you want glitzy belly dancing, try the **Belvedere** in the Nile Hilton, or the **Two Seasons Supper Club** in the **Ramses Hilton**, *1115 Comiche El-Nil*.

More authentic floorshows can be seen at the clubs along Pyramids Road, which cater to Egyptians.

The popular folk-dancing Rida Troupe performs at the **Balloon Theater**, *El-Nil Street, Agouza*.

If you'd rather spend a peaceful, romantic evening, take a *felucca* (small sailboat) on the Nile. Feluccas can be rented just south of the Kasr El-Nil Bridge on the east bank for about 20 Egyptian pounds ($6) an hour. Across the corniche from the Shepheards Hotel, boats are available from midnight to dawn for 26 to 33 Egyptian pounds ($4.50 to $7). It's felucca etiquette to bring food for a picnic to share with your navigator.

The best ways to get around Cairo

Getting around Cairo is simultaneously easy and bothersome. Overcrowded buses (commonly called VOAs, for Voice of America—they were bought with American aid) are cheap and run everywhere, but they can be recommended only to the most adventurous. They don't stop—they only slow down for you to jump on or off.

The newly built metro offers fast, inexpensive service, but only in the southern area of the city. The happiest traveler is the one who has mastered the art of Cairo taxis, which come either metered or unmetered. Either bargain the cost before you get into a cab or at the end of the ride pay the driver a fair amount—usually 15 to 20 Egyptian pounds ($2.50 to $3.50) for a ride within the city and 20 to 25 Egyptian pounds ($3.50 to $4.30) to travel from downtown to the pyramids.

Chaffeured cars can be hired for the day outside either Hilton. You also can rent a car to drive yourself around. This may be practical in the rest of Egypt, but in Cairo it's dangerous. The famous race-car driver Mario Andretti said that the one place he'd never drive is Cairo. Traffic lights here were built to be ignored. Cars speed through intersections, slowing only momentarily to warn pedestrians by honking their horns or flashing their headlights.

The World's Best Destinations

Giza: the best and the tackiest of Egypt

Not five miles west of Cairo, the pyramids of Giza are easily reached via Pyramids Road by taxi or buses 8 and 900. The best route is through Mena village. Toward the southern edge of this town is a broad plaza where tourist buses park. Here, clear of buildings, you have an uninterrupted view of the Sphinx with the pyramids behind and overhead.

The best time to visit Giza is at dawn, when sunlight makes the area glow and you feel the power that overwhelmed even Napoleon. If you show up before the tourists arrive, you can try to climb the outside of the Great Pyramid. It's necessary to hire a guide to take you up; you must pay him again to take you back down. Although technically illegal, this is common practice.

The greatest pyramid

The tallest pyramid in Egypt, the **Pyramid of Cheops** (or the Great Pyramid), was finished in 2690 B.C. and stands 448 feet tall. It contains 2.3 million separate blocks of stone, each weighing 2.5 tons. Millions have visited and climbed Cheops, from French novelist Gustave Flaubert to a Parisian wallpaper manufacturer, who left an advertisement on the top.

Scientists believe that Cheops (or Khufu) built the pyramid for some reason besides pure ostentation. Theories that the ancient Egyptians knew the earth was round and calculated the circumference are supported by the pyramid. Measurements taken in the 1930s revealed that the proportions of the Great Pyramid are the same as the proportions of the earth's Northern Hemisphere. Scientists don't know whether this information was used in ancient navigation and astronomy, but it suggests an advanced culture.

The Grand Gallery of Cheops, with its 28-foot ceiling, is unusually devoid of decoration. It is one of the main reasons for the Great Pyramid controversy—it is the largest chamber in Cheops but contains absolutely nothing to suggest worship or religion.

The gallery leads to the King's Chamber, which contains the bottom half of the sarcophagus. (A lid was never found.) The king was never buried here, because the passages in the pyramid were too narrow for the sarcophagus to be brought in after the pyramid was completed.

The most beautiful pyramid

Next to Cheops is the **Pyramid of Chepren** (Khafre), Cheops' son. This pyramid is actually about 10 feet shorter than the Pyramid of Cheops, even though it seems taller because it's on higher ground. Its construction is not symbolic—only the Great Pyramid is thought to have any astronomical significance.

Chepren, however, is the most beautiful of the pyramids, because part of its limestone casing remains. The interior is spacious, and the ornate sarcophagus sinks into the floor up to its lid.

The least-crowded pyramid

The **Pyramid of Mycerinus** (Menkaure) is a 15-minute walk south of Cheops and Chepren. Because it is "only" 210 feet tall, it attracts relatively few tourists. Mycerinus, Chepren's son, began the pyramid about 2472 B.C. but died before the outermost stones were placed.

The world's oldest boat

Next to the northern face of Cheops is the museum housing the ***Solar Barque***, the oldest boat in the world. Discovered in 1954, the 128-foot-long boat is presumed to have been built to carry Cheops to the Underworld.

The boat's construction is ingenious. Its hull is made from hundreds of jigsawlike pieces of wood that were fitted and then sewn together with rope. When the hull was put into water, the wet wood swelled while the rope shrunk, creating a watertight fit.

The world's greatest riddle

Northeast of the Great Pyramid crouches the most famous statue on earth: the giant **Sphinx**. Carved out of a single ridge of rock, it has the head of a man and the body of a lion and measures 240 feet long and 66 feet high. The face is missing its nose and beard, because the statue was used for target practice during the Turkish Occupation in the 1700s.

Because it is commonly believed that the face of the Sphinx represents Chepren, some conclude that the statue is 4,500 years old. Other scientists, however, believe it is much older. Geologists have concluded that the severe erosion of the body could not have been caused by wind and sand. Water, they say, must have been the cause. Egypt was flooded at the end of the last Ice Age, about 10,000 B.C.; therefore, the Sphinx must have been built prior to that time, which is thousands of years before mankind is thought to have had tools.

The Sphinx continues to crumble—it recently lost a chunk of its shoulder. Scientists are debating how to save it. See it while you can.

Also explore the **Valley Temple of Chepren** at the foot of the Sphinx. The core contains limestone blocks, each weighing more than 100 tons; the method used to lift these huge blocks into place is unknown. The floors of the temple are made of slabs of alabaster. Though small, the temple is well-preserved, and its construction is unique in all Egypt.

The most romantic views

Perhaps the most romantic thing to do in Egypt is to ride Arabian horses around the pyramids at dusk. Two stables near the Sphinx rent and lease horses.

The hokiest show

At night you can attend a sound-and-light show on the Giza Plateau. The pyramids and Sphinx are illuminated as the narrator tells the story of Egypt. It's as hokey as you'd expect, but few people regret attending. The English shows are held at 6:30 p.m. Mondays, Wednesdays, and Fridays.

The best hotels in Giza

Most people stay in Cairo and visit the pyramids from there; however, waking up to see the Great Pyramid catch the first rays of dawn outside your window is a special pleasure.

The best hotel in Giza is the **Mena House Oberoi**, *Pyramids Road*, which is within walking distance of the pyramids. It was once a weekend palace for the Khedives, the Turkish viceroys who governed the area from 1867 to 1914, then a meeting place for Churchill and Roosevelt. Since 1973, it has been a luxury hotel. The management has kept the old wooden balconies and added air conditioning, restaurants, bars, and a swimming pool.

A less expensive hotel is the **Holiday Inn Sphinx**, *P.O. Box 45*. It sounds like a motel that has fake pyramids in every room, but it's actually the most reasonably priced place to stay in Giza. The rooms are new and pleasant, and almost every one has a view of the pyramids.

Saqqara: the world's oldest stone complex

Saqqara, a necropolis 24 miles south of Cairo, is the oldest stone complex in the world, dating back to 2611 B.C. Although they'd never before worked with stone on such a grand scale, the Egyptians created a masterpiece here. As Egyptologist John West put it, "Starting architecture off with Saqqara is like starting automobiles off with the 1984 Porsche." The complex was designed by the legendary Imhotep, an Egyptian Leonardo.

The most important sight at Saqqara is the **pyramid complex of King Zoser**, which contains the world's oldest pyramid. Predating the Great Pyramid by a century, the 200-foot **Step Pyramid** was built of six *mastabas* (traditional rectangular tombs) of diminishing size. Inside are religious inscriptions.

The complex often uses stonework to imitate organic material; the ceiling of the entranceway to Zoser, for example, simulates a roof of split logs. And the colonnade contains columns that look like they're made of papyrus stalks. (These may be the first stone columns built.) The colonnade leads into the Great Court, where Zoser and his successors ran races as part of a ritual physical fitness test called *heb-sed*.

To the south of the complex are the ruins of the **Pyramid of Unas**. The dilapidated outer stones make you wonder at the people waiting in line to get in. However, once you're inside, you'll understand—the interior is decorated with the finest hieroglyphic reliefs in Egypt. The **Pyramid Texts**, as they're known, tell the story of—and give advice concerning—the trip to the after-life. Carved delicately out of slabs of white alabaster, the outstanding hieroglyphs in the tomb chamber are highlighted in blue paint dating back to 2330 B.C.

Surrounding the Pyramid of Unas are shacks covering stairways to the Persian tombs. (During Persian rule, mummies were buried in shaft tombs to prevent robbery.) See the Tomb of Ti, with its unusual wall decorations, and the Serapium, an ornate monument where the Persians buried sacred cows.

You can catch a minibus in Cairo to take you to Abu Sir in Giza Square at 6 a.m.; it drops you off about a mile from Saqqara. Or you can take a taxi directly to the site.

Luxor: ancient Thebes and modern city

Built on the site of ancient Thebes, **Luxor** remains one of Egypt's most popular cities. As in most Egyptian cities, the grand sights here are crowded with natives looking to hustle naive tourists.

Ancient Thebes was the capital of Egypt during the Middle Kingdom, when Amon was the most popular of the Egyptian gods. Today the metro-politan area comprises the east bank (Luxor) and the west bank (Thebes). Luxor is small enough that you can see it on foot. The three main thorough-fares are Sharia Al-Mahatta, Sharia El-Nil, and Sharia Al-Karnak.

The most noble temple

The principal sight in Luxor is the **Temple of Karnak**. *Noble* is the only word that aptly describes this gigantic building. Its unusual design stems from its history: From the beginning of the Middle Kingdom until the time of Alexander the Great, each pharaoh added something new to the temple's architecture. A double row of ram-headed sphinxes guards the entrance to the Great Court, the temple's largest room, built about 1000 B.C.

Pass through the mighty outer pylon (an entranceway between two flat-tened pyramids) into the corner of the Great Court, which is surrounded by huge columns and flanked by the Triple Shrine of Amon on one side and the Temple of Ramses III on the other.

Continue on through Hypostle Hall, which features the Obelisk of Queen Hathsheput, carved from exquisite pink granite, and enormous columns that have been imitated in several Egyptian temples. Next is Transverse Hall, with 134 monolithic columns.

Pass the southern buildings and pylons to the sanctuary. Filled with carved reliefs covering the mammoth stone blocks, this is the heart of the Karnak Temple. Past this are rooms, sarcophagi, and a sacred lake that is overshadowed by an enormous stone scarab. Take an entire afternoon to appreciate this.

The most unusual temple

The Avenue of the Sphinxes (which, as its name suggests, is lined with sphinxes) leads from Karnak to the most unusual temple in Egypt: the **Temple of Luxor**. Built with virtually no right angles, Luxor's rooms are set crookedly against one another. Six giant statues of Ramses II mark the main doorway, which is cut into the 80-foot Pylon of Ramses. Carved reliefs on the pylon illustrate Ramses' battle with the Hittites (tribes from Asia Minor who battled Egypt for control of Syria). Beside the pylon is a huge granite obelisk, the twin of one that stands in the Place de la Concorde in Paris.

Inside the temple court is the **Mosque of Abu el-Haggag**, a small building contrasting oddly with the general splendor of the temple. You'll pass the Colonnade of Amenhotep III, with its 14 pillars, on your way to the Sanctuary of Alexander the Great, which contains bas-reliefs of Alexander worshiping Amon.

A banana best

In the late afternoon, take a felucca to **Banana Island**, a palm-studded islet three miles upriver from Luxor. Here you can indulge in all the oranges, lemons, and, of course, bananas you can eat for next to nothing.

Luxor's best hotels

One of the two best hotels in Luxor is **Hotel Etap Luxor**, *Corniche El-Nil Street*, where every room has a Nile view. The other best hotel is the **New Winter Palace**, *Corniche El-Nil Street*.

The **Luxor Hotel**, *Maabed El Karnak Street*, is cheaper. It's decorated with bizarre Egyptian art-deco prints.

Luxor's best restaurant

The best restaurant in town is **Mont Azza**, overlooking Luxor near the Winter Palace.

The greatest collection of tombs

Across the Nile, in **Thebes**, is the greatest collection of tombs on earth. You can reach the hills of the west bank from Luxor via two tourist ferries. Once in Thebes, your best bet is to hire a taxi. Or consider a donkey. Thebes is too big and too hot to visit on foot. A donkey is certainly slower than a taxi, but it is also less than half the cost and can take you through areas too narrow for cars. (Also, it's much more fun.) The trail from the Valley of the Queens over the ridges to the Valley of the Kings makes an especially memorable donkey trip.

The best way to see the Valley of the Kings

Some 64 rulers are buried in the **Valley of the Kings**. Because the locations of the graves were selected haphazardly, a little effort is needed to see the seven most impressive tombs in chronological order.

Begin with the **tomb of Tuthmosis III**, the walls of which are covered with the complete text of the *Book of the Duat*, the most important guide to the afterlife. Next is the **tomb of Amenhotep II**. The walls here are covered with glare-producing glass.

You can skip the famous **tomb of Tutankhamon**. Although its discovery in 1922 was front-page news (and the mysterious deaths of the exploration team started the Curse of the Mummy lore), it is the smallest and plainest of all the tombs—all the treasure was moved to the Cairo Museum. In addition, this tomb is always ridiculously overcrowded.

Next are the Ramses tombs. The **tomb of Ramses I** is followed by the **tomb of Seti I**, which is possibly the best-preserved on the west bank. The lower section of the burial chamber displays an incredible vaulted ceiling decorated with the 12 signs of the zodiac.

The **tomb of Ramses III** contains 10 unusual side chambers that show scenes from daily life (which are not found in other tombs). The artwork in the **tomb of Ramses VI** is more garish and fantastic than that in earlier tombs—Ramses VI ruled during the decadent 20th dynasty. This tomb also is noted for its ancient Greek and Coptic graffiti. One marking translates roughly as "Hermogines of Amasa was here."

The best of the Valley of the Nobles

The **Valley of the Nobles** is divided into five ticket regions. To see the best tombs, buy tickets 6, 7, and 8. The **tomb of Khaemet** has some of the best detail. The **tomb of Ramose** shows the radical departure Egyptian art took under Akhnaten. Reliefs show the pharaoh in scenes from family life, displaying affection, and showing his physical deformity.

The **tomb of Nakht** contains well-preserved paintings, some biographical, some inexplicable. The **tomb of Usheret** is notable for female figures, defaced by a Christian monk who lived in the burial chamber in the seventh century. The **tomb of Intefoger** has strangely insulting portraits. One shows an adult yelling at a child, "Your mother was a female hippopotamus!"

The Ramasseum

The **Colossi of Memnon**, two 70-foot statues, guard the **Temple of Ramses II**, also known as the Ramasseum. The temple contains the fallen Colossus of Ramses, which the poet Shelley described as "two vast and trunkless legs of stone, half sunk, a shattered visage." However, even the ruins are impressive—one ear measures three-and-a-half feet. The rest of the Ramasseum is in better condition, with relics depicting the Battle of Kadesh, astronomical charts, and rituals.

The tomb of the eight primordials

According to legend, beneath the **Temple of Medinet Habu**, which contains temples of Ramses III and Thutmose III, are buried the **eight primordials**—the Egyptian gods that existed before creation (as did the Greek gods Rhea and Kronos). Ramses' temple has pictures chiseled eight inches into the stone.

"The Most Splendid of All"

North of the Ramasseum is the cliffside **Temple of Hatsheput**, known in Arabic as **Deir El-Bahari**, which translates as "The Most Splendid of All." Considered one of the most important architectural wonders of the world, Deir El-Bahari is the only monument to have been built partly against the cliff and partly into it. This is also the only temple in Egypt, and the first building in history, made to blend with and complement the landscape.

Hatsheput (circa 1473 B.C.) was the only queen to dare crown herself pharaoh. The temple's broad walkway, the chapels to Anubis and Hathor, and the inscriptions here depict her descent from the god Amon.

Hathor: the magnificent temple

About 35 miles north of Luxor lies Dendera and the magnificent **Temple of Hathor** (the cow goddess and deity of healing), built about 200 B.C. A massive gate leads into the great courtyard of the temple, where the ceilings are decorated with the signs of the zodiac. Pass into the column-filled Hypostle Hall, the walls of which are covered with reliefs carved by priests seeking to preserve secret texts when Egyptian culture fell to the Roman Empire. The results are hieroglyphics so complex that archeologists cannot decipher them. A staircase leads to two rooftop chapels. One contains the famous circular zodiac.

The Mysterious Corridor surrounds the sanctuary, opening off into 11 chapels, one of which has a small opening in the floor that leads to the crypts. The purpose of this subterranean hallway is unknown, but its highly stylized reliefs are fascinating. If the crypts are closed, a guard will open them for you if you offer *baksheesh*.

Abu-Simbel: the most remote temple

At the far end of the Nile, 150 miles south of Aswan in the Nubian desert, is an awe-inspiring temple that seems to rise out of nowhere. Four 65-foot colossi of Ramses II guard the entrance to the structure, which was originally cut out of a cliff. Between and beside his legs are smaller statues of his queens and daughters.

As remarkable as the temple itself is the fact that it was taken apart and moved. In the 1960s, it was dissected stone by stone and moved by archeologists after they learned it would be flooded by the new High Dam at Aswan.

The still beautiful temple lost some of its magnitude with the move. Formerly, it was part of a cliff overlooking the roaring Nile. Today, it is set beside calm Lake Nasser.

Scientists took great pains to place the temple exactly as its original builders did so that during equinoxes the rising sun shines directly through the entrance, lighting statues 180 feet back in the sanctuary. Unfortunately, the statues have been badly mutilated. (No one knows by whom.)

Travel like Cleopatra

The best way to explore Egypt is aboard a **felucca**, the traditional sail-boat that glides along the Nile. Because the river cuts through most of Egypt's towns and villages, following it gives you a complete view of the country. As you bob along, you'll pass women doing wash in the river, fishermen pulling in their nets, and children playing along the river's bank.

Between Aswan, where most felucca journeys begin, and Luxor, where most of them end, the Nile passes many of Egypt's most important ancient monuments and temples. During this 140-mile sail, a felucca stops at one monument a day.

Of course, on a felucca journey, you must be prepared to rough it. Usually, you have no bathroom facilities—other than the Nile. And meals, while hearty and usually tasty, are prepared over a campfire. Your bed is on board, beneath the stars.

Spring and fall are the best times to sail. Be sure to bring sunscreen, a hat, toilet paper, and a flashlight. Women should not wear bikinis or skimpy bathing suits—they cause problems in an Islamic country. It takes about three weeks to cruise the entire length of the Nile. However, the Aswan-Luxor stint takes only about five days.

Feluccas can be cheap or expensive. Shop around, and don't be afraid to bargain.

Feluccas line the riverfront in Aswan and Luxor. Ask around on the waterfront at the Cataract Hotel in Aswan. Hotel clerks often can recommend a place to rent a boat. It is a good idea to get references.

Alexandria: the least Egyptian city

Alexandria was a very un-Egyptian city when it was founded by Alexander the Great in 330 B.C. It flourished as the cultural center of the world for 300 years, until the great library accidentally burned down during the reign of Julius Caesar, destroying more than a half-million irreplaceable manuscripts. Modern Alexandria is an international city, small and clean and known for its Greco-Roman relics and its sandy beaches.

The **Greco-Roman Museum**, *Sharia el-Mathaf*, houses a collection of artifacts from the days of Greek and Roman rule, including bas-reliefs, pottery, statues, jewelry, and marble pieces. Don't miss Room 9, which displays relics of the cult of the crocodile god Pnepheros, including a mummified crocodile. The museum is open daily except Fridays from 9 a.m. to 4 p.m.

At the western end of town are the **catacombs of Kom el-Shoqafa**, burial chambers carved into rock 100 feet below ground. Built in the second century for a wealthy family that still practiced the ancient religion, the catacombs represent the last burst of native Egyptian sacred art. However, because the artisans were trained in Italy, the Egyptian gods have unmistakably Roman bodies. Reliefs depict a Roman-style Osiris making an offering to the deceased. Lesser gods hold bunches of grapes and Medusa heads. One statue of Anubis is even dressed in Roman armor. The museum is open daily from 9 a.m. to 4 p.m.

Near Nasr Station is a beautifully preserved white marble **Roman amphitheater**, the only known Roman era amphitheater remaining in Egypt. Behind it lie a cistern and Roman bath. In 1963, when construction workers were building the foundation of an office building, the ruins were unearthed; archeologists continue to uncover artifacts here.

A relatively modern attraction in this ancient city of Alexandria is the 19th-century summer residence of the Egyptian royal family, the **Ras el-Tin Palace**. King Farouk forfeited its Throne Room, Gothic Hall, and Marble Hall when he abdicated in 1953 for a life of exile in Italy.

The **Fine Arts Museum**, *18 Menasha St.*, contains both a collection of modern Egyptian art and Alexandria's public library. Not far from the Mosque of Abul Abaas, along the corniche, it is the largest Islamic building in the city and has a beautiful courtyard. According to legend, the priest Abul Abaas rose from his tomb here to catch bombs falling on Alexandria during World War II.

At the western end of the corniche, where the Lighthouse of Pharos (one of the original Seven Wonders of the World) once stood, is the **Fort of Qait Bay**. Built by Sultan Bay in the 15th century from the remains of the lighthouse, the fort commands a sweeping view of Alexandria. Inside are a scale model of the 400-foot lighthouse and a naval museum.

The best case of mistaken identity

A 98-foot granite column erected in Alexandria in 297 A.D. was named **Pompey's Pillar** by Crusaders during the 13th century. Actually, the rose-colored column is a monument to the emperor Diocletian that was built by his troops. The most famous monument of ancient Alexandria, the pillar sits in a small public park on a hill where Diocletian once had a temple dedicated to the bull god Serapis.

The best way to get to Alexandria

Located 110 miles north of Cairo, bordering the Nile Delta, Alexandria can be reached easily by bus, plane, train, or car. Golden Rocket buses carry you between Cairo's Giza Square and Alexandria's Zaghloul Square. Make reservations if you plan to use the daily air-conditioned trains that travel between Cairo's Ramses Station and Alexandria's Masr Station. Shared taxis take the same route, but they cost more. EgyptAir's flight from Cairo departs daily.

The best dining in Alexandria

Alexandria has several excellent restaurants. **Morgan**, *El-Gueish Boulevard*, is an elegant seafood restaurant on the shore.

Lord's Inn, around the corner from the San Stefano Hotel, offers continental cuisine in a gourmet setting.

For the best Pakistani food outside Pakistan, try **Tikka Grill**, located on the water-front near the Abul Abaas Mosque.

Santa Lucia, *40 Safia Zaghoul St.*, is a good French restaurant. **Restaurant Elite**, *43 Safia Zaghoul St.*, has inexpensive pizza and strong espresso. Ignore the menu and opt for the daily specials, which are written on the wall.

Egypt's best seafood restaurant

For the best seafood in Egypt, drive to the small town of Abu Kir, about 10 miles east of Alexandria. Here, four blocks from the central mosque, on the waterfront, is a famous restaurant called **Zephyrion**. In business since 1929, Zephyrion has fresh fish, large salads, imported beer, and succulent shrimp.

Alexandria's best hotels

The best hotels in Alexandria are inexpensive. You won't have as great a choice as in Cairo, but you won't have to fight the crowds either.

The **Ramada Renaissance**, *544 El Gueish St., Sidi Bishr*, has a pool, great views, and air conditioning.

Two rival beachfront hotels are the **Sheraton Montazah**, *Corniche Road, El Montazah*, and the **Palestine**, *Kasr El Montazah*.

More modest accommodation can be had at **El Alamein**, *PLM Azur*. **Al Haram**, *162 El Gueish St., Cleopatra*, is in a nice old stone building.

It isn't wise to stay too cheaply in Egypt; budget hotels must be chosen carefully. However, we do recommend the **Hotel Marhaba**, *10 Orabi Square*. It's quiet and immaculate. Another cheap but acceptable place is **Hotel Leroy**, *25 Talaat Harb St.*, located on the top floors of an office building. Rooms are clean; some have breezy balconies.

Sinai: the most unusual landscape

Four wars have been fought between Israel and Egypt on the **Sinai Peninsula**. The southern Sinai Peninsula, with its high granite mountains and deep chasms, has some of the most unusual landscapes in the world. It's also the site of two popular beaches and one of the most famous mountains in history.

The Sinai is heavily militarized. Police want you to keep to the main roads, but you can obtain permission to visit parts of the desert interior with a Bedouin guide. (You might even catch a glimpse of military exercises.) The Sinai heat can be unbearable, sometimes reaching 110 degrees Fahrenheit.

Buses are the most affordable way to get to the Sinai. They depart Abassiya Station in Cairo for St. Catherine, Nuweiba, and Dahab. Most stop at Sharm El Sheikh, the southernmost town on the peninsula, where you won't find anything much to do or see.

A car allows you more flexibility when exploring the Sinai. The main roads are well-maintained, but the drive from Cairo to Nuweiba is a good seven hours—and you won't find anywhere to stop along the way for gas or water.

Flying is fastest and easiest. **Air Sinai**, *15 Kasr El Nil St.*, flies from Cairo to St. Catherine.

Dahab: a golden town

When the Israelis occupied this town, they named it **Zahav** (Gold). It is split into two parts: a terrific beach and a Bedouin village of thatched huts and palm trees. The beach is never crowded and almost always sunny. In town, you can rent scuba gear for exploring the coral reefs.

Villagers allow travelers to stay with them in their huts for as little as 30 Egyptian pounds ($5). This is a great way to get to know the people and to experience firsthand their lifestyle. But remember, the huts have neither toilets nor running water, and Bedouins are superstitious about having their pictures taken.

More luxurious accommodation is available at the **Dahab Holiday Village**, with air-conditioned beachfront rooms. The hotel restaurant also serves dinner.

Nuweiba: the best beach

Nuweiba, a tourist village about 10 miles north of Dahab, has an even better beach. That's good, because this town doesn't have much else to offer, and the nearby Bedouin villages don't invite visitors. The bus to Nuweiba lets you off at the tourist office.

You can rent scuba gear or sailing equipment at the Sailing Club. The best reefs are along the southern part of Nuweiba's beach. For more secluded diving, walk a quarter-mile south to what the locals call the Stone House.

Mount Sinai: the most commanding mountain

God gave Moses the Ten Commandments atop **Mount Sinai**, a remote mountain in the Sinai desert. A religious landmark, the mountain is dotted with tents and small chapels.

The most interesting and difficult route to the 7,000-foot peak that the Arabs call Gebal Musa is up the 3,500 **Steps of Repentance**, supposedly carved out by just one monk to fulfill his pledge of penitence. An easier way to reach the peak is to take the camel path that begins directly behind the monastery. When the path and steps meet, look down at the 500-year-old cypress tree that marks Elijah's Hollow, where the prophet Elijah heard the voice of God. (There are now two chapels in the hollow.) At the mountain's summit is a small church, usually surrounded by dozens of tourists and pilgrims in sleeping bags.

You, too, can bring a sleeping bag and sleep on the mountain (but remember—it gets chilly). When you awaken, you'll see both Africa and Asia from the peak.

More comfortable places to stay include the monastery's hostel and **St. Catherine Salam**, a hotel in town. A national tourist office is located in this hotel.

A Byzantine best

At the base of Mount Sinai is **St. Catherine's Monastery**, the oldest unrestored Byzantine complex in the world. Emperor Justinian had it built in 342 A.D. on the site of the Burning Bush, where God first recruited Moses to lead the Hebrews out of Egypt.

Fortresslike walls protect St. Catherine's Monastery (named after the saint martyred in Alexandria). Inside are jewel-studded crosses, hand-carved furniture, and the Chapel of the Burning Bush. The monastery's library contains enough early Christian manuscripts to rival the Vatican, and the marvelous mosaic of the *Transfiguration of Christ* is one of the great treasures of early sacred painting. Don't miss the Ossary, a separate building containing the bones of all the monks who have died at St. Catherine's over the centuries.

The best snorkeling in the Middle East

The best snorkeling in the Middle East is at **Yemenieh Reef**, off Aqaba, a Jordanian town just across the gulf from Nuweiba. Here, you can see 40 kinds of coral not found anywhere else in the world. Scuba and skin divers commonly cross the gulf to Aqaba (captured from the Turks in 1917 by the legendary Lawrence of Arabia), which has beautiful beaches and an excellent aquarium in its Marine Research Center. Ferries depart daily from Nuweiba for Aqaba at 11 a.m. and 3 p.m. You'll need a passport, of course, to make the crossing.

The **Nuweiba Holiday Village**, near the ferry terminal, has comfortable lodgings.

Hurghada: Egypt's best coral reefs

The sleepy little town of **Hurghada**, which lies 240 miles south of Suez and about 350 miles from Cairo, is one of the best places in the world for unspoiled scuba and snorkeling expeditions. The coral reefs here are the most beautiful in Egypt, and dozens of boats are available to take you to any one of the tiny reef islands. At Giftun El Saghir, a small island off Hurghada, the water is so clear that you can see 100 feet down to the rocky bottom. At the offshore island of **Shaab Um Qamar**, divers sometimes catch lobsters at night with their bare hands.

Everything in Hughada centers around two landmarks: **Al-Dhar Mosque** and **Ugly Mountain**, which is, indeed, ugly. Hurghada is a good place to fish; it is teeming with barracuda, swordfish, sailfish, and tuna. You can rent bikes for a few dollars a day from a shop just north of the Al-Dhar Mosque. And about two miles north of that is the Red Sea Museum, which has a large collection of sea life, including sharks and sea lions.

The most comfortable place to stay in Hurghada is the **Hurghada Sheraton**, *48 B Giza St., Oman Tower Building*, which has air-conditioned double rooms.

What the cheaper places lack in air conditioning they make up for in personality. At **Hurghada Happy House**, between the Al-Dhar Mosque and the main avenue, Captain Muhammed Awad tells the best fishing stories in town. The captain will take you on his boat to the House of Sharks, a reef pulsating with lionfish, sharks, eels, and other sea creatures.

Tips on baksheesh

Baksheesh is a way of life in Egypt. Although only a minority of Egyptians pester foreigners, those who do, expect *baksheesh* for the slightest things—opening a door, for example—and even more *baksheesh* for doing nothing. In a bazaar, you will be followed by a half-dozen children with outstretched palms.

You should always travel with a pocketful of loose change and one-pound notes. However, give *baksheesh* only for services rendered.

Two useful terms concerning *baksheesh* are *Shukran* (Thanks) and *Emshee!* (Get lost!).

THE BEST OF MOROCCO

Morocco is a land of casbahs, veiled women with painted toenails, belly dancers, minarets, and ancient *souks*. Its ancient cities have modern European sections, with tree-lined avenues, Parisian boutiques, sidewalk cafés, and luxury hotels. But each also has a *medina*, or old quarter, where you must navigate your way through a maze of narrow, twisting, cobblestoned steets, arabesque archways, and cluttered bazaars.

Tangier—Morocco's port city

The port of **Tangier** on the country's northwestern tip attracts French, German, British, American, and especially Spanish travelers, who come via the hovercrafts that make daily trips between Tangier and Gibraltar and southern Spain. Its commanding position on the Straits of Gibraltar has made it a strategic military state, coveted by everyone from the Phoenicians to modern-day Spanish, British, French, and Germans. In 1923, Tangier was declared an international zone. In 1957, it became part of Morocco. Ask anyone who knows Morocco well, however, and he will tell you that Tangier is not Morocco. Its customs and culture, which retain vestiges of all those who have invaded it over the centuries, are too diverse to be truly Moroccan.

In addition to cafés, where Arabs and tourists alike sit for hours over cups of strong black coffee or sweet mint tea, Tangier has miles of uncrowded, golden beaches fringed by the Mediterranean to the north and the Atlantic to the west.

The legendary Garden of Hesperides, Tangier was once a haven for black marketeers and smugglers. Today, because of its low income tax and favorable climate, it has become a refuge for the world's wealthiest citizens.

The best marketplace

Tangier's casbah, or walled fortress, is very much the center of life here. It is built on the highest point of the city and juts up against the *medina*. You can reach it from the **Bab el Assa**, at the end of Rue Ben Raisouli in the *medina*. The white arched gateway into the casbah leads to an open court-yard called **Tabor Square**, which leads to Dar al Makhzen, the former sultan's palace (now a museum).

The casbah is really a huge marketplace. It is packed with people—vendors, shoppers, tourists. It is noisy. And it is filled with the smells of mint, spices, fresh camel meat, and fruits and vegetables.

The best place to stay

A relaxing and intimate place to stay in Tangier is **El Minzah Tangier**, *85 Rue de la Liberte*.

The best castles

On the outskirts of the city are the splendid villas of Gianni Agnelli (Italy's Fiat magnate) and the late Malcom Forbes.

The late dime-store heiress Barbara Hutton lived for years in a storybook palace tucked away in a corner of the mysterious casbah. The palace has been made a museum and is one of the city's major attractions.

The most magnificent city

Rabat, the present-day capital of Morocco, is home to one of the magnificent palaces of King Hassan II. Its entrances are protected by the personal guard of the royal family. You can see the full splendor of the guard on Friday morning, the Muslim holy day. It escorts the king, who rides in a gilded coach drawn by four white horses, across the palace grounds to the mosque. The weekly ritual is a dramatic reminder that King Hassan is not only the head of state but also the religious leader of the country.

Ancient Fez

The old walled city of **Fez**, wrapped in a pink fog, is four hours by car from Rabat. Founded in A.D. 800, Fez is a renowned religious center. For 11 centuries, it was the epitome of cultural, artistic, and religious life in Morocco.

The *souk* of the woodcarvers in Fez is filled with the pleasant scent of cedar. Not so the *souk* of the tanners. Here, young men in short pants, standing thigh-high in steaming cauldrons of red, yellow, and purple dye, leap from vat to vat, dipping, pulling, and kneading the sodden camel, goat, and sheepskin pelts in the noxious liquids.

The world's oldest university

Karaouine University, which dates to A.D. 859, is the oldest university in the world. Today it is a mosque that attracts Muslims in droves. They believe that seven pilgrimages to Karaouine are the spiritual equivalent of one trip to Mecca.

The best place to stay

The best place to stay in Fez is the **Palais Jamai**, *Bab El Guissa*, a former sultan's palace located at the entrance to the bustling *medina*. It is one of Morocco's most luxurious hotels. Lavish tile murals, fine cuisine, and an unbeatable situation above the city combine to produce an extraordinary hotel in a former 19th-century palace.

The biggest palace

Mekès, less than 40 miles from Fez, is home to the sultan's gigantic palace, complete with storerooms, gardens, military barracks, and stables. At the beginning of the 18th century, this unbelievable complex housed the court and the imperial family of 600 wives and 1,500 children, as well as at least 50,000 slaves, servants, and eunuchs. The stables accommodated 12,000 horses, each with its own stall and valet. All this splendor is now mostly in ruins, destroyed by an earthquake in 1755.

The most imperial city

The imperial city of **Marrakech** was chosen by the sultans as capital of the 1,200-year-old Sheriffien Empire, which stretched from Spain to Timbuktu. Founded on the arid Haoux plain in the 11th century, Marrakech was a caravansary, a major port of call on the Sahara desert for camel caravans that linked Ghana with Fez and Algiers.

Today Marrakech is a city of brownish-pink houses, towering ramparts, and graceful minarets. This capital city boasts a dry, warm climate, luxurious hotels, colorful marketplaces, and an old walled quarter.

The liveliest spot in town

The heart of Marrakech is a vast public square adjacent to the *medina* known as **Djemma El Fna**, or Place of the Dead, which is in fact the liveliest spot in town. Long ago, the sultans displayed the heads of criminals and enemies defeated in battle around this huge square. Today it is filled with bazaars where you can shop for almost anything.

But more than a market, Djemma is the largest outdoor show in all North Africa. Storytellers, mimes, medicine men, sword swallowers, male belly dancers, and snake charmers perform for the crowds, each competing for the small coins that spectators toss in appreciation.

The most colorful festival

One of the most striking spectacles in the Arab world takes place in Marrakech in June. The **National Folklore Festival**, which draws visitors from all over the world, is held amid the red-ochre ruins of the El Badii Palace.

The performers in the National Folklore Festival are not professionals. They are villagers, country people from the Sahara desert and the Atlas Mountains who have been selected by the festival directors to take part in the two-week extravaganza.

For the performances, the stage is covered with layers of intricately woven Moroccan carpets spread to create an *Arabian Nights* setting. On either side of the stage, huge striped tents are set up to house the performers waiting their turn. In the foreground, separating the stage from the audience, is the outer edge of a rectangular pool, where, centuries ago, sultans frolicked with their harem favorites.

The performances begin suddenly, with lines of colorfully garbed dancers surging forward from both sides of the stage, their shoulders twitching to the beat of the drums. Soon, the desert air is filled with their songs and hypnotic chants. Spotlights accentuate the splendid costumes and coined headpieces and necklaces. All the images are reflected in the pool.

Black dancers from the Sahara dressed in white pantaloons and red vests leap and whirl frantically to the rhythm of the shrill reed flutes. They are

The World's Best Destinations

followed by barefooted acrobats in green trousers, who somersault high in the air as cymbals crash. The stage seems to explode with motion and song.

The best mint teas

Mint, in Moroccan, means *hospitality*. No guest gets away from a Moroccan household without several glasses of hot mint tea. Actually a mixture of green tea, anisette, vervain, marjoram, and mint, the tea is made according to strict rules. First, two to three teaspoons of green tea are placed in a pot. The pot is held high to aerate the tea, which is then served in tiny glasses. Guests must, according to custom, have three glasses.

One of the best places for tea in Marrakech is the **Dar Marjana**, *15 Derb Ettir, Ang Bab Doukkada*. And tea is served with formality in the ornate courtyard of the elegant **Arab Palace**.

The best silver factory in Morocco

Situated south of Agadir, along a caravan crossroads in south Morocco, is **Tiznit**. This tiny town is best known for its silver jewelry, which is made by local Berbers from the silver mined nearby.

The rooms in what the townspeople refer to as their "silver factory" are filled with handmade silver jewelry, serving trays, pots, and trinkets. In the front of the rooms sit small boys, apprentices who work in the factory in the morning and go to school in the afternoon. Expect to haggle, but you'll end up with good silver at cheap prices.

The tiny, muddy passageways that make up Old Town are crowded with street vendors offering rugs, pottery, jewelry, and spices. Everything is for sale. (Nothing is refrigerated.)

THE BEST OF ALGERIA

Algeria, Africa's second-largest country, is a sea of sand drifts. It is also a place where anything Western is in high demand; Algerians are willing to pay handsomely for Western goods of all kinds. The chief black market commodity is whiskey; you can resell a bottle of whiskey for six times your purchase price.

There is still a definite discrimination against women in Algeria; men eat at the table, while women cook and remain in the kitchen, for example. Change is coming slowly here, giving travelers a rare opportunity to experience a centuries-old culture.

The most fundamentalist town

In the very fundamentalist town of **Ghardaïa**, the few women on the streets are clothed and veiled from head to foot. They have one eyehole, through which they peer cautiously. Ghardaïa is the most prosperous town in the country and is inhabited, as it has been for more than 900 years, by the Mozabites, a strict Muslim sect that broke from the mainstream of Islam in the seventh century. The people use the same underground irrigation canals, live in the same cubelike houses, and worship in the same mysterious mosques as did their ancestors.

The world's biggest sandpile

The golden sand in the west is called the **Grand Erg Occidental**. Its white counterpart in the east is called the Grand Erg Oriental. Erg can be translated as "sand sea" or "desert of sand dunes." Either way, you get the idea. The vastness of it all will overwhelm you at times.

The best way to see Algeria

The **Trans-Algerian Highway** is the only road that crosses Algeria from border to border. It passes through the Sahara desert and covers the 1,100 miles from Morocco to Tunisia. The Highway is well-maintained. Gas stations are adequately spaced along the road. (But don't ever pass one without filling up.) Spare auto parts are a rare commodity, however, so carry with you anything you think you might need.

The greatest attraction of traveling the highway is the chance it gives you to see the Sahara desert. Great sand dunes, with ridges perfectly carved by the wind, seem to go on forever, dwarfing the occasional camel train or group of palm trees.

A best for horse lovers

Horse lovers can spend two weeks in the saddle in Algeria. Riding is English-style, luggage is carried by a support car, and nights are spent at hotels, inns, private homes, or camps. Most tours involve four to six hours of riding a day. The best tours are arranged by an American company, **FITS Equestrian**, *685 Latten Road, Solvang, CA 93463*.

THE BEST OF AUSTRALIA

The world's oldest and smallest continent, Australia offers something for everyone. Nature lovers are fascinated by the Outback, with its rugged terrain and unusual animals. Divers explore the Great Barrier Reef, the largest coral reef in the world, stretching 1,260 miles along Australia's northeast coast. This coast is also the place to enjoy the world's best surfing. Sydney and Melbourne have big-city restaurants, nightlife, and shopping. And enormous cattle stations cover the interior of the country.

Australia is the world's most isolated country. Because of this, animals, birds, insects, and plants unknown to the rest of the world have evolved here. Nowhere else will you see kangaroos and koala bears, for example. Also because of the country's isolation, the aborigines, who have one of the most intriguing and ancient cultures in the world, were able to continue their way of life—living in harmony with nature—for thousands of years before Europeans arrived. Still largely uninhabitable and unexplored, this continent's vast desert heartland, known as the **Red Centre**, is made up of four great deserts that together occupy 1.2 million square miles.

Australia was formed when Europe and North America were still evolving. The last great geological shifts here took place 230 million years ago. However, some places in Australia date back 1 billion years. Ancient artifacts are stored in the **Great Western Plateau**, in the heart of Australia. A rock found near Marble Bar contained the remains of 3.5 billion-year-old organisms, the oldest forms of life yet discovered. And a dinosaur left his footprint in the rock near Broome.

Only slightly more than 15 million people live in this area roughly the size of the continental United States. Yet this is one of the most highly urbanized nations in the world—almost 85% of all Australians live in or around the cities. Furthermore, Australia boasts one of the world's highest standards of living.

✴SYDNEY: THE NUMBER-ONE SIGHT

Sydney—a huge city sprawling across 670 square miles—is the largest, oldest, and most cosmopolitan city in Australia. It is also naturally beautiful, built around a harbor and cradled by the fabulous "Blue Mountains."

Light-colored buildings and red-tile roofs stand out against the blue water and sky. Flowers bloom year-round. And the ocean laps at 150 miles of shoreline.

Life revolves around the harbor and the sea, where thousands of boats vie for space. Scantily clad sun worshipers flock to the city's 30-odd beaches, where topless bathing is the norm. (Three beaches also allow nude bathing.) But Sydney's beaches are never as packed as those at U.S. resorts.

During the Australian summer (from November through February), the city is hot and the humidity is suffocating—which is fine if you intend to spend all your time on the beach but uncomfortable if you are want to explore the city. Sydney's many hills, combined with the heat, are hard on visitors who aren't familiar with the transport system. However, during the winter, Sydney is mild and pleasant.

The summer heat brings Sydneyites outdoors and forces them to shed their clothes. At night, the inner streets of Sydney are overflowing with people, who eat outdoors and often party on until dawn.

The best view of Sydney

The best view of Sydney is from the 48th-floor, glassed-in skywalk at the **Australia Square Tower**. You'll be able to see the entire city, the Blue Mountains, and Botany Bay. What's more, the tower (which isn't square but round, constructed of steel, cement, and glass) has the fastest elevators in the Southern Hemisphere.

While you are in the building, stop off at the sixth-floor **Opal Skymine**, where you can see films about life in the Australian opal mines and supposedly buy gems at field prices.

If you can afford it, lunch at the **Summit Restaurant**, on the 47th floor, the largest revolving restaurant in the world. Needless to say, the view is superb—even if the fare isn't.

The best way to see Sydney

The **Sydney Pass** is the best bargain for sightseeing in Sydney. The pass allows you three days of unlimited use of the Sydney Explorer bus, the harbor shuttle, three different harbor cruises, all other Sydney ferry services, all Sydney buses, and the airport express bus.

The world's most unusual opera house

When work began on Sydney's ultramodern winged **opera house** in 1957, local residents, who called it the New South Whale and the Operasaurus, said it wouldn't fly. Much to its critics' chagrin, the opera house turned out to be the most beautiful in the world, praised from London to Hong Kong.

Designed by Danish architect Joern Utzon, the A$102 million ($80 million) structure on Bennelong Point, surrounded by Sydney's harbor, is topped by interlocking wing-shaped roofs that glitter with more than one million Swedish ceramic tiles. The acoustics are the best in the world.

Take a tour of the building to see the treated timber panels, the tinted glass through which you have a view of the harbor, and the bright blue curtains. The opera house has a total of 980 rooms, four of which are performance halls, where concerts, operas, ballets, plays, and recitals are held. Rock'n'roll groups perform as well as symphony orchestras. Tours are available from 9 a.m. until 4 p.m. Book through **Visitor's Services**.

Sydney's oldest quarter

The **Rocks**, a renovated area on the west side of Circular Quay, was notorious for its rough residents in the mid-1800s. Convicts, sailors, prostitutes, soldiers, whalers, and gangsters gathered on this rocky ridge, known as the Cradle of Sydney. For a map of the no-longer-seedy area, visit the **Information Center**, *104 George St.*, near the Overseas Passenger Terminal.

At the heart of The Rocks is **Argyle Place**, a peaceful park surrounded by pastel houses dressed with wrought-iron grills and balconies. The **Church of the Holy Trinity**, better known as the Garrison Church, was built in 1840. The second-oldest church in Sydney, it is the earliest example of Gothic architecture in Australia, with Gothic arches, mullioned windows, and a red cedar pulpit.

Sydney's oldest house, **Cadman's Cottage**, built in 1816, is just off Argyle Street. Circular Cove once came nearly to the door of this little homestead, built by John Cadman, superintendent of government boats.

The **Argyle Arts Centre**, *18 Argyle St.*, was built in 1820 by convicts as a three-story warehouse. Today the sandstone building houses craft shops and antique stores. Notice the hand-hewn timber. (Convict labor came cheap.) You can buy hand-blown glass, beeswax candles, and pottery here. The center is open from 10 a.m. until 5:30 p.m.

From Argyle Street, take the **Argyle Cut**, a dank 300-foot tunnel hollowed out of solid stone by prisoners 140 years ago. It leads to Miller's Point.

The best picnicking

The best places to get away from the cement and steel that make up Sydney are the **Domain** and the **Botanic Gardens**, separated from each other by a highway. The Domain is a park with an emerald lawn perfect for picnics and naps on Sunday afternoons. Soapbox orators harangue crowds here with their personal views of the world. The Botanic Gardens are known for their exotic flora, including giant Moreton Bay fig trees and hothouses filled with orchids and ferns.

Australia's best art gallery

Near the Botanic Gardens is the **Art Gallery of New South Wales**, *Art Gallery Road*, divided into two sections, one housing Renaissance to 20th-century art, the second housing Impressionist and modern works. The new

Australia   447

wing, with its angled white walls and views of the harbor, is more attractive. Look for works by Australian artists William Dobell, Sidney Nolan, and Russell Drysdale. The gallery is open Mondays through Saturdays 10 a.m. until 5 p.m. and Sundays noon until 5 p.m.

The Southern Hemisphere's best private gallery

Holdsworth Galleries, *86 Holdsworth St.*, is the biggest art gallery south of the equator, with a great collection of contemporary Australian artists that changes every three weeks. Among the displays are paintings and sculptures by Sidney Nolan, Sali Herman, Margaret Olley, and Arthur Boyd. The gallery is as lovely as the works it contains. Admission is free. It is open daily until 5 p.m.

The world's most beautifully situated zoo

Taronga Zoo and Aquarium, on a peninsula jutting into Mosman Bay, has the most beautiful setting of any zoo in the world. It offers a view of the harbor (**Taronga** means *water view* to the aborigines) and 75 acres of bush-land. Among other strange creatures, you can see koala bears, emus, platypuses, dingoes, kookaburras, and wombats. A special underground part of the zoo houses nocturnal animals, which you can see under red light. The rain forest aviary is also worth seeing. The zoo is open 9 a.m. until 5 p.m.

The worst prison

Fort Denison, on a little island in the harbor, was known as Pinchgut among Australia's early convicts, because of the starvation rations meted out here. The fort was never actually used to protect Sydney, although that was its original purpose when it was built in 1857. You can still see cannons and cannonballs in the round Martello Tower, which is used as a tidal observation station. Tours of the fort depart Wharf Two on Circular Quay three times a day Tuesdays through Sundays.

The best times to visit

Each year, Sydney hosts a number of different festivals. The entire month of January is one big festival, with plays, exhibitions, operas in the parks, sailboat races, and food and wine fairs. Then come the Royal Sydney Easter Show, which is a huge country fair with animal exhibitions; Royal Gardens Week; Carnivale; and the Blessing of the Fishing Fleet. And don't miss the Gay Mardi Gras, one of the biggest gay festivals held anywhere in the world.

Sydney's favorite pastimes

Surfing (which many schools teach as a physical-education course) and windsurfing are the two passions of Sydneyites. A sign on trains admonishes, "Surfers, be considerate. Don't block aisles with your boards."

Australia's best restaurant

Outside Sydney is the **Berowra Waters Inn**, *Berowra Waters*, the finest restaurant in Australia. Chef Gay Bilson produces innovative Australian dishes. Unfortunately, you can't get here by road; you must fly or take a boat.

The restaurant is open for lunch Friday through Sunday and for dinner Friday and Saturday.

Sydney's best dining bets

Sydney's best restaurant is **Oasis Seros**, *495 Oxford St., Paddington*, a simple but stylish place that serves light food made from fresh ingredients. The china, crystal, and cutlery are elegant, and an enormous bouquet of flowers adorns the mantelpiece.

A small Italian restaurant known as **No Name**, *81 Stanley St.*, has delicious food, an unpretentious atmosphere, and low prices. It's located in a little house on Chapel Street, a short street in East Sydney near the intersection of Crown and Stanley streets.

The best place for seafood is **Doyle's on the Beach**, *11 Marine Parade, Watson's Bay*. Enormous plates full of battered fish are served. And the setting is lovely—a sandy beach lined with little boats. The only drawback is that the restaurant's charms are known, and it's crowded.

Also at Watson's Bay is the **Fisherman's Lodge**, a pleasant restaurant housed in a 19th-century mansion. The **Endeavor at Mosman**, across the Harbor Bridge, is in an old ship.

Bellevue Hotel, *159 Hargrave*, in Paddo, has a back-garden barbecue and live entertainment.

Sydney's top hotels

Sydney's finest hotel is the **Regent**, *199 George St*. Overlooking the opera house and the harbor, it has luxurious rooms and an attentive staff. In the United States, make reservations through **Leading Hotels of the World**, *tel. (800)223-6800*.

Three close seconds are the **Sheraton-Wentworth**, the **Inter-Continental**, *117 Macquarie St.*, and the **Parkroyal Hotel**.

Outside the business district, near King's Cross, is the discreet and elegant **Sebel Town House**, *23 Elizabeth Bay Road, Elizabeth Bay;* (also represented by Leading Hotels of the World). This place is popular among celebrities, whose signed photographs paper the walls at the bar.

Another attractive small hotel is the **Russell**, *143a George St.*, where Rachel Ward stays when she's in town.

The hottest nightlife

Although Sydney's drinking laws are strict, the local residents manage to have a rowdy good time anyway. Bars close at 11 p.m. during the week, and after midnight on weekends and holidays (depending on the area). But many Sydneyites belong to private clubs, where you can get beer into the wee hours of the morning. The clubs often have live shows, slot machines, and food.

Sydney's chic set—good-looking models, visiting rock stars, and well-dressed socialites—makes a point of being seen at **Arthur's Bar and Restaurant**, *155 Victoria St., Potts Point;* **The Cauldron**, *207 Darlinghurst Road, Darlinghurst;* and the **Freezer**, *11 Oxford St., Paddington.*

If you'd like to barhop but don't want to drive or risk getting lost, go to the **Holiday Inn Menzies**, *14 Carrington St.,* where 20 pubs share one roof. Each has its own character and clientele, from snooty and expensive to cheap and blue-collar.

The liveliest neighborhood at night is **King's Cross**, a combination of Greenwich Village and red-light district, where Darlinghurst, Potts Point, and Elizabeth Bay meet. Darlinghurst Road and Macleay Street are the main thoroughfares. Sydney's best bar is here, the **Bourbon and Beefsteak**, *Darlinghurst Road.* The piano bar provides entertainment in the early evening, and jazz combos jam later on.

Sydney's oldest pub is in the **Hero of Waterloo Hotel**, *81 Lower Fort St.,* in The Rocks. Built in 1804 as a jail, it became a rousing pub in the rip-roaring 1800s. Today it is a peaceful place to have a drink while sitting beside a fireplace.

The **Manzil Room**, *15 Springfield Ave., King's Cross*, has live music until dawn all week.

The bluest mountains

The **Blue Mountains** really are a vivid blue. Oil released by the mountains' eucalyptus trees reflects the blue light rays of the sun on these saw-toothed peaks, just 50 miles from Sydney. Head for **Katoomba**, where you can take the Scenic Railway, the steepest in the world, up the mountains. Or you can ride the Scenic Skyway, a cable car dangling above a deep chasm. Nearby are the enormous Jenolan Caves and the giant waterfall at Govett's Leap, near Blackheath.

The world's most imaginative water festival

Surf Carnivals are hosted by the Surf Lifesaver's Association; they are perhaps the world's most imaginative water festivals. Not only do the macho members of the Surf Club compete in paddling wooden boats against a crashing surf, diving for plastic batons, and squatting on surfboards while hand paddling their way across the finish line, but the senior members of the Lifesavers Association, in units of 12, are judged for posture, pace, and unity. For more information, contact the **Surf Lifesavers Association of Australia**, *128 The Grand Parade, Brighton-le-Sands, New South Wales 2216.*

✳ CAPITAL CANBERRA

Canberra, the national capital, is a city planner's dream. Designed to function expressly as Australia's capital, it is free of traffic and unsightly shopping malls. At its heart is a large man-made lake. Throughout the city are parks, and the broad avenues are lined with trees. An American named Walter Burley Griffin designed the city in 1913, after winning an international competition for the job. However, Australia's parliament didn't actually meet here until 1927.

While it is not on the coast and doesn't have sunny beaches, Canberra is fast becoming an artistic and intellectual enclave. It boasts the new National Gallery, one of the finest art museums in Australia, and great restaurants and bars.

Canberra's top sights

The city's best-known landmark is the Captain Cook Memorial Water Jet, which shoots six tons of water 450 feet into the air from 10 a.m. to noon and 2 p.m. to 4 p.m. every day. Part of the fountain is a nine-foot globe illustrating the routes followed by Captain Cook. ✳

More important, however, is the **Australian War Memorial**, on Anzac Parade, a beautiful structure honoring the 100,000 Australians who died fighting in the world wars. Bronze panels inscribed with their names cover two enormous walls. The memorial contains excruciatingly realistic paintings of the wars, as well as old biplanes, tanks, and bombs. The **Australian ✳ National Gallery**, on the shores of the lake, has an outstanding collection of works by both Australians and foreigners. It also has a good restaurant with a lovely view of the lake. The memorial is open daily.

Canberra's **carillon** is one of the largest in the world, with 53 bells, the largest weighing more than six tons. A gift from Britain, the tall white pillar stands at the northern end of the Kings Avenue Bridge. Recitals are given on Sundays and Wednesdays.

The **Institute of Anatomy** on the campus of the Australian National University has a good museum illustrating the culture of the aborigines and the natives of New Guinea.

The **Botanic Gardens**, *Clunies Ross Street*, is a maze of footpaths and bridges that guide you over little ponds and through gardens with carefully labeled Australian plants and flowers.

For a glimpse of Australia's early pioneer life, visit **Blundell's Farmhouse**, *Wendouree Drive*, off Constitution Avenue. Built in 1858, the cottage's three rooms are filled with pioneer furnishings. It is open from 2 p.m. until 4 p.m. daily and 10 a.m. until noon on Wednesdays.

Twenty-five miles southwest of Canberra is the 12,000-acre **Tidbinbilla Nature Reserve**, where you can see local flora and fauna and feed the kangaroos. This unspoiled bushland is open daily from 9 a.m. to 6 p.m.

The best eating and sleeping

Charlie's, *Bunder Street*, is an elegant restaurant with French cuisine and especially good soups. Politicians eat here when Parliament is meeting.

Rascals, *33 Petrie Plaza*, is a restaurant with the atmosphere of a disco. A good place for after-theater supper, it stays open until 2 a.m. The decor is pleasant, with low ceilings and stained-glass windows. Prices are moderate.

Gus's Café, *Bunda Street*, is a tiny place with a pleasant outdoor terrace surrounded by flower boxes. You can linger over a meal here, reading Gus' selection of magazines and newspapers. Save room for the cheesecake, which is out of this world.

Tall Trees, *21 Stephen St., Ainslie*, two miles from Canberra, is an inviting lodge named for the tall trees that surround it. All rooms have views of the gorgeous gardens and are supplied with electric blankets. (It gets cold here during the winter.) The lodge has a laundry room and a lounge with a television and tea-making equipment.

Chelsea Lodge, *526 Northbourne Ave.*, is a bed-and-breakfast in a villa with a pleasant veranda. Breakfast is good. All rooms have televisions; two have private bathrooms.

✳ THE BEST OF MELBOURNE

Melbourne rivals Sydney as Australia's most attractive city. Both coastal cities have three million residents. However, Melbourne is more of a European city and offers more cultural opportunities than Sydney; it also has fewer tourists and lower prices.

Melbourne's weather is less pleasant than Sydney's. It rains more frequently, and winters can be grim, drizzly, and gray, without the excitement of snow. While Sydney's beauty is natural, Melbourne's is man-made. Because it is a planned city, Melbourne's road network forms a grid pattern, making travel within the city easy. The city's architecture is sophisticated, especially along wide and gracious **Collins Street**, the banking capital of Australia. Lush parks and the Yarra River add greenery to the cityscape.

Although Melbourne was founded in 1835 by a group of Tasmanian entrepreneurs, it didn't actually take off until 1851, when it became the center of Australia's biggest and longest gold rush. A product of the time, Melbourne is mostly Victorian in appearance.

Melbourne's must-sees

The National Museum, the Museum of Science, the state library, and LaTrobe Library are combined in one huge, interconnected complex between Swanston and Russell streets. The strangest sight in the entire complex is the stuffed body of a well-loved Australian racehorse, Phar Lap, who died a mysterious and shady death in the United States. Also look for Australia's first car and first airplane.

Melbourne's creepiest sight is the **Old Melbourne Gaol**, *Russell Street*. Built in 1841, it was used as a prison until 1929. More than 100 prisoners were hanged here. The somber building is now a museum, with death masks of notorious criminals and records of the early convicts transported to Australia from Britain. (Some were exiled for incredibly minor crimes.)

The **National Gallery**, housed in the Cultural Centre Complex on St. Kilda Road, has a good art collection and exhibits from overseas. The Great Hall has a beautiful stained-glass ceiling, and fountains fill the central courtyard. The gallery is closed Mondays.

King's Domain is an enormous park that houses the Shrine of Remembrance, a World War I memorial; Governor LaTrobe's cottage, the original Victorian government house prefabricated and sent from England; and the Sidney Myer Music Bowl, an outdoor concert hall.

The **Royal Botanic Gardens**, also within King's Domain, are the most beautiful in Australia. Laid out beside the Yarra River, they include lakes, a rainbow of flowers, and a surprising number of wild animals, including water fowl, cockatoos, and possums. You can have tea and scones by the lake.

The best bets for fitness freaks

On weekends, you can rent a bicycle at the Botanical Gardens or Como Park and then bike the trail along the Yarra River.

If canoeing is more your style, you can rent a canoe or a rowboat at Studley Park in Kew. The **Studley Park Boathouse** is open from 9:30 a.m. until 5:30 p.m.

The best place to jog is the two-and-a-half-mile running track around King's Domain Park. The Tan Track, as it is known, is where Melbourne's fitness freaks race at dawn and dusk.

The world's strangest football game

Australian football—a game all its own that is based on Gaelic football—is a strange combination of soccer and rugby.

You can see this one-of-a-kind game at the Melbourne Cricket Ground in Yarra Park, one of Australia's biggest sports stadiums. The best football game, if you can get tickets, is the Grand Final in September, Australia's biggest sporting event.

Melbourne's best restaurants

Without question, Melbourne beats Sydney when it comes to restaurants. **Fanny's**, *243 Lonsdale Street*, is one of the best restaurants in Australia, a cozy little place with international fare. If you want an elegant night out, eat upstairs. If you'd rather save your Australian dollars, eat in the little bistro downstairs. It is less chic but serves the same food at much lower prices.

The city's best seafood restaurant is **Jean Jacques by the Sea**, *40 Jacka Blvd., St. Kilda*.

Mietta's Melbourne, *7 Alfred Place*, is a lovely restaurant in an old Victorian building. A piano bar is located downstairs. **Stephanie's**, *405 Tooronga Road*, is another romantic place, in an elegant historic mansion.

Melbourne is famous for its ethnic cuisine. Chinatown (Little Bourke Street), for example, is a thriving neighborhood with pagoda-style buildings. The aroma of hanging ducks and ginseng fills the air. The best restaurant here is **Flower Drum**, *17 Market Lane*.

Turkish and Mideastern restaurants are sprinkled along Sydney Road. The Richmond district, just east of downtown Melbourne, off Swan Street, is also heavily ethnic, with Greek, Turkish, Argentine, Indian, Vietnamese, and Mexican restaurants. Lygon Street, near the university, is a busy row of Lebanese and Italian restaurants.

The best hotels

One of the great landmarks of Melbourne is the **Windsor Hotel**, *Spring Street*. Recently restored, the Victorian hotel has a domed Grand Dining Room, decorated with silk wallpaper and crystal chandeliers. Visiting statesmen stay here.

The **Regent**, *Collins Place, 25 Collins St.*, is a work of modern art, with a sky-lit atrium filled with little white bulbs. Occupying the top 15 floors of a 50-story building, the hotel has panoramic views of the city. Jackie Collins stayed in the Kensington Suite on the top floor, which has windows from floor to ceiling.

Rockman's Regency, *Lonsdale and Exhibition streets*, has suites with private Jacuzzis that hold five people at a time. The bar is nice, but it's open only to guests. John McEnroe stays here.

The dullest nightlife

In Melbourne, lights generally go out well before midnight. However, you can enjoy the arts at the city's theater complex and concert hall. Luciano Pavarotti praised the Melbourne concert hall as the finest in the world.

Melbourne does have one New York-style dance spot. **Inflation**, *60 King St.* has a gigantic video screen and a huge dance floor. The crowd is lively.

Palace, *Lower Esplanade, St. Kilda*, is also a fun place.

THE BEST OF PERTH

Perth, the largest city on Australia's west coast, is the most isolated city in the world. Adelaide, the closest town, is more than 1,000 miles away. It takes three days to get to Perth by train from Sydney. Because of their isolation, the one million residents of Perth are close-knit and friendly.

Perth has many parks and wide-open spaces, miles of great beaches, good hotels, and a wide variety of ethnic restaurants. But best of all, it has the most ideal weather in Australia, more like the Mediterranean than Down Under. Although it's not as hot as Sydney, it offers more continuous hours of sunshine.

Perth's pride

King's Park, a 1,000-acre wilderness area, tops Mount Eliza and offers panoramic views of Perth. At its heart is a fountain dedicated to pioneer women. If you lose track of the time, check the floral clock.

King's Park is a place to stroll at your leisure, enjoying some of Australia's exotic flora and fauna. When you tire, stop for a snack at the park's restaurant.

Other top sights

The **Art Gallery**, *47 James St.*, is one of the best art museums in Australia. It is a dramatic modern building that cost $10 million to build. Masterpieces by Van Gogh, Cézanne, Picasso, and Monet are displayed, as well as works by contemporary Australian artists. Look for the "Art of the Western Desert," created by the Panunya, a tribe of aborigines.

The **Old Mill**, at the end of Narrows Bridge in South Perth, ground flour during the gold rush in the 1800s. Today it houses colonial tools and artifacts.

Perth's best restaurants

The best Chinese food in Perth is **Choi's Inn**, *68 Roe St.* The restaurant serves Mandarin fare and is located in Perth's Chinatown.

Perth's best seafood restaurant is **Jessica's Fine Seafood**, *Shop 1, Merlin Centre, 99 Adelaide Terrace; tel. (61)89-325-2511*, which has a view of the Swan River. Try the grilled dhufish, a firm, sweet fish found only in Western Australia.

Other good bets are the **River Room** at the Sheraton Perth; the **Oyster Bar**, *20 Roe St., Northbridge*; **Lombardo's**, *Fishing Boat Harbor, Fremantle*; and **Oyster Beds**, on the Swan River at Fremantle. Oyster Beds is especially nice because the Swan River flows directly under the restaurant.

Perth's most pleasant hotels

Celebrities stay at the **Parmelia Hilton**, *Mill Street; tel. (61)89-322-3622*. Excellent service is the main attraction.

The **Hotel Rendezvous**, *Esplanade, Scarborough; tel. (61)89-245-1000*, was built on the beach and has spectacular views.

Other good hotels are the **Orchard**, the **Parkroyal**, the **Langley**, and the **Sheraton Perth**.

Perth's best bets

Burswood Restaurant and Casino, *Great Eastern Highway; tel. (61)89-362-7777*, is the largest resort complex in the Southern Hemisphere and the second-largest gaming floor anywhere in the world.

THE BEST OF QUEENSLAND

Queensland, Australia's northeastern province, is a diverse land made up of many different worlds: the fluorescent Great Barrier Reef in the Coral Sea, the aboriginal reservations; the Daintree Rain Forest, the gold and opal mines in the desert fringe, and the sacred natural art galleries in the pitiless Outback.

The best of Brisbane

Complete with a surfing subculture (at nearby Surfer's Paradise on the Gold Coast), Brisbane is often compared to Los Angeles. Homes in Queensland's sprawling capital city sport red-tile roofs and blue swimming pools. The hot sun fosters a casual dress code—men often wear shorts, knee socks, and ties to work. In the fields they wear kepis, military hats with wide brims that snap to the crowns on one side.

Founded as a penal colony for convicts supposedly too tough to be sent to Sydney, Brisbane originally was home to Australia's mining and agricultural industries. Today, tourism is making a bid for first place in the local economy.

While in Brisbane, stop by **Queensland Aboriginal Creations**, *135 George St.*, run by the Department of Aboriginal and Islanders Advancement. You can buy tribal masks, musical instruments, weapons, and bark paintings.

For a boost to your patriotic ego, stop by the memorial called **They Passed This Way**, *Lyndon B. Johnson Place, Newstead Park*, erected as a tribute to the United States after General MacArthur made his headquarters here during World War II.

Forest Park is an oasis of eucalyptus trees and tropical birds just outside Brisbane. Carefully designed walking paths lead through the park and its Botanical Gardens. Stop by the **Sir Thomas Brisbane Planetarium**, the largest in Australia.

The best place to see cuddly koalas is the **Lone Pine Sanctuary**, *Fig Tree Pocket*, west of Brisbane. About 100 of the little bears live here, along with kangaroos, emus, and other Australian animals. You can hold the koalas and feed the kangaroos by hand.

The place to stay in Brisbane is the **Sheraton Brisbane Hotel**, *249 Turbot St.* Rooms are beautifully furnished and offer views of the Brisbane River.

Another good bet is the **Hilton International Brisbane**, *190 Elizabeth St.*

CAIRNS: A TROPICAL BEST

Cairns is a beautiful fully-restored tropical town filled with the aromas of coffee, sugarcane, and orchids. You can walk from one end of Cairns to the other. The jungle encroaches wherever someone hasn't mowed his lawn or raked pesky mangoes from his yard.

A languid town, Cairns sprawls along the northern fringes of the Great Barrier Reef, overlooking blue Trinity Bay. The ramshackle houses, surrounding jungle, and fields of sugarcane lend the town its colonial mystique. Palm trees sway in the wind, and tropical fruits are mainstays of the local diet. Trading ships line the oceanfront.

Cairns can be a best or a worst for women, because it is home to many more men than women. Pubs are often partitioned into separate rooms for men and women, and signals can get crossed if the boundaries are violated.

Cairns' real attraction is the nearby Great Barrier Reef, which is described below.

Cairns' best hotels

Cairns does have a celebrated hotel or two, including **Harbourside Village**, *209 The Esplanade*; the **Pacific International**, *43 The Esplanade*; and the good old **Hilton International**, *Wharf Street*.

Palm Cove, not far from Cairns, has a jet-set resort called the **Reef House**, where bougainvillea scents the air and palm trees rustle in the wind. The resort's restaurant is good.

Australia's best caravan park

Australia's best — and most exotic — caravan park is **Ellis Beach**, 15 miles north of Cairns. It is situated among coconut palms, with views of Double Island and right next to the rain forest.

The Great Barrier Reef

Extending 1,260 miles, from New Guinea to the Tropic of Capricorn, the **Great Barrier Reef** passes along the coast of Queensland. Containing more than 2,000 coral reefs, coral islands, and cays, the reef is home to the world's greatest variety of marine life, nearly 1,400 kinds of sea creatures. It is a must-see if you are in Australia. The coral forms stunning natural patterns, and clear and brightly colored fish swim in unison.

Scuba divers from around the world come here to swim among the exotic fish. If you'd rather, you can walk across much of the reef at low tide, when the water recedes. (Wear tennis shoes, the coral is sharp.) Or you can go beyond the danger zones around this coral paradise and swim to your lungs' content.

Australia's best island

Green Island is the best place to stay while exploring the reef. You can see the submarine world through windows at the island's **Underwater Coral Observatory** or from one of the glass-bottom boats that depart the island regularly.

The beaches that edge the mile-square island are empty except for drift-wood trees. Cool coconut palm groves offer refuge from the hot sun. Blue and white herons prance along the sand paths. Even the pigeons here are beautiful—they're green and yellow, not the soot color of North American pigeons. Between the chirping crickets and slapping palms, Green Island is a lively spot.

The cheapest way to get to the island is to book a trip with Great Adventure Tours in Cairns. You get a boat ride to and from the reef. If the six-hour stay is too short, you can rent a bungalow from **Hayles Resort.**

Another beautiful reef resort is **Dunk Island**, where you can sleep in a beach-front cottage and spend your days snorkeling, swimming, walking in the rain forest, and playing golf and tennis.

Queensland's best market

Take the train from Cairns to **Kuranda**, which has an outdoor market selling Indonesian batiks, native opals, and sapphires. The town is a short walk from the market, past the reconstruction of a settlers' village and an aboriginal art gallery that sells bark paintings. (These barks cost less and look better than those in Sydney or Melbourne.)

Tarzan's favorite: Queensland's rain forests

Not far from Brisbane are misty rain forests where orchids scent the air and parrots sing from thick canopies of leaves hundreds of feet in the air. More than 800 kinds of trees grow in these forests, many with buttressed trunks that form church-size caves. Giant ferns, orchids, ginger plants, and organ-pipe fungi grow together in a thick web that blocks out the sun. You can swing like Tarzan from thick vines. Butterflies, tree frogs, snakes, and bugs make their homes here. (The best time to visit is during the less-buggy dry season, from May to November.)

The rain forest closest to Brisbane is at **Mount Glorious**, a 45-minute drive away. Slightly farther on, at **Mount Tamborine**, are six rain forest parks. While hiking here, stop at the Maiala Rain Forest Café to enjoy English tea served with fresh scones, jam, and thick cream, while savoring the fragrance of jasmine and watching colorful parrots. Just two-and-a-half hours south of Brisbane is the **Lamington Plateau**, where you can stay at Binna Burra or O'Reilly's Lodge.

The densest and least-spoiled rain forests are 1,000 miles north of Brisbane (closer to Cairns): Kurando, Lake Eachem, Lake Barrine, Daintree River, and Cape Tribulation.

The World's Best Destinations

Hayles Tours runs a private bus service from Cairns to Cape Tribulation. The one-store town is near a good youth hostel with compound huts that surround a free-form swimming pool and a patio of logs sliced in cross sections. The restaurant serves fresh fish on ginger rice topped with coconut milk and flanked by mango strips.

Peacocks and parrots roam Cape Tribulation, which begins the **Daintree Rain Forest**, said to be the oldest on earth. The controversial new road that cuts through the forest is threatened by roots reaching down from branches to reclaim the red mud.

Wear long pants, long sleeves, and a hat to protect yourself from bugs and thorny plants. (Look out for ticks, which are unusually tenacious here; the wait-a-while plant, which has savage thorns; snakes; and leeches.)

For information on transportation to the rain forests, contact the **Queensland Government Travel Centre**, *196 Adelaide St., Brisbane, Queensland 4000.*

AUSTRALIA'S OLDEST RESIDENTS

The aborigines lived in Australia for at least 39,000 years before Britain sent its prisoners to colonize the country. On the shores of Lake Mungo in western New South Wales, evidence remains of a cremation that took place 30,000 years ago. And caves on the Nullabor Plain and a Bass Strait island were occupied 20,000 years ago. Anthropologists estimate that 300,000 aborigines lived in Australia before 1770. They spoke 500 different languages.

The aborigines believe in Dreamtime, an age that existed at the dawn of creation and is still present, a timeless otherworld linking the past, present, and future. Mythological characters from Dreamtime, painted by the aborigines on rocks, can be seen in the **Nourlangie Rock Northern Territory** and at other places throughout the country.

North of Cairns, in Laura, is the **Quinkon Reserve**, which boasts three rock galleries. Some of the paintings date from 13,200 B.C. The cracked and overhanging rocks were chosen because they face east and the rising sun.

The best of the three galleries is the **Split Rock Gallery**, a natural gallery displaying ancient aboriginal cave paintings. Two routes lead from Cairns to the gallery. The easier of the two is through the Outback; the more interesting but riskier route is via the well-named Cape Tribulation through the jungle. You will need an odometer to find the rock walls that are decorated with the murals, because all traces are invisible from the road.

Aborigines continue the artistic ways of their forefathers, decorating weapons, tools, and totems with colorful religious patterns and figures. Tribal dancers hold on to the steps and music symbolizing events in Dreamtime. The best-known dance is the Corroboree, performed by dancers covered with white paint and wearing leafy pompoms around their knees.

Australia's 160,000 aborigines maintain their tribal traditions mainly in northern and central Australia. (Queensland is populated with more aborigines than any other state.)

About two-thirds of the aborigines are living a relatively modern lifestyle in the big cities. They are the poorest group in Australia, plagued by health problems, alcoholism, and culture shock.

Wujal Wujal, an aboriginal reserve, is in the Daintree Rain Forest, 30 miles from the nearest town of Helensvale. This village of impoverished shacks is littered with crashed cars, mysteriously parked on end, nose down, against trees. This position represents the ritual return to Dreamtime in aboriginal paintings.

The world's most mysterious rock

An island-size red monolith called **Ayer's Rock** lies in the heart of Australia. The largest rock on earth, it draws thousands of curious visitors and is part of a national park run by tribal elders and white officials. Situated in the Northern Territory, 200 miles southwest of Alice Springs, it could be considered the navel of the Australian Outback.

The Pitjantjatjara tribespeople call the rock Uluru and attach religious significance to it. On the north surface of the rock is a series of caves and grooves known as the Skull. Tribespeople believe this area of the rock served as the camp of their ancestors in Dreamtime before the world began. They perform initiation ceremonies here.

Resorts have been built near the rock. The best is the **Sheraton Ayers Rock**, *Yulara Drive*. Painted in the red hues of Ayer's Rock, it is kept cool by a huge white awning that stretches over the entire complex.

Yulara, 15 miles from the rock, has the **Four Seasons Hotel** and campgrounds.

Between Alice Springs and Ayer's Rock are the **Desert Oaks Resort Centre**, the **King's Canyon Frontier Lodge**, and the **Curtin Springs Roadside Inn**.

The best time to visit Ayer's Rock is during the Australian winter, from May through September, when rain makes the desert flower. Temperatures are in the 70s, rather than 140 degrees Fahrenheit as they can be in the summer.

A TASTE OF THE OUTBACK

Australia's great **Outback**, a vast, hot, wilderness land in the heart of the continent, is inhabited by leathery stockmen and ancient aborigines. A little-known land, it stretches from the heart of Australia to the northwest. It was once known as the Back of Beyond. Cattle graze on million-acre ranches, or stations as they are known, on dusty turf that conceals diamonds, iron, aluminum, and uranium.

To really get to know the Outback, arrange a farm or ranch stay. For more information, contact **Bed and Breakfast Australia**, *15 Yarabah Ave., Gordon, Sydney, New South Wales 2072.*

Or live like a ranch hand at **Escott Lodge Resort**, *Escott Station, Burketown,* a rambling cattle ranch in the wilds of northern Queensland. You'll stay in a rustic guest cottage on the homestead, eat with the ranch hands, and get acquainted with the cattle.

Don't expect a luxurious, California-style dude ranch. The place has a bar, a swimming pool, and electricity, but you are not pampered with resort-type service. You won't spend your days enjoying planned recreational activities — life on a ranch involves hard work. If you're up to it, tag along with the stockmen and watch the bulls being castrated. Or you can help out with more palatable jobs, such as breaking horses, catching crocodiles, and fishing. You also can canoe on the Nicholson River and go on a wild-pig shoot.

The most gem-studded land

The Outback, in places, is paved with gems. Towns in the region have such names as Sapphire, Rubyvale, and Emerald and are connected by dirt roads made from piles of earth heaped up by old-time miners. From time to time, valuable gems overlooked by miners are found in the dirt.

Finding a sapphire, emerald, or ruby could turn a vacation into a jack-pot. A book on Australian gems advises that "although it's not recommended that gem hunters should begin to dig up roads in search of stones, many fine gemstones have been found on the sides of roads." The odds against finding a gem on the road are like those against winning big in Las Vegas. But in the road, you don't have to pay to play.

It's not as easy as stepping from your vehicle and picking up a rock or two along the road; however, you could get lucky. Roy Spencer, a 12-year-old boy, did. He picked up the Black Star of Queensland, a 1,156-carat sapphire, in a field. It was cut to a 733-carat star sapphire valued at $450,000.

It's hard to see stones in the road. That sparkle you spy is most likely quartz or shards of glass from countless windshields that have been shattered along the way. Giant road trains — tractor trailers that tow huge dollies packed with freight or cattle — roar along the dirt tracks, shooting up rocks that demolish windshields. Because of this, most Australian vehicles that travel through the bush are outfitted with wire windshield guards or curved plastic shields.

The best way to set off on an Outback mining journey is to rent a camper in Sydney and then head north for the gem fields. Vans are well-equipped, but you will need a few extra items, such as a shovel, a block and tackle, a spare gas can, a thermos, and some plastic bowls. Small refrigerators that run on 220 volts, generators, or porta gas are provided. Finding water can be a problem. The bore water brought up by windmills is drink-able, but it acts as a laxative. Carry your own supply.

Mining licenses cost $15, but you don't need one for just a few days. Just don't try your luck on any claims you see pegged out.

Emerald is the first of the gem-field townships. Beyond this town are the fields near the mining village of Sapphire, a dingy huddle of slapped-together shacks and tents. The main post office is a tiny one-room shanty. The Rough and Ready Pub is just down the dirt road.

If you don't manage to find a gem on your own, you can buy some in this region and sell them in the United States for a fine profit. One Yankee miner recently gave up on the quest for gems and bought one instead—a star sapphire (in Sapphire, of course) for A$30 ($23). Back in the United States, the stone was appraised at twice that.

If you'd rather search for the world-famous Australian opal, head for Coober Pedy or Lightning Ridge, in the center of the country, where 90% of the world's opals are mined. Coober Pedy is an underground town on the edge of the formidable Simpson's Desert. Miners in this 120-degree desert live in underground caves, where the temperature is an even 65 degrees Fahrenheit.

Opal buyers throng to this settlement to buy wholesale opal rock clusters or polished opals. Dutch buyers predominate.

WESTERN AUSTRALIA—THE MOST FARAWAY LAND

Western Australia, the westernmost province, is about as far from Sydney and the east coast as you can get. This gigantic region's beauty is natural. Only 300,000 people live outside Perth, in an area four times the size of Texas.

The hottest town in Australia is in this province. **Marble Bar** has an average annual temperature of 96 degrees Fahrenheit.

The most beautiful sights in Westralia, as this region is known, are the fields of wild flowers. No ordinary fields these. They roll to the horizon, a patchwork quilt of blue, purple, red, and orange. Between August and October, more than 7,000 native species (some not found anywhere else on earth) blossom here. The most famous fields are near Albany on the southern coast and Geraldton, north of Perth.

Westralia also houses Australia's best ghost town. **Coolgardie**, once home to 15,000 rowdy, brawling gold miners, is now deserted except for tourists. Old covered wagons remain on the main street, where 29 hotels and bars once thrived. **Goldfields Exhibition**, *Bayley Street*, displays memorabilia from the gold rush of the 1890s, which brought nearly 200,000 miners to Westralia.

Kalgoorlie was the area's largest mining town, with two stock exchanges, seven newspapers, and some of the most expensive real estate in the country. Kalgoorlie still mines gold, but the pace has slowed.

The **Kimberley Plateau** raises its flat head in the northern corner of Westralia, covering a region larger than California but home to only 6,000 brave souls. The green Fitzroy River carves a gorge through the limestone plateau, its water filled with sharks, crocodiles, and stingrays. Caves once used by the aborigines as burial grounds can be seen at Windjana.

Australia's best foods

Australia's culinary delights often have strange names—but don't let that stop you from trying them. Look for Moreton Bay bugs and Victorian yabbies (both are crustaceans, not insects); Queensland snapper, coral trout and Red emperor; Sydney rock oysters; barramundi; John Dory fish; Tasmanian scallops; and shrimp from anywhere along Australia's 35,000-mile-long coastline. If you can find it, try some kangaroo-tail soup. For dessert, order pavlova, a delicious fruit, whipped cream, and meringue concoction.

Australian wines can be good. They have been compared favorably to those produced in France. The Baroosa Valley near Adelaide and Hunter Valley near Sydney are the prime wine-producing regions. The whites are superior to the reds.

Top travel tips

The best way to save on the cost of rail travel within Australia is to purchase an Austrailpass, similar to the Eurailpass, before you leave home. First-class and economy versions are available, and the cost depends on class and the length of your stay rather than distance traveled. For more information, contact the **Australian Travel Service**, *100 N. First St., Suite 301, Burbank, CA 91502.*

The best way to see the Outback is by train. Two routes are especially scenic.

The transcontinental **Indian-Pacific** runs from Sydney on the Pacific Ocean to Perth on the Indian Ocean. This route cuts through the Great Dividing Range and the pasture country to the west, the mining country around Broken Hill, along the shores of the Great Australian Bight, and across the vast expanse of the dry Nullabor Plains. The trip takes three days. Book a few months in advance—berths are in demand, particularly in September and October, when the wild flowers are blooming.

The **Ghan** runs from Adelaide on the south coast to Alice Springs in the center of Australia, skirting the beautiful Simpson Desert and its dry salt lakes. The train has an entertainment car with slot machines, a hairdresser, a gift shop, VCR rentals, and video games for children.

THE BEST OF NEW ZEALAND

New Zealand is a land of spectacular scenery: shooting geysers, cloud-shrouded mountain peaks, bubbling hot springs, deep blue fiords, and scheduled coves. It is also a land of extremes, with both tropical beaches and icebergs.

The Kiwis, as the people of New Zealand are affectionately known, love their land and are among the most ardent conservationists in the world. They are as varied and interesting as the landscape they seek to preserve. The Maoris, a Polynesian people who lived here long before the Europeans arrived, maintain their ancient traditions. The Europeans, too, preserve their old ways. Scottish dances seldom seen even in Scotland are danced by kilted sheep farmers.

This is the best place in the world for nature lovers, thrill seekers, and sports buffs. You can raft down a wild mountain river, battle a fighting rainbow trout, explore magnificent fiords, climb or ski the Southern Alps, or hike the awe-inspiring Milford Track.

New Zealand, which is made up of three main islands (North, South, and Stewart) and a number of smaller ones, stretches 1,000 miles along the southern tip of Polynesia. Its nearest neighbor is Australia, 1,300 miles to the northwest.

NEW ZEALAND'S LARGEST CITY

Auckland, huddled on an isthmus separating Waitemata and Manukau harbors, has 14 volcanos, each with tremendous views. The best panorama is from **Mount Eden**, the highest point in the city. Hike up the cow path or road and picnic in the volcano's grassy bowl while enjoying the view.

Known as the Queen City among is inhabitants. Auckland has restaurants, cinemas, shops, theaters, concerts, and art galleries. It also has 102 mainland beaches and 23 secluded islands. The Hauraki Gulf is a favorite among boaters (and Auckland has a lot of boaters — one in every four homeowners also owns a boat).

The world's best Polynesian museum

The **War Memorial Museum**, built in memory of the New Zealanders who died fighting in World War I, houses the world's best collection of

Maori and Polynesian artifacts, some dating back to A.D. 1200. The pièce de résistance is a 98-foot war canoe carved from a giant totara tree. It carried 80 Maori warriors at a time.

The best Kiwi art

The world's biggest collection of paintings by New Zealand artists is at the **Auckland City Art Gallery**, *Kitchener and Wellesley streets*. Especially worth seeing are works by John Webber and William Hodges, both of whom accompanied Captain Cook on his voyages in the South Pacific in the 18th century. The gallery is open 10 a.m. until 4.30 p.m.

Animal bests

Animal lovers should make time to visit the **Auckland Zoo**, where the nocturnal, flightless kiwi bird can be seen, as well as **Lion Safari Park** in Massey.

Auckland's best picnicking

The best places to picnic are the **Domain**, a large shaded park, and **Albert Park**, which adjoins the University of Auckland. Pack your picnic basket with mango juice, which is as common here as orange juice is in the United States, and good local cheeses.

The best bargains in town

Lamb is as cheap in Auckland as Kentucky Fried Chicken is in the United States. It can be found on cafeteria lunch menus, on the dinner table several nights a week, and at restaurants.

Good, inexpensive shops are located downtown, near Quay and Queen streets. Just east of the intersection is the **Old Customhouse**, which has been converted into a mall with a movie theater, arts and crafts shops, a tavern, and a bookstore. Built in 1889, the Customhouse is one of the few examples of Victorian architecture in Auckland.

A 10-minute walk west from the corner of Queen and Quay is the **Victoria Park Market**, located in the city's former trash dump. (It's quite picturesque, believe it or not!). You can buy kiwifruit for a few cents apiece, fresh fish, and inexpensive clothing. The market is open every day.

Polynesian bests

Karangahape Road (known as K Road) is where Auckland's Polynesian population shops. You can buy brilliantly colored cloth and tropical foods here alongside matrons from Samoa, Fiji, Tonga, and the Cook Islands.

(Auckland has the largest Polynesian population of any city in the world. More than 70,000 residents have Maori ancestry, and 58,000 Pacific islanders have immigrated here.)

Auckland's best dining

Most of the better restaurants in Auckland don't have liquor licenses. But you usually can bring your own wine (which brings down the price of dinner considerably).

Auckland's best restaurant is **Antoine's**, *333 Parnell Road; tel. (64)9-798-756*, a French restaurant in a sun-drenched colonial house with linen-covered tables. Wine is served here. Ring the doorbell to enter.

Other bests include **Harbourside Seafood Bar and Grill**, *First Floor, Ferry Building, 99 Quay St; tel. (64)9-307-0556*, **Cin Cin On Quay**, *Ferry Buildings, 99 Quay St; tel. (64)9-307-6966*, and **Sails**, *The Anchorage, Westhaven; tel. (64)9-789-890*.

Other good New Zealand and Polynesian restaurants are located on Ponsonby Road, near K. Road.

The best hotels

Aucklands only five-star hotel is the **Regent of Auckland**, *P.O. Box 3938; tel. (64)9-309-8888*.

Other good hotels are the impersonal but efficient **Hyatt Auckland**, *Waterloo Quadrant and Princes Street; tel. (64)9-797-22*, and the **Sheraton Auckland**, *83 Symonds St; tel. (64)9-795-132*. If you need to stay close to the Akl airport, book a room at the **Hotel du Vin**, *Lyons Road, Mangatawbiri Valley; tel. (64)9-233-6314*. It's only 35 minutes away.

The best place to argue politics

The bar at the **Abbey Hotel**, *Wellesley and Albert streets*, is known as the watering hole for Auckland's literati. A British-style lounge, it is frequented by sociable intellectuals, always looking for a lively battle over ideology. If you plan to get involved in the nightly squabble (it's all in good fun), be sure to read up first. The Kiwis have a good grasp of current events.

The Quay, a key travel hub

The Quay, in addition to offering a view of Harbour Bridge, is a transportation center. You can get a "Bus-About" pass here that allows you to ride public buses at reduced fares. You also can catch a ferry here to take you to the islands and beaches in Hauraki Gulf.

New Zealand's best train trip

If you want to see the beautiful countryside of New Zealand in first-class comfort and style, buy a ticket on the **Silver Fern**, one of the best trains in the world. The Silver Fern runs daily from Auckland to Wellington and back. For more information, contact **Frangipani Tours**, *tel. (800)458-1130* in the United States.

CAPITAL WELLINGTON

The growing city of **Wellington**, the capital of New Zealand, sprawls along the southern tip of North Island. For a view of Wellington's harbor and skyline, ascend Mount Victoria. (A Maori burial ground was bulldozed to make room for the viewing platform.) White wooden houses cover the green hills surrounding the city. The beaches of the Inner Harbor are popular, and on summer weekends the harbor is filled with yachts.

Wellington is a cultural center, with two professional theater companies, numerous amateur dramatic and musical societies, the New Zealand Symphony Orchestra, and the Royal New Zealand Ballet Company. The recently completed Michael Fowler Center and St. Paul's Cathedral (built in 1866) both sponsor plays and concerts.

From **Lambton Quay**, bright red cable cars carry pedestrians 397 feet over the suburbs to the beautiful **Botanical Gardens**.

The **National Museum and Art Gallery** in the suburb of Newtown has superb Maori artifacts, items used by Captain Cook, geological collections, colonial history displays, and works of art by national and international masters.

Wellington's best restaurants include **At the Bay**, *Marine Parade, Days Bay; tel. (64)4-562-8882*, which offers a variety of New Zealand specialties; **Grain of Salt**, *232 Oriental Parade, Oriental Parade; tel. (64)4-384-8642*, which is one of the top—and most expensive—restaurants in the city; and **Il Casino Restorante**, *108 Tory Street, TeAro; tel. (64)4-385-3947*, which has good Italian food.

The city's best French restaurant is the **Petit-Lyon Restaurant**, *8 Courtney Place; tel. (64)4-384-9402*.

The best place to stay in Wellington is the **Intercontinental**, *corner of Grey and Featherstone streets; tel. (64)4-472-2722*.

THE HIGHLIGHTS OF NORTH ISLAND

North Island is the cradle of New Zealand. It was here that the Europeans first landed and faced off with the native Maori. The island's beauty belies its violent past—it is fringed with beautiful, palm-shaded beaches and blessed with hospitable weather year-round. Explore it from north to south.

New Zealand's northernmost point

Cape Reinga, the country's northernmost point, affords a magnificent view of the Pacific Ocean and the Tasman Sea. Its graceful white lighthouse seems frail and vulnerable, facing the rage of two great bodies of water from the ridge of a narrow point of land.

The Maoris believe this is where spirits of the dead depart for their journey back to the ancestral land, which they call Hawaiki.

The cape is a pleasant three-and-a-half-hour drive on Highway 1 or a one-hour flight from Auckland. It is a great place to spend the night if you enjoy camping—the area lacks hotels. Try the campgrounds at Houhora and Taputupoto bays.

The best boating

Whangaroa Harbor, with its rocky pinnacles with biblical names, is the place to go for boating and deep-sea fishing. This is where the Royal Massacre occurred in 1809. A local tribe did away with the passengers and crew of the *Boyd*, the shell of which still can be seen here.

The largest private museum

The **Wagener Museum**, *tel. (64)9-409-8850*, at Houhora Heads, is the country's largest private museum, containing rare pre-European Maori artifacts, an excellent natural history display, and extensive exhibits from the Victorian era.

Best view, best springs

Kailohe has spectacular views of both the Tasman and Pacific coasts, as well as a museum called Pioneer Village. Nearby is **Ngawha Springs**, with waters that have the highest mineral content in the world and are known for their curative qualities.

The most magnificent trees

Magnificent native kauri trees stand along the road that runs through the 6,100-acre **Waipoua Kauri Sanctuary**. The largest is the mighty Tane Mahuta (Lord of the Forest), which is estimated to be 1,200 years old. The oldest is the 2,000-year-old Te Matua Ngahere (Father of the Forest).

Waikato: the best of the Maoris

North of **Hamilton**, which is the capital of New Zealand's rural Waikato region and the largest inland city, is the center of Maori culture. **Turangawaewae Marae** is the focal point of a Maori revival movement organized in the 1920s by Princess Te Puea Herangi, who established a complex of buildings on the river. The complex includes traditionally carved meetinghouses and a concert hall. It is not generally open to the public, but you can see it from across the river at the bridge downstream.

The sacred burial ground of the Waikato Maoris is two-and-a-half miles downstream at **Mount Taupiri**.

The scene of the last battle of the Wakato Land Wars in 1864 is southwest in **Orakau**. Maori Rewi Maniapoto and 300 men, women, and children fought off 1,400 colonial soldiers for three days before they lost their fortified village.

The finest Maori carved meetinghouse is in Te Kuiti in southern **Waitomo**. Maori leader Te Kooti Rikirangi built the wooden structure to thank the local Maniapoto people, who gave him refuge when he was in danger.

King Country, as the region is known, is largely a resort for outdoor enthusiasts. Tour companies based in Te Kuiti and Taumarunui offer canoeing, horseback riding, hunting, jet boating, and fishing expeditions. Safari expeditions operate from Te Kuiti.

The rose of New Zealand

The magnificent rose gardens of **Te Awamutu**, southwest of Hamilton, have earned this town the title Rose Town of New Zealand. The roses are best seen in November during the annual Rose Festival. New Zealand's oldest and loveliest church is here; **St. John's Anglican Church** was built in 1854.

New Zealand's largest lake

Lake Taupo, at the heart of North Island, is the largest New Zealand lake, extending over 232 square miles and filling an old volcanic crater. The trout fishing is terrific in the lake and the rivers and streams that feed it. You can fish here year-round.

One of New Zealand's most attractive lodges is on the banks of Lake Taupo. **Huka Lodge**, *Huka Falls Road, Taupo; tel. (64)7-378-5791*, is a five-star hotel with a rustic atmosphere.

The best adventures

At the southern end of Lake Taupo are the renowned trout-fishing and river-rafting waters of the Tongariro and Wanganui rivers, Kaimanawa State Forest Park, and Tongariro National Park, all accessible from Turangi.

Tongariro National Park, with its snow-capped mountain peaks, is a superb ski resort in winter and a scenic place to hike in summer. An extensive network of paths and huts makes it easy to explore the park and its historic Maori sights. The volcanic peaks of Tongariro, Ruapehu, and Ngauruhoe are the focal points.

The **THC Château**, *Mount Ruapehu; tel. (64)7-892-3809*, is a luxurious hotel at the heart of the park's spectacular mountains.

On the Wanganui River, you can embark on boat trips, guided canoe treks, and white-water rafting expeditions. This is also the site of an annual motorboat race. A luxury paddle boat travels along the river to the Holly Lodge Estate Winery, where wine tastings are held.

Rotorua: a heavenly Hades

"I was pleased to get so close to Hades and be able to return", said playwright George Bernard Shaw after visiting the area around **Rotorua City**—

the boiling, bubbling, steaming center of North Island.

Located on the volcanic rift that once inspired great fear, Rotorua is New Zealand's number-one tourist spot, surrounded by thermal springs, Maori villages, and 10 trout-filled lakes. Boiling mud, erupting geysers, steaming terraces of sulfur, and colorful silica deposits combine to create an other-worldly landscape.

Rotorua has the greatest concentration of Maori residents of any New Zealand city. The historic Maori village of **Ohinemutu**, on the lake, has a 19th-century traditional meeting house that took 12 years to carve. The Christian church, **St. Faith's** built in 1910, has a window with a Maori Christ, elaborate carvings, and a bust of Queen Victoria presented to the Maoris by Britain for their loyalty to the crown.

On Geyser Flat in Whakarewarewa is New Zealand's greatest geyser, Pohutu (Splashing), which shoots 100 feet into the air several times a day. The smaller geyser next to it usually erupts just before Pohutu does.

Rotorua is popular among trout fishermen. Professional fishing guides are available. If fishing isn't your thing, you can visit wildlife sanctuaries, government gardens, the Buried Village, and the Agrodome, where sheep- and dog-handling demonstrations are given.

Rotorua City was established as a sanatorium in 1880, when the New Zealand government leased the land from the Maoris. **Tudor Towers**, which houses a museum and an art gallery, was the original bathhouse. To its right are the **Polynesian Pools**, whose sulphurous waters are still at the Queen Elizabeth Hospital to treat rheumatism and arthritis. Another good hot pool is **Hinemoa**, on Mokoia Island, in the middle of Lake Rotorua.

The world's only mainland gannet reserve

The world's only mainland gannet (a large yellow-headed seabird) sanctuary is to the south of **Cape Kidnappers**, where large flocks can be seen between April and October. The reserve can be reached by four-wheel-drive vehicles or on foot.

The world's best sheep-shearing contest

Masterton, on the southern tip of North Island, hosts the annual Golden Shears competition—a sheep-shearing contest that attracts shearers from all over the world. For details, contact **Mr. N. Grieve**, *P.O. Box 40, Masterton*.

NAPIER: THE ART DECO CAPITAL

Napier is the Art Deco capital of the world, having been re-built after the devastating 1931 earthquake in the prevalent Art Deco style. People come from all over the world for special events and 1930s dress-up style, many in re-conditioned old cars, for the Art-Deco weekend each February.

SOUTH ISLAND: THE MOST BEAUTIFUL

New Zealand's most spectacular scenery is on **South Island**. At **Punakaiki**, for example, nature has carved limestone rocks into what looks like giant stacks of pancakes. The Tasman Sea rushes into bore holes in these oddly shaped rocks, making great shuddering booms. The island's most memorable sights are described below, starting at the north end, following along the Pacific coast, crossing the Southern Alps, and then following the Tasman coast.

The best boat charters

Ferries from North Island land in **Picton**, a busy little port in South Island's incredibly beautiful Marlborough Sounds, 597 miles of waterways sheltered by bays and coves. Picton is the base for charter boat companies that takes you cruising, fishing, and diving.

The best places to stay on South Island

The **Timara Lodge**, *Road #2; tel. (64)3-572-8276*, is the best place to say in Blenheim, but it's not cheap. The **Californian Guesthouse**, *29 Collingwood St., Nelson; tel. (64)3-548-4173*, about 50 miles from Blenheim, in Nelson, is another good place to stay on South Island. It's also less expensive.

The least-traveled trail

New Zealand is crisscrossed by well-marked trails leading through spectacular scenery. One of the least known, and therefore least crowded, is the **Nydia Trail**, along the Marlborough Sounds. Passing through genuine wilderness, the trail has no access road. A mail boat that serves farms and vacation homes also delivers hikers to any starting point along the 80-mile trail. If prearranged, the mail boat will pick you up again farther north. Check with the ranger station or public information office in the harbor town of Havelock for maps and to arrange transportation.

One of the best routes along the trail begins at Shag Poing in Kauma Bay. Heading north, you cross two fast-running jade-green rivers near a deer farm. (The Japanese buy the velvet of the deer antlers and use it as an aphrodisiac). The trail then climbs the first of several 1,000-foot saddles with a view of the valley below. You can quench your thirst at a waterfall before continuing across a stretch of private property. Keep an eye out for wild goats and boars—and take cover if you spot any.

At intervals of about five hours, the trail passes a series of bays: Stanley, Duncan, Penzance, and Elaine. The last is a good place to meet the mail boat and return to Havelock.

Don't attempt to travel the Nydia without an accurate map and a compass. The trail is barely marked and rarely tramped.

The wildcat coastline

South of Picton, at **Kaikoura**, the Pacific coast is at its wildest. The town is on a narrow peninsula buffeted by the ocean and protected by rocky cliffs and a narrow beach. Nearby are limestone caves and seal colonies. The Kaikoura Mountains are a dramatic backdrop. The peninsula is popular among fishermen and known for its large crayfish.

The most English town

Nestled at the base of Banks Peninsula on the edge of the Canterbury Plains is the garden city of **Christchurch**, a very English town. The river that meanders through its center, past old stone buildings and terraced houses, is called the Avon.

The best hotel in Christchurch is the **Parkroyal Christchurch**, *corner of Durham and Kilmore streets; 1544 Christchurch*. The food is exceptional and served with a smile.

The **Cotswold Inn**, *88-90 Papanui Road; tel. (64)3-355-3535*, is pleasant, with authentic period furnishings.

Two other good places to stay are the **Elizas Manor House**, *82 Bealey Ave.*, and the **Riverview Lodge**, *361 Cambridge Toe*.

New Zealand's only castle

The Edwardian and Victorian houses of **Dunedin**, on the southernmost Pacific coast, embrace Otago Harbor, a 12-mile fiord. On one of the hills overlooking the city is New Zealand's only castle, **Larnach**, built in 1871 by J.M. Larnach, minister of the crown. The castle took 14 years to build, its ceilings 12 years to carve. The strangely European edifice was built to impress Larnach's French wife. Perhaps it didn't work; she committed suicide in Wellington's Parliament building years later. The castle has been restored, and its 43 rooms are open to the public.

Dunedin has several good restaurants, including the elegant **La Scala**, and **Blade's**, an inexpensive place where you bring your own wine.

The world's largest flying bird

The world's largest bird of flight, the rare royal albatross, can be seen in all its glory at Taiaroa Head, at the tip of Otago Peninsula near Dunedin. The graceful bird has a 10-foot wingspan and hovers above the sea like a kite. The oldest-known wild bird in the world is an albatross. Since 1937, when she was banded, this albatross has returned here each year.

About 20 pairs of royal albatross circle the globe each year, at speeds of up to 66 miles per hour, to roost at Taiaroa. They mate for life and produce one chick every two years. You can observe the birds up close from a newly opened lookout. For more information, call the **Dunedin Visitor Center**, *tel. (64)3-44-3300*.

The world's largest marbles

North of Dunedin, on a beach near the fishing village of **Moeraki**, are the intriguing Moeraki boulders known as **The Devil's Marbles**, strange spherical rocks weighing several tons. The huge round stones were formed 60 million years ago by the accumulation of lime salts.

The shortest route across the Alps

The shortest route across the Southern Alps passes through the Alpine playground that is **Arthur's Pass National Park**. The picturesque mountain village of Arthur's Pass is a great base for mountain climbing, hiking, hunting, skiing, and breathing fresh mountain air.

If you'd like to savor the area, stay a few nights at the **Chalet**, *P.O. Box 5, Main Road*, a Swiss Alpine-style chalet with five rooms.

The Tasman Coast—a nature lover's best

The **Tasman Coast**, on the other side of the island, is a good place to go if you like hiking, mountain climbing, rafting, or watching animals. It has three major national parks and is flanked by rugged mountains and washed by turbulent rivers.

New Zealand's best glaciers

The 217,000-acre **Westland National Park** has New Zealand's two most beautiful glaciers: Fox and Franz Josef. Arrange a (strenuous) guided hike across the icy masses at the park headquarters in the town of Franz Josef. (The native forest is crisscrossed with 68 miles of trails.) Or take a helicopter or ski plane over the shining glaciers.

New Zealand's highest peak: Mount Cook

Mount Cook, at 12,349 feet, is New Zealand's highest mountain. Sir Edmund Hillary, the first man to climb Mount Everest, trained here. The mountain is at the heart of **Mount Cook National Park**, which also features the beautiful 18-mile Tasman Glacier (and four other very high, very large glaciers). Ski planes operate regular flights to the head of Tasman—an exhilarating experience.

The most spectacular park

Fiordland National Park, at the southern tip of South Island, is one of the largest national parks in the world. Much of it remains unexplored. Lonely fiords lap at the mountains, while waterfalls tumble thousands of feet into the densely forested valleys. The fourth-largest waterfall in the world, **Sutherland Falls**, drops 1,873 feet through the forest. The gateway to the park is the town of **Te Anau**, which is the place to go for hotels and restaurants.

Real Journey's Te Anau Visitors' Center, *P.O. Box 1, Te Anau, New Zealand; tel. (64)3-249-7416*, offers boat and bus tours of Doubtful Sound that take you to see Lake Manapouri, the Wilmot Pass, and many beaches in Fiordland Park.

The eighth wonder of the world

According to Rudyard Kipling, the **Milford Sound**, which leads from Fiordland National Park to the sea, is the eighth wonder of the world. And who are we to argue with Kipling? The scenery is indeed spectacular: misty peaks, white waterfalls tumbling down green cliffs, and cottony clouds reflected in the mirrorlike water. The sound is dominated by 6,247-foot **Mitre Park**, a pyramidlike mountaintop. And it is fed by the spectacular **Bowen Falls**, which drop 531 feet.

The most beautiful walk in the world

The 33-mile **Milford Track**, which makes its way through Fiordland National Park to the Milford Sound, is the most beautiful walk in the world. To get here, take a boat across Te Anau Lake to Glade House. Leading through rain forests, meadows, and mountain passes, the trail passes wild rivers, deep fiords, and crashing waterfalls. The clearly marked track takes five days to hike; it is suitable even for the novice.

You can hike independently or join a group. Accommodation is in shelters along the way. Only a limited number of hikers (82) are permitted on the trail each day, so write to the **Independent Hikers**, *Department of Conservation, P.O. Box 29, Te Anau*, as far in advance as possible (up to one year) to make arrangements. Reservations also can be made by travel agents in the United States through the New Zealand Central Reservations Office in California or through the **Southern Pacific Hotel Corporation**. The hiking season is late October through mid-April.

The most southerly Alpine pass

Haast Pass is the most southerly, and the most historic, of the trans-Alpine passages, following an ancient Maori route through a rugged, breathtaking landscape. The contrast between the east and west sides of the pass is dramatic—**Westland** is lush; **Otago**, on the other side of the pass, is a dry region, relieved by lakes.

The pass runs through **Mount Aspiring National Park**, a 100-mile reserve that covers most of the southern Alps. Looming above the park is 9,961-foot Mount Aspiring. Many of the park's activities (hiking and fishing, for example) are centered in its headquarters at Lake Wanaka.

The most beautiful lakes

Mackenzie Country (named for a Scottish shepherd who tried to hide stolen sheep in this isolated area at the heart of South Island) is a rural area known for its six glacial lakes, the largest of which are Tekapo, Pukaki, and Ohau. Lake Tekapo is an unbelievable turquoise color (the result of powdered rock ground by the glaciers feeding the lake). All the lakes offer great fishing.

Queenstown: the most sophisticated resort

Nestled on the shores of clear blue Lake Wakatipu is Tyrolean-style **Queenstown**. Once a sleepy lakeside town, Queenstown has become the country's most sophisticated resort, with restaurants, hotels, an airport, and ski slopes. Any adventure is possible here: jet boating, white-water rafting, canoeing, sailing, Jet Skiing, water skiing, horseback riding, snow skiing, back-country safaris, and helicopter flights. You can cruise Lake Wakatipu on the TSS Earnsblaw steamer or follow its southern border aboard the Kingston Flyer steam train.

The **Quality Inn A Line**, *27 Stanley St.*, is a nice hotel with a restaurant overlooking Queenstown Bay.

The **Lakeland Regency**, *Lake Explanade*, has scenic views, its own restaurant, a pool, and private bathrooms.

The **Nugget Point Club**, *Arthurs Point Road*, is a luxury sporting resort.

STEWART ISLAND, THE MOST UNSPOILED

Across Foveaux Strait from South Island is **Stewart Island**, an untouched haven of dense forest with birds, animals, and flowers. (Its Maori name is Rakiura, which translates as *Heavenly Glow*). The tiny fishing village of **Oban** is the main town on the island. Bush walks and paths spread out from it to strategically placed huts throughout the northern part of the island.

Stewart Island is a bird watcher's paradise. You can see tuis, bellbirds, wekas, tomtits, and wood pigeons. And you can hear their songs year-round from the woods and meadows. **Codfish Island**, off the west coast of Stewart Island, is also a great place to view birds.

Buffeted by both the Arctic and the Pacific oceans, Stewart Island's early settlers had a hard life. Many abandoned the island, fed up with the harsh storms and the cold winters, and left behind their homes, sawmills, tin mines, and whaling stations.

The place to stay is the **South Seas Hotel**, in the middle of Oban, where the island's inhabitants meet for a beer. If you're not interested in a beer, just enjoy the view of the harbor.

NEW ZEALAND'S WOOLIEST BARGAINS

New Zealand supports a flock of 70 million sheep. So it shouldn't be a surprise that fleece is a way of life for many and the backbone of the New

Zealand economy. An army of home knitters stands by to turn the raw material into sweaters, gloves, hats, and scarves. The handiwork of New Zealanders pays off in apparel that is sturdy and well-designed.

The wool varies from breed to breed, but most is incredibly dense and full of lanolin, which makes it water-resistant (and gives knitters baby-soft hands).

For those who like their wool still on the hide, New Zealand is also one of the world's greatest marketplaces for sheepskin.

THE BEST OF THE UNITED STATES

Americans go to great lengths and expense to travel to the far corners of the earth in search of the world's bests. The irony is that they can find many of them right in their own back yards. People from around the world flock to the United States to see New York, Washington, D.C., San Francisco, New Orleans, the Rocky Mountains, the Grand Canyon, and Niagara Falls.

New York is one of the most exciting cities in the world. California is where the world's trends are set. The Grand Canyon is one of the world's major wonders. Texas is a world unto itself. Hawaii has the world's best surfing. Alaska is one of the world's last frontiers. And decisions affecting the entire globe are made in Washington, D.C.

Where to begin? If you like big cities, go to New York or Chicago. If you prefer nature, go to Yellowstone and Yosemite national parks. Beach lovers should head for Southern California.

We will begin our look at the United States on the East Coast with New York City, continue on to New England, and then head south along the East Coast. Next we will head west through Texas and the Southwest. Then we will explore the Rockies and California, before heading north on the Pacific Coast. We won't overlook the Midwest, including Chicago. And last, but not least, we will describe the bests of Alaska and Hawaii. (This order is not meant as a rating.)

✴ NEW YORK CITY: AMERICA'S NUMBER-ONE SIGHT

Ask any foreign visitor where he would most like to go in the United States and his reply most likely will be New York City. People around the globe dream of visiting New York, America's great melting pot, a stew of colorful traditions and peoples. New York is also the creative center of the United States. Ambitious young Americans hoping to make it big make their way to the Big Apple—the country's best dancers, artists, writers, musicians, and fashion designers. This mixture of exotic, ambitious, and energetic people makes New York electric.

✴ Manhattan: the heart of the City

Manhattan Island, the liveliest of New York's five boroughs, is the heart

479

of the City, as New Yorkers call their town. The famous **Midtown** area, stretching from 34th to 59th streets, contains the most important sights, including the Museum of Modern Art, Rockefeller Center, St. Patrick's and St. Bartholomew's cathedrals, Times Square, Grand Central Station, the United Nations, Macy's and Bloomingdales (two of the most important department stores in the world), and the Empire State Building.

The southern tip of the island houses most of the city's historic sights, as well as the financial district. Farther north are ethnic neighborhoods: Little Italy, Chinatown, and the Lower East Side. SoHo, an artists' haven, is west of Little Italy. North of SoHo is Greenwich Village, the famous student and artist district, which has become more polished and expensive in recent years. Andy Warhol and Arthur Miller frequented Chelsea, just north of the Village. East of Chelsea is Gramercy Park, with its 19th-century mansions and brownstones.

The **Lower East Side**, between Houston and Canal streets and Allen and Essex streets, is a Jewish and Latino community with great bargain clothing stores. The best are on **Orchard Street**. For Jewish treats, visit **Yonah Schimmel's Knishery**, *137 E. Houston St.; (212)477-2858*, or **Moishe's Bakery**, *181 E. Houston St.*, open every day.

Chinatown, surrounding Mott Street, is the largest Chinese community east of San Francisco, with hundreds of Chinese restaurants and stores. The **Chinese Museum**, *8 Mott St.*, explains the history and culture of New York's Chinese community and leads tours through the neighborhood.

SoHo's best galleries are the **Museum of Holography**, *11 Mercer St.*, and **O.K. Harris**, *383 W. Broadway*. The shops along Canal Street, especially **Canal Jean**, have the best and most interesting buys.

Greenwich Village is filled with homes and haunts of American writers and artists. Louisa May Alcott once lived at 132 MacDougal St. Anarchists from the 1920s met at 137 MacDougal St. in the Liberal Club. Eugene O'Neill saw his first plays produced at the Provincetown Playhouse. Edgar Allen Poe lived at 85 W. Third St. Look for Picasso's colossal sculpture Sylvette on Bleecker Street.

Washington Square Park is the place to go to see first-class street performances. For a bit of spare change, you can watch comedians, musicians, and other performers do their stuff here. (You'll also see sunbathers, drug pushers, office workers, and lovers.)

If money interests you, visit the **Financial District**. Tour the Federal Reserve Bank (The Fed), located between Nassau and William streets, and the New York Stock Exchange (free), where you can see the trading floor from the visitors' gallery. Federal Hall, facing the Stock Exchange, is where George Washington took his oath of office.

The symbol of freedom

The **Statue of Liberty**, on an island off the tip of Manhattan Island, has become a symbol of America at its best—welcoming with open arms immigrants from poor and oppressive nations. The best view of the statue, a gift from France, is from the **Staten Island Ferry**, which leaves from the ferry dock on South Street. For a trip to the statue itself, take a ferry from **Battery Park**.

The best city park: Central Park

New York's **Central Park** is the best city park in the world—and one of the biggest. Here, New Yorkers escape the pace of their frenetic city. This playground for all ages has a zoo, a carousel, an ice-skating rink, a boating lake, gardens, soccer fields, horseshoe courts, baseball diamonds, tennis courts, jogging paths, basketball courts, wading pools, bird-watching, bike rentals, marionette shows, concerts, lawn bowling, horse-and-buggy rides, and refreshment stands. Free Shakespearean plays are performed during the summer.

The top sights

The **Empire State Building**, *Fifth Avenue*, between 33rd and 34th streets, was for years the tallest building in the world. Designed by Shreve, Lamb, and Harmon, it was built in 1930 to 1931. From the top of this 102-story building, you have a breathtaking view of New York. The building is open from 9:30 a.m. to midnight daily.

Radio City Music Hall, *50th Street and Sixth Avenue*, next to Rockefeller Center, is New York's most extravagant theater. The long-legged, feathered Rockettes and their cancan are the main attractions. The interior is art deco.

St. Patrick's Cathedral, *51st Street and Fifth Avenue*, is the largest Roman Catholic cathedral in the United States. Built between 1858 and 1879, it was designed by James Renwick. This Gothic Revival church has 12 side chapels and contains the shrine of St. John Neumann (1811-1860), the first American male to be canonized.

The **United Nations**, *between 42nd and 48th streets*, on the East River, is a large complex with a garden and an esplanade. Free tickets to General Assembly meetings are available in the lobby 30 minutes before each 10:30 a.m. and 3 p.m. meeting (weekdays). Tours are held daily.

Former Beatle John Lennon lived in the **Dakota Apartments**, Central Park West, between 72nd and 73rd streets, until his murder there Dec. 8, 1980. This elegant apartment building, home to many celebrities, was built in 1884.

New York's best museums

The **Metropolitan Museum of Art**, *Fifth Avenue and 82nd Street; tel. (212)535-7710 or (212)879-5500*, houses more than three million works of art, including the Rockefeller Collection of Primitive Art, European paintings, and Egyptian art. The Met, as it is known, is New York's number-one museum and a must-see. The museum is closed Monday.

The **Museum of Modern Art**, *11 W. 53rd Street*, has the best collections of modern art in the world. Permanent shows range from Impressionist to contemporary. It is closed Wednesday.

The **Cloisters**, *Washington Avenue and West 193rd Street; tel. (212) 923-3700*, in a rebuilt medieval monastery in Fort Tryon Park in upper west Manhattan, displays Romanesque and Gothic art. Highlights are the Unicorn Tapestries, the Cuxa Cloister, and the Treasury. It is closed Monday.

The **Guggenheim Museum**, *Fifth Avenue and 89th Street; tel. (212) 360-3500*, a modern spiral building designed by Frank Lloyd Wright, displays the best of contemporary art, including works by Kandinsky, Miró, Calder, and Klee.

The **American Museum of Natural History**, *Central Park West at 79th Street; tel. (212) 769-5000*, houses the fossilized remains of prehistoric animals, as well as reconstructed homes of present and past civilizations. See the show of stars at the planetarium.

The **International Center of Photography**, *1130 Fifth Ave. at 94th Street*, is America's only major museum of photography. The **Jewish Museum**, *Fifth Avenue at 92nd Street*, has a comprehensive collection of Jewish ceremonial art. The Jewish museum is closed Friday and Saturday.

The **Museum of the American Indian**, *3753 Broadway and 155th Street*, is the largest Indian museum in the world.

El Museo del Barrio, *1230 Fifth Ave. at 104th Street; tel. (212) 831-7272*, is devoted to Latin American art and culture.

The **Museum of the City of New York**, *103rd Street and Fifth Avenue; tel. (212) 534-1672*, illustrates the city's past.

The **Museum of Broadcasting**, *1 E. 53rd Street*, is one of the least known and most interesting museums in the city, showing old television shows and playing old radio recordings.

The **Whitney Museum**, *945 Madison Ave. at 75th Street; tel. (212) 570-3676*, is a futuristic structure housing modern American art by Hopper, Soyer, de Kooning, Motherwell, and Warhol. The Whitney is known for its innovative special exhibits.

The best way to see a live television show

Free tickets to live television shows are offered occasionally at the **New York City Visitors Bureau**, *2 Columbus Circle; tel. (212) 397-8200*.

The best entertainment

Midtown, on the west side, is New York at its most entertaining. You'll see everything from Broadway shows to X-rated movies. The **Theater District** stretches from 44th to 54th streets on Broadway. The most beautiful theaters are the **St. James**, *246 W. 44th St.*, the **Shubert**, *44th Street*, the **Booth**, *45th Street*, and the **Majestic**, *44th Street*.

Lincoln Center is the hub of New York's haute couture. More than 13,000 spectators can be accommodated in the center's six buildings: Avery Fisher Hall, the New York State Theater, the Metropolitan Opera House, the Library and Museum of Performing Arts, the Vivian Beaumont Theater, and the Julliard School of Music. The **Metropolitan Opera House** is spectacular, with gigantic Chagall murals, a beautiful central fountain, and glittering chandeliers.

The best on and off Broadway

If you're looking for lights, luster, and glitter, see a show on Broadway. For a more intimate or avant-garde evening, see an off-Broadway show. In either case, you'll be seeing some of the world's best theater.

At **TKTS**, *Duffy Square, 47th Street and Broadway*, you can get tickets to on- and off-Broadway shows for half-price — but you have to buy tickets for shows that same day. **Hit Shows**, *630 Ninth Ave.; tel. (212)581-4211*, sells "two-fers" for a discount. **QUIKTIX** at **Joseph Papp's Public Theater**, *425 Lafayette St.; tel. (212)539-8500*, sells tickets at half-price at 6 p.m. on the night of a performance (as do many other theaters, on and off Broadway).

Joseph Papp's New York **Shakespeare Festival** performs at the Delacorte Theater in Central Park from June through September. Tickets are given out free at 6:15 p.m. for the 8 p.m. performance. Arrive at 5 p.m. and bring a picnic to ensure a good place in line.

The world's best opera company

The **Metropolitan Opera Company**, *tel. (212)362-6000*, is the largest in the world, with a cast that sometimes includes Joan Sutherland and Luciano Pavarotti. The sets are incomparable. From September through April, the company performs at the Metropolitan Opera House in Lincoln Center. During the summer, free performances are given in city parks.

The best dance and music

The **New York City Ballet**, *tel. (212)870-5570*, is the oldest ballet company in the United States. It presents classics, including the Nutcracker Suite at Christmas, at Lincoln Center.

The **American Ballet Theater**, *890 Broadway; tel. (212)477-3030*, directed by Mikhail Baryshnikov, engages such stars as Baryshnikov himself.

The **Joffrey Ballet**, *tel. (212)265-7300*, and the **Alvin Ailey Dance Company**, *tel. (212)767-0590*, are innovative troupes that perform in the City Center, *130 W. 56th St.* Joffrey does classic revivals. Ailey concentrates on modern dance.

The **New York City Opera**, *tel. (212)870-5570*, managed by Beverly Sills, presents bold productions, often in English. Foreign-language operas have supertitles.

The **New York Philharmonic**, *tel. (212)875-5000*, is well-respected, performing works from Bach to Bernstein from September through May at Lincoln Center.

The best jazz joints

New York's best places to hear jazz include the **Blue Note**, *131 W. Third St; tel. (212)475-8592;* **Sweet Basil**, *88 Seventh Ave. S.; tel. (212)242-1785;* the **Village Vanguard**, *178 Seventh Ave. S.; tel. (212)255-4037;* the **Bottom Line**, *15 W. Fourth St. at Mercer Street; tel. (212)228-6300* (all in Greenwich Village); and the **West End Café**, *2909-011 Broadway; tel. (212)662-8830*, near Columbia University.

The best contemporary music

The **Ritz**, *119 E. 11th St; tel. (212)956-3731*, rocks with the tunes of such musicians as Chuck Berry.

The **Lone Star Café**, *240 W. 52nd St; tel. (212)245-2950*, has good country-western and blues music, a surprise in the middle of such a cosmopolitan city.

The **Back Porch**, *488 Third Ave.; tel. (212)685-3828*, has a terrific pianist.

Brazilian music is played at **Sounds of Brazil**, *204 Varick St.; tel. (212)924-5221*.

New York's best restaurant

The **21 Club**, *21 W. 52nd St.; tel. (212)582-7200*, in the heart of midtown Manhattan, has an elegant dining room for those who wish to keep a low profile. Dr. Armand Hammer and Aristotle Onassis have been patrons.

This establishment began as a speakeasy during Prohibition; Jack Kriendler and Charlie Berns opened the club on New Year's Day in 1930. Away from the scrutiny of federal agents, it became a haven for politicos, actors, and journalists. Tallulah Bankhead once said there wasn't much point in getting up on Sunday, because 21 is closed. Dinner for two at 21 is about $100, not including drinks.

Other superb restaurants

The **Quilted Giraffe**, *550 Madison Ave.; tel. (212)593-1221*, serves the innovative creations of Barry and Susan Wine. The beggar's purses are especially good, little crepes filled with crème fraîche and caviar. The restaurant is closed Sunday and Monday.

The **Four Seasons**, *99 E. 52nd St.; tel. (212)754-9494*, is a popular place for lunch. The menu varies with the season, a combination of classic and contemporary cuisines. Save room for the chocolate-chocolate mahogany cake.

Lutece, *249 E. 50th St.; tel. (212)752-2225*, is the best French restaurant in New York. Only the finest ingredients are used, and the preparation is imaginative.

Café des Artistes, *1 W. 67th St.; tel. (212)877-3500*, has been a New York institution since the 1930s. Try the potted and roasted duck confit. The restaurant is open daily for dinner and Sundays for brunch.

Le Cirque, *58 E. 65th St.*, is one of the best French restaurants in Manhattan, an elegant, spacious place with impeccable cuisine. Its crème brulée is the best in the United States. Reservations are required. Le Cirque is closed Sundays.

Enoteca Iperbole, *137 E. 55th St.*, has the largest wine cellar in the United States. Try the pheasant with your wine. The restaurant is closed Sundays.

The best ethnic restaurants

The best Mexican restaurant in New York (and one of the best in the United States) is **Rosa Mexicana**, *1063 First Ave.; tel. (212)753-7407*. Try the red snapper in cilantro sauce. The restaurant is open every night.

Benito's II, *163 Mulberry St.; tel. (212)226-9012*, in Little Italy, is one of the city's best Italian (Sicilian) restaurants. **Elaine's**, *1703 Second Ave.*, is also good, especially popular among publishers and writers. And **Sandro's**, *420 E. 59th St.*, should not be overlooked. Chef Sandro Fioriti goes all out with spices and imagination when preparing his pasta. The fried ricotta with tomato sauce is tasty. Sandro's is open daily after 3 p.m.

The **Russian Tea Room**, *150 W. 57th St.; tel. (212)265-0947*, near Carnegie Hall, has Russian specialties and a glamorous clientele. Try the blini with caviar, the borscht, and the icy vodka drinks. The restaurant is open daily.

The **Ukrainian Restaurant**, *140 Second Ave.*, is humble and cheap—but the food is excellent.

Darbar, *44 W. 56th St.; tel. (212)432-7227*, is the best Indian restaurant in town, an elegant place with white-linen tablecloths and correct service.

New York's best hotels

The best place to stay is the **Carlyle**, *35 E. 76th St.; tel. (212)744-1600*, an old-fashioned, Old World hotel with perfect service. The attention to detail is remarkable. **Morgans**, *237 Madison Ave.; tel. (212)686-0300*, is an exclusive hideaway for celebrities, including Margaux Hemingway and Rod Stewart. An enthusiastic young staff (owner Steve Rubell says he hired no New Yorkers) takes care of guests' needs. Andy Warhol paintings adorn some of the rooms. Guests are guaranteed admission to the Palladium.

The **Algonquin**, *59 W. 44th St.; tel. (212)840-6800*, is a first-class, old-fashioned hotel.

The **Helmsley Palace**, *455 Madison Ave.; tel. (212)888-7000*, is a modern skyscraper rising out of a 19th-century mansion. The lobby and dining rooms are elegant old rooms with antiques. Bedrooms are spacious and modern, with fantastic views of New York.

The **Ritz Carlton**, *112 Central Park S.; tel. (212)757-1900*, is a very English, very luxurious modern establishment with views of Central Park and a central location near the main shopping areas. The popular Jockey Club dining room is here.

The **Pierre**, *Fifth Avenue at 61st Street; tel. (212)838-8000*, is a peaceful place, where celebrities stay when they want privacy. The view is of Central Park.

The **Michelangelo Hotel**, *152 W. 51st St.; tel. (212)765-1900 or (800)237-0990*, is a bit of old Europe in the middle of Manhattan. Each of the 180 rooms is decorated differently, but all have bathrooms of Italian marble. Hotel services include courtesy limousine service to Wall Street and use of nearby health-club facilities. The concierge is especially helpful.

The best budget hotel

The best hotel for your money in New York is the **Paramount**, *235 W. 46th St.; tel. (212)764-5500*, with a progressive European atmosphere and decor and first-class service. The Paramount is becoming the place to stay in the City.

THE BEST OF NEW YORK STATE

Don't spend all your time in the City; **New York State** also is worth seeing. Unspoiled forest and rolling farmland still exist in this fertile state, which is watered by lakes Champlain, George, Erie, and Ontario, as well as the Hudson River. The Adirondack and Catskill mountains offer retreat from the noise and pollution of New York City.

The best of the Adirondacks

You can hike in the **Adirondacks** for days without leaving the wilderness. The most beautiful area is between lakes Placid and Saranac, where the forest is untouched and the streams are pure.

Adirondack National Park is the largest wilderness area east of the Mississippi, bordered by lakes George and Champlain. One of the most beautiful sights in the park is the **Ausable Chasm**, on Route 9 near Interstate 87, a mile-long gorge near Lake Champlain.

Fort Ticonderoga, used during the French and Indian War and the Revolutionary War, guards the junction of lakes Champlain and George. A museum today, it is open May through October.

Lakes Placid and Saranac, at the heart of the Adirondacks, offer canoeing, boating, and fishing. Lake Placid has tremendous skiing—good enough for Olympic athletes, in fact, who competed here in 1980.

The best place to stay on Saranac Lake is **The Point**, *Star Route, Saranak Lake, Box 65; tel. (518)891-5674*, an 11-room inn with a private beach.

Originally a camp, The Point is elegant now, decorated with fine paintings. The bedrooms are enormous. You can sail or canoe on the lake, hike or cross-country ski through the woods, or play tennis, golf, badminton, billiards, Ping-Pong, or croquet.

High Peaks Base Camp, 13 miles from Lake Placid, *Springfield Road*, is situated on 200 acres ringed by the Sentinel Wilderness Range and the Hurricane Mountain Primitive area. It has miles of cross-country ski trails and is just five miles from the downhill ski slopes at Whiteface Mountain. Enjoy a home-cooked meal in the Wood Parlor.

The **Rose Inn**, *Route 34N, P.O. Box 6576, Ithaca; tel. (607) 533-7905*, is also a charming place to stay, 10 minutes outside of Ithaca. The light-rose, Italianate mansion is set on 20 acres of gardens, a pond, and an apple orchard. All the rooms are decorated differently, with a variety of antiques and Victorian furniture. The cuisine here is fabulous. Each guest chooses his appetizer and entree at the time of booking.

The Baseball Hall of Fame

Cooperstown, in central New York state, is a small town with a big drawing card — the **Baseball Hall of Fame**. Three floors of baseball memorabilia fill this museum, a mecca for baseball fans. You can see enlarged photographs of the world's best baseball players, sculptures of Babe Ruth and Ted Williams carved from single pieces of laminated basswood, and roughly 1,000 artifacts and photos from the early Negro baseball leagues. Also on display are baseball cards from 1900, Lou Gehrig's uniform, and Joe DiMaggio's locker.

Cooperstown has several good restaurants. The best is the **Dining Room**, *171 Main St.; tel. (607) 547-2211*, where you can indulge in homemade fare and rich desserts.

Our favorite place to stay is **Angelholm**, *14 Elm St.; tel. (607) 547-2483*, a restored home built nearly 175 years ago. This bed-and-breakfast has only four bedrooms, and baths are shared. But a complete breakfast is included in the price of a room.

Lake Champlain's bests (and beasts)

Between New York, Vermont, and Quebec lies **Lake Champlain**, where more than 200 sightings of a controversial monster called Champ have been reported. Champ's existence is debatable, but the beauty of the lake and its islands is not.

Lake Champlain's major islands — North Hero, South Hero, and Isle La Motte — are dotted with sugar maple and oak trees, red barns, and silos. Although they look serene, they have had a tumultuous history. The French, British, and Americans warred over the lake, because of its importance as a natural highway from New York to Canada.

Samuel de Champlain discovered the islands in 1609, claiming them for the French. Later, the British claimed them, and finally the Americans. The turning-point battle of the War of 1812 was fought at Pittsburgh, where nearly 30,000 British troops were defeated by 2,000 Americans.

Isle La Motte is the site of the first settlement in Vermont, **Fort St. Anne**, which was built by the French in 1666 for defense against the Indians. Today open-air Masses are held here. **Fort Blunder**, built by the Americans in 1777, was so named because its builders didn't realize it was on Canadian soil.

THE BEST OF NEW ENGLAND

One of the oldest and most historic areas of the United States is **New England**, where quaint, shingled homes and simple churches have a unique charm. Boston harbors intellect, art, ethnic variety, and beauty. Cape Cod has the most beautiful coastline on the Atlantic. And the mountains of northern New England are green and rolling.

The best of Boston

Boston, one of the most livable cities in America, is a collection of interconnected small towns. Despite its folksy atmosphere, it is sophisticated, with a large intellectual community and many universities and colleges. It is also the best place to trace American colonial history. Historic figures, such as Samuel Adams, Paul Revere, and Ben Franklin, lived here. Walk by the **Old North Church**, where lanterns were hung to signal an attack by the British during the Revolutionary War. Or climb **Bunker Hill**, the site of one of the war's major battles. And visit the place where Boston Tea Party participants dumped British tea into the harbor.

American writers Ralph Waldo Emerson, Henry David Thoreau, Louisa May Alcott, and Daniel Webster found inspiration in Boston. In more recent years, Boston has spawned the Kennedys. And many of America's best minds have graduated from nearby Harvard University.

The easiest way to see the best of Boston

The easiest way to see Boston is to follow the **Freedom Trail**—a red brick or painted line that leads past the city's greatest landmarks. The trail takes you past the **Old State House**, where the Boston Massacre occurred; the **Old North Church**, where the light was hung to signal Paul Revere; the **Old South Meeting House**, where the Boston Tea Party was planned; the **Boston Tea Party Ship and Museum**; and the **Granary Burial Ground**, where the victims of the Boston Massacre are buried.

Boston's must-sees

The best view of the city is from **Bunker Hill**, but you'll have to climb 294 steps to enjoy it.

Beacon Hill is an elegant neighborhood with trees, cobblestoned streets, and beautiful old brownstones. Louisa May Alcott once lived at 10 Louisburg Square. Blue bloods now live where Puritans originally settled.

The 1 passes 16 important landmarks of black history over the past 300 years.

The **State House**, a gold-domed building in Beacon Hill, is open to visitors.

The world's oldest public library

Boston's **Public Library** is the oldest in the world, founded by Benjamin Franklin and decorated with paintings by Sargent.

Boston's best museums

The **Museum of Fine Arts**, *tel. (617)267-9377*, near Northeastern University, has Egyptian, Impressionist, and Americana collections.

The **Isabella Stuart Gardner Museum**, *280 Fenway; tel. (617)734-1359*, is a small Venetian-style palace filled with great works of art, including Titian's The Rape of Europa, Raphael's Pieta, and paintings by Rembrandt, Sargent, Whistler, and Matisse. The museum is closed Monday.

Boston's **Institute of Contemporary Art**, *955 Boylston St.*, in a former fire station, displays works by contemporary artists.

The museum at the **John F. Kennedy Library**, *Morrisey Boulevard*, contains photos and documents about John and Robert Kennedy.

The world's largest fish tank

The **New England Aquarium** on Central Wharf is the world's largest fish tank, containing the world's greatest collection of sharks.

Boston's best parks

Boston is a city of parks. The best is the **Boston Common**, with its inviting green lawns, sunbathers, Frisbee players, musicians, picnicking families, and swan-filled ponds.

Boston's **Public Gardens**, between Arlington, Boylston, Beacon, and Charles streets, are just across from the Boston Common.

The **Arnold Arboretum**, a 265-acre park on the Arborway in Jamaica Plain, is one of America's oldest parks, containing 6,000 varieties of trees.

The most festive times to visit

Patriot's Day (April 19) is celebrated with the re-enactment of Paul Revere's ride. The hero sets out from the North End and gallops past the

Old North Church yelling, "The British are coming, The British are coming." In Concord, Minutemen re-enact the battle of the Old North Bridge. This is also the day of the Boston Marathon.

Boston's best ice cream

Every Boston-area neighborhood has its favorite ice-cream parlor. The best is **Toscanini's**, *899 Main St.; tel. (617)491-5877*, in Cambridge, a small shop serving 16 homemade flavors, including ginger, grape-nut raisin, Vienna finger cookie, and Belgian chocolate.

A roster of great restaurants

The best seafood restaurant in Boston is **Anthony's Pier 4**, *140 Northern Ave.*, which is decorated with pieces of scrimshaw and old navigational equipment. Order the lobster.

The most elegant restaurant in town is **Aujourd'hui**, in the Four Seasons Hotel, *200 Boylston St.; tel. (617)338-4400*, where New England fare is spiced up with European and Asian accents. White linen and Royal Doulton china dress the tables.

The most romantic restaurant is **Café Budapest**, *90 Exeter St.*, where exotic flowers decorate the Old World dining rooms, and spicy Central European dishes scent the air.

One of the oldest restaurants in Boston is the **Locke-Ober Café**, *3 Winter Place; tel. (617)542-1340*, which opened in 1875. Try the filet of lemon sole *bonne femme*.

The best value seafood and prime rib

The **No-Name Restaurant**, *Boston Fish Pier, Northern Avenue; tel. (617)423-2705*, is a little out of the way, but still easily accessible from downtown Boston, especially if you are near Quincy Market or Faneuil Hall. The menu is limited to fried or broiled seafood, and usually a catch of the day. The portions are enormous, and the atmosphere a little crazy. You sit at long tables which seat about 18 people, so this is not the place to go if you're looking for intimacy. It *is* the place to go if you are looking for great food and cheap prices. Bring your own wine, as they do not serve alcohol here. Reservations are not accepted, so be prepared to stand in line. Credit cards are not accepted.

Durgin Park, *340 Faneuil Hall Marketplace; tel. (617)227-2038*, serves the best prime rib for the money in Boston. Its atmosphere, too, is a little crazy. The portions are enormous—hanging over the edge of the platters—and prices are inexpensive. The decor is rustic or early colonialist.

Boston's finest hotels

The oldest hotel in America and Boston's best is the **Omni Parker House Hotel**, *60 School St; tel. (617)227-8600*. Dickens, Emerson, and

Longfellow all stayed here. The famous Parker House roll was first baked here more than a century ago. Ho Chi Minh once worked at the Parker house as a busboy.

The **Ritz Carlton**, *15 Arlington St.; tel. (617)536-5700*, is an elegant place with a dignified staff and luxurious rooms. The hotel restaurant offers exquisite meals and lovely views of Boston's Public Gardens.

The **Copley Plaza**, *138 St. James Ave.; tel. (617)267-5300*, is an elegant 460-room hotel opened in 1912. While it is grand, it has an intimate air, with a library where you can take tea. The bedrooms are spacious and richly furnished. The Copley has three restaurants, three bars, and shops.

The best of Cambridge

Across the Charles River from Boston is **Cambridge**, a charming area encompassing Harvard University (the oldest in the nation), the Massachusetts Institute of Technology (MIT), and lots of bookstores and movie houses.

The trendiest shops and restaurants are on **Harvard Square**, where you'll also find street performers, five ice-cream parlors, and seven bars. **Harvard Yard**, part of the campus, is quieter and more dignified.

The **Harvard University Museum**, *24 Oxford St.*, is actually four museums: the Peabody Museum of Archeology and Ethnology, the Museum of Comparative Zoology, the Mineralogical and Geological Museum, and the Botanical Museum. The museum's Ware Collection of glass flowers is the finest array of decorative glasswork in the world.

The **Fogg Art Museum**, *32 Quincy St.*, is the best university art collection, a formidable assortment of Oriental and late 18th-century European art.

One of the largest comic book stores in the United States is the **Million Year Picnic**, *99 Mount Auburn St.*

The **Grolier Bookstore**, *6 Plympton St.*, is the oldest poetry bookstore in the country.

Two historic towns

Just outside Boston are two towns that played essential roles in American history: Lexington and Concord.

Paul Revere rode through **Lexington** the night of April 18, 1775, warning that British troops were approaching. On Lexington Green, the first shots of the Revolutionary War were fired and the first blood was drawn.

Founding fathers Samuel Adams and John Hancock slept at the **Hancock-Clarke House**, *36 Hancock St.*, today a museum.

Concord is the town next door, where Minutemen gathered to head off the British. The **Old North Bridge** over the Concord River is the site of the Revolutionary War's first battle. It was made famous by these words: "Here once the embattled farmers stood and fired the shot heard round the world."

Concord produced some of America's most famous writers. Louisa May Alcott lived with her family at the Wayside and wrote *Little Women* at the Orchard House. You can visit the **Ralph Waldo Emerson House**, *28 Cambridge Turnpike*. Nathaniel Hawthorne rented the **Old Manse**, *Monument Street*, but bought **Wayside**, *Lexington Road*.

The **Concord Museum**, *Lexington Road and Cambridge Turnpike*, displays possessions of Emerson and Thoreau.

Cape Cod: the most beautiful coastline

Cape Cod, a hook-shaped sandy peninsula in southeast Massachusetts, has the most beautiful coastline on the Atlantic: sand dunes covered with sea oats, silvery driftwood, seagulls basking in the sun, huge rocks, and the crashing ocean. The Cape Cod National Seashore protects 44,600 acres of the cape from development.

The liveliest town

Provincetown, at the northern tip, is the cape's hot spot, a maze of clapboard houses, some dating back to the 18th century, galleries, guesthouses, and shops. Popular and busy, it draws artists, the gay community, and families. The town lies within the Cape Cod National Seashore and is surrounded by dunes, ocean beaches, marshes, and woods.

Commercial Street, the main thoroughfare, is lined with art galleries, shops, and crowds of pedestrians, bikers, cars, horse-drawn buggies, hawkers, and skateboarders. Here, also, is the **Provincetown Playhouse**, where Eugene O'Neill spent a lot of time.

Provincetown has a long history. Although Plymouth claims to be the oldest colony, the pilgrims actually landed at Provincetown first, before heading on to Plymouth, where they settled. A monument to these hardy souls sits atop a 100-foot hill at the heart of town. The 252-foot granite column can be climbed via 116 steps. From the top, you can see for 50 miles on a clear day.

Provincetown boasts one of the few links-style golf courses in the United States, the **Highland Golf Club**, *Highland Road, Truro; tel. (508)487-9201*.

For dancing, go to **Captain John's**, *Shankpainter Road*. More novel entertainment can be found at the **Surf Club**, *MacMillan Wharf*, where you can marvel at the Provincetown Jug and Marching Band—four musicians who play 20 instruments, including washboards, jugs, and kazoos.

The **Moors**, *Bradford Street*, has good Portuguese dishes and fresh seafood, but it is a seasonal restaurant.

Our favorite inn is **Snug Cottage**, *178 Bradford St.; tel. (508)487-1616*, built in 1820, one block from the beach. The two-story main house and the four additional cottages are decorated with fireplaces and old-fashioned furnishings. The hotel is seasonal, so call before arriving.

New England's oldest settlement

Plymouth, where the *Mayflower* landed in December 1620, is the oldest European settlement in New England. Half the colony died the first terrible winter here. **Plymouth Rock**, the landmark boulder marking the spot where the pilgrims disembarked, is kept behind bars at **Pilgrim Hall**, *Water Street*. The Plymouth of 1627 and the Wampanoag Indian summer campsite have been recreated here in a Williamsburg-style complex called Plimouth Plantation, where actors play the parts of the pilgrims and Indians. Explore the *Mayflower II*, a reproduction of the original.

The **Sleepy Pilgrim**, *182 Court St.*, is a pleasant 12-unit motel. It is open April through December.

The best whale watching

Whale-watching cruises depart Plymouth and Provincetown for the Stellwagen Bank north of Cape Cod, one of the few areas in the United States where great whales can be seen on a regular basis. Each year, thousands of these beautiful giants take up residence on the 20-mile-long shoal. Fifteen kinds of whales have been seen in these waters, as well as dolphins, porpoises, and rare birds. Marine biologists accompany the cruises to identify and describe the fish and birds and explain their behavior.

Groups offering cruises from Plymouth include **Captain Tim Brady & Sons**, *tel. (508) 746-4809*. Whale-watching cruises from Provincetown include **Portuguese Princess**, *tel. (508) 487-2651*, and **Provincetown Whale Watch**, *tel. (508) 487-3322*.

Provincetown Inn, at the tip of Provincetown, *tel. (508) 487-9500*, offers a whale-watching package that includes a cruise, two dinners, two breakfasts, and two nights lodging.

Also visit the **Whale Discovery Museum** in Plymouth.

The most beautiful island

Martha's Vineyard Island, off the coast of Cape Cod, is the most beautiful on the Atlantic Coast, protected by bluffs and dunes. Rocky and sandy beaches edge the island. Inland are pine forests and peaceful lakes and ponds, where you can canoe among rare seabirds. At the far end of the island are the brightly colored cliffs of Gay Head and a small Indian reservation. Shingled Cape Cod houses nestle among the island's rolling hills, and bayberry scents the air.

You can catch a ferry to Martha's Vineyard from the Cape Cod town of **Woods Hole**. If you plan to bring a car, make reservations well in advance; you'll have to wait in line for hours if you don't.

Edgartown is the most elegant town on the island, its narrow streets lined with expensive shops and guesthouses.

Oak Bluffs is a honky-tonk town, less stuffy than most of the towns on the island. Gingerbread houses make this slightly seedy town look quaint. The largest carousel in the world, the Flying Horses, is here.

Gay Head is the most beautiful spot on Martha's Vineyard. It is also home to the remaining Indians on the island, who live on a reservation nearby. An Indian-operated lunch counter at the top of the cliffs serves the best milk shakes anywhere. The view from the patio is the best on the island.

Seafood is fresh and plentiful on Martha's Vineyard. For lobster, go to the **Homeport** restaurant, *Menemsha; tel. (508) 645-2679*. Bring your own wine. Reservations are advised.

If you're feeling more adventurous, buy your own fresh lobster and a steamer in Menemsha, a small fishing village, and prepare your own feast. Or stop in at any of the restaurants in these towns frequented by the local fishermen; most all of them offer lunch specials including one or two small lobsters, french fries, and salad.

Edgartown is home to the island's two most elegant restaurants: L'Etoile and Warriners. The seafood at **Warriners**, *Post Office Square; tel. (508) 627-4488*, is good, and the wine list is extensive. But it's a bit stuffy, and it's closed Wednesday nights. **L'Etoile, Charlotte Inn**, *27 S. Summer St.; tel. (508) 627-5187*, is pretty, and the service is superb.

Our favorite inn is the **Kelly House**, *121 N. Water St.; tel. (508) 627-4394*, in Edgartown. A cozy place decorated in the style of the 1890s, it is open year-round. The dining room is good and inexpensive.

The **Captain Dexter House**, *100 Main St., Vineyard Haven*, is a good inn with reasonable prices. This old sea captain's home was built in 1843 and is filled with antiques. But it is seasonal, so call ahead.

Nantucket—the most exclusive

Nantucket is a lovely island east of Martha's Vineyard. This wealthy resort has long, sandy beaches and quaint, cobblestoned streets. If you love to shop, you'll love Nantucket. Look for Nantucket woven baskets and scrimshaw jewelry (carved from whale teeth). **Seven Seas Gifts** is a good gift shop with an enormous variety. The best way to see Nantucket is by bike. Pedal out to **Seaskonset Beach** (pronounced Skonset) and check out the island's many old lighthouses.

Nantucket was the greatest whaling town in the United States during the 18th and 19th centuries. Visit the **Nantucket Whaling Museum** and **Hadwen House** and **Peter Foulger House**, old whaling homes that are open to the public.

The island's best restaurant is the **Jared Coffin House**, *29 Broad St., tel. (508) 228-2400*, which is internationally acclaimed. It is open April through December.

Two pleasant old inns are the **Carriage House**, *5 Ray's Court; tel. (508) 228-0326*, in a converted 1865 carriage house, and the **Ships Inn**, *13*

Fair St.; tel. (508)228-0040, in a sea captain's house built in 1812. Both have antique furnishings. Both are seasonal.

New Hampshire's bests

The highest peak on the East Coast is **Mount Washington** in the White Mountains of New Hampshire. Located in the **White Mountain National Forest**, this 6,288-foot mountain is a popular ski resort. Take the train to the top. **Crawford Notch State Park**, nearby, has sparkling waterfalls. Take Route 3 to the flume at the southern end of Franconia Notch. This glacier-covered chasm has 70-foot walls. A rock formation called The Old Man of the Mountains looks over Profile Lake.

Mount Washington Hotel and Resort, *Bretton Woods; tel. (603)278-1000*, is the most peaceful of the White Mountain resorts. Excellent stables, a championship golf course, fishing, skiing, and tennis are offered.

Maine's main sights

The best thing about **Portland, Maine**, is the area surrounding it. Casco Bay, the Casco Bay Islands, and Sebago Lake are typical New England areas, with quaint houses and good boating and swimming. Portland also has great lobster, good nightlife, and the poet Longfellow's house. **Cap'n Newick's Lobster**, *740 Broadway St., South Portland; tel. (207)799-3090*, is the best place in town for lobster (although the decor isn't much).

Bar Harbor

Bar Harbor, Maine, once a mecca for the wealthy, welcomes a broader spectrum of visitors today. The quaint harbor town shares **Mount Desert Island** (so named by Champlain in 1604 because of its rocky summit) with **Acadia National Park**, an expanse of mountains, spruce forests, rugged coastline, and deep lakes. Along the shore is Somes Sound, the deepest fiord on the East Coast. The air is pure, and the drinking water is the best we have ever tasted. The local restaurants serve fresh lobster for next to nothing.

Acadia National Park is surrounded by a 10-mile park road loop. Along the road are **Thunder Hole**, where waves rush into a rocky canyon producing a thundering boom and sending up towers of foam; **Jordan Pond**, an idyllic, mirrorlike pond reflecting the Bubbles, two rounded mountains; **Jackson Memorial Library**, the world's largest center for mammalian genetic research; and **Sand Beach**, the island's only sandy swimming area.

It's worth rolling out of bed early to see the sun rise from the summit of **Cadillac Mountain**, a windswept bald spot, the highest on the island, with views of forests, ocean, and neighboring islands. If you do get here at dawn, you are the first person in the United States to see the sun rise.

The best place to dine on the island is the **Jordan Pond House**, *Park*

Loop Road, Acadia National Park, a rambling old house. You can dine on the lawn when it's warm or by the fireplace when it's not.

A good place to stay is the **Bluenose**, *90 Eden St., Bar Harbor; tel. (800)445-4077*, set on a cliff just outside town. Rooms have French doors that open onto private balconies overlooking Frenchman's Bay. The pool is heated, a real asset in chilly Maine. And there is also an indoor pool.

Newport: best jazz, best sailing

✳**Newport, Rhode Island** has New England's finest mansions (which belong to such families as the Astors and the Vanderbilts), as well as the region's top music festival and sailing events. (Before the America's Cup was won by Australia, the regatta began here, at the mouth of the Narragansett Bay.)

For two weeks every July, Newport hosts a music festival with concerts featuring premier and recently discovered works and thematic programs, such as "Emperor's Court," works composed in Austria-Hungary during the reign of Franz Josef. The spectacular mansions of Newport are converted to concert halls for this 21-year-old event. The long list of debuts by major talents at this festival is indicative of its quality. You can get tickets through the **Music Box**, *tel. (401)849-6666*.

The best restaurant in town is the **White Horse Tavern**, *Marlborough and Farewell streets; tel. (401)849-3600*, America's oldest tavern. Built in 1673, it later became a tavern run by a notorious Red Sea pirate. It doesn't open for lunch on Tuesdays.

A good place to stay the night is **Mill Street Inn**, *75 Mill St.; tel. (401)849-9500*. The most interesting inn in the area is the **Jail House Inn**, *13 Marlborough St.; tel. (401)847-4638*. Built in 1772, it served as the Newport jail for over 200 years. The 22 "cells" have been converted into modern, sunny suites with views of downtown Newport.

Classic New England in Vermont

Rural Vermont offers the rolling Green Mountains, lovely Lake Champlain, covered bridges, bridle trails, farmland, and little villages.

Stowe, in northern Vermont, is the state's biggest vacation center. It is best visited during its Winter Carnival in mid-January, which includes ice sculpture and winter sport competitions. **Mount Mansfield** provides downhill and cross-country skiing and hiking on its Long Trail.

Arlington, in southwestern Vermont, is home to the Norman Rockwell exhibition and to our favorite inn in the area, the **Arlington Inn**, *Historic Route 7A, P.O. Box 369; tel. (802)375-6532*. The feel and decor of the Arlington is pure Victorian; the exterior architecture is Greek Revival. Each of the 13 rooms has a fireplace, as well as a reading chair or sitting area.

The quintessential New England town is **Newfane**, Vermont. North of

Brattleboro, this town is gorgeous in the fall, when autumn leaves splatter it with color and the air smells of apples. In winter, neighbors gather around the potbelly in Union Hall.

The **Old Newfane Inn** (1787), *Court Street; tel. (802)365-4427*, dates back to when Vermont was a republic. **Union Hall**, built in 1832, was once a house of worship. The **Newfane Store** sells homemade cider and fudge. The famous **Marlboro Music Festival** is held nearby each summer, on the campus of Marlboro College.

One of Vermont's best resorts is **Stratton Mountain Resort**, *tel. (802)297-2200*, in the Green Mountains. Lessons are given in downhill and cross-country skiing, golf, tennis, and fishing.

Said to be the most photographed village in Vermont, **Lower Waterford** is home to one of the best places to stay in the entire state. The **Rabbit Hill Inn**, *Route 18; tel. (802)748-5168*, makes you feel right at home. When you arrive, tea or cider is served in the formal dining room, and dinner is served by candlelight. Many of the rooms include four-poster beds, sitting areas, and fireplaces.

NEW JERSEY: THE MOST MALIGNED STATE

New Jersey is the most maligned state in the Union, probably because most people know only the long and ugly turnpike. Despite odorous industrial cities, such as Newark and Elizabeth, New Jersey does deserve its description as The Garden State. A patchwork quilt of farm communities and historical parks, New Jersey offers the top per-acre value for agricultural production.

The state's beaches are natural and white and extend the entire length of the coast. At the heart of New Jersey are the **Pine Barrens**, an unspoiled wooded area. Northern New Jersey has pretty lakes, and in the northwest are mountains leading into the Poconos. Along the Delaware border are historic towns dating back to the Revolutionary War.

More than 100 clashes occurred on New Jersey soil during the Revolutionary War, including pivotal battles in Trenton, Princeton, and Monmouth.

Princeton: New Jersey's prettiest town

Princeton, a beautiful, historic town founded in the 17th century, is the site of an Ivy League university, stately private mansions, and an intimate downtown area. In addition to housing **Princeton University**, the town is the home of the Institute of Advanced Study founded by Einstein, the Princeton Theological Seminary, and Westminster Choir College, famous for its choir.

Built around Princeton University, a center of thought since 1756, the town has been embellished by such wealthy benefactors as Andrew Carnegie (who funded the building of a lake used as a training area for the Princeton rowing crew and as an ice-skating rink in winter). Another benefactor refurbished the central downtown square (called **Palmer Square**) in a Tudor motif, complete with an old-fashioned inn. Palmer Square is especially lovely at Christmas, when the giant pine at its center is decorated. Princetonians gather around the tree to sing carols.

Nassau Hall at the university was the seat of the Continental Congress from June to November 1783.

Buy a gourmet picnic lunch from the **Squire's Choice**, *Palmer Square*, and enjoy it on **Princeton Battlefield**, where George Washington's army won a victory on Jan. 3, 1777, against the British, or in **Marquand Park**, which has more variety than most botanical gardens. Late in the summer, community theater groups stage plays on the battlefield beside the four marble columns left standing from a home burned down during the Revolutionary War. The cool pines protect the audience from the summer sun.

The **Annex Restaurant**, *Nassau Street*, is an Italian restaurant where you can get a relatively inexpensive but delicious meal. After 10 p.m., you can mingle with professors and students at the bar.

The **Nassau Inn**, *10 Palmer Square; tel. (609)921-7500*, at the center of town, has several dining rooms, including the Yankee Doodle Tap Room, which offers live music. Initials carved in the inn's tabletops date back to 1919.

THE BEST OF THE JERSEY SHORE

One hundred miles of boardwalk and beaches trim the New Jersey coast, offering both honky-tonk towns and quiet enclaves.

Atlantic City: a gambler's best

Almost every American knows the streets of **Atlantic City**, a honky-tonk town famous for its gambling, by heart—they are on the *Monopoly* game board. Before the Civil War, Atlantic City was the seaside getaway for the high society of New York and Philadelphia. The town fell on hard times during the mid-20th century. However, in 1978, Resorts International opened the first casino here, and since then the town has been revived. A dozen casinos have opened along the boardwalk and on the bay.

The former Million Dollar Pier has been reborn as **Ocean One**, a shopping and dining arcade. Like visitors of 100 years ago, you can ride a canopied wicker chair on wheels from one end of the boardwalk to the other, stopping to see saltwater taffy being pulled.

The best restaurant in town is the **Knife and Fork**, *Pacific and Albany avenues*, near Bally's Grand. Service is fabulous; customers are treated like royalty. The seafood dishes are excellent, especially the bouillabaisse, which is chock-full of fish, including large pieces of lobster.

Cape May: a Victorian surprise

At the southern tip of the Jersey shore is a Victorian surprise: **Cape May**. Victorian mansions with wide porches, gables, and elaborate woodwork line the streets. Many are guesthouses. The wide sandy beach is inviting.

The **Barnard-Good House**, *238 Perry St.; tel. (609) 884-5381*, is a Victorian house with a wraparound porch decorated with lacy wood trim. The parlor has an antique pump organ and a hand-carved and tiled false fireplace. An iron, pewter, and brass gasolier hangs above the dining room table. The breakfast served here is delicious—fresh juice, omelets, croissants, home-made breads, and crepes. Each of the six bedrooms is decorated differently; some have four-poster beds, others have bathrooms with antique tubs. It is seasonal.

The **Summer Cottage Inn**, *613 Columbia Ave.; tel. (609) 884-4948*, was built in 1867 as a summer home. Verandas and tall ceilings keep the house cool. This Victorian bed-and-breakfast is decorated with walnut- and oak-inlaid floors and period wallpaper. Afternoon tea is served in the sitting room, where wicker furnishings are placed around the fireplace. Three of the bed-rooms have private baths.

New Jersey's best inn

The **Woolverton Inn**, *Woolverton Road, Stockton; tel. (609) 397-0802*, is on the New Jersey/Pennsylvania line at the Delaware River. Shaded by two spacious front porches and big old trees, this stone manor house was built in 1793 by John Prall, who ran a quarry in what is now the garden. In 1957, Sir John Terrell, the owner of the popular Music Circus, bought the property, and many of the celebrities performing in the Music Circus have stayed here. Every room is filled with antiques. Some bedrooms have canopied beds, others have four-poster beds.

PHILADELPHIA: A HISTORIAN'S BEST

Philadelphia is the most historically important city in the United States. Founded in 1681 by William Penn as a Quaker colony, Philadelphia is where Thomas Jefferson wrote the Declaration of Independence, signed at Independence Hall, and where the Bill of Rights was adopted at Congress Hall. The Continental Congress met in Philadelphia, which was the national capital from 1777 to 1800.

All the city's major historic sights are in **Independence National Historic Park**: Independence Hall; the Liberty Bell; Carpenter's Hall, where the First Continental Congress met in 1774; City Tavern, a reconstruction of the tavern where delegates of the Continental Congress gathered; Congress Hall; Graff House, where Thomas Jefferson lived; Old City Hall; and the Betsy Ross House.

Bordering the one-mile-square park is **Society Hill**, Philadelphia's oldest neighborhood, which has been completely restored. Society Hill was named for the Free Society of Stock Traders, a company created by William Penn. However, most people presume it was named for the somewhat snooty residents.

The most important sights

The Declaration of Independence and the Constitution were signed at **Independence Hall**, *Chestnut Street*. Half-hour tours are offered. Across the street is the **Liberty Bell Pavilion**, where you can touch the cracked bell that rang out in July 1776 to proclaim the Declaration of Independence. (The bell cracked in 1835 and again in 1846.)

The **Betsy Ross House**, *Arch Street between Second and Third streets*, is where musket balls were made for the Continental Army and flags were made for the Pennsylvania Navy. In the house are Betsy Ross' spectacles, snuffbox, and Bible.

The **National Portrait Gallery**, *420 Chestnut St.*, houses paintings of great American figures, many painted by artist Charles William Peale. It is open 9 a.m. until 5 p.m. daily; admission is free.

Penn's Landing is the largest freshwater port in the world. You can visit several ships here, including the *Gazela Primeiro*, a Portuguese square-rigger built in 1883; the *Moshulu*, the largest all-steel sailing ship afloat; and the *SS Olympia*, Admiral Dewey's flagship for the battle of Manila Bay during the Spanish American War.

The **Edgar Allan Poe House**, *532 N. Seventh St.; tel. (215)597-8780*, is where Poe wrote The Raven, The Tell-Tale Heart, and The Murders in the Rue Morgue.

Germantown: the most historic neighborhood

Philadelphia's most historic neighborhood is **Germantown**. In 1688, its residents made the first formal protest against slavery in this country. The British quartered their troops here during the Revolutionary War. In the 18th century, Philadelphian society built mansions in the area. The most elegant is **Cliveden**, *6401 Germantown Ave.; tel. (215)848-1777*, built in 1763 for Benjamin Chew, a friend of the Penns. The mansion is open to visitors Tuesday through Saturday 10 a.m. until 4 p.m. and Sunday 1 p.m. until 4 p.m.

The **Wyck Mansion**, *6026 Germantown Ave.; tel. (215)848-1690*, and the **Stenton Mansion**, *Windrim Avenue and 18th Street; tel. (215)329-7312* (which served as Washington's headquarters for a time), are also beautiful. The Wyck Mansion is open 1 p.m. until 4 p.m. Tuesday, Thursday, and Saturday, April through December. The Stenton Mansion is open Tuesday through Saturday 1 p.m. until 4 p.m. April through Christmas.

The city's best museums

The **Philadelphia Museum of Art**, *26th Street and Benjamin Franklin Parkway; tel. (215)763-8100*, houses one of the best art collections in the United States. Especially good are the John G. Johnson Collection of European old masters and the paintings by Eakins. The building is a 1928 reproduction of the Parthenon. See Ruben's *Prometheus Bound*, Van Eyck's *St. Francis Receiving the Stigmata*, and Brueghel's *Village Wedding*. The museum is open Tuesday through Sunday 10 a.m. until 5 p.m. and until 8:45 p.m. Wednesday.

The **Barnes Foundation Museum**, *300 N. Latches Lane, Merion Station; tel. (215)667-0290*, displays a superb collection of Impressionist paintings, including works by Renoir, Cézanne, and Matisse. The museum is open Friday and Saturday 9:30 a.m. until 4:30 p.m. and Sunday 1 p.m. until 4:30 p.m. It is closed in July and August. Children under 12 are not admitted.

The rare book department of the **Philadelphia Library**, *Logan Square; tel. (215)686-5322*, is a treasure trove of letters, manuscripts, and original prints, including letters by Dickens, folios by Shakespeare, and Edgar Allen Poe manuscripts.

The **Franklin Institute**, *20th Street and Benjamin Franklin Parkway; tel. (215)448-1200*, is a hands-on science museum founded in 1824, where you can walk through a giant human heart, check out a steam engine, or watch a giant clock that works by gravity. This is the best museum for children in the entire country.

The **Norman Rockwell Museum**, *601 Walnut St.; tel. (215)922-4345*, in the Curtis Building, houses more than 600 reproductions of the painter's works and 324 of his Saturday Evening Post covers. The museum is open daily 10 a.m. until 4 p.m. and Sunday 11 a.m. until 4 p.m.

The **Pennsylvania Academy of Fine Arts**, *Broad and Cherry streets; tel. (215)972-7600*, contains famous American paintings, including Benjamin West's *Penn's Treaty With the Indians* and Winslow Homer's *Fox Hunt*. The Academy is closed Monday.

The **Rodin Museum**, *22nd Street and Benjamin Franklin Parkway*, has the most complete Rodin collection outside Paris. It is closed Monday.

The **Rosenbach Museum**, *2010 Delancey Place; tel. (215)732-1600*, has the Rosenbach family collection of rare books, antiques, paintings, and drawings. The original manuscript of James Joyce's *Ulysses*, first editions of *Don Quixote*, a rough draft of *Lord Jim*, and Keats' famous love letters to Fanny Brawne are kept here. The museum is closed Monday; the last tours of the day begin at 2:30 p.m.

Three tip-top restaurants

Le Bec-Fin, *1523 Walnut St.; tel. (215)567-1000*, is an elegant restaurant with only 14 tables. The prix-fixe menu includes six courses and changes with the season. Seatings are at 6 p.m. and 9 p.m. The restaurant is closed Sunday.

The **Garden**, *1617 Spruce St.*, as its name implies, has a lovely garden for dining outdoors. It also has five inviting dining rooms. Try the roast chicken flambé. The restaurant is closed Sunday.

Old Original Bookbinders, *125 Walnut St.; tel. (215)925-7027*, is the place for seafood. This Philadelphia fixture was founded at the end of the Civil War by Samuel Bookbinder and has always been popular. Nearly every president since Lincoln has eaten here.

Philadelphia's best hotels

The crème de la crème of Philadelphia hotels is the **Four Seasons**, *18th and Benjamin Franklin Parkway; tel. (215)963-1500*, an elegant institution with 24-hour room service, a health spa, an indoor pool, complimentary shoeshines, valet parking, a restaurant, and a lounge.

The **Sheraton Society Hill**, *One Dock St.; tel. (215)238-6000*, is centrally located in Society Hill, near the historic sights. Facilities include an indoor pool, a health spa, a restaurant, an entertainment lounge, and 24-hour room service.

✯ THE BEST OF WASHINGTON, D.C.

Washington, D.C. has more open space than any capital city in the world. At its heart is the **Mall**, a two-mile expanse of lawn stretching from the Capitol to the Lincoln Memorial and from the George Washington Monument to the Jefferson Memorial. The city's main roads are wide as well, giving a sense of that valued American commodity—elbow room.

Capital sights

The **Capitol**, a domed white building topped by a statue of an Indian symbolizing freedom, is Washington's bull's eye. The main avenues begin here and head out toward the suburbs like spokes on a bicycle wheel. The building is open to the public; you can sit in on congressional hearings. Free tours are offered every 10 minutes to the congressional visitors' galleries of the Senate and the House of Representatives.

From the visitors' gallery of the **Supreme Court Building**, behind the Capitol, you can watch as the laws of the United States are shaped. Sixteen marble columns line the front of this classic Greek-style structure. Six-ton bronze doors guard the main entrance, which is flanked by two huge statues: *The Contemplation of Justice* and *The Guardian, or Authority, of Law*. The court is in session from October through April.

The ✴White House is the nation's number-one residence. The best way to see the president's house is to have your congressman arrange a tour. If that's not possible, take one of the regular (and free!) tours conducted in the morning. Be prepared for a long wait. You'll see the public rooms, not the rooms where the first family actually lives. For more information, call *(202)456-2200.*

The **Library of Congress**, *First and Independent streets S.E.*, is one of the world's most comprehensive libraries, with 83 million books, magazines, maps, photos, and films. It is made up of one main building and two annexes and grows at a rate of 7,000 items per day. The original Library of Congress building opened in 1897, a grand Italian Renaissance structure with a dome, columns, murals, and carved balustrades. Three Gutenberg Bibles, a collection of Stradivarius violins, and rare books and prints are kept here. All adults can use the facilities for research, but you cannot take books out. A librarian can explain how to find materials.

✴**Ford's Theater**, *511 10th St. N. W.; tel. (202)347-4833*, where Lincoln was assassinated, is still in use. Plays are presented October through May.

The Smithsonian: America's treasure-house

The stated purpose of the **Smithsonian Institute**, founded by Congress in 1846, is "the increase and diffusion of knowledge among men." In its quest to fulfill this goal, the institution has expanded many times and now comprises 15 museums, galleries, a theater, and a zoo. All the Smithsonian museums are open daily 10 a.m. until 5:30 p.m.; admission is free.

The most fascinating of the Smithsonian museums is the **National Air** ✴ **and Space Museum**, *606 Independence Ave. between Sixth and Seventh streets*. It houses the Wright brothers' *Kitty Hawk*, Lindbergh's *Spirit of St. Louis*, and spacecraft. Don't miss the three-dimensional movies on flight.

The **Hirshorn Museum**, *Eighth Street and Independence Avenue N. W.*, contains the most comprehensive collection of modern sculptures in the world. The circular building has ramps that lead upward in a spiral past works of art. Outside the Hirschorn, on the Mall, is the museum's sculpture garden, which contains works by Rodin.

The **Freer Gallery of Art**, *12th Street at Jefferson Drive S. W.*, displays Far Eastern art and artifacts and a splendid collection of works by James Whistler. The president's inaugural reception is held in the garden.

The ✴**National Gallery of Art**, *Sixth and Constitution avenues N. W.*, hosts first-rate art shows. The East Wing, opened in 1978, is an architectural feat, a triangular shape that comes to a perfect point. The West Wing houses one of the world's greatest collections of 19th-century European paintings. It is open Monday through Saturday from 10 a.m. until 5 p.m. and on Sundays from 11 a.m. to 6 p.m.

The ✴**National Museum of Natural History**, *10th and Constitution avenues*, has dinosaur skeletons and the Hope Diamond.

The **National Museum of African Art**, *950 Independence Ave.*, has one of the best collections of African art in the world, as well as an extensive collection of photos and films about Africa.

The **National Museum of American History**, *12th Street and Constitution Avenue N.W.*, displays the earliest American bicycles, the ruby slippers worn by Judy Garland in *The Wizard of Oz*, a 240-pound brass pendulum, tapes of the Watergate hearings, tapes of old *Superman* television shows, recordings of radio shows from the 1940s, and reproductions of log cabins.

The nation's greatest monuments

The **Washington Monument** is the tallest and can be seen from most places in the capital. To enjoy the view from the top, you'll have to wait in a seemingly endless line.

The **Lincoln Memorial** is the most impressive of the monuments. This imposing statue of Honest Abe looks over the reflecting pool. The words of the Gettysburg Address are engraved in the marble walls around him. It is most beautiful at night, when spotlights bring out Lincoln's craggy features.

The **Jefferson Memorial** is the most beautiful, a white marble structure softened by a dome and reflected in the Tidal Basin. It is loveliest in the spring when the cherry trees surrounding it are in bloom.

The **Kennedy Center for the Performing Arts** commemorates President Kennedy. Tour the building and its many theaters even if you don't see a show.

The most moving monument is the **Vietnam War Memorial**, a long black marble wall sunk into the earth, on which the name of every American soldier killed in Vietnam is inscribed. War veterans from around the country make pilgrimages to the site.

The grandest cemetery

Arlington National Cemetery is the final resting place of thousands of soldiers and famous Americans. The tomb of the Unknown Soldier and the graves of John and Robert Kennedy, Pierre L'Enfant (the architect who designed the city), and Chief Justice Oliver Wendell Holmes are also here. The cemetery is located across Memorial Bridge.

Mount Vernon: the most beautiful home

George Washington's home, **Mount Vernon**, is located in a beautiful spot along the Potomac, in Virginia. The pillared colonial mansion house of the tobacco plantation has a gorgeous view of the river. See the slave cemetery, a sad reminder of the days when some Americans were not free. To get to the house, drive south from Alexandria. The house is open daily from 9 a.m. to 4 p.m.

The most beautiful parks and gardens

Dumbarton Oaks Museum and Garden, *1703 32nd St. N.W.*, has the city's most beautiful gardens. The museum has a choice collection of Roman and Byzantine art and a display of Columbian jewelry. The French and Italian gardens become more informal as they descend the hill toward woods. The museum is closed Mondays.

The **National Zoological Park**, *the 3000 block of Connecticut Avenue N.W.*, is one of the largest zoos in the country. And it's free. The giant pandas were a gift from China. In warm weather, the monkeys play outside on jungle gyms.

Joggers, bikers, hikers, and horseback riders get away from the city in **Rock Creek Park**. If you follow the wooded trails, you will find yourself alone in the forest. It's hard to believe you're in the middle of the city.

The **Chesapeake and Ohio Canal National Historic Park** provides 185 miles of biking and hiking trails along the Potomac River.

The capital's finest fare

Jean-Louis, at the Watergate Hotel, *2650 Virginia Ave.; tel. (202)298-4488*, is the most elegant restaurant in Washington, a favorite of former President Reagan. Chef Jean-Louis Palladin prepares prix-fixe meals with an endless array of courses. As you might expect, it's expensive.

The Palm, *1225 19th St. N.W.; tel. (202)293-9091*, is an elegant restaurant, the best in town for steak.

Dominique's, *1900 Pennsylvania Ave. N.W.; tel. (202)452-1126*, serves exotic and tasty game dishes. It offers a prix-fixe menu as well as an a la carte menu.

Washington's best ethnic food

Au Pied du Cochon, *1335 Wisconsin Ave. N.W.*, is a good, inexpensive French bistro.

Le Gaulois, *Pennsylvania Avenue*, near George Washington University, is a popular French restaurant. Make reservations, or you'll wait in line forever.

Thai Taste, *Connecticut Avenue at Calvert Street*, is a good Thai restaurant with reasonable prices. Expect to wait in line if you come here on a weekend.

The **Iron Gate Inn**, *1734 N St. N.W.*, has terrific Mideastern food. The outdoor courtyard is charming.

Washington's most elegant hotels

The **Sheraton Carlton**, *525 New Jersey Ave. N. W.; tel. (800)325-3535* or *(202)638-2626*, on 16th and K streets, is only two blocks from the White House.

The **Four Seasons**, *2800 Pennsylvania Ave. N.W.; tel. (202)342-0444*, in Georgetown, is the oldest and, until recently, the most elegant hotel in Washington.

The **Wyndham Hotel**, *1400 M St. N.W.; tel. (202)429-1700*, is built around a 14-story atrium. This hotel's facade is a 130-foot-high window. The six floors of suites were personally decorated by Givenchy.

The **Washington Plaza Hotel**, *Massachusetts and Vermont avenues; tel. (800)424-1140*, is five blocks from the White House and five blocks from the Convention Center. Oriental art decorates the lobby of this nine-story building, which has one of the nicest swimming pools in Washington.

The **Stouffer Mayflower Hotel**, *1127 Connecticut Ave. N.W.; tel. (800)468-3571*, was one of the greatest hotels in the world when it opened in 1925. John F. Kennedy, Lyndon B. Johnson, and Harry S. Truman stayed here.

The **Capitol Hilton**, *16th and K streets N.W.; tel. (202)393-1000*, was renovated recently but still has its old marble walls. Trader Vic's, a well-known restaurant in the same building, serves seafood and fancy alcoholic drinks.

The **Hay-Adams**, *H and 16th streets; tel. (800)424-5054*, facing the White House, is the best-situated hotel in Washington. The lobby has rich walnut paneling and two 17th-century tapestries.

The **Omni Shoreham**, *Calvert Street and Connecticut Avenue N.W.; tel. (800)843-6664 or (202)234-0700*, is surrounded by 11 acres of parks and woods. Built in 1930, the hotel's 770 rooms have been renovated.

The **Watergate Hotel**, *2650 Virginia Ave. N. W.; tel. (800)424-2736 or (202)393-0930*, was the scene of the famous Watergate burglaries during the Nixon years. Museum-quality Oriental art and top-class restaurants draw visitors.

The best nightlife

Blues Alley, *1073 Wisconsin Ave. N.W.; tel. (202)337-4141*, in Georgetown, is a great place to see big-name acts. Because the room is so small, you are sure to have a good view of the stage.

One Step Down, *2517 Pennsylvania Ave. N.W.*, has good jazz musicians on weekends.

The Bayou, *K Street*, in Georgetown, has live local and national bands.

You can hear live jazz at **Lautrec's**, *2431 18th St.* On the weekends, there is tap dancing atop the bar.

Kilimanjaro, *1724 California Ave. N.W.*, in Adams Morgan, offers live bands, reggae, and steel drums.

Cities, *18th Street*, in Adams Morgan, is a restaurant with a really hot disco upstairs, where everyone is dressed to the hilt. The restaurant is fun. The decor, which revolves around a city theme, changes monthly; one month the place looks like Nairobi, the next month like Paris.

If you prefer a quieter evening, see a Shakespearean play at the **Lansburgh Theater**, *450 Seventh St. N.W.* Or take in a show at the **Kennedy Center**, *North Hampshire Avenue and F Street; tel. (202)467-4600*; the **National Theater**, *1321 Pennsylvania Ave. N.W.; tel. (202)628-6161*; or **Arena Stage**, *Sixth Street and Maine Avenue S.W.; tel. (202)488-3300*.

THE BEST OF DIXIE

The **U.S. South** offers a traditional yet laid-back lifestyle all its own. Southern hospitality is alive and well below the Mason-Dixon Line.

Williamsburg: America's best colonial town

Williamsburg, Virginia, is a completely reconstructed colonial town. Originally, Williamsburg was an outpost of Jamestown, the first permanent English settlement. By the late 1600s, it was the capital of Virginia. However, when the capital was moved to Richmond during the Revolutionary War, Williamsburg was forgotten. In 1926, John D. Rockefeller had the town restored. Today, costumed actors act out the roles of Williamsburg's early settlers.

William and Mary, the second oldest college in the country, is located in Williamsburg. The Sir Christopher Wren Building is the oldest classroom building in the United States.

Old plantations line the banks of the James River near Williamsburg, remnants of colonial days. **Carter's Grove** is the most beautiful. A dirt road leads from Williamsburg through plantation fields to this Georgian mansion, located on U.S. Route 60.

Berkeley Plantation—not Plymouth—between Williamsburg and Richmond on Route 5 was the site of the first Thanksgiving in 1619. Both Benjamin Harrison and William Henry Harrison were born here.

Charlottesville

Charlottesville, Virginia, sits in the foothills of the Blue Ridge Mountains. Its softly rolling countryside is peppered with acres of mature forests. It is less than 20 minutes from the Shenandoah National Park and Skyline Drive and just around the corner from the University of Virginia, founded by the area's most famous resident, Thomas Jefferson. Although the Charlottesville of today has been "discovered" by the world's rich and famous, the city remains at heart a small, Southern town—a place where Southern hospitality, gentility, and even chivalry are alive and well.

The South's best inn

Just 10 minutes from downtown Charlottesville is the **Clifton Inn**, *Route 13, Box 26; tel. (434) 971-1800.* The 40-acre estate was once part of the Shadwell Plantation, birthplace of Thomas Jefferson. The Clifton possesses not only beauty and history but also a certain charm that truly sets it apart from other inns and hotels. At the Clifton, you are greeted as an old friend and invited to make yourself at home. The main floor of the house is entirely open to guests, who can help themselves to a snack from the kitchen's always-full cookie jar and guest refrigerator.

ATLANTA: THE SOUTH'S MOST IMPORTANT CITY

Atlanta, the city that suffered the most during the Civil War, has become the South's most prominent city. The federal headquarters of Reconstruction following the war is modern and bustling.

Reverend Martin Luther King Jr. began his crusade against racism in Atlanta, which became one of the first southern cities to erase the vestiges of the old slave system. King and his father were pastors at **Ebeneezer Baptist Church**, *407 Auburn Ave. N.E.* King's tomb is in the churchyard there.

Paces Ferry Road is one of the prettiest residential sections in the area. Magnificent estates line the road. The finest is the **governor's mansion**, *391 W. Paces Ferry Road*, with its antiques, gardens, and fountains. The **Atlanta Historical Society property**, *3101 Andrews Drive*, includes the Swan House, an elegant mansion; the Tullie Smith House, a restored antebellum farmhouse and McElreath Hall, which has historic exhibits.

The Margaret Mitchell Room in the **Fulton Public Library**, *Carnegie Way and Forsythe Street; tel. (404)730-1700*, houses autographed copies of *Gone With the Wind*.

Uncle Remus fans should see the **Wren's Nest**, *1050 Abernathy St.; tel. (404)753-7735*, where Joel Chandler Harris lived.

Atlanta's best restaurants and hotels

The **Abbey**, *163 Ponce de Leon Ave.; tel. (404)876-8831*, is meant to look like an abbey, with stained-glass windows and waiters wearing monks' robes. The food is sinfully good and rich. Try the *feuilleté d'agneau* (lamb in a pastry crust).

The **Dining Room**, *3434 Peachtree Road N.E.; tel. (404)237-2700*, just outside Atlanta in Buckhead, has uncompromising service and scrumptious food and wine. Afternoon tea is served and all meals are served with dessert.

Two of the finest hotels in the South are the **Westin Peachtree Plaza**, *Peachtree Street and International Boulevard; tel. (404)659-1400*, and the **Hyatt Regency**, *265 Peachtree St.; tel. (404)577-1234*. The Plaza has a lake, birds, and floating cocktail lounges. The Hyatt has a 27-story atrium and revolving bars.

Savannah and Charleston: the best of the Old South

Savannah and Charleston retain the charm of the Old South, with pastel houses and near-tropical greenery. **Charleston** is a museum, with old homes, historic monuments, and gardens. Mansions line Church, Meeting, and Battery streets. The two most splendid are the **Nathaniel Russell House**, *51 Meeting St.*, and the **Edmonston-Allston House**, *21 E. Battery St.*

The **Charleston Museum**, *360 Meeting St.*, is the oldest in America. The **Gibbes Gallery**, *135 Meeting St.*, has a collection of works by American artists. Also visit **Fort Sumter**, where the Civil War began when South

Carolina attacked the Union stronghold.

Stay at the **Maison Du Pre**, *317 E. Bay St.*, in the historic district of Charleston. A double room includes Continental breakfast, afternoon tea, and newspapers.

Savannah, Charleston's sister city, has a pirate past but an aristocratic Southern ambience. For two centuries, piracy and shipping flourished here. Today, mansions and gardens dot the town, and the renovated waterfront is filled with shops and restaurants.

Visit the **Ships of the Sea Museum**, *503 E. River St.; tel. (912)232-1511*, which displays ship models and figureheads. Also see the **Owens-Thomas House**, *124 Abercom St.; tel. (912)233-9743*, and the **Davenport House**, *Columbia Square; tel. (912)236-8097*. The Owens-Thomas House was built in 1816 and has formal gardens and a restored kitchen. The Davenport House is older and has a beautiful china collection. The grave of Tomochichi, the Indian who allowed settlement in the area, is at Wright Square.

The **First African Baptist Church**, *Franklin Square*, built in 1788, is one of the oldest black churches in the country.

Savannah's best restaurant is **Wilkes Dining Room**, *107 W. Jones St.* Mrs. Wilkes says grace at each table. Long lines wait to enjoy the food at this inexpensive place.

The **Johnny Harris Restaurant**, *1651 E. Victory Drive*, serves the best barbecue in the South. Stay at the **Gastonian**, *220 E. Gaston St.; tel. (912)232-2869*. With two adjoining mansions built in 1868, the Gastonian is the epitome of Southern innkeeping.

The best swamp: Okefenokee

This huge wildlife sanctuary is home to rare birds and alligators. Immense cypress trees spread their roots in the black water. Known as the Land of the Trembling Earth by Indians, Okefenokee is surrounded with legend. The northern entrance is south of Waycross, Georgia. For information on swamp excursions, call *(912)283-0583*.

The country-western capital: Nashville

Nashville, the town from which most of America's greatest country musicians hail, is a mecca for country music fans.

The **Grand Ole Opry** is where country music achieved its fame. The Opry opened in 1943 at the Ryman Auditorium, drawing country music fans from far and wide. In 1974, it moved to the newer, bigger **Grand Ole Opry House**, *2802 Opry Lane Drive, just off I-40; (615)889-6700*. The best seats in the house are in high demand, so call early for reservations.

Nashville's top sights

Centennial Park is the place to laze as you listen to local jazz musicians do their thing. The 140-acre park, located on the fringe of downtown Nashville, has a lake and a rose garden and is always filled with people throwing Frisbees and playing soccer.

Centennial Park's reproduction of the Greek Parthenon gave Nashville its nickname, the Athens of the South. This impressive structure was built in 1897 to celebrate Nashville's centennial. Housed inside the Parthenon are a collection of oil paintings by American artists from the late 1800s and a statue of Athena—a Nashville sculptor's rendering of a demolished statue described in a fifth-century B.C. critique. For more information on the park, call *(615) 862-8431*.

The **Hermitage**, *4580 Rachel's Lane, off Old Hickory Boulevard near I-40; (615) 889-2941*, was the home of Andrew Jackson, the seventh president of the United States, built in 1819. Here, Jackson made the decision to move the Cherokee from their homeland to Oklahoma. Some 18,000 Indians passed not far from his house as they marched the Trail of Tears in 1838. The house escaped harm during the Civil War; it was guarded by Federal troops. The house is open daily.

The **Country Music Hall of Fame**, *4 Music Square E.*, houses Elvis' solid gold Cadillac and other memorabilia. Across the street is a pool shaped like a guitar.

Fort Nashborough, *First Avenue below Church Street*, is a recreation of the original settlement of Nashville. It's open from 9 a.m. to 4 p.m. daily.

Top entertainment

Although Nashville is home to country music, that's not the only kind of entertainment you'll find here.

The **Tennessee Performing Arts Center (TPAC)**, *505 Deaderick St.*, offers Broadway road shows and performances by the Nashville Ballet and the Tennessee Repertory Theater.

For live music (including blues, jazz, rock, and country), go to the **Bluebird Café**, *4104 Hillsboro Road; tel. (615) 383-1461*. Get here early or reserve a table. There is a cover charge after 9 p.m.

The best restaurants

Julian's, *2412 W. End Ave.; tel. (615) 327-2412*, offers the best a la carte classic French cuisine in Nashville. Because the rooms are small, with only one table per room, privacy is ensured. **Arthur's**, *1001 Broadway in the Union Station Hotel; tel. (615) 255-1494*, in the mall at Green Hills, is an elegant four-star restaurant with a prix-fixe seven-course meal. Princess Anne, President Ford, and country music stars have dined here. Arthur's won the 1988 Travel-Holiday magazine award for the best restaurant.

The best hotel

The most luxurious accommodation in town is at the **Hermitage**, *231 Sixth Ave. N.; tel. (800)251-1908 or (615)244-3121*, built in 1910. This hotel, voted the most romantic in Nashville, offers only suites: Choose from contemporary, traditional, and Oriental. Hotel limousines will meet you at the airport.

Memphis—home of the king of rock'n'roll

Memphis, located on the banks of the mighty Mississippi, was home to Elvis Presley (known affectionately as The King) and is the cradle of blues music. The music lives on, on Beale Street and at Graceland, Elvis' home.

Take a guided tour of **Graceland**. You'll see the King's vast car collection, his trophy room, and the Meditation Gardens, where he and his family are buried. Elvis paid $100,000 for the house in 1957, when he was 22 years old. Die-hard Elvis fans come here to mourn at the singer's grave, often wearing Elvis costumes (white pantsuits, dark glasses, and slicked-back hair). For more information, call *(901)332-3322 or (800)238-2000*.

New Orleans: the best party town

New Orleans is famous for its outrageous Mardi Gras, when residents don splendid costumes and hold all-night parties and balls. But it also has some of the nation's best food. And it is one of the prettiest cities in the country.

The **French Quarter** is the oldest, loveliest, and zaniest section of town. Wrought-iron balconies and railings decorate French- and Spanish-style buildings. Female impersonators dance in the bars. Artists, musicians, and partiers roam the streets. Jackson Square, the heart of the French Quarter, is marked by St. Louis Cathedral and a statue of Andrew Jackson. The **Moonwalk** provides a view of the river. Streetcar tours along the Mississippi are available and excellent river tours are available on the *Cajun Queen* and the *Creole Queen, tel. (504)524-0814*. You can choose either a day cruise or a dinner and jazz cruise. The **French Market** has colorful shops with local crafts and fruits for sale.

The **Garden District**, above Canal Street, is also a good place to visit. This was the center of 19th century American aristocracy, and the homes in the area are of Victorian and Greek Revival design.

Most of the city's bars, which stay open 24 hours a day, are located along **Bourbon Street**. College students, transvestites, bums, tourists, and locals stroll up and down the street in a never-ending, colorful parade. **Royal Street** has good art galleries and shops.

Lafitte's Blacksmith Shop, on Bourbon Street, is New Orlean's most historic saloon. It originally belonged to the pirate John Lafitte, who sold his booty here and plotted to rescue the exiled Napoleon.

Also visit **Café du Monde**, *800 Decatur St; tel. (504)581-2914*, and treat yourself to its famous beignets and café au lait.

The best museums in New Orleans

The **Cabildo**, near Jackson Square, houses a death mask of Napoleon. This building was at various times the seat of French, Spanish, and American rule of the Louisiana Territory. It is closed at this time but will reopen Labor Day weekend 1993.

The **Chalmette National Historic Museum**, *St. Bernard Highway*, is the site of the Battle of New Orleans (1815), where Andrew Jackson defeated the British.

The **Musee Conti**, *917 Conti St.*, is one of the world's finest. The voodoo display and the haunted dungeon are the best.

The **Voodoo Museum**, *724 Dumaine; tel. (504)523-7685*, has a voodoo altar and educational displays.

Mardi Gras: the biggest party

Mardi Gras—a famous celebration that includes balls, parades, and a costume contest—begins shortly after Christmas and lasts until Lent. Most of the activity is in the French Quarter and along Canal Street. The most popular event is a transvestite **He Sheba Contest**. Make reservations well in advance.

The best jazz festival

The **New Orleans Jazz and Heritage Festival** lasts for 10 days in late April and early May, featuring jazz, blues, gospel, and Cajun music. Big-name performers, such as Fats Domino, the Fabulous Thunderbirds, and Wynton Marsalis, have played. For information, contact the **New Orleans Jazz and Heritage Foundation Inc.**, *P. O. Box 53407, New Orleans, LA 70153; tel. (504)522-4786*.

Booklovers' favorite festival

The **Tennessee Williams/New Orleans Literary Festival** is a must for all booklovers. It takes place in the middle of March.

The best way to dine

The **Grill Room**, at the Windsor Court Hotel, *300 Gravier St.; tel. (504)523-6000*, is the most elegant place in town. It has hosted Nancy Reagan and Princess Anne. The menu and wines are superb. The restaurant is open daily for lunch and dinner.

Arnaud's, *813 Bienville St.; tel. (504)523-5433*, in the French Quarter, is the best Creole restaurant. The decor glitters: crystal chandeliers, antique ceiling fans, beveled windows, and delicate china. Try the oysters Bienville, and save room for the crepes suzette.

The best bars

In the **Napoleon House**, *500 Chartres St.; tel. (504) 524-9752*, pictures of the emperor hang on the wall beneath ceiling fans.

The **Old Absinthe House**, *240 Bourbon St.*, once served absinthe, an extract of wormwood that is now outlawed because it causes insanity. Here pirates, artists, and gentlemen drank absinthe from a fountain. Today, the bar offers a tasty Absinthe Frappe made with anisette or Pernod.

Pat O'Brien's, *718 St. Peter St.; tel. (504) 525-4823*, has a pianist, lots of singles, and an unusual fountain.

Antoine's, *713 St. Louis St.; tel. (504) 581-4422*, has New Orleans' best wine cellar. **K-Paul's Louisiana Kitchen**, *416 Chartres St.; tel. (504) 524-7394*, serves gin marinated with jalapeno peppers. At the **Maple Leaf**, *8316 Oak St.*, you can hear zydeco, Jex-Mex, blues, and ragtime. And the **Preservation Hall**, *726 St. Peter St.*, is famous for its Dixieland Jazz. (The Hall doesn't serve drinks; although you can bring your own with you.)

The best hotels

Pontchartrain, *2031 St. Charles Ave.; tel. (504) 524-0581*, is the most romantic hotel in town.

A pleasant, more affordable place to stay, is the **Frenchmen Inn**, *417 Frenchmen St.*, in two townhouses built in 1860. Rooms are decorated with antiques and have balconies overlooking the courtyard, the pool, and the patio.

Soniat House, *1133 Chartres St.; tel. (504) 522-0570*, is one of the most elegant and delightful of New Orleans' little hotels. The rooms have all the amenities of luxury hotels, with such added touches as antiques, Oriental rugs, fireplaces, and polished hardwood floors. Rooms are expensive, though.

⚹ FLORIDA: THE MOST TROPICAL STATE

Florida is the closest most North Americans get to the tropics. Thousands of Yankees and Canadians descend on the Sunshine State during the winter and spring to escape the snow and cold of their home states. It's the easiest winter escape, complete with sandy beaches, palm trees, tropical drinks, resort hotels, seafood restaurants, and lively crowds.

(See more about Florida's best beaches in Section 3: The World's Best Beaches.)

⚹ The Keys: Florida at its best

The 100-mile chain of gorgeous islands known as the Florida Keys stretches into the Gulf of Mexico from Florida's southern coast. Beaches in the Keys are less commercial, less spoiled, and more relaxed than most of Florida's other beaches.

Four towns dot the islands: Key Largo, Islamorada, Marathon, and Key

West. **Key West**, at the tip of the Keys, is known as a place for all-out parties; **Key Largo** is peppered with beaches in small coves; **Smathers** is the longest; **Memorial** has a 100-yard pier over the water; and **South** is the most peaceful. Tavernier and Plantation islands have pretty Atlantic beaches. Big Pine Key has white sand coves on the Gulf side.

The best place to stay in the Keys is the **Marriott Casa Marina**, *1500 Reynolds Ave., Key West; tel. (305)296-3535* or *(800)228-9290*, literally the last resort in the United States, situated at the south end of the southernmost city in Florida. Originally, it was a stopover for travelers heading to Havana, Cuba. This posh four-story resort hotel has vaulted ceilings, polished mahogany, arched windows, sea views, and landscaped gardens. Hemingway liked this hotel, as did Harry Truman. During the Cuban Missile Crisis in 1962, the hotel housed American troops. In 1978, it was renovated and returned to its original splendor.

St. Augustine: America's oldest settlement

Decades before Plymouth or Jamestown, the Spanish established **St. Augustine**, America's oldest permanent settlement, in 1565. In 1740, the fortified town fought off the English. Its fortress, **Castillo de San Marcos**, built in 1672 of coquina rock, has been preserved and can be visited. The courtyard is surrounded by guardrooms, storerooms, a jail, and a chapel.

The **Oldest Store Museum**, *4 Artillery Lane*, has tools and machines from the 1800s, including high-wheeled bicycles, a steam-powered tractor, a Gibson Girl corset, and animal-powered treadmills.

The **Kenwood Inn**, *38 Marine St.; tel. (904)824-2116*, is a charming old inn in the historic section of St. Augustine. Built in 1865, it has been restored and is furnished with antiques and reproductions. Guests can use the inn's pool.

Wakulla Springs—America's deepest

Johnny Weissmuller grappled with alligators at **Wakulla Springs** in his famous Tarzan role. Located 10 miles south of Tallahassee, this deep spring has no bottom, or so divers claim, which is why the water is so incredibly cold. If you want to get away from the Florida heat, this is the place. Mastadon bones have been found in this spring.

A beautiful old resort hotel, the **Wakulla Springs Lodge**, overlooks the spring, surrounded by giant oaks draped with Spanish moss. The lodge is decorated with wood-beamed ceilings, marble floors, massive doors, and antiques, and the food in the dining room is good.

TEXAS: THE LONE STAR STATE

Texas, the second-biggest state (after Alaska), is a land of extremes. Here, the J.R. Ewings of the world gamble great fortunes, while the women dress in furs, despite the scorching heat, and keep the makeup manufacturers of the world in business. At the same time, cowboys roam the stark, wide-open ranges. And Mexicans risk their lives to cross the border illegally. Going to Texas can be as much a cultural experience as visiting a foreign country.

Houston: the fastest-growing city

Houston has grown faster than any other American city, sprawling across 532 miles. Twenty-five oil companies have their headquarters in the city's skyscrapers.

The coolest way to tour hot, humid Houston is through the **Houston Tunnel System**, a series of air-conditioned passageways that connect all the major buildings downtown. For a map of the tunnels, which are lined with shops and restaurants, stop by the Houston Library, Penzoil Place, or the Texas Commerce Bank. ·

Penzoil Place is Houston's cultural showpiece. Designed by the prominent architect Philip Johnson, this glass complex includes the Jesse H. Jones Hall for the Performing Arts and the Alley Theater. The Jesse H. Jones Hall is home of the Houston Symphony Orchestra, the Grand Opera, and the Houston Ballet Company. Its lobby features Richard Lippold's *Gemini II* sculpture.

Hermann Park contains the Museum of Natural Science and Burke Baker Planetarium, the Houston Zoological Gardens (where you can see a colony of vampire bats), and the Miller Outdoor Theater. Nearby are the **Museum of Contemporary Arts**, *5216 Montrose Blvd.*, which is free, and the **Museum of Fine Arts**, *1001 Bissonet*.

Also worth seeing are the **Bayou Bend**, *1 Wescott St., off Memorial Drive*, the former home of Ima Hogg, daughter of the first native-born Texas governor, and the **San Jacinto Museum of History**, *3800 Park Road*, located at the base of the San Jacinto Monument (which is taller than the Washington Monument) on the San Jacinto Battlegrounds.

One of the world's greatest sports complexes is Houston's immense **Astrodomain**, which includes the Astrodome.

The **Menil Collection**, *1515 Sul Ross St.; tel. (713) 525-9400*, is a wide-ranging gallery with prehistoric to modern art and special exhibits on tribal cultures. The gallery is closed Monday and Tuesday.

Houston's best rodeo

Every February, the **Houston Livestock Show and Rodeo** is held in the Astrodome. The largest show of its kind in the world, it draws cowboys from all over North America.

United States   515

Houston's best restaurants

Brennan's, *3300 Smith; tel. (713)522-9711*, is a well-loved Houston institution with fine food and bargain prices. Try the eggs Creole or the catfish with roasted pecans; save room for praline parfait.

Charley's 517, *517 Louisiana; tel. (713)224-4438*, has imaginative fare, including fresh venison and buffalo. The wine list is extensive.

La Reserve, *Inn on the Park, Four Riverway; tel. (713)871-8181*, is an elegant restaurant surrounded by reflecting pools where black swans glide. Inside are beveled ceiling mirrors, antiques, and crystal chandeliers. The menu changes daily but always includes fresh fish, beef, game, and produce.

Houston's best hotel

The best hotel in town is the **Saint Regis**, *Post Oak Park, 1919 Briar Oaks Lane; tel. (713)840-7600*, a beautifully decorated place with a homey feel. Little extras make it special: handmade soaps, fresh fruit and chocolates in the bedrooms, and brass razors.

Dallas: fact is better than fiction

Dallas is famous for J.R. Ewing of the television series Dallas, the Dallas Cowboys and their cheerleaders, and the assassination of John F. Kennedy. What many people don't know is that it is the most sophisticated city in the South.

Be prepared for the **Dallas-Fort Worth Airport**, the world's largest—larger than Manhattan Island.

The saddest sight

The most sobering sight in Dallas is the spot where John F. Kennedy was shot, a grassy knoll at Market and Main streets marked by a large black granite marker. The **John F. Kennedy Museum** opened in November 1988 to mark the 25th anniversary of his assassination. It is located on the sixth floor of the School Book Depository, where Lee Harvey Oswald hid and took aim at the president.

Dallas' best sights

Dallas City Hall, *1500 Manila*, rises 560 feet and surrounds a pleasant plaza.

The **Dallas Zoo**, *621 E. Clarendon Drive; tel. (214)946-5154*, has the finest collection of rare birds in the nation. It is open daily.

Thanksgiving Square has a bell tower, the Chapel of Thanksgiving, and the Hall of Thanksgiving, which exhibits costumes and artifacts from seven continents.

The **Museum of Fine Arts**, *1717 N. Harwood St.; tel. (214)922-1200*, displays classic, pre-Columbian, European, and American paintings and sculpture. The museum is closed Mondays; admission is free.

The best collection of museums

State Fair Park, *off I-30 East*, has five museums within walking distance of one another. **Science Place** is one of the best science museums in the United States, housing exhibits on astronomical phenomena, human anatomy, shells, and the workings of radios. The **Dallas Hall of State** covers 400 years of state history. The **Age of Steam Railroad Museum** exhibits an old Dallas depot, a streetcar, an old passenger train, and the world's largest steam locomotive. The **Museum of Natural History** features the wildlife of the Southwest. The **Dallas Aquarium** and the **Dallas Planetarium** are favorites with children.

Dining bests in Dallas

Lawry's The Prime Rib, *3008 Maple Ave.*, serves the best roast beef in Texas, carefully dry aged 14 to 21 days and then roasted on a bed of rock salt. It is carved and served warm at your table. When it was founded 50 years ago, Lawrence Frank and Walter Van de Kamp agreed that their restaurant should be elegant but friendly—no snooty waiters and no foreign languages on the menu.

The **Routh Street Cafe**, *3005 Routh St.*, has a five-course prix-fixe menu that includes American, Mexican, and Continental cuisine. This renovated prairie-style house has an art deco decor. Reservations are required.

Dallas' best digs

Mansion on Turtle Creek, *2821 Turtle Creek Blvd.; tel. (214)559-2100* or *(800)527-5432*, a 1920s mansion-turned-hotel, is cozy, with wood fires, leaded windows, and a good dining room. The lobby has polished floorboards, a domed ceiling, and tall arched windows.

Austin: the most laid-back city in Texas

A large student population and a rebellious history make Austin the most laid-back and freethinking city in Texas. It is also one of the prettiest.

Austin's top sights

The **Texas State Capitol**, *Congress Avenue*, built in 1888, is colossal. It is open 24 hours a day when the legislature is in session, and free tours are conducted from 8:30 a.m. to 4:30 p.m. The Texas Archives and Library Building is located on the capital grounds.

The **Laguna Gloria Art Museum**, *3809 W. 35th St.; tel. (512)458-8191*, has the city's best art collection. Concerts, plays, and festivals are held on the grounds, which are lovely. The museum is closed Mondays.

The **Lyndon Baines Johnson Library**, *2313 Red River St.*, contains the former president's speeches.

Austin's Area Garden Center, *2220 Barton Springs Road*, in Zilker Park, has gardens, a 19th-century pioneer cabin, a log-cabin school, and an old blacksmith shop.

A country-western Hollywood

Young country-western musicians flock to Austin to try to make it big. Willie Nelson and Jerry Jeff Walker are among those who have succeeded. **The Terrace**, *200 Academy Drive*, was formerly owned by Willie Nelson and now is rented out for occasional events. The **Broken Spoke**, *3201 S. Lamar*, is the best place for foot stompin'.

A bed for the night

The best place to stay in Austin is the **Driskill Hotel**, *604 Brazos St.; tel. (512)474-5911*, a renovated 19th-century building.

San Antonio: the best of Tex-Mex

San Antonio is the site of the battle of the **Alamo** between 200 Texans (including Davy Crockett) and 4,000 Mexicans led by Commander Santa Anna. The Texans turned a mission building into a fort and fought to free Texas from Mexico. When the siege ended, all but six Texans were dead. Crockett survived, but he was later killed on the orders of Santa Anna. "Remember the Alamo" became a battle cry. The people of San Antonio still commemorate March 6, the day the siege ended.

Founded in 1718 as a Spanish military mission, the city is now more than half Mexican-American. The Tex-Mex atmosphere is thick and spicy.

The best Mexican food north of the border is prepared in San Antonio. Try **The Hacienda** at Los Patios, *2015 N.E. Loop 410*, which has the best location, or **Casa Rio**, *430 E. Commerce St.*, which is the oldest and most popular.

The best of the missions

Spanish Franciscan missionaries built five missions in San Antonio to convert local Indians to Christianity. Two of them, the Alamo and Mission San Jose, are downtown.

The **Alamo**, *Alamo Plaza*, is actually the Mission San Antonio de Valero, with a chapel and barracks. The **Mission San Jose**, *6539 San Jose Blvd.*, is the largest. It has its own irrigation system, built by the Spaniards, and a beautiful rose window. Mass is still held here, and a mariachi band plays on Sundays.

The **Mission San Francisco de la Espada**, *10040 Espada Road*, has a beautiful chapel. A mile-long aqueduct, built between 1731 and 1745, supplies it with water. The **Mission San Juan Capistrano**, *9102 Grof Road*, built in 1731, differs from other, more architecturally elaborate missions in its simplicity.

The best museums

The **San Antonio Museum of Art**, *200 W. Jones Ave.*, is housed in the restored Lone Star Brewery building, which has towers, turrets, ornate columns, and huge rooms. The collection includes pre-Columbian, American Indian, Spanish Colonial, Mexican, and European art and Texas furniture.

The **Lone Star Brewing Company**, *600 Lone Star Blvd.*, displays animal heads, horns, and antlers, as well as birds and fish. You can sample free beer at the Buckhorn Bar.

The best restaurant and hotel

San Antonio's best restaurant is **La Louisiane**, *2632 Broadway*, which is beautifully decorated and has good French cuisine.

Amerisuites, *11221 San Pedro Ave.*, is a good, inexpensive hotel with a heated pool and a whirlpool.

THE SOUTHWEST: NATURE AT ITS MOST POWERFUL

The **Southwest** region of the United States is an area of awe-inspiring natural beauty, much of which is preserved in the region's national parks. The most famous is the **Grand Canyon** in Arizona. If you think the reality can't possibly match the Grand Canyon's reputation, you're wrong. This is a sublime place, carved over the course of eons by the Colorado River. The descent to the bottom is rugged. From the base, the canyon looks like some otherworldly Shangri-La, a rainbow of colors and powerful bastions.

The best place to stay while you explore is **El Tovar Hotel**, on the South Rim, an elegant but rustic lodge perched on the edge. All other hotels are outside the park limits and do not have views of the canyon. For more information, contact the **Grand Canyon South Rim Visitors Center**, *tel. (602)638-7888*.

Zion National Park, in Springdale, Utah, is less famous. It is so named because its beauty reminded Mormon pioneers of paradise. The best view in all the Southwest is from **Angel's Landing**, a two-and-a-half-mile trail from the Grotto picnic area in the park.

Bryce Canyon National Park, five hours south of Salt Lake City, has a delicacy that differentiates it from other canyons. Some consider it the most beautiful, with its lacy rock formations. For information, contact the **Visitors Center**, *tel. (801)834-5322*.

⋇ Phoenix—the best oasis

The power of nature in the Southwest—the giant rocks and the lack of water—is unrelenting. **Phoenix** is a welcome oasis in the middle of this desert. The capital of Arizona is actually a chain of resort towns. The Valley of the Sun, ringed by mountains, is inhabited by one-and-a-half million people—many of them wealthy retirees. Outside Phoenix are 23 reservations, home to 50,000 Indians.

Both the best view and the best meal can be found at **Etienne's Different Point of View**, *Pointe Tapatio Resort, 11111 N. Seventh St.; (602)866-6350*. This restaurant at the top of a mountain has a 360-degree view of the city and the surrounding desert. Try to dine at sunset.

Frank Lloyd Wright designed the valley's greatest hotel, the **Arizona Biltmore**, *24th Street and Missouri; tel. (800)228-3000 or (602)955-6600*. Gold leaf lines the ceilings. The color scheme and decor are Southwestern, with stained glass, murals, paintings, and Indian tapestries. The Biltmore has two 18-hole golf courses, 18 tennis courts, three swimming pools, a health club, and a sauna.

⋇ The best of Tucson

Tucson, surrounded by the Sonora Desert, has both the easygoing atmosphere of a small town and the cultural offerings of a big city, including opera, a symphony, theater, and art. With an influx of newcomers from the East Coast, Tucson is losing some of its Hispanic and Southwestern flavor. But old Spanish festivals are still held, and good Mexican restaurants can be found throughout the town.

Most of Tucson's sights are within walking distance of the University of Arizona campus. The **Arizona State Museum**, for example, has a collection of Southwest Indian artifacts and exhibits on area plants and animals. It is open daily and is free. The **Arizona Historical Society**, *949 E. Second St.*, illustrates the state's history, with colorful exhibits about early settlers and outlaws.

El Presidio is a walled fortress built by Spanish settlers. Nearby are the **Spanish Colonial Pima County Courthouse**, built in 1928, and the **Tucson Museum of Art**, *140 N. Main Ave.* The museum is closed Monday.

Old Town Artisans, *186 N. Meyer St.*, next to El Presidio, displays Western handicrafts, including Navajo rugs, in a 19th-century adobe building. It is open daily.

Fourteen miles west of Tucson is the **Arizona-Sonora Desert Museum**, where you can see jaguars, mountain lions, beavers, and bighorn sheep, as well as a cave and a garden with 300 kinds of plants.

The **Mission of San Xavier del Bac**, nine miles south of Tucson on Mission Road on the Tohano O'Adham Indian Reservation, was founded in 1692 by the Jesuits. It is one of the most beautiful churches in the

The World's Best Destinations

Southwest, a white Mexican Renaissance structure surrounded by brown desert. Visit during the Mariachi Mass, held at 12:30 on Sundays during the winter. This adobe structure has frescoes, carved figurines of saints, and two lions that wear satin bow ties.

Tuscon's best restaurant is the **Tack Room**, *Rancho Del Rio Resort, 2800 N. Sabino Canyon Road*, in an old adobe hacienda in the desert. Try the veal or the rack of lamb Sonora. Breads and desserts are homemade.

The best place for closet cowboys

If you've always dreamt of riding horses across the desert, visit the **Tanque Verde Guest Ranch**, *14301 E. Speedway Blvd.; tel. (602)296-6275.* Located 12 miles from Tucson, this hostelry, a working ranch until the 1920s, welcomes you into ranch life. You can eat well, swim in the indoor pool, and ride horses.

The best cliff dwellings

Most travelers travel to Machu Picchu and Chichen Itza to see ancient Indian ruins. However, the most extraordinary pre-Columbian ruins are to be found in the United States. The mysterious Anasazi Indians built beautiful, complex cliff dwellings in the **Four Corners** region of the American Southwest long before Europeans arrived. Great cities were carved out of reddish-gold sandstone cliffs by these unknown people, whom the Navajo named the Anasazi, or Ancient Ones. Their civilization flourished from the time of Christ until 1300, then disappeared without a trace.

No one knows exactly what became of the Anasazi, but you can explore their ancient dwellings, perched in gigantic cliffside caves on plateaus in the open plain, at times five stories high with as many as 800 rooms. (The caves are tiny as compared with the sheer cliffs that loom above them.) The caves went unseen by the white man until December 1888, when they were discovered by two cowboys searching for stray cows.

The most extensive cliff dwellings (4,000 in all) are in the 52,000-acre **Mesa Verde National Park** in Colorado. The largest and most famous cliff dwelling is **Cliff Palace**, where about 250 people lived in the 13th century. Its towered ruins look like a fantasy castle protected by a gigantic cave 100 yards wide and 30 yards deep, almost perfectly preserved because it is shielded from the elements by the cliff overhang. It is one of the five dwellings in the park that you can visit.

Hiking is limited in the park, but you are permitted to walk along five marked trails. The best is the loop called **Petroglyph Trail**.

During the winter season, ranger-guided tours of **Spruce Tree House**, one of the cliff dwellings, are conducted daily. And the **Archeological Museum** is open from 8 a.m. to 5 p.m. For more information, contact the **Park Superintendent**, *Box 8, Mesa Verde National Park, CO 81330; tel. (303)529-4461.*

Mesa Verde National Park is a two-hour drive from the airport at Durango, Colorado, where rental cars are available.

The best place to stay is the **Far View Lodge**, *Box 277, Mancos, CO*, near the cliff dwellings. Each room has a private balcony with a view.

You also can see Anasazi dwellings at the Navaho National Monument in **Monument Valley Tribal Park**, near Kayenta, Arizona. Unfortunately, overuse is wearing down the three dwellings there—Inscription House, Betatakin, and Keet Steel. Inscription House has been closed, and entrance to Betatakin and Keet Steel houses is limited.

The best of modern-day Indian country

Modern-day Indians maintain their traditions throughout the Southwest. Their pueblos are living communities, not museums.

The **Navajo reservation** in Monument Valley covers 16 million acres, mostly in northeastern Arizona. Over 260,000 people make up the Navajo nation. They are shepherds, silversmiths, weavers, and tour guides. One of the oldest (active) Navajo trading posts in the area is **Hubbell's**, a national historic site. For more information on the Navajos, contact **Recreational Resources Department**, *Navajo Tribe, Box 308, Window Rock, AZ 86515*.

The **Hopi** reservation is enclosed by Navajo country. The 10,000 Hopis (whose name means *Peaceful Ones*) occupy 1.4 million acres of land. Believed to be the descendants of the Anasazi, the Hopis are farmers and crafts-people. They believe spirits live in the nearby San Francisco Peaks.

The Hopis live on three main mesas. The Indians on **First Mesa** produce the best pottery. Those on **Second Mesa** create beautiful baskets, kachina doll carvings, and silver jewelry. The Hopis on **Third Mesa** are known for decorative wicker plaques.

Old Orabi on Third Mesa vies with Acoma Pueblo as the oldest inhabited town in the United States. The centuries-old village of **Walpi**, high on the edge of First Mesa, has tiny winding streets and houses crowded into the cliffs. For more information, contact the **Hopi Cultural Center**, *Box 67, Second Mesa, AZ 86043*.

Santa Fe: the nation's oldest capital

Set atop a 7,000-foot plateau at the base of the Sangre de Cristo Mountains in northern New Mexico is *Santa Fe*. The air is pure, the adobe homes are ancient, and the people are a mixture of Spanish, Indian, and Anglo.

The oldest capital in the nation is inhabited by families who have been here for 14 generations. Outside the city are weathered mountains and old Indian pueblos. The desert is dotted with cacti and piñon pines.

Spanish conquistadors arrived here 400 years ago and named the town La Villa Real de la Santa Fe de San Francisco. The Spanish town was built on the site of abandoned Pueblo Indian villages that had been built 300 years before the arrival of the conquistadors.

The central plaza of Santa Fe was laid out by the Spanish in 1610. The **Palace of the Governors**, built of adobe in 1610, is the oldest public building in North America. It houses the **Museum of New Mexico** and occupies the entire north side of the plaza. Along its porch, Indians spread blankets and sell handmade jewelry and pottery.

An inn has existed at the site of the **Hotel La Fonda**, off the plaza, since before the opening of the Santa Fe Trail. A faded sign on the hotel wall marks the end of the trail.

Around the corner is **St. Francis Cathedral**, completed in 1886. The two gold towers of this stone structure glow in the sun. Inside is a 16th-century wooden statue called *La Conquistadora*, said to be the oldest madonna in North America. A block away is the Loretto Chapel, which houses the circular miraculous staircase built without nails or other visible means of support by an unknown carpenter. Legend says the carpenter was St. Joseph. The chapel itself was modeled after the Ste. Chapelle in Paris.

The best fiesta

The **Fiesta de Santa Fe**, held in September, has music, dancing, and candlelight processions that begin at the cathedral. Zozobra, a 40-foot puppet representing Old Man Gloom, is burned to the delight of the crowds.

The biggest bomb

The scientists responsible for the atomic bomb met at 109 E. Palace St. beginning in 1943. Members of the **Manhattan Project** entered here and then went out a back way to Los Alamos. A plaque on the wall says, "All the men and women who made the first atomic bomb passed through this portal to their secret mission at Los Alamos. Their creation in 27 months of the weapons that ended World War II was one of the greatest achievements of all time."

The best restaurants

The **Pink Adobe**, *406 Old Santa Fe Trail; tel. (505)983-7712*, in a 300-year-old adobe building, serves native specialties with creative variations. It is closed on major holidays.

Arturo Jaramillo and his family serve some of the region's best traditional food at **Rancho de Chimayo**, *tel. (505)351-4444* or *(505)351-4375*, in the village of Chimayo. Reservations are advised.

The best accommodation

The **Bishop's Lodge**, *Bishop's Lodge Road; tel. (505)983-6377*, is set on 1,000 acres in the foothills of the Sangre de Cristo Mountains and offers horseback riding, tennis, swimming, and a fine dining room. Archbishop Latour in Willa Cather's *Death Comes for the Archbishop* retreated here. In reality, the archbishop's name was Lamy, and he left his little chapel with painted glass windows. At the turn of the century, the archbishop's retreat was purchased by newspaper tycoon Joseph Pulitzer, who added two houses to the estate before selling it to James R. Thorpe. Thorpe turned it into a dude ranch.

Taos: an artists' best

Artists and writers flock to **Taos**, the most picturesque town in the Southwest. About 3,000 people live here at the foot of Mount Wheeler, the highest peak in the state. **Taos Plaza**, built in 1617, became an artists' colony in the 1890s and is still inhabited by artists today. Museums around the plaza include the 200-year-old **Blumenschein House**, *LeDoux Street*, where pioneer artist Ernest Blumenschein lived from 1919 to 1962. The **Harwood Foundation Museum and Library** contains the paintings of the first Taos artists. The **Kit Carson Museum** was bought by the scout in 1843. Also on the plaza are the **Millicent Rogers Museum of Southwestern Arts and Crafts** and the **D.H. Lawrence Shrine and Ranch**, where the writer lived in the 1920s.

Just north of Taos on Route 68 is the most striking and best-preserved adobe pueblo in New Mexico. This town, which dates from 1100, is home to about 2,000 Taos Indians. Wooden ladders lead to the five-story tiered homes. For more information, contact **Taos Pueblo Tourism Director**, *P.O. Box 1846, Taos, NM 87571; tel. (505) 758-8626.*

The best place to stay in the area is the **Sagebrush Inn**, *tel. (505) 758-2254*, where Georgia O'Keeffe painted some of her best canvases. The adobe walls are 24 inches thick, and the interior ceilings are supported by log beams. Spanish-tile floors and fireplaces give the inn a rustic look. Navajo Indian rugs and works by Taos artists decorate the lounge. The inn has a swimming pool and tennis courts.

THE BEST OF THE ROCKIES

Glacier National Park, in northwest Montana contains some of the most spectacular and least-touched scenery in the **Rocky Mountains**, including glaciers, high peaks, lakes and streams, and a great variety of wildlife (including grizzly bears, so be careful). The park straddles the Continental Divide. **Going to the Sun Road** is a 50-mile stretch leading to hiking trails.

Glacier Park Lodge, in the park, draws nature lovers, fishermen, hikers, and backpackers. This scenic resort also offers naturalist programs, golf, horse-back riding, swimming, cruises, and nightly entertainment.

Rocky Mountain National Park is the best place in Colorado for hiking and horseback riding. Two hours from Denver, the park has 20 peaks rising more than 12,000 feet. You'll see bighorn sheep, deer, and elk on the park grounds. Admission to the park is $5.

Yellowstone National Park is the world's greatest geyser area, with more than 200 geysers and 10,000 hot springs. The most famous geyser is **Old Faithful**, which erupts at regular intervals. Steamboat is the largest geyser in the world, lasting 20 minutes and shooting higher than 300 feet.

The **Yellowstone River** has carved a canyon through the rock at Yellowstone National Park. Waterfalls and lakes reflect the blue sky. More than 1,000 miles of trails crisscross the park. Be careful if you hike the back-country; grizzly bears have become a problem. You'll also see moose and bison. Park employees say swimming in the warm waters of Firehole River can be exhilarating; however, this isn't encouraged, because you can be scalded. Yellowstone is the oldest national park in the United States, established in 1872.

THE BEST OF CALIFORNIA

During the past century, Americans have flocked to **California** with visions of fame, fortune, and freedom. They have been drawn by dreams of striking it rich or of making it big in Hollywood. The energy created by these imaginative and ambitious people has made this state one of the most productive in the Union—and one of the most unusual.

The best of San Francisco

San Francisco is the most inviting city in the United States—even if it also is one of the most expensive. It's beautiful, surrounded on two sides by water—the Pacific Ocean and San Francisco Bay. When the fog rolls in, the city becomes mysterious and soft. When the sun shines, the city glitters. Situated atop steep hills, San Francisco has been the setting for many a chase scene in the movies. Nearly every neighborhood has a hill with a spec-tacular view. This city is remarkably clean—and very cosmopolitan.

The **Golden Gate Bridge**, which crosses the Golden Gate Strait between the Pacific Ocean and San Francisco Bay, is the city's most famous land-mark. Actually a reddish color, the bridge is especially beautiful when partially shrouded in fog. The bridge connects the city to exclusive Marin County, home of Sausolito's artists' colony. It is also one route to the Napa Valley wineries.

The **Golden Gate Promenade** in Aquatic Park is a three-and-a-half-mile hike to the bridge that passes beaches, a yacht harbor, the Palace of Fine Arts, the Presidio Army Museum, and Fort Point.

Golden Gate Park offers 1,017 acres of hiking trails and bridle paths. Free concerts are held in the **Music Concourse** on Sundays at 2 p.m. One of the city's major art museums, the **MH de Young Memorial Museum**, which has a splendid Rodin collection, is in the park. Next door is the **Asian Art Museum**. The **California Academy of Sciences**, which features the Wattis Hall of Man, the Steinhart Aquarium, and the Morrison Planetarium, is also located here.

The most interesting neighborhoods

San Francisco's **Chinatown** is the largest Chinese community in the United States. Walking these streets, you can actually imagine you are in China. Most of your fellow pedestrians are Oriental. The signs are in Chinese. Little shops sell silk Chinese jackets and little black slippers. Food stores have unidentifiable items in their windows. And the architecture of the buildings is Chinese; many were built long ago by the first Chinese immigrants, brought to America to help build the railroad. The best time to visit is during the Chinese New Year celebration in January or February. The highlight is the Dragon Parade, but there also are marching bands, fireworks, and a beauty pageant.

Nob Hill, an area with plush hotels and a lovely park, is San Francisco's most elegant neighborhood. The **Stanford Court Hotel**, *905 California St.; tel. (415)989-3500*, serves high tea and delicious dinners. Leland Stanford, a railroad mogul, once owned this mansion. **Huntingdon Park**, between Taylor and Mason streets, with a lovely view of Grace Cathedral, is the most romantic place for a picnic.

North Beach, between Chinatown and Fisherman's Wharf, is home to hippies, the Italian community, and many of the city's best restaurants and bars. The Cathedral of Saints Peter and Paul looms above the neighborhood, making sure its residents keep their faith. You are likely to see elderly men playing boccie in the parks. The most colorful time to visit is during the Blessing of the Fishing Boats, the first weekend in October, when the community parades from the cathedral to Fisherman's Wharf.

Superb restaurants

Nob Hill Restaurant, *The Mark Hopkins, Number One Nob Hill, 999 California St.*, is the best in San Francisco. It has a gentlemen's club atmosphere, with wood paneling and a quiet dining room.

Le Castel, *3235 Sacramento St.*, in an old San Francisco home, has delicious poached salmon. Make reservations at this popular restaurant, which is closed Mondays.

The **Mandarin**, *900 N. Point St.; tel. (415)673-8812*, is the city's best Chinese restaurant. And it has a spectacular view of San Francisco Bay. This is the place to get Peking duck. Save room for the mandarin glazed bananas for dessert.

McCormick & Kuleto's, *tel. (415)929-1730*, is decorated like a steamship, with a wood and brass decor. Tables have excellent views of the bay.

Favorite inns

Our favorite inn in San Francisco, home to some of the best inns in the United States, is the **White Swan**, *845 Bush St.; tel. (415)775-1755*, in the heart of town. Each room is individually decorated, with four-poster beds, fireplaces, antique chairs and desks, and shelves and shelves of books. Guests are provided with thick terry bathrobes, and at night the sheets are turned down and chocolates are left on the pillows. Soft teddy bears lounge on the beds, and the air smells of the homemade cookies being baked in the kitchen. Breakfasts are enough to keep you going until dinner. Afternoon cocktails and hors d'oeuvres are served in the cozy sitting room. The young staff is extremely helpful and friendly.

La Petite Auberge, *863 Bush St.; tel. (415)928-6000*, has a French motif. Fresh flowers scent the rooms, and floral wallpaper, French country antiques, quilts, handmade pillows, and working fireplaces make them cozy. Continental breakfast and afternoon tea are served in the dining room.

The **Archbishop's Mansion Inn**, *1000 Fulton St.; tel. (415)563-7872*, is the lavishly restored home of the archbishop of San Francisco. In 1934, the pope spent the night here. Rooms, which are named after operas, are decorated with carved beds, fireplaces, and antiques. Breakfast and a complimentary cocktail are included in the cost of the room. Smoking is permitted only in the drawing room.

The **Mansion Hotel**, *2220 Sacramento St.*, is the most amusing place to stay, owned and operated by zany Bob Pritikin, who entertains visitors with his musical saw on weekend evenings. The hotel is decorated with oddball antiques and is set in a grand old home that was built in 1877 by Senator Chambers. His daughter Claudia haunts the house, or so they say. The art collection is museum-worthy, the furniture Victorian, and the service first-class.

The **Sherman House**, *2160 Green St.*, was originally the home of 19th-century music publisher Leander Sherman. The hotel is complete with marble fireplaces and butlers to light them, canopy drapes on the feather beds, and thick terry bathrobes next to whirlpool baths.

The best side trip

Sausalito, across Golden Gate Strait by bridge or ferry, is a pretty port and beach resort. The population of this former Bohemian haven doubles on summer weekends. Situated between San Francisco and Mount Tamalpais, Sausalito has lovely views, unusual crowds, great bars and restaurants, and a profusion of shops.

Sausalito's two best hotels are the **Alta Mira**, *tel. (415)332-1350*, and the **Casa Madrona**, *tel. (415)332-0502*.

Los Angeles: the most eclectic city

Although **Los Angeles** is often obscured by smog and deafened by the din of traffic, it has the stuff of which dreams are made: Hollywood, Beverly Hills, Malibu, and Marina del Rey. This is the stage for the jet-set world of the Beautiful People.

Hollywood: the best of the limelight

Northwest of downtown Los Angeles is the center of the entertainment world: **Hollywood**. Major film and television studios are here, as well as great cinemas and theaters. **Hollywood Boulevard** is a fascinating mishmash of shops and people. **Grauman's Chinese Theater** is a garish building. Outside the theater, in the cement, are the foot- and handprints of famous Hollywood movie stars. **Sunset Boulevard**, or The Strip, is lined with nightclubs, bars, and performance halls, and **Melrose Avenue** is lined with pleasant restaurants, where you can stargaze. Hollywood is seedy at night, frequented mainly by prostitutes.

The best studios

Universal Studios, *Universal City; tel. (818) 508-9600*, the birthplace of box-office hits and prime-time television shows, offers the most elaborate tour, lasting seven hours.

NBC Television Studios, *3000 W. Alameda Ave., Burbank*, is smaller, but you can sit in on TV tapings free.

Free tickets to some show tapings are offered by all the television studios on a first-come, first-served basis. You can get them at the Visitors Information Center in the Greater Los Angeles Visitor and Convention Bureau. Or send a self-addressed, stamped envelope to **ABC-TV**, *4151 Prospect, Hollywood CA 90027;* **CBS-TV**, *7800 Beverly Blvd., Hollywood CA 90036;* or **NBC-TV**, *3000 W. Alameda Ave., Burbank CA 91523.*

L.A. sights

The oldest buildings in the city are in the **Pueblo de Los Angeles State Historical Park**, a 19th-century area in the northwest section of downtown. The **Old Plaza**, with 100-year-old trees, stands at the center. You can tour the Avila Adobe, the Pico and Sepulveda houses, and ancient Chinese gambling and opium dens.

Visit the **Huntington Library, Art Gallery, and Botanical Gardens**, *1151 Oxford Road, San Marino, CA*. The library houses one of the world's most important collections of rare books, including a Gutenberg Bible and original editions of *The Canterbury Tales*, Thoreau's *Walden*, and Benjamin Franklin's autobiography. The art gallery contains 18th- and 19th-century British paintings, including Thomas Gainsborough's *Blue Boy* and Sir Thomas Lawrence's *Pinkie*. The botanical gardens are immense, with desert, Japanese, and Elizabethan sections. The library and gallery are closed Monday.

The **J. Paul Getty Museum**, *17985 Pacific Coast Highway*, in Malibu, is located in the mansion of the late billionaire, a replica of a first-century Roman villa situated on a cliff overlooking the coast. Inside are pieces of Greek and Roman sculpture, 18th-century French decorative art, and European paintings. The museum is open Tuesdays through Sundays, 10 a.m. until 5 p.m.

The **Watts Towers**, *1765 E. 107th St.*, are eight spirals of varying heights, taking on the shape of a boat, built single-handedly by Simon Rodia out of pieces of trash. The old man took 33 years to build these works.

Disneyland: the world's best theme park

Disneyland, outside Los Angeles, is the world's original theme park. (Walt Disney World outside Orlando, Florida, was built later.) The oldest and still the best, it brings Mickey Mouse to life, offers trips through the stars, and creates a disconcertingly convincing haunted house. By 1992, Disneyland had had an estimated 320 million visitors.

The best song and dance

The **Los Angeles Philharmonic** plays at the **Hollywood Bowl**, *2301 N. Highland Ave., Hollywood*, during the summer. The rest of the year, it plays at the Dorothy Chandler Pavilion in the **Music Center**, *First Street and Grand Avenue*.

Troubadour, *9081 Santa Monica Blvd., West Hollywood*, hosted Linda Ronstadt, Miles Davis, Joni Mitchell, and Blood, Sweat, and Tears before they hit the big time.

The **Roxy**, *9009 Sunset Blvd., West Hollywood*, is a fashionable night spot and a testing and recruiting ground for the music industry.

The **Comedy Store**, *8433 Sunset Blvd., Hollywood*, hosts well-known comedians, including Richard Pryor, Steve Martin, and Robin Williams. There is usually a cover charge.

The best restaurants

The **Polo Lounge**, in the Beverly Hills Hotel, *9641 Sunset Blvd.*, is where celebrities are made—and then fade. The many windows of this fishbowl offer views of a swimming pool and tropical plants. The Polo Lounge attracts the likes of Barbra Streisand, Gore Vidal, and Joan Collins. If the celebrities don't interest you, concentrate on the food, which is scrumptious.

Le Dome, *8720 Sunset Blvd.*, serves better down-home French country cooking than you'll find in France. The *choucroute garnie* is delicious, and the wine list is good. The restaurant is closed Sundays and Saturdays at lunchtime.

The **Dynasty Room**, *Westwood Marquis, 930 Hilgard Ave.*, is a gourmet restaurant, with classic Continental cuisine. The decor is lovely, with crystal chandeliers and T'ang Dynasty pottery.

Scandia, *9040 Sunset Blvd., West Hollywood,* is the best Scandinavian restaurant in the United States. Have brunch or a late supper after the theater at this popular place.

L.A.'s heavenly hotels

Celebrities who don't live in Beverly Hills stay at the Beverly Wilshire or the Beverly Hills hotels. The **Beverly Wilshire Hotel,** *9500 Wilshire Blvd.,* has cobblestoned pavements and Louis XIV gates. The older wing, called the Wilshire, is a lavish neo-Renaissance building. The newer Beverly Wing is decorated with French tapestries, Spanish furniture, and Italian marble. Prince Charles stayed in the most opulent suite, the Christian Dior.

The **Beverly Hills Hotel,** *9641 W. Sunset Blvd.,* a pink-stucco Spanish villa, is surrounded by palm-shaded lawns where movie stars lounge. Less-famous folks have a hard time getting a room here.

The **Bel Air,** *701 Stone Canyon Road, Bel Air,* is a pink mission building with red-tiled roofs and a courtyard fountain. Despite its old-fashioned appearance, it has many modern luxuries. Dolly Parton likes the Bel Air.

The **Terrace Manor,** *1353 Alvarado Terrace,* is a Tudor-style house built in 1903 by the owner of a glass factory, who fitted the windows with art nouveau leaded stained glass. Victorian antiques look stately against the mahogany and oak wall panels. Caruso recordings are played while cocktails are served in the parlor in the late afternoon. The price of a room at the Terrace includes dinner and the entrance fee to the Magic Castle.

Bacchus' favorite: Napa Valley

The beautiful **Napa Valley,** 40 miles north of San Francisco on Highway 101, produces America's best wines. September through November, the area's wineries are busy harvesting grapes. More than 60 wineries in Napa and Sonoma counties invite visitors to tour their facilities and sample their wines. The best tour is the three-hour exploration of the **Robert Mondavi Winery,** designed for people who already know something about wine.

A lovely place to stay in the valley is **Beazley House,** *1910 First St., Napa,* a two-story shingled residence built in 1902. The Beazley House is noted for its woodwork and stained-glass windows. Sherry, coffee, and tea are served to guests in the living room, next to a large fireplace.

The tallest tree in the world

Redwood National Park in northwest California contains the world's tallest tree, 367 feet high. Magnificent stretches of virgin redwood forest, many of the trees 2,000 years old, are the main attraction. The park borders the Pacific coastline, where sea lions, seals, and birds live unthreatened.

The highest falls in North America

The falls located in Yosemite National Park, in east central California, are the highest in North America (dropping 2,425 feet). They are among many natural spectacles in the **Sierra Nevada**, the cliffs and pinnacles of which were formed by glaciers. The famous photographer Ansel Adams took many of his best-known photographs in this park.

The **Ahwahnee Resort** in Yosemite, built in 1927, has views of the falls and Glacier Point. The six-story pseudo castle is decorated with Western and Indian motifs. Movie stars and heads of state have stayed here. The 77-foot Great Lounge has two fireplaces. Facilities include a pool, tennis courts, horseback riding, hiking trails, and winter sports.

THE NORTHWEST: NATURE AT ITS BEST

The **Pacific Northwest** has managed to keep its natural beauty from being commercialized and overdeveloped. The rugged, untouched coasts of Washington and Oregon are breathtaking. The mountains are protected by national parks. The cities are lively without polluting the countryside.

The Northwest gets a lot of rain. If you can put up with the drizzle, you'll love its result. This is the greenest place in North America. Grass is an emerald color. Pine trees grow straight and tall, to heights unheard of on the East Coast.

Seattle: where the grass is greenest

Seattle is one of the nation's most gorgeous cities. Surrounded by mountains on nearly all sides, it sits on Puget Sound and Lake Washington. The Cascade and Olympic mountains are only two hours away, and the lone white peak of Mount Rainier can be seen from anywhere in the city. In addition to all its natural wonders, the city also offers restaurants, bars, and cultural activities.

The best view of the city is from the **Space Needle** in Seattle Center, a remnant of the 1962 World's Fair.

The most bizarre place in Seattle is **Ye Olde Curiosity Shop**, *Pier 54*, where shrunken heads and mummified humans are displayed

The best place for restaurants and nightlife is **Pioneer Square**, the renovated section of Old Seattle. **Grand Central Arcade**, *First Avenue and Occidental Street*, has the best shops.

The best tour of the city is the **Underground Seattle Tour**, which leaves from 610 First Ave. and shows you the remains of the original city, which burned in 1889.

Seattle's finest food

Pike Place Farmer's Market, *First Avenue and Pike Street*, has stalls filled with colorful fresh vegetables and fruits. It also has good restaurants. One of Seattle's best is **Chez Shea**, *tel. (206)467-9990*, a cozy room on the top floor of the Corner Market Building. You can enjoy gourmet food while looking out over Puget Sound and the Olympic Mountains. **Café Sport**, at the north end of the Pike Place Market, is a casual restaurant with good seafood.

Le Gourmand, *425 N.W. Market St.*, is an intimate restaurant with three-course prix-fixe meals. It is open Wednesday through Saturday.

The **Georgian Room**, *Four Seasons Olympic Hotel, 411 University*, is a stately dining room serving nature's best.

Seattle's best inn

Chambered Nautilus Bed and Breakfast Inn, *5005 22nd Ave. N.E.; tel. (206)522-2536*, is a rambling old house on a steep hill with views of the Cascade Mountains. Country antiques are sprinkled throughout the house, and most rooms have their own porches. Wine and tea are served by the fireplace in the parlor. Breakfast is served in the dining room and usually includes fresh-baked bread or muffins.

The best of the wilderness

Mount Rainier, a 14,410-foot mountain in **Mount Rainier National Park**, has more glaciers than any other mountain on the U.S. mainland. The four-and-a-half-mile **Skyline Trail** is the longest loop trail on the mountain. From Panorama Point, you can see glaciers and the summit. Mount Rainier was sacred to the Yakima and Klickatt Indians, who believed evil spirits inhabited a crater lake at the summit and caused storms and avalanches.

You can stay in Mount Rainier National Park at the **Paradise Inn**, *Highway 706*, which looks out over Mount Rainier and the valley below. This rustic inn was built in 1916 of notched cedar logs, with no nails. The open-beamed lobby has 50-foot cathedral ceilings and two stone fireplaces. The inn is open May through October.

The **Olympic National Forest** has wildly beautiful beaches along the Pacific Ocean. Inland, the Hoh, Queets, and Quinault river valleys have nontropical rain forests. Up to 140 inches of rain fall here each year, and moss covers everything. **Mount Olympus** rises 7,915 feet, challenging mountain climbers.

Stay at **Quinault Lodge**, a big lodge on Lake Quinault in Olympic National Park. Facilities include a pool, sauna, boats, hiking trails, and fishing areas.

To truly understand the power of nature, visit **Mount St. Helens**, a volcano that erupted in 1980 causing mass destruction. You can tour the barren, burned-out area around the mountain. This peak is 50 miles northwest of Portland, Oregon.

America's deepest lake

Crater Lake in Oregon, which fills a 1,932-foot crater, never freezes, because of its depth. Located 6,000 feet above sea level, it is surrounded by snow-capped mountains. This beautiful, deep blue lake is five hours south of Portland. While the park is open year-round, only the south and west entrance roads are open during the winter. And Rim Drive is open only from July 1 through late September or October, depending on the snowfall. For more information, call *(503)594-2211.*

You can spend the night by the lake in cottages operated by **Crater Lake Lodge**, *tel. (503)594-2511.* The cottages are equipped with cold running water, blankets, and electricity.

THE BEST OF THE GREAT LAKES

In the middle of America's northern prairies are the **Great Lakes**. Surrounding these five mammoth, freshwater lakes are some of the nation's best farmland and most prosperous cities. **Lake Superior** is the deepest, the most treacherous, and the most beautiful. **Lake Michigan** is the best for fishing, swimming, and sailing. And its high western dunes are excellent for hang gliding.

Chicago: the biggest city

The greatest thing about this rough-and-tumble town is its beautiful, clean beaches. Its architecture is memorable also, showing off the genius of Frank Lloyd Wright and his ilk. The second-largest city in the United States, **Chicago** has three of the world's tallest buildings. And its neighborhoods are varied, filled with ethnic groups.

The best architecture

Chicago was the birthplace of modern architecture as developed by Louis Sullivan, his disciple Frank Lloyd Wright, and other members of the unofficial Chicago School of Architecture. Many of this group's first skyscrapers are still standing, next to taller, more modern buildings designed by the likes of Mies van der Rohe and Helmut Jahn. The **Archicenter**, *224 S. Michigan Ave.; tel. (312)922-3432*, is the place to learn about Chicago's diverse architecture. For tour information, call *(312)922-TOUR.*

The tallest building

Standing proudly over Chicago is the **Sears Tower**, *233 S. Wacker*. Its 110 stories are reached by 103 elevators and lit by 16,000 windows. It covers an entire block. You can visit the sky deck on the top floor, from which, on a clear day, you can see as far as Wisconsin to the north, Indiana to the south, and Michigan to the east.

The most magnificent mile

The 16-block stretch of Michigan Avenue between the Chicago River and Oak Street is called the **Magnificent Mile**—with good reason. Here are Chicago's best and most exclusive department stores, as well as hundreds of small specialty shops and many of the best restaurants in Chicago.

Along the Magnificent Mile is **Water Tower Place**, *835 N. Michigan Ave.; tel. (312)440-3165*, by far Chicago's best—and most beautiful—indoor shopping mall, eight stories of shops and restaurants.

The **Chicago Water Tower and the Pumping Station**, *Michigan and Chicago avenues*, were the only buildings that survived the Great Chicago Fire of 1871.

The best museums

The **Art Institute of Chicago**, *Michigan Avenue at Adams; tel. (312)443-3600*, is a world-class art museum with the finest collection of Impressioinist paintings in this country and an outstanding collection of Renaissance, Oriental, and post-Impressionist art.

The **Field Museum of Natural History**, *Roosevelt Road and South Lake Shore Drive; tel. (312)922-9410*, is a huge museum with a collection of jewels, Egyptian mummies, and freestanding dinosaur skeletons.

The **Museum of Broadcast Communications**, *800 S. Welk; tel. (312)987-1500*, pays tribute to Chicago's glory days, when many national radio and television broadcasts originated here. You can watch or listen to more than 400 classic radio shows and over 900 television shows.

The **Museum of Contemporary Art**, *237 E. Ontario; tel. (312)280-2660*, features art being created today. The museum is closed on Mondays.

With more than 2,000 displays—including a coal mine, a World War II German submarine, and the Apollo 8 command module—the **Museum of Science and Industry**, *57th Street and South Lake Shore Drive*, is the most popular in the city. The Omnimax Theater features a five-story domed screen that puts the viewer in the middle of the action. Admission to the museum is free.

The **Oriental Institute**, at the University of Chicago, *1155 E. 58th St.*, is a first-rate museum of artifacts from the ancient Near East (Egypt, Mesopotamia, Iran, and the Holy Land). Highlights are Egyptian mummies, fragments of the Dead Sea scrolls, and a huge winged bull from the throne room of King Sargon II of Assyia. Admission is free. The institute is closed Monday.

One of Chicago's newest museums, the **Terra Museum of American Art**, *666 N. Michigan Ave.; tel. (312)664-3939*, which opened in 1987, has a strong collection of works by American Impressionists.

The most colorful neighborhoods

Hyde Park, the home of the University of Chicago, is an intellectual's dream, with six bookstores (four new, two used) and hundreds of people itching for a good conversation. Hyde Park is also home to the Museum of Science and Industry, the Oriental Institute, and Frank Lloyd Wright's famous Robie House. Every June, Hyde Park hosts its annual **57th Street Art Fair**.

The wealthiest part of town, known as the **Gold Coast**, is an area of old mansions and luxury apartment buildings, conveniently close to Lake Michigan, Oak Street Beach, and the Magnificent Mile.

Chicago's old Bohemia was Old Town, where many of the city's artists and hippies lived. But as Old Town gentrified, rising rents drove the artists, actors, and writers out. The new Bohemia is **Lake View**, the neighborhood around Belmont and Clark, which is filled with restaurants, bookstores, small theaters, coffee shops, and used-clothing stores.

Chicago's newest neighborhood is **River North**, an old warehouse district that in the past 10 years has become a chic loft area. Bounded by the Chicago River on the south and Chicago Avenue on the north, River North is an area of fashionable shops, trendy nightclubs, and popular new restaurants.

An art gallery district—not unlike SoHo in New York City—thrives along West Erie, Huron, and Superior streets, between Wells and Sedgwick.

The best parks and zoos

Chicago has 29 miles of lakefront parks. Lake Michigan offers clean water and pleasant swimming. The most popular beaches are **Lincoln Park** and **Oak Street**. Smaller, rockier, and less crowded are the beaches in **Hyde Park**, between 49th and 57th streets.

Grant Park, on the waterfront between Roosevelt Road and Randolph Street, east of Michigan Avenue, is attractive. The Grant Park Orchestra gives free outdoor concerts here on Wednesday, Friday, and Saturday evenings. At night, a light display dances across the Buckingham Fountain, which sprays 90 feet into the air.

On the grounds of the **Lincoln Park Zoo**, *2200 N. Cannon Park*, are beaches, yacht harbors, and the Lincoln Park Conservatory, which is the city's music capital. Good music can also be heard in the bars and theaters along Clark Street and Lincoln Avenue. Look out for muggers.

The **Brookfield Zoo**, *First Avenue and 31st Street; tel. (708)485-2200*, in Brookfield, recreates the Sahara Desert and the Australian Outback, as well as the habitat of the Siberian tiger. Admission is free on Tuesdays and Thursdays.

The best town for theater

Thirty years ago, Chicago had no live theater to speak of. However, today more than 100 groups perform in the city. In fact, Chicago's theater scene rivals even those of New York and London. Although many are shoe-string operations performing in storefronts and church basements, Chicago also has a respectable number of strong, well-established theaters.

No other Chicago theater group comes close to the **Steppenwolf Theater**, *1650 N. Hoisted; tel. (312)335-1650*. Many of its best shows have gone on to perform off-Broadway in New York City.

Chicago's best laughs

For about 30 years, **Second City**, *1616 N. Wells; tel. (312)337-3992*, the best comedy theater in the city, has provided Chicago with consistently pop-ular comedy revues. John Belushi, Shelley Long, Gilda Radner, and Alan Arkin all began their careers here. If you want to go, make reservations at least a week in advance.

Second City recently opened a second stage, **Second City ETC**, *1608 N. Wells*.

The most outrageous entertainment

Believe it or not, one of Chicago's most popular night spots is the **Baton Lounge**, *436 N. Clark*, an outrageous club, where funny, ravishing female impersonators attract an eclectic crowd. Straight and gay, young and old all come to see such local legends as Chili Pepper and Leslie. Reservations are essential. The Lounge is closed Monday and Tuesday.

The best jazz and blues

For music lovers, Chicago is synonymous with jazz and blues. And **Joe Segal's Jazz Showcase**, in the Blackstone Hotel, *636 S. Michigan Ave.*, has been the place to hear great jazz in Chicago for decades.

No blues bar comes close to the **New Checkerboard Lounge**, *423 E. 43rd St.*, where such blues greats as Buddy Guy and Junior Wells perform regularly and rock stars such as Mick Jagger and Keith Richard drop by. (Sometimes they even jam with the old bluesmen.) The club itself is friendly and safe, but it is located in a dangerous neighborhood—so park near the club or take a cab. Don't take a bus or the subway—Chicago's South Side is rough.

If you love the blues but prefer to stay in a safer neighborhood, visit the **Kingston Mines**, *2548 N. Halsted*, in the heart of Lincoln Park. The Kingston Mines attracts many of the acts that play at the New Checkerboard Lounge as well as newer bands during the week.

The best classical music and opera

Under the leadership of its conductor, Daniel Barenboim, the **Chicago Symphony Orchestra** (CSO) has become a world-class orchestra, popular not only in its home city but also in Europe and the Orient. The CSO performs in **Orchestra Hall**, *220 S. Michigan Ave.*, across the street from the Art Institute of Chicago.

The **Lyric Opera**, *20 N. Wacker Drive; tel. (312)332-2244*, is world-famous for its grandly staged operas.

The best deep-dish pizza

A quick way to start an argument in Chicago is to ask who has the best pizza in town. Everyone has his favorite place for pizza. The world-famous Chicago-style pizza was first served in the late 1940s at **Pizzeria Uno**, *29 E. Ohio Ave.; tel. (312)321-1000*. And everyone agrees (even in Chicago) that Pizzeria Uno and sister restaurant **Due**, *619 N. Wabash Ave.; tel. (312)943-2400*, still serve great pizza.

The best barbecued ribs

Chicago, not the South, has the best barbecued ribs in the world. At **Ribs 'n Bibs**, *East 53rd Street*, you can get a whole slab of hickory smoked ribs with BBQ sauce, fries, coleslaw, and bread for $12.75.

The best ethnic restaurants

A city of ethnic groups—Poles, Irish, Lithuanians, Serbs, Croatians, Italians, and Hispanics—Chicago has hundreds of great ethnic restaurants. The best is a Serbo-Croatian restaurant called the **Golden Shell**, *10063 South Ave. N.*, on Chicago's far southeast side. The food is great, and on weekends authentic folk bands and belly dancers perform.

The best gourmet restaurant

In a city of excellent restaurants, **Le Francais**, *269 S. Milwaukee Ave.*, in the nearby suburb of Wheeling, is la crème de la crème. Close to O'Hare International Airport and a 45-minute drive from the Chicago Loop, Le Francais serves a classically French menu that will please the most finicky gourmet palate. The restaurant is closed Sunday.

The best grand hotel

The **Mayfair Regent**, *181 E. Lake Shore Drive; tel. (312)787-8500*, is Chicago's first-class hotel, the place where important businessmen want to be seen. The penthouse restaurant has a wide view of the lake, as do most of the rooms.

The best little hotel

The **Tremont Hotel**, *100 E. Chestnut St.; tel. (312)751-1900*, just off the Magnificent Mile, is one of Chicago's most elegant little hotels. A short walk from Michigan Avenue and the Oak Street Beach, the Tremont couldn't be more conveniently located.

The Great Lakes' best resort

Mackinac Island, Michigan, where Lake Huron meets Lake Michigan, is a beautiful, peaceful place with no automobiles, just horse-drawn carriages and bicycles. Indians once lived here in lodges that are preserved in an open-air museum. During the Revolution, British forces built a fort here, now restored and open to the public. The island became a fashionable resort in the late 19th century, and it was the second area (after Yellowstone) to become a national park.

Today, the island is a refuge for city dwellers, a place for sailing, golfing, horseback riding, and tennis. Victorian homes and white church steeples dot the town. Sailboats bob in the lakes, and the waterfront is filled with shops and restaurants.

The **Grand Hotel**, *tel. (906)847-3331* (call collect for reservations), on Mackinac Island, was built in 1887 by railroad and steamship companies. Constructed in Greek Revival style, with a long veranda supported by columns, it has a lovely pool (where Esther Williams swam in *This Time for Keeps*), as well as a golf course and tennis courts. The food is good, but the main dining room is stuffy. Tea is served in the parlor.

The **Island House**, *tel. (906)847-3347*, is an old Victorian resort on Mackinac Island. The enormous white building is fringed with shaded porches and topped with corner turrets and dormer windows. Built in 1852, it is the island's oldest hotel. Breakfast and dinner are served in the hotel dining room. You can sleep late and then have cocktails on the front porch while savoring the view of the straits.

Mission Point Resort, *tel. (800)833-7711*, is set on 18 acres of Lake Huron shoreline. It has a heated outdoor swimming pool, two hot tubs, three tennis courts, a fully equipped health and fitness center, a pool hall, and an arcade. The main lobby is a spacious circular room with five huge stone fireplaces and a soaring, vaulted ceiling of 40-foot hand-hewn timbers. Rooms overlook Lake Huron.

ALASKA: THE WILDEST (AND COLDEST) STATE

Alaska is the last frontier in the United States. Having more unexplored territory than the rest of the 49 states combined, Alaska's virtues lie not in its few major cities but in the beauty of its frozen landscape, home to only 300,000 fishermen, prospectors, and Eskimos. Our largest state has excellent fishing, unlimited trails, and an endless reserve of wildlife.

Alaska is a land of superlatives. **Mount McKinley**, at 20,320 feet, is the tallest mountain in North America. Astounding amounts of gold and oil have been discovered in this state. And Alaska is the last area in the country where native populations keep their traditional ways, undisturbed by the white man. Alaska has the longest winter in the United States, lasting from October to April. June and July have days of continuous light. This is the best time to visit—unless you really like the snow.

Alaska's most spectacular sight

The most spectacular sight in Alaska is **Glacier Bay National Monument**, where myriad of ice boulders float in fiords bordered by thick forests. The park was covered by ice thousands of feet deep until just 200 years ago. Nowhere else can you get so close to glaciers. In this ever-changing area, humpback and killer whales spout, porpoises and seals play, and bears, mountain goats, and more than 200 species of birds, including the bald eagle, live. The waters are filled with trout, salmon, and halibut. During the summer, Glacier Bay is a rainbow of flowers.

The top of the world

Across the **Arctic Circle** is the land of the Eskimo, where the sun never sets during summer. All you can see for miles is vast, gently rolling tundra.

Barrow is the northernmost point of the continent, located 330 miles north of the Arctic Circle. North America's largest Eskimo settlement is here—Barrow covers 88,000 square miles. This is also the whaling capital of the Arctic.

Kotzebue is the trading center of the Arctic. Part of the ancient land bridge that once joined Siberia and North America, it has been a major settlement and trade center for 6,000 years. **Front Street**, the city's main street, is also the beach, where fishing boats pull up and fish and meat are hung on racks to dry. You can shop here for jade, ivory carvings, furs, native handicrafts, and artifacts.

The Pribilof Islands

The **Pribilof Islands**, in the Bering Sea, are home to North America's largest seal herd and the biggest seabird colony in the world. (More than 190 bird species have been sighted.) Each summer, 1.7 million northern fur seals migrate here to bear their young.

The best of the Alaskan panhandle

The history of Alaska began in its panhandle, a scenic fishing, timber, and mining area filled with thousands of wooded islands, mountains covered by glaciers, and waterfalls. The entire southeast of the state is the huge, wild

Tongass National Forest. One of its glaciers, the Malaspina, is as big as Rhode Island. Lonely, isolated towns are blocked from the mainland by the Coastal Mountains.

Juneau, the capital

Juneau, the capital of Alaska, was founded 100 years ago as a fishing and gold-mining town. It has 18,000 residents, who are watched over by Mount Roberts and Mount Juneau. Behind the state capitol is **Gold Creek**, where a mining museum shows what it was like to tunnel through the mountains. North of town is the splendid **Mendenhall Glacier**.

Juneau's best hotel is the **Westmark Juneau**, *51 W. Egan Drive; tel. (907) 586-6900*, across from the waterfront. Beautifully carved wood decorates this hotel, which has modern furnishings, cable television, and a good restaurant and lounge.

Luxury in Alaska

The most luxurious place on the panhandle is a hot-springs resort on Chichagof Island called **Tenakee Springs**. The springs (about 107 degrees Fahrenheit) are therapeutic. The town is made up of wooden houses on stilts connected by plank walkways. Stay at the **Victorian Tenakee Inn and Tavern**.

Sitka: where Russia meets America

Alaska's tourist center is **Sitka**, at the base of Mount Edgecumbe. When Alaska was part of Russia, this was its capital. You can still see the Slavic influence, especially in the Russian Orthodox cathedral. Visit the **Sitka National Historical Park,** at Lincoln Street and the Indian River. Here, Russians captured a Tlingit Indian stronghold in 1804. You can see totem poles, the battlefield, and a museum with displays of Tlingit and Russian culture.

The **Westmark Shee Atika**, *330 Seward St., Sitka; tel. (907) 747-6241*, is decorated with native art, including a wall mural illustrating Tlingit history. A sunken living room surrounds the fireplace. The best views are from the rooms on the fifth floor.

Where the people are: Anchorage

Half of Alaska's population (about 180,000 people) lives in **Anchorage**. This big city boasts two daily newspapers, performances by celebrities and internationally recognized orchestras, theater, fast-food joints, glass and steel buildings, supermarkets, and department stores.

The best thing about Anchorage is its nightlife. This is where those with cabin fever go to let off steam. Bars, massage parlors, restaurants, nightclubs, and strip joints keep the money changing along Fourth Avenue and Spenard Road.

Visit the **Anchorage Museum of History and Art**, *121 W. Seventh Ave.; tel. (907)343-4326.*

Shop for native crafts at the **Alaska Native Arts and Crafts**, *333 W. Fourth Ave.* Look for the soft, warm clothing of Alaska at the **Oomingmak Musk Ox Cooperative**, *604 H St.; tel. (907)272-9225.*

The best time to visit Anchorage is during the **Winter Carnival**, held each year in mid-February.

Alaska's best restaurants and hotel

Even hotel restaurants in Alaska, which is known for its seafood, are surprisingly good. The best restaurant is the **Crow's Nest**, at the Captain Cook Hotel in Anchorage. Other good restaurants include **Elevation 92,** *Third Avenue and K Street*, and **Simon and Seaforths**, *410 L St.*

The state's best hotel is the **Anchorage Westward Hilton**, *tel. (907)272-7411*, which will seem like paradise after the rough cold of the Alaska wilderness.

The largest island: Kodiak (with the biggest bears)

Kodiak, the largest island in the United States, is also the largest fishing port and the home of the king crab. This island, where you will see Russian architecture, has the oldest European settlement in Alaska. The Kodiak bear is the world's largest species of bear.

A heavenly sight

One of the most beautiful sights in Alaska can be seen from anywhere in the state. Electromagnetic fluctuations in the atmosphere and the magnetic pull of the North Pole create the magnificent spectacle of the **Aurora Borealis**, a rainbow of colors that glimmers on the horizon.

✻ HAWAII: AMERICA'S PARADISE

The most beautiful place in the United States is halfway around the world—**Hawaii**. Long, sandy beaches, palm trees, jungles, exotic people, luxurious resorts, and the some of the world's best surfing combine to make this state a true paradise.

✻**Maui**, the second-largest of the Hawaiian Islands, has both luxury resorts and large undeveloped areas. The **Kaanapali Beach Resort** has restaurants, shops, and hotels. The **Hyatt Regency Maui** is splendid. Its open-air lobby is decorated with antique Asian vases. The **Kapalua Bay Hotel** is more subtle.

On the east coast of Maui is **Hana,** a ranch town (the drive here is breathtaking). Maui's best adventure is a helicopter ride over the **Haleakala volcano.** You will see waterfalls and sacred pools, as well as the grave of

Charles Lindbergh. You also can join a bicycle tour down Mount Haleakala. A van carries you to the rim of the volcano, where you enjoy breakfast and the sunrise. Then you coast downhill for 38 miles.

The most civilized island is **Oahu**, where Honolulu is located. The **Kahala Hilton** is superb, as is the **Halekulani**. Visit the Iolani Palace, the Bishop Museum, and Pearl Harbor.

Hawaii, the biggest island

Waterfalls, black-sand beaches, cliffs, surf, soft trade winds, and beautiful views make **Hawaii** gorgeous. The Big Island, as it is known, is also the most historic, settled by Polynesians more than 1,000 years ago. The island has plantation towns, royal homes, missionary churches, and burial grounds. Its extraordinary resort hotels, which draw people from around the world, lie on the **Kohala Coast**.

Hawaii is a 93-mile-long diamond-shaped island with four active volcanos. A trip around the island leads past fields of sugarcane, rain forests with wild orchids, steam vents, volcanos, black-sand beaches, petroglyphs, ancient temples, coffee trees, shacks, grasslands, and cacti.

While exploring Hawaii, you may also see the Night Marchers, ghost warriors who chant along the ancient **King's Trail**, which winds through several resorts. The **Puuhonua O Honaunau National Historical Park** was a place of refuge, where Hawaiians could escape the king's wrath in ancient times. Near the town of **Hawi** is the birthplace of Kamehameha, the first king to rule all the islands. Nearby is the **Mo'okini Heiau**, a temple dating back to A.D. 480, still cared for by the Mo'okini family, which has watched over it since it was built.

The beach town of **Kailua** has reasonably priced hotels, fishing charters, shops, and stone churches built in the 1800s. **Hulihee Palace**, now a museum, provides a view of the harbor. Built as a summer palace for Hawaiian royalty, its architecture is a curious blend of elements from New England, France, England, and Hawaii.

Hawaii Volcanos National Park encompasses the island's two active volcanos: **Kilauea** and **Mauna Loa**. An 11-mile drive circles Kilauea's huge collapsed summit, or caldera, which passes near man-size lava tubes and the **Halemaumau**, a fire pit where the goddess Pele is said to live. The most beautiful drive is along the **Chain of Craters Road**, which winds 25 miles down Kilauea and takes you as close as you are permitted (and as close as you would want to get) to **Puu Oo Vent**, which erupts regularly.

Mauna Kea is the best place on earth to conduct infrared studies. This peak is 13,796 feet above a huge, dark ocean, protected from the lights of civilization; it is also above 40% of the earth's atmosphere. The **Manua Kea Observatory** has six astronomical telescopes.

If you can afford it, stay at the **Kona Village Resort**, *P.O. Box 1299, Kailua-Kona; tel. (808)325-5555.*

Kauai: the lushest isle

Kauai, the fourth-largest Hawaiian island, is the most beautiful. *The Thorn Birds, Raiders of the Lost Ark*, and *South Pacific* were filmed here. The **Na Pali Coast**, which can be reached by helicopter, is the island's most spectacular area.

The air seems green on this lush island. Waterfalls cascade down sharp peaks into the **Hanalai River**. Orchids and ginger line the river, which meanders through taro fields toward the sea. Three beautiful parks line Hanalei Bay: Hanalei Beach Park, Hanalei Pavilion, and Waioli Beach Park. Two large peaks, Hihimanu and Namolokama, watch over the valley.

Waimea Canyon is often called the Grand Canyon of the Pacific. It is 3,600 feet deep and 10 miles long. Its valleys are green, and its ridges are blanketed with flowers. The **Kukui Trail** leads down 2,000 feet to the fertile canyon floor, where you can explore ancient Hawaiian ruins.

The wettest place on earth is **Mount Waialeale**, where 450 inches of rain fall each year. On the western slope of this 5,080-foot peak lies the **Alakai Swamp**, a 10-mile area where birds and plants (but no mosquitoes) flourish. The **Pihea Trail** (which translates as *Din of Voices*) leads to the swamp, where giant ferns and tree-size violets grow.

Hawaii's most luxurious resorts

Honolulu has two grand hotels: the **Moana**, *2365 Kalakaua Ave.; tel. (808)922-3111,* and the **Royal Hawaiian**, *2259 Kalakaua Ave.; tel. (808)923-7311* or *(800)325-3535.*

The **Moana**, one of Hawaii's first hotels, opened in 1901. Robert Louis Stevenson came here to write. The 75-room white clapboard hotel is of classic South Seas design, with some verandas furnished with wicker furniture. It is on the beach.

The **Royal Hawaiian** is a pink Moorish-style palace built in the 1920s. The hotel's first guest was Princess Kawanakoa, who would have been queen of Hawaii if the islands had been left alone. The hotel is on the beach and has a pool.

The **Kahala Hilton**, *5000 Kahala Ave., Honolulu; tel. (808)734-2211,* is a first-class hotel with a beach and a swimming pool. It also has a pool filled with dolphins. The hotel's beach-front restaurant is good.

The **Mauna Kea Beach Hotel**, *1 Mauna Kea Beach Drive, Kohala Coast; tel. (800)882-6060,* was built in July 1965 by Laurance Rockefeller on the white sands at Kaunaoa Bay.

Kona Village, *P.O. Box 1299, Queen Ka'ahumanu Highway, Kailua-Kona; tel. (800)367-5290,* is on a kipuka, an area of land left untouched by surrounding lava flows. This recreation of a South Seas island community was built by Johnno Jackson. Jackson sailed to this protected cove for years before opening the resort, where coats and ties are banned. You stay in individual thatched huts in a tropical setting.

THE BEST OF CANADA

Canada, which covers 3.8 million square miles, is the second-largest country on earth. Within its wide boundaries are a rainbow of cultures and a kaleidoscope of natural sights. To the west are cloud-piercing mountain peaks, the rugged Pacific coastline, and cities with large Chinese communities. In the east are quaint British towns, French-speaking Quebec, and secluded islands. The interior is home to cowboys, rodeos, and ranches.

Canada is a nature lover's dream, offering some of the world's best skiing, fishing, boating, hiking, bird-watching, and hunting. But it offers the best of big-city life as well. Montreal, Toronto, Edmonton, and Vancouver are metropolises with fine restaurants, high-fashion boutiques, cosmopolitan populations, artistic communities, and good theater and dance companies.

THE BEST OF MONTREAL

Montreal is the world's second-largest French-speaking city (after Paris). Parisian sophistication and Canadian friendliness blend here. The air smells of good coffee and French cooking.

Located on Montreal Island in the St. Lawrence River, the city faces the entrance to the St. Lawrence Seaway. Dominating the city is Mont Réal (Mount Royal), for which the city is named.

The city is informally split in two: the English section in the west and the French section in the east. Street names reinforce this division.

The oldest section

The oldest section, which hugs the waterfront, is called, appropriately, **Vieux Montreal** (Old Montreal). The seed of the city was an Indian village called Hochelaga. French settlers took it over in 1642 and called their town Ville Marie de Montreal. The French town was surrendered to the British 118 years later, in 1760. For one year (1775 to 1776), the British ceded the town to the Americans. The quarter has been patiently restored and is filled with antique shops, cafés, and boutiques. The cobblestoned alleyways are lined with artists and their easels on summer evenings. It's a pleasant place to wander or stop for a snack.

A futuristic contrast

At the other end of the time scale is **Man and His World**, a permanent miniversion of the international exposition EXPO '67. Situated on an island in the St. Lawrence River, it is a fascinating, ultramodern collection of spheres and towers, some of which are slowly rusting and falling apart.

Montreal's prettiest churches

The **Basilica of Notre Dame**, *Place d'Armes*, is an elaborate neo-Gothic affair with two tall spires. Built in 1829, the church houses an immense organ with 5,772 pipes. The altar, too, is monumental. And the woodcarvings are carefully detailed. The basilica was designed by New York architect James O'Donnell, whose grave is in the church. The **Sacred Heart Chapel**, adjacent to the basilica, has stained-glass windows illustrating the history of Montreal. The church is open daily.

Notre-Dame-de-Bonsecours, *400 St. Paul St. E.*, in Vieux Montreal, is the city's oldest church, built in 1657, destroyed by fire, then rebuilt in 1771. The facade is from 1895. Located near the water, it is also known as the Sailor's Chapel. It is closed Monday.

The best of Montreal at night

Montreal doesn't close until 3:30 a.m., a liberty that spoils other cities for many Montrealers. The center of the city's nighttime activity is charming and sophisticated Crescent Street, Montreal's version of the Latin Quarter in Paris. Prince Arthur, Duluth, and St. Denis streets are also lined with bars, cafés, and restaurants.

On summer nights in early July, you can take in the jazz festival at the Theatre St. Denis, and in late August you can enjoy the film festival at cinemas throughout the city.

For something unique, go to a *boîte a chanson*, a Quebec-style café with French folk music.

The finest French cooking

The best restaurant in Montreal is **Les Mignardises**, *2037 rue St. Denis; tel. (514) 842-1151*. Chef Jean Pierre Monnet creates masterpieces, and the service is superb. The restaurant is closed Sundays.

Chez la Mère Michel, *1209 Guy St.; tel. (514) 934-0473*, is cozy, with an outstanding French provincial menu and a pretty garden patio. Try the *homard soufflé Nantua* (fresh lobster added to mousseline potatoes and served on a bed of spinach). The restaurant is closed Sundays and Monday mornings.

Les Chênets, *2075 Bishop St.; tel. (514) 844-1842*, is decorated with original works of art. The dishes, too, are masterpieces, smothered in delicious sauces. The selection of Cognac and Armagnac brandies is the best in the Americas.

The best hotels

Montreal's best hotel is the **Ritz Carlton**, *Sherbrooke West; tel. (514)842-4212.* A luxurious, Continental-style hotel, it is near fashionable boutiques, restaurants, and galleries.

Less expensive hotels include **L'Hôtel de la Montagne**, *tel. (514)288-5656*, and the **Hotel Château Versailles**, *tel. (514)933-3611*.

But we think the best (and certainly the most affordable) accommodation in Montreal is at the city's bed-and-breakfasts. For a list, contact **Downtown Bed and Breakfast**, *3458 Laval Ave., Montreal H2X 3C8; tel. (514)289-9749.*

✴ QUEBEC: THE FRENCH HEART — AND THE ONLY WALLED CITY

Quebec City, the capital of the French-speaking province of Quebec, is the focal point of French Canadian nationalism. It is also the first French settlement in North America (95% of the population is French) and the oldest city in the New World (the walled fortress was founded by Champlain in 1608). Quebec is the only walled city in North America. It is set high on Cape Diamond, 350 feet above the St. Lawrence River.

The best of Vieux Quebec

In **Vieux Quebec** (Old Quebec), you'll see 17th- and 18th-century stone houses similar to those in the villages of Normandy and Brittany in France.

The heart of Vieux Quebec is the beautiful **Place d'Armes**. A good introduction to the history of Quebec is the sound-and-light show at the **Musée du Fort**. The Seminary, dating from 1663, houses a museum containing a rare collection of Canadian money, including Indian wampum and playing cards used as legal tender in colonial times. In the museum at the **Hotel Dieu**, you can see the stone vaults where Augustinian nuns took refuge during the 1759 siege. The skull of French general Montcalm is on view at the **Ursulin Convent Museum**.

Looming over the Place d'Armes is the **Château Frontenac**, *tel. (418)692-3861*, a magnificent Victorian hotel with turrets and towers. Built in 1892, it perches at the top of Cape Diamond, a 300-foot bluff.

Next door is the **Jardin des Gouverneurs**, originally the private garden of the Chateau St. Louis. It is best known for its statue of General James Wolfe and Marquis de Montcalm, erected in 1828. On it is written, "Their courage gave them the same lot; history, the same fame; posterity, the same monument."

Canada's most important battlefield

The **Plains of Abraham** in Quebec were the site of a battle that determined the fate of Canada. On Sept. 13, 1759, the British army under Wolfe defeated the French under Montcalm, and Canada was turned over to the British. (However, the French inhabitants held on to their language and culture.) Both Wolfe and Montcalm were killed during the battle. According to legend, at the end of the battle, a voice was heard across the plains crying, "*Je me souviens*" (I remember), which became the motto of the province of Quebec.

Today the battlefield is part of the 230-acre **Pare des Champs de Bataille**. From the observation post, you'll have a wide view of the field and the river.

The **Quebec Museum**, *tel. (418)643-2150*, is also on the park grounds. It contains displays illustrating Quebec's history, paintings by Quebecois artists, and a section devoted to 17th-century decorative arts. The museum is open 10 a.m. until 5:45 p.m. daily except Monday, when it is closed.

The oldest section

The oldest section of the city is around Place Royale in a district known as **Lower Town**. When Champlain started his colony here, it was a trading post, with a store, a few houses, and fortifications. In later years, Place Royale became the center of the fur-trading industry. As colonists and missionaries arrived, the settlement gradually moved uphill, to Vieux Quebec.

Today, Lower Town is a busy port. Designated a historic area by the Canadian government, the section surrounding Place Royale is being restored. It has the greatest concentration of 17th- and 18th-century buildings in North America.

The oldest church in Quebec, **Notre Dame des Victoires**, is located on Place Royale. This small stone church built in 1688 is decorated inside with elaborate woodwork. The altar is carved in the shape of an old fort. The church is open daily.

A funicular will take you from Place d'Armes down to Place Royale, where you can walk along cobblestoned streets past 17th-century buildings and sunny squares. **Rue de Trésor** is the best place to stroll; painters sell their masterpieces along here.

The best French architecture

Quebec's **Assemblée Nationale** (parliament buildings)—bounded by rue Dufferin, boulevards St. Cyrille and St. Augustin, and Le Grande Allée—are imposing French structures built in 1877 and 1886. Twelve bronze statues commemorating famous Canadians rest in niches in the facade. They are the works of the Quebec sculptor Hubert. Guided tours are conducted daily during the summer and on weekdays during the winter.

The most romantic train ride

The sunset steam train dinner trip from Gatineau to Wakefield, Quebec, is the most romantic train ride. To pass by the emerald green Gatineau river, the bright colorful wild flowers and magnificent scenery of rolling Gatineau mountains, and at the same time be served gourmet food and entertained by classical musicians is one of the world's most romantic experiences.

The best time to visit

The **Carnival de Quebec**, a 10-day celebration beginning on the first Thursday in February, is the most festive time to visit the city. A huge party to commemorate the end of winter, it includes two parades, fireworks, and winter sports. The official mascot is a seven-foot snowman called Le Bonhomme Carnival.

If you plan to visit during Carnival, you will be competing for hotel rooms with more than a half-million people from all over North America. Make reservations. If you can't find a room, contact the **Carnival Lodging Committee**, *tel. (418)524-8441*.

Quebec's best restaurants

The best restaurant in town is **À le Table de Serge Bruyère**, *Livernois Comples (upstairs), 1200 rue St. Jean*, where a special prix-flxe menu of seven courses is served. Try the filet of Quebec lamb with green shallots and fresh tomatoes. Reservations are required. The restaurant is open daily.

Restaurant Louis Hebert, *668 Grande Allée Est*, is also good, serving light French fare. Set in a 17th-century fieldstone building, it has a French provincial atmosphere, with calico lampshades and an outdoor terrace. It is open daily.

The best place for local French-Canadian fare is **Aux Anciens Canadiens**, *34 rue St. Louis*. Located in the former home of the 19th-century historical novelist Philippe Aubert de Gaspé (which was built in 1675), the restaurant serves Canadian yellow pea soup, *tourtière* (meat pie), and maple syrup pie with heavy cream. Reservations are suggested. The restaurant is open daily.

The best hotels

The most elegant place to stay is **Le Château Frontenac**, *1 ave. des Carrières; tel. (418)692-3861*. It is grand, historic, and expensive. The cocktail lounge and many of the rooms have views of the St. Lawrence. However, because this is a tourist hotel, expect to be one of many Americans.

Auberge du Trésor, *20 rue Ste. Anne; tel. (418)694-1876*, is a 300-year-old inn on the Place d'Armes. Its 20 guest rooms have private bathrooms, televisions, and air conditioning. Prices are moderate.

Le Château de Pierre, *17 ave. Ste. Geneviève; tel. (418)694-0429*, is a 15-room mansion built in 1853. Its large rooms all have color televisions and air conditioning.

THE BEST OF PROVINCIAL FRENCH CANADA

Most American visitors, smitten by Quebec City's charms, overlook the nearby countryside (unless they snow ski in the Laurentides, Quebec's Little Switzerland). This is a big oversight. Farmstays are available in fascinating villages, where people wake up with the roosters.

An island lost in time

Nearby **Ile d'Orléans** is a lovely island with historic Quebecois homes, old farming villages, and French restaurants. Until 1935, the island could be reached only by boat. Because of this, it retained its old French ways longer than its neighbors. Many of the houses here are from the 17th and 18th centuries. Most residents are farmers and descendants of French immigrants from Normandy and Brittany.

Miraculous cures

Farther on is the village of **Ste. Anne de Beaupré**, whose massive cathedral is a famous Catholic shrine. Invalids from all over the world come here to be cured—the fountain in front of the church is said to cure many diseases. There must be something to this claim, to judge from the plethora of crutches, canes, and walkers left behind by cured believers—some of the paraphernalia is hung from the church's ceiling. Built in 1922, the cathedral holds 10,000 people.

A best for Les artistes

Just an hour north of Quebec City, on the north shore of the St. Lawrence River, is a bustling resort for artists and patrons called **Baie St. Paul**. Dozens of galleries display works of the Group of Seven—painters who portray the Charlevoix region.

The Gaspe Peninsula

An hour northeast of Baie St. Paul, the port of Rivière du Loup marks the beginning of the **Gaspe Peninsula**, a French fishing and farming region. The Gaspe begins dramatically. Mountains plunge into the sea. Little fishing towns brave the pounding surf. Although rugged, the peninsula is accommodating—many manor houses have been converted to inns.

Gaspe is an old French fishing village, three hours north of Riviere du Loup on the northern tip of the peninsula. The French spoken here, *joual*, sounds to the French of France as Middle English would sound to us. Gaspe is where Cartier first stepped ashore in North America in 1534. A large granite cross marks the spot. The Gaspe Museum has exhibits on the history and folklore of the area.

Around the point from Gape is **Bonaventure**, founded by French-speaking Acadians fleeing British troops in 1755. Nearby are limestone rock formations that reach out of the sea—popular among small-boat sailors and seabirds. You can walk to **Percé Rock** at low tide. **Ile Bonaventure** is a boat ride away. This bird sanctuary was once a pirate hideout.

One of Quebec province's best restaurants perches 1,000 feet above Perce Rock. **L'Auberge du Gargantua**, *tel. (418) 782-2852*, serves excellent French provincial cooking. Specialties include periwinkles in court bouillon, fresh fish, and giant crab. But the best dish is the bouillabaisse Cargantua. Reservations are required. The restaurant is open daily.

OTTAWA, A CAPITAL CITY

Canada's capital, **Ottawa**, is a small beautiful city with only 303,747 inhabitants. Set high on a bluff overlooking the confluence of the Ottawa, Gatineau, and Rideau rivers, it has lovely views in all directions. Man has added to the scenery: the Gothic parliament buildings create a romantic sky-line. The Rideau Canal is pretty, cutting through the city.

Ottawa has a British flavor. The language is predominantly English, and you're more likely to be served scones than croissants. Established by Queen Victoria in 1858 as the capital of the United Provinces of Canada, the city is filled with elaborate Victorian architecture. It became the capital of modern Canada in 1867.

Ottawa's top sights

Parliament Hill, on a bluff over the Ottawa River, is the pedestal for the spectacular parliament buildings, with their tall copper roofs. The 302-foot **Peace Tower** dedicated to Canadians who lost their lives in World War I forms part of the main entrance to the buildings. Its walls and floors are made of stones from the battlefields. Its tower contains a 53-bell carillon. You can go to the Visitor's Galleries in the House of Commons and the Senate. Or take a tour of the Center Block, which passes through the Memorial Chamber, the library, and the Peace Tower lookout. During the summer, you can watch the changing of the guard on the lawns of Parliament Hill daily at 10 a.m.

The **National Gallery of Canada** is located in the **Lorne Building**, *Elgin Street*, between Albert and Slater streets. It contains six floors of galleries devoted to European and Canadian art, displaying works by Canada's Group of Seven, including Paul Kane's paintings of Indians and Cornelius Kreigoff's paintings of pioneers. European masters Rembrandt, Chardin, El Greco, Cézanne, Van Gogh, Monet, and Picasso are also represented.

Bytown Museum, near the junction of the Rideau Canal and the Ottawa River, is filled with artifacts of the Ottawa Indians: furniture, clothes, guns, tools, and toys.

Ottawa's best hotels

The best hotel in town is **Château Laurier**, *Confederation Square*. An institution in Canada since 1912, it is a favorite among politicians and big-time businessmen. The hotel's restaurant, the Canadian Grill, is dignified.

The **Sheraton Hotel**, *150 Albert St.*, has all the modern luxuries: whirlpool baths, tanning rooms, and saunas. The rooms have been renovated recently, and the dining room and wine bar are popular. This is one of Ottawa's most expensive hotels.

The **Ramada Hotel**, *111 Cooper St.; tel. (613)238-1331*, is a moderately priced hotel.

THE BEST OF SHAKESPEARE

Try to make it to Stratford's annual summer **Shakespearean Festival**. The town, which is modeled on Stratford, England, has swans, green lawns that sweep down to the river, and pretty cottages. You can picnic in **Queen's Park** beneath tall shade trees. Past the Orr Dam and the 90-year-old stone bridge is the **Shakespearean Garden**, a formal English garden with a sundial that was presented to the town by a former mayor of England's Stratford-upon-Avon. For more information, contact the **Stratford Festival Office**, *P.O. Box 520, Stratford, Ontario N5A 6V2; tel. (519)273-1600*.

The most curious place to dine in Stratford is **The Church**, *Brunswick and Waterloo streets; tel. (519)273-3424*, which has delicious food and churchlike decor—organ pipes, an altar, a vaulted roof, and stained-glass windows. Reservations are required.

NIAGARA FROM THE OTHER SIDE

Just 20 minutes from Niagara-on-the-Lake, down Niagara Parkway, is the Canadian side of **Niagara Falls**, which is both prettier than the U.S. side and less crowded. You can take an elevator below the falls at Table Rock House. And the ship *Maid of the Mist* takes you practically under the falls. Boats leave from the dock on the parkway just down from the Rainbow Bridge.

THE BEST OF TORONTO

Toronto, situated on the Great Lakes, is the largest city in Canada. Towering buildings, such as the CN (Canadian National) Tower, the world's tallest freestanding structure, punctuate the city's dramatic skyline. Canada's most modern city, Toronto boasts avant-garde architecture, especially on Eaton Square and at the O'Keefe Center.

Despite its modern appearance, Toronto is old, occupying the site of a

French fort (1749-1759) in an area purchased by the British from the Indians in 1787. It was settled largely by Loyalists who left the Thirteen Colonies during and just after the Revolutionary War. Americans raided the city twice, destroying parts of it during the War of 1812. Then known as York, it was renamed Toronto in 1834.

Toronto is an Indian word meaning *place of meeting*, which is appropriate considering the huge and varied ethnic groups that populate the city. Because of the diversified population, the choice of restaurants is astounding.

Toronto is second only to New York in number and variety of stage productions. It has a progressive urban spirit and a sophisticated cosmopolitan outlook, without the big-city problems of Chicago and New York.

Toronto's top sights

The best place to begin exploring the city is at its heart: **City Hall**, a modern superstructure that looks something like the landing pad for a spaceship. Topped with a white dome and flanked by 20- and 27-story curved towers, the building's twin clamshell design won an international competition for Finnish architect Viljo Revell, one of 530 contestants.

The nine-acre plaza in front of City Hall, called **Nathan Phillips Square**, was named after the Toronto mayor responsible for the project. It provides a community meeting place for concerts and self-appointed orators. In the winter, the reflecting pool doubles as a skating rink. The focal point of the square is a Henry Moore sculpture called *The Archer*. When city fathers balked at buying it, the people of Toronto raised the money to buy it themselves. Moore was so touched by their enthusiasm that he donated many of his works to the Art Gallery of Toronto.

Across the street is **Old City Hall**, an imposing Romanesque fortress that houses the Provincial Courts. Built in 1899, it has marble columns, stained glass, and grained flooring from Georgia. The building is embellished with carved gargoyles, said to be furtive caricatures of city councilors with whom the architect battled in the 1890s.

In Queen's Park, the **Provincial Parliament Building** stands on the site of a former lunatic asylum. Wander through the pink sandstone complex and listen to the lawmakers, debating in the legislative chambers.

Casa Loma is a 98-room medieval-looking castle created by financier Sir Henry Pellant. Built between 1911 and 1914, this extravagance boasts gold-plated bath fixtures, a gigantic pipe organ, and one of the largest wine cellars in North America. An 800-foot underground tunnel leads to stables furnished in marble, mahogany, and Spanish tile.

Old Fort York, *Garrison Road*, was built in 1793, destroyed during the War of 1812, and then rebuilt. The officers' quarters, center blockhouse, and battlements have been refurbished. Members of the Fort York Guard are dressed in uniforms of British troops of the era.

Also visit the city's new baseball stadium, the **Skydome**. It has a retractable roof, several restaurants—including a Hard Rock Café, and a hotel. You can even get McDonald's food from the vendors in the bleachers.

The finest art

The **Art Gallery of Ontario** is renowned for its collection of works by Canadian artists and for its important collection of Henry Moore sculptures.

The **Royal Ontario Museum**, *Avenue Road and Bloor Street West*, displays Chinese art and artifacts, extensive ethnological collections, dinosaurs, fossils, and minerals.

The **McMichael Canadian Collection of Art**, in Kleinburg, about 25 miles north of Toronto, has 30 gallery rooms constructed from timbers that once enclosed pioneer homes and barns. More than 1,000 paintings by the Group of Seven and their contemporaries are on display, along with West Coast and Woodland Indian and Inuit works.

The most inviting parks

Toronto has 15,000 acres of parkland displaying signs that say "Please walk on the grass." **Toronto Islands Park** can be reached by ferry from across the harbor. **Exhibition Place**, *Lakeshore Boulevard West*, is the site of the Canadian National Exhibition, held from the third week in August to the first Monday in September. **High Park**, near the west end of the Queen streetcar route, is a lovely place for sailing, picnicking, and strolling.

The best entertainment

Ontario Place, along the lakefront, is an overwhelming futuristic entertainment complex built over the water on three man-made islands. It includes a disco, a roller rink, a marina, numerous restaurants, and snack bars. The main attraction is the **Cinesphere**, a ball-shaped theater where films are projected on a six-story curved screen, the world's tallest.

Harborfront, another recreational development, stretches one-and-a-half miles from York Street to just past Bathurst. Divided into four sections, the attractions include antique shops, art galleries, cafés, studios, theaters, picnic facilities, and a multicultural media center.

Toronto has its own symphony and is home to both the Canadian Opera Company and the National Ballet. The **O'Keefe Center**, *Front and Yonge streets*, is a modern hall with seating for 3,200. The **St. Lawrence Center**, *Front and Scott streets*, contains an 830-seat theater that accommodates a resident repertory company, visiting theater groups, and opera and dance companies.

Incomparable cooking

Canada's best Thai restaurant is **Bangkok Garden**, *18 Elm St.; tel. (416) 977-6748*, a beautifully decorated place. Try the steamed gingerfish or the mussels in spicy coconut sauce. The restaurant is closed Sundays.

The most charming restaurant in town is **Le Bistingo**, *349 Queen St. W.; tel. (416)598-3490*, a fashionable French restaurant with scrumptious desserts. It is closed Sundays and major holidays.

The best place for French Continental cuisine (with a touch of California) is **Chiaro's**, *37 King St. E.; tel. (416)863-9700*, in the newly renovated King Edward Hotel. Dishes are not only light and delicious but also beautifully presented. Try the tea-smoked Atlantic salmon and fruit ices. Chiaro's is closed Sundays and holidays.

Il Posto, *York Square, 148 Yorkville Ave.; tel. (416)968-0469*, is Toronto's best Italian restaurant, with imaginatively prepared pasta dishes. The restaurant is closed Sundays.

The best hotels

The **Royal York Hotel**, *100 Front St. W.; tel. (416)368-2511*, is the biggest hotel in the British Commonwealth. A landmark since 1929, it is a favorite among royalty, movie stars, and visiting prime ministers. Service is superb.

Toronto's most charming hotel is the **King Edward**, *37 King St. E.; tel. (416)863-9700*. This Edwardian-style classic was recently renovated.

The **Sheraton Center**, *123 Queen St. W.; tel. (416)361-1000*, outdoes itself with imaginative decor. A three-story waterfall cascades in the lobby, and the hotel complex houses 40 stores, two theaters, 10 restaurants, and six bars. Outside are lovely gardens. And, of course, modern luxuries, such as saunas and indoor and outdoor pools, have not been forgotten.

A pleasant moderately priced hotel is the **Delta Chelsea Inn**, *33 Gerrard St. W.; tel. (416)595-1975*, between Yonge and Bay streets.

THE BEST OF NEW BRUNSWICK

Along **New Brunswick's** 1,400-mile shoreline are some of the oldest cities and towns in Canada, founded by Loyalist refugees from the American Revolution. The coast is also home to small Acadian French towns. Forests cover 84% of the province. Life is serene. Along the **Fundy Coast**, residents pass the time predicting the weather and discussing the price of seafood.

Campobello Island, a president's favorite

Campobello Island is where President Franklin Roosevelt retreated from the tensions of his job. His house is open to the public. The **Roosevelt Campobello International Park**, a joint Canadian-American preservation effort, is open May to October from 9 a.m. to 6 p.m. Benedict Arnold also lived on Campobello Island for a time, at Snug Cove.

St. Andrews, a moving town

St. Andrews is a Loyalist settlement with a unique history. The first settlers built their town at Fort George (later Castine, Maine). When that area became part of the United States, the townspeople actually lifted their homes and moved them to the Canadian side of the border. Today St. Andrews is a peaceful summer haven with swimming, golfing, and tours of Passamoquoddy Bay.

St. Andrews Blockhouse National Historic Site, at the northwest end of Water Street, is the only surviving wood fortress of several built for the town's defense during the War of 1812. Also see **Greenock Church**, a pretty church built in 1824.

Visit the aquarium at Huntsman Marine Laboratories, northwest of town on Brandy Cover Road, and the **Ross Memorial Museum**, *188 Montague St.,* in an old house filled with antiques, paintings, and curios.

The best place to stay in town is the quirky **Rossmount Inn**, *tel. (506) 529-3351.* The Victorian house is decorated with a mishmash of Persian rugs, English wallpaper, and French art. Smoking is not permitted on the grounds. Credit cards are accepted, but it is seasonal, so call before you go.

The best bird-watching

New Brunswick is an excellent place for bird-watching. More than 350 species of birds can be seen; you need only a pair of binoculars and a North American field guide. During the winter, New Brunswick attracts such rare birds as the Bohemian waxwing, pine grosbeak, common redpoll, and purple finch.

For bird watchers, the event of the year is the **Christmas Bird Count**, sponsored by the National Audubon Society. As many observers as possible are needed on the count day, which usually falls during the last two weeks of December. Write to the **New Brunswick Museum**, *Natural Science Department, 277 Douglas Ave., St. John, New Brunswick E2K 1E5*, for the names and addresses of count compilers.

The New Brunswick Federation of Naturalists sponsors field trips several times a year. For more information, write to the **New Brunswick Museum**, *address above*.

St. John: the oldest town

St. John is the oldest incorporated town in Canada, inaugurated in 1785. Actually, it was founded by Samuel de Champlain on St. John the Baptist Day (June 24) in 1604. The Loyalists turned this city into one of the world's greatest shipbuilding ports. Vessels from every country call here.

The St. John River's **Reversing Falls** will leave you wondering. The falls, which appear to flow backward, are actually rapids beneath the bridge on Highway 100. A Tourist Information Center here shows a film explaining the phenomenon. Usually the river empties into the Bay of Fundy. But as the tide rises, the estuary water reverses the river current, creating climbing rapids.

New Brunswick's best seafood

Shediac, which holds a six-day Lobster Festival every July, is known for its incredibly fresh and inexpensive lobster. The city is also known for having New Brunswick's warmest water, thanks to sand bars and shallow depths.

Paturel Shore House, *tel. (506) 532-4431*, on the ocean next to a seafood-packing plant, is the best place in the area to get seafood. Take Highway 15 east from Shediac and watch for signs to Cape Bimet and Paturel. Lobster is caught locally and prepared to your specifications. The lobster stew can be a meal in itself.

The best place to stay is **Chez Françoise**, *93 Main St.; tel. (506) 532-4233*.

Nova Scotia: more Gaelic than Scotland

Nova Scotia, a 375-mile peninsula separated from New Brunswick by the Bay of Fundy, is more Gaelic than its grandfather, Scotland. The province, which is made up of two main sections, Nova Scotia proper and **Cape Breton Island**, drew boatloads of Scotsmen during the wave of immigration from the Highlands in the 18th century. The Cape Breton immigrants left before they felt the full impact of King James VI's law of 1616, which prohibited the use of Gaelic and the wearing of kilts. Today, even in such remote regions of Scotland as the Isle of Skye, the use of Gaelic is rare. However, on western Cape Breton Island, most adult residents have Gaelic-speaking parents. (Nova Scotia is actually a better place to learn Scottish Gaelic than Scotland. You can take summer classes at St. Anne's in Cape Breton. For more information, contact the **Scottish Studies Department** in Ontario, *tel. (519) 824-4120*.)

Fiddlers in this province retain a Scottish style abandoned by most Scottish musicians long ago. The stretch along the coast of Cape Breton from the causeway at Port Hastings to Margaree Forks, known as the **Ceilidh Trail**, is the place to go to enjoy traditional music and dance. Check with the proprietors of pubs in the area for details.

Every July, Antigonish hosts the annual **Highland Games**, during which contestants compete in the cabor (log) toss, among other things. For more information, contact the **Nova Scotia Department of Tourism**, *tel. (800) 341-6096*.

The Micmac Indians also sponsor annual summer games, which have evolved from a reunion, lasting three months, held since the 18th century.

Originally, a continental Indian congress met and planned survival tactics against the encroaching Europeans. It succeeded at least to a degree—to this day, the Micmacs on rural reservations retain their native language.

The Micmac summer games include tributes to St. Ann, such as dances to the beat of the sacred drum, and field games, including archery, canoeing, and *waltes*, a dice game.

The best treasure hunting

Oak Island, Nova Scotia, has frustrated treasure hunters for nearly 200 years. Convinced that Captain Kidd and his fellow pirates hid their loot here, many fortune seekers have tried the hunt and failed. Millions of dollars have been spent and six lives lost trying to find the treasure. So far, nothing has been found.

THE OLDEST COLONY: NEWFOUNDLAND

Newfoundland is at once the newest of the Canadian provinces and the oldest of the British colonies. Sir Humphrey Gilbert landed on this North Atlantic island in 1583 and claimed it for Queen Elizabeth. But it didn't become part of Canada until 1949.

Legions of hunters, hikers, fishermen, campers, boaters, and photographers take advantage of the natural bounties of this northern province's 47 provincial park wilderness areas and two national parks: Terra Nova in the east and Gros Morne in the west.

The **Marine Atlantic Reservations Bureau**, *121 Eden St., Bar Harbor, ME 04609; tel. (800)341-7981*, operates a year-round vehicle and passenger ferry service between North Sydney, Nova Scotia, and Port-aux-Basques, Newfoundland. During the summer, an additional service operates between North Sydney and Argentia, 78 miles from St. John's.

Gros Morne: the most beautiful scenery

Gros Morne National Park is a jaw-dropping wilderness area on the west coast of Newfoundland. The 750-square-mile park has the most spectacular fiords in North America. Gros Morne (which translates as *Big Knoll* in French) is a flat-topped extinct volcano rising 2,000 feet front the Gulf of St. Lawrence. Climb the two-and-a-half-mile **Names Callaghan Trail** to the top of Gros Morne for the best view of the tundra and the roaring sea below. Look for moose, caribou, bald eagles, black bears, and beaver.

Hike along the elevated boardwalk through the marshes to **Western Brook Pond**. At the end of the path is a dock, where you can catch a tour boat and cruise the pond. (You can register for a boat tour at the park's visitor center.) Boats sail beneath towering rocky cliffs to a misty 2,000-foot waterfall. Three boat trips depart daily, weather permitting, from mid-June to mid-September. Boat capacity is 25 to 30 people. To get to the pond, drive north of the visitor center on Highway 430 for about 18 miles, past Sally's Cove.

Canada's best archeological sites

The Great Northern Peninsula is the site of some of Canada's most interesting archeological sites. **Porte-aux-Choix** has a 5,000-year-old Red Paint Indian burial mound and the remains of later Inuit cultures. Three Red Paint burial mounds have been excavated here, uncovering the remains of 100 people, weapons, and artifacts. The relics can be seen in the visitor center, which is open from June through Labor Day. (The Red Paint lived here about 2340 B.C. Later, Dorset Eskimos, known for their fine stone tools, lived here for 2,000 years. About A.D. 1100, the Beothuck Indians took over the region.)

At the tip of the Great Northern Peninsula is **L'Anse aux Meadows National Historic Park**, the site of a Viking settlement dating from A.D. 1000 (492 years before Columbus). These early Norse settlers built six thatched houses, three of which have been reconstructed. Historians believe the first European child born in America was Snorri Thorfinnson, born here to Icelandic trader Thorfinn Karlsefni in A.D. 1005. The child is mentioned in Viking sagas.

While visiting the park, stay at the **St. Anthony Motel**, *P.O. Box 465, St. Anthony, NF, A0K 4S0*.

The best of the Beothucks

For a glimpse of the life of the Beothuck Indians, head east on the **Trans-Canada Highway** (Highway 1) to Grand Falls. The **Mary March Museum**, *Cromer Avenue*, is dedicated to the study of these people, who inhabited the region when the first European settlers of the 1600s came ashore. Mary March was the last of the unassimilated Beothucks, and her knowledge was the foundation of the museum.

While in Grand Falls, stay at the **Mt. Peyton Hotel-Motel**, *214 Lincoln Road, Grand Falls, NF A2A 1P8; (800)563-4894* (for reservations only) or *(709)489-2251*.

Terra Nova: the best wildlife

Terra Nova National Park, *tel. (709)533-2801*, southeast of Gander, is famous for its Atlantic beaches and its wildlife (including moose, black bear, red fox, Canada geese, beaver, and lynx). Keep an eye out for the park's unusual pitcher plant, which is carnivorous. You can rent cabins, canoes, and bikes at the park headquarters.

The best of France in the New World

Off the southern coast of Newfoundland are two French islands: **St. Pierre** and **Miquelon**. You must clear customs to travel to these islands, but a passport is unnecessary if you have identification.

Both islands truly feel like forgotten French towns, with French architecture, fashion, and culture. French wines are a good buy here, even though the islands lost their tax-free status.

The best place to stay on St. Pierre is **Hôtel Robert**, a small old-fashioned hotel. For reservations at any of the hotels in St. Pierre, contact **SPM Tours**, *tel. (709) 722-3892.*

The most romantic town

St. John's, a natural rockbound harbor on the Avalon Peninsula, is Newfoundland's most romantic town. Quaint houses with brightly colored facades recall the town's wild past, when pirates raided and great feasts were held. While St. John's is one of the oldest towns in North America, inhabited by fishermen since the 15th century, its buildings are Victorian. Earlier dwellings all were destroyed by fire.

Signal Hill, which looms above the harbor, was the site of the first trans-Atlantic reception of a radio signal, sent by Guglielmo Marconi on Dec. 12, 1901. About two-thirds of the way up Signal Hill is **Queen's Battery**, built in the late 18th century. Across the narrows from Queen's Battery is **Fort Amherst**. The battery and the fort, together with a chain that stretched across the narrows, were effective in closing the port to enemies.

St. John's has two beautiful churches: the twin-spired **Roman Catholic Basilica** and the **Anglican Cathedral**, one of the best examples of Gothic architecture in North America.

If you're looking for restaurants, shops, and people, stroll downtown along Duckworth and Water streets. (**Water Street** is known as the "oldest main street on the continent," because it served as a pathway for the early explorers.)

To dine in an old-time colonial atmosphere, visit the **Woodstock Colonial Inn**, *tel. (709) 722-6933.*

Most hotels in St. John's are expensive. The best are the **Hotel Newfoundland**, *tel. (709) 726-4980 or (800) 268-8136 in Canada*, located on Cavendish Square, and the **Stel Battery Hotel**, *tel. (709) 576-0040*, which has panoramic views.

THE BEST OF ALBERTA

The peaceful and vast prairies of **Alberta** retain much of the open space and freedom that drew settlers into the Canadian wilderness a century ago. Alberta's prairies stretch for miles, a flat quilt at the foot of the Canadian Rockies.

While Alberta does have thriving, colorful cities, most of this vast 255,285-square-mile province is unpopulated—it has fewer inhabitants than the city of Philadelphia. And most of the population (more than half) lives in Edmonton and Calgary.

Calgary: the best cow town

Calgary is both a colorful remnant of the Wild West and a huge, modern city. Known as Cowtown, because of its cattle industry, Calgary is a thriving business center located less than an hour from the Rockies. This lively, crazy town is best known as the home of the **Calgary Stampede**, a wild rodeo of horse racing and high jinks.

Calgary got its start as a Royal Canadian Mounted Police post in 1875, back in the days when buffalo hunters, whiskey traders, pioneers, and Indians required the likes of Sergeant Preston of the Yukon to keep them in line. The post was founded at the junction of two rivers, the Bow and the Elbow. Colonel J.F. Macloud, the commander of the Mounties who founded the post, named it Calgary after his favorite fishing spot on the Bay of Mull in Scotland. The log fort attracted 600 settlers.

Four years later, the Canadian Pacific Railway reached Calgary in its rush to "save the West from the Yankees." The population of the post promptly doubled, as Chinese were brought in from the Pacific to lay railway tracks and European settlers—mostly English—poured in from the Atlantic Coast.

Tremendous beef herds were built up around Calgary, and it soon became a cattle metropolis. With the discovery of oil at nearby Turner Valley in 1914, Calgary boomed.

Outside the downtown area, Calgary is beautiful. The Rocky Mountain foothills begin to the west. The prairie stretches forever to the east. Northeast of Calgary are the **Drumheller Badlands**, where dinosaur skeletons have been found. Southwest is the **Glenmore Reservoir**, surrounded by parks and trails. Farm towns and huge cattle ranches begin south of the city.

The best rodeo

If you want to brave the **Calgary Stampede**, make sure you have reservations—the city swells with participants and spectators. (To make reservations, contact **Calgary Exhibition & Stampede**, *P.O. Box 1860, Calgary, AB T2P 2M7; tel. (403)261-0101.*)

The stampede is big and rough, drawing an immense and enthusiastic crowd. Cowboys from all over the continent ride bucking broncos and bulls, rope calves, and wrestle steers for prizes. The **Stampede Stage Show** features chorus girls, clowns, bands, and glamour. The funniest event is the **Chuckwagon Race**, in which old-time cowboy chuck wagons race around the track.

The best view of the city

The revolving restaurant at the top of the 626-foot **Calgary Tower**, *Ninth Avenue and Center Street; tel. (403)266-7171*, has the best view in town. You can see the Rockies when it's clear. If you don't want to pay for dinner, enjoy the view from the observation deck.

Calgary's top sights

Fort Calgary, *750 Ninth Ave. S.E.; tel. (403)290-1875*, is a 40-acre natural history park on the site of the original Mounted Police fort. Exhibits explain the history of Calgary. The fort is open daily year-round. Tours can be arranged for a nominal fee.

The **Glenbow Museum**, *130 Ninth Ave. S.E.; tel. (403)264-8300*, has extensive displays of Indian and Inuit art and artifacts. The art gallery has carvings and ceramics from all over the world. The museum is closed Mondays.

Explore **Heritage Park**, *west of 14th Street and Heritage Drive S.W.; tel. (403)255-1182*, an authentic pre-1915 Alberta town. Original pioneer buildings from all over Alberta have been transported here, including a log church, a blacksmith's shop, a newspaper office, and a bakery. The park is open May through mid-October.

The best shopping

If you have a secret urge to look like Roy Rogers, head to **Western Outfitters**, *128 Eighth Ave. S.E.* (If you're planning to attend the Calgary Stampede, this is the place to pick up your spurs!)

The best food

The most elegant restaurant in Calgary is the **Owl's Nest**, *320 Fourth Ave. S.W.; tel. (403)266-1611*. Before dinner, women are given roses. Have the British Columbia salmon, Beluga caviar, lobster, or quail. Reservations are suggested. Major credit cards are accepted.

The finest of Alberta's beef is served at the **Rimrock Room**, *Palliser Hotel, Ninth Avenue and First Street S.W.; tel. (403)262-1234*.

Calgary's best hotel

The **Palliser**, *133 Ninth Ave. S.W.; tel. (403)262-1234*, is an institution in Calgary, built in 1914 by the Canadian Pacific Railroad. The gracious old hotel has brass doors, marble pillars, and chandeliers.

Canada's most beautiful national parks

Banff and Jasper national parks, on the border between British Columbia and Alberta, are among the most beautiful nature reserves in the world. Together, they comprise 6,764 square miles in the Rocky Mountains.

Imagine snow-topped peaks, deep-green forests, cascading rivers, mountain sheep, bears, and silent blue lakes.

Banff is the older of the parks, Jasper the larger. They run together and stretch from Mount Sir Douglas in the south to the Resthaven Mountains in the far north. Many nature trails climb into their remote valleys and peaks. Banff lies 81 miles from Calgary via Highway 1; Jasper is 225 miles from Edmonton on Route 16.

Highway 93, from Banff to Jasper, which passes the Athabasca glacier, is spectacular. You'll see bighorn sheep, mountain goats, and bears from the road.

The 160-square-mile **Columbia ice fields** spread across Jasper. Rent a snowmobile in the park and take off to explore them. Jasper also boasts Alberta's highest peak, **Mount Columbia** (12,294 feet), and the spectacular **Athabasca Falls**, which rush through a narrow gap.

The **Banff Springs Hotel**, *Spray Avenue; tel. (403)762-2211*, which has views of the mountains and two rivers, is the best place to stay while exploring the parks. Established in 1928 to bring visitors to the nearby hot springs, the castlelike hotel has four dining rooms, an espresso bar, cocktail lounges, and a post office. Its golf course is considered one of the most scenic in the world.

Edmonton: the best boomtown

Edmonton has been a boomtown three times in its life: The fur trade brought hundreds of trappers and trackers in the 18th century, the gold rush attracted thousands in the 1890s, and the discovery of oil and natural gas brought industrial development in the 1960s. Despite its spurts of sudden growth, Edmonton is well-designed, with 11,000 acres of parks. And city leaders have made a tremendous effort to preserve historic buildings.

Edmonton's best festival

Klondike Days, which celebrate the days of gold prospecting, take place in late July. Everyone must dress in period costumes (those who don't may find themselves temporarily incarcerated in the Klondike clink!), the streets are filled with performers, and parades make their way through the streets. The new coliseum hosts rock'n'roll and Western entertainment.

Edmonton's best sights

Fort Edmonton, a replica of the fur-trading post established in 1795, stands in a 158-acre park off Whitemud Freeway in the suburbs. It is complete with a stockade, a fur-processing plant, a clay oven, McDougall's General Store, the Northwest Mounted Police Jail, and a Masonic temple. The original trading post has been replaced with **Alberta's Legislative Building**, *109th Street and 97th Avenue*, which was built in 1912.

The **Muttart Conservatory and Horticulture Center**, *98th Avenue and 96th Street*, is a complex of four ultramodern pyramid-shaped greenhouses that act as a botanical incubator. Each pyramid has a specific climate and is filled with flora of appropriate regions. The complex is open daily.

The **Edmonton Civic Center**, *100th Street and 102nd Avenue*, is a gigantic structure containing the Edmonton Art Gallery, City Hall, a convention center, the law courts building, and the Centennial Library.

Edmonton's best restaurants

Hy's Steak Loft, *10013 101st Ave.*, serves superb steaks. (Alberta is famous for its beef.) The restaurant is closed Sundays. Reservations are required.

Vi's, *9712 111th St.*, has good, hearty food for a reasonable price. Try the thick homemade soup; finish your meal with the chocolate-glazed pecan pie. The restaurant is open daily.

The best hotel

The **Westin Hotel**, *100th Street at 101st Avenue; tel. (780)426-3636*, is where Princess Di and Prince Charles stayed when they visited in 1983. The swimming pool and sauna are inviting, and the restaurant is one of the best in the city.

THE BEST OF BRITISH COLUMBIA

British Columbia, Canada's westernmost province, has snow-capped mountains that rise out of the Pacific, providing backdrops for Vancouver and Victoria. In the north of this region are tiny settlements lost in a stark wilderness; in the center are wide-open ranchlands that cowboys call home. Throughout the area, glacier ice fields jut into birch and maple forests.

More than one million acres of British Columbia have been set aside for five national parks. The area also contains 11 million acres of provincial parks.

Throughout this coastal province are **petroglyphs**, rock drawings made by unknown tribes long ago, which are carefully preserved by the government. Mementos of the early fur traders, explorers, and pioneers can be seen at **Fort Langley**, a restored fur trading post in Fort Defiance on Vancouver Island, and at **Fort James**, near Prince George. Artifacts of the Cariboo gold rush of the 1860s are preserved at **Barkerville**. And the Royal Mounted Police left its mark at **Fort Steel**.

Vancouver: a best city

Vancouver is surrounded on all sides by snow-capped mountains, and glass-sided skyscrapers are reflected in the glittering blue harbor. The air is pure, and the climate is mild. At the western edge of the city, cliffs drop to the sea. Totem poles stand near the Strait of Georgia, a reminder of the Northwest Indians, who were the first inhabitants of this region. Canada's third-largest city, Vancouver has 1.3 million residents.

The city's main thoroughfare is **Georgia Street**, where you'll find the old Hotel Vancouver, the Vancouver Art Gallery inside an old granite court-house, and entrances to underground shopping malls.

Near Georgia Street, between Howe and Hornby, is **Robson Square**, a three-block complex designed by Arthur Erickson. Inside the square are international kiosks, a skating rink, and terraced gardens with pools and waterfalls. At the edge of the square is a seven-story glass pyramid—the **Law Courts Building**. During the week, you can wander into an open courtroom, sink into an upholstered chair, and watch a hearing.

Stanley Park, just north of downtown, is a wilderness playground with performing whales and a zoo. The best way to see this immense, 1,000-acre preserve is by bike. (A six-mile scenic drive circles the park.) **Stanley Park Rentals**, *676 Chilco St.*, just outside the park, rents 10-speed and tandem bicycles.

Gastown, east of the Sea Bus terminal, is the birthplace of Vancouver. This renovated 19th-century area is filled with pubs, restaurants, galleries, and boutiques. Stop by **Hill's Indian Crafts**, *Water Street*, for baskets, moc-casins, carvings, jewelry, prints, and sweaters.

South of Gastown, along Pender Street, is **Chinatown**. Sidewalk stalls sell Chinese food and knicknacks, and herbalists offer deer horns, dried sea horses, and exotic teas. The **Chinese Cultural Center**, *Pender Street*, has maps of the area. Stroll through the **Dr. Sun Yat-Sen Classical Garden**, two-and-a-half acres of miniature fountains, pavilions, ponds, and bridges.

Granville Island has galleries, theaters, cafés, and an open market. Have dinner at Bridges. Afterward, stop by Granville Island Hotel's **Pelican Bay Lounge** to enjoy some jazz. Return downtown from Granville aboard the False Creek Ferry, which departs from a dock near Bridges.

The stern-faced totem poles in the **Museum of Anthropology** at the University of British Columbia are a sharp contrast to the modern lines of the museum itself, which was designed by Erickson.

The best restaurants

Chartwell, *Georgia and Howe streets; tel. (604)689-9333*, in the Four Seasons Hotel has a superb menu that features game and seafood. The wine list is extensive. The restaurant is closed Sundays. Reservations are highly recommended.

Umberto's is an institution in Vancouver, with three restaurants serving three different cuisines. The original, *1380 Hornby St.; tel. (604)687-6316*, spe-cializes in northern Italian cuisine. **Al Porto Umberto**, *321 Water St.;*

tel. (604)683-8376, has fresh local seafood. And **Il Giardino**, *1382 Hornby; tel. (604)669-2422*, serves fowl and wild game. All three are excellent.

The **Only**, *20 E. Hastings St.; tel. (604)681-6546*, serves the freshest seafood in town. A cheap, informal place in a down-at-the-heels neighborhood, it has booths and counter seats, all with views of the gas burners and frying pans where the fish is cooked. No liquor is served, and credit cards are not accepted. The restaurant is closed Sundays.

Vancouver's best beds

Vancouver's best hotel is **Delta Place**, *645 Howe St.; tel. (604)687-1122*, which offers every luxury and convenience imaginable, from a gourmet restaurant to a health club.

The **Bayshore Inn**, *1601 W. Georgia St.; tel. (604)682-3377*, once hosted Howard Hughes, who took over the top two floors. Yachtsmen stay here, mooring their boats at the hotel dock. Doormen in red jackets and tall fur hats guard the doors. Rooms have floor-to-ceiling windows with lovely views of the water and the city. Shops, lounges, restaurants, and a pool are available to guests.

If you're watching your budget, stay at the **Sylvia Hotel**, *1154 Gilford St; tel. (604)681-9321*. This nine-story hotel, which has a good dining room, is popular, so make reservations in advance.

Vancouver Island: the most beautiful

Vancouver Island, which stretches 170 miles along the western coastline of British Columbia, is sheltered along its southern border by the state of Washington's Olympic Peninsula. You can take a ferry from Vancouver City to Nanaimo.

Most of the half-million people on Vancouver Island live along its east coast, which is rich in timber, farmland, and fishing streams, or at the southern tip in the city of Victoria. The wild and rugged west coast is sparsely inhabited, with few villages. It is deeply cut by fiords and piled high with mountains. The south end of the island is mountainous, reaching a height of 7,200 feet; the north end is flat.

Victoria, the provincial capital, was first settled by Europeans in 1843. It has been the site of coal mining, logging, fur trading, and fishing.

One of the most beautiful sights on the island is **Butchart Gardens**, near Victoria, across the Saanich Peninsula from Sydney. Originally (in 1905), this area was a limestone quarry; today it offers entertainment on summer evenings.

Victoria, the most British city

"A tweedy, daffodilish, green-fingered sort of place, a golfish, fly-fishing, 5 o'clock teapot place." That's how Canadian author Bruce Hutchinson described Victoria, which feels more British than any other city in the Americas. While it is the largest city on Vancouver Island, the atmosphere is relaxed. The air smells of flowers and the sea. The climate is mild, less rainy than on the island's west coast.

Go behind the **Tweed Curtain**, as it is known, along Oak Bay. Enjoy the thick British accents and stop for tea at the Oak Bay Beach Hotel, the Blethering Place Tearoom in Oak Bay Village, or the dining room in the Butchart Gardens Mansion.

Activity in Victoria centers around the harbor, which is surrounded by Victorian buildings, including the Empress Hotel, the Provincial legislative buildings, the old steamship terminal (now a wax museum), and the Belmont Building. The Visitors and Convention Bureau, an art deco building, offers maps and information.

Victoria's **Provincial Museum** traces life before and after glaciers covered Vancouver Island with a sheet of ice three-and-a-half miles thick. Walk through the rain forest, which includes a reconstructed 19th-century town and an Indian longhouse.

Outside the Provincial Museum complex is **Thunderbird Park**, which has a collection of coastal Indian totem poles. You can watch Indian craftsmen carving reproductions of traditional designs. Just beyond the park is the **Helmcken House**, the oldest house still standing in British Columbia.

The **Tong-Ji Men** (Gate of Harmonious Interest), at the corner of Fisgard and Government in Chinatown, is a 30-foot arch with 4,500 ceramic tiles and 1,008 decorative panels that was made in Taiwan.

Craigdarroch Castle, *Joan Crescent*, was built in 1885 by the multimillionaire coal baron Robert Dunsmuir for his wife Joan. A nonprofit society is refurbishing the castle, which was auctioned off for a dollar after Joan's death.

Along Rockland Avenue is the **Government House**, where the lieutenant governor of British Columbia resides. Its gardens are more than 100 years old.

Most restaurants in Victoria serve mostly bland English fare—fish and chips and the lot. Two exceptions are **Periklis**, *531 Yates St.*, where you can enjoy Greek food, and **Foo Hong**, in Chinatown, a popular and inexpensive lunch spot.

Stay at the **Gothic Empress Hotel**, *721 Government St.; tel. (604)384-8111*, which is great fun but rather touristy and expensive. Built in 1906 on the harbor, it has lovely views as well as a bar, a restaurant, and a disco. Have high tea in the afternoon.

A good, moderately priced hotel is **Helm's Inn**, off Government Street, near the Provincial Museum, *tel. (604)385-5767*.

The most shopping space

Nanaimo, the second-largest city on Vancouver Island, has the largest amount of retail shopping space per capita of any city in Canada. The city is also filled with preserved pioneer buildings and sites, which you can see on the historic walking tour.

Stroll around Nanaimo's waterfront, where you'll see the **Bastion**, the former Hudson's Bay Company Fort, erected in 1852 by settlers as protection against raiding Indians. **Fishermen's Wharf** has an abundance of fresh seafood. The **Georgia Park Promenade** leads to the modern seaplane base and on to Swy-A-Lana Lagoon and Maffeo Sutton Park.

Georgia Park is dedicated to the Indian tribes who first inhabited this area and features a display of authentic Indian canoes and totem poles. **Swy-A-Lana Lagoon** features a man-made tidal pool. Next to the lagoon, native Indians operate a traditional carving shed, where you can watch craftsmen carving masks and other artifacts.

The world's best bathtub race

Nanaimo's annual **Bathtub Race** in mid-July is a zany spectacle. Hundreds of daring tubbers challenge the wild waters of the Georgia Strait in a 30-mile race to the beaches of Vancouver. It's hilarious.

The best whale watching

You can track the great gray whale each spring as it migrates northward along the west coast of Vancouver Island. The first migrants appear in late February; by mid-April, the waters are filled with hundreds of them. As many as 40 or 50 gray whales like the area so much that they spend the summer here.

The best time for whale watching is from late February through June. The whales can be spotted from the headlands of Pacific Rim National Park, from the restaurant at Wickaninnish Bay, or from the rocky shores of Little Beach, Big Beach, or Amphitrite Point in Uduelet. However, the best way to watch is from the deck of a charter boat that specializes in whale-watching trips.

You'll usually see only a small portion of the whale. When spouting, whales roll forward and seem to lift partly out of the water, revealing their scarred gray backs and the bumps of their vertebrae, which are known as knuckles. While diving in deep water, they occasionally show their graceful, barnacle-encrusted tails, displays called fluking. When they poke their heads out of the water for a look around, they are spy-hopping. The most breath-taking sight is when whales breach, jumping almost completely out of the water to land on their backs with a huge splash.

Canadian Princess Resort offers whale-watching cruises that depart from Vancouver and Victoria. For more information, contact the resort at **Oak**

Bay Marina Ltd., *1327 Beach Drive, Victoria, BC V8S 2N4.*

Subtidal Adventures, *P.O. Box 253, Uduelet, BC VOR 3A0; tel. (604)726-7061* or *(604)726-7336*, also offers a whale-watching cruise.

The highest city

British Columbia boasts the highest city in Canada: **Kimberley**, in the Rocky Mountains just north of the U.S. border. This mining town-turned-ski resort resembles a Bavarian Alpine village. The townspeople sponsor a **Julyfest** modeled after the German Oktoberfest (but held earlier in the year) that includes parades, folk dances, beer tents, and international entertainment.

Kimberley's real claim to fame is its excellent downhill skiing. The city's mountain rises 2,300 feet and has 32 runs served by chair lifts and T-bars. The mountain also has one of North America's longest lighted ski runs (1,600 feet). For information on ski packages, contact **Kimberley Ski Resort**, *P.O. Box 40, Kimberley, BC VIA 2Y5; tel. (604)427-4881.*

Canada's only desert town

Osoyoos is a Spanish-influenced desert town in a 252-mile desert pocket east of Vancouver. It is watered by deep Lake Osoyoos, where you can fish for trout and bass. You can swim here, too, if you don't mind sharing the water with painted turtles. Try your luck panning for gold in the Okanagan Valley above Osoyoos.

The most authentic Indian village

Hazelton (known as Kiran-maksh among the Indians), in the heart of British Columbia, is a modern Indian town next to a reconstructed Gitskan Indian village built to look as it did before the arrival of the white man. The village, called **Ksan**, has six longhouses, totem poles, and birchbark canoes. The House of Treasures contains the tribal regalia of Gitksan chiefs. A campground and trailer park adjoin the village.

THE WORLD'S BEST FISHING

Some say Canada, which is bordered by three oceans and the Hudson Bay and dotted with thousands of lakes, rivers, and streams, has the best fishing in the world. Inland waters are filled with major freshwater fish, while the Atlantic and Pacific coasts run with striped bass, bluefin tuna, shark, and other deep-sea fish. Generally, the farther north you go, the better the fishing. In the Yukon and Northwest Territories, the open-water fishing season runs from June to late September. Water in these Arctic regions is ice-cold, and the fish fight harder, making the sport more challenging and exciting.

British Columbia: the best fishing year-round

In British Columbia, which many claim has the best fishing in Canada, you can fish year-round. With so many miles of streams and rivers and thousands of lakes spread across a sparsely populated land, it is a fisherman's paradise. Despite all this, the region isn't crowded.

Five species of salmon can be caught in the coastal waters off British Columbia. Pacific-Gulf Charters offers three-day packages in British Columbia which include accommodation, fishing equipment, and meals. Contact **Oak Bay Marine Group**, *1327 Beach Drive, Victoria, BC V85 2N4; tel. (800)663-7090.*

Fred Kuzyk is one of the best fishing guides in the business. His company, **Coho Fishing and Guiding Services**, *104 E. 49th Ave., Vancouver, BC Canada V5W 2G2; tel. (604)324-8214,* can organize every detail of your trip, including all the necessary fishing licenses. All packages include transportation, accommodation, meals, equipment, tackle, and guide.

THE HAPPIEST HUNTING GROUNDS

Canada has a profusion of wildlife: brown bears and grizzly bears in British Columbia and the Laurentian Mountains of Quebec, buffalo in Alberta, and elk and moose in Saskatchewan. The Northwest Territories and the Yukon have polar bears, musk oxen, caribou, seals, walruses, and penguins. Most of the animals are protected. Hunting laws are detailed and involve specific seasons and registrations. For more information, contact the Ministry of Natural Resources of the area where you want to hunt.

The most adventurous hunt

Adventurous and experienced hunters can track polar bears in the Northwest Territories with the help of Eskimo guides. However, the total quota of polar bears that can be hunted is 400 a year, and the local Eskimos decide how many of these are to be shot by tourists. You must use an Eskimo guide, and you can't use mechanical vehicles in your hunt. Plan on two weeks of travel over huge ice ridges via dogsled.

If the polar bear quota is filled, plenty of other game can be hunted in the Northwest Territories: musk ox, caribou, reindeer, wolf, wolverine, mink, lynx, otter, beaver, seal, walrus, and whale.

The best hunting camps and lodges

For a real wilderness adventure, stay at an Indian camp in Ontario, where a sure-footed Indian guide can show you the trails. **Big Trout Lake Indian Band** operates a lodge, where you can hunt moose, bear, and grouse. Access is by aircraft. For more information, contact **Tom Morris**, *Bugg River Camp, Big Trout Lake, Ontario POV 1G0.*

Sylvester Jack, *P.O. Box 210, Atlin, BC V0W 1A0*, operates a big-game hunting camp in northwestern British Columbia. He can guide you on sheep, bear, and moose hunts.

CANADA'S BEST SAILING

Nova Scotia is a Shangri-La for boaters. Its calm harbors and rolling hills are a perfect refuge for Atlantic sailors. Boaters can dock at **Armdale Yacht Club**, *Halifax, North West Arm;* **Bedford Basin Yacht Club**, *Halifax;* **Bras d'Or Yacht Club**, *Baddeck;* **Canadian Forces Sailing Association**, *P. O. Box 280, Shearwater;* **Chester Yacht Club**, *PO Box 290, Chester;* **Dartmouth Yacht Club**, *Bedford Basin;* **Lennox Passage Yacht Club**, *D'Escousse;* **Lunenburg Yacht Club**, *P.O. Box 820, Lunenburg;* and **Royal Western Nova Scotia Yacht Club**, *Montague Row, Digby.*

The rugged island is filled with boat charter and rental companies. **Whale Cruisers Cheticamp Ltd.** (Capt. Bill Crawford), *P.O. Box 10, Grand Etang, Nova Scotia B0E 1L0; tel. (902)224-3376*, offers whale-watching cruises and scenic boat tours and charters that depart Government Wharf at Cheticamp Harbor at 9 a.m., 1 p.m., and 6 p.m. during July and August. Special group rates and charters can be arranged.

THE MOST EXCITING RAFTING

Aventures en Eau Vive, *RR 2, Calumet J0V1B0; tel. (819)242-6084*, arranges rafting groups on the Rouge River from April through October.

THE BEST ON HORSEBACK

What better way to see the wilds of Canada than on horseback? The best way to go is with **Trail Riders of the Canadian Rockies**, *P.O. Box 6742, Station D, Calgary, Alberta, Canada T2P 2E6*, a nonprofit group that leads riders through the uninhabited valleys of Banff National Park. A six-day trip includes accommodation in Indian tepees, horses, saddles, meals, and guides.

THE BEST OF THE CARIBBEAN

The Caribbean Sea is speckled with dozens of beautiful little worlds—islands rimmed with white sand, coral reefs, and palm trees. Each is unique. Some have volcanos, others are as flat as pancakes. On some, residents speak French; on others, the people speak Spanish, Dutch, or English. A few of the islands have luxurious resorts with gambling casinos and fine restaurants that draw the jet set. Others are remote, with thick jungles and few inhabitants. Although technically not in the Caribbean, the Bahamas and Bermuda have been included because of their tropical lifestyle and beaches.

(See more about the Caribbean's best beaches in Section 3: The World's Best Beaches.)

THE PUREST OF THE U.S. VIRGINS: ST. JOHN

St. John, the smallest of the U.S. Virgin Islands, seems to be escaping the fate of its overdeveloped sisters. Two-thirds of its mere 20 square miles are set aside as national parkland. Campsites dot the park, just a few yards from the surf.

The favorite pastime on St. John is snorkeling. One of the best places to watch the fish is **Watermelon Bay**, past the ruins of the Annaberg sugarcane factory near Leinster Bay.

At the tip of Frances Bay is **Mary's Point**, a haunted promontory. Legend has it that during the revolt against the Danes in 1733, slaves leapt to their deaths from the cliff above to avoid being captured. They believed their souls would return to Africa.

Maho Bay—a 14-acre private campground—is our favorite place to stay on the island. When Maho Bay was first built, materials were carried to the site by hand to keep the natural beauty intact. Innovative water and sewage systems help to conserve precious supplies.

The 102 cottages at Maho Bay are actually canvas tents on 16-foot platforms connected by a labyrinth of walkways. Each includes a sleeping area with two beds, a living room with one bed, a cooking area, and a porch with a table and chairs. Electric lamps, bed linens, blankets, and towels are provided.

The most luxurious place to stay

The most luxurious place to stay on St. John is **Caneel Bay Plantation**, *tel. (809) 776-6111*. The 170-acre, 18th-century sugar plantation is dotted with tennis courts and exotic plants. Cottages are clustered around seven beaches. The posh cottages don't have air conditioning or telephones.

THE BEST OF ST. THOMAS

The island of St. Thomas is 32 square miles of lush tropical paradise. Exploring the island will take you up winding hills and along mountainous roadways where each breathtaking panorama is more dramatic than the one before. Visit **Drake's Seat**, the vantage point where Sir Francis Drake used to sit and observe his fleet.

Finest dining in St. Thomas

Built as a residence by a French sea merchant, **Hotel 1829**, *tel. (toll free in U.S.) (800) 524-2002, (outside U.S.) (340) 776-1829; website: www.hotel1829.com*, is now a registered National Historic Site. Converted into a hotel with a bar and restaurant in 1906, the entire structure—public rooms, terraces, and guestrooms—reflects the architectural style of the Caribbean of the past. Steps and archways lead to landscaped garden patios and delightful nooks where you can enjoy a cool drink and watch the harbor views.

Best place for the kids

Located on the grounds of the Renaissance Grand Beach Resort, **Blazing Villas**, *tel. (800) 382-2002; website: www.blazing-villas.com*, is a unique group of studio suites, each with up to three bedrooms and full kitchens. With full access to the hotel's facilities—white sand beach, pools, tennis courts, a spa, and dining facilities—Blazing Villas combines the best of a luxury condo with the best of a resort hotel. This is the best place to stay if you're traveling with children.

The best of Old St. Thomas

Located at the west entrance to the St. Thomas harbor in the historic district of Frenchtown, The **Admiral's Inn**, *tel. (340) 774-1276*, is a 12-room bed and breakfast. Frenchtown, a collection of multicolored houses and buildings that gets its name from the French settlers who came from Martinique over 150 years ago, is now the spot where the French fishing boats dock with supplies of seafood for St. Thomas. It's a good place to get a feel for the St. Thomas of the pre-cruise ship era. Plus, some of St. Thomas' finest restaurants are located in this Frenchtown area.

ANGUILLA—THE MOST PEACEABLE ISLAND

On **Anguilla**, one of the Caribbean's least-discovered islands, you apologize shyly if you pass someone on the beach. Anguilla has no discos, no casinos, no highrises—just lots of beach and solitude.

The Anguillans are a peaceful people with a peaceful history. Slavery didn't pay here. Cotton and bananas won't grow, and the workers were a strain on the water supplies. So plantation owners left the islanders to lead their own lives.

In 1969, when the English Parachute Regiment landed in Anguilla to put down what was thought to be a revolt, the parachutists were met by Anguillans waving Union Jacks. The islanders wanted to remain a Crown Colony.

Serene beaches border the island. The best is at **Shoal Bay Villes**, a two-mile stretch that is popular but still uncrowded. The ocean bottom is evenly sloped to a distant string of rocks that attracts sea creatures and snorkelers. Underwater, you can look around for coral gardens, reefs of elkhorn, and star and flower coral, as well as squirrelfish, sergeant fish, and damselfish. Snorkeling and rafting equipment can be rented at **Happy Jack's**, *tel. (809)497-2051*, a restaurant in the Shoal Bay Villes complex.

The **Malliouhana Hotel**, *Meads Bay; tel. (1-264)497-6111; website: www.malliouhana.com*, is the most exclusive and expensive hotel in the Caribbean. (Guests have included Kissinger and Onassis.) The hotel has Mediterranean and Far Eastern furnishings, hardwood floors, brass fixtures, and balconies off every room. The 30 acres surrounding the hotel are dotted with swimming pools perched high on the cliffs.

A more rustic, less expensive place to stay is the **Mariners**, *Sandy Ground; tel. (809)497-2671*. The hotel complex is made up of nine gingerbread cottages on the beach, each with trellised doorways and tiled floors.

Caribbean's best bird watching

You can expect to see 136 species of birds in Anguilla: the White-tailed tropicbird, Least Bittern, Tricolored Heron, Killy-killy, Lesser Scaup, Killdeer, Greater Yellowlegs, and, of course, the Zaneida Dove, which is the national bird.

ANTIGUA: A BEACH FOR EACH DAY
OF THE YEAR

There are 365 beaches on Antigua—one for each day of the year—and all are open to the public.

Antigua has warm steady winds, a complex coastline of safe harbors, and a protective, nearly unbroken wall of coral reef. The trade winds that once blew British men-of-war safely into English Harbor now fuel one of the world's foremost maritime events—Sailing Week.

Best hotel in Antigua

Jumby Bay, *tel. (1-268)462-6000; website: www.jumbybayresort.com*, the playground of the super-rich and second home for Robin Leach, is at the top of the line in terms of cost and includes all the expected luxuries. Located on its own 300-acre island reachable by private ferry, 50 suites and villas are offered on an all-inclusive, per-room basis.

Best inexpensive restaurant

Built as a typical West Indian home—edged with white bric-a-brac and a sloping light blue roof—a toothsome salad of seafood poached in vermouth, delicately topped with a lime and honey dressing, can be enjoyed at **Coco's**, *tel. (1-268)460-2626*. Pumpkin soup, Cajun crab puffs, even a tasty liver paté are other lunch options. The best part is that when the bill comes, no gasping or fainting is necessary, for the bill rarely goes beyond $12. Dinner is flawless, the sea red tuna with roasted crab and fennel, and the potpourri of island seafood with squid ink pasta, are highly recommended. Coco's also has 12 West Indian ginger bread cottages, nestled on the hillside, for rent. Charmingly decorated, each has its own romantic veranda, perfect for glorifying in the orange-pink sunsets. Prices, per person, are all inclusive.

The best of Guadeloupe

Along with a shimmering aquamarine sea, Guadeloupe has more than 50 beautiful crescent beaches, sleepy rural villages...and wonderful diving and snorkeling.

Best topless bathing in the Caribbean

Don't expect to hear many American or Canadian accents on the beaches of Grand-Terre. Most visitors are from mainland France. Some guidebooks aimed at North Americans take quite a stern moralistic tone. They warn potential visitors that many women sunbathe topless. And, (horror of horrors!), some beaches are "clothing-optional."

Best place to shop for swimwear

On weekend afternoons, the beach at **Saint-Francois** transforms itself into a Parisian catwalk. Nubile wenches from local boutiques arrive with big straw baskets packed with elegant swimwear, sarongs and floppy harem pants. Donning different outfits, they slowly parade like supermodels up and down the water's edge. And they seem to do a roaring trade amongst the captive customers. You can try before you buy—if you don't mind doing it in front of an interested audience!

Most pathetic four star hotel in the Caribbean

Le Meridien, a good hotel in the past, was sold to a company called Kalenda Resorts. Avoid it. The rooms and reception areas are shoddy, there are practically none of the facilities you'd associate with a four star hotel, and the only word for the breakfast is pathetic.

Most romantic hotel in Guadeloupe

In Basse-Terre, **Le Domaine de Malendure**, *tel. (590)98-92-12*, a hideaway set in a jungle-like garden with stupendous views over the Pigeon Islands, is the most romantic hotel in Guadeloupe. Accommodation is in duplexes, built in the style of Creole cottages. Room furnishings are simple, but there's a lovely pool, breakfast is good, and plenty of Creole specialties appear on the restaurant menu.

THE BEST OF MARTINIQUE

Martinique is the most sophisticated and developed island in the Caribbean, with gourmet restaurants and nude beaches. It is lush, covered with flowers. Fort-de-France is known as the Paris of the western Atlantic, with the same wrought-iron grillwork and narrow-street charm as the European city. And Martinique (along with Guadeloupe) has the best Creole food in the region. French luxury goods are sold at bargain prices, and luxury to rock-bottom accommodations are available.

(See more about Martinique's best beaches in Section 3: The World's Best Beaches.)

Most flowery island of the Caribbean

Martinique must boast at least $100 worth of fabulously scented blossoms to the square yard. The island's original Carib Indian inhabitants called their lush island *Madinina*, the Island of Flowers. The name is still apt — more than a thousand varieties grow here.

Martinique's most powerful mountain

Climb Martinique's extinct volcano, **Mount Pelée**. Ask for a guide at the town hall. Needless to say, the view from the mountain is spectacular. For a glimpse of the fierce power of Mount Pelée, visit the ruins of the town of St. Pierre, destroyed by the volcano in 1902.

The island's most famous resident

La Pagerie, on the Southwest peninsula, is the birthplace of Empress Josephine. A museum here contains mementos and love letters to her from Napoleon.

Best hotel in Martinique

The best place to stay in Martinique is **Hôtel Plantation de Leyritz**, *tel. (596)589-785-392*, an isolated 18th-century French-colonial plantation that has been made into a hotel with a first-class health spa that offers beauty and health therapy, horseback riding, and French food.

Montserrat — The Best Refuge

Montserrat is a lush green island that was colonized primarily by Irish Catholics from nearby St. Kitts in the early 17th century. (Because of its Irish heritage, Montserrat is known as the Emerald Isle. It is now a British colony, but Irish influences remain.)

Plymouth, the island's largest town, is remarkably quiet. Chickens cross the road here as often as people do. Shops along **Parliament Street** sell handmade cotton goods and local fruits. Stop by **Anthony's Church** to see its exquisite interior, as well as the 200-year-old tamarind tree outside. Try Montserrat's rum liqueur punch at **Perk's Factory**.

(See more about Montserrat's best beaches in Section 3: The World's Best Beaches.)

The best walks

Montserrat has miles of hiking trails across its mountains. The most spectacular is the one to the **Great Alps Waterfall**, a 70-foot cascade. A slightly more difficult walk takes you along **Galway's Soufrère**, where water bubbles out of the ground.

The best for cultural diversity

The Carib Indians supplied Montserrat's earliest recorded name "Alliouagana," meaning the land of the prickly bush. When Christopher Columbus finally saw the island during his second trip in 1493, its jagged peaks reminded him of the Monastery of Montserrate just outside of Barcelona, Spain — so he renamed it Santa Maria de Montserrate. Over 150 years later, in 1632, Sir Thomas Warner led a group of English settlers to colonize the island. Many Irish, disgruntled at their treatment on St. Kitts, decided to join him. Soon other Irish immigrants arrived from Virginia as well. The settlers concentrated on tobacco, indigo, cotton, and sugar plantations with African slave labor supplying the manpower. With nary a Spaniard in sight, it still took until 1783 for Montserrat to become an English possession by virtue of the Treaty of Versailles.

The best St. Patrick's Day in the Caribbean

Art and music festivals and competitions are held throughout the year. Of particular interest is March 17, when both St. Patrick's Day and the slave revolt of over 100 years ago against the wealthy plantation owners are celebrated simultaneously. It's not unusual to find the wearing of the green combined with calypso, soca, and iron-pan music, and the Emerald Singers appearing on the same program as Jumby dancers.

The best recording studio in the Caribbean

Rock stars Elton John, Phil Collins, Sting, Stevie Wonder, Paul McCartney, and James Taylor have been drawn to Montserrat by George Martin's recording studio, **Air Studios**, recognized as one of the best in the world.

The Caribbean's most active volcano

The **Soufrière Hills** volcano, overlooking Plymouth and the southern end of the island, lurched back to life in 1995. The rumblings increased until 1997, when a violent, ash-filled explosion rose 30,000 feet into the air. Plymouth was evacuated along with all the villages south of Belham Valley…and Montserrat was forever changed.

THE BEST OF ST. KITTS AND NEVIS

Nevis offers a gorgeous landscape…stunningly rich green clad mountains (dormant volcanos, thousands of years old), azure seas, balmy breezes, elegant plantation inns…

Best places for a night out on Nevis

Tuesday nights, **Oualie Beach** has live music, while **Eddie's** (a popular hangout for both locals and expats) in Charlestown is the place to be on Wednesdays for a DJ, karaoke, and dancing. Thursdays, people head for the live electric band at **Booby's Beach Bar** or, for something more subdued, the live band at the **Nisbet Beach Club**. Fridays, rock at **Booby's**, or you can choose a DJ at **Sand Dollar**, or live band at **Banana's**. Saturday offers a live string band at **Oualie Beach Hotel** or the **Golden Rock**, with an electric band at **Banana's**. Then it's church on Sunday and refuel on Monday.

Best hotel on Nevis

The **Four Seasons Resort**, *tel. (1-869)469-1111; website: www.fourseasons.com*, the crème de la crème of the Caribbean, provides the largest and arguably most elegant rooms on the island. You can also book gingerbread-trimmed cottages, a duplex, or even a private villa. Infinity pools provide an alternative to the sugar-sand beach. With 196 rooms, a world-class golf course, tennis, an old English gaming room, and private beach massage, you'll want for nothing.

Oualie Beach Hotel, *tel. (869)469-973; website: www.oualie.com*, is perfect for a romantic getaway if you request one of the cottages farthest from the dining area. Or it's perfect for your whole family. The open-air restaurant and bar offer good Caribbean and continental food, and occasional live entertainment. The informal ambience makes it easy to meet other guests and locals.

Fanciest place to eat on Nevis

The most entertaining evening you'll find on Nevis is at **Miss June's Cuisine**, *tel. (869)469-5330*. Miss June cooks at home three times a week by reservation. Limited to 25 guests, diners assemble around 7:30 p.m. for cocktails and hors d'oeuvres in the lounge. At 8:30 p.m., a five-course dinner, with Trinidadian, Caribbean, Indonesian, and European influences is served at formal tables set with fine crystal and pure white napery. The first course is soup and sherry, followed by fish. A tempting buffet beckons and your wineglass is kept full. After dessert, guests retire to the veranda to savor coffee and liqueurs. Miss June joins her guests and the evening sometimes lasts until the wee hours. The price includes all you can eat and drink.

Best rainforest on St. Kitts

The 68 square miles of St. Kitts are mountainous and blessed with expansive soil-rich valleys, natural spring-fed water, and jungle-like rain-forests laden with wild bananas, breadfruit, papayas, and mangoes. The highest point is 3,792-foot Mt. Liamuiga, also called "Mt. Misery" by the locals—try to climb it, and you'll probably agree. The island's rich rainforest is the last in the world to be actually increasing in size.

Best shipwrecks for exploration

You can explore one of over 400 wrecks (sunk between 1493 and 1825). St Kitts has more than any other island in the Caribbean.

ST. MARTIN/SINT MAARTEN: THE MOST DIVIDED ISLAND

The French and Dutch **St. Martin/Sint Maarten** is the most varied of the Caribbean islands. It has tropical scenery and a European culture. In fact, it has two European cultures.

Sint Maarten, the Dutch half of the island, has luxurious Dutch inns frequented by the royal family of the Netherlands. Cruise ships dock in the Philipsburg Harbor to allow passengers to take advantage of duty-free prices on jewelry, linens, crystal, and cameras.

The French half of the island is more affordable (although several of the large new hotels tend to be expensive) and has better restaurants. Artists come to **Marigot**, St. Martin's waterfront square, to set up their easels. Small fishing boats pull into port with the day's catches; vendors sell their wares under brightly colored umbrellas; and travelers meet at La Vie en Rose to chat over fresh, exquisitely prepared seafood. Accommodation ranges from luxury resorts in the French-Mediterranean style to downright cheap guesthouses.

Away from the main towns, you'll find secluded bays and long sandy beaches protected by coral reefs. In the center of the island, mountain peaks rise sharply. Palm trees grow alongside orange bougainvillea and magenta hibiscus. The sun shines year-round, and temperatures hover around 80 degrees Fahrenheit. The only international golf course is at Port de Plaisance on the Dutch side. The course runs across the island to the French side.

Thanks to the island's French legacy, dining is a pleasure and worth taking time to enjoy. More than 150 restaurants are spread over both sides of the island. Our favorite is **La Caravelle** in Philipsburg. The entrance is on Front Street opposite the Caribbean Hotel. The romantic covered terrace is candlelit and looks out over the ocean.

The best hotels on the island are La Samanna, Mullet Bay, Caravanserai, Oyster Pond, and L'Habitation. La Belle Creole is one of the island's most charming hotels, built in the form of an old Mediterranean village.

The best way to get a hangover

Guavaberry liquor is a national drink whose secret lies in the rum it's combined with. Stop at the **Guavaberry Emporium**, *tel. (599) 542-2965*, in Philipsburg to learn how to make it—your lesson comes with a free sample. While on the booze trail, you're apt to come across a Rum Jumbie hut on the Dutch side—they also offer a free taste. Local lore says that "Jumbies" are celestial spirits who possess the man who's drunk too much rum, forcing him to dance to the conga drums 'til dawn. You've been warned. By this point on the trail, if you still want a monstrous headache, head over to the Rum Museum on the French side for the finishing touch.

The best way to avoid a hangover

After the Rum Jumbie hut, if you feel you've had enough, save the Rum Museum for another day and visit **La Ferme des Papillons** (Butterfly Farm), *tel. (590) 590-873-121*. Over 1,000 winged beauties in Pucci-like colors (the Blue Morpho is a favorite) fly free, attracted by the many tasty fruits and flowering plants. This is a sure way to avoid any headaches in the morning.

The best French restaurant

Rainbow, *tel. (590) 590-875-580; website: www.rainbow-cafe.com*, arguably the finest restaurant on the French side—many say on the island—is French perfection. Occupying an old house with balconies open to the beach and

Atlantic, Rainbow is found along restaurant row in Grand Case. Start with perfectly spiced crab cakes with lemon buerre blanc followed by an endive, mixed greens, walnuts, and blue cheese salad, dressed with meaux mustard vinaigrette.

The best nightlife

There's no end to the nightlife—well, actually there is when the sun comes up—on both sides of the island, but especially on the Dutch side, where many people start their evening at the raucous **Sunset Beach Bar** on Maho Bay. (Check out their web cam at *www.sunsetbeachbar.com*). Next, people head to the **Greenhouse Café**, *tel. (599)542-2941*, for dinner and disco, or to the popular **Boat House**, *tel. (599)544-5404*, an ex-pat hangout by day, a jumping open-air night-club with live band by night. The glitterati make the private **Q-club**, *tel. (599)545-2632*, their stomping ground. Situated above the Casino Royal in Maho Bay, the huge disco features a VIP section, live 80s music, and dancing till dawn. If the noise level gets to you, cross the street and go upstairs to **Sopranos**, *tel. (599)522-7088*, a perfect place to end an evening. The colorful, intimate bar features live piano music (Sinatra to the Beatles), romantic booths, and fine cigars.

✳ THE DOMINICAN REPUBLIC—
THE FIRST SETTLEMENT

Columbus called the **Dominican Republic** the most beautiful island in the world when he landed here in 1492. One year later, his brother Bartholomeo established here the first permanent European settlement in the Americas, New Isabella (known today as Santo Domingo). Historic monuments, monasteries, and fortresses remain from the colonial days, giving the island a Spanish air.

Unlike most Caribbean islands, where English is widely spoken, few locals in the Dominican Republic outside of the tourist areas speak anything but Spanish. Be sure to learn a few bare essentials.

The Dominican Republic covers 1,900 square miles, approximately two-thirds of the island of **Hispaniola**, which it shares with Haiti. It has lovely beaches, lively nightlife, excellent restaurants, and many hotels. The tallest mountains in the Caribbean (more than 10,000 feet) are here.

The oldest city in the Americas

In Santo Domingo, you can visit **Zona Colonial**, the oldest European settlement in the Americas. Columbus landed here in 1492, after stopping in Cuba, where he believed he had found a shortcut to Japan. In Santo Domingo, Columbus, his brother, and later his son ruled the Spanish colony in the early 1500s. From Santo Domingo, the Spanish launched their conquests of Central and South America. If you're looking for historic colonial architecture in the Americas, it doesn't get any better than this. The colonial district contains the oldest European fort in the Americas, the oldest monastery, the first paved street, ruins from the first hospital, the oldest church…and dozens of buildings that date from the 16th and 17th centuries.

The most posh resort in the Caribbean

The poshest resort in all the Caribbean is the **Casa de Campo**, *website: www.casadcampo.com*, at La Romana in the Dominican Republic. Frank Lloyd Wright designed the main building, and the interior was designed by Oscar de la Renta. A few celebrities have mansions on the grounds.

Accommodation at the resort includes private villas along the golf course and sea. You can hire a horse and buggy to take you dining. The nephew of the maharaja of Jodphur introduced polo to the Dominican Republic, and you'll find the best riding horses in the Caribbean at the Casa de Campo resort.

The best whale watching

The town of Samana is located on the southern coast of the peninsula. It is built along the water, and up onto the surrounding hills, around a sail-boat-filled natural harbor, the Bay of Samana. For several weeks every year (in January, February, and the beginning of March), more than 4,000 humpback whales migrate several thousand miles from distant northern feeding grounds in the Gulf of Maine, the East Coast of Canada, Greenland, and Iceland to breed in the bay's warm, sheltered waters. The 30-ton mammals put on quite a show…males breach 30 feet or more in the air and splash back to the surface. You can watch from shore with binoculars…but will be better off hiring the services of one of the local tour companies.

THE BEST OF THE BAHAMAS

Just a few hours from New York or Miami are the 700 islands of the **Bahamas**, an idyllic chain of islands stretching from Bimini, just 50 miles off the coast of Florida, toward Haiti. The islands are mostly flat and bordered by white-sand beaches. Only 20 of them are inhabited. **Nassau**, the biggest tourist center, acts as the seat of government. It is not particularly attractive, plagued by crime, unemployment, and resentment.

However, Nassau does have a splendid health club, the **Royal Bahamian Hotel**, *tel. (809) 327-6400*. This first-class hideaway offers guests use of a gym, a whirlpool, a sauna, steam baths, a massage room, tennis courts, swimming pools, and a private white-sand beach.

The best hotel in Nassau

If you must stay in Nassau, make reservations at the **Carnival Crystal Palace Resort and Casino**, *tel. (800)222-7466*, an oceanfront hotel 10 minutes from the airport downtown. It is on three-quarters of a mile of property, with 13 restaurants, (four of them gourmet), discos, spas, and sports facilities.

The world's best planned paradise

The best thing to do when you get to Nassau is leave. Cross the bridge from Nassau to **Paradise Island**, leaving the shabby, graffiti-stained city behind. You will be engulfed in growth as green, thick, and dark as a jungle.

This is a planned playland for vacationers. All the trappings are here: quick and easy access from the United States; a benevolent June-like climate year-round; accommodation of every degree of luxury; sandy beaches and calm, clear water; a championship golf course; tennis courts; restaurants and nightclubs; and a large casino.

One of the most beautiful places on Paradise Island is **Versailles Gardens**, located behind the Ocean Club Hotel. This landscaped series of terraced gardens stretches across the island from the hotel grounds to the water's edge. Work on the gardens began years ago when Dr. Axel Wenner-Gren, who owned the island, set out to recreate the gardens at the Château de Versailles in France. When Wenner-Gren sold the island in 1960, the new owner, Huntington Hartford, continued to develop the gardens, adding statues, fountains, and—the crowning touch—a 14th-century Augustinian cloister transported all the way from France.

Nightlife on Paradise Island is Las Vegas revisited. Most of the action is at the **Paradise Island Resort and Casino**, a loud and gaudy place with a casino and nightclubs. Your best bet is the variety show at the **Tradewinds Lounge**, located within The Paradise Island Resort and Casino. The show is corny but worth seeing for Bill Bonaparte, a steel drummer.

The finest (and oldest) hotel on Paradise Island is the **Ocean Club**, *tel. (809)363-2501*. It's a small, tasteful 71-room place. A doorman, in top hat and tails, stands by to greet you. The hotel's restaurant, the Courtyard Terrace, is beautiful and romantic.

The **Paradise Resort**, *tel. (809)363-2542*, attracts a young, lively crowd with free water sports.

To make reservations at the above hotels from the United States, call *(800)321-3000* or *(305)895-2922*.

The most comfortable hotel on the Exumas

You'll be treated like family at the **Peace and Plenty Hotel**, *P.O. Box 55, Georgetown; tel. (809)336-2551* or *(809)336-2552*. The rooms are comfortable and each one looks over Elizabeth Harbor.

TRINIDAD — THE CARIBBEAN'S BEST CARNIVAL

Trinidad, a cosmopolitan island, oil-rich and industrialized, rivals Rio as host of the world's best **Carnival**. Its Carnival parades have developed into an art form, as carefully choreographed and costumed as any Broadway musical. They have casts of thousands.

Participants in Trinidad's spectacular parades are grouped into theme bands. As many as 3,000 people can be part of one costume band, while steel bands have 80 to 100 musicians, playing up to 500 steel pans.

The steel band competition begins about three weeks before the Carnival and culminates on the Saturday before, when the champions are chosen from the island's 100-odd bands. The musicians are so talented (and their drums so well tuned) that they have been known to play classical symphonies with expertise.

The Carnival activities climax in the big parade on Shrove Tuesday. Revelers work themselves into a frenzy and join the bands in their dances.

The best place to stay in Trinidad and Tobago is at the **Man of War Cottages**, *Charlotteville; tel. (809)660-4327*. This facility offers truly exceptional accommodation right in the rain forest. Bird watching and hiking are at your fingertips.

Best place to stay in Tobago

Though not on a beach, the small hotel, **Kariwak Village**, *tel. (868)639-8442; website: www.kariwak.co.tt*, more than makes up for this with a serene warmth and friendliness. Most guests are repeaters, preferring the simply decorated half moon shaped rooms without TV (never missed), and whole and natural foods served from the well-run kitchen. There are 24 rooms, 18 of which are poolside, with six bordering the garden. A thatch-roofed, open-air *Ajoupa* sits quietly apart, bordered by leafy pathways where daily Hatha Yoga and Qi Dong classes are given.

The best hotel

For something more upscale, try the **Coco Reef Resort and Spa**, *tel. (868)639-8574; website: www.cocoreef.com*, winner of the 2002 World Travel Award for "Best Caribbean Hotel." Near Scarborough, the resort nestles in 10 acres of tropical gardens bordering a beach on the Atlantic side. Of the 135 rooms, suites, and villas, 114 have ocean views.

Best seafood restaurant in Tobago

The **Seahorse Inn**, *tel. (868)639-0686*, is considered the best seafood restaurant in Tobago — and besides great food, it's the only place where your dinner may be interrupted by a cry of "turtles sighted." Everyone troops out to watch the six-foot-long leatherbacks come ashore to lay their eggs. Nick Hardwicke, owner and chef, actively protects the glorious creatures during their nesting period of April to August. The restaurant also has four decorative guestrooms, each with an ocean view of Stonehaven Bay.

St. Margarite — the World's Best Windsurfing

Playa El Yague, on Margarite's southern shores, is the world's best windsurfing beach and attracts world-class competitors—a lot of them. Five years ago, there were three hotels here; today there are 15, plus eight or more windsurfing clubs. The bay is calm and wide, the sea less than waist deep for 1,000 feet out, and the trade winds blow steadily at 15 to 20 mph—qualities made to order for windsurfing.

South America's largest amusement park

There is a "swim with the dolphins" attraction near Pampatar, called **Diverland**. Touted as South America's largest amusement park, it features 16 attractions including a giant Ferris wheel, roller coaster, and water toboggan.

The Grenadines — the Tahiti of the Caribbean

St. Vincent and the Grenadine Islands are billed as Tahiti of the Caribbean, because of their tropical beauty. Here, Captain Bligh brought the breadfruit that survived the mutiny on the *Bounty*. The 100 islands making up the grenadines are connected by local mail boats, and all offer inexpensive accommodation.

Mustique is the Grenadine hideout of celebrities, including Princess Margaret. Try the **Cotton House**, *tel. (809)456-4777*, a hotel in an 18th-century cotton warehouse built of stone and coral. Rooms are expensive, but the hotel restaurant, Roft, and the Basil's Bar are good.

The crown jewel of the Grenadines

Somehow **Bequia**, the crown jewel of the Grenadines, has avoided becoming another traffic-choked stop on cruise ship itineraries. Its seven square miles of lush, hilly terrain and wide, empty beaches are home to about 6,000 full-time residents who welcome visitors with the friendliest smiles on the planet. And why not? If you're blessed with such near-perfect weather all year-round, you're bound to be happy.

Most of the island's activities center around Port Elizabeth on Admiralty Bay, where ferries from St. Vincent come and go and most yachts drop anchor. It's a relatively busy harbor, with several grocery stores, a thriving vegetable market, and a handful of bars and restaurants by the sea. But getting out of Port Elizabeth and exploring around here is easy. If you're in good shape, you can hike the small but well-paved network of roads and see the whole island in just a few leisurely hours. Alternatively, you can get a rental car or hire a local taxi to take you on a two- or three-hour tour for about $40 to $50, plus tip. Rates should be negotiated in advance, and you can check the tourist office for recommended fares. Bequian taxi drivers are a friendly bunch, so if you choose to take this mode of transportation, be prepared to form a solid friendship during your stay.

The best beds on Bequia

Bequia boasts a handful of luxury accommodations, most notably the **Gingerbread Hotel** and the **Frangipani**, both of which are located on Belmont Walkway, a narrow, paved path that skirts Admiralty Bay. Well-appointed suites with gorgeous views can be upward of $200 or more, but the comfortable economy rooms are a reasonable $60 to $80. On the more remote Friendship Bay, the **Blue Tropic Hotel** has some spotlessly clean doubles with balconies overlooking the Atlantic for about $50 to $60, including breakfast—a great bargain. For more about visiting Bequia, go to: *www.bequiatourism.com*.

THE EASIEST—AND CHEAPEST— CARIBBEAN DESTINATION

Puerto Rico boasts the most extensive air service in the Caribbean, with daily flights from all major North American cities. And because it is a U.S. territory, American visitors don't have to worry about passports or changing money.

The island's beaches are lined with modern, self-contained resorts, as well as budget hotels and charming guesthouses. But the island also has a huge modern city with a historic core—**San Juan**. Old San Juan, a cluster of cobblestoned Spanish streets with old houses and churches, is built in and around a fort. The city offers posh boutiques, horse races, cockfights (if your tastes run in this direction), casinos, flamenco dancing, Las Vegas-style shows, discos, and brothels.

The most historical hotel in Puerto Rico

El Convento, *website: www.elconvento.com*, located in San Juan, is in a beautiful Spanish-style building with many antiques but modern facilities. A convent dating from 1600, it is a historical landmark in Old San Juan, now restored with most of the original architecture, tiles, and beams left intact.

Puerto Rico's best town

Puerto Rico's most charming town is **Rincon**, on the unspoiled

Southwest coast. A friendly fishing town, it draws American retirees, with its easygoing pace and low prices. Panoramic roads curve down from the green hilltop farms to the beaches. Trade winds from the east dump moisture on the 4,500-foot-high rain forest. In the morning, you can help fishermen pull their nets onto the beach. While the main plaza has a supermarket, a bakery, a tropical bar, and restaurants, the town does not have highrise hotels, casinos, gourmet food, fancy boutiques, or tourists.

Rincon's beach is shaded by palm trees and backed by squatters' shacks surrounded by mango, banana, citrus, papaya, and breadfruit trees.

The best hotel in town is the **Villa Antonio**, *tel. (809)823-2645*.

Puerto Rico's best-kept secret

Puerto Rico's best-kept secret is **Vieques**, a little known 21-mile-long island due east of the big island. A U.S. naval base is located here, and from time to time bomb tests are held.

Despite this, Vieques is a nice vacation cove. Wild horses and cattle roam on the roads and empty beaches. Small boats cruise to **Phosphorescent Bay** on moonless nights, allowing you to see the brilliant streaks emitted by the phosphorescent organisms. Mahogany and rubber trees reach through the ceiling of the small rainforest. And white-sand beaches, some near coral reefs, slip into clear calm waters.

Home to 8,000 Spanish-speaking natives and 100 U.S. sailors and Marines, Vieques is an informal, low-key, and low-cost hideaway. You can hire a ketch for scuba diving through **Vieques Divers** in Esperanza.

To get to Vieques, either take a plane from San Juan or drive from San Juan to Fajardo and then take the ferry to Vieques.

The most central place to stay on Vieques is **Parador Villa Esperanza**, *tel. (787)741-8675*, in the little fishing village of Esperanza. The Marina has mooring facilities and tennis courts. To the right of the front door is a restaurant row.

Landlubbers might prefer **Casa del Frances**, *P.O. Box 458, Vieques, PR 00765; tel. (809)741-3751*, a guesthouse that features horseback riding. This former plantation has French doors, pillars, balconies, an atrium, a large pool, and an outdoor bar with tropical plantings. It is a mile or so from the beach and Esperanza.

HAITI: THE MOST EXOTIC ISLAND

It's unfortunate that Haiti is politically unstable and dreadfully poor, because it is the most unique island in the Caribbean. The Haitians' exotic culture is a blend of French, African, and voodoo traditions. You can see African dances, attend one of the most colorful Mardi Gras celebrations, and indulge in Creole feasts. Accommodation ranges from luxury villas and antique mansions to quaint hostelries, including **Habitation Leclerc**, the West Indian palace of Napoleon's sister Pauline. Jackie Onassis and Catherine Deneuve have stayed here. **Cap Haitien** is one of the most beautiful cities in the West Indies, with artists' studios and a port.

The voodoo capital

Haiti's dramatic mountains and flawless black and white beaches set the stage for the true drama of the island: **voodoo**. Haitians believe the island gods are all around you, moving through the air and living in the mountains, rivers, seas, rocks, caves, and sacred trees.

Spirit-worship rituals are performed by priests or priestesses, known by their followers as *hungans*. Accompanied by the hypnotizing rhythm of sacred drums, bells and rattles, the *hungans* dance and chant, beckoning spirits to possess them and their followers.

The climax is always the blood sacrifice, when an animal's sacred powers are believed to be released. The adorned and painted animal, typically a chicken, is mutilated, dismembered, and placed on the altar as an offering to the gods. Sometimes the blood is collected and drunk by the worshipers to sate the thirst of the spirit. As the frenzy of the drumbeats and the singing increases, the believers become possessed, and their bodies begin to convulse and contort. Once the believers are in the trance state, the spirits speak through them, giving advice and threatening evildoers in the assembly.

To display the miraculous powers of the spirits, called *loas*, the possessed may repeatedly stab themselves, handle red-hot coals or bars of iron, or eat broken glass, apparently causing themselves no harm.

The best hotel in Haiti

Haiti's best hotel is the **Grand Hotel Oloffson**, *tel. (509)234102*, where rooms are named after the celebrities who have stayed in them — Mick Jagger, Marlon Brando, Graham Greene, and Anne Bancroft.

CURAÇAO — THE BEST OF HOLLAND IN THE CARIBBEAN

Curaçao, the largest island in the Netherlands Antilles, is a bit of old Holland in the New World. **Willemstad**, the capital, resembles Amsterdam, complete with canals and 17th-century canal houses; the tallest pontoon bridge in the Caribbean (named after Queen Juliana); Indonesian restaurants; and a museum featuring wooden shoes and Delft tiles.

History buffs should visit the Willemstad forts. **Fort Nassau** is situated in the ramparts above town. **Fort Amsterdam**, on the sea, is the site of the Governor's Palace and the 18th-century Dutch Reformed Church, which still has an English cannonball embedded in its walls.

See **Ronde Klip** in the northeast, a privately owned *landuis*, or plantation, and Jan Kok Landhuis, built in 1650 and used as a restaurant.

The prettiest natural sight in Curacao is in **St. Christoffelberg**, where wild orchids grow. To see this, you must climb 1,213 feet to the highest spot on the island.

The oldest Jewish settlement in the New World

The Dutch tradition of religious tolerance spread early to the New World, and in 1651 a group of Jews established the oldest Jewish settlement in the Americas on this island. The Jewish graveyard **Beth Haim** is also the oldest in the Americas.

Most exotic cuisine in the Caribbean

Curaçao features a mélange of Dutch, Latin American, and Indonesian cuisines. The great seafood restaurants on the island can be found in **Westpunt**, a fishing port just outside Willemstad. Dutch-French food is also served at **De Taveerne**, near Willemstad, in an 18th-century manor house complete with antiques of the period.

SABA: THE MOST SCENIC

Although **Saba**, a five-square-mile volcanic island, has no beaches, it is incredibly scenic. This rugged mountainous island is a wall of jagged black and gray rock that shoots up 3,000 feet from the white caps of the surf. Its summit is lost in the clouds. Roads snake through picturesque villages with such names as Hell's Gate and The Bottom. Because most of the houses are built on slopes, each one has a magnificent view. Cultivated crops cut into the sides of hills like steps.

Saba has no casinos and no highrises, and you won't find air-conditioning. But lush rainforests hug the mountainsides, mist shrouds the summits, and gabled Dutch architecture distinguishes the small towns.

The best places to eat in Saba

After scuba diving and hiking around the beautiful mountains, you'll want a good meal. Try **Scout's Place** or **Lime Time**, which is located in The Bottom. Local specialties are curried barbecued goat and lobster.

Saba's most popular hotel is **The Captain's Quarters**, *tel. (599)4-2201*, formerly the residence of a famous Saban sea captain. This comfortable hotel has one of the few swimming pools on the island. The food at the restaurant is delicious and moderately priced.

Bermuda — a perfect family getaway

Although most people visit the Caribbean to lie in the sun, this may not be your primary objective if you are traveling with children. If you want to travel in the Caribbean — and you plan to have your family in tow — head for Bermuda, the best place in the Caribbean to entertain kids. Following is a guide to the best things on Bermuda to do with your family.

- Ride the ferry. Ferries run from Hamilton Harbor to Somerset and the Royal Naval Dockyard, at the southern tip of the island. They depart Hamilton from 6:15 a.m. until 6 p.m. Monday through Friday, 8:50 a.m. until 11 p.m. Saturday. The ride to the Dockyard takes an hour and costs $1. This is one of the best ways to see the harbor and southern section of the island. And children are welcome.
- Take the bus to St. George's, at the other end of the island. This is the most historic spot in Bermuda. Settled in 1609, St. George's was the capital of the island until 1815.
- Take a ride in a glass-bottomed boat. Many are offered; all depart from Hamilton Harbor.
- Ride in a horse-drawn carriage through Hamilton and the surrounding suburbs. Carriages pull up in front of Hamilton Harbor beginning at noon each day and wait for passengers.
- Visit the aquarium, the zoo, and the national History Museum, all in Hamilton Parish.

The best way to punish your nagging wife

While at St. George's, you might want to forego a photograph at the stocks and pillory (unless you don't mind waiting in line behind every other tourist on the island), but don't miss the **ducking stool** — a fiendish contraption used to punish nagging wives. Any wife found guilty of spreading rumors or engaging in the crime of gossiping was sentenced to the appropriate number of ducks in the harbor. For the poor disgraced woman, it was a punishment worse than death.

Cuba: waiting to be discovered — again

Until Fidel Castro came to power, Cuba was traditionally the Caribbean's most popular vacation destination. Less than 100 miles from Florida, Cuba is also the largest island in the region and has a population of more than 10 million.

Today this island awaits a new influx of tourists. Canadians and Europeans are already enjoying some of the most beautiful beaches in the hemisphere. Five-star hotels have been built on Varadero Beach by Spanish and Jamaican investors.

Most historical hotel in Cuba

The Internacional (today the **Varadero Internacional**), *tel. (534)566-7038*, in Havana, was the place to stay before Castro. Built in the 1950s, it was a world-famous hotel for the jet set, and it was reopened in renovated splendor in 1992.

THE BEST OF JAMAICA

Jamaica is a sensuous place, a land of sunshine, ganja, reggae, colonial houses with verandas, and thick tropical jungle. The pace is slow and laid-back. The sexiest place on the island is the **Blue Lagoon**, where Brooke Shields starred in a romantic movie by the same name.

Most beautiful sunset in the Western Hemisphere

At the westernmost point of the island is **Rick's Café**, propped 10 feet from the edge of a cliff. The water below is deep and clear, prompting thrill seekers to dive from the top of the cliff into the water 30 or 40 feet below. Try to get there in time for the sunset, the most fantastic in the Western Hemisphere.

The most beautiful house

The most beautiful of Jamaica's great houses (mansions left from the colonial days) is **Rose Hall**, in Montego Bay, once inhabited by the infamous white witch Anne Palmer. It was bought by John Rollins, the former lieutenant governor of Delaware, in the 1960s and restored with meticulous attention to the original detail.

The best places to hear reggae

Jamaica's reggae is an urban outgrowth of the Rastafarian religion, which grew up on this island among a group of escaped African slaves called Maroons. To hear Reggae in a perfectly safe tourist environment, visit **Montego Bay** and **Negril**. Appearances by the top reggae artists are advertised in local newspapers. Outdoor concerts are held every Friday at Cornwall Beach in Montego Bay.

If you have Jamaican friends, ask them to take you to clubs outside tourist areas. These are cheaper and feature smaller reggae bands. But you shouldn't frequent these clubs unless you are accompanied by a Jamaican (and don't object to the ever-present ganja).

The best hotel in Jamaica

The best place to stay in Jamaica is the **Sans Souci**, *tel. (954)925-0925*. The décor is casual—white rattan and wicker furniture on a tile floor in the foyer, overhead fans, and a mahogany bar fancifully done up as the Ballroom

Bar. The hotel has its own band that performs Bob Marley tunes with the same ease and grace as it handles Elvis hits. When the band takes a break, the pianist in the bar, who is a dead ringer for Sam in the movie **Casablanca**, takes over. You'll hear **As Time Goes By** at least once during the course of the evening.

The world's most expensive coffee

Blue Mountain Coffee, the world's most expensive, is grown in Jamaica on the Blue Mountain range. It's also sold here, for far less than you'd pay anywhere else in the world (but still pricey). Be sure to enjoy at least one cup.

THE BEST WAY TO EXPLORE THE ISLANDS

What better way to explore the Caribbean islands than by sailboat? And you don't have to sell the family jewels to afford a trip like this. Prices for bareboats (where you bring your own provisions and sail the boat yourself) can be surprisingly affordable.

Unlike Greece and its islands, the Caribbean knows no winter. And unlike their counterparts in the South Pacific, the Caribbean islands are close enough to each other to make knowledge of the sextant unnecessary.

A charter company will check your sailing skills to make sure you can operate its expensive vessel safely before agreeing to rent to you. The company may decide to appoint a professional skipper to accompany you (at an extra cost) or refuse to rent you a vessel altogether if you don't have enough experience handling sailboats.

If you want relatively calm waters and a few hours of sailing each day, consider the British Virgin Islands. The entire chain is only 50 miles long, and large charter fleets are based on St. Thomas, in the U.S. Virgin Islands, and Tortola, in the British Virgin Islands. The islands are small, with scores of quiet bays off sandy beaches. One of the nicest places to anchor is **Cane Garden Bay** on Tortola's north shore, a narrow fiord cut into tall, steep hills. You can row a dinghy ashore for dinner of fresh lobster and a steel drum concert at **Stanley's Welcome Bar**, right on the beach.

If you are in for more adventurous sailing and more diversion, consider the Leeward or Windward islands. Beginning with St. Martin, about 80 miles east of the Virgin Islands and the Lesser Antilles island, the chain turns south. Distances between the islands are greater here than in the Virgins, and the ocean swells that roll in from Africa can make the inter-island passes wet and rough.

The months from July through November are hurricane season. High season is from mid-December to mid-April, when the weather tends to be settled, the trade winds reliable, and prices high.

The Moorings, *tel. (284)494-2332; website: www.moorings.com*, is the oldest and most reliable bareboat outfit operating the Caribbean. Marinas are located in the British Virgin Islands and St. Lucia.

North South Charters, *tel. (284)494-0096; website: www.nsyv.com*, is a good company also located in the British Virgin Islands. It rents bareboats, with or without skippers.

THE BEST OF BELIZE

Belize is a very diverse little nation. And because it's so small, it means you can be on the beach and very quickly get into the highlands. Belize's interior hides Mayan ruins, tall waterfalls, rainforests, and rivers you can explore. Down near Sittee Point, in fact, is a jaguar preserve where you can venture into the jungle in search of the elusive cats. Bird watching in Belize's interior is a treat; you'll be able to spot parrots, toucans, flycatchers, and herons in their natural habitat.

THE WORLD'S SECOND LARGEST REEF

No longer a secret to the adventurous traveler, Belize is most famous for its virtually unspoiled coast. Just off the shores of its beautiful beaches is a 176-mile barrier reef, the largest coral reef in the Western Hemisphere and second only to Australia's Great Barrier Reef. Belize's reef has long been a mecca for skilled divers, snorkelers, and fisherman.

YOUR BEST CONTACTS IN BELIZE

If you're planning on traveling to Belize, the best contact to make is with Lascelle and Serita Tillet, who own S & L Travel. These two are friendly and reliable people who are forever going out of their way to help people navigate their way through Belize. Whether you want to rent a car, book an in-country flight, find a driver to take you from point A to point B, locate the perfect hotel, or learn which excursions are worth the trouble…these two can help you out. Contact them at **S & L Travel**, *91 North Front Street, P.O. Box 700, Belize City; tel. (501)2-77593 or (501)2-75145, e-mail: sltravel@btl.net.*

THE BELIZE CITY GUIDE

If you fly into Belize, your first taste of the country will most likely be **Belize City**. It has suffered more than its share of bad press, but not all of it is on the mark. It's true that women, especially, would be foolish to walk the streets alone at night; petty street crime is widespread, and the area is generally run-down and dirty. Still, there is a redeeming charm about this dilapidated city. The grand colonial houses rival those anywhere in Central or South America, and residents always have a kind smile for visitors.

Where to stay in Belize City

The **Radisson Fort George**, *2 Marine Parade, Belize City, Belize*; reservations from the U.S. *tel. (800)333-333*, in Belize *tel. (501)2-33333; fax (501)2-73820, e-mail: rdfg@btl.nut, website: www.radissonbelize.com* is one of two larger hotels in town. This is a very hospitable hotel. The **Fort Street Guesthouse**, *4 Fort Street, Belize City, Belize; tel. (501)2-30116; fax (501)2-78808, e-mail: fortst@btl.net; website: www.fortst.com* is a guesthouse in an old building in the colonial section of the city. A double room costs about $40 including breakfast.

The best places to eat in Belize City

There are many good restaurants in Belize City. These include **The Grill**, *164 Newton Street*, which has excellent food and a nice lounge, **Macy's**, *18 Bishop Street*, is a good Creole restaurant, and **El Centro Restaurant** on Bishop Street has good local food.

Belize's best shopping

If you're looking for souvenirs to bring home, walk through the **National Handcraft Center**, *tel. (501)2-33636*, open Monday to Friday 8 a.m. to 6 p.m. and Saturday 8 a.m. to 1 p.m. The selection isn't great, but some very nice, carved picture frames as well as paintings by local artists are available.

The best cigars

U.S. travelers, in particular, seem often to be in the market for Cuban cigars. You can't legally buy them in the U.S. or bring them home with you (not with the labels on them, anyway). But they are for sale in Belize. To find them in a state-of-the-art, walk-in humidor, take a taxi to the *Aficionado* where you'll find cigars from all over Central and South America.

The zoo: a local landmark

A good way to get familiar with the wildlife of Belize would be to visit **The Belize Zoo and Tropical Education Center**, *P.O. Box 1787, Belize City, Belize; tel. (501)81-3004; website: www.belizezoo.org*. It looks as if the zookeepers have thrown nets over portions of a jungle, and many of the zoo's inhabitants were wild animals that have been domesticated or injured and nursed back to health.

THE MOST UNSPOILED CAYES

Hundreds of uninhabited, palm-lined Cayes dot the coast of Belize. Of the inhabited ones, **Ambergris Caye** is the largest and most populated. Caye Caulker, Caye Chapel, and St. George's Caye, located just south of Ambergris Caye, are less developed but just as beautiful and offer accommodation and dive packages. Southwater Caye and other islands on the lower reef, accessible by boat from Dangriga, are truly undiscovered, unspoiled treasures.

The best cave diving

Half Moon Caye Natural Monument lies in the midst of the Lighthouse Reef atoll, 60 miles east of Belize City. The reserve features a lighthouse and sanctuary built in 1848, as well as a sanctuary for the red-footed boobie and more than 100 other bird species. The Lighthouse Reef atoll is also host to the circular Great Blue Hole, a natural phenomenon, which stretches 1,000 feet in diameter and 400 feet below the sea's surface and offers spectacular cave diving.

The best of Ambergris Caye

San Pedro, the main town on Ambergris Caye, even with its seaside restaurants, handful of souvenir shops, and three nightclubs, is an easygoing village of guides, fishermen, families, and expatriate Americans and Britons. In the evening, the main plaza is alive with strollers and volleyball players, and hermit-crab races are held at the Pier Lounge every Monday night.

The best hotels

The **Victoria House**, *tel. (501)26-2067 or (800)247-5159; website: www.victoria-house.com*, is a nice, quiet, and secluded hotel with a popular beachside bar. **Paradise Resort Hotel**, *tel. (501)26-2033; website: www.ambergriscaye.com/paradiseresort*, is a hotel right on the beach.

Ambergris' best seafood

Elvi's Kitchen has a sand floor and there is a huge tree growing out through the roof. Sample, in season, the best lobster on the planet. **Little Italy** is another good restaurant; the snapper here comes highly recommended. **Pier Lounge** is a good place to grab a drink and chat with the locals.

Where to shop on Ambergris

Kimara's Gift Shop in town is a good one to try. Also, **Eden Art** across from the airstrip has quality products from around Belize. **Belizean Arts** has two locations, one next to the church and another under the archway at Fido's. In both you'll find top-quality products—sculptures, pottery, jewelry, as well as the largest local collection of paintings and prints by Walter Castillo whose colorful work has made him Belize's best-known artist.

THE BEST OF THE CAYO DISTRICT

The "high jungle" of the **Cayo District** is known for its broad-leaf rainforest and its slight elevation, which means few bugs and cool nights.

Overflowing with pine trees, tall waterfalls, low mountains, and breathtaking views, it is a good base from which to explore the Mountain Pine Ridge (practically inaccessible to motor vehicles) and the vast Mayan ruins in the area.

San Ignacio—a favorite inland escape

San Ignacio is a town built in Cayo's hills where the Macal and Mopan Rivers converge to form the Belize River. An old metal one-way elevated bridge crosses the Macal in town—"the loudest bridge in Central America," as it is known by the locals.

The best traveler's rest

Eva's is the local hangout, a restaurant where every traveler in the region travels eventually. There you can eat lunch or dinner for a few dollars or simply order a beer, have a seat, and discover all you need to know about what's going on in the region.

The best of nature's remedies

Rosita Arvigo, a naprapathy doctor, uses her 35 acres of jungle land to create medicines from the plants. These medicines, marketed as Rain Forest Remedies, can be used to treat everything from skin irritations to arthritis, including the common cold and impotence. They sell for $7 to $12.50 a bottle and can be purchased at Rosita's farm, in stores in Belize, or through the mail. **Rain Forest Remedies**, *Ix Chel Farm, San Ignacio, Cayo, Belize, C.A.; fax (501)92-3870*. People are also able to visit the farm and indulge themselves in the medicinal plant culture.

Where to stay in the jungle

Twelve miles south of Belmopan lies the **Caves Branch Jungle Lodge**, *tel. by radio phone (501)8-22800*. Three underground river systems allow guests to float on inner tubes through miles of river caves, where they pass magnificent stalagmites sparkling like diamonds. Here you can camp for $5 per person, share a bunk room for $15 per person, rent a cabana for $68 per night, or stay in a cabana suite for $108 per night.

Chaa Creek Inland Expeditions, *tel. (501)92-2037, e-mail: chaacreek@btl.net; website: www.chaacreek.com*, is a lovely piece of land owned by Mick and Lucy Fleming that has been turned into a sort of retreat. The cottages here range in price from $140 to $365 per night and are well worth the money.

An equestrian's dream

Mountain Equestrian Trails, *tel. (501)9-3310; e-mail: awztrav2bz@aol.com; website: www.metbelize.com*, is a small resort that specializes in horseback riding and offers trail rides throughout the region to visit caves, waterfalls, and the jungle. A double room here rents for $85 to $120 per night, depending on the season.

The best butterflies

Green Hills Butterfly Ranch and Botanical Collection, *tel. (501)91-2017; e-mail: meerman@btl.net*, is a research facility that is open to the public from 9 a.m. to 5 p.m. every day between Christmas and Easter. If viewing butterflies flying freely in a net enclosure landscaped with a collection of tropical plants is your thing, then this is the place.

THE MOST CARIBBEAN

This is technically Central America, but **Placencia Village**, located on Placencia Peninsula in the south of Belize, has an easy pace of living and a laid-back vibe that feels very Caribbean. The folks are friendly, and the Maya, Gafiruna, and Creole cultures blend yet remain distinct and unique. After just a few days biking Placencia's one road or walking its one sidewalk, which runs between the road and the sea, bordered by restaurants, beachside bars, gift shops, and guesthouses, local faces and places become familiar quickly. The nightlife here is casual, and when something is going on, maybe a live band one night or a dj the next, everyone in town can be found there, because, well, that's usually the only thing going on that night. It's easy to settle in.

Placencia's best hotels

Singing Sands Inn, *tel. (501)6-37017; e-mail: ssi@btl.net; website: www.singingsands.com*, is a lovely hotel that sits on a perfect piece of the beach. A double costs $85 to $115 a night, depending on the season. **Robert's Grove**, *tel. (501)6-23565; e-mail: info@robertsgrove.com; website: www.robertsgrove.com*, is another great place to stay. Room rates range from $79 to $135 depending on the season.

THE BEST OF COSTA RICA

What you'll find most surprising when visiting Costa Rica is that, despite all its natural beauty, despite all the favorable press it has received for years now, despite its low cost of living, despite its Edenic climate, and despite its friendly populace, this tropical paradise has not yet been overrun with tourists. Yes, there have been many more visitors to Costa Rica in recent years than a couple of decades ago, for example. But, compared with the world's other tropical paradises, Costa Rica remains largely undiscovered.

The country boasts some of the best-preserved countryside in Latin America. There are acres upon acres of pristine forest and jungle. And there are long stretches of totally deserted and undeveloped beaches, on both the Caribbean and the Pacific coasts.

Two other characteristics set Costa Rica well apart from its Central American neighbors: a high literacy rate (one of the highest in the world) and the absence of an army.

SAN JOSÉ: THE BEST MODERN CITY IN COSTA RICA

The primary drawback to **Costa Rica** is its capital city, **San José**, which is crowded, noisy, run-down, polluted, and crawling with pickpockets. At one time, though, San Jose must have been beautiful. The old sections of the city are filled with large, ornate buildings that were originally residences but have been converted into office space.

One thing you should take time to see in San José is the **Téatro Nationale**, a beautiful building inside and out. When you walk into the lobby, be sure to look up, to see one of the most beautifully painted ceilings outside Rome.

The best way to get around San José

The best way to see San José is by foot. The city is arranged in a grid, with calles running from north to south and avenidas running from east to west. However, if you do decide to walk your way around San José, we offer one caveat: Don't assume that pedestrians have the right of way. Costa Rica has the highest number of traffic fatalities per year of any country in the world. And when you step off a curb in San José, you'll understand why.

The best place to eat in San José

Bar Centrale, *Calle Centrale and avenida 6; tel. (506)22-52-52*, is small and simple. The food and service are good. Beer at the Bar Centrale, as at most places throughout the country, is served with a *boca*, a piece of barbecued meat and a little salad.

The best beds in San José

The best place to stay in the city is the **Amstel**, *tel. (506)22-49-92*, where the service is first-rate and the food at the hotel restaurant is good.

Another good place to stay is the **Costa Rican Inn**, *tel. (506)21-27-62*. The décor is nicer than most Costa Rican hotels.

San José's best English bookstore

Casey's Book Exchange, *Calle Centrale between avenidas 7 and 9; tel. (506)21-79-95*, stocks hundreds of used paperbacks and attracts dozens of expats who come in to browse and chat. Casey himself may offer you a cup of coffee and exchange gossip with you about literary and local matters.

SARCHI: THE BEST WOODEN CRAFTS

Sarchi, a small artisan's town, filled with the shops of local craftsmen, exists solely as a tourist attraction. However, the wooden furniture here is so well made and so affordable that touristy Sarchi is worth the visit. Prices are often higher for gringos than for Ticos so, if possible, have your guide or hosts do your buying for you. Haggling is discouraged.

THE MOST DEVELOPED BEACH

Jaco, south of San José, is the most developed beach in the country. Jaco is especially popular with Canadians, who have invested heavily in development here. Construction is evident everywhere; new hotels, restaurants, souvenir shops, and surf shops are springing up every month.

THE COUNTRY'S ONLY JACUZZIS

The **Flamingo Marina Resort Hotel and Club** is the only hotel in the country that boasts Jacuzzis in some of the suites. Other amenities include tennis courts, a swimming pool, and a poolside bar. A double room can cost as much as $135 a night during the high season. The hotel can be contacted at e-mail: *flamingo@centralamerica.com*.

THE COUNTRY'S ONLY TRAIN TRIP

At one time, trains traveled from one coast to the other, with connections in all the major towns. Today, a single train runs from San José to Puntarenas. It departs the **Pacific Coast Train Station** every day at 7 a.m. and 3 p.m. It is slow-going, but it is also a chance to see some of the country's most picturesque landscapes.

THE BEST OF
HONDURAS

THE BEST OF THE BAY ISLANDS

The **Bay Islands** today call to mind The Bahamas in the early 1970s.
Sufficient infrastructure—phone lines, paved roads, regular flights in and
out, restaurants, dive shops, grocery stores—makes life here comfortable.
But the beaches remain pristine and not overrun with tourists. Vast swaths
of land sit lush with greenery...not a home in sight.

Roatan and Utila boast long, white beaches and lush, green interiors.
This is quintessential Caribbean with crystal-clear turquoise waters and fiery
sunsets. The snorkeling and diving along this hemisphere's largest barrier
reef is among the best in the world, and here you avoid the crowds that
regularly invade Cozumel, Grand Cayman, Barbados, and the rest.

THE BEST OF ROATAN

Roatan's high green hills, lush with hardwood trees and palms, provide
picture-postcard views to the warm, turquoise waters shimmering below.
Bright bougainvillea and hibiscus fill gardens, and passion fruit vines
tumble over porch railings. Wide ribbons of white sand cling to the coast in
protected coves. Elsewhere, towering rocks jut out into the sea, forming
dramatic perches for magnificent homes.

The most affordable diving

Most visitors to Roatan come here to dive. The traveler on a budget
heads for **West End**—nice beaches, pleasant posadas, and experienced dive
shops; you'll find beautiful beaches and higher-end accommodations at West
Bay, a few miles down the road. Diving off Roatan is popular because it's
part of the Belizean Barrier Reef, the second longest barrier reef in the
world, abundant with wildlife—schools of colorful fish, sea turtles, sharks,
and even octopi—and the intensely beautiful and colorful coral reef.

Staying at West End costs from $15 for a basic room to $50 for a posada
with a kitchenette. Many posadas have private beaches with tables and
chairs for lounging. If you're self-catering, be sure to stock up on groceries
in Coxen Hole, where you'll pay 50% less.

The shuttle from West End to Coxen Hole runs regularly each day ($1.50)—but avoid traveling on Tuesday and Wednesday when the cruise ships dock as it's nearly impossible to get a lift back.

Several small bars offer a daily meal for around $8, usually including lobster. Conch soup is an island specialty at $3 to $5 a bowl, and it's always a filling meal.

Open water diver certification courses start at $150, making Roatan one of the world's most affordable places to obtain your certification. A typical course includes classroom instruction, contained water dives, and several open water dives. Following certification, additional dives are available from $15 per tank. Specialty night dives may run closer to $45. If you are already certified, you'll still pay under $25 per tank.

THE BEST OF UTILA

Utila has a different feel altogether. Much smaller and flatter, its beaches are just as striking—arguably more so—than those on the big island. Perhaps the swaths of sand here appeal so because they tend to take you by surprise. You encounter them, for the most part, by boat. (Precious few roads traverse the island.) So as you round a bend in the coast, squinting in the sun and spray, the tat-tat of the engine and the sound of sloshing water below, you discover in front of you these impossibly picturesque scenes.

The small town, with its sand roads and curving pathways, is built of colorful gingerbread houses with well-kept gardens. There you will find a bank, little shops, a cinema, small restaurants, and bars.

GUANAJA: THE PERFECT TROPICAL GETAWAY

Guanaja is the most laid-back of the three Bay Islands...the perfect tropical getaway for people who crave the simple life and a return to nature. Thirteen miles long and three miles wide, this is also the tallest island, with mountain peaks crowding the center. The Honduran government declared the central area a national forest.

The island is split into unequal halves by a manmade channel, which you can traverse by water taxi. Next to the channel is a paved airstrip, rated for daytime landings only, with daily service to mainland La Ceiba and an occasional connection through Roatan.

There are no roads and little nighttime entertainment, besides diving. What do you do here? Hike...ride horses...explore the miles of deserted beaches...and enjoy the silence.

THE BEST GOLF CLUB IN HONDURAS

Our favorite golf club in Honduras is in **La Ceiba** (a two-hour ferry crossing—or an even shorter flight—from Roatan). Membership costs $600 plus annual dues of $195 (this fee allows you to play other courses in Honduras too). The club also has a swimming pool and tennis courts. Tee off by 8.30 a.m. if you travel from Roatan by ferry, or 7 a.m. if you fly. At that time of the morning you'll have the course to yourself.

La Ceiba's golf course is only nine holes but there is a second set of tee boxes that makes it 18 holes (only one of Honduras' six golf courses is an 18-hole course). The fairways are tree-lined and the greens are surrounded by plenty of sand. Like all Honduran golf clubs, wearing shorts is acceptable.

We also recommend the course at **Tela** (60 miles west of La Ceiba). The drive from La Ceiba to Tela is a relaxing one, through pineapple plantations and palm groves.

Remember, though, this is Honduras: These aren't U.S. championship-quality courses, but they're good nonetheless. La Ceiba club was recently host to the Honduran equivalent of the U.S. open, a big event for the town.

THE BEST OF MEXICO

AFTER MEXICO, I SHALL ALWAYS ASSOCIATE BALCONIES AND POLITICIANS —
PLUMP MEN WITH BLUE CHINS WEARING SOFT HATS AND GUNS ON THEIR
HIPS. THEY LOOK DOWN FROM THE OFFICIAL BALCONY IN EVERY CITY ALL
DAY LONG WITH NOTHING TO DO BUT STARE WITH THE EXPRESSION OF MEN
KEEPING AN EYE ON A GOOD THING.

—Graham Greene, 1939

Mexico is a North American's best choice for an inexpensive vacation in
a warm and exotic foreign country. It is also perfect for sun worshipers,
hardy adventurers, high rollers, and those on a tight budget. Mexico offers
beautiful beaches, unexplored wilderness, cosmopolitan cities, historic
monuments, and good food—all for next to nothing.

MEXICO CITY: THE WORLD'S LARGEST LANDLOCKED CITY

Mexico City is the cultural, political, and commercial hub of the country.
Located on a plateau, it is surrounded by mountains. Colonial architecture
gives it a Spanish air. The best place to put the city in perspective is from
the rooftop bar on the 44-floor **Latin American Tower**, *Eje Central
Lázaro Cárdenas*.

The best museums

The best place to begin your tour of the city is the **Museo de la Ciudad**
(City Museum), *Pino Suarez 30*. Formerly the Palace of the Counts of
Santiago (early Spanish conquistadors who came to the New World seeking
their fortunes), it documents Mexico City's history in chronological order
from the Aztecs through the 20th century. The museum is open Tuesdays
through Sundays from 9 a.m. until 5 p.m., and a small admission fee is
charged. Tours in English are conducted every day.

The **National Museum of Anthropology**, *Paseo de la Reforma*, in
Chapultepec Park, houses most of Mexico's excavated pre-Columbian treasures, including artifacts from the Palenque tombs, Mexico's most spectacular
Mayan site. The architecture and figurines at Palenque strangely resemble
those at ancient Oriental sites in Cambodia, which is possible evidence of a
direct ancestral link.

The museum also houses an Aztec calendar stone that divides the year accurately into a 52-week cycle, providing evidence of early Indian civilizations' ability to use astronomy to divide time. On the second floor, a display depicts present-day Indian lifestyles in Mexico. Bilingual guides are available for tours. The museum is open Tuesday through Friday 9 a.m. until 5 p.m. and Saturday and Sunday 10 a.m. until 6 p.m. Tours in English are conducted daily.

The **Bellas Artes Museum**, *Lázaro Cárdenas*, has a permanent collection of Mexico's world-famous murals, including a duplicate of the Diego Riviera mural commissioned for the Rockefeller Center in New York City. (Because Rivera depicted John D. Rockefeller as a greedy capitalist, the copy in New York is now covered by another less provocative mural.)

If you visit the Bellas Artes Museum on a Sunday or a Wednesday, you can see a performance by **Ballet Folklórico**, a lively folk ballet company. The glass curtain that hangs across the stage was commissioned from Tiffany's. The museum is open 10 a.m. until 6 p.m. daily except Monday.

The best of the Hapsburgs in Mexico

In **Chapultepec Park**, once the royal hunting grounds of the Aztecs, is Chapultepec Castle, once the imperial residence of the Hapsburgs, whose quarters are now on display. This unlikely bit of Austria-Hungary in the heart of Mexico was engineered by Napoleon III of France, who in 1864 installed the Hapsburg prince Maximillian as governor of Mexico. Needless to say, this ill-thought-out bit of colonialism didn't work. In 1867, this outpost of Napoleon's empire collapsed, Maximillian was killed, and his widow went mad.

The castle, which is a museum today, also displays a collection of 19th-century art and costumes. It is open to the public 9 a.m. until 6 p.m. daily except Monday. A small admission fee is charged.

The best handicrafts

Mexico is known for its regional crafts, including leatherwork, furniture, blown glass, ceramics, pottery, textiles, tinwork, and woodcarving. At the **National Museum of Art and Popular Industry**, *avenida Juarez 44*, you can inspect the country's handicrafts and then purchase your favorites at the museum shop. Prices are relatively cheap, and the quality is usually good. The museum is open daily.

The zocalo: the heart of the city

Many of Mexico City's attractions are on the zocalo, the main city square. The grandest is the **National Palace**, which houses most of Mexico's government offices. It is a beautiful example of colonial architecture, especially dramatic when illuminated during Mexico's many holidays. Inside are Diego Rivera murals depicting this country's history through the Revolution of 1910. The National Palace is open 9 a.m. to 6 p.m. daily except Monday.

Mexico's grandest cathedral

The **Cathedral of Mexico**, the largest in the country, is also on the zocalo. Built over a 200-year period beginning in the 16th century, the cathedral incorporates many architectural styles. Its massive sanctuary houses 16 chapels, 27 altars, and a valuable collection of religious artwork from the Spanish colonial period.

The **Altar of the Kings** is a highly ornamental creation built in the wild baroque style known as churrigueresque, which was introduced by Spanish architect and artisan Jose Churriguera. Popular in the late 17th century, this style ignored the restraint employed by Renaissance artists and used elaborate designs and rich materials, such as gold and silver.

The greatest archeological find

Located just off the zocalo is the greatest accidental archeological find of the last century: the **Great Temple of Tenochitlán**. Unearthed in 1978 by the Mexican Power and Light Company, it was once the holiest temple of the Aztecs. Although many of the artifacts found here are displayed in museums around the country, the site is still impressive, with intricate, artistic wall sculptures. Admission is free. The site is closed Mondays.

The city's best house

The 17th–century **Casa de los Azulejos** (House of Tiles), *Calle Madero 4*, which is completely covered in tiles, was built by the son of one of the counts of Orizaba. The young man became wealthy despite his father's prediction that he would never have a house of tiles (A Spanish saying that meant he would never be successful). To spite his father, he bought a house and had it completely covered in tiles.

The House of Tiles is now a department store called Sanborns.

Mexico City's best restaurants

Hosteria Santo Domingo, *tel. (952) 5-510-1434*, serves traditional Mexican food and wonderful desserts. The best part about this restaurant is that it is located in a perfectly preserved 19th-century building with beautiful decoration.

The **San Angel Inn**, *tel. (52) 5-548-6840*, is the most beautiful restaurant in Mexico, situated in a 250-year-old building that has been completely restored. It has hosted Pancho Villa, Pavlova, Caruso, and Gershwin. Chef Manual Lozano cooks up a good *pompano en papillote*. Men are required to wear jackets.

The **Hacienda de los Morales**, *tel. (52) 5-540-3225* is an elegant, reasonably priced restaurant specializing in both Continental and Mexican cuisine. Reservations are a must at this beautifully restored 16th-century hacienda.

La Fonda el Refugio, *Liverpool 166; tel. (52) 5-525-8128*, is decorated with primitive art and locally blown glass. The Tuesday special is delicious: *mole poblano* (thin tortillas fried and stuffed with shredded chicken and covered with *mole*, a rich sauce made with 25 ingredients, including hot peppers, tomatoes, raisins, and chocolate). Finish your meal with *café de olla* (black coffee served with brown sugar, cinnamon, and cloves). Reservations are recommended.

Meson del Cid, *Humboldt 61; tel. (52)5-521-1940*, is a three-level dining room that serves open-hearth cooking. Baby suckling pig *à la segovia* is the house specialty. The pheasant *à la maison del cid* is good, too.

The **Del Lago Restaurant**, *Nuevo Bosque de Chapultepec; tel. (52)5-515-9585*, has a clear view of Chapultepec Lagoon through its grand windows. Trees and hanging plants give the interior an outdoor look. The seafood is good. Save room for dessert, and order the *mango flambé au tequilla*.

The capital's best hotels

Camino Real, *Mariano Escobedo 700; tel. (52)5-203-2121*, is located at the edge of Chapultepec Park, its seven-acre spread includes pools, tennis courts, three entertainment bars, a disco, a coffee shop, and two restaurants.

Gran Hotel Howard Johnson, *ave. 16 de Septiembre #82, Colonia Centro, 070000, Mexico City; tel. (52)5-510-4040*, is centrally located, comfortable and has excellent service. It has cage elevators and a Tiffany glass ceiling in the lobby.

The **Hotel Majestic**, *Francisco Madero 73; tel. (52)5-521-8600*, is another good hotel. From its rooftop terrace, the view of the city is panoramic. The Mexican color guard marches by the hotel every day at 6:30 p.m.

Hotel de Cortes, *ave. Hidalgo 85; tel. (52)5-585-0322*, a restored 18th-century hacienda, is a moderately priced hotel that is clean, comfortable, and efficient. It is also popular, so make reservations well in advance.

The **Maria Cristina**, *Lerma 31; tel. (52)5-546-9880*, is a small hotel with a pretty garden and a piano bar.

The hottest nightlife

El hijo del Cuervo, *No. 1 Francisco Sosa at Jardin Centenario*, has live music, a local crowd, and a young style. **Las Coronelas**, *1765 Insurgentes sur Ave.*, inside the Guadalupe Inn, is staged as a country-style Cantina. **La Guadalupana**, *Higuera St. and Caballocalco*, is known for its toreros ambience and has a wide variety of drinks.

The best day-trips

Midway between Mexico City and Tula, the capital of the ancient Toltec Indians, is the **Tepotzotlàn Monastery**, a beautiful example of Spanish architecture, encrusted with intricate gold carvings made by local Indians. You can visit Wednesday through Sunday 11 a.m. until 6 p.m.

Cholula was the site of thousands of human sacrifices. In fact, although it was built long before the Aztec civilization flourished, this gory monument was still in use when the Spanish came. Hearing that they were to be killed here, Hernan Cortes and his entourage killed thousands of Aztecs. The site is open daily.

The pyramids of **Teotihuacan**, built sometime between A.D. 400 and A.D. 800, make up the largest, most complete archeological site in this hemisphere, covering more than 35 square miles. The Indians who built the pyramids, probably Mayans or their predecessors, marked time in 52-year cycles, building a new pyramid on top of the old one every cycle. The site includes hundreds of small temples, two large ones (the Pyramid of the Sun and the Pyramid of the Moon), and a large enclosed arena that was probably used for religious spectacles or ceremonial ball games. From mid-October to mid-May, a narrated sound-and-light show begins at 7 p.m. in English and at 8:15 p.m. in Spanish. The site is open daily. A small admission fee is charged.

SAN MIGUEL DE ALLENDE: THE BEST ARTISANS' TOWN

Situated in a small valley surrounded by hills, **San Miguel de Allende** has retained its colonial charm while blossoming into a center for the arts. *Burros* line the streets, and flowers fill every corner. Homes are hidden behind tall, bougainvillea-draped stucco walls. And art galleries, cafés, and restaurants serve the thriving expatriate community.

Located on the high central plateau about 250 miles northwest of Mexico City, San Miguel is in the agriculturally rich Bajio region on the colonial route. The entire town is a historic national monument; all architecture conforms to the colonial style.

La Parroquia, the imposing pink cathedral on the main zocalo, is a 19th-century Indian mason's interpretation of a French Gothic cathedral. The bells chime every 15 minutes.

Instituto Allende: largest Latin American fine arts school

San Miguel earned its reputation as an international arts center in 1938, with the opening of the first English-speaking school, the **Instituto Allende**, *Bellas Artes, Centro Cultural El Nigromante*. The institute is now the largest Latin American fine arts school for English-speaking students.

Buying handicrafts and antiques

This is one of the best places in Mexico to buy handicrafts. Most shops are within three blocks of the main square. It's a good idea to visit several shops before buying—quality varies. Although you can do some bargaining, most of the prices are set.

Casa Maxwell, *Canal 14*, and **Llamas Brothers**, *Zacateros 11*, are two of the best handicraft shops in San Miguel. They're also both quite expensive. Two cheaper shops are **La Ventana**, *Canal Street*, and **La Balaiza Mercantil**, *Mesones 42*.

San Miguel is also a good place to buy antiques. Although no pre-Columbian antiques may be sold legally in Mexico, you can buy Spanish antiques from the colonial period. Try the antique shops that line the main square but be careful because many items offered are merely convincing reproductions.

The world's best facelift

It is possible to get a 10-day cosmetic surgery vacation package to San Miguel de Allende, with the surgery performed at a private hospital just outside town. The hospital has 20 specialists on staff and surgery is performed in a state-of-the-art operating room, with an M.D. anesthesiologist attending. You are in a private hospital room for three days following surgery, not an outpatient, as is the case in the U.S. The trip is fully escorted, including round-trip transfers by private car from Leon airport. The price of $6,000 for a complete facelift is one-third the price in the States. And the quality is superior. The cost of the 10-day holiday is an additional $775. For more information, visit *www.faceliftmexico.com*.

The best restaurants

The best restaurant in San Miguel de Allende is the **Villa Jacaranda**, *Aldama 53; tel. (52)465-21015*. The food is superb, but the atmosphere alone makes the place worth a visit. Set in a vast stone hacienda, the quiet and relaxing restaurant is surrounded by gardens filled with flowers and trailing vines. Try the house specialty, drunken chicken, which is breast of chicken sautéed in onions and peppers. At brunch, try the **chilis nogadas**, a tangy blend of peppers covered in a sweet cream sauce. Order the crisp, dry local white wine called Calafia.

The restaurant at the **Casa de Sierra Nevada**, *Hospicio 35; tel. (52)465-20415*, is the most elegant in town.

La Posada Carmina, *Cuna de Allende 7; tel. (52)465-20548*, set in a cool, inviting courtyard filled with flowers, is also good. On Thursdays, try the specialty, a cheese and vegetable salad, or the *paella Valenciana*. You don't need to make reservations.

El Patio, *Correo 10*, is a good place for lunch. Although the food is ordinary, the setting is pleasant. You can enjoy live music in the bar.

The sweetest dreams

La Posada San Francisco, *Plaza Principal 2*, right on the main square, is within walking distance of just about everything in San Miguel.

Casa de Sierra Nevada, *Hospicio 35*, is an old Spanish villa. The hotel has an excellent restaurant.

The spiciest nights

Cantinas, nightclubs, and cocktail lounges in San Miguel stay open until 1 a.m., and many will stay open later at the request of guests. **The Ring**, *Calle de Hidalgo 25*, is a disco popular with the over-35 crowd. **Laberintos Discoteque**, *Calle Ancha de San Antonio 7*, is popular with a younger set and has loud music. You must pay a cover charge.

Mama Mia, *Umaron 8*, has live music, from Andean folk to jazz, Wednesday through Monday on its patio. **La Princesa**, *Recreo 5*, is a quiet place, where you can listen to music while enjoying an early evening drink.

The steamiest side trips

Just a few miles from San Miguel, in **Taboada**, you can soak in steaming hot springs while a waiter serves you drinks. And at **La Gruta** you can swim in an Olympic-sized heated pool or take a steam bath in a cave of hot mineral water.

The best place to hear the flutter of butterfly wings

A three-hour drive from San Miguel de Allende is the colorful old mining town of **Angangueo**. And only an hour from Angangueo, up a steep, unpaved road, is the **Monarch Butterfly Sanctuary**. The park's 12,000 acres became a protected area in 1986 and now there is no worry that the butterflies' habitat and migration site will ever be destroyed. For information about organized tours to the sanctuary, contact **Rocamar Tours**, *tel. (1)866-ROCA-MAR; e-mail: rocamar@rocamar.com.mx*.

TAXCO: THE SILVER CAPITAL

Taxco is a mining town in the mountains. About a day's ride outside of Mexico City and off the main tourist route, it is less crowded than Guanajanto or Cuernavaca. It is also *the* place to buy silver jewelry.

William Spratling introduced silversmithing to Taxco in 1929. Now the town has more than 300 fine jewelry shops. And the mines show no signs of cutting off the supply of metal.

Original Spratling pieces are difficult to come by, but most of the jewelry sold throughout Taxco is styled upon his original models. All silver products, from jewelry to candelabras, cost about 25% less than American counterparts and about 50% less than European pieces.

The best jewelry shops are **Los Castillos**, *Plazeula Bernal 10*, and **La Mina**, *Avenida J.F. Kennedy*, on the site of an old silver mine.

The most colorful times to visit Taxco are during Holy Week and the National Silver Fair, at the beginning of December. Make reservations far in advance.

Taxco's best tables

La Ventana de Taxco, *Hotel Hacienda del Solar*, in a pink stone house on a hill just south of town, serves delicious Italian food for reasonable prices. Tables look out at the red-roofed houses of Taxco and the mountains beyond. The view is loveliest at sunset. Hollywood publicist Ted Wick, who lives in town, once owned this building—he still plays the grand piano in the lounge.

La Pagaduriá del Rey, *Calle H. Colegio Militar*, serves steaks, seafood, and Mexican food. The menu is limited, and the restaurant opens whenever the staff feels like it, but the food is good.

The best hotels

Rancho Taxco-Victoria, *tel. (52)762-20210*, is a lovely hotel with large rooms, a pleasant restaurant, a bar, a swimming pool, and beautiful gardens.

Hotel de la Borda, *tel. (52)762-20025*, is cozy with a pool, restaurant overlooking the city, and large bathrooms.

Fiesta Montetaxco, *off Route 95; tel. (52)762-2-1300*, a mountainside hotel on the north side of town, has 160 rooms and 50 villas and suites. It offers color television, air conditioning, a pool, spa facilities, a golf course, a tennis court, horseback riding, and a restaurant with nightly entertainment.

CUERNAVACA, WHERE SPRING
SPRINGS ETERNAL

Cuernavaca is the city of eternal spring, with temperatures that hover around 75 degrees Fahrenheit year-round and lush vegetation. The Mexicans were not the first to recognize this city as an ideal resort. The Aztecs also used Cuernavaca (or Cuauhnáhuac, as the city was originally called) as a retreat.

Cortes recognized its appeal as well. He built **El Palacio de Cortés**, his personal residence, here. This massive fortress is now home to the **Cuauhnáhuac Historical Museum**, which houses murals by Rivera, Siquieros, and Orozco.

Cuernavaca has become expensive by Mexican standards, in part because of the year-round expatriate community. Prices are substantially higher than in Taxco or San Miguel de Allende, and the area is more touristy than other cities.

See the cathedral that Cortes founded in 1529, the summer palace of the Hapsburgs, and the beautiful Borda Gardens, where a botanical festival is held each year in April.

The best hotels

The most luxurious place to stay in Cuernavaca is the **Hotel Hacienda Cortes**, *tel. (52)73-15-8844*. Amenities include tennis courts, spa facilities, pools, lounges, two restaurants, and weekend concerts. **Las Mañanitas**, *tel. (52)77-7314-466*, is another luxurious hotel with all of the amenities, but rooms here are a bit more expensive.

OAXACA: THE BEST INDIAN RUINS

Oaxaca, the most Indian region, is the best place to explore present-day Indian culture as well as ancient Indian ruins. The colonial city of Oaxaca is a good base. Plan to stay at least a few days—there is a lot to see.

The age-old tradition of weaving lives on in the village of **Teotitlán del Valle**. You can watch weavers at work and then buy decorated carpets and serapes.

About eight miles outside Teotitlán del Valle is the **Yagul** site, dating from about A.D. 700. Earlier this century, precious Zapotec artifacts were taken from this series of multiple tombs. The site includes a hill fortress, a group of palaces and temples, and a ball court.

Mitla, the City of the Dead, is 26 miles outside Oaxaca. Built by the Zapotecs, Mitla was later enlarged by the Mixtecs. Although this is a touristy spot (Indian women mill around trying to sell souvenirs), it is also impressive, with intricate mosaics and strange stone carvings on the walls.

In the opposite direction from Oaxaca is another impressive archeological site: **Monte Albán**. This massive group of Zapotec ruins covers 15 square miles. The Temple of Dancers and the ceremonial ball court are the two most impressive sites. However, you can spend hours wandering among literally hundreds of ceremonial altars, winding staircases, and stone carvings. The site is open daily from 8 a.m. until 6 p.m.

To see what was found in the tombs of Mitla and the ruins of Monte Albán, visit the **Regional Museum in Oaxaca**, *Calle M. Alcalá*, where most of the treasures are kept.

Keep in mind that, when exploring the region of Oaxaca, you should use your camera respectfully; the natives don't like to have their pictures taken.

Oaxaca's best buys

The region of Oaxaca is a good place to shop. Prices for textiles, jewelry, and handicrafts are much lower than those in Cuernavaca and Mexico City. Visit the village of **Tlacolula** on a Sunday, when a huge market is set up by

Indian vendors and artisans selling clothing, pottery, rugs, wall hangings, and gold jewelry styled upon the original Zapotec and Mixtec patterns. Visit the village of **Atzompa** on a Tuesday for superb green-glazed ceramics. The village of **Ejutla** is famous for its intricately carved knives, **San Bartolo Coyotepec** for its black pottery, and **Octolan** for its straw baskets.

If you prefer to shop in stores rather than open markets, visit **Casa Brena**, *Pino Suarez 58*, or **Aripo**, *Garcia Vigil 809*.

Oaxaca's best food and lodging

El Asador Vasco, *Portal de Flores 10; tel. (52)951-6-2092*, overlooking the zocalo, is the best restaurant in town. Chef Juan Hernandez takes cuisine seriously, and his restaurant is worth a special trip. Both Spanish and Mexican dishes are served. Try the house specialty, *cazuelas*, small casseroles of baked cheese, mushrooms, and garlic. The restaurant is closed Sundays.

El Sol y La Luna, *Murguia 105; tel. (52)951-6-2933*, is a combination coffeehouse, restaurant, and gallery. Although the restaurant is small and you may have to wait for a table, it's worth the wait. The restaurant is closed Sundays.

No matter where you eat, your meal will probably include chocolate. Oaxaca is known for it. Try the famous *mole* sauce (a mixture of chocolate, cinnamon, chili peppers, and bananas), which is served on meat and poultry.

Although hotels here do not have the amenities of those in the resort cities, they are clean, comfortable and cheap. The **Victoria**, *tel. (52)951-52633*, atop a hill overlooking town, is one of the best, with a heated pool, tennis courts, a disco, and large breakfasts.

El Presidente, housed in the former Santa Catalina Convent, *Cinco de Mayo 300*, is comfortable and serves an excellent luncheon buffet that is open to both guests and visitors.

GUADALAJARA: MEXICO AT ITS BEST

Guadalajara is the home of the Mexican hat dance, mariachi bands, tequila, Mexican horsemen, and rodeos. It is also a bustling, sophisticated city with a large American community, attracted by the easy lifestyle and pleasant climate.

This is a good place to admire Spanish colonial architecture. Many of the buildings in the **Plaza Tapatía** have been restored to their former glory. Hospicio Cabanas, built in 1801 as an orphanage, has been renovated and converted into the Cabanas Institute, a center for the arts. Its chapel contains Orozco's famous mural, *Four Horsemen of the Apocalypse*. Other colonial buildings of interest include the cathedral at the center of the city, the Jalisco Supreme Court, the Government Palace, and the Legislative Hall.

Guadalajara is a city of parks. The largest, **Parque Agua Azul**, *Gonzales*

Gallo and avenida Independencia, has an open-air theater, a bird sanctuary, and special sections designed for children and the blind. The park also houses the House of Handicrafts, which contains superb examples of colonial furniture, ceramics, blown glass, tinwork, and textiles produced in the state of Jalisco. Most of the products are for sale at reasonable, fixed prices.

Mexico's largest open-air market

The huge **Libertad Market**, *Calzada Independencia*, is the largest open-air market in Mexico. After shopping, retire to the **Plaza de los Mariachis**, across the street, and listen to the strolling musicians while sipping a cool drink.

The best place to eat

If you find yourself hungry in Guadalajara, look for the green building on the corner at 5645 Pedro Simon Laplace. The green is for good luck—and, in this case, good food and good value.

Las Arboledas, *5645 Pedro Simon Laplace*, is one of four restaurants whose owner—affectionately known as *"La Gorda,"* or "The Fat One"—was recently recognized for 45 years spent preserving the traditional culinary arts of Jalisco, the state where Guadalajara is located. Over the years, the *papel picados* (cut paper banners) hanging out front have welcomed a varied and even illustrious clientele, including Mexican president Vicente Fox, who poses with the owner in a proudly displayed photo.

Through hard work, perseverance, and lots of good food, the original La Gorda kitchen has grown from a street stand to four restaurants, including Las Arboledas, where you're greeted by the appetizing aroma of food bubbling in pots in the open kitchen. All the cooks line up behind the counter wearing white headscarves and aprons, ready to serve specialties such as *pozole* (hominy and pork soup), *mole* (a popular Mexican sauce of chili peppers, nuts, spices, and chocolate), and *pepian* (chicken in spicy green sauce). These cooks are an institution at the La Gorda restaurants, and they preserve the consistent deliciousness of the food.

Try the **horchata** (cold rice milk) served in clay pitchers, *tacos dorados* (tacos with a variety of fillings), and meat enchiladas. The *mole poblano* (a chicken dish made with mole sauce) is the best you'll ever eat. The *sopes fritos de pollo*—thick little tortilla pies filled with chicken, is a favorite with the kids.

Whatever you decide on, you can afford to eat a lot of it. The traditional plates at Las Arboledas cost a very reasonable 54 pesos (about $4.85 at the time of writing), with specialties of the house from 21 pesos ($1.90) to 40 pesos ($3.60). Drinks will set you back 17 pesos ($1.50) to 86 pesos ($7.75), desserts from 19 pesos ($1.70) to 26 pesos ($2.35), and your after-dinner coffee a mere 12 pesos ($1.10).

Mexico

The best places to dine to music

For a late lunch, try the **Guadalajara Grill**, *tel. (52)36-31-56-22*, where the band strikes up around 3 p.m. and then again at about 10 p.m The Guadalajara serves Mexican food. Another favorite is the **Cazuelas Grill**, *tel. (52)36-31-57-80*, a family run, traditional restaurant. There are two shows daily, at 1:30 p.m. and 6:30 p.m.

The best day-trips

Tlaquepaque, a suburb of Guadalajara, has a wide selection of artisans' shops selling textiles, blown glass, and brass. Have lunch at the **Restaurant Sin Nombre**, *tel. (52)36-354520*, which serves a creative mixture of Provençal and Mexican food. Dress is casual and daily entertainment includes a vocal trio, singing waiters, and mariachis.

JALAPA: THE FLOWER GARDEN OF MEXICO

Jalapa, the capital of Veracruz, is known as the flower garden of Mexico, because of its many parks. This small and friendly colonial city is seldom visited by tourists of any kind.

The city is 4,700 feet above see level, and all the streets run at steep angles. Walking is thoroughly exhausting, so hire a taxi to take you sightseeing. Taxis are plentiful, and the rates are regulated.

Begin your tour in the main square. Visit the **Palacio de Gobierno** (Government House), which houses the famous *Liberation* mural by Diego Rivera, depicting man's struggle through life, and the massive colonial cathedral, built in 1773.

El Mercado Jauregui, one of the four local markets, has booths selling food, furniture, clothes, and flowers.

After the crush of the market, visit the small **Barrio Xalitic**, said to pre-date Christopher Columbus. Women scrub their clothes in the public water trough, and children play in a small park among tapped springs and small Christian shrines.

At centrally located **Parque Juarez**, vendors sell balloons, flowers, and food, and boys offer to shine your shoes. Steer clear of the food sold by vendors; it looks good but is known to cause Montezuma's revenge.

Try some of Jalapa's famous coffee at the café in the park, shaded by red-and-white striped umbrellas. The café serves an excellent *lechero*—hot milk poured into rich coffee extract and sweetened.

Mexico's best symphony

Jalapa boasts the best symphony orchestra in Mexico. You can listen to both classical music and contemporary creations in the modern **State Theater**, *tel. (52)281-74177*. During intermission, members of the audience are allowed backstage to meet the orchestra.

The best hotels

The **Maria Victoria**, *Zaragosa 6; tel. (52)281-86011*, is the best hotel in Jalapa. It has a good restaurant and a bar.

The **Hotel Villa del Mar**, *Boulevard Avila Camacho, Veracruz; tel. (52)29-313366*, is an attractive and inexpensive place to stay.

The **Hotel Jalapa**, *tel. (52)281-82222*, is also a good place to stay in the center of town.

CHIHUAHUA: HOME OF THE BEST BANDITO

Chihuahua was home to Pancho Villa (Doroteo Arranga), the Mexican Robin Hood. The house where the beloved bandito lived is a museum of the revolutionary era as well as of Villa's life. (In 1910, Villa joined rebels and fought for President Madero and against General Huerta and President Carranza. He and his men killed American citizens in Columbus, New Mexico in 1916 and were pursued unsuccessfully by the U.S. Army for 11 months.) Villa's house was inhabited until the late 80s by his aging widow. The featured artifact on display is the bullet-riddled Dodge in which Villa was assassinated in 1923.

Chihuahua's best sites

Also in Chihuahua is the **Museo de Arte Popular**, which has an exhibit on the Tarahuamara culture, with woven blankets, full-sleeved blouses, whirling skirts, carved wooden masks decorated with goat hair, and palm baskets. Adjacent to the museum is a gift shop, where you can buy copies of these items as well as books on the indigenous cultures of Mexico and Mexican history.

El Palacio del Gobierno (Government Palace) is noteworthy for its gorgeous murals by Pina Mora, depicting the history of Mexico, including the arrival of the first priests, the Spanish Conquest, and the Mexican Civil War and its heroes.

The **Museo Regional** is housed in a beautiful art deco mansion with well-preserved stained-glass windows and elaborately carved mantels. Parts of the mansion have exhibits of Mormon and Mennonite settlements in Chihuahua.

You can see a replica of an adobe house from the ancient Paquime Indian culture in the northern part of Chihuahua, at **Casa Grandes**.

The world's grandest canyon—and most exciting train ride

Chihuahua's Barranca del Cobre (Copper Canyon) is four times larger and 300 feet deeper than the U.S. Grand Canyon. Its mountain peaks rise 10,000 feet, and its valleys drop 1,500 feet.

Until 1961, when the Chihuahua al Pacifico train line opened, the canyon was inaccessible and known only to isolated Tarahumara Indians living in caves. The train line climbs from sea level at Los Mochis on the Pacific to 8,000 feet before descending to Chihuahua. It passes the most spectacular scenery in Mexico—sheer cliffs that change color as the sun sets, giant rock formations, deep gorges, and mountain peaks. You can catch the train every day in Chihuahua at 7 a.m. or in Los Mochis at 6 a.m.

The best place to stay in the canyon is **Hotel Cabañas Divisadero-Barrancas**, *Calle 7, No. 1216*, in Divisadero, midway along the route. This rustic log-cabin hotel is perched on the rim of the canyon and affords dizzying views. Several Indian families live in caves nearby. These timid people sell hand-woven baskets, woodcarvings, and necklaces. Surrounding the hotel are trails that the Indians follow to the bottom of the canyon, 5,000 feet below.

QUERETARO—MEXICO'S MOST BEAUTIFUL CITY

Queretaro's colonial core is crisscrossed with pedestrian walkways, which lead you past lavishly restored homes and shops. Second floors are adorned with iron balconies…from which great bunches of flowers tumble downward—pinks, fuchsias, purples, lavenders, and all seven shades of bougainvillea. European plazas, with manicured gardens and sidewalk cafés, punctuate the downtown.

The best opals in Mexico

Queretaro is famous for its opals—still mined there today—fire opals in particular, in reds and yellows. You can buy them, both set in jewelry and loose, at shops throughout the downtown. However, beware of street vendors hawking low-quality stones that are likely to crumble.

Queretaro's best hotel

La Casa de la Marquesa, *tel. (52)4212-0092; fax 4212-0098; e-mail: marquesa@albec.net.mx*, is a 300-year-old hotel, which was once a dilapidated mansion, and is absolutely resplendent today. From the rooms that are furnished with antiques, Persian rugs, and original paintings to the fabulous two restaurants that are housed in the hotel, La Casa de la Marquesa is a grand place to stay. The 25 suites range in price from $180 to $375, including continental breakfast and a welcome drink.

The second best hotel

The **Hotel Mesón de Santa Rosa**, *tel. (52)4224-2623; fax 4212-5522; e-mail: starosa@ciateq.mx*, another beautifully restored home on the tree-lined Plaza de Armas, has 21 guest rooms and some suites, as well as a heated swimming pool. Its lobby-courtyard, once used to house horse-drawn carriages, still contains a long water trough. The rooms here, with their extravagantly high-beamed ceilings and antique furnishings, are comfortable and inviting.

The Pacific at its best

Acapulco and Puerto Vallarta are busy resort towns, much changed from the sleepy fishing villages they once were. However, you still can experience the peaceful ways of the Pacific in **San Blas**, 40 minutes south of Mazatlan, off Highway 15.

This is a land of endless summer, with rain forests, orchids, and warm waves. Life is lazy, and no one worries about the time. The cafés serve giant shrimp and fresh fish roasted over coals. For a few cents, you can take a bus from San Blas to **Matanchin Bay**, the most beautiful beach on the Pacific, where the waves are giant and clear and carry surfers miles before breaking.

When you tire of the beach, take a jungle boat for a few dollars into the marshy forest. You will see iguanas, blue herons, and parrots. The boat stops at a little cantina overlooking a deep pool. Have a beer and a swim.

The best whale watching

In October, hundreds of gray whales migrate from the Bering Straits to the warm lagoons of the **Baja Peninsula** to mate and have babies. The best place to see them is **San Ignacio Lagoon**, halfway down the peninsula on the Pacific Coast. The whales are so friendly that they'll probably come right up to you.

The bright green lagoon is mirror-like, ringed with sandy hills and rocks. The hazy Santa Clara mountains stand in the background. Because whale watching has become so popular here, it is carefully regulated by the Mexican government. San Ignacio, Ojo de Liebre, and Guerrero Negro are official sanctuaries. Boats must have permits to enter, and only two are permitted in at a time.

Baja Discovery, *P.O. Box 152527, San Diego, CA 92195; (619)232-1600*, arranges camping and whale-watching expeditions in San Ignacio. Five-day trips include airfare, camping equipment, transportation, one night in the La Pinta Hotel in San Ignacio, and meals.

THE BEST OF THE MEXICAN CARIBBEAN

Until the early 1970s, Mexico's idyllic Caribbean coast was undeveloped, inhabited only by Mayan Indians. Then the Mexican government realized the area's potential as a resort and began developing the Yucatan Peninsula. The empty island of Kankune became *Cancun*—the trendiest resort town in Mexico. Its neighbors, Cozumel and Isla Mujéres, also have benefited from the exposure, sprouting luxury hotels and restaurants and attracting tourists in larger numbers each year.

Considering their temperate climate, white-sand beaches, and clear waters, it's amazing that these spots took so long to attract notice. The weather is mostly sunny from October through April, and, even during the rainy season (July through September), showers are often only brief afternoon events. If you tire of the sand and surf, you can visit the nearby Mayan ruins at Tulum, Coba, and Chichén Itzá.

While Cancun and Cozumel are developed resort towns, with superb restaurants, luxurious hotels, excellent beaches, and facilities for water sports, Isla Mujérès is less sophisticated—still a place for Mexican families on holiday. One recent visitor reported that some of the islanders were less than friendly. However, Isla Mujérès does have a Mayan temple and excellent scuba diving.

The best of the mysterious Mayans

Remnants of the great civilization of the Mayans, who mysteriously disappeared long before Europeans appeared in Mexico, can be explored near Cancun. Descendants of the Mayan workers can be seen on the streets of the city and in surrounding villages—friendly, small, dark-eyed people with round faces. Many live as they have for centuries in one-room, palm-thatched huts furnished with hammocks and a table.

However, no traces remain of the ancient Mayan priests and mathematicians, who designed and built the great monuments and developed a calendar more accurate than the Gregorian.

✗Chichén Itzá is worth the three-hour drive from Cancun. The most famous and complete of the ancient ceremonial sites, it was built by the Toltecs (an invading Indian group) on top of a smaller Mayan site. The 1,000-year-old temple complex includes burial grounds, sacrificial altars, and royal ball courts. Plan to get here early in the day, and wear low-heeled shoes and sunscreen.

The most impressive monument at Chichén Itzá is the **Temple of Kukulcan**, which is a perfect calendar as well as an engineering feat. The 91 steps to the top of each of the pyramid's four faces, plus the one step to the temple at the top, add up to 365, the number of days in a year. Fifty-two panels decorate the sides of the pyramid, one for each year of the Mayan century. The 18 terraces equal the 18 months of the Mayan year. During the spring and fall equinoxes, the sun creates a shadow on one face of the wall that resembles a serpent, the sign of the god Kukulcan.

Although the climb is steep, the view from the top of the pyramid makes it worthwhile. Ascending is actually easier than descending the tall, narrow steps. The easiest way to get back down to the ground is to walk sideways, holding onto the chain provided for that purpose. Experts say this is the correct way to descend anyway, as it is considered impolite to turn your back on the gods.

Another impressive sight at Chichén Itzá is the ceremonial ball court, used by the Mayans to play a game that was a cross between soccer and basketball. The goal was to get the ball through one of two hoops placed 25 feet high on opposing walls. The winning captain was beheaded as a sacrifice to the gods. However, before he was dropped down the 390-foot sacrificial well (which you can still see), the sacrificee was given hallucinogenic drugs and wine. And he was consoled by the fact that he was guaranteed a place in heaven.

To get to Chichén Itzá from Cancun, you can rent a car and drive your-self (but be careful of villagers and their animals, who cross the country roads with abandon). Or you can hire a taxi and a guide to take you there. Another alternative is to join a bus tour at your hotel. Beer and Coke are sold on the bus for a pittance.

The walled city of **Tulum** is on a cliff overlooking the sea. The piles of ancient rock are brightened by flowering trees. Parts date back to A.D. 500. Climb the steep, narrow steps to the top of the main pyramid, the **Temple of the Descending God**. Below, white-sand beaches stretch in either direction. Human sacrifices were once pushed over this cliff. Note the carving of the upside-down god. Some say it is the god of rain; others claim that it is a being from outer space descending to earth.

You can arrange a bus from Cancun to Tulum and Xel-Ha. Tours to Tulum and Chichén Itzá can be arranged from Cozumel.

The largely uncharted city of Cobá, about 30 miles west of Tulum, boasts the tallest pyramid in the Yucatan—at 1,150 feet, it is twice the height of El Castillo at Chichén Itzá. Once it has been completely studied, Coba may prove the most important Mayan city of all. It once had as many as 40,000 inhabitants, and more than 7,000 stone structures have survived. Carvings of the Descending God can be seen on the temple that tops the pyramid. From the summit you can see Cobá's five lakes, surrounded by jungle.

Uxmal is the best preserved of the Mayan cities on the Yucatan Peninsula. It's also one of the prettiest, with reservoirs rather than wells. Built and abandoned three times between A.D. 325 and A.D. 900, it boasts richly carved temples. One of the most intriguing buildings here was named the **Nunnery** by conquistadors, who knew little about the Mayans. Some scholars believe the name is almost correct, because the building housed priestesses, who would be sacrificed to the god Chac. Others say it was just an administrative center.

The ancient Mayan ways also linger in **San Cristobal de las Casas**. The former colonial capital is located 6,500 feet high in the mountains of the southern state of Chiapas. Besides market days, the best times to visit San Cristobal and its mountain villages are during religious festivals. Masked dancers perform to traditional music played on harps, flutes, and drums; farces are acted out mocking the forces of evil; and horse races and fireworks are staged. (Keep in mind that hotel prices are increased during these festival times. And you must make reservations at least a couple of weeks in advance.)

Major festivals are staged during Carnival and Holy Week. In addition, the following holidays are observed: **Martes (Tuesday) of Carnival**, when Chamula (a neighboring village to San Cristobal de las Casas) enacts a purification ritual, with dancers leaping over open fires; **July 22nd to July 24th**, when Chamula celebrates the festival of its patron saint, San Juan, in ceremonies that are both Catholic and Mayan; **July 24th to July 25th**, when San Cristobal honors its patron saint with a torchlight parade; and **Dec. 30th to Jan. 1st**, when ceremonies are held to mark the changing of village officials.

The best place to stay in San Cristobal de las Casas is the **Posada Diego de Mazaiegos**, *Calle Ma. Adelina Flores 2; tel. (52)967-81825*. All the rooms have fireplaces, and the hotel is located just off the main plaza.

A good starting point for more information on the Mayan civilization and how to visit their ruins is at *www.cancunsouth.com*.

A fisherman's paradise

Fishing is fabulous in the Mexican Caribbean. From March through mid-July, the sailfish run. From May through early June, the bonito and dolphin run. From May through September, it's the wahoo and kingfish. And barracuda, bluefin, mackerel, white marlin, and grouper can be fished year-round.

The best place to arrange a charter is in **Puerto Juarez**. Isla Mujeres also has good rates—you can arrange an all-inclusive deep-sea fishing expedition for four people through **Mexico Divers**. Rates are much higher in Cancun and Cozumel.

The world's best luthiers

Ask any guitar player in any Mariachi band where his guitar came from, and he won't tell you about Spain or Italy or New York—places you'd expect great guitar players to find great guitars. He won't even mention Guadalajara, the birthplace of Mariachi music. He'll simply say "Paracho" and expect you to understand.

The story goes that, in the 1600s, a Spanish priest named Vasco de Quiroga came to the Mexican state of Michoacan, high in the south-central mountains, to convert the local Purepecha Indian tribes and teach them economically viable crafts. He taught everyone in one village to make brass kettles. He taught another village to make tables and chairs. He taught yet another to cut stone arches and pillars. And he taught the people of Paracho to make guitars.

A cool story (and maybe it's even true) but, the fact is, today, the craftsmen of Paracho make some of the finest guitars in the world.

Paracho (30 minutes north of Uruapan) has a population of 30,000, including 2,000 luthiers, many from families who have been making guitars for three generations. Almost half the town's population earns a living in some way from guitar production. Everywhere you go, you see guitars hanging in shop windows; in the back streets, you find workshops in living rooms, old garages, and converted bodegas. Paracho is renowned for the handcrafted artistry that goes into its guitars. Craftsmen carve guitar components with ancient, trusted cuchillos, favored over modern equipment.

The result, at least from the best-known and highest-quality shops, is individual works of art composed of exotic woods like Brazilian jacaranda, German spruce, Indian rosewood (or the Mexican variety called Palo Escrito), Canadian cedar, and ebony from Sri Lanka and Cameroon. These instruments take weeks to complete and sometimes years to receive on back-order. Names like Francisco Navarro and Benito Huipe on a guitar can command thousands of dollars apiece. Good-quality Mariachi-style cutaways are easier to get and cheaper to own, as are dreadnaught styles, but these too are made one at a time by craftsmen who, in some cases, haven't had to refer to their stencils or cutting patterns for years. For them, it's all look, feel, and instinct.

Paracho produces about 80,000 guitars a year, ranging in price from $50 to $3,000 apiece. The best of these guitars are among the best in the world.

But the master builders of Paracho are an independent lot, unwilling to change the old ways or throw in with another shop to increase production or bargaining power. In a world where identical, precision-made, high-quality instruments can be produced by machine in a matter of days, many of the world's players are less inclined to wait for a one-of-a-kind guitar, preferring instead mass-produced models from Japan and China.

This means that more of Paracho's youth—the next generation of masters—are leaving to look elsewhere to make a decent living. If you're in the market for a unique, hand-carved guitar from a master craftsman, go to Paracho sooner rather than later.

The Best of
Nicaragua

Laguna de Apoyo: Nicaragua's best-kept secret escape

Laguna de Apoyo, or Lake Apoyo, is a four-and-a-half-mile-wide caldera—a crater formed when the Apoyo volcano exploded about 23,000 years ago during what was probably Nicaragua's strongest volcanic explosion in recent geological history. The steep caldera walls rise more than 300 feet on the eastern rim, and up to 1,600 feet on the western rim. The deep lake was formed and is maintained by a series of underground springs. Nicaragua has the largest number of tropical volcanic lake systems outside of Africa, and Lake Apoyo is the largest and cleanest of these crater lakes.

The most healing waters

The clear, turquoise, mineral-dense thermal waters of the lake are said to heal everything from rheumatism to arthritis. Underground vents from the nearly extinct volcano give the lake a high sulfur and mineral content, which helps to keep its water pure.

The best scuba diving in Nicaragua

Laguna de Apoyo is reported to be the cleanest lake in all of Central America. With visibility of up to 100 feet, and colorful fish and underwater wildlife found in very few other places on Earth, it offers the best scuba diving in the country.

The best place to stay on Lake Apoyo

The best place to stay on the lake is a great little getaway on the water's edge, called the **Norome Resort**. The resort is made up of eight handsomely furnished thatched cottages. Each cottage has a view of the lake and a little garden in the bathroom, fed with sun by a large skylight. The resort has a bar on the water, a restaurant, a spa offering everything from mud baths to massages, a secluded Jacuzzi next to a man-made waterfall, hammocks, and wooden swings in the trees. For reservations or more information *tel. (505)882-4816* or *(505)886-7123; e-mail: edulat@yahoo.com.*

GRANADA — NICARAGUA'S GRANDEST CITY

Granada is a city with history and charm and a large central plaza surrounded by old Spanish colonial buildings. The city has little streets for meandering, neighborhoods for exploring, and lots of style. Granada has character. It feels like a small town; friendly and safe.

Granada also offers good restaurants, good hotels, a movie theater, four internet cafés, and decent shopping (there's a big computer supply store, for example).

Granada's best hotel

The **Hotel Colonial**, *tel. (505)552-7299*, located a half-block off the main square, is a beautifully designed and decorated place with 26 rooms, including suites and condos for longer-term stays. For as little as $50 a night (for a single room), you can enjoy relative luxury and a prime location. The large, comfortable suites go for $100 a night.

The best place to stay—on a budget

The **Oasis** is the first budget hotel in Granada where you wouldn't mind actually spending the night. It has 56 beds, air conditioning, a restaurant, a bar, a swimming pool, a patio, a garden, and is just two blocks from the main square. You can stay in one of the dormitories for just $6 a night. For $8, you can move up to a room with bunk beds and air conditioning. These rooms have just four beds each and private bathrooms.

The best deal is the one and only double room. This has cable TV, air conditioning, a fan, and a private bathroom, and rents for just $28 a night. This is the best value accommodation in the city.

The Oasis also has a kitchen, complete with a small pizza oven. Breakfast of eggs, gallo pinto, bread, tortilla, cheese, and coffee, tea, or milk, is just $1.48. Lunch of Hawaiian pizza is $2.82. And for dinner, the typical Nicaraguan dish of broiled meat, gallo pinto, plantains, salad, and cheese will cost about $4.59. Wash all this down with a local beer at 70 cents or a glass of Chilean wine for $1.48.

For reservations, contact Maria Morell, e-mail: *msmorell@hotmail.com*.

Granada's best restaurants

The best restaurant in town is the **Mediterraneo**, *Calle el Caimito*. It has a good menu, with daily seafood specials.

The second best is **Restaurante Dona Conchi's**, *Calle Caimito de la Alcadia*. Dona Conchi moved to Granada with Enriqueta (the woman who owns the Restaurante Mediterraneo) and Enriqueta's daughter in the early 1990s. The three opened the Mediterraneo together. About a year-and-a-half ago, Dona struck out on her own and opened what is the second best restaurant in the city. The menus are very different. Mediterraneo, despite the name, features more typical Nicaraguan specialties. Dona's restaurant specializes in Mediterranean fare.

Conchi's is distinguished, though, primarily by the bullet holes in its walls. Legend has it that William Walker was captured here and stood up against these walls for execution. He stood just 5'2" tall. The marksmen ordered to carry out his execution, evidently, didn't allow for this fact. Or maybe they were just very bad shots. The holes their bullets left are all at the six-foot mark or higher. William handily escaped and fled. We sat at the table just beneath the bullet holes and the plaque that tells the story.

The **Estrada** restaurant, just off the main square, may be the most elegant spot in all Nicaragua, with 16-foot-high hardwood ceilings, ornate chandeliers, and a long garden patio.

Nicaragua's Running of the Bulls

Nicaragua has all the festivals of Mother Spain, including a "Running of the Bulls" event, which takes place in Granada. Both countries share the same date for this occasion: August 12th. The original festival was to mark the day in mid-August when the evenings began to get darker.

In Nicaragua it is referred to as the "Virgin of August Celebration." A half-dozen bulls are released at the cemetery (in consideration of the slow runners) where hordes of people on foot, and a dozen or so on horseback, chase them through the town to the lakefront.

This is not Spain's Pamplona by any stretch of the imagination. The bulls are timid and look frightened to death. Some wander off and run through houses and restaurants.

THE BEST VIEW IN MANAGUA

The **Coyotepe fort**, just five minutes from Managua airport, enjoys the best view in Managua. The fort was built in the 1800s, then used in the next century by the Sandinistas as a prison and, for a couple of years, as a place to train their secret police. (It's managed today by the Nicaraguan Boy Scouts. With the help of a flashlight, you can explore the dark, underground maze. Some cells in the interior of the underground sections of the fort are completely without access to light or air. Prisoners who singled themselves out in some way were kept in these cells and chained to the walls in a standing-up position, for up to a year at a time.)

Outside the fort, climb up onto the fort walls and you will be presented with a 360-degree view of Managua in one direction, Granada and its lake in another, and the mountains and volcanos of Nicaragua all around.

NICARAGUA'S FIRST RESORT

Two hours north of Managua, near the city of Matagalpa, is the **Selva Negra** resort (Spanish for *Black Forest*).

Owners Eddy Kuhl (a well-known Nicaraguan writer) and Mausi Hayn are descendants of a wave of German immigrants who came to Nicaragua in the late 1800s looking for gold, but found their fortune in coffee. When Eddy and Mausi built their German-style mountain lodge on an existing coffee plantation in the 1970s, it was Nicaragua's first real resort.

You can tour the coffee plantation and the impressive organic farm that goes with it. Bump down steep mountain roads, past orchards that produce shade-grown organic coffee, fields and pens filled with cows, pigs, chickens, and food crops, most of which end up on the restaurant menu. On the way back, you might even meet Baby, the ocelot that Selva Negra bottle-raised from a kitten after a guest left it behind.

The restaurant serves American, Nicaraguan, and German food, and the beautiful stone wedding chapel at the edge of the rainforest is available for weddings. All this is at Nicaraguan-style prices: rustic bungalows start at $50 a night, and you can get a five-bedroom chalet with its own wooded walkway for $150.

Selva Negra boasts an annual Oktoberfest celebration. If you're passing this way, it's easy to find: The resort's road marker is a wrecked tank left over from the civil war.

THE BEST OF PANAMA

BOQUETE: THE FRESH MARKET

At the weekend market in Boquete, farmers sell their just-picked vegetables, fruits, meats, and flowers from covered stalls. The papaya and other fruits are fresher than a French sailor, and good beef, chicken, and sausage are also a great buy at the market.

The adventure capital of Panama

You don't have to spend every day relaxing and soaking in the ambience that Boquete provides—this region is the adventure capital of Panama. There are hills for climbing, trails for horse riding, streams for fishing, and rivers for rafting.

The best bird watching

Flocks of elusive Resplendent Quetzal congregate, especially near wild fig and avocado trees, in Boquete, making it one of the best places in the world to go bird watching. These large, protected birds are among the most spectacular in the world. The males have emerald-green heads, bright-red bellies, and long and ostentatious green and white tails. In flight, especially, they are a glorious sight.

There are 944 different bird species that have been identified in Panama, more than in the United States and Canada combined. Of these species, 127 are migratory, and 23 are endemic. Panama's national bird is the harpy eagle, considered the most powerful bird of prey in the world. For birding tours, we recommend Willie Orates of **Nature Panama**, *tel. (507) 225-7325; e-mail: panabird@sinfo.net.*

SAN BLAS: PANAMA'S MOST
BEAUTIFUL BEACHES

San Blas is an autonomous region that stretches from the province of Colon to Colombia, along the Caribbean coast. It's governed by the Kuna Indian tribe and has been since the 1920s, when Panama agreed to the sovereign rule. Almost 400 islands make up the archipelago of San Blas. These islands, along with more than 125 miles of coastline, make up the Comarcade San Blas. Depending on whom you ask in this country, the region of San Blas is either the thorn in Panama's side, resisting development and modernization, or the most beautiful frontier, unspoiled and true to its traditions.

PANAMA CITY: THE CAPITAL CITY

The capital, and largest city, is the principal commercial center and lies on the Gulf of Panama, which opens onto the Pacific Ocean. The shopping, nightlife, and cultural events here rival that of any other large cosmopolitan city; Via España, the city's main shopping area, and the Avenida Central both offer a wide assortment of bazaars and boutiques.

The best cultural experience

The **Teatro Nacional** presents symphonies and plays, and the Panamanian Folkloric ballet presents dances and rituals of the native Kuna and Guaymi Indians. The **ATLAPA Convention Center** also hosts a plethora of concerts and conventions.

Three cities in one

Panama City is really three cities in one: Old Panama, Colonial Panama, and Modern Panama. In old Panama, you can explore the ruins of the old city, which was sacked and destroyed by the pirate Henry Morgan in 1671. Colonial Panama, with its narrow streets and decorative balconies, has been rebuilt. The San Jose Church's Golden Altar, the Flat Arch, the National Theater, the cathedrals, and las Bovedas promenade are all worth a visit.

The best fare

There are many restaurants to choose from in Panama City, and because Panama sits at the crossroads of the Americas, you can find just about every Central and South American cuisine here, plus a good mix of American and European fare. The best restaurants are **Café de Asis**, the most charming restaurant in the city, **Lemoncillo**, a sophisticated place with an excellent menu, and **Mi Ranchito**, which has a great view of the city.

Where to stay in Panama

There are many hotels to choose from in Panama City. Here we have it narrowed down to our favorite three: The **Bristol Hotel**, *tel. (507)265-7844; e-mail, bristol@psi.net.pa;* The **Continental Hotel**, *tel.(507)263-9999, e-mail: continental@hotelesriande.com,* a four-star hotel with an excellent location for business; and The **Caesar Park Hotel**, *tel. (507)270-0477, e-mail: info@ caeserpark.com,* a five-star hotel with nice facilities.

The best surfing and sailing

The popular surfing beaches are about 50 miles west of Panama City, on the Pacific coast. Try Rio Mar, near San Carlos.

At one of Panama's major yacht clubs you can find a crew prepared to go just about anywhere in the world…and a place to tie up your own boat. Try **Club de Yates y Pesca** (where you can also charter a boat through a group called Ocean Fun Tours), *tel. (507)227-0145;* the **Balboa Yacht Club**, *tel. (507)228-5794*, or the **Panama Canal Yacht Club at Cristobal**, *tel. (507)441-5882.*

If you want to join a tennis club, try **Club de Montana**, *tel. (507)230-1075* or *(507)230-1158.*

The best horse racing

The President Remon Racetrack in Juan Diaz has live racing every Thursday, Saturday, and Sunday.

Adventure-tour specialists

A handful of tour companies throughout the country specialize in adventure tours, such as climbing and repelling, surfing, diving, and river rafting.

- **Aventuras**, *tel. (507)263-3077.*
- **Iguana Tours**, *tel. (507)226-4516; e-mail: iguana@sinfo.net.*
- **Ecocircitos Margo Tours**, *tel. (507)264-4001; e-mail: ecocircuito@cwp.net.pa.*
- **Experience Panama Tours**, *tel. (507)264-4230; e-mail: eptours@ihpanama.com.*
- **Scuba Panama Tours, S.A.**, *tel.(507)261-3841; e-mail: rene.Gomez@wcom.com.*

THE BEST WAY TO GET AROUND

Driving in Panama City should only be attempted if you have mastered rush-hour Tokyo. Instead, take a taxi.

Few streets here have signs, so it's always helpful to have a guide. Plus, taxis are an inexpensive way to travel (with the exception of a government imposed tariff for transfers to and from the airport).

Here's a quick taxi-savvy guide:
- There are no meters and no initial charges; fares are determined on travel zones.
- Usually, the taxi will find you. Taxi drivers honk to indicate their availability and to attract potential fares' attention (and to indicate their appreciation of any remotely attractive female). But if you have to hail a taxi, lower your arm (yes, lower; not raise) and point to where you want the taxi to stop.

- Once the taxi has stopped, approach the passenger window and state your destination (a little prior practice with an accent helps). If you're male and the front passenger seat is available, take it; a female passenger should never sit in the front.
- If you really want to drive, make sure Sunday is your first day—the streets are mostly empty.
- After a while, you learn which signs and signals are respected and which are ignored; but if you see a transit police officer, be on your best behavior. (Not wearing your seat belt is against the law in Panama, as is talking on a cell phone while driving; both laws are enforced and carry a hefty fine.)

THE BEST OF
ARGENTINA

Argentina has historically suffered the curse of politics; Argentine politics have been characterized by cruel military dictators, pointless border disputes with Chile, civil strife, high inflation, corruption, and general instability. But the country still has its charms.

No country in the world is as naturally suited for farming as Argentina, the second-largest country in Latin America. It has more than a million square miles of territory. An extraordinary three-quarters of this is suitable for cultivation, and the topsoil is as much as a yard deep. Argentina is also an exporter of oil and gas (to Chile), and its mines offer an abundance of minerals.

THE RICHEST REGION

The richest 10% of Argentine terrain is in **La Pampa**, the only part of the country that is cultivated. (The Argentines are careful about protecting their lands and stingy about the areas they farm). La Pampa is a treeless plain of the central, temperate-climate zone, with richness other countries can only dream about.

BUENOS AIRES — THE PARIS OF THE POOR

Nobody lives in poverty with the style and flair of the Argentines; even in its impoverished state, Buenos Aires is as full of pizzazz as Paris itself. And Buenos Aires is a city of neighborhoods — that is what makes it so hospitable.

The **Plaza Dorrego**, in the heart of San Telmo, is Buenos Aires' answer to the Latin Quarter. Weekdays it is quiet, but on the weekends it is transformed into a bustling antiques market. Walk down avenida de Mayo to see the Casa Rosada, the pink presidential palace. It is here that thousands of workpeople cheered political leaders Juan and Evita Péron. The square is surrounded by monuments.

La Boca is the city's oldest Italian section. It is also the poorest neighborhood in the city, distinguished by its colorfully painted wooden houses. The heart of the neighborhood is a touristy walkway, **El Caminito**, where painters hang out. La Boca's side streets are jammed with bakeries and butcher shops.

The **Recoleta** neighborhood is one of the most desirable in **Buenos Aires**. Located in the northern part of the city, it is home to a fashionable residential area, elegant restaurants, deluxe hotels, fine museums, and some of the city's finest shops.

The best restaurants

Three of the best restaurants are **Milion**, *tel. (54)11-4815-9925*, **Central**, *tel. (54)11-4776-7374*, and **Sucre**, *tel. (54)11-4782-9082*. Milion used to be a gorgeous colonial-style mansion but it has been converted into a beautiful restaurant. Try to get a table upstairs.

Central is probably the hippest restaurant in Buenos Aires—it's where the celebrities go. It is ultra-modern and minimalist. Marble abounds. Try to get a table by the amazingly long sofa against the wall.

Sucre is probably the most popular restaurant in the city among rich Argentines. It has a log cabin feel about it and an immense bar. The food is great, too. And, of course, all the restaurants are incredibly cheap by Western standards—around $12 per person, including the wine.

Buenos Aires' best nightclub

The best electronic music club in Buenos Aires is **Clubland@Pacha**, *La Pampa and Avenida Costanera*, which takes place in a huge, pink-colored art deco building beside the River Plate, usually on a Saturday night. This club is not for the faint-hearted. It does not really get going until 3 a.m. (it finishes at 8.30 a.m.), and is heaving. It has a separate dance floor outside on the river, which is a bit more relaxed. You can also buy a table in the VIP area, where you can chill out with champagne and watch beautiful people dance around you. Many of the world's top DJs regularly perform at the club, which is rated by many DJs as their favorite club in the world.

The best antiques

The weekend market in Buenos Aires at **San Telmo's Plaza Dorrego** is an antique-lover's dream come true. Hundreds of vendors, many selling quality stuff, for a fraction of what you'd pay most anyplace else, gather here every Sunday from early morning until about 6 p.m.

Calle Defensa is packed with antique dealers; heirlooms of once-wealthy merchant families—their fine china, their brocade-upholstered chairs, and their fanciful English hunting prints—are for sale here. And the prices are so low that they would embarrass most antique dealers.

The best tango

The **San Martin Municipal Theater** is the best place in Buenos Aires to see a traditional tango.

The World's Best Destinations

THE WORLD'S SOUTHERNMOST SKIING

The southernmost skiing in the world is in **Ushuaia**, where you can choose from five small ski centers. It is a beautiful and safe place to ski. And its residents are gracious. But the best thing about skiing here is the cost. Lodging and dining are inexpensive.

THE BEST WATERFALL

Iguazu National Park has the most beautiful waterfalls in the world. Taller than Niagara Falls and twice as wide, there are over 275 individual cascades stretching across two miles of river. There are hundreds of butterflies as well as many other species of wildlife.

The **Iguazu River**, born high in Paraguay, crashes down multiple steep falls to the lower Iguazu at the border of Brazil and Argentina. The river winds up in the River Plate, just as Niagara Falls winds up in the St. Lawrence.

THE BEST OF BRAZIL

DELIGHT IS A WEAK TERM TO EXPRESS THE FEELINGS OF A NATURALIST WHO,
FOR THE FIRST TIME, HAS WANDERED BY HIMSELF IN A BRAZILIAN FOREST.
THE ELEGANCE OF THE GRASSES, THE NOVELTY OF THE PARASITICAL PLANTS,
THE BEAUTY OF THE FLOWERS, THE GLOSSY GREEN OF THE FOLIAGE, BUT
ABOVE ALL THE GENERAL LUXURIANCE OF THE VEGETATION, FILLED ME WITH
ADMIRATION. A MOST PARADOXICAL MIXTURE OF SOUND AND SILENCE
PERVADES THE SHADY PARTS OF THE WOOD. THE NOISE FROM THE INSECTS
IS SO LOUD THAT IT MAY BE HEARD EVEN IN A VESSEL ANCHORED SEVERAL
HUNDRED YARDS FROM THE SHORE; YET WITHIN THE RECESSES OF THE
FOREST A UNIVERSAL SILENCE APPEARS TO REIGN.

—Charles Darwin, 1832-1836

Brazil—the largest South American country—is watered by the Amazon rain forest, the largest in the world, and drained by the Amazon River, which carries more water than any other river in the world. The country's spectacular shoreline—which is lined with broad beaches and high mountains that circle the harbors—rivals any shoreline in the world. But Brazil has more to offer than spectacular scenery. It boasts the continent's most exciting city, Rio de Janeiro, and South America's largest industrial city, São Paulo.

Brazilians are beautiful, an exotic blend of Indian, African, and European ancestry. Half the population is under 25, adding to the beauty quotient, but creating social and economic problems.

A fun-loving nation, Brazil has the world's best Carnival, with glittering costumes, immense processions, mesmerizing music, and gala balls. And year-round, its beaches boast the world's most scantily clad sun worshipers.

Restaurants in Brazil are excellent and cheap. Food supplies are abundant and varied, and the chefs are talented. Once you have tried the national dish, *feijoada* (a spicy black-bean stew), take advantage of the international cuisine. You can enjoy gourmet meals for next to nothing.

RIO: BRAZIL'S CULTURAL CENTER

Rio de Janeiro is Brazil's most cosmopolitan city. It is famous for its pre-Lenten Carnival, but it has much more to offer than simply a festival. A beautiful city surrounded by low mountains, Rio hugs Guanabara Bay, which is rimmed with palm-lined beaches and dotted with 84 islands.

Jet-setters from around the world soak in the sun all day and dance in the nightclubs all night.

The world's best carnival

People from around the world flock to Rio for its **Carnival**, a four-day extravaganza that concludes on Ash Wednesday. Poor Cariocas (residents of Rio) often put a year's savings into their costumes for the round of wild parties and balls.

Carnival officially begins when the mayor hands the key to the city to King Momo, the mock king of the festivities, who appears at all major Carnival events (parades, balls, costume contests) and orders everyone to have fun. King Momo is elected every year by the residents of Rio; the primary requirement is that he be very fat.

Samba schools are the focus of glittering processions beginning at 6 p.m. Sunday and Monday and continuing until noon on Shrove Tuesday. These enormous groups compete for prizes and go to great lengths to come up with the most fantastic and outrageous costumes and themes. The competition is always passionate, and at times it gets violent.

Traditionally, each of the city's samba schools (which number up to 5,000 members each) paraded through the streets of downtown Rio displaying their floats and gaudy costumes. A few years ago, the rowdy parades were taken off the streets and put into the **Sambo'dromo**, a stadium about half a mile long and about as wide as a street. It is the equivalent in spectacle to a half-time show at the Super Bowl, but the majorettes are topless. And the show lasts 17 hours.

If you can't get tickets to the Sambo'dromo, just walk through the streets. Bandstands are erected on street corners, where samba bands give impromptu concerts and people in skimpy costumes shake their stuff.

Rio's elite, disguised in fantastic costumes, attend elaborate balls. The best are at the Canecão nightclub, the Yacht Club, the Flamenco Football Club, La Scala, and Sugarloaf Mountain. Local nightclubs also arrange elaborate parties, with samba bands and costumes.

Tickets for Carnival balls and parades go on sale in November and sell out early.

The most exotic New Year's celebration

As colorful as Carnival—but less known—is Rio's New Year's celebration. Just before midnight, thousands of white-robed worshipers carrying candles gather on the city's beaches to make offerings to the goddess of the sea, Lemanja. At midnight, fireworks go off, and crying, singing worshipers rush into the ocean carrying flowers and gifts for their deity.

The best view from Christ's feet

Rio's best-known landmark is the huge statue of **Christ the Redeemer**, overlooking the harbor from the top of Corcovado Mountain, 2,250 feet above sea level. A little train takes you to the statue.

From this vantage point on the top of the mountain, the view of the harbor is spectacular, particularly as the day turns to dusk, then dark, and the city below begins to glitter against the aquamarine blue of the sea. Have a drink in the café at the top of the mountain.

Another beautiful view of Rio is from the top of **Pao de Açucar** (Sugarloaf Mountain), a rock rising 390 feet above the bay. A cable car makes the trip from 8 a.m. until 10 p.m.

Rio's best garden

Rio's **Jardim Botânico** (Botanical Garden) has 7,000 varieties of tropical plants. Palm-lined paths wind their way past ponds covered with lily pads.

Rio's best museum

The **Quinta da Boa Vista** (National Museum), *Sao Cistovao*, in the former Imperial Palace, displays objects that once belonged to the royal family, along with the Bendego meteorite, one of the largest ever grounded on earth, an impressive Amazon Indian display.

The lawns, flowerbeds, and hothouses that surround the Quinta da Boa Vista can be explored by horse-drawn carriage.

Brazil's best books

The **National Library**, founded in 1810, has a collection of one million volumes in various languages, including a parchment copy of the Guttenberg Bible (one of four existing) and an astonishing collection of Hebraica.

The most authentic neighborhoods

Lapa, an old, slightly crumbling neighborhood, has narrow streets with wrought-iron balconies. The old townhouses have been converted into shops and pensions.

Santa Teresa, near Corcovado Mountain, gives a glimpse of Rio as it was at the turn of the century. Beautiful old houses, completely neglected, flank cobblestoned avenues shaded by broad, ancient trees. The neighborhood has no restaurants or nightclubs. Nor has any visible effort been made to restore or preserve this lovely part of the city.

Brazil's best cuisine, two hours north of Rio

Two hours north of Rio are the beaches of **Buzios**, the playgrounds of the elite. Called the jewel of the Brazilian Riviera, Buzios is filled with expensive boutiques. The pace is languid. People sleep until noon and dine in the wee hours of the morning. You can walk to the beach from anywhere in this little fishing village. Houses have no doors, and drums can be heard everywhere.

Buzios' cuisine is considered the finest in Brazil. An elaborate dinner for two at one of the town's best restaurants can cost more than a night in a local hotel. But it's worth it. Restaurants to try in Buzios include **Au Cherval Blanc** and **French Satyricon**, both of which serve local fish specialties and Italian food.

At Satyricon, you can enjoy a complimentary appetizer of eggplant roasted in garlic, quail eggs (hard-boiled), baked red and yellow peppers, and warm bread. Follow all of this with fresh marimba seasoned with hot red peppers you pluck from a plant on the table.

The world's largest stadium

Maracana Stadium, the world's largest sports arena, which holds more than 200,000 people, is the locale of Rio's wild soccer matches. The games are second in importance only to Carnival here. Buy a Cadierra Especial ticket—this allows you to enjoy the matches in an area fenced off from the mobs of raucous fans. Most hotels offer packages that provide transportation to and from the stadium as well as seats for the games.

Your best bet

The **Jockey Club** holds horse races Thursday nights and weekends. The most important is the Grande Premio Brasil, held the first Sunday in August. Everyone who is anyone shows up in fancy dress to watch South America's best horses run.

The best way to see the bay

The best way to see **Guanabara Bay** is to take a day or half-day cruise among its islands. Boats dock along avenida Nestor Moreira, next to the Sol e Mar restaurant. **Paqueta**, where Rio's lovers meet, is the loveliest island. Cars aren't allowed here, only bikes and carriages. A ferry to Paqueta takes about an hour-and-a-half; the hydrofoil takes about 30 minutes.

Rio's best restaurants

Rio has an endless list of outstanding eateries. The city's best gourmet restaurants include **Le St. Honoré**, *Meridien Hotel; tel. (55)21-275-9922;* **Le Pré Catalán**, *Rio Palace Hotel; tel. (55)21-521-3232;* and **Le Bec Fin**, *ave. Copacabana; tel. (55)21-542-4097.*

For authentic Brazilian food, the best restaurant in town is **Moenda**, *Trocadero Hotel Second Floor, ave. Atlantica 2064, Copacabana; tel. (55)21-257-1834.* The décor is not deluxe, but the food is scrumptious. Try the *feijoada completa.* Prices are moderate.

Ouro Verde, *tel. (55)21-542-1887*, attached to the hotel of the same name, is one of the best restaurants in Copacabana. The most romantic is **Copacabana**, *tel. (55)21-255-7070*, in the Copacabana Hotel. **Enotria**, *rua Constante Ramos; tel. (55)21-237-6705*, serves delicious northern Italian food.

In old Rio, try **Chale**, *rua da Matriz 54; tel. (55)21-286-9548*, or **Maria Thereza Weiss**, *rua Visconde Silva 152; tel. (55)21-286-3866*. Both are in old colonial houses full of Brazilian antiques.

In new Rio, try **La Tour**, *rua Santa Luzia*, a revolving restaurant at the top of the Aeronautical Club building near the U.S. Consulate.

Rio also has good barbecue restaurants, called *churrascarias*. These all-you-can-eat places serve grilled meats—pork, beef, marinated chicken livers—with salad and rice. The food is inexpensive and usually superb.

The best *churrascaria* is **Gaucha**, *rua Laranjeiras 114; tel. (55)21-285-5767*. *Porção Barra; tel. (55)21-521-0999*, past São Conrado, is also good.

Rio's best seafood is served at the **Sol e Mar**, *ave. Nestor Moreira 11; tel. (55)21-295-1896*, in Botafogo, which has a view of the bay. A string quartet entertains as you enjoy your South Atlantic fish.

The city's best Portuguese restaurant is the elegant **Antiquarius**, *rua Aristides Espindola 19; tel. (55)21-294-1496*, in Leblon. Inexpensive Portuguese food is served at a no-frills eatery called **Adegao**, *Campo de São Cristovão; tel. (55)21-580-7288*. A lunchtime favorite is **Penafiel**, *rua Senhor dos Passes; tel. (55)21-224-6870*.

Rio's best hotels

Rio's most inviting hotel, in a glitzy modern way, is the **Meridien**, *Copacabana; tel. (55)21-275-9922*. Other first-class hotels include the **Rio Palace**, *Copacabana Beach; tel. (55)21-521-3232*; **Caesar Park**, *Ipanema; tel. (55)21-287-3122*; and **Marina Palace**, *Leblon; tel. (55)21-259-5212*.

The **Copacabana Palace**, *ave. Atlantica 1702; tel. (55)21-255-7070*, is the grand old lady of Rio's hotels, the first major hotel built on Copacabana Beach. Until recent years, jet-setters from around the world returned here year after year. However, despite cosmetic surgery, the old girl can't match the attractions of newer hotels on Copacabana and Ipanema beaches, and the Copacabana Palace is not as popular as it once was.

The **Ouro Verde Hotel**, *ave. Atlantica; tel. (55)21-542-1887*, is on the beach in Copacabana and has a good French restaurant. It used to be the best hotel in Rio, with the atmosphere of a genteel British men's club. But it too has become a bit shabby.

The best budget hotel

The centrally located **Carlton**, *tel. (55)21-259-1932*, is recommended as a budget hotel, but it doesn't scrimp on service.

The hottest nightlife

Rio residents don't sit down to dinner until 9 p.m. or so. By the time dinner is finished, it's nearly 11 p.m. This is when the city's nightspots wake up.

The most popular *discotecas* (discos) are Hippopotamus, Caligula, and Help. They are like discos everywhere, with loud music, light shows, and lively crowds. Many are organized as private clubs; you need to make a reservation, and in some cases a reference, to get in. Ask the concierge at your hotel to make a reservation for you.

Rio's *gafieiras* are a better bet if you want to see authentic Brazilian nightlife. Thee large dance halls draw people of all ages. The places have little or no décor, the bands vary in quality, and the crowds are noisy. But the noise is distinctly Brazilian, and the crowds are charmingly unsophisticated. One of the more sophisticated *gafieiras* is **Asa Branca**, *ave. Meme de Sa 17; tel. (55)21-252-0966*, a fairly new dance hall owned by one of Rio's most energetic entertainment moguls, Chico Recarey.

One of the best clubs for live entertainment is **Karaoke de Canja**, *ave. Ataulfo de Paiza 375; tel. (55)21-511-0484*.

You'll find a more sophisticated piano bar and a live band at **Café Un, Deux, Trois**, *rua Bartolomeu Mitre 123; tel. (55)21-239-0198*. **Biblos**, *ave. Epitacio Pessoa 1484; tel. (55)21-521-2645*, is a good place to dance.

If you're in the mood for a quiet evening, try the **Bâteau Mouche Bar**, next to the Sol e Mar. The tunes date back to the 1940s, and there's dancing, of course.

For a Las Vegas-type show, take in the spectacles at **Plataforma**, *rua Adalberto Ferreira 32; tel. (55)21-274-4022*, or **Scala Rio**, *ave. Afranio de Melos Franco 296; tel. (55)21-239-4448*.

SOUTH AMERICA'S MOST MODERN CITY: BRASILIA

Brasilia is a futuristic fantasy situated in the middle of the great central plain of Brazil and the white buildings of the city are striking, as they are set against the rich red soil. The capital is laid out in the shape of an airplane, with government buildings down the middle and residential and commercial areas along the two wings.

Brasilia came into existence in 1960. President Juscelino Kubitschek decided the nation's capital should be in the center of the country, rather than on the coast, and began construction of the city, which took three years to complete. He drew on the talents of urban planner Lucio Costa, who designed the city, and architect Oscar Niemeyer, who designed the city's major buildings.

However, the seeds of Brasilia were sown in the 1800s by St. João Bosco, who wrote in his memoirs, "Repeatedly a voice spoke out, saying:

When they come to excavate the mines hidden in the breasts of these mountains (between the 15th and 20th parallels), here the promised land will arise, giving forth milk and honey. It will be of unimaginable riches, and this will happen before the second generation passes...before 120 years go by."

Bosco's vision inspired Brazilian leaders to stipulate in the constitution of 1891 that the new capital should be established in the area between the 15th and 20th parallels, the location of modern-day Brasilia. The saint is commemorated at **Dom Bosco Church**, which has tall and brilliant blue stained-glass windows.

Brazil's tallest tower

Brasilia has one of the tallest telecommunications towers in the world, the 600-foot **Torre de Televisão**. Take an elevator to a platform at 225 feet or another elevator to a restaurant and bar, both of which offer an extensive view of the city.

The best place to begin

Catetinho, the temporary residence of President Juscelino Kubitschek in 1956 and Brasilia's first building, is the best place to begin a tour of the city. The white, clapboard house on stilts was built in 10 days for the former president, when he and city planners were plotting the city's future. It is modestly furnished, with a bed and a plain wooden table, around which city planners gathered.

Brazil's ultramodern cathedral

The architecturally noteworthy **National Cathedral** is an ultramodern structure designed in the shape of the crown of thorns. A statue of St. Peter is suspended from the roof in the Passage of Reflection, which leads to the underground nave. A pool, which surrounds the concrete building, is reflected in the nave's glass roof panels, giving the interior an airy brightness.

The prettiest palace

One of Brasilia's most famous buildings is the **Itamarati Palace**, which rises out of the beautiful water gardens that hold the city's well–known sculpture, the Meteor. The reflecting pool is filled with yard-wide lily pads called Victoria Regia, native to the Amazon. Inside the palace is a splendid collection of Brazilian art, including works by Portinari, the country's premiere painter.

Brazil's boldest architecture

The **National Congress Complex** looks more like an outer-space colony than a political center. The long, narrow building is reached by ramp-like staircases and topped by two eggshell domes (one inverted) known as the cup and saucer. The building glows at sunset.

The **Planalto Palacio** is the city's most graceful building, its roof supported by marble arches, its façade mirrored in a reflecting pool. Next door, a man-made waterfall washes the face of the Justice Ministry.

The **Palacio dos Arcos** (the Ministry of Foreign Relations) is considered the city's most beautiful building.

The president's house

The **Palacio da Alvorada**, the home of the president of Brazil, is outside town on Lake Paranoá. The sumptuous building has glass walls, rosewood floors, and panels of gilded tile. To visit the palace, which is open to the public most weekends, obtain a pass from the **Palacio do Planalto**, *Praça Dos Tres Podres, Brisilia DS, 70150; tel. (55)61-211-1200*.

Modern masterpieces

Brasilia is known for its modern sculptures, displayed outdoors in public places. The most famous is the **Meteor**, at the Itamarati Palace, which was mentioned above. Also important are the **Warriors**, in front of the Planalto; the **Water Nymphs**, at the Alvorada; and the **Mermaid**, in front of the Navy Ministry on the Esplanada dos Ministérios.

Brasilia's best dining

The *churrascarias* along the lake are good places to eat. The best is **Churrascaria do Lago**, *tel. (55)61-223-9266*.

Good international cuisine is served at the **Piantella**, *tel. (55)61-224-9408*, which has live music.

First-class hotels

Brasilia's best hotel is the first-class **Nacional**, *Setor Hoteleiro, Sul Lote 1; tel. (55)61-321-7575*, which has a lovely central view of the government buildings.

Hotel Das Americas, *Setor Hoteleiro, Sol 4, Building D; tel. (55)61-321-3355*, in the southern hotel area, is air-conditioned. Rooms are supplied with refrigerators.

Brazil's best theater

The **Teatro Nacional** (National Theater) in Brasilia has one of the most flexible modern stages in South America, as well as two auditoriums. The building was designed to look like an elongated Aztec pyramid.

SÃO PAULO: SOUTH AMERICA'S RICHEST CITY

São Paulo, a city of nearly 20 million, is the industrial center of Brazil and the largest city in South America. It employs the largest labor force in

Latin America, with more than 400,000 workers, and it has the highest standard of living in Brazil. Also, it has the largest number of Japanese in the world outside of Japan.

South America's biggest cathedral

The **Catedralo Mertropolitano of São Paulo** is the largest cathedral—and one of the most beautiful in South America. The vaulted neo-Gothic structure holds 8,000 worshipers and dominates the **Praça da Sé** (Cathedral Plaza), where fountains gurgle and Paulistas gather. The cathedral's extensive underground crypt contains the remains of past ecclesiastical figures.

South America's biggest zoo

The **São Paulo Zoo**, *ave. Miguel Estefano 4241, Auga Funda*, expands across 204 acres and is home to about 2,700 animals of 366 species. The zoo is open daily from 9 a.m. until 6 p.m.

After visiting the zoo, you may find interest in stopping by the **Jardim Botanico** just down the street to view the 35,000 orchid species displayed here. The gardens are open Tuesday through Sunday from 9 a.m. until 5 p.m.

South America's best art gallery

The **Museu de Arte de São Paulo**, *tel. (55)11-251-5644*, has a collection of Western art from the Gothic Age to the present, the only such collection in South America. The museum has Raphael's *Resurrection*, painted when the 16th-century artist was just 17, a Rembrandt self-portrait, and 13 works by Renoir.

The closest thing to Japan in the Americas

São Paulo's **Liberdade**—south of Praça da Sé along Praça da Liberdade and rua Galvão Bueno—is the closest thing to Japan in the Americas. Entered through red lacquer gates, it has tranquil rock gardens, Japanese grocers, and herbal-remedy stores. To realize the importance of São Paulo's Japanese population (nearly 800,000 strong), visit the **Museu da Imigração Japonesa** (Japanese Immigration in Brazil Museum), where exhibits explain the 85-year history of Japanese immigration.

The world's second-best religious art museum

São Paulo's **Museu de Arte Sacra** (Sacred Art Museum), is second only to the Vatican when it comes to collections of Western religious art. Room after room of the museum is filled with carved altars, gold altarpieces, statues, and paintings.

The top sights

Ibirapuera Park was built for São Paulo's fourth centennial celebration. Inside the grounds is an exact reproduction of Japan's Katura Palace. Willows border the lakes, and eucalyptus groves scent the air.

Casa do Bandeirante, *Praça Monteiro Lobato*, is an 18th-century pioneer house preserved for tourists. You can see firsthand the Spartan lifestyles of early settlers, who slept in hammocks and used trunks as tables. On the grounds are oxcarts and three mills for sugarcane and corn. The house is open Tuesday through Sunday 9 a.m. until 5 p.m.

You can see how Brazil's wealthier colonists lived at the **Museu da Casa Brasileira** (Brazilian Home Museum), *ave. Brigada Faria Lima 774*. Built in 1945, the mansion contains photos and sketches of early homes, as well as antique furniture and religious pieces.

In the old center of town, near the financial district, several churches and a Byzantine Franciscan convent still stand, as well as São Paulo's oldest building, a Jesuit chapel built in 1554.

Another attraction (so to speak) is the largest snake farm on the continent, the **Instituto Butantã**, *ave. Vital Brasil 1500*, where venom is collected for medicinal uses.

The best restaurants

O Profeta, *Alameda Dos Aicas 40; tel. (55)11-549-5311*, serves food from all over Brazil. The specialties are fish and *feijoadas*.

The best place in São Paulo for *feijoadas* is **Bolinha**, *ave. Cidade Jardim 53; tel. (55)11-852-9526*, a popular place that usually has long lines (reservations not accepted). Have a drink at the bar and people watch while you wait.

If you tire of Brazilian food, you can have a good French meal at **Marcel's**, *rua Epitácio Pessôa 98; tel. (55)11-257-6968*. The restaurant is closed on Sunday. **Terraço Italia**, *ave. Ipiranga 344; tel. (55)11-257-6566*, has a spectacular view of the city as well as good food.

São Paulo also has good *churrascarias* (**Rodeio**, *rua Haddock Lobo 1498; tel. (55)11-883-2322*, which has a great cowboy atmosphere, is the best) and a great many ethnic restaurants. The city's Oriental section is five square miles and loaded with Asian restaurants. To the east is an area of typical Italian restaurants run by descendants of immigrants who came to Brazil to grow coffee and wine.

The best beds

Maksoud Palace, *Alameda Campinas 150; tel. (55)11-251-2233*, is the most luxurious hotel in São Paulo, with a swimming pool, a sauna, squash courts, eight restaurants, and a Scandinavian smorgasbord. Top floor rooms have a maid, butler, and valet service. Built in 1979, it is a 22-story structure surrounding an atrium, where a one-ton sculpture by the Brazilian artist Toyota hangs.

The chicest hotel in São Paulo is **Caesar Park**, *rua Augusta 1508;*
tel. (55)11-285-6622, surrounded by lush vegetation. The lobby is an elegant
place for a rendezvous. Breakfast is served in the garden, and at night a
band plays in the rooftop bar.

The **Mofarrej Sheraton**, *Alameda Santos 1437; tel. (55)11-284-5544*, is a
five-star European-style luxury hotel.

The **São Paulo Hilton**, *ave. Ipiranga 165; tel. (55)11-256-0033*, has a pool, a
sauna, four restaurants, five bars, and jewelry and gift stores. But it is
touristy and near the red-light district.

The **Othon Palace Hotel**, *rua Libero Badaro 190; tel. (55)11-239-3277*,
is reasonably priced and conveniently located in the center of the
financial district.

SALVADOR — CENTER OF VOODOOISM

Salvador de Bahía is the center of the **candomblé** cult, created by
African slaves who were forced to practice Catholicism but wanted to preserve their own religion. The slaves merged their gods with Christian saints
and biblical characters and worshiped both. The deity of lightning, Chong,
for example, was combined with St. Barbara, also associated with lightning.
And Iemanja is another name for the Virgin Mary. Candomble has become
an accepted part of Roman Catholicism. Salvador has 166 churches and
4,000 candomblé *terreiros* (temples).

You can attend a candomblé ceremony (as long as you don't bring a camera or cross your hands or feet, which is considered unlucky). The god to be
honored at the ceremony has a special costume, the colors of which are
donned by candomblé followers. Men and women are seated opposite each
other. As the ritual progresses, worshipers fall to the ground in convulsions,
their bodies apparently possessed by the spirits being conjured up. They
speak in voices completely unlike their own.

Most ceremonies begin at 8:30 p.m. and continue until 11 p.m. or midnight. Another ritual dating back to the days of slavery is the **capoeira**, a
dance-fight. This strange and beautiful performance was begun by slaves
who, forbidden to fight, learned to disguise their aggressions in the graceful
form of a dance.

Traditional Christianity is also colorful in Salvador. Celebrations of
regional Catholic holidays, including the Procession of Our Lady of the
Seamen, the Procession of Bonfim, and the Feast of the Second of July,
are elaborate.

The best place to enjoy Carnival

Carnival is even more colorful in Salvador than in Rio, although it is less
known. And it is longer, beginning one month before Lent. Participants pay

homage to Iemanjá, the goddess of the sea, and don the *mortalha*, a costume made of bed sheets. Groups, called *afoxes*, dance to drums and throw a powder called *efu*, which is made from the horns of sheep and supposedly possesses mystical powers.

The most beautiful church

Igreja da São Francisco, *Praça Pae. Anchieta 1; tel. (55)71-243-2367*, is one of the most beautiful baroque churches in the world. Built in the 18th century by Franciscans, the interior walls are covered with gold leaf and hand-carved rosewood. Portuguese stone was imported to construct the church and Portuguese tiles to illustrate the life of St. Francis. Men can visit the monastery next door, but women can only peer through the door.

Salvador's cathedral, **Terreiro de Jesus**, is massive and also covered in gold leaf. The Jesuits built the cathedral from 1657 to 1672, before they were ousted from Brazil. It is closed to the public during Carnival.

The most popular church in the city is the **Igreja de Nosso Senhor do Bonfim** (Church of Our Lord of the Good Ending), *Adro do Bonfim*. It is dedicated to Oxalá, the father of candomblé gods and goddesses, who is also known as Jesus. Worshippers often wear silver and white, the colors of Oxalá. A tiny room in the back of the church contains creepy testimonials to the power of faith—wax castings of injured or sick human body parts that have been miraculously cured.

A beautiful little Carmelite church, **Largo do Carmo**; *tel. (55)71-243-1935*, founded in 1585, has been made into a museum that displays religious objects in precious metals and stones and an exhibit explaining candomblé.

Igreja da Boa Viagen (Church of the Good Voyage), *Boa Viagen Beach; tel. (55)71-226-1800*, is known for its 18th-century Portuguese mosaics.

The oldest church in Salvador is **Igreja e Mosterio de Nossa Senhora da Graça**, *Largo da Graça; tel. (55)71-247-4670*. The 18th-century church includes part of a monastery built in 1557.

Igreja e Convento de Santa Tereza, *rua do Sodré 25; tel. (55)71-243-6310*, was built in the 17th century for the Shoeless Carmelites' Order of St. Teresa. It has been restored and made into the Museu de Arte Sacre. The museum is open Tuesday through Saturday 10 a.m. until 11:30 a.m. and 2 p.m. until 5:30 p.m.

The best shopping

Mercado São Joaquim, *avenida Jequitaia*, is the largest market in Salvador, selling everything from vegetables to magic herbs. You can find great bargains. The market is open from 6 a.m. to 6 p.m. daily except Sundays, when it closes at 1 p.m.

Mercado Modelo, *Praça Cairu*, is a great place to shop for gifts. Choose from silver and rosewood charms to ward off the evil eye, or you can buy *balagandãs*, little silver fruits once given to slave women who shared their masters' beds.

Salvador's best food

In addition to religion, African culture also has influenced local cuisine, most of which you'll find fantastic, some of which you'll find strange. It is characterized by creoles and jambalayas, spicy and served with rice. The primary ingredients are pork, seafood, and coconut.

Solar do Unhão, *avenida do Contorno; tel. (55) 71-321-5588*, is in an old stone sugarcane factory washed by the Bahía de Todo los Santos (Bay of All Saints), which gives Bahía its name. Brazilian politicos and jet-setters come here.

Casa da Gamboa, *rua Gamboa de Cima 51; tel. (55)71-321-9776*, is located in a colonial house with antique furniture and lace curtains. Bahían specialties are served. The restaurant is closed Sundays.

The best hotels

Luxor Convento do Carmo, *Largo de Carmo; tel. (55)71-242-3111*, is the most charming hotel in town, occupying the former convent of a 16th-century Carmelite church. Guests sleep in nuns' cells, which have been outfitted with decadent modern additions, such as air conditioning, color televisions, and refrigerator-bars. The central courtyard has a large pool. Although the hotel is not near the beaches, it is a convenient base for exploring town. The hotel restaurant, **Forno o Fogão**, serves good local fare.

Quatro Rodas Salvador, *Farol de Itapuã; tel. (55)71-249-9611*, is located on the beach 40 minutes from town. It has an ocean-view rooftop nightclub, two excellent restaurants, a bar, tennis courts, a concert hall, and satellite television.

The best moderately priced hotels in Salvador are the **Praia Mar**, *ave. 7 de Setembro 3577; tel. (55)71-247-7011*, and the **Grande Hotel da Barra**, *rua Forte de Sao Diago 2; tel. (55)71-247-6011*. Both have pools and restaurants.

Niagara's superior

Iguaçu Falls, at the border with Argentina and even bigger than Niagara Falls, is a spectacular sight. One of the world's greatest waterfalls, it is on the Igauçu River, near its confluence with the Paraná River. Iguaçu Falls is actually made up of 275 separate falls, some very tiny. The biggest is Devil's Throat, 330 feet high. (*Igauçu* means *great waters* in the language of the local Guaraní tribes, who were once cannibalistic and the subject of the movie *Missionary*.)

To best see the falls, take the elevator down to the river's edge and walk out onto the platform that reaches into the middle. From this angle, you will see rainbows glimmering through the water.

Nearby is the great **Itaipú Dam** and the world's largest hydroelectric power complex.

THE WORLD'S LARGEST RAINFOREST: THE AMAZON

The world's largest rainforest and the world's largest river share the same name: the **Amazon**. The river flows 3,550 miles, is fed by 1,000 smaller rivers and tributaries, and is home to 2,000 species of fish (including the life-threatening piranha, with its razor-sharp teeth, and the candiru, which swims up human orifices and lodges itself in the body).

The forest is home to exotic animals, such as the tapir and anaconda. You'll see colorful parrots deep in the jungle. About 158 Indian tribes live in the Amazon. When they first visited the New World, Christopher Columbus and Sir Walter Raleigh both reported hearing Amazon warrior women, who, like the characters in Greek legend, lived independently of men.

Encompassing an area of 2.3 million square miles, the Amazon is over-whelming. The only practical way to see it is by boat—few roads make their way through the dense jungle. Don't expect to see all the Amazon's mysteries when traveling down the river—at points the river is so wide that the shore cannot be seen on both sides.

The best ways to see the Amazon

If you are not one for wilderness, cruises down the river are available with amenities such as staterooms, dining areas, and air conditioning. However, if you are willing to sleep in a hammock on deck, riverboats depart weekly and allow for truly enveloping yourself within the feel of the Amazon.

It is best to plan these adventures from the United States. For more information contact one of the following tour operators: **LADATCO**, *tel. (800) 327-6162; website: www.ladatco.com;* or **Brazil Nuts**, *tel. (800) 553-9959; website: www.brazilnuts.com.*

The best medical advice

Take proper medical precautions against malaria before and during a trip to the Amazon. Anti-malaria pills, such as Aralen (chloroquinephosphate, 500 milligrams), are available with a prescription. Yellow fever shots are also required for travel in the Amazon.

The best of Belém, gateway to the Amazon

Belém—the gateway to the Amazon—is a modern city with vestiges of its colonial past. Nearby, at the mouth of the Amazon, is **Marajo Island**, which is bigger than all of Denmark. Archeologists are studying burial

The World's Best Destinations

grounds on Marajo, where remnants of a long-lost people can be seen. The island also has huge buffalo farms and herds of wild buffalo, whose ancestors escaped the captivity of earlier farms. Buffalo hunts are organized out of Belém.

The most expensive hotel in town is the **Hilton**, *ave. Presidente Vargas 862; tel. (55)91-223-6500* (or from the United States *(800)445-8667*), across from the Praça da Republica.

A block away, on avenida Presidente Vargas, is the **Excelsior Grão Para**, *tel. (55)91-222-3255*, with small, rather drab, but inexpensive rooms. The **Hotel Regente**, *ave. Governador José Malcher 485; tel. (55)91-224-0755*, is an inexpensive three-star place.

Manaus: at the heart of the rain forest

If you want to really experience the Amazon, go to **Manaus**. The architecture in this town is a mix of European styles and modern wooden structures that is blended into the jungle surroundings. The waterfront market sells live animals and birds and voodoo and Indian artifacts. Because Manaus is a free port, you can buy imported merchandise for at least two-thirds less than elsewhere in Brazil.

Manaus is the best base for taking day excursions upriver into narrow tributary channels. **Capitania do Porto** (Office of the Port Captain), *rua Marques de Santa Cruz*, has information on boat trips, including several one- and two-day trips up the River Negro. Hunting and fishing safaris also can be arranged.

The best hotel in Manaus is the five-star **Tropical**, *tel. (55)92-238-5757*, on the beach of Ponta Negra outside town. It is well worth its price. The Tropical is situated on a 10-acre site, cleared from virgin jungle, running along the River Negro from Manaus. It has a private zoo. Architect Adolpho Linden designed the hotel to look like a Portuguese colonial country house.

You can arrange expeditions to explore the Amazon River and the jungle from the hotel. The hotel's restaurant is first-class, known for its superb regional fish dishes.

South America's most spectacular wildlife

Pantanal, a region similar to the Florida Everglades, is located south of the Amazon in western Brazil. Pantanal has the most spectacular concentrations of wildlife in South America, if not the world. A tremendous place for birding and fishing, Pantanal can be reached from either Campo Grande or Cuiaba via a jeep safari or riverboat trip. The same groups that arrange trips to the Amazon organize trips to Pantanal.

The world's best colored gems

Brazil is the world's major purveyor of colored gems. Aquamarine, topaz, amethyst, and turmaline stones are abundant, and they cost 20% to 25% less in Brazil than in New York, for example. Emeralds are also in great supply; settings and mountings of these gems are also tremendous bargains because of the low cost of labor.

Two good places to shop for colored gems are **H. Stern**, *tel. (55)21-259-7442*, and **Amsterdam Sauer**, *tel. (55)21-210-3123*—the largest dealers in Brazil. H. Stern offers free round-trip transportation from all major hotels in Rio to its headquarters in Ipanema. It also conducts tours of its lapidary, goldsmith workshops, and gem museum, the latter of which features a 42-pound aquamarine.

THE BEST OF CHILE

Chile offers a mild climate, friendly people, excellent wines, and some of the best skiing and white-water rafting in the world. In addition, the political situation is stable and the prices are low.

THE BEST PLACE TO EAT IN THE CAPITAL

In Santiago, eat at **Aquí Está Coco**, *La Concepcion 236; tel. (56)465-985*. The seafood is especially good. The adventurous should try the national dish, called *erizos*, a mixture of sea urchins that can be quite tasty when prepared in the right sauce.

THE MOST ARID PLACE ON EARTH

North of Antofagasta is the small port town to **Taltal**. It lies at the edge of the **Atacama Desert**, which covers the northernmost end of Chile. Reputedly the most arid place on earth, there are whole stretches of this desert where rain does not fall for years at a time. In the interior of the desert, nothing lives—no grass, no cactus, no lizards, and no birds. It is a fascinating landscape.

THE BEST SURFING

Surfers should head to **Pichilemu**, site of the 1990 international surfing and body board championships. Watching from a cliff overlooking the beach, you'll see row after row of breaking waves, as many as 12 to 15 at a time.

A primitive beach town, travelers should not expect much as far as accommodation goes. There are two hotels located in Pichilemu; the **Gran Hotel Ross** and the **Chile-Espana Hotel**, which can both be booked by e-mail: *hotels@gotolatin.com*.

THE BEST OF THE LAKE DISTRICT

Chile's Lake District is north of Puerto Montt and far south of Santiago. Although Spanish is the official language in the region, many here speak German.

The most ambitious trip through the Lake District is to pick up a car in Santiago and drive all the way south to Puerto Montt. However, many car rental companies tack on one-way drop-off charges in the hundreds of dollars.

The better option is to fly into Puerto Montt, pick up a car there, and drive a circuit around the region. The main highways are paved and in good condition. The secondary roads vary greatly in condition, from smooth and paved to dirt and gravel. All of the roads are well marked.

In addition to lakes, the Patagonia region is filled with volcanos and rivers. Given all the waterways and all the rain, the region is incredibly green, reminiscent of New Zealand.

The Lake District's best bed and board

An idyllic bed-and-breakfast in Puerto Montt, **Leuterio Ramirez 415**, *Puerto Chico, Casilla 301, Puerto Varas*, opened by two German sisters now in their late 60s, offers the best accommodation in the country. Breakfast is served in a large country kitchen; before the meal, the sisters hold hands and give thanks in German song.

CHILE'S BEST LUXURY HOTEL

The luxury hotels in the south of Chile cater to Chilean and Argentinian vacationers. The **Hotel Termas**, *Puyehue, Osorno*, situated on Lake Rupanco, has elegant rooms, piped-in Beethoven music, an Olympic-size swimming pool, hot baths, and mud massages.

SOUTH AMERICA'S LONGEST SKI LIFT

The longest ski lift in the country is 8,200 feet; it takes 25 minutes to complete the trip. And **Termas de Chillan**, *tel. (56)2-251-2685*, the slope on which the ski lift operates, offers 15,000 acres of challenging runs, with the most varied terrain and snow conditions in Chile. There are volcanos above, while below are thermal springs belching steam from the mountainsides.

(For more information on skiing in Chile, see Section 4: The World's Best Sporting Destinations.)

THE BEST WHITE-WATER RAFTING

Though it begins as an emerald green stream, the rapids on Chile's **Rio Bio-Bio** include some of the most challenging stretches of navigable cataracts anywhere in the world.

The Bio-Bio is 400 miles south of Santiago; getting to the river is an adventure in itself. You travel on a 50-year-old train, decorated with mahogany and brass, that rattles slowly south and inland, toward Patagonia and the river.

The river begins high in the Andes. Rafters and kayakers meet up with it a few miles from the source, in a little cowboy town called **Lonquimay**. At first the Bio-Bio is little more than a stream, an emerald-green trickle flowing through a valley of flowered meadows and pine scented forests.

The most difficult rapids

When the river approaches **Nireco Canyon**, the narrow path becomes cluttered with boulders. And a few miles downstream from the entrance to the canyon, rising straight up from eye level, is a curving wall of solid basalt. Here are the rapids for which the Bio-Bio is famous: the Milky Way, Lost Yak, Lava South, and Cyclops. The rapids are big and rocky, and to make navigation even more difficult, the force of the river pushes you constantly toward house-sized slabs of volcanic stone. This section of the Bio-Bio has taken its toll, and rafting here is not for the inexperienced. Two Bio-Bio rafters have drowned, and another was impaled on a 10-foot oar.

Flush Canyon, (named after the poker hand, because rafting here is a real gamble) with its five rapids, also offers challenging runs. After the **Valley of the Thousand Waterfalls**, the river's pace slows down.

THE OLDEST LIVING THINGS ON EARTH

Chile's magnificent evergreen giants, called *alerce*, are the largest trees in the Southern Hemisphere. These trees grow only in the temperate rainforests of South America, where the ecosystem is different than in a tropical rainforest. Temperatures are much cooler, the growing season is shorter, and plants and animals must be well adapted to harsh living conditions — or perish.

All of these factors combined to produce an ancient (old growth) forest, with groves of giant old trees, some of which exceed 13 feet in diameter. This is especially amazing when you realize that each tree grows only about one millimeter in diameter each year. These trees were here long before Columbus discovered the Americas.

THE BEST OF ECUADOR

Ecuador is located between Colombia and Peru on the Pacific coast of South America, directly on the equator (*Ecuador* is Spanish for *equator*.) It offers an endless summer, with year-round temperatures between 65 and 89 degrees Fahrenheit.

It also offers good and inexpensive health care; many of the doctors in Quito have been trained in the Unites States or West Germany, but they bill in Ecuadorian prices.

GUAYAQUIL — ECUADOR'S LARGEST CITY

Guayaquil, Ecuador's largest city, bustling with activity year-round, is also one of the country's major exporting ports. Ecuador is the largest exporter of bananas and the second-largest exporter of shrimp in the world.

Guayaquil's best hotel

The best hotel in Guayaquil is the **Hotel Oro Verde**, *tel. (593)4-327-999.* Your only complaint will be the temperature; the Swiss management seems to use air conditioning to recreate an Alpine environment. Otherwise, the deluxe hotel is a pleasure.

The best markets

The city's major supermarkets, **Supermaxi** and **Mi Comisariato**, carry abundant fresh fruits, vegetables, fish, and seafood. Excellent fresh milk and European-style yogurt are available from the farmers' Co-op called **Civeria**. And Top Cream makes gourmet ice cream. To shop at either of the two supermarket chains, you must become a member. Simply purchase a *cupo* card, which also entitles you to a 10% discount.

The best day-trips

Within a couple of hours of Guayaquil are **Salinas** and **Playas**, two good weekend getaways. Playas was once a fishing village; today it is a popular beach resort. Salinas is more modern; it, too, is highly regarded by locals for it beaches. It also offers some of the best fishing in the country; for tuna, black marlin, and billfish.

Buses run from Guayaquil to both Playas and Salinas several times a day.

Cuenca, the country's third-largest city, is four hours away by car. The narrow, winding streets here are filled with artesinia shops. And the Old

Town area has churches that date from the 16th and 17th centuries.

THE BEST OF QUITO

Quito, today the capital of Ecuador, has the feel of an 18th century colonial town; much of its colonial architecture remains. It has been called the "Florence of the Americas."

The country's best crafts

About two hours north of central Quito is the town of **Otavalo**, situated among several Indian villages. The handiwork of these Indian craftsmen is respected around the world. A market is held every Saturday morning, where you can purchase the Indians' handiwork, including woven goods and gold jewelry.

Ecuador's highest mountain—and greatest adventure

The best adventure in Ecuador is a climb up the country's highest mountain, the 20,670-foot **Chimborazo volcano**. Start your journey on horseback in Pogyos. As you make your way up the mountain, you can make camp at Quebrada Colorado (Red Gorge); Abraspungo; Chuquipogyo, on the volcano's eastern slopes; Riobamba; the Valley of Totoras, on the mountain's southern slopes, and by the Edward Whymper Refuge, at the foot of the Thielman Glacier on the western slopes, where the British mountaineer began the first successful ascent of the Chimborazo volcano in 1880.

En route, your trek will take you across the Valley of Rubbish, where local Indians gather ice from the glacier, wrap it in hay, and then sell it in the mountain villages. Between the Whymper Refuge and the trek's end back at Pogyos, you follow part of the ancient Inca road through El Arenal (the Great Sand Pit), a vast, high desert.

Riobamba, one of the towns along your trek, is the center of an extensive Indian region. The Spanish established their first capital nearby, and Riobamba became the repository of an extraordinary collection of religious paintings, sculpture, and goldwork. (All of it was saved from the 1797 earthquake that destroyed most of the original city.) Riobamba is also famous for its Sunday market, where you can shop for ponchos, shawls, leather goods, and baskets.

La Mirage—the best spa

Just an hour-and-a-half north of Quito, **La Mirage** is designed in its every detail to eliminate the harsh sensations of everyday life and induce a state of restful, re-energizing calm. Owners Michel Duer and Jorge Espinoza have designed La Mirage's restaurant, bar, spa, and 23 private rooms and suites with an enlightened blend of European and indigenous architecture, art, and decoration. Rooms cost $220 to $250, suites from $260 to $550, and spa treatments from $25 to $75. For more information, contact **La Mirage Garden Hotel & Spa**, in the United States and Canada *tel. (800)327-3573;* in Ecuador, *tel. (593)6-915-237; e-mail: mirage1@mirage.com.ec; website:www.larc1.com.*

The best almost-free lunch

Quito is home to the *almuerzito*, the "little lunch" restaurant where security guards and office staffers fill up on local dishes at prices that would make Ebenezer Scrooge dance a jig. There is one every few blocks.

One of the best is **Restaurant Milanesa**, near the corner of Andalusia and Salazar. Despite the name, there is nothing vaguely Milanese about the place. Six small tables and a tiny service counter completely fill the space, but it's clean and well lit. There is no menu—the waiter asks if you want the *almuerzo*, and you either say "yes" or ask for something specific. If they have it, they'll serve it.

An *almuerzo* of fresh pineapple juice, a large bowl of beef and vegetable soup, a plate of tripe and potato stew with a mound of rice, a fresh salad topped with avocado, and a tangerine for dessert comes to a grand total of $1.15.

THE BEST PLACE TO RELAX

Ecuador is an inexpensive, healthful, safe country; one of Latin America's most popular destinations, with a spring-like climate year-round; and a friendly, polite, laid-back population. But if you already live "away from it all" full-time, where do you go for a vacation? Ecuadorians go to **Baños**.

A four-hour bus ride ($4) from Quito, Baños is famous for its hot baths, fed by thermal springs from the base of active volcano Tungurahua (literally little hell). Although most visitors come here to relax, there's plenty to do.

You can hike Volcán Cotopaxi, or watch Tungurahua erupt nightly, white-water raft on class III and IV rivers (from $30 per day), bike (you can easily cycle downhill to the jungle's edge and return to town by bus for $5), horseride along the river (from $14 for a four-hour tour to $240 for an overnight excursion), or take a rain forest expedition (two to seven days; $40 to $50 per day with meals, accommodations, and tour guides included).

Hostales (small hotels) start at $3 per night and double rooms with private bath cost $8 to $12 per night. For longer stays, consider renting an apartment. Some of the town's apartments are shared with private rooms that join a common living room, kitchen, and bath. Expect to pay $4 to $5 per night, per person.

You can get breakfast here for $2, lunch for $3, and a full dinner costs less than $6.

After a few days in Baños, you'll feel more relaxed than you've ever felt before.

THE BEST OF PERU

Peru is physically spectacular, caught between the Pacific and the stupendous Andes Mountains. Covering 60% of the country is the Amazon basin, located to the east of the Andes; the gateway to this region is the former missionary town of **Iquitos**.

In the southern half of the country is Cuzco, a Peruvian region high up in the Andes. From there, the Incas ruled much of South America. Using this as a base, the archeologically inclined can head for the mountains and Machu Picchu.

The most hidden city

Several hours from Cuzco lies **Machu Picchu**. Surrounded by thick jungle, this is the only Inca city that the Spanish invaders never found (although they knew of its existence). This is hardly surprising. Even today, the road to Machu Picchu is not easy. You can make the trip, either by foot or by train, for the most breathtaking scenery in all Peru. On foot, the trip is rugged, taking you along the Inca Trail through the Andean hills—but the view is worth it.

The best tours

Organize your tour arrangements with **Highland Peru Tours**, *tel. (51)1-242-7189; e-mail: highland@ddm.com.pe*.

THE BEST OF CUZCO

Cuzco is a small city nestled in a valley against the rugged backdrop of the Andes Mountains. It was once the capital of the Inca Empire, and many Inca vestiges remain. The Spanish retained the superb stonework after conquering the country—they built their homes on top of the original Inca foundations.

The finest church in the Americas

Cuzco's primary site is its Renaissance cathedral, which many believe is the finest church in the Americas. It was built on the site of an Inca temple to the god of creation, Viracocha. Situated in the main square, it is a hub of activity. Here, the people of Cuzco sell everything from handmade turquoise jewelry to hand-woven wool belts. Also see Cuzco's 328 shrines, marvels of masonry built by Indian craftsmen. The shrines correspond to former Inca religious sites (the Inca calendar had 328 days).

PERU'S MOST FAMOUS JUNGLE CITY

Iquitos sprang up overnight in this rainforest nearly 100 years ago, and it garnered such fame that European opera stars risked shipwreck and dysentery to perform in this Amazon city. Today, it is again Peru's largest jungle city, with modern shops, restaurants, and hotels. And it is becoming increasingly popular as a tourist destination.

THE WORLD'S MOST REMOTE JUNGLE

The **Manu National Park** is surrounded by the finest pristine jungle anywhere in South America—if not the world. Comprised of more than five million square acres, the park is located in the Mother of God (Madre de Dios) department in southeastern Peru, at the end of one of the Amazon's tributaries. This park is so remote that two tribes of Peruvian Indians yet to be contacted by the outside world dwell within it. Their villages have only been seen by plane.

THE BEST OF URUGUAY

We believe Uruguay is one of the most attractive countries in South America—and it's certainly one of the most undiscovered. This tiny country, especially its capital city of Montevideo, is reminiscent of European countries. There is one important difference however—the cost of living is considerably lower here than in any country on the Continent.

The Uruguayan countryside is lovely—long stretches of open fields planted with corn and wheat and peppered with cattle and sheep. And because of the tropical climate, palm trees, cacti, rubber plants, and ferns grow wild along the roadsides—along with the famous pampas grasses.

The beaches along the **Costa de Oro** (Gold Coast), which extends from Montevideo to **Punta del Este**, the country's major seaside resort, are beautiful—sandy and clean. The water of the **Río de la Plata** (which is so broad you'll think it's an ocean) is shimmering silver (hence the name). The people are friendly and welcoming. Even strangers are greeted with an embrace and kiss on the cheek.

MONTEVIDEO, THE BEST PORT

Montevideo is a port city; in fact, it is considered the best port in Latin America. Large freighters from around the world dock here, then transport their cargo to smaller ships that can make it into the other, smaller Latin American harbors. The large sprawling city has a single hill, from which it takes its name. (Montevideo means literally *I see a hill*. This was the phrase uttered by the first Spanish explorers to see these shores.)

The best sites

In the center of downtown Montevideo, in the middle of **Plaza Independencia**, is the tomb of the country's national hero, General Josef Artigas, who led the fight more than 100 years ago for Uruguay's independence from Spain. The tomb is guarded 24 hours a day by soldiers in red, white and black uniforms. Try to visit in the morning for the changing of the guards.

The streets of the city are lined with vendors selling all manner of junk, much of it worthless. The one thing you should shop for on the streets is a *mate*. This is a gourd made into a cup. You use it, along with a silver straw, to drink *yerba*, a kind of herbal tea that originated among the gauchos on Uruguay's frontier. (They had no tea, so they invented one from the grasses growing wild in the fields.) Everywhere you go, you'll see Uruguayan men and women sipping from their *mates*.

The best place to stay in Montevideo

The **Balmoral**, *tel. (598)2-902-3393; website: www.balmoral.com.uy*, is a first-class establishment; we recommend it as the best place to stay in the entire country. The bathrooms are large and modern, the beds have mattresses and box springs (a rarity here), room service is standard, and modern computers and printers whir in the lobby.

The world's best beef

Uruguay is known for its beef. The country's cattle produce some of the world's best beef—and the country's people consume this meat in tremendous quantities. Don't visit if you're a devout vegetarian—you'll starve. One of the most typical Uruguayan specialties is the *asado*, a barbecue that includes steak, ribs, sausages, intestines, and brains. The best place to sample the *asado* is at Montevideo's port market area.

The country's best spa

In **Piriapolis**, east along the coast from Montevideo, the place to stay is the **Argentino Hotel Casino**, *tel. (598)432-2796*, right on the water at Playa de Piriapolis. One of the hotel's wings is given over to the Centro PiriaVital, a health spa founded by a Romanian doctor who has trained local Uruguayans in ancient East European health and fitness techniques. Visitors to the spa are put on an eight- to 24-day program of exercise, hydrotherapy, mud baths, and massage. The cost is from $1,195 to $2,795, including accommodation at the hotel and all meals.

Uruguay's best hotel and restaurant

La Posta del Cangrejo, *tel. (598)42-7002*, the country's most internationally renowned hotel, is located in Punta del Este, northeast of Piriapolis. The hotel's restaurant, situated right on the water, is considered the finest in the country. It is expensive, but the food is worth the price.

The best fort

The **fortin de Santa Rosa**, *tel. (598)372-7376*, is situated along the Costa de Oro, just west of Atlantida. The small white fort is just off the highway, but you'll feel like you're miles from everything. The rooms are tastefully decorated and the beds are draped with mosquito netting (a necessity).

THE BEST OF VENEZUELA

Venezuela is a land of contrasts that has remained unchanged for thousands of years. The country boasts the world's largest falls, Angel Falls (3,212 feet), impenetrable rain forests, and an abundance of wildlife and lush vegetation. Then there's Caracas, Maracaibo, and other coastal towns, where the concrete and skyscrapers remind you that you are still in the 21st century.

THE FASTEST-GROWING CITY — CARACAS

Caracas, Venezuela's capital, is modern, boasting an efficient and inexpensive metro system, as well as theaters, concert halls, and sports arenas. See the **Casa Natal del Libertador**, *Calle Traposos*, the birthplace of Simon Bolivar and a museum; the **Museo de Bellas Artes**, *Plaza Morelos*, *Parque Los Caobos*, which has an excellent collection of contemporary art; and the **Museo de Arte Contemporaneo**, *edificio Anauco, Parque Central*, which has an exceptional display of cyber-kinetic art.

The best hotels in Caracas

The best hotels in Caracas are the **Caracas Hilton**, *tel. (58)2-574-1122*, and the **Tamanaco Inter-Continental**, *tel. (58)212-909-7111*.

The best cuisine in Caracas

For typical Venezuelan cuisine, try **El Porton**, *avenida Pichincha*, a restaurant decorated with Venezuelan handicrafts and featuring entertainment at the weekends. The goat and rabbit specialties are gourmet delights. Dress is casual, and the clientele is mainly Venezuelan. Another favorite is **Barba Roja**, *avenida Tamanaco*, in the Rosal section. The food is Spanish with an emphasis on fish dishes. Try the *hayaca navidena*, a pastry made of light corn flour.

MERIDA: VENEZUELANS' FAVORITE CITY

If you ask a Venezuelan what his favorite city is, nine out of 10 times he'll name **Merida**. The climate in this city, which is located about an hour west of Caracas at the foot of the Andes, is close to ideal. Merida lies in the

Chama River Valley, where small farms bordered with ancient stone walls are still cultivated by oxen. Local craftsmen who sell alpaca blankets, sweaters, and other handicrafts line the roads. Merida is also home to an impressive, though austere, cathedral and the University of the Andes.

THE BEST BONE-JARRING TRAILS— THE GRAN SABANA

The journey through **Canaima National Park** in Venezuela's Gran Sabana is a succession of surprises. There are no tour buses, no airplanes, and no schedules. There are also very few tourists. The only thing you can count on here is the scenery, which is world-class. The Gran Sabana is the remains of an ancient plateau in southeastern Venezuela. The heart of the savanna is almost uninhabited and is protected by Canaima National Park, the third largest national park in the world.

Journeying the Gran Sabana

Do not attempt to make your way through the Gran Sabana without a guide who knows his way across this unmarked and unmapped terrain. To arrange a trip through the Gran Sabana, visit *www.lastfrontiers.com* or contact **Turven Tropical Travel Service**, *tel. (58)2-95-11-176.*

ANGEL FALLS: THE WORLD'S LARGEST FALLS

The most famous landmark in Canaima National Park is **Angel Falls**, which plunges 3,280 feet from Auyan-Tepui (Devil's Mountain). Thousands of tourists fly by Angel Falls every year—or fly to stay at the comfortable Canaima camp a few miles from the falls.

SECTION 2:

THE WORLD'S BEST
HONEYMOON DESTINATIONS

*Paris • French Riviera • Amalfi Coast • Austria • England • Menorca
Niagra Falls • Vancouver Island • St. Thomas • Caribbean • Bahamas
Bermuda • Macau*

PARIS: THE WORLD'S MOST ROMANTIC CITY

Few would argue that Paris is not the most romantic city in the world, and one of the best destinations for lovers.

The three most romantic restaurants in Paris

The number-one most romantic restaurant in Paris is **Le Grand Vefour**, *17 rue de Beaujolais; tel. (33)1-42-96-56-27*, a three-star restaurant built in 1784 at the north end of the Palais Royal. Napoleon is said to have courted Josephine here. Chef Guy Martin's cuisine has been described as "inventive flights of fancy reaching new heights." Expensive...but a good ambience.

The Jules Verne, *tel. (33)1-45-55-61-44*, on the second level of the Eiffel Tower offers, without question, one of Paris' finest views. And the dark interiors are perfect for romance. Unfortunately, the food doesn't live up to the price, and you may be intruded on by tourists who don't know how to whisper. Nevertheless, the atmosphere is as romantic as it gets.

Bar Antoine, *17 rue Lafontaine; tel. (33)1-40-50-14-30*, is a tiny bistro on rue La Fontaine, in the corner of one of the most elegant art nouveau buildings in the fashionable 16th arrondissement. No more than ten people can dine in the main room at one time. The ceiling is hand-painted canvas covered in glass. The homemade *Millefeuille* is the best in Paris—a sensual experience to help set the mood. Plus, dinner is less than $20 per person.

THE MOST ROMANTIC TOWN ON THE FRENCH RIVIERA

Antibes, the center of the perfume market, has lovely beaches, a small port, and a colorful fruit and flower market.

The best place to stay in this romantic town is the **Hotel du Cap-Eden Roc**, *tel. (33)4-93-61-39-01*. It was a favorite of Scott and Zelda Fitzgerald because of its glamorous and romantic atmosphere.

THE MOST ROMANTIC HOTEL ON THE AMALFI COAST

Hotel San Pietro, *tel. (39)89-87-54-55*, is a cantilevered castle built into a cliffside on the Amalfi Coast. Every room faces the sea and has a sweeping view. While each room is different, they all have private gardens. Balconies with painted tiles, arches, antiques, and bouquets of flowers give you your own view of the foaming sea. You can descend through the mountain to swim and sunbathe, watch the fishermen come and go in their boats, shop for Italian pottery, or sit back and relax by the bay. A double room is $500 a night.

THE MOST ROMANTIC HOTEL IN AUSTRIA

The **Schloss Durnstein**, *tel. (43)2-711-212*, presides over a wide curve of the Danube River. Located deep in the wine district of Wachau, this magnificent castle is surrounded by distinctive vine-clad hills, age-old ruins, and timeless picturesque villages with one-lane streets. According to legend, it was here that the imprisoned Kind Richard the Lionhearted was reunited with his faithful minstrel, who had sung his way across Europe searching for his master.

Also intriguing is the wine cellar (which can accommodate 8,000 "buckets" of wine), the arch-crossed cobbled courtyard, and the 33 chandeliered chambers fronting the Danube.

ENGLAND'S MOST ROMANTIC B&B

Hope End, *Ledbury; tel. (44)1531-633-618*, is one of the most alluring B&Bs in England. Located in the coach house and stables of the house where Elizabeth Barrett Browning lived for 23 years, it is cozy and serves delicious meals. The B&B is closed November 30th through February and has eight rooms.

MENORCA, SPAIN'S MOST ROMANTIC ISLE

Menorca, the most romantic of the Balearic Islands, is the kind of spot you might want to escape to on your honeymoon, as Princess Grace and Prince Rainier did. Traveling from one end of the island to the other on its narrow, winding roads, you will probably encounter no one, save the unobtrusive sheep on the hillsides. Menorca is lush and hilly but not mountainous. Menorca is said to have 120 coves with beaches, most unpeopled. The most deserted beach is Sambal, which is four miles long.

Lobster and bouillabaisse are served at **Espla**, a restaurant famous for its breathtaking setting on the waterfront. Another good island restaurant is **Buccaneros**. The best hotel on the island is **Port Mahon**, *tel. (34)71-36-26-00*.

NIAGARA FALLS: AMERICA'S BEST
HONEYMOON SPOT

You'll hear **Niagara Falls** long before you see it. This 180-foot waterfall, which pours 40 million gallons of water a minute, is actually made up of three great torrents: **Canada's Horseshoe Falls**, the **American Falls**, and **Bridal Veil Falls**. Horseshoe is the most spectacular, so you should definitely see this natural wonder from both the U.S. and Canadian sides.

The best way to see Niagara is aboard the *Maid of the Mist*, which departs

Prospect Park and the landing on the American side. Another good way to see the falls is from the Observation Tower in Prospect Park.

You can also view the cascade from below. Take an elevator 125 feet down to the **Scenic Tunnels**, which lead to a two-level observation deck near Horseshoe Falls. Wear a slicker; it's wet.

Bridges and wooden walkways lead across the base of Bridal Veil Falls, within 25 feet of the river, to the **Cave of the Winds** below Goat Island. The roar of the water and the heavy spray are overwhelming.

THE MOST ROMANTIC TOWN ON VANCOUVER ISLAND

One of the loveliest places on the island is **Parksville**, a little town off Route 19 on the east coast. From the highway, the town doesn't look like much—a few trailers and gift shops. But behind the ever-present towering pines are wide beaches with calm, clear waters. On the horizon are purple, snow-topped mountain ranges. The beach extends out for nearly a mile at low tide, and sea lions cavort not far from land. The water is surprisingly warm as early as May.

Tigh Na Mara, *1095 E. Island Highway, V9P 2E5; tel. (604)248-2072*, has the most romantic accommodation on Vancouver Island. You stay in log cabins (with fireplaces) next to the beach and have use of a Jacuzzi, canoes, paddleboats, and rowboats.

THE MOST ROMANTIC RESORT IN ST. THOMAS

Each of the 25 rooms at the St. Thomas resort known as **Pavilions and Pools**, *tel. (800)524-200; website: http://pavilionsandpools.com*, has its own fresh-water pool set inside a private and secluded garden. All units are one-bedroom villas with kitchenettes, and all are within walking distance of two beautiful white-sand beaches. This is undoubtedly the best place on the island for a romantic getaway or honeymoon.

THE MOST ROMANTIC HOTEL IN THE CARIBBEAN

Tucked into Maunday Bay on Anguilla is the ultimate Caribbean hide-away. With its villas of soft white arches, tiled roofs, and covered terraces that face long, creamy beaches, **Cap Juluca**, *tel. (1-264)497-6666*, offers secluded island beauty. The sunset sail on Cap Juluca's yacht to offshore cays, with a silver service picnic prepared by seven members of the crew, is particularly recommended. Other noble pursuits include Sunfish sailing, Hobie cat voyages, windsurfing, deep-sea fishing, and water-skiing.

THE MOST ROMANTIC RESORT IN THE BAHAMAS

Fernandez Bay Village, *website: www.fernandezbayvillage.com*, one of only three establishments on Cat Island, is nothing less than spectacular. With no major towns, and only occasional hamlets on the island's one main road, Fernandez Bay is a focal point for the area. But it's more like a sailor's retreat than a social center. Before bags are unpacked, guests are pointed toward a thatched-roof circular bar and veranda just a few feet from the water's edge. The bar, like all the resort's facilities, happily goes unmanned most of the time. The Armbristers (the owners) invite guests to help themselves on the "honor system." The best part of the day is dinnertime. Just before nightfall, barefoot guests begin their nightly stroll to the dining area to join the Armbristers and staff for cocktails. Travelers from all over the world meet at the open-air restaurant by the sea to trade tales of the day's events. The food is delicious and served buffet-style in a relaxed atmosphere.

THE BEST HONEYMOON SPOT IN BERMUDA

The **Elbow Beach Hotel**, *tel. (441)236-8043; website: www.mandarinoriental. com/bermuda*, is a jet set—and romantic—place to stay on the island. You can choose either a spacious room in the main hotel or an ocean-view suite tucked away in the hotel's botanical gardens. A private ocean beach is at your doorstep, as well as a beautiful pool, a health club, and six distinctive bars.

THE BEST PLACE TO HONEYMOON IN MACAU

Pousada de Sao Tiago, *tel. (852)2736-0922*, became a hotel in 1980 and every historical feature was preserved during the transformation, including the Portuguese marble, hand-painted tiles, ancient stone walls, gentle cascades, hand-covered mahogany, and even the trees that shade the multilevel terraces. This hotel overlooks the South China Sea and is enveloped in warm, salty breezes.

SECTION 3:

THE WORLD'S BEST BEACHES

Britain • France • Germany • Sardinia • Spain • Croatia • Slovenia India • Greece • Africa • Israel • Australia • New Zealand • United States • Mexico • South America • Belize • Costa Rica • Caribbean Roatan • Venezuela

BRITAIN'S MOST REGAL BEACH RESORT

The seaside town of **Brighton** became popular with aristocrats in the mid-18th century. (It later lost standing and became a big favorite of P.G. Wodehouse's Jeeves, the butler, who liked to fish here.) Brighton was originally a tiny fishing village that is mentioned in the Domesday Book.

The best walks in Brighton are along Old Steine, which is the center of activity; out to the Palace Pier, a Victorian structure that juts nearly a third of a mile into the English Channel; and along the Marine Parade, an attractive promenade with 19th-century terraces.

The biggest attraction in the town is the restored **Royal Pavilion**, a pseudo-Oriental structure built by the Prince Regent, George, Prince of Wales (later King George IV) from 1787 to 1822. The pavilion graphically demonstrates the excesses and extravagances of the Regency period.

If you tire of the sun—or rain—the most inviting places for tea are the lounge of the Metropole and the veranda of the Grand Hotel (rebuilt after the Irish Republican Army bombed it in 1984 in an attempt on the life of Margaret Thatcher).

FRANCE'S MOST BEAUTIFUL BEACH

The most beautiful beach in France is **Etretat**, in Normandy. Two magnificent white cliffs loom above the wide, rocky beach. While the beach is gorgeous, it's not particularly comfortable but, because of this, it's never crowded.

GERMANY'S BEST BEACHES

Few visitors realize that, as well as medieval villages and deep forests, Germany boasts beautiful beaches. The **East Frisian Islands**, which fringe the North Sea coastline, have long sandy beaches guarded by dunes and frequented by nude sunbathers. The islands also have fishing villages, seal-covered rocks, and an ancient language and culture. For more information on the East Frisian Islands, visit the tourist office in the railroad station in Oldenburg.

THE BEST BEACH IN SARDINIA

La Costa del Sud, about 31 miles southwest of Cagliari, has unspoiled beaches and hidden coves. The water is turquoise and perfectly clear. Buses run to the coast from Cagliari as far as the beach near the Torre di Chia. But the next beach over, Capo Spartivento, is larger and has two lovely islands that are great for sunbathing.

SPAIN'S BEST BEACHES

Costa de Almería: the most peaceful beaches

Spain's most peaceful beaches are along the relatively undiscovered **Costa de Almeria**. Stretching 120 miles between Almeria and Cartagena on the southeastern edge of Spain, the coast retains much of its original charm and still has reasonable prices.

The best nude beach

The **Costa Brava** has a number of lovely secluded beaches perfect for nude sunbathing. **Cabo de Creus** has clean water and little caves hidden among the rocks.

CROATIA'S BEST BEACH

The nicest beach on the entire coastline is at the south end if the island of **Krk**, a half-hour boat ride from Rijeka. Krk is a strangely beautiful place with a barren valley surrounded by stern, stony hills. The island has a small hotel.

SLOVENIA—THE MOST GLAMOROUS BEACHES

The **Slovenian Riviera**—the area from the Italian border to the end of the Istrian Peninsula's west coast—is the most glamorous stretch along the coast. It feels like Italy. **Izola** and **Piran** are attractive resort towns along the Slovenian Riviera—both resemble old-style Italian resorts. **Potoroz**, a more modern resort, is the most expensive.

INDIA'S BEST BEACHES

Hugging the coast of the Bay of Bengal, **Marine Beach**, is the most beautiful beach in Madras, if not the world. It has fine sand and is lined with walkways and gardens.

Little Portugal: Goa

South of Mumbai is **Goa**, a Portuguese colony from 1510 to 1961. It has a mixture of local and Portuguese charms and the most beautiful beaches in India. In addition to all this, Goa has got beautiful weather (except during monsoon season from June through September). St. Francis Xavier was the first to come here and convert people to Catholicism in 1540. Although he died in China, his body was returned to Goa. His embalmed remains lie in a silver, gem-encrusted casket in the **Basilica of Bom Jesus** in Panaji.

Goa's delights are physical as well as spiritual. The silvery beaches along the Malabar Coast are incomparable. The best are near Panaji, the Capital. **Dona Paula** is the most chic.

GREECE'S BEST BEACHES

Skiathos has the best sand beaches (most beaches in Greece are pebbly), and its Old Town section is charming. Not as tourist-trodden as the other, better-developed islands, such as Corfu, Rhodes, and Mykonos, Skiathos is said to be the Greeks' favorite island. Its large British expatriate community colors its cultural atmosphere. A few of the resident artists are British. English pubs are sprinkled among the alleyways of the Old Town.

Vacation amenities include water-skiing, windsurfing, and boating; yet those who want to get away from it all will find a sense of privacy. Small boats gather on the town waterfront each morning to offer tourists excursions to nearby islands, beaches, and the Kastro, a castle ruin on the other side. The best-organized trip is to an uninhabited island across from the town, which has a beautiful beach with flowers growing in the sand and a myriad of butterflies.

THE BEST OF AFRICA'S BEACHES

Kenya's best beach

Kenya has 300 miles of glorious beaches along the Indian Ocean. The Swahili, a people of Arab and African ancestry and culture, live along the coast and for centuries have been astute traders.

The white-sand beaches, edged with palms, are protected from pollution and sharks by reefs. Beyond the palm trees is the forest, inhabited by leopards, Colobus monkeys, and brightly colored birds.

South Africa's best beaches

With more than 100 gorgeous white-sand beaches to choose from, the Cape Peninsula has some of the best coastline in Africa. Discerning sun worshipers prefer **Clifton** beach, with its mountainous backdrop. Another favorite is **Muizenberg**, a seaside resort town within 22 miles of beach.

Senegal's best beach

Cap Slurring in Joal is an unspoiled, dazzling white beach fringed by coconut trees. **Club Med** has a highly recommended outpost here. Watch out for sharks (not just the human kind). The resort is closed during the summer (monsoon season).

The least expensive place to stay is **Le Campement**, a government-run accommodation made up of little concrete huts on the water. For a few dol-·

lars, you can spend the night on foam pads under clean sheets and enjoy good local food.

The Egyptian Riviera

In the summer, Muslim Egyptians crowd Alexandria's beaches, where the temperature is an average 15 degrees cooler than in Cairo. The beaches are beautiful and the water clear, but Egypt's **Riviera** is crowded and cluttered. And remember, this is a Muslim beach, so don't wear bikinis or daring swimsuits.

Corniche, the 15-mile road along the coast, is lined with houses, hotels, shops, and palm trees. At the eastern tip of Alexandria's stretch of beaches is the **Montaza Palace and Gardens**, a huge complex that includes gardens, beaches, and hotels. Just east of Montaza is **Ma'amura**, a cleaner, relatively isolated beach where the people have more Western tastes in swimwear. However, true beach lovers will best enjoy Egypt's beach resorts along the Sinai and Red Sea.

The best beaches in Morocco

Agadir, in southwest Morocco, is the country's playground. It has a white-sand beach and all the sun and water sports anyone could want. And, unlike most of the world's beach towns, Agadir doesn't scream commercialism and tourism.

Destroyed by an earthquake in 1960, Agadir has been completely rebuilt. But its main attraction is still its beach, which is a pleasant 10-minute walk from the center of town. To get there, you meander down a terraced hillside covered with greenery and flowering plants. Along the beach runs a wide walk of marble, which is lined with open-air cafés facing the water. In the background are the **Anti-Atlas Mountains**.

Agadir enjoys more than 300 days of sun a year. And the temperature is always between 66 and 82 degrees Fahrenheit. Its white-sand beaches are as beautiful as you'll find anywhere, and its water as blue. It is easy to see why European sun seekers flock here year-round.

Agadir can be expensive and crowded because of its thriving tourist industry, however. If you're looking for space and a bit of private beach, head north from Agadir, where you'll find sandy coves every few miles.

ISRAEL'S BEST BEACH

Akko is one of the oldest (it existed more than 3,500 years ago) and most picturesque cities in the world. Surrounded by thick seawalls on the tip of a point of land, the city is fringed with palm trees and punctuated with minarets. Only 14 miles north of Haifa, it was an important Phoenician port and later served as a capital for the Crusaders.

On the southern edge of Akko is the **Argaman**, or purple beach, the most beautiful beach on the coast, with crystal-clear water.

Akko was the site of the largest prison break in history. On May 4, 1947, 251 prisoners were freed from the prison known as the Fortress by Jewish underground fighters. The movie *Exodus*, which is about the escape, was filmed here. Part of the prison, known as the Museum of Heroes, contains Jewish memorabilia and the cell where Bahaullah was imprisoned in the 1860s. The other part of the prison is a mental hospital.

Most of Akko's sights are in the Old City, including the remains of an underground Crusader town, the Al-Jazzar mosque (the third largest in Israel), caravanserais, and Oriental markets. If you admire architecture, you will be dazzled by the ramparts, minarets, spires, and domes. The city's high walls, alleys, and stairways are thick with fragrances from the Arab market.

Akko is considered the holiest place on earth by people of the Baha'i faith. Their prophet, Bahaullah, is buried here, at the shrine at Bahji. He was brought to the Ottoman-Victorian house here to die after spending two years in the Fortress. His ornate tomb is covered with flowers and gold designs. The house (now his shrine) contains memorabilia of the leader. The surrounding gardens are lush and peaceful.

Concerts are held from time to time at Knights' Hall in **Crusader Castle**. The Haifa Symphony Orchestra performs here, 10 feet below ground because of the good acoustics. During mid-October, the Knights' Hall hosts the **Akko Theater Festival**.

The **Argaman Motel**, *P.O. Box 153, Akko Beach*, has one of the most beautiful views of the sea in Israel, with the walls of the Old City in the foreground. Rooms are spacious, with air conditioning, balconies, telephones, and modern bathrooms. The hotel is located next to the gas station on the Road of the Sea, near Argaman Beach.

THE BEST BEACHES IN AUSTRALIA

Sydney's best beach

Sydney has 34 ocean beaches, each with its own style. If you are looking for peace and quiet, try Whale, Avalon, or Bilgola. But if you want to see a Sydney beach at its best—filled with perfect bodies, sun-streaked blonds, surf bums, and joggers, all in a sunny mood—go to Bondi.

Bondi (pronounced Bond-Eye) has produced many world-champion surfers. The half-mile crescent of sand and surf is filled from dawn to dusk with surfers, sunbathers, and swimmers. Snacks and drinks are available at Bondi Junction, near the beach.

Bondi's neighbor, **Tamarama Beach**, is smaller, prettier, and more peaceful.

SURFER'S PARADISE: THE BEST OF THE GOLD COAST

Just south of Brisbane is **Surfer's Paradise**, the largest and liveliest resort on Australia's 20-mile Gold Coast. The sandy beaches are perfect, the water warm, the surf, as you would expect, terrific—and behind it all are the MacPherson Mountains. Believe it or not, the beach here is even better than in Hawaii. However, the crowds can be unbearable, especially around Christmas and Easter.

A good place to stay is the **Hub Hotel**, *21 Cavill Ave.*, actually a motel near the beach. Each unit has its own balcony, bathroom, refrigerator, and television.

NEW ZEALAND: NORTH ISLAND'S BEST BEACHES

Doubtless Bay is a crescent of perfect sandy beaches that draws throngs on holidays. Houhora is a beach favored by fishermen, picnickers, campers, and smugglers.

Ninety Mile Beach (which is only 57 miles long) is a seemingly endless stretch of golden sandy beaches lined with dunes and embroidered with seashells. This is the scene of a popular fishing contest each summer and the prime spot to find toheroa, a much sought-after shellfish.

The hottest beach

The **Coromandel Peninsula**, on the east coast of North Island, has New Zealand's hottest (and strangest) swimming spot: **Hot Water Beach**. Named for the hot springs that seep through its sand, the beach literally steams. You can create your own thermal pool by digging into the sand.

The peninsula is also a mecca of alternative lifestyles and naturalists. The back-to-nature movement remains as healthy here today as it was in the United States in the 1960s. You can see how hippies have evolved over the past 40-odd years—bringing communal life into the electromagnetic age by constructing recording studios on their farms, for example. The marijuana smoked in New Zealand allegedly originates on this peninsula.

THE BEST OF THE U.S.A.'S BEACHES

New York's best beaches

While New York isn't known as a beach town, it does have 20 miles of beaches. The best are **Rockaway Beach** (not Far Rockaway, which is seedy) and **Jones Beach**; the worst is **Coney Island**, which has become a slum.

Take the A or CC subway train to Rockaway, the Long Island Railroad to Jones. **Brighton Beach** is a Russian enclave called Odessa by the Sea.

Florida's most peaceful beaches

Most people think of the Atlantic Coast when they think of Florida. But some of the prettiest and least crowded beaches are along the Gulf of Mexico. **Pensacola Beach**, on the panhandle, has fine, white sand and temperate, clear water. **Fort Walton Beach** is attractive and has a 1,200-foot observation pier. Farther south are the white sand beaches of **Belleair** and **Clearwater**. The finest sand is at **Madeira** and **Redington** beaches. **Long Boat Key** is posh and not too crowded. **Point O'Rocks**, an isolated beach near Siesta Key, is famous for its colorful rocks. **Venice Beach** is known for the sharks' teeth that wash up on shore. **Fort Myers Beach** has the most beautiful sunsets. And **Sanibel** and **Captiva** islands are the best places in the state to look for seashells.

Our favorite hotel on the Gulf of Mexico is the **Don CeSar** on St. Petersburg Beach, an amazing pink Spanish-style castle surrounded by palm trees overlooking the ocean. Once the hideaway of F. Scott Fitzgerald, it is the playground of celebrities.

The **Belleview Biltmore**, *25 Belleview Blvd., Belleair-Clearwater; tel. (800)237-8947 or (800)282-8072*, is a spa. Here you can soak in whirlpools and Swedish showers and work up a sweat in the exercise room.

The **Buccaneer Inn**, *595 Dream Island Road; tel. (813)383-1101*, is the best restaurant on Longboat Key, situated on a marina. The house specialty is prime rib cooked very rare and then roasted over live charcoal.

Where the action is: the Atlantic Coast

The Gulf of Mexico is nice, but the surf and the crowds are more exciting on the Atlantic. **Daytona Beach** has 23 miles of sandy beach and a boardwalk. Highrise hotels and condominiums line the ocean. Alas, cars can drive on the beach (a real nuisance).

The most beautiful dunes and beaches along the Atlantic Coast are at **Ponte Vedra** and **South Ponte Vedra** beaches, where two exclusive resorts are located: the Sawgrass and the Ponte Vedra Inn.

The quietest East Coast beach is **New Smyrna**, between Daytona Beach and Titusville. One of the state's last unspoiled beaches is **Playalinda**, part of the Canaveral National Seashore.

Southern Florida's Atlantic Coast has some of the world's most famous resort towns: **Palm Beach**, **Fort Lauderdale**, and **Miami Beach**. College students flock here for spring vacation, and Americans in general migrate here during the winter.

Our favorite place to stay on Florida's Atlantic Coast is the **Breakers**, *South County Road, Palm Beach*. The lobby of this grand Italianate resort has frescoed vaulted ceilings and 15th-century Flemish tapestries. The original Breakers, built in 1903, burned, as did the second. The present building was built in 1926. The National Register of Historic Places lists the Breakers as "culturally significant in its reflection of 20th-century grandeur." It has two 18-hole golf courses, a private beach with cabanas, 14 tennis courts, an outdoor saltwater pool, a sauna, lawn bowling, croquet, and programs for children. The hotel dining room is large, and its 100,000-bottle wine cellar is one of the world's biggest.

Fort Lauderdale has some of the finest beaches south of Daytona—and the best nightlife.

The **Bonaventure Resort Spa**, *250 Racquet Club Road*, is surrounded by palm trees and waters. You can put your body through a Swiss needle shower, a Shiatsu massage, or an herbal wrap.

Miami Beach is the most famous resort, drawing 13 million visitors each year to its luxurious beachfront hotels. South Beach's **Lummus Park** is the best beach area. Eighth Street in **Little Havana** is lined with great Cuban restaurants. The affluent **Coral Gables** neighborhood has more elegant restaurants. And in the middle of Coral Gables sits a gem of a hotel, the **Hotel Place St. Michel**; *162 Alcazar Ave.; tel. (305)444-1666.*

Venice: Los Angeles' craziest beach

Venice, a crowded, crazy, somewhat seedy beach area on the edge of Los Angeles, is the best place in the city to people watch. **Ocean Front Boulevard**, a coastal walkway, is lined with vendors, street musicians, roller skaters, drug addicts, lovers, beach boys, gay people, senior citizens, artists, and tourists from all over the world. Venice was so named because of its many canals and Italian-style buildings. Abbot Kinney attempted to build an American Riviera here at the turn of the century, with canals and gondoliers.

MEXICO'S BEST BEACHES

Acapulco: Mexico's most sophisticated resort

Since the 1920s, the rich and famous have retreated to **Acapulco** every winter. The tropical Pacific Coast resort is famous for its fine beaches, luxury hotels, and deep-sea fishing facilities. Slim, tanned bodies line the beach, and colorful parasails float above it.

Acapulco isn't quite as nice as it used to be. It has become a smoggy, crowded city with bumper-to-bumper traffic. And on the hills above the city, crowded, dirty barrios have developed that house the cheap labor serving the many hotels and restaurants.

But you can forget all that, if you choose, by not driving and by frequenting such places as the **Crazy Lobster**, a seafood restaurant on La

Condesa Beach, where the langostas and margaritas are as perfect as the view.

Blackbeard's, *Costera Miguel Aleman; tel. (52)74-84-25-49*, also on La Condesa Beach, is another popular restaurant. Have the fish kabobs and the house rum with pineapple juice. **Villa Demos**, *ave. Del Prado 6*, serves good Italian food in a tropical garden.

The place to stay, if you can afford it, is **Las Brisas**, *Carretera Escenica Clemente Mejia 5255; tel. (52)748-41650*. Guests stay in individual casitas on a hill overlooking Acapulco Bay, surrounded by bougainvillea and hibiscus. Each little cottage has its own pool.

Another good—and slightly more affordable—hotel in Acapulco is the **Villa Vera**, *Lomas del Mar 35, P.O. Box 560*. Originally a private home, this hotel stresses service and intimacy. It is private; it is discreet; it is charming. Its décor is white stucco, old stonework, fountains, and grottos, with touches of deep blue. The rooms are furnished with touches of old Mexico and the Orient.

Puerto Vallarta: the most charming resort

Puerto Vallarta, that sleepy little fishing village discovered by Hollywood in 1964, has developed into one of Mexico's foremost resort towns. And unlike Acapulco, Puerto Vallarta hasn't yet lost its traditional charm. Native vendors push their wares in barrows up cobblestoned streets. Local fisherman roast pompano and red snapper on the beach. And Indian women pound their laundry on rocks by the stream.

The town doesn't have fine examples of Spanish architecture or a preponderance of pre-Columbian ruins, but it does have 25 miles of beaches, superb restaurants, and luxurious hotels.

The fishing is good here, too. Marlin season is November through January. And an international fishing competition is held every November off the coast of Manzanillo. You can charter a deep-sea fishing boat in town at the bay.

Puerto Vallarta was carved out of the jungle, which still encroaches on the town. You can join a jungle tour—most involve a three-hour van ride through backcountry. Douse yourself with insect repellant—these mosquitoes eat gringos.

The best places to eat

La Perla, *tel. (52)322-30123*, is the best restaurant in town, with an international cuisine and a fine wine list. You can try gourmet treats, such as poached quail eggs with red caviar. La Perla is open 7 p.m. until 11 p.m. **Carlos O'Brian's**, *tel. (52)322-21444*, is a popular restaurant—long lines form hours before the 7 p.m. opening. The food is delicious and the margaritas are strong.

The best breakfast in Puerto Vallarta is at **Memo's Casa de los Hot Cakes**, *Basilio Badillo 289*. This place is no secret; it's not uncommon to wait for a seat. There are 60 types of pancake to choose from, including Black Forest, Bananas 'n' Cream, and Chocolate Peanut Butter. They also have cheese blintzes, waffles, many typical Mexican breakfast dishes, and fresh squeezed orange juice. And the fare is cheap—breakfast ranges from $2 to $5.

The best hotels

The best hotel in Puerto Vallarta is **Garza Blanca**, *tel. (52)322-21023; website: www.garza-blanca.com*. You can stay in suites right on the beach or in a villa with its own garden and pool.

El Camino Real, *tel. (52)322-30123 or (800)228-3000 in the United States*, two miles south of Puerto Vallarta, is also an area best. Rooms are expensive but spacious, with two double beds, a large bathroom, a fully stocked refrigerator, and a small lounging area.

Mexico's most secluded beach

The most secluded, pristine stretch of white powder beach is at the **Si'aan Kaan Biosphere**, a nature preserve just outside of Tulum, on the Yucatan peninsula. These deserted beaches—dotted with coconut palm trees, populated by curious iguanas and sea birds, with azure blue water and total silence but for the roar of the surf—cannot be matched for tranquility and natural beauty.

The most seductive beaches

The Caribbean side of Cancun has the best beaches, with sand as soft as talcum powder, aquamarine water, and exhilarating waves. The beach in front of the **Hyatt Caribe** is especially pretty, shaded by coconut palms and studded with lounge chairs that can be used by anyone, not just guests at the hotel. If you tire of the beach, splash in the Hyatt's series of pools connected by a canal that is crossed by a little bridge.

Cancun's best beach playground is at the **Camino Real**, *tel. (52)988-30100*, a hotel on a point of land. On one side, the Caribbean crashes against an inviting beach; on the other is the calm Bahia de Mujéres, where you can snorkel among fluorescent fish. The hotel has a saltwater pool fed by the bay and inhabited by giant tortoises and tropical fish. You can snorkel here or sun on the raft in the middle. Then wash the salt off your body in the ice-cold futuristic freshwater pool. (You don't have to be a guest to use the pools here either.)

On Cozumel, the beaches north and south of San Miguel are superb. Most of the island's hotels hug these beach coves, so guests walk directly from their rooms onto the beach each morning. Because the currents off Cozumel are so unpredictable, you should never swim alone.

Isla Mujéres' most beautiful beach is **El Garrafón**. The beaches at Tortugas and Marias are less crowded, though.

SOUTH AMERICA'S BEST BEACHES

Rio de Janeiro in Brazil has spectacularly beautiful beaches—Botafogo, Copacabana, Ipanema, Leblon, São Conrado—where women, wearing the world's skimpiest bikinis, bask in the sun. Called tangos, the bikinis here consist of three tiny triangles of fabric held in place by lengths of string.

The prettiest beach is the one most distant from the center of the city, **São Conrado**, where the Hotel Intercontinental has taken root. This beach is not as crowded as Copacabana and Ipanema, and the water is cleaner.

São Conrado is also the best place to go hang gliding—or just to watch the colorful gliders hover in the air for hours, held aloft by updrafts coming off the ocean and up the mountainside. They look like huge butterflies leisurely enjoying the afternoon sun.

Copacabana, lined with luxury hotels, restaurants, and nightclubs, is the chicest beach in South America. It is the longest and widest in Rio. Stroll along **avenida Atlântica**, which is tiled with mosaics and lined with first-class hotels and expensive shops.

Close rivals of Copacabana are Ipanema (which is less congested and draws a younger crowd), Leblon, and Barra da Tijuca. The southern part of Ipanema is a fashionable residential area.

About 90 miles north of Rio is Cabo Frio, where forts and a 17th-century convent provide a dramatic backdrop to a wide, almost deserted beach.

A word of caution: never take valuables to the beach—leave them in your hotel safe. Thieves from the nearby *favelas* (slums) roam the beaches looking for easy pickings, and they move quickly.

THE STANN CREEK DISTRICT: BELIZE'S
NICEST BEACHES

If you're looking for a relaxing getaway where you won't see many other tourists and where you can sun yourself on the nicest beaches in the country, go to **Placencia**. The one dirt road that runs the length of the peninsula helps to make the area seem far away and a real escape.

COSTA RICA'S BEST BEACH

Cahuita beach is notable for its split personality: it has one beach of white sand and one of black sand. A wrecked Spanish galleon lies on a nearby coral reef; you can swim out to explore it.

The best place to eat in Cahuita

The **Cahuita National Park Restaurant**, *tel. (506)58-15-15, ext. 201*, situated right on the beach, is nothing more than a platform with a straw roof and wooden tables and chairs, but the view is spectacular, the service friendly, and the food good. Island music plays in the background for student-age clientele.

The best place to stay in Cahuita

Down the road from the Cahuita National Park Restaurant is a place called **Cabinas Atlantida**. It's hidden back off the road but worth going out of your way to find. Each of the 30 cabins comes with a private bathroom, breakfast, and the use of a bicycle (necessary for beach hopping). Picnic tables and hammocks are set up on the grounds. There's even a mascot—a spider monkey who roams freely.

The Best Beaches in the Caribbean

St. Barthélemy—the beaches of the rich and famous

St. Barthélemy has the most gorgeous beaches in the Caribbean. This millionaire's island is dotted with vacation homes of such illustrious families as the Rockefellers and the Rothschilds. Mick Jagger, Peter Jennings, Beverly Sills, Mikhail Baryshnikov, and Billy Joel frequent this island. They are drawn to St. Barts (as the island is affectionately known) by the seductive languor of its lifestyle and its sophisticated French atmosphere.

The island's most beautiful beach is **Anse du Gouverneur**, on the south coast. The sand is as soft as talcum powder, and jagged cliffs protect the beach on two sides, giving it a secluded air. It is never crowded.

Despite the jet-setters who frequent the island, life on St. Bart's is homey and small scale. However, it has become pricey. One of the island's most exclusive resorts is **Sapore di Mare**, *tel. (590)276173*, founded by a financier on the board of the American Ballet.

St. Barthélemy is one of only two completely free trading ports in the Caribbean (the other is St. Martin), and it sells French perfume and champagne at prices lower than in Paris.

St. Thomas's most beautiful beach

Magens Bay Beach, below Drake's Seat, is one of the most beautiful beaches in the world, according to *National Geographic*.

Martinique's best beaches

Martinique has both silvery beaches and rocky cliffs. Inland are rain forests and a volcano. The island's most appealing beaches, as well as several

The World's Best Destinations

petrified wood savanna forests, are in **Ste. Anne**. The church in the center of town is planted with beautiful tamarind trees. Ste. Anne has two good restaurants: Chez Jack and l'Etoile de Mer.

Off Martinique's coasts are the wrecks of 13 ships, which can be explored by scuba divers. For equipment, visit the Carib Scuba Club in Carbet.

Montserrat's best beaches

Montserrat's black-sand beaches (which set it apart from other Caribbean islands) were formed from volcanic ash. The only white-sand beach is also one of the best (and least accessible): **Rendezvous Beach**. To get to the beach, board a local charter from the **Vue Point Hotel**, *tel. (809)491-5210*. The Vue Point is also a lovely place to stay.

Aruba—the world's most beautiful beaches

The southwest coast of the island of Aruba is fringed by seven miles of white-sand beaches, considered the most beautiful in the world. In fact, *Sports Illustrated* was so impressed that it featured the beaches in past Swimsuit Issues.

The best hotels in Aruba

The **Hyatt Regency Hotel**, *tel. (297)586-1234*, is an elegant and dramatic-looking hotel. Though expensive, it definitely offers Aruba's best beds.

Also outstanding are the **Sonesta Hotel Beach Club and Casino**, *tel. (297)8-36000*, and the **La Cabana All-Suite Hotel**, *tel. (297)8-3900*.

Best restaurant in Aruba

The **Waterfront Crabhouse**, *tel. (297)583-5858*, is an upscale seafood restaurant. It's a good idea to make reservations.

The most beautiful beach in Jamaica

Jamaica's longest, most beautiful white-sand beach is **Negril**, discovered by hippies almost two decades ago. The hippies have gone, but Negril is still a place for the younger crowd. Nude sunbathing is allowed on a section of the beach.

ROATAN'S BEST BEACH

West Bay Beach is arguably the best beach on the island...maybe the best beach in all the Bay Islands. The aqua blue water that is home to a large population of tropical fish surrounds the crescent-shaped, two-mile-long, gleaming white stretch of sand. Accommodation on this beach can be found by contacting Emiliana and Claudio Miconi, *tel. (504)995-4468;*

e-mail: lascupulas@earthlink.net; website: www.westbayvillage.com. They can also arrange scuba diving and car rentals for you.

VENEZUELA'S BEST BEACHES

The beaches of **Tucacas** on the Caribbean coast are part of Morrocoy National Park, and finding a nearly deserted stretch of sand is not a problem. **Cumana** has an isolated coastline protected by Mochimo National Park and is an important fishing center of Venezuela. Here you can find many undiscovered beaches while adventuring. Other great beaches in Venezuela include Cauataro, Cautarito, Los Matos, Puerto la Cruz, and Margarita Island. Rocky cliffs make them accessible only by sea.

SECTION 4:

THE WORLD'S BEST SPORTING DESTINATIONS

Skiing: *Austria • Innsbruck • St. Anton • Zürs • French Alps German Alps • Italian Alps • Western Europe • St. Moritz • Zakopane Hokkaido • Australia • New Zealand • United States • Canada • Chile*

Golf: *Scotland • Ireland • Portugal • India • Thailand • United States*

Diving: *Israel • Palau • Belize • Cayman Islands • Guadeloupe Saba • Mexico*

Fishing: *Australia • New Zealand • Isle of Man*

The world's best skiing

Austria's best skiing

The **Arlberg** region of Austria is the best place in the world for skiing. It offers a combination of features not duplicated anywhere else: a high altitude, which guarantees good snow; slopes for skiers of all levels of experience; interconnected villages that range from quaint to crowded to exclusive; serious ski instruction; and a cheery dose of Gemutlichkeit, or coziness. Some of the villages are large, such as Lech or St. Anton; others, including Zurs, are small and exclusive.

Innsbruck: the prettiest Alpine city

One of the prettiest Alpine cities, Innsbruck is also one of the biggest ski centers in Europe. The towering Alps can be seen from almost every street corner. Miles of cross-country skiing can be found outside Innsbruck, as well as the Olympic bobsled run, a ski jump, and a large ice-skating rink and hockey arena.

Stubai Glacier, 25 miles from Innsbruck, is said to be the most exciting summer skiing around. For tickets, prices, and other information, view their website: *www.stubai-gletscher.com*.

The best ski school

St. Anton is the best place to go for ski instruction, thanks to tradition and the city's 300 instructors. This is the cradle of modern skiing, where Hannes Schneider began teaching the now-accepted Arlberg School ski technique. The runs from the top of the Galzig and the Valuga (9,216 feet) are superb—as are the views.

St. Anton is also a good place to go for nightlife. The Hotel Hospiz has a fine restaurant.

The most exclusive resort

Zürs is a first-class ski resort where tour groups are discouraged. This place is for the skiing purist who also likes fine living.

All the hotels in Zürs are first-class or better. The **Zorserhof**, *tel. (43) 5583-25130*, is an expensive five-star deluxe establishment that regularly attracts celebrities. It may be the best ski hotel in Austria.

The French Alps: the mightiest Alp and best resort

The mightiest Alp is **Mont Blanc**, Europe's highest peak, which rises 15,772 feet into the sky. A good place to stay while you enjoy the Alps is **Chamonix**, a convenient train ride from Paris. Many hiking trails and cable car rides radiate from this posh and expensive ski resort. For more information, *tel. (33)4-50-53-00-24* (Tourist Office); *e-mail: info@chamonix.com*.

The best ride is from the téléphérique to the Aiguille du Midi. You'll hover thousands of feet above rocky drops and seas of ice. Try to take the ride in the morning, when the view is clearest. Wear warm clothes because it's chilly at the top! If you'd rather hike through the mountains, you can follow the miles of signposted trails. For more information, contact **Compagnie des Guides**, *Maison de la Montagne, 190 place de l'Eglise; tel. (33)50-53-00-88*.

Chamonix, *place d'Eglise; tel. (33)53-00-88*, is the most popular ski resort in the French Alps. The deep-powder snow and the variety of runs in the 13,000-foot mountain range attract experts from all over the world. The 12.4-mile glacier run down the Vallée Blanche is one of the most exciting in the world.

For those who find skiing too tame, Chamonix also offers one of the newest thrills: parapente, which involves parachuting off steep vertical cliffs high in the mountains. You can also hang glide in the mountains.

The best skiing in the German Alps

Garmisch-Partenkirchen, the most popular resort in the German Alps, offers Germany's best skiing. The powdery peaks are accessible via an assortment of lifts. Trails are geared toward every level of skier. A pretty town with gaily-painted alpine houses, Garmisch has après-ski entertainment, a casino, and concerts. Proximity to the American Army base, however, is causing the town to lose some of its Germanic charm. Nearby are Ludwig II's Linderhof Castle and the domed Benedictine abbey of Ettal.

The best place to stay is the **Schneefernerhaus**, *tel. (49)8821-58011*, a miracle of engineering perched at 8,692 feet atop the Zugspitze. The view is absolutely incredible, but the hotel is basic and inexpensive.

The best bargain skiing in the Italian Alps

Cortina d'Ampezzo, in the eastern Dolomites, is Italy's most popular ski resort. Although it is very crowded, it has some of the best ski facilities in Italy. The area is huge—you can ski for days without doubling back to redo the same runs. When you tire of skiing, you can ice skate in what remains of the Olympic Stadium, shop in the town's many boutiques, or dine in one of its many restaurants.

Accommodation here is more expensive than in Mount Livata or Pescasseroli, nearby. The **Cristallo Hotel**, *via R. Menardi 42, 32942; tel. (39)436-4281*, has spacious, well-appointed rooms and a good restaurant. It is open from mid-December through March and during late summer.

In **Courmayeur** and **Cervinia**, you can ski in the summer as well as the winter. These towns are well known—and pricey for Italy. The Val dAyas is undiscovered and has lower lift prices (and more challenging runs).

Colfosco, a small, quiet ski village with numerous runs, attracts ardent downhill skiers. The area is best suited to beginning and intermediate skiers—it offers little cross-country skiing and no deep-powder skiing. Its major advantage over the larger, more crowded ski resorts is that it is part of the **Alta Badia**, a five-village ski association. With a Colfosco lift ticket you have access to 75 miles of trails and 53 lifts. You can also buy the Super Dolomite lift pass, which gives you access to 10 major ski areas that include 650 miles of trails and 430 lifts. For more information, contact **Azienda Autonoma di Soggiono e Tourismo Corvara-Colfosco**, *tel. (39)471-836-171.*

Hotel Colfosco Hof, *39003 Colfosco, Corvara, Badia; tel. (39)471-836-188*, at the first curve of the Grodner Pass, is the most pleasant hotel in the area. It has good hearty food, a pool, a sauna, and a squash court.

The cheapest skiing in Western Europe

Spain is famous for sunshine and bullfights, not snow-covered mountains and ski slopes. However, the skiing in Spain can be quite good, and it's far less expensive and less crowded than in the Alps.

Although the Spanish Pyrenees many not have the kudos of the Alps resorts of France, Italy, Switzerland, and Austria, that is also one of its advantages, for it remains pretty much off the radar of the package holiday firms. Instead, the slopes are almost wholly for the locals.

The most popular ski resort is **Baquiera-Beret**, in Lerida province in the Pyrenees. The long ski season here lasts from late November to late April. You can choose from seven slopes of varying difficulty. Facilities include six chair lifts, eight ski lifts, and one baby lift. Ski instruction and equipment rental are available.

Hotels are open from Dec. 1 to May 1. **Hotel Montarto**, *tel. (34)73-64-50-75*, is comfortable, has spectacular views of the slopes, and is near the lifts.

The largest of the string of resorts that run along Spain's border with France is Alp 2500, just a two-hour drive north from the mild Mediterranean climes of Barcelona. Strictly speaking, it is two resorts—**La Molina** and **Masella**—occupying adjacent pine-clad valleys which have been linked by lifts to form a combined ski area of 68 runs, totaling 67 miles of pistes.

The two-star **Hotel Solineu** in La Molina village is a leisurely five-minute walk from the cable car station. Though basic, the rooms are clean and comfortable, and the eat-as-much-as-you-like dinner in the restaurant is a definite hit after an appetite-inducing day on the slopes. While more stars and lower prices can be found in the hotels in and around the town of Puigcerdà at the base of the mountain, the half-board daily rate of $205 per couple—which includes ski passes for the La Molina valley—is still good value in comparison to rival European and North American resorts.

Up on the slopes there is also plenty to entice. Both Alp 2500 resorts offer a good range of pistes that will test all skill levels, from beginner to advanced. There are also the additional attractions of a cross-country circuit, dog-sledge track, and quad bike area around the winter-wonderland setting of la Molina's lake. Alp 2500 boasts a good snow record, too, with more than 600 artificial snow cannons on standby in case of any shortfall.

St Moritz: the world's most famous ski resort

St. Moritz, Switzerland, is the most famous, most elegant ski playground in the world. Princess Ira von Furstenberg and Gunther Sachs are among the celebrities who ski here. And it's easy to understand why—the five mountains at St. Moritz have great slopes. However, as you might expect, skiing here in peak season is expensive.

Where to stay on the mountain

Badrutt's Palace, *tel. (800)223-6800* in the U.S. or *(41)82-21101* outside the U.S., is the finest hotel in town and, in February, the most elite skiers stay here. A less expensive and more charming hotel is the **Hotel Chesa sur l'En**, *tel. (41)82-33144*. This hotel is a Swiss chalet surrounded by pines; it has a massive front door, a stone-flagged entrance hall, and a richly paneled ornate main hall.

Zakopane: Poland's best ski resort

Zakopane, in the Tatra Mountains near the Czech border, a half-hour south of Nowy Targ, is the top ski resort in Poland. At 2,625 feet, it has good ski conditions November through May. Zakopane is also a center for sheep-herding mountaineers and has been a mecca for sports and nature enthusiasts since the turn of the century. Summer is for rafting, hiking, fishing, and mountain climbing. And the numerous health spas are popular regardless of the season.

The place to stay in Zakopane is **Orbis Kasprowy**, *tel. (48)1-654-011*, a 300-room hotel with a restaurant, a nightclub, an indoor pool, a sauna, an ice-skating rink, and a mini-golf course. All rooms have private baths.

The *Kawiarnia Miś, Bukowina Tatrzanska, Ulica Dluge 154*, is a small country restaurant with six tables for six. It is the creation of Hendryk Kolbusz and his wife and deserves its high-flown reputation.

Hokkaido: Japan's best skiing

The 1972 Winter Olympics were held in **Hokkaido**, Japan's northernmost district. It was then that the world discovered the region's ideal skiing conditions.

Skiing in Japan is luxurious. Everything is civilized and efficient. For your après-ski enjoyment, try a relaxing *o-furo* (hot bath) with a massage and hot sake.

The two best places to ski are **Teine**, good for slalom skiing, and **Eniwa**, good for downhill skiing. **Mount Moiwa**, 30 minutes southwest of the city by bus, is also popular, overlooking the capital and the Sea of Japan.

The best places to stay

The region's best city is **Sapporo**, which has a wide choice of hotels, as well as taxis and buses to take you to the slopes. The **Akakura Kankon Hotel**, *tel. (81)255-87-2501*, in Niigata prefecture, is one of the best in Sapporo, with an excellent restaurant. **Yamagat Grand**, *tel. (81)236-412-611*, is a wonderful place to stay. **Sapporo Park**, *tel. (81)11-511-3131*, and **Sapporo Grand Hotel**, *tel. (81)11-0261-3311*, both are excellent places to stay, with a warm and inviting atmosphere.

Numerous lodges and *minshuku* (guesthouses) are located throughout Japan's ski country. Accommodation is Japanese-style—which means you sleep on a futon and share a room with three or four other people. Rooms are heated and often have televisions. Baths are communal and toilets are down the hall. The food, Japanese country cooking served boarding house-style, is plentiful and good.

You can rent ski equipment at most Japanese resorts, and it is easy to book a ski trip once you are in Japan.

Australia's best skiing

The **Snowy Mountains**, 300 miles southwest of Sydney, are much higher than the Blue Mountains. Covered with snow from June to late August, they are a great place to ski. Australia's highest peak is here, Mount Kosciusko (known as Mount Kozzie locally), which rises 7,314 feet.

Although skiing in Australia is as spectacular as skiing in the Alps (Australia has more snow than Switzerland), it is much less expensive. And it's one big party. Aussies drink until dawn, and then manage to ski the 25 miles of trails flawlessly.

The Snowy Mountains are worth a visit off-season as well, when prices are even lower and you can take a mile-and-a-half chair lift to the top of Mount Crackenback. The fishing, swimming, and hiking can't be beat.

New Zealand: the world's best summer skiing

Summer skiing in New Zealand is much cheaper than winter skiing in the United States or Europe. Lift tickets are about half the price of those at U.S. or European ski resorts. And hotels and restaurants are much less expensive.

The largest ski area

The largest and most popular ski area in New Zealand is the **Whakapapa Skifield** in Tongariro National Park on North Island. The slopes descend from Mount Ruapehu, a dormant volcano. Skiers are warned that part of the ski area is in a mudflow danger zone.

The park is a comfortable one-day drive from Auckland. Head south on State Highway 4 and then turn onto Provincial Highway 48, which takes you into the park and eventually up to the slopes. If you arrive early in the morning, the road to the top of Ruapehu is usually clear of snow and ice, allowing you to drive all the way to the parking area. Midday, however, usually brings fresh snow, and you may be forced to leave your car below and ride up the hill on a goat (a comfortable, four-wheel-drive bus).

Lift ticket fees allow you to use the platter lift, four chair lifts, four T-bars, two pomas, and seven rope tows. With a capacity of 10,000 skiers per hour, these lifts provide access up to 7,200 feet. Whakapapa has slopes for every level of skier, including a superb national downhill course for experts.

Skiing across the top of the last face of the High Traverse, you can look up into the chimney at the end of the run. The chimney isn't very long, but when you drop in from the top you can't see the slope below—and you have no retreat. It's a bit like stepping into an empty elevator shaft—a thrill for even the most jaded of skiers.

On the flanks of **Mount Ruapehu**, accommodation ranges from the luxurious Château Tongariro to the rustic cabins at Skotel, from high-class hotels and club chalets to a trailer park. If you want to stay at the Château, make reservations well in advance. An elegant restaurant in the basement serves delicious steak and seafood specialties.

The longest ski season

Mount Hutt, *tel. (64)3-302-8811*, on South Island, has New Zealand's longest ski season, extending from May through November. It boasts the earliest operating date of any ski field in the Southern Hemisphere. The field itself is set in a huge bowl that collects snow. Early in the season is the best time to ski powder snow; little patches of powder hide in the shadow of ridges.

Mount Hutt has several great routes that offer almost 2,300 vertical feet of skiing and a range of slopes and snow types. Facilities include one chair lift and four T-bars. You can heli-ski here, too, with the help of Methven Heliski, which flies to the upper Rakai Ranges.

The best skiing in the United States

Taos, New Mexico, and **Jackson Hole, Wyoming**, are challenging ski areas that are remote enough to not attract big crowds. Both have serious ski schools, but neither has much après-ski activity. Taos does have French-run inns and an Indian culture. Jackson Hole has views of the magnificent Tetons, and from time to time you'll see a graceful elk leaping through the snowfields. **Grand Targhee**, the backside of the Tetons, offers world-class powder and empty slopes. The resort at **Sun Valley, Idaho**, has all the amenities but little charm. Snowbird, Utah, has the best powder skiing in the country.

Canada's best skiing

Skiing in Canada is as exhilarating as skiing in the Alps. British Columbia and Alberta have some of the most spectacular peaks in the world, beginning on the Pacific coastline. The Canadian Rockies are rugged, wild, and challenging. And Quebec's Laurentians offer aprés-ski activities with a French flavor.

The best heli-skiing

Heli-skiing, a relatively new sport, uses helicopters instead of chair lifts to allow you to avoid lift lines and to reach empty slopes in remote places. Canada boasts some of the best heli-skiing opportunities in the world.

Kootenay Heli-skiing, *P.O. Box 717, Nakusp, BC VOG 1R0; tel. (604)265-3121* or *(800)663-0100*, offers trips into the open bowls and steep treelined runs of the unspoiled Selkirk and Monashee mountains. (Because the terrain is difficult, you must be an accomplished skier to participate.)

Whistler Heli-skiing, *P.O. Box 368, Whistler, BC VON 1B0; tel. (604)932-4105*, offers packages out of Whistler and Bralorne that take you into the four surrounding mountain ranges.

Mike Wiegele Helicopter Skiing, *P.O. Box 249, Banff, Alberta, Canada TOL OCO; tel. (403)762-5548* or *(800)661-9170*, takes you to the Cariboos and Monashees in the Canadian Rockies.

The best powder skiing: British Columbia

British Columbia's ski slopes are a sparkling, powder-covered paradise. And they are varied, including the Rockies, Bugaboos, Purcells, Selkirks, Chilcotin, Cariboo, and Monashees. The longest fall-line runs in North America are here, as is the highest serviced vertical drop.

Whistler, a trendy, fast-growing resort with gorgeous powder-bowl skiing above the tree line, has the longest vertical drop in the Americas (4,278 feet). Nearby **Blackcomb Mountain**, *tel. (604)932-3141*, opened recently. For more information, contact **Whistler Resort Association**, *4010 Whistler Way, Whistler, BC VON 1B4; tel. (604)932-4222*.

Alberta's best slopes

Calgary, Alberta, the jumping-off point for some of the world's finest downhill and cross-country skiing, hosted the 1988 Winter Olympic Games. About an hour from Calgary are the magnificent Rocky Mountains and **Mount Allan**, the site of many Olympic events. Thirty minutes farther into the mountains is **Banff National Park**, with beautiful terrain reminiscent of Lake Tahoe and Yosemite National Park.

Banff, the best resort

Banff is the area's best ski resort, with both the easiest and most difficult trails as well as superb facilities. **Mount Norquay** has some of the best beginner trails in the park, as well as three of the most difficult runs in North America: the North American, the Bowl, and the Lone Pine. The **Lone Pine** is a favorite among residents of Calgary, but it often intimidates tourists. The North American and the Bowl have acted as training grounds for many of Canada's world-class downhill racers. The mountain rises from 2,680 feet to 7,005 feet; the longest run measures 1.6 miles.

The best time to visit Banff (unless you dislike crowds) is during the winter festival, which has been held every January since 1917. Teams from around the country meet for the Mountain Madness Relay Race—a pentathlon of downhill skiing, running, skating, snowshoeing, and cross-country skiing.

The Banff Springs Hotel is the best ski lodge in Canada. Built in 1888, it was once the world's largest hotel. Not only does it look like a castle, but it operates like one, too. A medieval banquet—complete with period costumes and mead—is staged once a week in the imposing two-story Mount Stephen Dining Hall.

The longest season

Another ski area popular among Calgarians is **Sunshine Village**, about 20 minutes from Mount Norquay. Located at the tree line in an Alpine bowl, it is known for its powdery snow. It has the longest ski season in the region, lasting through mid-June—due to an average annual snowfall of 30 feet. Trails range from tight tree-lined runs to open bowls at the top. Sunshine's runs cover 1,200 acres, with a vertical drop of 3,420 feet to an on-the-mountain village. Stay at the **Sunshine Inn**.

Sunshine Village's **Nordic Center**, which opened in 1982, offers excellent high-country touring and programs for the novice and the telemark cross-country skier. Tracks to look for include the Spray River Loop, the Cascade Fire Road, the Red Earth Creek, the Pipestone Loop, and a telemark trail on Moraine Lake Road.

The world's biggest ski jump

The world's biggest ski jump is in **Thunder Bay, Ontario**, the newest hot spot for ski-jump fans. Four major Alpine areas have scores of slopes, including dozens of cross-country trails, for both beginners and experts. Canada's famous ski-jump champions practice here. Daily air service is available from Toronto, Winnipeg, Sault Ste. Marie, and Minneapolis.

North America's oldest ski slopes

The **Laurentians** (*Laurentides* in French), 40 minutes north of Montreal, boast the oldest ski areas in North America. The world's first rope tow was installed here in 1932 in the Quebec village of Shawbridge. Since then, these mountains have catered to skiers from around the world.

Mount Tremblant, the highest peak in the Laurentians, has a spectacular view of lakes, valleys, and forests. Its 3,000-foot vertical drop makes all kinds of skiing possible.

Gray Rocks also offers tremendous skiing. **St. Sauveur** is the place to ski and be seen.

If you're looking for accommodation in the Laurentians, try **Station Mount Tremblant**, which can handle up to 800 guests. **Manoir Pinoteau** has the best view of Tremblant and serves excellent food.

Chile: South America's best summer skiing

In Chile, the snow begins to fall in June and July, and from mid-August through September the weather and snow conditions are dependable, the slopes are not crowded, and all the ski resorts offer their lowest prices of the year. Furthermore, the scenery of the Andes is as spectacular as any in the Alps.

The safest slopes

At **La Parva**, only 35 minutes from Santiago, you can ski right from your door to the base of the lift. From there you can choose from nine poma lifts and two chair lifts. Wide-open and friendly, this is a safe place to be adventurous. Snowboarders can twist and turn over the edges of wind-curled cornices, and the miles of treeless mountains are perfect for heli-skiing.

The biggest slopes

Valle Nevado is the biggest, newest, and most talked about ski resort in South America, with 33 square miles of skiable terrain. These slopes offer the solitude of cross-country skiing **and** the conveniences of a downhill resort.

The granddaddy of ski resorts

The first skiers at **Portillo**, the granddaddy of South American ski resorts, were Norwegian mountaineers who arrived in 1890 to study the construction of a railroad between Chile and Argentina. The first lift was built in 1937 and had wooden towers. In 1947, this was replaced by a chair lift, and in 1949 the first hotel was built.

Portillo offers some of the most challenging terrain and ski lifts in South America. Because avalanches periodically wiped out lift towers on the steep upper slopes (where the best skiing is), the French invented the Va et Vient lift. Also known as the Sling Shot, this contraption shoots people standing four abreast on a poma lift, straight up 2,442 feet.

The World's Best Golfing

Scotland's best golfing

The **Gleneagles** in Perthshire has a guest list that comprises the who's who of golfing and is a favorite with golf-loving celebrities. Gleneagles has four courses: the nine-hole Wee Course, the King's Course (tricky), the Queen's Course (beautiful), and the PGA Centenary Course (stunning), designed by Jack Nicklaus. It cost more than $11 million, so it's not surprising that it's rated one of the best in the world. The **Gleneagles Hotel**, *Auchterarder, Perthshire, Scotland PH3 1NF; tel. toll free in the U.K. (0800)389-3737; toll free in the U.S. (44)1866-881-9525; fax (44)1764-662134; e-mail: resort.sales@ gleneagles.com; website: www.gleneagles.com.*

The world's oldest golf course

The **Old Course** in St. Andrews, Scotland, is the oldest and most venerable golf course in the world. It dates back to the 15th century and has been the site of 24 British Opens. It is a difficult course, with ever-changing winds and sandy greens. Contact the **Links Management Committee of St. Andrews**, *tel. (44)1334-475-757*. You will need a certificate of handicap or a letter of introduction from your club. The Old Course is closed on Sundays and for two weeks in February and two weeks in November.

Ireland's best golfing

Ireland is internationally recognized as a major golfing destination, and in recent years has hosted such major competitions as the American Express World Championships and the Ryder Cup.

Ireland is best known for its wonderful links courses. Links land is literally the ground that connects (or "links") the sea to the farmable soil. It's sandy, treeless, and windswept. This is the kind of terrain on which golf was first played by the Scots in the middle of the 19th century. Because no trees or crops could grow on the sandy soil, Scottish farmers used it to play golf. In Ireland, the game was introduced by the ancestors of British aristocrats, who supplanted Irish peasants to make way for their games. Links courses are common in the western regions of Ireland, mainly Sligo and Donegal.

Ireland possesses 40% of the world's links courses, but also has a range of parkland courses that offer a real test of golfing skills.

Europe's best golf course

Portugal's Algarve has the best golfing in Europe, combining emerald greens and perfect weather year-round. And the best of the Algarve's many courses is **Quinta do Lago**, *tel. (351)89-394-271*. Lush fairways of Bermuda grass invite international golfers. The clubhouse and the pool are both welcoming.

Dona Filipa, *Vale do Lobo; tel. (351)89-394-141*, is a grand hotel with views of the greens and the sea. It has a pool and tennis courts for those who tire of golf.

Hotel Dom Pedro Golf, *8125 Vilamoura, Quarteira; tel. (351)89-389-650*, has a swimming pool and tennis courts. It is popular with golfers.

The world's highest golf course

The highest golf course in the world is at **Gulmarg** (8,700 feet), in India, once a summer hill station popular with British colonialists. Gulmarg's seven-mile Circular Path offers a dizzying view of the Vale of Kashmir and Srinagar.

Thailand's best golf course

Thailand is fast emerging as a favorite year-round venue for the world's golfers. The country already boasts some 50 courses, and additional courses are in the works.

The best golf course in Thailand is the **Rose Garden Golf Course**, 45 minutes from Bangkok. It has been awarded a Silver Medal by *Golf Magazine USA* for being one of the best golf courses in the world. It is renowned as Thailand's best managed and most attractive, and the caddies are exceptionally well trained and savvy.

America's best golf resort

Pebble Beach, 120 miles south of San Francisco and 337 miles north of Los Angeles, has America's best golf course. **Pebble Beach Golf Links** has hosted three U.S. Open golf tournaments (1972, 1982, and 1992), two U.S. Amateur Golf Championships, and the annual AT&T Pebble Beach National Pro-Am. It is 6,357 yards long, very narrow, and draped across a magnificent landscape.

The **Cypress Point Club**, also in Pebble Beach, is the most exclusive golf course in the world and one of the prettiest. You must be invited to play here.

This area is worth a visit even if you aren't a golfer. **Carmel**, a quaint beach town with chic shops and inviting inns, is nearby. The best view of the sun setting over the Pacific Ocean is from the beach in Carmel. Residents flock here each evening to watch the red orb sink behind the sea. And the **Del Monte Forest**, stretching along the coast, offers some of the most scenic—and expensive—real estate in the world. The forest is surrounded by **17-Mile Drive**, a loop that passes beaches, sea lions, blowholes, grand estates, and scenic overlooks.

The **Lodge at Pebble Beach**, *17 Mile Drive, Pebble Beach*, is a gorgeous resort with tennis, swimming, horseback riding, saunas, hiking, fishing, and hunting.

The premier auto show in the world is the **Pebble Beach Concours d'Elegance**, held on the lawn of the Lodge at Pebble Beach.

THE WORLD'S BEST DIVING

Eilat, Israel—the world's best scuba diving

During the winter, fashionable Israelis flock to this port town at the southernmost tip of Israel, on the coast of the Red Sea. The beaches are filled with tanned bodies; the water just offshore is filled with marine life that exists nowhere else—tropical fish the origin of which is lost in time. The Red Sea is part of the African Rift, which runs through East Africa to the gold mines of the Rand in South Africa. **Eilat** has marvelous facilities for skin and scuba diving. One of the best places to rent gear is the **Lucky Divers' Eilat Scuba Center**.

Eilat has one of the best underwater observatories in the world for viewing exotic aquatic life. In spring, the city becomes a bird watcher's paradise, as dozens of migrating species make a stopover here. The colorful annual festival at Eilat (usually held in March) is marked by water sports and moonlight pageants.

If you're a nature lover, explore the Eilat zoo and **Hai-Bar**, an 8,000-acre wildlife preserve where animals from Biblical times are being returned to their natural habitats. Hai-Bar also contains the ruins of Nabataean cities (Nabataea was a small kingdom from 200 B.C. to 300 B.C.) and remnants of the oldest Christian churches in the world. Your hotel should be able to arrange tours or give you directions.

Neviot, Israel's only nude beach, about 30 miles south, is less crowded than Eilat's beaches.

Palau's best dive sites

Scuba divers in Palau should head straight for the outer reefs, including the Big Drop-off, Blue Corners, Blue Hole, and Turtle Cover, where you can descend to incredible depths in search of dazzling coral formations and exotic sea life.

The best dive shop

Koror has no shortage of dive shops or tour operators, but you can't go wrong with **Sam's Tour Service**, *tel. (680)488-1720; fax (680)488-1471.* Sam Scott is the American stepson of Ibedul, high chief of Koror. He can help you arrange it all—diving in the coral reefs of Rock Islands, exploring shipwrecks from World War II, sightseeing, fishing, boat charters, or even a night search for alligators in the mangrove swamps of Babeldop.

The best diving and snorkeling in Belize

In Ambergris, Belize, you'll find some of the very best diving and snorkeling in the world. Our favorite diving captain is **Captain Rene**, *tel. (501) 26-2819*. But if he's not available, don't despair. Ask at your hotel for a captain they recommend. Fishing is worthwhile, too. A good guide will know all the secret spots to try, and you'll come back with dinner, guaranteed.

The almost perfectly round "Blue Hole" of Belize, in the center of the Lighthouse Reef Atoll, is one of the world's most intriguing dive destinations. At more than 400 feet deep and 1,000 feet in diameter, it's visible from outer space.

The Blue Hole, a two-hour boat ride off the island of Caye Caulker, used to be a cave that rested atop the sea, and was made famous by Jacques Cousteau in the 1970s. Melting ice from the end of the last Ice Age engulfed the cave, which now delves 480 feet into the sea.

The dive begins as your group descends to a sandy beach floor about 16 to 19 feet below the surface. From there you wiggle your way over to the edge—a daunting sight as you look down hundreds of feet into a dark and scary hole.

At this point, the group begins the real descent to 130 feet (the depth limit for recreational divers). Once at the depth limit, divers are able to swim around massive stalactites and stalagmites, the size of which most have never seen. Because of the depth of the water, and the fact you are in a former cave, visibility is limited to around 30 feet. If you are lucky, as our group was, you may catch a glimpse of the reef sharks that live and hunt in the cave.

The cost of the dive is $130 to $140, including food, drink, and three dives.

The Cayman Islands—a mecca for scuba divers

The most varied scuba diving in the Caribbean is off the Caymans, three islands (Grand Cayman, Cayman Brac, and Little Cayman) surrounded by almost continuous rings of reefs. This spectacular underwater frontier contains 325 coral-encrusted shipwrecks, some rumored to contain pirates' treasure. The water is crystal clear, with a visibility of 200 feet. Craggy coral formations extend to the North Canyon Wall, where the ocean floor drops off a mile deep.

More than 20 diving companies offer scuba-diving lessons and gear rental in the Caymans. The oldest and largest on Grand Cayman is **Bob Soto's Diving**, *tel. (809) 949-2022*, run by owner Ron Kipp out of four locations, including the Holiday Inn on Seven Mile Beach.

The inhabitants of the Caymans are among the best seamen in the world and are heavily recruited by international freighting companies. Until tourism became their bread and butter (beginning in the 1960s), every able-bodied man went to sea at age 18.

Aside from scuba diving, the national pastimes are barhopping and churchgoing. Barefoot Man (a local legend—reminiscent of Jimmy Buffet) and other island bands play nightly except Sunday at the **Grand Cayman Holiday Inn**.

Another popular nightspot is Silver's Nightclub at the **Treasure Island Hotel**.

Blue laws close bars at midnight on Saturday. Bars can open again at noon on Sunday; however, on Sunday, live music can't be performed.

The **Tortuga Club**, *tel. (809)947-7449*, is the most romantic place to stay. It offers reasonably priced package tours.

Our other choice for the best place to stay on Grand Cayman is the Hyatt, an incredible property that includes three restaurants, gift and specialty shops, and a charter boat company.

The best diving in Guadeloupe

Underwater explorer Jacques Cousteau once described Basse-Terre's western coast as being among the world's top 12 dive sites. Attracting a daily pilgrimage of divers and snorkelers, the **Pigeon Islands** lie just off Malendure village. Warmed by hot springs, the bright turquoise seas around these three islets boast some of the Caribbean's most varied marine life. The islets are protected as part of the Cousteau Marine Reserve, but even non-divers can see the corals, sponges, and vividly colored shoals of tropical fish. A glass-bottomed boat, the Nautilus, sails from Malendure four times daily. The first boat leaves at 10.30 a.m. and the trip takes 90 minutes.

Saba's best diving

The Caribbean island of **Saba** is world-famous for its scuba diving, with more than 25 different diving areas. Diving instruction and certification are offered at **Saba Deep**, a diving shop at the LAI Chance Harbor, which is owned and operated by two Americans.

Mexico's best diving and snorkeling

Outside Cancun, on the road to Tulum, is an idyllic lagoon called **Xel-Hà**, where you can enjoy the best snorkeling in the Mexican Caribbean. Netting keeps the sharks out, while letting all the colorful fish in. You can glide among rocks, circle around the edge, or explore coves on the far side. You will see electric-blue fish, yellow fish with black stripes, and schools of tiny darters moving in unison. Although the lagoon is deep, the water is so crystal clear that you can see to the bottom. You can rent equipment here, but the flipper sizes are limited.

The best scuba diving is off the coast of Isla Mujéres, which is surrounded by reefs. You can rent equipment at **Mexico Divers**, *avenida Rueda Medina*, on the waterfront.

About 500 yards off Cozumel, along **El Cantil**, is a series of reefs where you can dive to see tropical fish and underwater wrecks. Water visibility averages 100 feet, perfect for photographs. You can rent diving equipment in San Miguel from **Aqua Safaris**, *ave. Melgar 39A; tel. (52)987-2-0101*, or **Dive Cozumel**, *tel. (52)988-2-0002*. Tanks and weights rent by the hour.

Most hotels charge higher prices for their diving facilities, but the on-site convenience is sometimes worth it. And some hotels offer scuba lessons. At the Stouffer Prezidente in Cozumel, for example, a two-hour lesson or four-day progressive scuba diver seminar with a certified instructor are available. A one-day guided diving tour from Cozumel to Palancar Reef includes equipment.

Cancun's best scuba diving is in the waters off its southern point. You can arrange guided diving expeditions and equipment rental through your hotel.

The world's best fishing

Australia's best fishing

For decades, Cairns has been a fishing capital of the world, abounding in barramundi, shark, and marlin. It's also the stepping-off point for the world's best black marlin fishing grounds. Although they aren't particularly good eating, black marlin put up one heck of a fight, making for a good battle.

New Zealand's best fishing

The **Canterbury** region, especially the town of Methven, is a mecca for salmon and trout fishermen. During the summer, quinnat salmon run in the Rangitata and Ashburton rivers near Geraldine. Three major salmon-fishing contests are held each year on the Rangitata, Rakaia, and Waitaki rivers.

Man's best fishing

Sports fishermen adore the Isle of Man because of its variety of fishing: surf casting, river fishing, and deep-sea fishing. The best place to go surf fishing is the **Point of Ayre**, where you can fish at any tide. The best time however is low tide.

SECTION 5:

THE WORLD'S BEST SHOPPING

Singapore • Athens • Rome • Florence • Bologna • Lisbon • Zurich Beijing • Tokyo • Hong Kong • Delhi • Calcutta • Nairobi • Dakar Israel • Sydney • Melbourne • New York City • Montreal • Toronto Rio • Mexican Caribbean • São Paulo • Caymen Islands

SINGAPORE: THE WORLD'S GREATEST SHOPPING

There are two reasons Singapore offers the best shopping in the world. First, a better selection cannot be found anywhere else. Second, the government's harsh policy toward unscrupulous merchants makes this a safe place to spend your money.

Tanglin, **Orchard**, and **Scotts** roads are the obvious places to begin a shopping spree. Prices are fixed, charge cards are welcome, and shopkeepers are friendly and speak English. Bring your walking shoes—or better yet, buy a pair at one of the shops in the area.

The best place to buy a carpet

The best place to buy a carpet in Singapore is at an auction. Open to the public, auctions are announced in the local paper. They are usually held in hotel ballrooms. Attend several auctions before purchasing anything; it pays to listen and learn. The carpets sold are from Afghanistan, Turkey, and Pakistan. Weavers tend to depict their everyday experiences in their works.

ATHENS' BEST SHOPPING

The **Plaka**, where you can buy any kind of handicraft made in Greece, is the best place for shopping. However, if you're heading out to the islands, where goods are cheaper, wait.

Monastiraki, better known as the Athens flea market, is a special part of the Plaka. It runs from Monastiraki Square to Ifestou Street and includes shops offering both antiques and old junk. The best time to visit is Sunday morning.

Kolonaki has posh boutiques, modern art galleries, expensive antique shops, and good dress designers.

Omonia Square is where the locals shop. The Greek-style department stores here offer better prices than Kolonaki. Goods are sensible rather than stylish.

Pandrossou, the Street of Shoes, also has shops selling brassware, peasant costumes, Greek dolls, and good imitation antiques. (You can't take real ones out of the country.)

The **National Archeological Museum** sells copies and castings of Greek museum pieces.

THE BEST SHOPPING IN ROME

Luxury shops fill the Piazza di Spagna and line the adjoining streets. Less expensive shops can be found along via del Corso, and there are also department stores that employ their own designers and feature stylish collections. Leather goods, gloves, shoes, purses, wallets, belts, and luggage displayed in windows draw credit cards from the pockets of passersby like magnets.

FLORENCE: THE MOST INTERESTING SHOPPING

The **Oltrarno**, or artisan quarter on the left bank of the Arno, is a maze of streets spreading out from the Pitti Palace and around the Church of Santo Spirito. Stop in at the workshops, where picture frames are gilded, furniture is restored, and metals are forged.

BOLOGNA'S BEST FOOD SHOPPING

Tamburini, *website: www.tamburini.com*, in via Caprarie, has been in business for over 70 years purveying over 150 foods, including the best of the region's delicious cheeses, pastas, sausages, hams, patés, preserves, balsamic vinegar, Vignola cherries, and wines. There's an attached *bistrot* too, with a vast lunch menu.

Around the corner from the Tamburini is the thriving **Mercato di Mezzo** food market for meat and fish, fresh fruit and vegetables, and the ubiquitous parmesan cheese. Make sure your parmesan is marked Parmigiano-Reggiano to prove it's the genuine article from Bologna's Emilia-Romagna region.

LISBON'S BEST SHOPPING

Veer off the grand avenida da Liberdade onto the rua do Carmo and rua Garrett. This is **Chiado**, Lisbon's shopping district, where you'll find jewelry, Portuguese tiles, leather goods, and wine for reasonable prices.

Lisbon's other main shopping area, **Baixa**, is located between Rossio Square and the river. Here are old bookshops and antique stores. The best place for gold and silver filigree is **Sarmento**. **Por-fi-ri-os Contraste** sells the skimpiest bikinis around. **Helio Cinderela** has good prices on Charles Jourdan shoes and smart leather bags. **Saboia** sells fine men's suits. Brightly colored *azulejos* are sold at **Fabrica Sant'Anna**.

Where to find a real steal

A cheap, offbeat place to shop is the **Feira da Ladra** (Market of Female Thieves). This 300-year-old market is similar to huge flea markets in Rome and Paris. Originally, it was literally a market of *sovaqueiras*, or female thieves. The *sovaqueiras* hid illegal wares in their armpits and sold them at stalls then located in Lisbon's central Rossio Square. You can buy just about anything you want at this market. Be on the lookout for bronze, copper, and gold—sometimes you can find great bargains.

Zurich's best shopping

The Bahnofstrasse is also known as **Luxury Mile**, because of its expensive, first-class shops. While it's fun to look at 18-carat gold shoehorns and watches, you're better off doing your shopping in Zurich's department stores or along **Marktzplatz Oerlikon**, a pedestrian district near Bahnhofstrasse.

Beijing's best shopping

Qianmen-Dashalan Business Street lies in the southern city of Beijing. It is to the south of Zhengyangmen and to the west of the central line. This is an old shopping street with a long history. It has a lot of famous shops, such as Liubiju sauce and pickle shop, Tongrentang drugstore, Ruifuxiang silk shop, Neiliaansheng shoe shop, and Zhangyiyuan teashop.

Wangfujing Business Street lies in Dongcheng District, the center of Beijing. It is a beautiful walking street. On this street are the well-known Beijing Department Store, the famous Dong'an Market, the biggest arts and crafts shop in China, the biggest Xinhua Bookstore, the Foreign Languages Bookstore, Lisheng Sports Shop, and a Medical Appliances Shop. Also here are some famous old shops, such as Shengxifu hat shop, Tonghesheng shoe shop, New World silk shop, Hengteli watchmaker's shop, Baicaoshenrong drugstore, and Jiguge historical relic shop.

Xidan Business Street is in Xicheng District, the center of Beijing. This district is where the famous Xidan Market, Xidan Shopping Center and some old shops, such as Shengxifu hat shop and Jingyi glasses shop, are located.

Some popular shopping centers are **Yansha Friendship Shop**, *No.52 Liangmahe Road*, **Chaoyang District**; *Saite Shopping Center, Jianwai Street, Chaoyang District*; **Friendship Shop**, *No. 17 Jianwai Street, Chaoyang District*.

Flea and antique markets are also very popular. Some good ones to attend are the **Panjiayuan Flea Market** (the third eastern and southern circle), **Haiwangcun Flea Market** (Liulichang), **Hongqiao Flea Market** (the northern gate of the Temple of Heaven).

For arts, pearls, and jewels, China's Arts and Craft Shops are lovely. **Yuanlonggu Silk Shop**, *No. 55 Tiantan Road*, is a famous old shop, where you can buy original color silks, green satins and brocades, as well as carpets and tapestries.

The world's most exotic market

In China, Guangzhou's **Quingping Market**, just over the bridge from Shamian Island, has an incredible assortment of animals intended for the table. It is divided into two sections: one for vendors of traditional Chinese medicines and one for vendors of produce, meats, and live animals to be butchered. Dogs hang from hooks. Kittens are sold by the pound. Dead rats are sold as food. Wild boars are caged. Owls, mice, and snakes await slaughter. Small, Bambi-like deer are slaughtered before your eyes. And internal organs you have never heard of are for sale.

THE GINZA: TOKYO'S BEST SHOPPING

The **Ginza district**, southeast of the center of the city, is world-famous for its enormous department stores and exclusive little shops. Cars and trucks are barred from this area on weekends, when shoppers take over the streets and merchandise is moved onto the sidewalks. Ginza (which translates as *Silver Mint*) is named for the Japanese mint, which was once located south of Kyobashi Bridge.

In addition to the usual fare, Takashimaya, a department store in the Ginza, has restaurants, tearooms, boutiques, a kimono department, and an art gallery that exhibits shows from top international museums. The best time to experience the formal hospitality of this store is at 10 a.m., when it opens and the salespeople line up and bow to you.

For an experience in high-tech shopping, visit Seibu. In addition to designer clothes and imported ice cream, Seibu has 177 closed-circuit televisions that entertain shoppers with rock music videos, breaking waves, and cherry blossoms.

The most colorful place to shop in the Ginza is the Tsukiji fish market, a 50-acre stretch of wholesale fish stalls. This is a great place to take photos. You will see all the fish that make their way into Tokyo's sushi bars, some familiar, some not. Wear waterproof shoes.

THE BEST SHOPPING FOR GEMS

Hong Kong boasts more jewelry shops per square mile than any other city in the world, and it's the world's third-largest diamond-trading center. You'll find good buys on not only diamonds but also on gold, pearls, emeralds, sapphires, coral, jade, and lapis lazuli.

The best-known street market

The most famous of Hong Kong's many street markets is the **Stanley Market**, on the south side of the island. Stanley is an old fishing village with a large expatriate community. Silk dresses, sunglasses, fresh fruits, rattan furniture, porcelain ware, shoes, and luggage are available for bargain prices.

DELHI'S BEST SHOPPING

Chandni Chowk, the city's marketplace, is a web of narrow streets that surround the Red Fort. Here you can shop for shoes, cows, pungent oriental spices, jewelry, ivory carvings, and rich brocades, and then have your stars read or your hair cut.

THE BEST SHOPPING IN CALCUTTA

New Market is one of the largest markets in India, with 2,500 stalls selling everything from cheap tin pots to fine silks. The market's real name, the Sir Stuart Hogg Market, is, not surprisingly, seldom used. The market is open from early morning until about 8 p.m.

NAIROBI'S BEST SHOPPING

In the center of Nairobi is the **Nairobi City Market**, where you can barter for animal carvings and usually come out ahead. The **African Heritage Shop**, *Kenyatta Avenue*, sells animal carvings, textiles, and jewelry. **Colpro Outfitters**, *Kenyatta Avenue*, is the place to go for safari gear.

Here are some of the Swahili words that may prove useful: *Bei gain* (How much?); *Ni ghali* (It is expensive); *Taf adhali nipunguzie bei* (Please give me a discount).

THE MOST INTERNATIONAL SHOPPING

Dakar, in Senegal, Africa, is filled with fascinating markets that combine African, Arabian, and European traditions. The one drawback is that all the city's markets are expensive.

The most colorful is **Sandaga**, an enormous place covering several city blocks with little stalls selling everything from fruit and meat to cloth and sandals. This is where the locals shop—it is about as authentic as you'll get. Another typical market is **Marché Tilène**, *avenue Blaise Diagne*.

Local designers create garments decorated with batik and embroidery and then sell their clothing in boutiques throughout the city. Recommended boutiques include **Fara**, *rues Assane N'Doye and Wagane Diouf*, and the **Deco Shop**, *rues Carnot and Blanchot*.

Marché Kermel, *near place de l'Indépendence*, is Dakar's European-style market, where you can buy high-quality imported goods, as well as clothing and souvenirs. Haggling is not recommended. The market is open daily.

Caritas Tissage Traditionnel, *Route de Ouakam*, is a weavers' workshop that sells belts, bedspreads, purses, and clothing. Prices are reasonable. Again, haggling is not recommended.

ISRAEL'S BEST SHOPPING

Tel Aviv's main streets, Allenby, Ben Yehuda, and Dizengoff, are lined with cafés and boutiques. A connoisseur's choice of Israeli handicrafts, including chunky silver jewelry, pottery, and embroidered caftans, is available at **Maskit**, *Ben Yehuda Street off Frishman Street*. Dizengoff Street, lined with trees and cafés and bistros that rival those of Paris, is the place to shop for high fashion and diamonds (cut and polished in Netanya, 19 miles to the north).

SYDNEY'S BEST SHOPPING

Paddington, or Paddo as it is called, is the best place to shop in Sydney. The area is much like Washington, D.C.'s Georgetown, with restored town houses and colorful little shops.

The major draw is the **Village Bazaar**, held each Saturday from 9 a.m. to 4 p.m. on the grounds of the Uniting Church in Australia. The bazaar feels for all the world like California in the 1960s, filled with lots of long-haired youths. But look closer and you also will see busy matrons searching for dinner. More than 120 stalls sell handicrafts, antiques, clothing, imported goods, and art. This is one of the best places in Australia to find authentic Australian-made goods at bargain prices.

Although the bazaar can be a shopping spree in itself, it should be considered only the starting point of a shopping journey through Paddington. Along Oxford Street, the main thoroughfare, and its side streets, you will discover antique shops, boutiques, art galleries, bookstores, craft shops, jewelers, and record shops.

Paddo's best shops include **Jack O'Beans**, *264 Oxford St.*, an elegant antique store; the **Australian Centre for Photography**, *257 Oxford. St.*, for Australian and international photo art; **Game Birds**, *108 Oxford St.*, for made-to-order leather and lace fashions; **Cooee Australian Emporium**, *98 Oxford St.*, for custom-designed jewelry; and **Angelo's**, *112 Oxford St.*, for handmade boots and shoes.

Sample homemade Russian chocolates at **W. Pulknownik's**, *Oxford and Elizabeth streets*.

To get to Paddington from downtown Sydney, take the 380 bus from Circular Quay to Oxford Street or bus 378 from Railway Square.

MELBOURNE'S BEST SHOPPING

Melbourne's center for shopping buffs is located between Swanston and Elizabeth streets, on Collins and Bourke. This is where you'll find **Myers**, Australia's biggest department store. Bourke Street is a pedestrian mall, but be careful; trams pass through here at alarming speeds.

Aboriginal Handicrafts, *Ninth Floor, 125 Swanston St.*, is the best place for honest-to-goodness handicrafts made by Australia's oldest residents. It is open daily from 10 a.m. until 4:30 p.m.

NEW YORK CITY'S BEST SHOPPING

Fifth Avenue is lined with some of the world's chicest and most expensive stores. Look at the gigantic gems in Tiffany's windows. Take stock of the latest fashions on display at Bergdorf Goodman and Saks. Or stop in at F.A.O. Schwartz, where you can spend from $20 to $20,000 for a toy. Also look for Cartier, Gucci, Steuben Glass, Godiva Chocolates, and the famous Trump Tower.

Other elegant shopping streets include Madison, Park, and Seventh avenues and 39th, 56th, and 57th streets.

If you prefer bargains over elegance, go to Orchard and Delaney streets. **Annemarie Gardin Inc.**, *498 Seventh Ave.*, where prices are very low, is open Monday through Friday only from 9 a.m. to 5 p.m. The **Better Made Coat and Suit Company**, *270 W. 38th Street*, has designer labels for less than designer prices.

The world's best diamond market

The **Diamond Exchange**, *47th Street and Sixth Avenue*, is responsible for more than 80% of the world's wholesale diamond trade. The exchange is dominated by the Orthodox Jewish community.

New York's best food markets

Zabar's, *2245 Broadway; tel. (212) 787-2000*, has the greatest variety of delicacies and the biggest crowds, attracting 30,000 customers per week. The coffee is roasted by Saul Zabar himself. Twenty-six kinds of salami, 42 kinds of mustard, and 30 varieties of honey are sold. Zabar's is open every day.

Balducci's, *424 Avenue of the Americas*, has fresh produce and herbs, pasta, homemade dishes, and candy. Prices are high.

Dean & Deluca, *560 Broadway; tel. (212) 431-1691*, is another deli with an incredible variety, including edible ferns in season. The Italian foods are good. The Dean & Deluca café is located at 121 Prince Street.

UNDERGROUND MONTREAL: THE WARMEST SHOPPING

Because Montreal can be buried in as much as 100 inches of snow during the winter, many of the city's shops have taken refuge in a seven-mile mall beneath the city. Designed by architect I.M. Pei and developer William

Zeckendorf in the 1950s, the underground complex has shops, sports facilities, theaters, exhibits, restaurants, apartments, hotels, and banks. Best of all, it's all heated.

The nucleus of the complex is **Place Ville Marie**, where shops surround a sculptured fountain. Corridors link Ville Marie with similar complexes at Place Bonaventure and Place du Canada. The three areas together contain 280 shops, 20 restaurants and bars, and entrances to three hotels.

Place des Arts is a lavish performing-arts center, home of the Montreal Symphony Orchestra and the Montreal Opera. To get there, take the metro to the Place des Arts stop.

TORONTO'S BEST SHOPPING

The hub of downtown shopping is **Eaton Center**, an 860-foot-long shopping center docked on Yonge Street. The mall is shaped like a large ocean freighter, with a series of railings, big exposed ducts, greenhouse glazing, and three-dozen sculptured geese swooping from the glass-domed ceiling. The Eaton Center does more gross sales than any other shopping mall in North America.

The retail giants Simpsons and Eaton's are anchored at each end of the mall, with 300 shops, banks, boutiques, and fast-food outlets on three levels in between.

RIO'S BEST SHOPPING

The best shopping in Rio is for leather goods. You'll find good deals at all the city's department stores, including **Rio Sul**, on the west side of the tunnel leading from avenida Princesa Isabel. Or stroll along avenida Atlantica in the evening, where you'll find a wide assortment of leather products.

Feirarte (formerly known as the Hippie Market) is a good place to buy arts and crafts. It is held Sundays at Praça General Osorio in Ipanema.

THE BEST SHOPPING IN THE MEXICAN CARIBBEAN

Shopping in the Caribbean takes patience, persistence, and a poker face. The basic rules of haggling apply. First ask the price of something and then offer half as much. The shopkeeper inevitably will reply that what you're offering won't even cover the costs of the materials. Your best response is to shrug your shoulders and walk away. The shopkeeper will probably follow you.

In Cancun

Cancun's major market area is downtown along avenida Tulum. As you

The World's Best Destinations

walk by this open-stall market, which stretches for about two blocks, the shopkeepers call to you—some even reach out and grab you by the arm as you pass. Blankets, sweaters, silver bracelets, and straw hats are thrown in boxes and tables in the stalls, and nothing is marked with a price. Feel free to rummage, but wait to ask for help until you're sure of what you want to buy. Once you have the attention of a salesperson, you won't get rid of him easily.

The sweaters and blankets at this market are good quality, but the gold and silver may be less so. Buy a piece of jewelry (if you can get a good price) because you like it, not because you think you're investing in gold. Real silver is marked with a government symbol that shows an eagle with a snake in its mouth leaning against a cactus.

If you'd rather avoid the market, good shops are located along avenida Tulum. **La Casita**, for example, stocks traditional Mexican clothes as well as silver and coral jewelry.

El Parian, Cancun's main square, also is a good place to shop. One store there, **Anakena**, sells Mayan art.

Little boys on the streets sell marionettes dressed in Mexican costume that make good gifts for children and cost next to nothing.

In Isla Mujéres

The place to go for handmade, brightly embroidered cotton dresses is **Isla Mujéres**. As you step from the boat onto the deck, you'll be bombarded by people selling blankets, lace tablecloths, necklaces, and conch shells. However, the better merchandise is in the shops in town. These shops keep their doors open to the sun, and the maracas and hats seem to pour from the shops onto the streets and sidewalks.

In Cozumel

In Cozumel, **Bazaar Cozumel**, *Boulevard Rafael E. Melgar*, sells high-quality Mexican art, including silverwork, tapestries, and pottery, at good prices. And **Plaza del Sol** has about a dozen craft and jewelry shops.

SHOPPING BESTS IN SÃO PAULO

São Paulo is known for its shopping. The best buys include clothing, antiques, and Brazilian jewels. The steep rua Augusta, lined with little boutiques selling native art and unusual clothing, is a good place to begin your shopping spree. In addition, the city has many large shopping malls, which offer a glittering array of high-quality merchandise. The two biggest are **Iguatemi** and **Ibirapueraon**. The jeweler Henry Stern has an office in São Paulo as well as in Rio.

A huge Sunday fair is held along the **Praça da Republica**. A colorful street fair is held Tuesday and Thursday through Saturday in Pacaembú Stadium.

Unrecognizable tropical fruits and vegetables are sold, as well as such exotic items as octopus and orchids.

THE CAYMAN ISLANDS: THE WORLD'S BEST DUTY-FREE SHOPPING

The Cayman Islands have recently expanded into a bargain center for high-quality goods. Shopping centers have arisen to accommodate the needs of the Caymans' relatively affluent population—and to cater to tourists. You'll find fashion boutiques, scuba equipment shops, beauty salons, and gift stores. Better yet, prices of goods in duty-free shops are often as much as 40% cheaper than those in U.S. shops.

SECTION 6:

THE WORLD'S MOST SCENIC DRIVES

Ireland • Scotland • French Riviera • Amalfi Coast • Germany
Nairobi • New Zealand • United States • Canada • Rio • Costa Rica

IRELAND'S MOST BEAUTIFUL DRIVES

County Kerry is known for the spectacular **Ring of Kerry**, a 110-mile drive that hugs the coast of the Inveragh Peninsula. Highlights of the drive include **Rossbeigh Beach**, near Glenbeigh on the north coast, which offers the best view of Drung Hill; **Glencar**, near Caragh Lake, a good place to hike; cells carved from solid rock by monks escaping the Vikings at **Skellig Rocks**; **Ballaghisheen Pass**, which takes you through scenic mountains; and the peaceful beaches that line the southern half of the ring. You can make the drive in a day, but don't be surprised if you take longer—all the beautiful sights along the road make it hard to pull yourself away.

Wild and Gaelic **Dingle Peninsula** is another beautiful drive in County Kerry. Begin the drive in the town of Dingle, on the ocean. Surrounded by hills, this fishing town is protected by an ancient wall. From Dingle, take the road to Ventry, which has an inviting beach. Outside **Ventry** are beehive huts built by monks of early Irish monasteries. Slea Head, at the tip of the peninsula, has a lovely view of the seven Blasket Islands. And the beach at **Slea Head** has water warm enough for swimming, thanks to the Gulf Stream.

Northeast of Slea Head is **Gallerus Oratory**, an unmortared stone building from the ninth century. After 1,000 years, it is still watertight. From the **Conair Pass**, you can see the lakes and Brandon, Tralee, and Dingle bays. **Sybil Head** has high green-sodded cliffs topped by thatched cottages and washed by the Atlantic below.

While in Kerry stay at the **Ballyseede Castle Hotel**, *tel. (353)66-25799*. Acres of greenery surround this 15th-century castle. Or stay at the ideally situated **Parknasilla Great Southern**, *tel. (353)64-45122*. It offers outstanding atmosphere, great service, beautiful room décor, and extensive facilities, including swimming, tennis, golf, and horseback riding, all on 300 acres of beautiful grounds. The hotel overlooks Kenmare Bay.

SCOTLAND'S MOST SCENIC DRIVES: THE HIGHLANDS

The Road to the Isles, A830, follows the spectacular Atlantic coast. One of the most beautiful passes en route is **Glenfinnan**, where in 1745 Bonnie Prince Charlie, the 25-year-old son of the exiled Stuart Pretender, launched his campaign to reclaim the British crown. The statue of a Jacobite Highlander tops Glenfinnan Monument on the shore where the prince raised the Stuart standard.

The tiny town of **Arisaig** is also steeped in history. Bonnie Prince Charlie landed here to begin his uprising. He hid in a cave in the region. The rocky coast is a short walk away. While here, stay in **Arisaig House**, *Beasdale*,

Arisaig PH39 4NR, an outstanding hotel with a walled rose garden. Prices are moderate.

On the route to Mallaig from Arisaig is an unpaved track leading to a remote and beautiful hamlet called **Bracora**. The road follows Loch Morar, Scotland's deepest lake, which is 1,017 feet.

THE BEST DRIVE ON THE FRENCH RIVIERA

The drive along the **Grande Corniche**, the high road along the crests of the mountains, is spectacular. At times you will see the high snow-covered peaks of the Alps. At other places, you will see the sea. On the way down, visit Roquebrune, where a chateau was hewn from the rock.

The Corniche is where the Monte Carlo Grand Prix car races are held and where the spectacular chase in *Casino Royale* was filmed.

ITALY'S MOST SPECTACULAR DRIVE: THE AMALFI COAST

The **Amalfi Coast**, a mountainous peninsula between the Gulf of Naples and the Gulf of Salerno, is a land of legends. Pirates once used the secluded inlets as hideouts. Spectacular views can be enjoyed from the dizzying summits of the mountains. Serpentine roads wind through cliffside villages. Olive groves and grapevines dot the plains.

In July or August, the Amalfi Coast becomes a madhouse, and it is nearly impossible to drive. The spring and fall are idyllic—warm and uncrowded.

The best coastal views

One of the most breathtaking views on the coast is from the old **Capuchin Monastery** perched on a cliff above Amalfi. An elevator takes you up to the 12th-century building, which today is an inexpensive hotel. Theodore Roosevelt and Henry Wadsworth Longfellow have stayed here.

You still can visit a chapel and cloisters within the hotel. The foundations of the convent, which is perched on a sheer cliff, date back to A.D. 1000. Bus service connects the hotel with the beach. If you ask, the staff will pack you a picnic lunch.

Another spectacular view is from the little town of **Ravello**, above Amalfi. A bus will take you to this summit via narrow, twisting roads. **Hotel Rufolo**, *via San Francesco 4, 84010 Ravello (Salerno); tel. (39)89-85-71-33*, is a lovely 11th-century building now used as a hotel. It has gorgeous gardens filled with hydrangeas and a Moorish cloister overgrown with flowers. During the summer, concerts are staged here. The villa was once the residence of Pope Adrian IV, the only English pope, who reigned from 1154 to 1159. Lord Byron, Greta Garbo, and composer Richard Wagner have stayed here.

The cathedral in Ravello has sculptures of strange-looking animals and contains a reliquary with the skull of Santa Barbara. The blood of the town's patron saint, San Pantaleone, is preserved in a cracked vessel that never leaks (or so it is said).

The **Hotel Caruso Belvedere**, *via San Giovanni del Torro 52, 84010 Ravello (Salerno); tel. (39)89-857-111*, set 900 feet above the Mediterranean coast, has sweeping views of the sea through its arched terrace. This well-known hotel is in the 11th-century d'Afflito Palace. Wines from surrounding vineyards are served in the restaurant. Most rooms have private bathrooms and private balconies.

Hotel Palumbo, *via S. Giovanni del Toro 28, 84010 Ravello (Salerno); tel. (39)89-857-244*, perched 1,200 feet above the coast, also has tremendous views. The 12th-century building was once the Palazzo Confalone. It is a pretty building, with arch and pillar vaulting, stone staircases, tile-inlaid floors, and good paintings. The hotel restaurant serves its own Ravello wines. Three-day stays are requested.

THE MOST SCENIC DRIVES THROUGH GERMANY

Germany is known for its beautiful scenic drives. The longest is the **Alpen-Ostsee**, stretching from the Baltic Sea island of Fehmarn to the Bavarian village of Berchtesgaden. The most unusual is the Windmill Road in the marshy area of Minden/Lubeck. The roads overlap in many of the most picturesque places. For instance, the Romantic and the Alpine roads both lead to Mad Ludwig's castle Neuschwanstein.

The Romantic Road

The **Romantic Road** runs from Wurzburg in the north to Fussen in the south. The road, which follows a medieval trade route, is about 200 miles long and passes vineyards, ruined castles, and wooded hills.

Begin by heading east from Heidelberg along the Neckar River on the Castle Road (Route 37). At Nedkarelz, turn left on Route 27 and go through Mosbach. Take Route 292 to Bad Mergentheim. Stop in Weikersheim to visit the town's castle, which has a marvelous Hunting Hall and baroque gardens.

The German Alpine Road

The **Deutsche Alpenstrasse** (German Alpine Road) leads from Bodensee through the Bavarian Alps. It passes Germany's highest peak, the Zugspitze; the limestone massifs of the Alpine National Park; the ski resorts of Garmisch-Partenkirchen; Berchtesgadener Land, where the mighty

Watzmann Mountain drops down suddenly to the deep-blue Konigsee; Mittenwald; and the castles of Hohenschwangau and Neuschwanstein, where Mad King Ludwig lived out his fantasies. The natural scenery along the route is consistently awe-inspiring.

The best place to stay along this route is the Posthotel Partenkirchen, Ludwigstrasse 49, near Garmisch. This 15th-century family-run hotel overflows with Bavarian atmosphere. The exterior of the three-story building is covered with paintings. Inside are oil portraits, dark wood furniture, beamed ceilings, and wood paneling. Many of the rooms have balconies, and a roof garden affords a view of the Zugspitze.

The Road of the Nibelungs

The **Nibelungenstrasse** (Road of the Nibelungs) is a favorite among devotees of the Siegfried sagas. (Wagner used these tales for his Ring operas.) The route, which goes from Worms to Wertheim, passes through the Odenwald, an inhospitable forest region in the time of the Nibelungs. Today, the hilly, wooded region is much more welcoming, with a series of health spas (Amorbach, Bad König, Beerfelden, Erbach, and Michelstadt). The **Bergstrasse-Odenwald Nature Park** is a good place to stop and appreciate the rocky forest. The park is covered by an extensive network of footpaths.

The Fairy-Tale Trail

The **Fairy-Tale Trail** leads from Bremen through Hamelin to Steinau, the home of the brothers Grimm. The road leads 360 miles south, through medieval towns and past castles, palaces, and seemingly enchanted forests. It takes you to the 13th-century castle of Neustadt, where Rapunzel was locked in a tower by a witch; the town of Schwalmstadt, where Little Red Riding Hood lived; and Kassel, where the brothers Grimm collected their first book of fairy tales in 1812.

The most magical place to stay en route is Sleeping Beauty's castle (or one of them) in **Sababurg**. Built in 1334 to protect pilgrims heading for Gottsbüren, the castle has two massive towers. The hotel is closed January through March.

THE LOVELIEST DRIVE FROM NAIROBI

The best way to see the countryside around Nairobi is by car, at your own pace. Following is the best itinerary, recommended by an old Kenya hand.

Drive three hours north of Nairobi to **Nayuki**, stopping along the way to see the grave of Lord Baden Powell, founder of the Boy Scouts, in Nyerere. On his tomb is a circle with a dot in the middle, the scout symbol for "gone home."

Nanyuki is situated 8,000 feet high on the slope of snow-topped Mount Kenya, which sits smack on the equator. Once you have become acclimated to the altitude, you will find this an ideal base for observing Kenya's wildlife.

Take time to stay at either the **Sportman Arm's Club** or the **Mwingo Gate Hotel** (formerly the safari Club). Visit Africa's most exciting racetrack.

From Nayuki, head north to **Archer's Post**, a spring in the middle of the desert. If you are traveling independently, this is the end of the line. Solo travelers are not permitted to venture farther out into the Northern Frontier district. (This is for your own protection).

To venture deeper into the desert, join an organized tour and continue north to **Marsabit**, a tree-covered mountain in the middle of the Kaisul desert; this is where game animals come to drink during the dry season.

Backtrack to Nanyuki and then take the road to **Nakuru**, which runs along the edge of the Rift Valley. You will see flamingos and views of mountains and the plain. This is where early traces of man were discovered.

En route, stop at the **Nyahururu waterfall** (formerly called Thomson's Fall). Stay at the **Thomson's Fall Lodge**, a bit of old England, where you can take tea on the lawn while watching the waterfall. A few miles away is the courthouse where Jomo Kenyatta, leader of the independence movement, was tried.

NEW ZEALAND'S MOST BEAUTIFUL DRIVE

The road around the **East Cape** on North Island is one of the most rugged yet beautiful coastal drives in New Zealand, passing small historic settlements, pleasant coves and beaches, and wild countryside that remains rich in Maori tradition and culture. Some of the finest Maori carvings can be seen in the traditional meetinghouses of this district, which is the first in the world to greet the morning sun.

AMERICA'S MOST BEAUTIFUL DRIVE

The drive along the Pacific Coast from San Francisco south to Big Sur is the most spectacular in the United States. **Highway 1** is a dizzying twisting ribbon edging high cliffs above the pounding surf. Many movie chase scenes have been filmed on these precipitous roads. Stop from time to time to look over the edge at the deep blue water and empty beaches below. Because the undertow along the coast is so fierce, swimming is usually forbidden. In places, you'll hear colonies of sea lions barking on the rocks. The most spectacular scenery is at **Big Sur**. Waves crash through holes worn in giant rocks, and fierce winds whip along the sand. When you get here, ask how to get down to the beach. The roads often aren't marked.

The **Ventana Inn**, *Highway 1, Big Sur*, is a modern cedar structure. Rooms have carved arched headboards and handmade Nova Scotian quilts. Some have fireplaces, saunas, and Japanese hot tubs. The hotel has a heated swimming pool. Continental breakfast is served in the lobby, and a complimentary cheese and wine buffet is offered in the afternoon. The inn's restaurant has good food and a view of the ocean and mountains.

Alaska's best drive

The most spectacular drive from Juneau is north to **Haines**. Forty miles of road wind through the mountains to the border. **Klukwan**, near Haines, has the largest concentration of bald eagles in North America. The **Chilkoot Trail**, which begins in the gold-rush town of Skagway, is littered with wagon wheels, horse skeletons, and commemorative plaques that trace the steps of gold-crazed miners.

CANADA'S LOVELIEST DRIVE

Canada's most beautiful drive is **Highway 430,** north of Gros Morne, on the coast of the **Great Northern Peninsula.** The waters of jagged fiords lap at the steep Long Range Mountains. At the northern tip of the peninsula, hundreds of icebergs rise as much as 300 feet out of the water. You can get more information from the Information Center in Wiltondale, which is open 9 a.m. until 9 p.m. in the summer.

RIO'S BEST DRIVE

The road that winds through Rio's mountain backdrop, passing through Itatiaia National Park toward Visconde de Maua, is breathtaking. En route is **Petropolis**, once the emperor's summer palace, which has been preserved complete with royal belongings, including the Brazilian imperial crown. You must remove your shoes to visit the interior of the palace, which is open to the public from noon until 5:30p.m. daily except Monday. About an hour farther along is **Teresopolis**, a national park that attracts mountain climbers.

COSTA RICA'S MOST BEAUTIFUL DRIVE

Bone-rattling though it is, a ride across the Inter-American Highway from San Jose to Limon takes you through some of the most startlingly beautiful scenery in the world, including the state-protected **Braulio Carrillo National Park**, dense with wet and tropical forests and acres of banana and coffee plantations. Winding up and down these mountainsides, snaking through these lush valleys, you'll begin to wonder how this tropical paradise has managed to escape a huge influx of tourists.